Lecture Notes in Computer Science 8013

Commenced Publication in 1973
Founding and Former Series Editors:
Gerhard Goos, Juris Hartmanis, and Jan van Leeuwen

Aaron Marcus (Ed.)

Design, User Experience, and Usability

Health, Learning, Playing, Cultural, and Cross-Cultural User Experience

Second International Conference, DUXU 2013
Held as Part of HCI International 2013
Las Vegas, NV, USA, July 21-26, 2013
Proceedings, Part II

 Springer

Volume Editor

Aaron Marcus
Aaron Marcus and Associates, Inc.
1196 Euclid Avenue, Suite 1F
Berkeley, CA 94708, USA
E-mail: aaron.marcus@amanda.com

ISSN 0302-9743   e-ISSN 1611-3349
ISBN 978-3-642-39240-5   e-ISBN 978-3-642-39241-2
DOI 10.1007/978-3-642-39241-2
Springer Heidelberg Dordrecht London New York

Library of Congress Control Number: 2013941914

CR Subject Classification (1998): H.5, H.3, K.3, K.4, J.3, H.4, K.8.0

LNCS Sublibrary: SL 3 – Information Systems and Application, incl. Internet/Web
and HCI

Typesetting: Camera-ready by author, data conversion by Scientific Publishing Services, Chennai, India

Printed on acid-free paper

Springer is part of Springer Science+Business Media (www.springer.com)

Foreword

The 15th International Conference on Human–Computer Interaction, HCI International 2013, was held in Las Vegas, Nevada, USA, 21–26 July 2013, incorporating 12 conferences / thematic areas:

Thematic areas:

- Human–Computer Interaction
- Human Interface and the Management of Information

Affiliated conferences:

- 10th International Conference on Engineering Psychology and Cognitive Ergonomics
- 7th International Conference on Universal Access in Human–Computer Interaction
- 5th International Conference on Virtual, Augmented and Mixed Reality
- 5th International Conference on Cross-Cultural Design
- 5th International Conference on Online Communities and Social Computing
- 7th International Conference on Augmented Cognition
- 4th International Conference on Digital Human Modeling and Applications in Health, Safety, Ergonomics and Risk Management
- 2nd International Conference on Design, User Experience and Usability
- 1st International Conference on Distributed, Ambient and Pervasive Interactions
- 1st International Conference on Human Aspects of Information Security, Privacy and Trust

A total of 5210 individuals from academia, research institutes, industry and governmental agencies from 70 countries submitted contributions, and 1666 papers and 303 posters were included in the program. These papers address the latest research and development efforts and highlight the human aspects of design and use of computing systems. The papers accepted for presentation thoroughly cover the entire field of Human–Computer Interaction, addressing major advances in knowledge and effective use of computers in a variety of application areas.

This volume, edited by Aaron Marcus, contains papers focusing on the thematic area of Design, User Experience and Usability, and addressing the following major topics:

- Cross-Cultural and Intercultural User Experience
- Designing for the Learning and Culture Experience
- Designing for the Health and Quality-of-Life Experience
- Games and Gamification

The remaining volumes of the HCI International 2013 proceedings are:

- Volume 1, LNCS 8004, Human–Computer Interaction: Human-Centred Design Approaches, Methods, Tools and Environments (Part I), edited by Masaaki Kurosu
- Volume 2, LNCS 8005, Human–Computer Interaction: Applications and Services (Part II), edited by Masaaki Kurosu
- Volume 3, LNCS 8006, Human–Computer Interaction: Users and Contexts of Use (Part III), edited by Masaaki Kurosu
- Volume 4, LNCS 8007, Human–Computer Interaction: Interaction Modalities and Techniques (Part IV), edited by Masaaki Kurosu
- Volume 5, LNCS 8008, Human–Computer Interaction: Towards Intelligent and Implicit Interaction (Part V), edited by Masaaki Kurosu
- Volume 6, LNCS 8009, Universal Access in Human–Computer Interaction: Design Methods, Tools and Interaction Techniques for eInclusion (Part I), edited by Constantine Stephanidis and Margherita Antona
- Volume 7, LNCS 8010, Universal Access in Human–Computer Interaction: User and Context Diversity (Part II), edited by Constantine Stephanidis and Margherita Antona
- Volume 8, LNCS 8011, Universal Access in Human–Computer Interaction: Applications and Services for Quality of Life (Part III), edited by Constantine Stephanidis and Margherita Antona
- Volume 9, LNCS 8012, Design, User Experience, and Usability: Design Philosophy, Methods and Tools (Part I), edited by Aaron Marcus
- Volume 11, LNCS 8014, Design, User Experience, and Usability: User Experience in Novel Technological Environments (Part III), edited by Aaron Marcus
- Volume 12, LNCS 8015, Design, User Experience, and Usability: Web, Mobile and Product Design (Part IV), edited by Aaron Marcus
- Volume 13, LNCS 8016, Human Interface and the Management of Information: Information and Interaction Design (Part I), edited by Sakae Yamamoto
- Volume 14, LNCS 8017, Human Interface and the Management of Information: Information and Interaction for Health, Safety, Mobility and Complex Environments (Part II), edited by Sakae Yamamoto
- Volume 15, LNCS 8018, Human Interface and the Management of Information: Information and Interaction for Learning, Culture, Collaboration and Business (Part III), edited by Sakae Yamamoto
- Volume 16, LNAI 8019, Engineering Psychology and Cognitive Ergonomics: Understanding Human Cognition (Part I), edited by Don Harris
- Volume 17, LNAI 8020, Engineering Psychology and Cognitive Ergonomics: Applications and Services (Part II), edited by Don Harris
- Volume 18, LNCS 8021, Virtual, Augmented and Mixed Reality: Designing and Developing Augmented and Virtual Environments (Part I), edited by Randall Shumaker
- Volume 19, LNCS 8022, Virtual, Augmented and Mixed Reality: Systems and Applications (Part II), edited by Randall Shumaker

- Volume 20, LNCS 8023, Cross-Cultural Design: Methods, Practice and Case Studies (Part I), edited by P.L. Patrick Rau
- Volume 21, LNCS 8024, Cross-Cultural Design: Cultural Differences in Everyday Life (Part II), edited by P.L. Patrick Rau
- Volume 22, LNCS 8025, Digital Human Modeling and Applications in Health, Safety, Ergonomics and Risk Management: Healthcare and Safety of the Environment and Transport (Part I), edited by Vincent G. Duffy
- Volume 23, LNCS 8026, Digital Human Modeling and Applications in Health, Safety, Ergonomics and Risk Management: Human Body Modeling and Ergonomics (Part II), edited by Vincent G. Duffy
- Volume 24, LNAI 8027, Foundations of Augmented Cognition, edited by Dylan D. Schmorrow and Cali M. Fidopiastis
- Volume 25, LNCS 8028, Distributed, Ambient and Pervasive Interactions, edited by Norbert Streitz and Constantine Stephanidis
- Volume 26, LNCS 8029, Online Communities and Social Computing, edited by A. Ant Ozok and Panayiotis Zaphiris
- Volume 27, LNCS 8030, Human Aspects of Information Security, Privacy and Trust, edited by Louis Marinos and Ioannis Askoxylakis
- Volume 28, CCIS 373, HCI International 2013 Posters Proceedings (Part I), edited by Constantine Stephanidis
- Volume 29, CCIS 374, HCI International 2013 Posters Proceedings (Part II), edited by Constantine Stephanidis

I would like to thank the Program Chairs and the members of the Program Boards of all affiliated conferences and thematic areas, listed below, for their contribution to the highest scientific quality and the overall success of the HCI International 2013 conference.

This conference could not have been possible without the continuous support and advice of the Founding Chair and Conference Scientific Advisor, Prof. Gavriel Salvendy, as well as the dedicated work and outstanding efforts of the Communications Chair and Editor of HCI International News, Abbas Moallem.

I would also like to thank for their contribution towards the smooth organization of the HCI International 2013 Conference the members of the Human–Computer Interaction Laboratory of ICS-FORTH, and in particular George Paparoulis, Maria Pitsoulaki, Stavroula Ntoa, Maria Bouhli and George Kapnas.

May 2013   Constantine Stephanidis
                                         General Chair, HCI International 2013

Organization

Human–Computer Interaction

Program Chair: Masaaki Kurosu, Japan

Jose Abdelnour-Nocera, UK
Sebastiano Bagnara, Italy
Simone Barbosa, Brazil
Tomas Berns, Sweden
Nigel Bevan, UK
Simone Borsci, UK
Apala Lahiri Chavan, India
Sherry Chen, Taiwan
Kevin Clark, USA
Torkil Clemmensen, Denmark
Xiaowen Fang, USA
Shin'ichi Fukuzumi, Japan
Vicki Hanson, UK
Ayako Hashizume, Japan
Anzai Hiroyuki, Italy
Sheue-Ling Hwang, Taiwan
Wonil Hwang, South Korea
Minna Isomursu, Finland
Yong Gu Ji, South Korea
Esther Jun, USA
Mitsuhiko Karashima, Japan

Kyungdoh Kim, South Korea
Heidi Krömker, Germany
Chen Ling, USA
Yan Liu, USA
Zhengjie Liu, P.R. China
Loïc Martínez Normand, Spain
Chang S. Nam, USA
Naoko Okuizumi, Japan
Noriko Osaka, Japan
Philippe Palanque, France
Hans Persson, Sweden
Ling Rothrock, USA
Naoki Sakakibara, Japan
Dominique Scapin, France
Guangfeng Song, USA
Sanjay Tripathi, India
Chui Yin Wong, Malaysia
Toshiki Yamaoka, Japan
Kazuhiko Yamazaki, Japan
Ryoji Yoshitake, Japan
Silvia Zimmermann, Switzerland

Human Interface and the Management of Information

Program Chair: Sakae Yamamoto, Japan

Hans-Jorg Bullinger, Germany
Alan Chan, Hong Kong
Gilsoo Cho, South Korea
Jon R. Gunderson, USA
Shin'ichi Fukuzumi, Japan
Michitaka Hirose, Japan
Jhilmil Jain, USA
Yasufumi Kume, Japan

Mark Lehto, USA
Hiroyuki Miki, Japan
Hirohiko Mori, Japan
Fiona Fui-Hoon Nah, USA
Shogo Nishida, Japan
Robert Proctor, USA
Youngho Rhee, South Korea
Katsunori Shimohara, Japan

Michale Smith, USA
Tsutomu Tabe, Japan
Hiroshi Tsuji, Japan

Kim-Phuong Vu, USA
Tomio Watanabe, Japan
Hidekazu Yoshikawa, Japan

Engineering Psychology and Cognitive Ergonomics

Program Chair: Don Harris, UK

Guy Andre Boy, USA
Joakim Dahlman, Sweden
Trevor Dobbins, UK
Mike Feary, USA
Shan Fu, P.R. China
Michaela Heese, Austria
Hung-Sying Jing, Taiwan
Wen-Chin Li, Taiwan
Mark A. Neerincx, The Netherlands
Jan M. Noyes, UK
Taezoon Park, Singapore

Paul Salmon, Australia
Axel Schulte, Germany
Siraj Shaikh, UK
Sarah C. Sharples, UK
Anthony Smoker, UK
Neville A. Stanton, UK
Alex Stedmon, UK
Xianghong Sun, P.R. China
Andrew Thatcher, South Africa
Matthew J.W. Thomas, Australia
Rolf Zon, The Netherlands

Universal Access in Human–Computer Interaction

Program Chairs: Constantine Stephanidis, Greece, and Margherita Antona, Greece

Julio Abascal, Spain
Ray Adams, UK
Gisela Susanne Bahr, USA
Margit Betke, USA
Christian Bühler, Germany
Stefan Carmien, Spain
Jerzy Charytonowicz, Poland
Carlos Duarte, Portugal
Pier Luigi Emiliani, Italy
Qin Gao, P.R. China
Andrina Granić, Croatia
Andreas Holzinger, Austria
Josette Jones, USA
Simeon Keates, UK

Georgios Kouroupetroglou, Greece
Patrick Langdon, UK
Seongil Lee, Korea
Ana Isabel B.B. Paraguay, Brazil
Helen Petrie, UK
Michael Pieper, Germany
Enrico Pontelli, USA
Jaime Sanchez, Chile
Anthony Savidis, Greece
Christian Stary, Austria
Hirotada Ueda, Japan
Gerhard Weber, Germany
Harald Weber, Germany

Virtual, Augmented and Mixed Reality

Program Chair: Randall Shumaker, USA

Waymon Armstrong, USA
Juan Cendan, USA
Rudy Darken, USA
Cali M. Fidopiastis, USA
Charles Hughes, USA
David Kaber, USA
Hirokazu Kato, Japan
Denis Laurendeau, Canada
Fotis Liarokapis, UK

Mark Livingston, USA
Michael Macedonia, USA
Gordon Mair, UK
Jose San Martin, Spain
Jacquelyn Morie, USA
Albert "Skip" Rizzo, USA
Kay Stanney, USA
Christopher Stapleton, USA
Gregory Welch, USA

Cross-Cultural Design

Program Chair: P.L. Patrick Rau, P.R. China

Pilsung Choe, P.R. China
Henry Been-Lirn Duh, Singapore
Vanessa Evers, The Netherlands
Paul Fu, USA
Zhiyong Fu, P.R. China
Fu Guo, P.R. China
Sung H. Han, Korea
Toshikazu Kato, Japan
Dyi-Yih Michael Lin, Taiwan
Rungtai Lin, Taiwan

Sheau-Farn Max Liang, Taiwan
Liang Ma, P.R. China
Alexander Mädche, Germany
Katsuhiko Ogawa, Japan
Tom Plocher, USA
Kerstin Röse, Germany
Supriya Singh, Australia
Hsiu-Ping Yueh, Taiwan
Liang (Leon) Zeng, USA
Chen Zhao, USA

Online Communities and Social Computing

Program Chairs: A. Ant Ozok, USA, and Panayiotis Zaphiris, Cyprus

Areej Al-Wabil, Saudi Arabia
Leonelo Almeida, Brazil
Bjørn Andersen, Norway
Chee Siang Ang, UK
Aneesha Bakharia, Australia
Ania Bobrowicz, UK
Paul Cairns, UK
Farzin Deravi, UK
Andri Ioannou, Cyprus
Slava Kisilevich, Germany

Niki Lambropoulos, Greece
Effie Law, Switzerland
Soo Ling Lim, UK
Fernando Loizides, Cyprus
Gabriele Meiselwitz, USA
Anthony Norcio, USA
Elaine Raybourn, USA
Panote Siriaraya, UK
David Stuart, UK
June Wei, USA

Augmented Cognition

Program Chairs: Dylan D. Schmorrow, USA, and Cali M. Fidopiastis, USA

Robert Arrabito, Canada
Richard Backs, USA
Chris Berka, USA
Joseph Cohn, USA
Martha E. Crosby, USA
Julie Drexler, USA
Ivy Estabrooke, USA
Chris Forsythe, USA
Wai Tat Fu, USA
Rodolphe Gentili, USA
Marc Grootjen, The Netherlands
Jefferson Grubb, USA
Ming Hou, Canada

Santosh Mathan, USA
Rob Matthews, Australia
Dennis McBride, USA
Jeff Morrison, USA
Mark A. Neerincx, The Netherlands
Denise Nicholson, USA
Banu Onaral, USA
Lee Sciarini, USA
Kay Stanney, USA
Roy Stripling, USA
Rob Taylor, UK
Karl van Orden, USA

Digital Human Modeling and Applications in Health, Safety, Ergonomics and Risk Management

Program Chair: Vincent G. Duffy, USA and Russia

Karim Abdel-Malek, USA
Giuseppe Andreoni, Italy
Daniel Carruth, USA
Eliza Yingzi Du, USA
Enda Fallon, Ireland
Afzal Godil, USA
Ravindra Goonetilleke, Hong Kong
Bo Hoege, Germany
Waldemar Karwowski, USA
Zhizhong Li, P.R. China

Kang Li, USA
Tim Marler, USA
Michelle Robertson, USA
Matthias Rötting, Germany
Peter Vink, The Netherlands
Mao-Jiun Wang, Taiwan
Xuguang Wang, France
Jingzhou (James) Yang, USA
Xiugan Yuan, P.R. China
Gülcin Yücel Hoge, Germany

Design, User Experience, and Usability

Program Chair: Aaron Marcus, USA

Sisira Adikari, Australia
Ronald Baecker, Canada
Arne Berger, Germany
Jamie Blustein, Canada

Ana Boa-Ventura, USA
Jan Brejcha, Czech Republic
Lorenzo Cantoni, Switzerland
Maximilian Eibl, Germany

Anthony Faiola, USA
Emilie Gould, USA
Zelda Harrison, USA
Rüdiger Heimgärtner, Germany
Brigitte Herrmann, Germany
Steffen Hess, Germany
Kaleem Khan, Canada

Jennifer McGinn, USA
Francisco Rebelo, Portugal
Michael Renner, Switzerland
Kerem Rızvanoğlu, Turkey
Marcelo Soares, Brazil
Christian Sturm, Germany
Michele Visciola, Italy

Distributed, Ambient and Pervasive Interactions

Program Chairs: Norbert Streitz, Germany, and Constantine Stephanidis, Greece

Emile Aarts, The Netherlands
Adnan Abu-Dayya, Qatar
Juan Carlos Augusto, UK
Boris de Ruyter, The Netherlands
Anind Dey, USA
Dimitris Grammenos, Greece
Nuno M. Guimaraes, Portugal
Shin'ichi Konomi, Japan
Carsten Magerkurth, Switzerland

Christian Müller-Tomfelde, Australia
Fabio Paternó, Italy
Gilles Privat, France
Harald Reiterer, Germany
Carsten Röcker, Germany
Reiner Wichert, Germany
Woontack Woo, South Korea
Xenophon Zabulis, Greece

Human Aspects of Information Security, Privacy and Trust

Program Chairs: Louis Marinos, ENISA EU, and Ioannis Askoxylakis, Greece

Claudio Agostino Ardagna, Italy
Zinaida Benenson, Germany
Daniele Catteddu, Italy
Raoul Chiesa, Italy
Bryan Cline, USA
Sadie Creese, UK
Jorge Cuellar, Germany
Marc Dacier, USA
Dieter Gollmann, Germany
Kirstie Hawkey, Canada
Jaap-Henk Hoepman, The Netherlands
Cagatay Karabat, Turkey
Angelos Keromytis, USA
Ayako Komatsu, Japan

Ronald Leenes, The Netherlands
Javier Lopez, Spain
Steve Marsh, Canada
Gregorio Martinez, Spain
Emilio Mordini, Italy
Yuko Murayama, Japan
Masakatsu Nishigaki, Japan
Aljosa Pasic, Spain
Milan Petković, The Netherlands
Joachim Posegga, Germany
Jean-Jacques Quisquater, Belgium
Damien Sauveron, France
George Spanoudakis, UK
Kerry-Lynn Thomson, South Africa

Julien Touzeau, France
Theo Tryfonas, UK
João Vilela, Portugal

Claire Vishik, UK
Melanie Volkamer, Germany

External Reviewers

Maysoon Abulkhair, Saudi Arabia
Ilia Adami, Greece
Vishal Barot, UK
Stephan Böhm, Germany
Vassilis Charissis, UK
Francisco Cipolla-Ficarra, Spain
Maria De Marsico, Italy
Marc Fabri, UK
David Fonseca, Spain
Linda Harley, USA
Yasushi Ikei, Japan
Wei Ji, USA
Nouf Khashman, Canada
John Killilea, USA
Iosif Klironomos, Greece
Ute Klotz, Switzerland
Maria Korozi, Greece
Kentaro Kotani, Japan

Vassilis Kouroumalis, Greece
Stephanie Lackey, USA
Janelle LaMarche, USA
Asterios Leonidis, Greece
Nickolas Macchiarella, USA
George Margetis, Greece
Matthew Marraffino, USA
Joseph Mercado, USA
Claudia Mont'Alvão, Brazil
Yoichi Motomura, Japan
Karsten Nebe, Germany
Stavroula Ntoa, Greece
Martin Osen, Austria
Stephen Prior, UK
Farid Shirazi, Canada
Jan Stelovsky, USA
Sarah Swierenga, USA

HCI International 2014

The 16th International Conference on Human–Computer Interaction, HCI International 2014, will be held jointly with the affiliated conferences in the summer of 2014. It will cover a broad spectrum of themes related to Human–Computer Interaction, including theoretical issues, methods, tools, processes and case studies in HCI design, as well as novel interaction techniques, interfaces and applications. The proceedings will be published by Springer. More information about the topics, as well as the venue and dates of the conference, will be announced through the HCI International Conference series website: http://www.hci-international.org/

General Chair
Professor Constantine Stephanidis
University of Crete and ICS-FORTH
Heraklion, Crete, Greece
Email: cs@ics.forth.gr

Table of Contents – Part II

Cross-Cultural and Intercultural User Experience

A Novel Reading Technique Application: Exploring Arabic Children
Experience 3
 *Maram S. Alhafzy, Ebtesam A. Alomari, Hind H. Mahdy, and
 Maysoon F. Abulkhair*

Observation Analysis Method for Culture Centered Design – Proposal
of KH Method 11
 Kaho Asano and Kazuhiko Yamazaki

Lessons Learned from Projects in Japan and Korea Relevant for
Intercultural HCI Development 20
 Martin Blankl, Peter Biersack, and Rüdiger Heimgärtner

Usability Evaluation of Two Chinese Segmentation Methods in
Subtitles to Scaffold Chinese Novice 28
 Chih-Kai Chang

Young Egyptians Use of Social Networks and the January 2011
Revolution 38
 Ghada R. El Said

Designing for a Thumb: An Ideal Mobile Touchscreen Interface for
Chinese Users 44
 Qian Fei

Examining Interdisciplinary Prototyping in the Context of Cultural
Communication 54
 Michael Heidt

Intercultural User Interface Design – Culture-Centered HCI Design
– Cross-Cultural User Interface Design: Different Terminology or
Different Approaches? 62
 Rüdiger Heimgärtner

User-Experience and Science-Fiction in Chinese, Indian, and Japanese
Films 72
 Aaron Marcus

Two Solitudes Revisited: A Cross-Cultural Exploration of Online Image
Searcher's Behaviors 79
 Elaine Ménard, Nouf Khashman, and Jonathan Dorey

Usability Assessment in the Multicultural Approach 89
   Maria Lúcia L.R. Okimoto, Cristina Olaverri Monreal, and
   Klaus-Josef Bengler

Lessons from Intercultural Project Management for the Intercultural
HCI Design Process 95
   Yvonne Schoper and Rüdiger Heimgärtner

Localization beyond National Characteristics: The Impact of Language
on Users' Performance with Different Menu Structures 105
   Christian Sturm, Gerhard Strube, and Sara Gouda

Tracing Technology Diffusion of Social Media with Culturally Localized
User Experience Approach 115
   Huatong Sun

The Interactive Media between Human and the Sacred: An Example
for Taiwanese Spiritual Practice 121
   Pi-Fen Wang

Banner Evaluation Predicted by Eye Tracking Performance and the
Median Thinking Style 129
   Man-Ying Wang, Da-Lung Tang, Chih-Tung Kao, and
   Vincent C. Sun

Intercultural Design for Use – Extending Usage-Centered Design by
Cultural Aspects 139
   Helmut Windl and Rüdiger Heimgärtner

A Usability Testing of Chinese Character Writing System for Foreign
Learners 149
   Manlai You and Yu-Jie Xu

Designing for the Learning and Culture Experience

A Cross-Cultural Evaluation of HCI Student Performance - Reflections
for the Curriculum 161
   José Abdelnour-Nocera, Ann Austin, Mario Michaelides, and
   Sunila Modi

Desirability of a Teaching and Learning Tool for Thai Dance Body
Motion 171
   Worawat Choensawat, Kingkarn Sookhanaphibarn,
   Chommanad Kijkhun, and Kozaburo Hachimura

Improving User Experience in e-Learning, the Case of the Open
University of Catalonia 180
   Eva de Lera, Magí Almirall, Llorenç Valverde, and Mercè Gisbert

Math Fluency through Game Design 189
  Wanda Eugene, Tiffany Barnes, and Jennifer Wilson

Musical Experience Development Model Based on Service Design
Thinking.. 199
  Sunyoung Kim and Eui-Chul Jung

Investigation of Interaction Modalities Designed for Immersive
Visualizations Using Commodity Devices in the Classroom 209
  *Kira Lawrence, Alisa Maas, Neera Pradhan, Treschiel Ford,
  Jacqueline Shinker, and Amy Ulinski Banic*

Legibility in Children's Reading: The Methodological Development of
an Experiment for Reading Printed and Digital Texts 219
  Daniel Lourenço and Solange Coutinho

PALMA: Usability Testing of an Application for Adult Literacy
in Brazil 229
  Francimar Rodrigues Maciel

Setting Conditions for Learning: Mediated Play and Socio-material
Dialogue 238
  Emanuela Marchetti and Eva Petersson Brooks

The Learning Machine: Mobile UX Design That Combines Information
Design with Persuasion Design.................................. 247
  Aaron Marcus, Yuan Peng, and Nicola Lecca

Information Accessibility in Museums with a Focus on Technology and
Cognitive Process 257
  Laura B. Martins and Felipe Gabriele

Luz, Câmera, Libras!: How a Mobile Game Can Improve the Learning
of Sign Languages... 266
  *Guilherme Moura, Luis Arthur Vasconcelos, Aline Cavalcanti,
  Felipe Breyer, Daliton da Silva, João Marcelo Teixeira,
  Crystian Leão, and Judith Kelner*

Toward Social Media Based Writing 276
  John Sadauskas, Daragh Byrne, and Robert K. Atkinson

Participatory Design for Mobile Application for Academic Management
in a Brazilian University 286
  *José Guilherme Santa Rosa, Andrei Gurgel, and
  Marcel de Oliveira Passos*

YUSR: Speech Recognition Software for Dyslexics 296
  *Mounira Taileb, Reem Al-Saggaf, Amal Al-Ghamdi,
  Maha Al-Zebaidi, and Sultana Al-Sahafi*

Measuring Usability of the Mobile Mathematics Curriculum-Based
Measurement Application with Children 304
    Mengping Tsuei, Hsin-Yin Chou, and Bo-Sheng Chen

Teachers and Children Playing with Factorization: Putting Prime
Slaughter to the Test 311
    Andrea Valente and Emanuela Marchetti

Towards a Common Implementation Framework for Online Virtual
Museums 321
    Katarzyna Wilkosinska, Andreas Aderhold, Holger Graf, and
    Yvonne Jung

Designing for the Health and Quality of Life Experience

Towards an Arabic Language Augmentative and Alternative
Communication Application for Autism 333
    Bayan Al-Arifi, Arwa Al-Rubaian, Ghadah Al-Ofisan,
    Norah Al-Romi, and Areej Al-Wabil

Improving Autistic Children's Social Skills Using Virtual Reality 342
    Omaima Bamasak, Roa'a Braik, Hadeel Al-Tayari, Shatha Al-Harbi,
    Ghadeer Al-Semairi, and Malak Abu-Hnaidi

Lazy Eye Shooter: Making a Game Therapy for Visual Recovery in
Adult Amblyopia Usable 352
    Jessica D. Bayliss, Indu Vedamurthy, Mor Nahum,
    Dennis Levi, and Daphne Bavelier

Designing Supportive Mobile Technology for Stable Diabetes 361
    Katherine S. Blondon and Predrag Klasnja

Application of Rhetorical Appeals in Interactive Design for Health 371
    Sauman Chu and G. Mauricio Mejía

Addressing Human Computer Interaction Issues of Electronic Health
Record in Clinical Encounters 381
    Martina A. Clarke, Linsey M. Steege, Joi L. Moore,
    Jeffery L. Belden, Richelle J. Koopman, and
    Min Soon Kim

Designing Co-located Tabletop Interaction for Rehabilitation of Brain
Injury 391
   Jonathan Duckworth, Patrick R. Thomas, David Shum, and
   Peter H. Wilson

Paindroid: A Mobile Tool for Pain Visualization and Management 401
   Tor-Morten Grønli, Gheorghita Ghinea, Fotios Spyridonis, and
   Jarle Hansen

Usability Testing Medical Devices: A Practical Guide to Minimizing
Risk and Maximizing Success 407
   Chris Hass and Dan Berlin

Exploring the Need for, and Feasibility of, a Web-Based
Self-management Resource for Teenage and Young Adult Cancer
Survivors in the UK 417
   Louise Moody, Andy Turner, Jane Osmond,
   Joanna Kosmala-Anderson, Louise Hooker, and Lynn Batehup

Avatar Interfaces for Biobehavioral Feedback 424
   Tylar Murray, Delquawn Hardy, Donna Spruijt-Metz,
   Eric Hekler, and Andrew Raij

Participatory Interaction Design for the Healthcare Service Field 435
   Takuichi Nishimura, M. Kobayakawa, M. Nakajima,
   K.C. Yamada, T. Fukuhara, M. Hamasaki, H. Miwa,
   Kentaro Watanabe, Y. Sakamoto, T. Sunaga, and Yoichi Motomura

Virtual Environment to Treat Social Anxiety 442
   Ana Paula Cláudio, Maria Beatriz Carmo, Tânia Pinheiro,
   Francisco Esteves, and Eder Lopes

Development and Evaluation of a Knowledge-Based Method for the
Treatment of Use-Oriented and Technical Risks Using the Example of
Medical Devices 452
   Simon Plogmann, Armin Janß, Arne Jansen-Troy, and
   Klaus Radermacher

Interactive System for Solving Children Communication Disorder 462
   Wafaa M. Shalash, Malak Bas-sam, and Ghada Shawly

Game-Based Interactive Media in Behavioral Medicine: Creating
Serious Affective-Cognitive-Environmental-Social Integration
Experiences 470
   Alasdair G. Thin and Marientina Gotsis

A Mobile Prototype for Clinical Emergency Calls 480
   Cornelius Wille, Thomas Marx, and Adam Maciak

Games and Gamification

The Design in the Development of Exergames: A New Game for the
Contribute to Control Childhood Obesity 491
    Marina Barros, André Neves, Walter Correia,
    Marcelo Marcio Soares, and Fábio Campos

Case Study: Identifying Gamification Opportunities in Sales
Applications.. 501
    Joëlle Carignan and Sally Lawler Kennedy

Interactive Doodles: A Comparative Analysis of the Usability and
Playability of Google Trademark Games between 2010 and 2012 508
    Breno José Andrade de Carvalho, Marcelo Marcio Soares,
    Andre Menezes Marques das Neves, and Rodrigo Pessoa Medeiros

Exploring Adjustable Interactive Rings in Game Playing: Preliminary
Results 518
    Leonardo Cunha de Miranda, Heiko Hornung, Roberto Pereira, and
    Maria Cecília C. Baranauskas

Gamification at Work: Designing Engaging Business Software.......... 528
    Janaki Kumar

Stand Up, Heroes!: Gamification for Standing People on Crowded
Public Transportation 538
    Itaru Kuramoto, Takuya Ishibashi, Keiko Yamamoto, and
    Yoshihiro Tsujino

Applying Gamification in Customer Service Application to Improve
Agents' Efficiency and Satisfaction 548
    Prerna Makanawala, Jaideep Godara, Eliad Goldwasser, and
    Hang Le

Perception of Gamification: Between Graphical Design and Persuasive
Design... 558
    Cathie Marache-Francisco and Eric Brangier

Interactive Rock Climbing Playground Equipment: Modeling through
Service 568
    Mikiko Oono, Koji Kitamura, Yoshifumi Nishida, and
    Yoichi Motomura

Work and Gameplay in the Transparent 'Magic Circle' of Gamification:
Insights from a Gameful Collaborative Review Exercise 577
    Răzvan Rughiniş

Augmenting Yu-Gi-Oh! Trading Card Game as Persuasive Transmedia
Storytelling 587
    Mizuki Sakamoto and Tatsuo Nakajima

How Gamification and Behavioral Science Can Drive Social Change
One Employee at a Time..   597
   Susan Hunt Stevens

Bridging the Gap between Consumer and Enterprise Applications
through Gamification...   602
   Tim Thianthai and Bingjun Zhou

Gamification: When It works, When It Doesn't   608
   Erika Noll Webb

Author Index..   615

Part I
Cross-Cultural and Intercultural User Experience

A Novel Reading Technique Application:
Exploring Arabic Children Experience

Maram S. Alhafzy, Ebtesam A. Alomari, Hind H. Mahdy, and Maysoon F. Abulkhair

Faculty of Computing and Information Technology, King Abdulaziz University,
Jeddah, Saudi Arabia
{maram.alhafzy,ebtesam07}@yahoo.com, hind_mahdy_07@hotmail.com,
mabualkhair@kau.edu.sa

Abstract. Computers and many of their applications are extremely vital and play a crucial role in the children's education and knowledge building. This paper discusses the results of a study about Arabic-speaking children's interaction with an Arabic application. Then, researchers collected information to study how these children reacted and felt when they were interacting with this Arabic reading application.

Keywords: Children, Reading, Arabic Application.

1 Introduction

A child's reading skills are definitely essential to his or her success in school and work. Reading can be an entertaining activity for children, and it helps them to recognize new words from the atmosphere around them. This skill may be improved through different techniques such as traditional and technical. In the technical method, children can use computers, specialized devices and other tools to support them in reading.

Most of the earlier researches, presented that computers and many of their applications, which support and target children, are truly important and play a crucial role in the children's education and knowledge building. However, there are some problems and weaknesses in those software tools and applications offered for kids. This problem is that there are few Arabic websites and applications.

Some Arabic applications' and websites' interfaces are crowded with numerous images and sounds, which distract the attention of the child from the educational content. In addition to that, some of them focus only on text more than images and sounds. Furthermore, some children's applications provide difficult terms and vocabularies without considering their age which lead to non-attractive and ineffective application for children.

On the other hand, some of the children's websites do not have an appropriate format. Their designers use different font types and sizes; consequently, children face difficulties while navigating among their windows and activities. Moreover, most of

A. Marcus (Ed.): DUXU/HCII 2013, Part II, LNCS 8013, pp. 3–10, 2013.

Arabic tools are old, traditional, and not built based on new studies. In contrast English tools motivate children to learn and enjoy their time through fun activities.

It is certainly important to measure and determine the reading level of the children. However, depending on our knowledge, there are no software applications to assess the kid's reading skills. Additionally, the early assessment will help to detect the child's reading difficulties and help the parents and teacher(s) to know the child's educational progress level.

This paper is organized as follows; next section presents reading strategy. Section 3 displays brief description about the application. Section 4 discusses the literature review. Section 5 illustrates the research questions. Section 6 explains the methodology. The results and discussion are presented in section 7 and 8. The last section is the conclusion.

2   Reading Strategy

The "Let's Read" application designed for kid's ages from 3-7 years old. Application activities are based on experts in childhood department. These activities include the following: phonics awareness, character recognition and word recognition, as shown in fig.1.

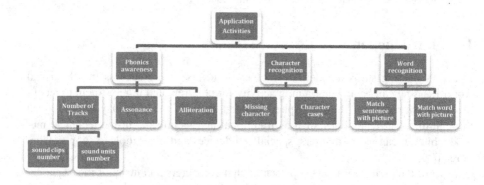

Fig. 1. Activities Hierarchical

3   "Let's Read" Application

The child will interact with application by using the mouse, because developers note from previous studies that using the mouse in movement and selecting objects will be more efficient for children and easier than using the keyboard. As well, through the designing process, designers consider designing and selecting pictures that are suitable for the content and that are in a good size as shown in fig.2, 3.

Fig. 2. Activities' Main Window

Fig. 3. Phonics Awareness's Main Window

Furthermore, they try to design large icons, which are clear, easy to select, and help child to navigate easier; they provide an option to return to the previous activity. When children do not solve the activity correctly, the application will give him/her another chance to try. Also, activities' questions are asked by a clear sound instead of written question. Therefore, children who do not have high reading skills can use this application as shown in fig.4, 5.

Fig. 4. Example1 of activity

Fig. 5. Example2 of activity

There are two interactive characters: girl (Basmah) and boy (Basem), as shown in fig.6. Each time children can select which character they would like to help and guide the character to solving the activities' questions.

Fig. 6. Application's Characters the: girl (Basmah) and boy (Basem)

4   Literature Review

It has become obvious that as children's wishes, prerequisites, desires, and needs increase when it comes to technology. To design an attractive application for children, children must be involved in the designing process in a meaningful way. Then again, there are limitations for involving children in all aspects of the designing process, as children often have a difficulty in expressing ideas. The real issue is not whether involving children is advantageous or disadvantageous but how increase their effective engagement in the design process [1].

Websites designed for children are preferred to be convivial, beautiful, vividly colorful, stimulating ,captivating, and memorable. In Designing Websites for Kids: Trends and Best Practices article, Louis Lazaris found best practices that are exclusive to Web design for children's sites. These practices will be explained in the following paragraphs [2].

The website should contain bright, vivid colors, because bright colors will hold a child's attention for a longer period of time, and visually stimulate them in an unforgettable way. Also, it should place the child in a high-spirited, exuberant mood.

The website's interface is preferred to have elements from nature because children's experiences in life are limited; some of the things they are most familiar with are found in nature. Large animated speaking characters are a captivating way to grab a child's attention [2].

Children's website designers can oversimplify navigation and call-to-action areas so that children can navigate easily. One of the most important ways for a children's website to succeed, is to include elements that allow a child to interact with the site in some way, like animation, sound, video and games [2].

According to the analysis of the children's cognition features and combines the basic principle of the software interface designed by X. Pan, he gets the following revelation. The layout is mainly on single window, reducing the disturbing elements of the interface and the operation procedure should be simplified [3].

For children's websites and applications larger font sizes are generally preferred. Bernard, Mills et al found that kids 9 to 11 years old prefer 14-point fonts over 12-point fonts [4].

Research has indicated that input devices are important for the usability of any educational software. Study by A. Donker and P. Reitsma aim to investigate the suitability of the mouse as an input device for young children. The results show that young children are clearly capable of using a computer mouse. It is evident that they can click very accurately on targets, even though they need a lot of time to aim on objects. This indicates that objects in educational software do not have to be much larger than objects in software for adults, unless children are required to respond quickly [5].

A study by S. Atkinson et al about non-keyboard input device (NKID) users. It is recommended that the users should be able to use a combination of methods in order to carry out standard tasks e.g. shortcuts, icons, device buttons to reduce NKID dependency; besides, users should be encouraged to incorporate a mix of screen and non-screen work in their daily work routine [6].

5   Research Questions

In order to study the Arabic-speaking children's interaction with the "Let's read" application, this study addressed the following questions:

1. How much is this application's design and interface suitable for children from 3-7 years old and how far does it help them to improve their reading skill?
2. How much the interface, pictures, characters and their encouragement statements, which are related to the Arabic culture, can affect the Arabic-speaking children and increase their willingness to use the application?

6   Method

Observation and interviews were conducted with children to observe their interactions and their comprehensibility while using "Let's Read" educational application. Five children were interviewed and asked to use the application and perform some tasks.

6.1   Participants

The participants in the study were five children between 3 and 7 years old. All the participating children had a normal vision and 2 out of 5 were boys. All of them knew how to use iPads and iPhones but they had no idea about the new reading strategy that was implemented in this application. Moreover, 2 out of 5 are three year olds; thus, they did not know the alphabet and reading basics.

6.2   Procedure

The study was divided into two phases, which were the testing phase and the interview phase. During the testing phase, children asked to play by selecting the characters that helped them, and then they selected their choice of activity. Prior to that, a brief description and explanation were given so that they understood that they could start playing and answering the questions by selecting any activity without any restrictions.

The time given was approximately 20-25 minutes for each child. After the testing phase, the interview phase was conducted immediately to get details on their background and how they felt after using this application.

7   Result

Basically the results presented that the children showed positive attitude towards using the application. Although they liked cartoon characters like SpongeBob and Tom and Jerry, they found the characters in this application more attractive. They liked their names, 'Basmah' and 'Basem' because they are relevant to their culture. In addition, researchers noticed that girls always selected the girl character (Basmah), they said: "she is beautiful", and one child said: "I like her dress and shoe color". Also, we noticed that they tried to act out the characters' way of movement and dancing when they solved the activity correctly.

In addition, most of the children enjoyed listening to the positive feedback when they got correct answers and completed a task. They liked the sound of the character that encouraged them by articulating Arabic sentences. They tried to repeat their sentences because even if they failed in solving the task; the characters encouraged them to try again and told them that they are able to solve it correctly.

Most of the participants knew how to navigate between; for example, they knew how to go back to the previous window or go to the next window. Also, most of them knew how to solve the exercises by clicking on one of the three picture choices after they listen to the exercise's question.

However, we noticed two of participants who were three years old faced some difficulties in using the mouse because they were used to dealing with touch screen devices. Similarly, they do not understand some activities because they still did not learn alphabets. Yet, they understood the functions of the icons such as the repeat the question icon. Additionally, we noticed they wanted to continue playing because they found the colors and pictures very attractive.

Furthermore, most of the participants knew how to use the application from the first time and found it easy to use. They were pleased when they played, and they wanted to continue playing as one child said, "I want to play again at home" and another child found it is very helpful and asked, "Can I have it on my iPad?".

8 Discussion

From the study, it shows that the application is easy to use and very eye-catching, the pictures' size and color are suitable for children in this age; moreover, they encourage them to use the application, which helps to improve their reading skills.

Furthermore, the characters' name and design attracted the children because they were related to their culture, and each time they can select the character that they prefer. As well, the characters' interactions and encouragement statements motivated the children to continue.

Although all the questions in this application do not need drag and drop or any tough mouse movements and the icons were large and easy to select, children who are three years old faced struggles while using the mouse as mentioned above in section 7. Consequently, researchers suggested improving the application in order for it to function on touch screen devices, which will make it easier to use and transport than on a laptop or desktop computer. This makes it more available to a large percentage of children that use iPads or other touch screen devices.

9 Conclusions

Computers and many of their applications play a fundamental role in the children's education and knowledge building. This paper presents a study to analyze the usability of using "Let's Read" application, which aims to improve the reading skills for pre-school children. The results of this study showed that the application is easy to use, very attractive and the pictures' colors and sizes were suitable for children in this age. Besides, characters' names and the design were related to their culture and motivated children to use the application. Still, as future work, researchers suggest to improve the application to make it operate on touch screen devices.

References

1. Nesset, V., Large, A.: Children in the information technology design process: A review of theories and their applications. Library & Information Science Research 26(2), 140–161 (2004)
2. Lazaris, L.: Designing Websites for Kids: Trends and Best Practices (2009), http://www.smashingmagazine.com/2011/07/06/best-
3. Pan, X.: Research of iphone application UI design based on children cognition feature. In: 2010 IEEE 11th International Conference on Computer-Aided Industrial Design & Conceptual Design (CAIDCD), vol. 1. IEEE (2010)

4. Bruckman, A., Bandlow: HCI for Kids. In: Jacko, J., et al. (eds.) The Human-Computer Interaction Handbook: Fundamentals, Evolving Technologies, and Emerging Applications (2002)
5. Donker, A., Reitsma, P.: Young children's ability to use a computer mouse. Computers & Education 48(4), 602–617 (2007)
6. Atkinson, S., et al.: Using non-keyboard input devices: interviews with users in the workplace. International Journal of Industrial Ergonomics 33(6), 571–579 (2004)

Observation Analysis Method for Culture Centered Design – Proposal of KH Method –

Kaho Asano and Kazuhiko Yamazaki

Chiba Institute of Technology, 2-17-1 Tsudanuma, Narashino-shi, Chiba 275-0016 Japan
kaho.asano@gmail.com

Abstract. Product development has advanced for developing countries with their economic growths. It must have a priority to learn their culture when developing a product for people having different background. This study focuses on observational method, which is important for designing an overseas product, and provides author's original method from observation to output named KH method. KH method aims at making basement of ideation figured out deeply their experience through culture centered thinking in the phase of Observation, Analysis and Ideation.

Keywords: Culture Centered Design, Observational method, Storyboarding.

1   Introduction

Developing country's economic growth has been booming therefore we need to develop a product and service for countries that have completely different cultures and religions such as Indonesia, India, Africa and Brazil from countries, which we used to target to in the future. Most of companies in Japan try to apply the same business model, which was used when Japan was still developing, however, it's essential to make a product based on understanding their background for penetrate into developing countries.

2   Purpose

The purpose of this study is suggesting the ethnography method for developers to design a product and service based on taking into account of cultural trait to users that have different background.

3   Approach of Culture Centered Design

To step into a local community overseas and study its life, observe experientially, find some questions and create hypothesis are required. Based on this process, we stayed and observed Japanese and Brazilian community in Japan. Moreover, we focused on the phase of analysis and ideation after observation to figure out how cultural trait can influence designing.

A. Marcus (Ed.): DUXU/HCII 2013, Part II, LNCS 8013, pp. 11–19, 2013.

4   Suggesting a Design Method

This chapter describes the original design method we suggest named KH method.
KH method is named after the author's first name, Kaho.

4.1   Features of KH Method

It's divided into Observation and Analysis phases as features of this method.

At the phase of Observation, there is a place where it's easy to step into the community when you go on a field trip. To give some examples, Japanese people get along more easily at Japanese style bar, Izakaya where we can get a drink than only sitting and interview. As for Brazilian people in Japan, there is a Brazilian market of Mercado in the city where they live mostly. This market has a small food court outside and they gather together to chat and eat Churrasco, which is Brazilian cuisine every weekend there, which means that it can be a good opportunity to get closer with them.

Besides, we take tons of photos of everything that we see. The quantity of photos is important, therefore the skill of photography isn't required. Compared with video shooting, when you want to see a part of scenes, it takes time to fast-wind and forward, in contrast, photos are accessible to overlook the whole object of observation with project members together.

At the phase of Analysis, the photos from fieldwork are organized in chronological order with using Storyboarding method to get their culture and life contextually. The findings from the analysis need to be investigated with Video Ethnography, Shadowing and some observational method.

As described above, KH method is that step into the specific community based on culture for observation and figure out cultural trait contextually with using Storyboarding method for analysis. Moreover, these findings can be the foundation of idea.

4.2   Comparison with other Observational Method

This is the table shows the difference between KH method and other observational method such as Shadowing, Found-Behavior and Rapid Ethnography.
The utility of KH method were as follows:

1. Only taking tons of photos in the process is required which means that you don't need a skill and preparation so much.
2. As F. Kato points out, you can go on a field trip lightly without big preparation by functions of smartphone which people daily use such as camera, memo and map.
3. Unless there are many observers, Story shows contextually the whole image of observation, therefore project members who didn't do fieldwork also can get a findings and share the result well.

Method	Shadowing	Found-Behavior	Rapid Ethnography	KH method
Summary	Spending time with an examinee and observe at the same time like a shadow.	Record examinee's whole activity with video and interview him with showing it after observation.	Examine rapidly hypothesis in planning stage. It's required to collect and analysis data repeatedly after do ethnography promptly.	Based on cultural trait, observe with taking tons of photos and share them with Storyboarding contextually.
Advantage	You can see contextually how to use the targeted object with examinee's activity.	Precise memory can be drawn out by showing video of the observation in an interview	Having chances to get a finding in observation sharing and analysis phase.	It's easy to step into the community and possible to understand people empirically.
Weakness	It has difficulty for examinee to act naturally because of being observed.	The presence of observer can be noise and intervening is difficult.	Sharing information is difficult because of the limit of number of observers and it makes data bias.	Learning a rule how to take a photo of the target and how to share is required.
Form	Face-to-face	Face-to-face	Face-to-face (Sometimes Indirect.)	Face-to-face (Sometimes Indirect.)
Number of Observer	Multiple	Multiple	A couple of people	Multiple
Required Time	Not too long	Not too long	Not too long	Not too long
Place	Local area	Local area	Local area	Local area
Facility	Normal	Difficult	Normal	Normal
Examinee's Load	Hard	Hard	Low	Low
Observer's Interposition	Difficult	Difficult	Normal	Easy
Tools for Documentation	Video	Video	Video / Camera	Smartphone camera

Fig. 1. Comparison KH method with other observational ones

Difficulty of Sharing data	Normal	Normal	Difficult	Easy
Culture Considered	Proper	Proper	Proper	Proper

Fig. 1. (*continued*)

4.3   Practical Example

We practiced 3 observations, "The stay with a Brazilian family in Yamanashi, Japan", "Tohoku kindergarten reconstruction project in Miyagi, Japan" and "Fieldwork at Brazilian town in Gunma, Japan"

Implementation of Observation

According to 3 observation examples, we used the way to take many photos in the process of fieldwork.

In this process, two examples are about Brazilian people and the other is Japanese people and we learnt 4 Hofstede Cultural Dimensions that are Power distance, Individualism, Uncertainty avoidance and Masculinity so that we compared Japanese culture with Brazilian one to figure out cultural trait clearly.

This chapter's results were follows:

1. We found that there is a place where you can see their activity naturally and step into their life rapidly every culture. For examples, as Hofstede stated that Japanese generally never show their expression but talk a lot like release their inner self with drinking at bar. It's like a different person. Thus For Japanese community, you can be the part of member in their community with having alcohol which means that the start of fieldwork depends on culture.

2. In the case of observing with several people, objects that you missed in the field can be captured by someone, moreover we can get tons of photos taken by them which is more helpful to make non-observers understand and share the result clearly. Therefore we describes that having several observers are better to improve quantity and quality of information of observation.

Implementation of Analysis

We held 6 workshops with 13 students to ideate based on observation after "Tohoku kindergarten reconstruction project in Miyagi, Japan". Storyboarding and Card sorting method were used to learn how photos taken by observers could be shared effectively in this practice. Workshops we held are one of them are with using Storyboarding, another one is with Card sorting and the other is with both methods from sharing and ideation.

Workshop with Storyboarding

It was held with 13 students and a total 3 times at Chiba Institute of Technology and Tama Art University in June 2012. The purpose of this workshop is to analysis the utility of sharing observation objects with Storyboarding. Besides, we used printed A4 sized photos of observation (Fig.2) and participants, post-it with story, map and if you did interview, you need to visualize what people said with storyboard. (Fig.3)

 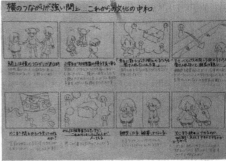

Fig. 2. Sharing with Storyboard   **Fig. 3.** Storyboard that visualized interview

This chapter's results were follows:

Not only sentence but showing large photos on the wall makes observation result give more impact which is you can have findings more easily and Storyboarding shows generally small sized font on paper and it's hard to recognize the story, however, you can remember the story from the big images.

Furthermore, Non-observers can easily understand and review observation result by story-lined.

We still need to figure out to make preparation easier and make a rule what point you need to take a photo.

Workshop with Card Sorting

It was held with 4 students at Tama Art University in June 2012. The purpose of this workshop is to analysis the utility of sharing observation objects with Card sorting. In this workshop, we used business card-sized photos (we called this "photo card") (Fig.4), a large paper for discussion on the table, post-it and map made by photo cards (Fig.5).

Fig. 4. Sharing with many photo cards   **Fig. 5.** Explain with a map made by photo cards

This chapter's results were follows:

1. Compared with Storyboarding, which you can explain contextually what you did in the field, Card sorting isn't suited for it, nevertheless it was useful to ideate on the

table which means that we supposed that you need to divide using tools between analysis and ideation phase.

2. We learnt that using photo cards, as a map was helpful for understanding the field more.

3. Discussion with a big paper on the table urged you to visualize what you think, thus we can share and understand each other easily.

4. Object you should take a picture of in the field depends on what your design target is.

- If you design a kindergarten, you'd better not to take a photo of existing kindergarten but a photo of environment around it.

- If you design communication design in a kindergarten, photos of place where children actually spend time and play.

Workshop with Both Methods

Fig. 6. Environment to share data   **Fig. 7.** Ideation with tools (photo cards, storyboard)

It was held with 13 students at Chiba Institute of Technology and Tama Art University in July 2012. The purpose of this workshop is to analysis the utility of sharing observation objects and ideation with Storyboarding and Card sorting. In this workshop, we used A4 sized photos, photo cards, post-it with story, a large paper and the map.

This chapter's results were follows:

Using both photos with story and map made by photo cards to explain made us more understand the local environment and life. Moreover, it was possible to check the result of observation and make ideas have more reality and attractive when working in the place you can see those 2 tools, however, you need to get to used to how to use those tools.

Conclusions of This Chapter

1. In the phase of analysis, storyboarding with A4 photos and map of photo cards were the most effective to figure out the context of fieldwork.

2. Project members who didn't observe was able to understand more what the field looks like and how people live by sharing the result of fieldwork with having a story.

3. In the phase of ideation, it was effective to use business card sized photos and express member's idea with a big paper on the table for discussion.

5   Proposal

We created new kindergarten in a area of northeastern Japan, Tohoku where Tsunami hit on March 11 based on the process of observation and analysis from one of the practice example, "Tohoku kindergarten reconstruction project"

Fig. 8. Environment design of Wakaba Kodomo En

Title: "Wakaba Kodomo En"
Concept :
Children do gardening to create green in Yuriage area in Tohoku where broken down by disaster and there is only concrete all over the ground with elderly people together who lost everything and are living alone in temporary housing, thence this attitude keeps other disaster victim's spirit up and urge people to restore.

Branding
- Logo (Fig.9)

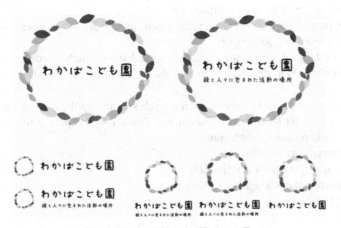

Fig. 9. Logo of Wakaba Kodomo En

We keep the picture of young leaf from previous logo that the principle of this kindergarten made and we combined an image that people hand in hand with each other with it.

- Color

We take care of matching between environment and color, moreover we put some bright color to express power of children.

Fig. 10. Customer Journey Map of Wakaba Kodomo En

System (Fig.10)

This kindergarten has 2 facilities, a main hall and a gardening space that build in the affected area.

- A main hall "Wakaba Kodomo En"

This building opens up for children in the daytime and for parents and local people to communicate at night. It aims at getting the disaster victims who separate to gather together also get along with people who absorb the victims.

- A gardening space "Yuriage no Midori En"

Place where people get together and create greens to activate the disaster area.

Activity of "Yuriage no Midori En"

It provides to do gardening with local people, to have a lunch to communicate with them and for children to discuss and to be a shelter for affected animals.

Online Service

This kindergarten put online service such as web site and application of tablet device into practice. It won't be lost by Tsunami and disaster by keeping a record of children's activity and newsletters on online.

Suggesting service were follows:

1. You can check your kid's activity at home
2. Teacher share today's kid aspect with tablet

6   Conclusions

In this paper, KH method was provided by 2 steps, Observation and Analysis with a culture centered view.

Summary of KH method were follows:
1. Starting observation at a place based on cultural trait is helping to step into the community easily.
2. Going on a field trip easily and rapidly can be provided by taking tons of picture of the local information with several observers which is you can get various of views at the place without any photo shoot skill.
3. It's important to start a field trip at a place based on cultural trait for observation and figuring out the result of observation with Storyboarding contextually at the phase of analysis. For this reason, it can be a culture-centered method.

In this study, we found the effectivity of this method as a germinating research.
    Moreover, taking account of this utility in a developing country actually is the subject of further study.

References

[1] Sato, I.: FieldWork, Revised edn. Shinyosha (2006)
[2] Terasawa, H., Taura, T., Nagai, Y.: Found Behavior-Interface Design Originated from Interactive Experience. In: Proceedings of the 52nd Annual Conference of JSSD (2005)
[3] Kushi, K.: Rapid-Ethnography for HCD Process Human Centered Design (HCD) (2011)
[4] Kato, F.: Camp theory: A new fieldwork. Keio University Press, Tokyo (2009)
[5] The project is to reconstruct a kindergarten in Natori-shi, Miyagi which broken down by 3.11 Tohoku earthquake and tsunami from the aspect of environment design and communication design
[6] Hofstede, G.: Cultures and Organizations: Software of the Mind. Yuhikaku (1995)
[7] Beyer, H., Holtzblatt, K.: Contextual Design: Defining Customer-Centered Systems (Interactive Technologies). Morgan Kaufmann (1997)
[8] Quesenbery, W., Szuc, D.: Global UX: Design and Research in a Connected World. Morgan Kaufmann (2011)

Lessons Learned from Projects in Japan and Korea Relevant for Intercultural HCI Development

Martin Blankl[1], Peter Biersack[2], and Rüdiger Heimgärtner[3]

[1] M-Sys GmbH
Isarberg 4, 94522 Wallersdorf, Germany
mb@msys-gmbh.de
[2] Maschinenfabrik Rheinhausen GmbH
Falkensteinstraße 8, 93059 Regensburg, Germany
p.biersack@reinhausen.com
[3] Intercultural User Interface Consulting (IUIC)
Lindenstraße 9, 93152 Undorf, Germany
ruediger.heimgaertner@iuic.de

Abstract. This paper describes pitfalls experienced during intercultural human-machine interaction (HMI) development projects in Japan and Korea and how they can be explained from a scientific point of view with the goal of deriving recommendations to avoid them in future intercultural human-computer interaction (HCI) development projects.

Keywords: Cultural differences, culture, communication, understanding, empathy, intercultural communication, intercultural, design, HCI, HMI, intercultural HCI design, intercultural HMI design, lessons learned, Japan, Korea, design/evaluation for cross-cultural users, globalization, localization, management, processes, software, project.

1 Motivation and Objective

Several levels of intercultural know-how contribute to successful intercultural human-computer interaction (HCI) design (cf. [1]). The communication level represents the basis, followed by the levels of project management, software and usability engineering and HCI design itself on the way to successful intercultural HCI design. Hence, on all levels, intercultural communication skills at the basic level can contribute to solve the problems raised on the higher levels by cultural differences. For successful (intercultural) usability engineering, an adequate engineering process is necessary to ensure good usability (i.e. when the user understands the developer's device and is thus able and content to operate it with ease). It is necessary that the developer understands the user ([2], [3]). At least the following aspects of the user must be analyzed in detail before the product can be developed:

- World view, Weltanschauung (metaphysical approach) of the end-user,
- General knowledge (procedural and factual knowledge) of the end-user,

A. Marcus (Ed.): DUXU/HCII 2013, Part II, LNCS 8013, pp. 20–27, 2013.
© Springer-Verlag Berlin Heidelberg 2013

- The context in which the product will be used by the end-user,
- The tasks the end-user intends to accomplish by using the product.

Only by considering these aspects, intercultural communication can be successful, which is as an essential prerequisite for intercultural usability engineering and user interface design, which in turn can therefore lead to successful international product design and user experience. This presupposes the capability to distance oneself from other persons and exploit the chance to recognize the differences to them and then to put oneself in their position. Within the intercultural context this requires being aware of one's own cultural standards before it is possible to compare and recognize differences to other cultures ([4]).

This paper describes pitfalls experienced during projects in Japan and Korea and how they can be explained from a scientific point of view. Finally, the lessons learned are presented to take the wind out of the sails of those detractors challenging the successful accomplishment of future human-machine interaction (HMI) development projects.

2   Projects and Cultural Background

2.1   Experiences during Two Projects

The first project example concerns the development of driver navigation systems for the Asian market, i.e. the experiences come directly from intercultural human-machine interaction (HMI) projects. Car manufacturers are in a global market where they demand a worldwide infotainment solution from one supplier (cf. [5]). However, European navigation systems do not work in countries like Japan or Korea because structure of a street address is completely different (cf. [6]). For example, in Japan, there are seven layers for a street address in opposition to a European one where you can locate any address using the country, town/city, street and house number. In Japan the house numbers are not registered in a row, but sequentially according to their building date. This makes orientation difficult even for natives. Therefore, navigation addresses are often entered by phone number and an algorithm must match the number to the relevant address and retrieves the related data from a huge database. Furthermore, traffic messages are also handled in a different way, which is only available for the members of the particular association. All these differences made the "worldwide" solution of a navigation system become very adventuresome.

The second project example comes from a German company which is active in the area of energy technology in Japan. It's core business is the regulation of power transformers by so-called on-load tap-changers, which adapt the transmission ratio of the primary to secondary windings to changing load ratios and, together with additional, innovative products and services, ensure an interruption-free power supply. The Japanese market is not easy to enter because of different reasons. One of them is cultural hurdles which often aggravate and delay projects. Japan has the image of being a "premium market". Therefore Japanese customers are prepared to pay for "premium" products, quality and services. In addition, in East Asia, Japan plays the role of a technology leader in the view of many other Asian countries.

Therefore the effort to enter this market is very worthwhile. Once you are accepted in Japan, the business in other Asian countries will also benefit from Japan's image: It is well known in Asia that Japan in general has very high requirements in terms of quality and security. What is accepted in Japan will in many cases also be accepted in other Asian countries (cf. [7]).

2.2   Cultural Background

Standards

While in 192 countries in the world the IEC (International Electro Technical Commission) standard is accepted, the Japanese insist on having their own JEC (Japanese Electrical Committee) standard for testing and approving products in the energy industry (cf. [8]). Even though the German manufacturer's in-house rules for product validation are much tougher than the requirements of IEC or JEC, and even though the Japanese are also members in the IEC, the tests must be done and accurately documented exactly according to what the JEC standard says.

Trust

To build trust is essential in Japan in order to improve business performance (cf. [9] and [10]). For this purpose you need many meetings to present and explain quality assurance and supplier evaluation systems. Also a deep understanding of the product is requested by the Japanese OEMs and end-users. Sometimes their curiosity comes close to compromising corporate secrets. Visits in the German manufacturer's work shop are serious for Japanese delegations. They are also very helpful for building trust. "To see is to believe", as one of the Japanese visitors used to say.

Quality View

Approval tests, witnessed by end-users, are required to document the quality and to prove that the specifications are fulfilled. This is also an important requirement of the end-users in the Japanese energy business. Although a complete type test according to the JEC standard cannot be witnessed, to see parts of such a test, to be eye witness and to see the results of that partial test is decisive.

3   Identified Intercultural Challenges during the Projects

The projects confronted not only technical challenges, but also collaboration challenges. The easiest headache to solve was with the display language and could be solved by technical translators. But this could not solve the intricacies of communication. Therefore, sensitiveness is required.

3.1   Formalized Communication in Japan

The technical project leader from Germany got into deep technical discussions with a senior expert from the Japanese company. Since the Japanese expert was several years older, the acceptance of the young German project leader's position was rejected. Obvious problems could not be discussed directly, but the traditional formal path of data exchange had to be followed.

3.2   Interactive Learning in Japan

The Japanese Partner Company had to be taught the new technologies. During the lessons the teacher asked several times, if everything were understood. All these questions had been answered with "Yes". After dedicated inquires it came out that the lessons where not understood. The German teacher changed his strategy and let the participants make exercises at the desk. But this was not accepted by all participants. About 20 % felt blamed and did not accept the exercises. They simply "disappeared" the next day. The remaining participants appreciated it more and more and had fun with the lessons.

3.3   Concept of Quality in Korea

The Korean supplier had another concept of quality. A reset (boot procedure triggered by watchdog) or misbehavior (functional errors) was not a big problem. But for a German car manufacturer, this could not be tolerated. This concept had to be transferred to the Korean supplier.

3.4   Dynamic Korea

The Korean supplier had a very pragmatic working style. When hardware parameters did not match the expectations, they changed components on short notice – also without considering EMC aspects. After intense examination, the changes have been accepted.

3.5   Font Problem in Japan

Since the Asian branches were not considered from the very beginning, several subsequent adaptations were necessary. A big problem was the font, since the specialist for the primary unit was no longer available. Therefore, all the font determinations had to be re-investigated. Afterwards, unplanned effort became necessary for checking the text length and adaption of the layout.

3.6   Asian Look and Feel vs. German Objectiveness

For German understanding, Asian navigation systems have too many unnecessary features. For example, the "carsor" (symbol of one's own car on the map) in Germany is only an arrow. In Asia, you can choose between dozens of different car bitmaps. Therefore, the German car manufacturer demanded an adaptation of the user interface to the conservative German style.

3.7 Higher Efforts and Investment for Testing Specific to Japan

Performing the type test for on-load tap-changers according to JEC is an "absolute necessity", even though the technical requirements for this test are far below the German manufacturer's in-house requirements for testing. And to perform the test it is not enough to understand the document issued by the JEC just linguistically. The intricacies in semantics and the relevance for action can only be uncovered with the help of Japanese supporters, coming from this business and knowing the technology in detail.

To plan and to perform the tests requires great efforts and appreciable investments. Many people were involved and the resources in the manufacturer's test centre were blocked for months by occupying engineers as well as test stands and test and measurement equipment as the JEC tests need painstaking preparation by engineers and the pure testing time for completing all the required mechanical and electrical tests summed up easily to half a year.

3.8 Isolation of Manufacturer from End-Customer

In many countries worldwide it is quite normal that the service and maintenance of tap-changers is done by the manufacturer. This has the advantage that the experience of thousands of service jobs is bundled and the end-customer profits from this experience. In Japan the transformer maker feels responsible for the complete transformer, including the tap-changer which is supplied from Germany. He is the only one who does the maintenance, for the transformer and for the tap-changer as well, and this is what the end-user actually expects.

What for the Japanese is a traditional way of customer relationship appears as being held off from the end-customer for the German manufacturer. It may not be done intentionally, but in fact and as a result it is protecting the market from Foreign Service providers.

4   Possible Explanations Drawn from Culture Studies and Derived Lessons Learned for Intercultural Projects

Ad 3.1: Japanese culture is well defined and organized. Honor is strongly respected. Everything has to follow a certain rule. Lessons Learned: Accept the cultural characteristics of the cooperation partners and try to follow their rules.

Ad 3.2: The Japanese school system is basically *ex cathedra* teaching. Therefore, interactive learning is not trained. Lessons Learned: Accept the cultural characteristics of the cooperation partners and try to follow their rules. Furthermore, also take dependent thinking into account because of the resultant high uncertainty avoidance (cf. [11]).

Ad 3.3 and 3.4: For the Korean, time to market is the most important aspect in order to be the first with highest market share. Therefore, they do accept minor errors in the product, when overall improvement results and the product find customers. Besides, also the customers are more tolerant of failures. Lessons Learned: In the case of insisting on one's own guidelines explain carefully why you are insisting on them.

Ad 3.5: Under project pressure, documentation and knowledge management is always neglected. Lessons Learned: Plan a buffer for completing the work.

Ad 3.6: This is a mentality difference. Lessons Learned: Also consider seemingly minor aspects in the project planning.

Ad 3.7 and 3.8: There is a consensus between all of the 10 Japanese Electrical Power Companies and the ca. 14 Japanese transformer manufacturers about how to approve the quality of tap-changers and it deviates from the rest of the world. t The Japanese market thereby has been protected for decades. A kind of "comfortable" win-win-situation for both sides has existed for a long time: for the transformer manufacturers, who could charge relatively high prices, but also for the end-users, the power companies. They undoubtedly got good service and could retrieve the high costs for it from their customers. This refinancing was supported by the very special Japanese system in the energy market. It allows the energy companies to charge all costs to their customers, plus a defined margin (cf. [12]). These structures seem to be softening. A forceful change of mind is evident, especially after the Fukushima disaster with its enormous costs for repairing or replacing damaged transformers and for compensation payments to the victims, as well as for gigantic energy imports while nuclear power plants are down. The government, holding high shares in energy companies, advised them to open the tenders and to also consider foreign, economically priced suppliers, as long as the quality meets the requirements.

Lessons Learned: There are basic requirements to fulfill. If a supplier does not accept that or wants to discuss the sense or nonsense of Japanese rules, he will not be successful. The specifications must be fulfilled and the tests must be performed. Not always because they make sense, but because they are written in the specification and the specification is the "bible", the common understanding of all involved (Japanese) parties. Market entry in Japan is longsome. It requires patience, strain and may not to be shy of investment. The yield of these efforts is loyal partners, many small feelings of success and many new adorable friends for the involved members of the German project teams.

In addition, it is essential to establish relations, not only to the OEM, but also to the end-users. It is not easy to bring decision makers to the German factory, but once they are there, they might be convinced that even non-Japanese companies have high quality standards, high manufacturing and assembling skills, highly skilled staff. Once the end-user is convinced he will ask his Japanese supplier to make the German product available for him. And there is one thing that can help and open the door: German culture and traditions, as well as German and especially Bavarian food and beer are very popular among the Japanese. And therefore Japanese people at least like to see Germany. German companies can use this affinity for inviting decision makers.

5   Recommendations for Intercultural HCI Development

5.1   Pay Attention to the Implications of Cultural Differences in the HCI Design Process

Analyze the cultural characteristics of the desired target groups and take them into account in intercultural HCI development. Take into account cultural differences in thinking from developers, manufacturers, producers, designers, users and customers. Plan enough buffer time to manage the additional effort caused by integrating teams from different cultures. Determine very exactly the user and customer requirements and accept them. Get into contact and establish good relationships before starting with the project. Ensure that you are familiar with the characteristics of the desired cultures and establish empathic communication.

5.2   Consider the Additional Effort for Adapting Technologies to Different Cultures

The integrated system must be adapted to the look and feel of the car manufacturer and the system's environment (e.g. a "head unit", which steers several sub devices) must be adapted to the Asian requirements. The information provided by the sub devices should be displayed by the "framing" head unit on the same touch screen display. Furthermore, a remote control should be used to operate the integrated box. The final solution is a "hybridized" infotainment system. The navigation and communication part can be provided by a local supplier integrated as separate hardware within the standard infotainment system. The entertainment part, the car interfaces and the touch screen for the user interface can be delivered by the "worldwide" Tier-1 supplier.

6   Conclusions

International projects are challenging. But in total, it is great fun and the experience lets a person grow mentally. When respecting each other, success is possible. And international friendships arise. From the analysis of the lessons learned during intercultural projects in Japan and Korea useful recommendations for the intercultural HCI development process as well as for the adaptation of technologies to the relevant cultures can be drawn. Nevertheless, this paper just touches on a tiny part of the problem and with it only a few aspects on its surface. Therefore, future research is necessary to study the issues in detail and to integrate them into the overall intercultural HCI development process.

References

1. Heimgärtner, R., Tiede, L.-W., Windl, H.: Empathy as Key Factor for Successful Intercultural HCI Design. In: Marcus, A. (ed.) HCII 2011 and DUXU 2011, Part II. LNCS, vol. 6770, pp. 557–566. Springer, Heidelberg (2011)

2. Honold, P.: Culture and Context: An Empirical Study for the Development of a Framework for the Elicitation of Cultural Influence in Product Usage. International Journal of Human-Computer Interaction 12, 327–345 (2000)
3. Nielsen, J.: Usability engineering. Kaufmann, Amsterdam (2006)
4. Thomas, A., Kinast, E.-U., Schroll-Machl, S.: Handbook of intercultural communication and cooperation. Basics and areas of application. Vandenhoeck & Ruprecht, Göttingen (2010)
5. Heimgärtner, R.: Research in Progress: Towards Cross-Cultural Adaptive Human-Machine-Interaction in Automotive Navigation Systems. In: Day, D., del Galdo, E.M. (eds.) Proceedings of the Seventh International Workshop on Internationalisation of Products and Systems (IWIPS 2005), pp. 97–111. Grafisch Centrum Amsterdam, The Netherlands (2005b)
6. Dr. International: Developing International Software (2003)
7. Lippert, S.S., Marcus: Premiummarkt Japan? Preisstrategie und Profitabilität deutscher Unternehmen in Japan. Nexxus Communications K.K. (2008)
8. Japanese Electrotechnical Committee (JEC), http://www.spsp.gov.cn/DataCenter/Standard/PDFView.aspx?ca=AeFU7jn6zeY= (last access March 03, 2013)
9. Matsumoto, D., Hwang, H., Yamada, H.: Cultural Differences in the Relative Contributions of Face and Context to Judgments of Emotions. Journal of Cross-Cultural Psychology 43, 198–218 (2012)
10. Sako, M.: Does Trust Improve Business Performance? In: Kramer, R.M. (ed.) Organizational Trust: A Reader, pp. 88–117. Oxford University Press (1998)
11. Hofstede, G.H., Hofstede, G.J., Minkov, M.: Cultures and organizations: software of the mind. McGraw-Hill, Maidenhead (2010)
12. Onishi, N.F., Martin: A frustrated push to break grip of Japanese utilities. International Herald Tribune (2011)

Usability Evaluation of Two Chinese Segmentation Methods in Subtitles to Scaffold Chinese Novice

Chih-Kai Chang

Department of Information and Learning Technology
National University of Tainan, Taiwan
chihkai@mail.nutn.edu.tw

Abstract. Recently the number of people who learn Chinese as a Foreign Language (CFL) increased. New comers, international students, and denizened spouses all need to improve their Chinese reading fluency and listening comprehension for daily communication and work requirements. However, not everyone gets opportunity for formal education in a language school. Thus, informal learning is very important for CFL learners in Taiwan. For novice Chinese learners, they should first master a skill to grouping Chinese words into meaningful chunks, i.e. Chinese segmentation. For instance, "老師對教育的貢獻" (teachers' contribution in education). After Chinese word segmentation, the sentence becomes "老師 (teachers)/ 對 (P)/ 教育 (education)/ 的 (DE)/ 貢獻 (contribution)" from "老/師/對/教/育/的/貢/獻". Consequently, this study used two Chinese segmentation methods to highlight meaningful and important word chunks in subtitles of Chinese videos and evaluate its usability for CFL learners. The first method adopted the top 800 and 1600 high-frequency words from an analysis report based on Academia Sinica Balanced Corpus of Modern Chinese to identify proper word segmentation in video subtitles and analyze its performance based on the forward maximum matching method. The statistical results show that most Chinese subtitles still remain unsegmented (62.3%) which means the Chinese subtitles in the videos are not appropriately segmented based on the corpus that contains the top 800 high frequency words. However, with the integration of the top 1600 high frequency words in the corpus, approximately 60% of the subtitles in each video are effectively segmented, and numerous unknown words still remain. Active phrases, idioms, and short phrases in Chinese subtitles may lead to the difficulty in word segmentation; moreover, the usability testing result of using high frequency words to conduct word segmentation is not significant.

The second method used natural language processing technique to split Chinese subtitles into its separate morphemes. The study adopted CKIP Chinese parser, which is a word segmentation tool for Chinese, to split subtitles according their part-of-speech tagging (i.e. grammatical tagging). The statistical results show that 97.26% subtitles are split, but the usability testing shows that subjective satisfaction is not good enough. To further investigation, we asked subjects to identify the "improper" word segmentation. For instance, the subtitle "接受治療很久了" (treated for a long time) will be split into "接受/治療/很/久/了", but most novices think that the proper segmentation should be "接受/治療/很久了". The "improper" rate is about 22.30% on average. In other words, the

A. Marcus (Ed.): DUXU/HCII 2013, Part II, LNCS 8013, pp. 28–37, 2013.

segmentation results from Chinese parser based on natural language processing technique are not best scaffolding for Chinese novice while watching videos with Chinese subtitles. The preliminary results of usability testing show that the second method can provide effective scaffolding for novice, but the granularity of chunked words may be too fine to read fluently sometimes (i.e. less than thirty percentage in results). Consequently, adaptation mechanism is required for learners to achieve the balance point of provided scaffolding between aforementioned two methods. For example, the Chinese function words, such as 很 and 了, serve only grammatical functions (i.e. they have no meaning by themselves). Those function words should not be separated out from subtitles for learning purpose. Further work is necessary to find out the proper granularity for chunking words, design adaptation mechanism of segmentation, and prevent segmentation errors in new or unknown words.

Keywords: Chinese as a foreign language, Chinese segmentation, subtitle manipulation, natural language processing, computer-assisted language learning.

1   Research Background

The study aims to design and develop a system for people who learn Chinese as a foreign language (CFL learners). In recent years, the rapid economic development in the Chinese region brings the worldwide craze of learning Chinese becoming the second international language after English. In addition to the formal education, learning Chinese is not limited to regular educational settings and textbooks. Many scholars pointed out that the development of technology makes the way of learning a second language or foreign languages become more diverse. The integration of technology in teaching Chinese internationally and the application of multimedia in language learning are booming. Currently, learning from watching videos is a popular trend; subtitles of the videos can effectively benefit second language learners' reading, vocabulary, and listening comprehension [1, 2, 3]. Researches indicated that the integration of subtitles in audiovisual teaching materials has been verified as an effective teaching strategy to promote listening and reading comprehension of a second language [4, 5, 6, 7]. Subtitles can aid learners to visualize messages of what they hear, especially for people whose language ability is unable to comprehend those messages; subtitles can increase learners' language comprehension ability. Moreover, subtitles can assist language learning because audio and visual messages of the brain can be transformed into a message map which is also a process of language learning [8]. Since 1980, subtitles have been considered a tool to enhance concentration, reduce anxiety, increase motivation, and help learners to instantly confirm messages of what they hear [9, 10, 11, 12]. Therefore, many studies verified that whether watching videos with subtitles can benefit learners more than those without subtitles [13, 14, 15, 16]; the results showed that learners who watched videos with subtitles performed better than those who didn't on the comprehension test at the time. With the features of the rapid spread of the network and the convenience of the subtitle software, many universities combine traditional language teaching methods with online resources in the U.S. [17, 18, 19, 20]. Therefore, learners can learn vocabulary and syntax under a natural and relaxed environment to lower cultural shock, reduce learners' psychological panic and anxiety, and minimize the feelings of rejection by integrating features of multimedia [21]. Chinese language and videos with subtitles respectively have great potential for development; it is anticipated that combining those two elements together will have the synergistic effect of increasing the pleasure, motivation and learning ability of the learners.

With different cultures and language proficiency levels, learners may have difficulty to understand the contents of movies and learn a language. The basic semantic unit of movie subtitles, machine translation, full-text search index, and sentence comprehension is a word which plays an important role in understanding of words and reading comprehension for learners. However, Chinese sentences are sequences of words delimited by white spaces; in Chinese text, sentences are represented as strings of Chinese characters without similar natural delimiters. Learners must possess the word segmentation ability to identify the sequence of words in a sentence and mark boundaries in appropriate places. Word segmentation is to divide a string of written sentences into component words so that readers can accurately understand its meaning. For instance, "老師對教育的貢獻"(teachers' contribution in education). After Chinese word segmentation, the sentence becomes " 老 師 (teachers)/ 對 (P)/ 教 育 (education)/的(DE)/貢獻(contribution)" from "老/師/對/教/育/的/貢/獻" (Fang, 2008). "Word ambiguity" and "unknown word" are two major segmentation problems that affect the accuracy of Chinese word segmentation performance. The first problem is associated with typical ambiguity problems that may lead to unexpected segmentation results [22]. For example, the sentence, "下雨天留客天留我不留", has several explanations because of the different ways of word segmentations. Therefore, word segmentation becomes the first task when processing Chinese text. The text of the Chinese corpus has been segmented, and words are separated by white spaces which can enhance and increase learners' ability to identify words and help learners to combine those words after understanding their meanings to solve the inability of recognizing words.

The study uses the maximum matching algorithm and the top 800 and 1600 high-frequency words from the Academia Sinica Balanced Corpus of Modern Chinese to segment Chinese subtitles in videos so that learners can understand the meaning of Chinese subtitles and learn Chinese language [23]. The Maximum Matching (MM) algorithm, a most commonly used dictionary-based approach, is used to initially segment the text by referring to a pre-compiled dictionary. The algorithm starts at the first character in a sentence and attempts to find the longest matching word in the text starting with that character. If a word is found, the maximum-matching algorithm marks a boundary at the end of the longest matching word, then, begins the same longest match search starting at the character following the match. If no match is found in the text, the MM algorithm simply skips that character and begins the search starting at the next character to obtain an initial segmentation. The accuracy of the MM algorithm is expected to be more than 90%. The forward maximum matching method starts with the beginning of the sentence which is from left to right, attempting to find the longest matching word in the given sentence and then repeating the process until it reaches the end of the sentence. The backward maximum matching approach starts with the end of the sentence, finding the longest matching word in the database and repeating the process until it reaches the beginning of the sentence (See Table 1). Since the MM algorithm segments words based on a pre-compiled dictionary, it is unable to deal with unknown words, not listed in the dictionary. For example, "亞洲巨星五月天" (Asian superstar Mayday) is segmented as "亞洲(Asia)/巨星(superstar)/五(five)/月(month)/天(day)" (See Table 1).

Table 1. Forward and backward maximum matching examples

Example	Forward MM	Backward MM
才能夠完成	才能/夠/完成	才/能夠/完成
家庭和諧	家庭/和諧	家庭/和諧
亞洲巨星五月天	亞洲/巨星/五月/天	亞洲/巨星/五/月/天

The completeness of the dictionary to a large extent determines the degree of success for segmenting words using this approach. Therefore, learners can easily understand the contents of the videos when the Chinese subtitles have appropriate word segmentations so that their learning effectiveness of Chinese language can be increased.

2   Research Method

2.1   The System Design

The study uses a programming language, Python, to develop a word segmentation system to segment Chinese subtitles according to the corpus that contains the top 800 and 1600 high frequency words so that learners can understand the contents of Chinese videos and learn Chinese language. Figure 1 displays the framework of the system. The system functions are to select subtitles, segment words, select high frequency words, display segmented subtitles, collect and analyze data. The users (CFL learners) learn Chinese as a foreign language. They can select Chinese subtitles from the given videos for word segmentation, and the system displays the segmented subtitles so that they can easily comprehend the contents of the videos and increase their motivation to learn Chinese.

The study randomly selected two videos with Chinese subtitles that introduce Taiwan as samples from a university's library. The CFL learners can select one of the two provided videos with the SRT subtitle format. The study adopts the top 800 and 1600 high frequency words from the "Word List with Accumulated Word Frequency in Sinica Corpus" from Institute of Linguistics of Academia Sinica to develop a corpus for Chinese word segmentation [24, 25]. The SRT subtitle format mainly consists of three parts, serial numbers, timelines, and texts of the subtitles. The function of "select subtitles" can extract serial numbers and timelines and then process the

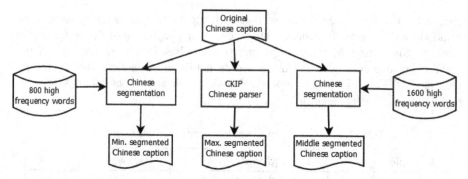

Fig. 1. The flowchart of the process to generate adaptive Chinese captions

remaining strings of subtitles. Subtitles within each timeline may have multiple lines of texts required to separate them into multiple strings of subtitles for further word segmentation in each subtitle file. The study adopts the forward maximum matching method to carry out word segmentation of subtitles in Chinese videos. The algorithm starts from the a given point in the sentence, finding the longest string of words that matches a word entry in a corpus and then repeating the process until it reaches the end of the subtitles. For example, if a string of words is "相當重要的生態資源" (a very important ecological resource), the system matches it with the longest word entry in the corpus. If the system cannot find a match, the system repeats the process until it finds the string of words, "相當", in the corpus. Then, the system removes it, "相當", from the original sentence and starts to match the remaining string of words, "重要的生態資源", with the word entries in the corpus until the end. The anticipated result is "相當/重要/的/生態/資源". The corpus for Chinese word segmentation is developed based on the "Word List with Accumulated Word Frequency in Sinica Corpus" from Institute of Linguistics of Academia Sinica. The word lists of the corpus allows users to search for the word frequency ranking, the frequency by words, the words by frequency, and the cumulative frequency; the searching results display information with regard to the high frequency words, their rankings, frequencies, percentages, and cumulative percentage (See Table 2).

Table 2. Example of modern Chinese word frequency ranking from 792 to 800

Rank	Word	Frequency	Percent	Cumulation
792	教師(Na)	748	0.015	56.482
792	要(VE)	748	0.015	56.498
792	否則(Cbb)	748	0.015	56.513
795	重視(VJ)	747	0.015	56.528
795	工具(Na)	747	0.015	56.543
797	實施(VC)	746	0.015	56.559
798	臉(Na)	745	0.015	56.574
798	節目(Na)	745	0.015	56.589
798	法(Na)	745	0.015	56.605

The study adopts the Chinese Natural Language Statistical Toolkit (CNLSTK), a natural language processing search tool for character-based texts, to calculate word frequency. The CNLSTK tags texts and develops a corpus for supporting researches on Chinese language. The corpus is a research resource used for processing natural Chinese language and providing tools for retrieving, mining, and analyzing. In comparison with the Natural Language Toolkit (NLTK), the CNLSTK mainly focuses on statistical functions and places less emphasis on semantics, pronunciation, and part of speech correction. The CNLSTK currently supports UTF-16 encoding; other encodings should be converted to UTF-16. Before manipulating the system, users need to create a folder for saving one or multiple files or folders for saving multiple files. Then, users create indexes (建立索引|標籤) for retrieving information. The current search functions of the toolkit are to search for string frequency, to list all files' names, to get the frequency distribution of the given string in files, to retrieve the full text by file names, to retrieve the backward sequence of full text by file names, to get a concordance of strings, to get a backward concordance of strings, to narrow concordance down of the given files, to narrow down backward concordance results, to search for previous or next characters, to get statistical information of previous or next characters, and to have the distribution of two strings in all files. The study uses the CNLSTK to process the corpus that contains the top 800 and 1600 high frequency words to match words of the subtitles in the videos. If the words of the corpus don't match the words of the subtitles at all, those words are removed from the corpus. Therefore, the words of the subtitles match those in the corpus at least once or more times. The remaining words in the corpus are less than the original quantity of the words that may increase the speed of segmenting the subtitles. In addition, the toolkit provides information of the frequency, concordance, location, and distribution of the words showed in the subtitles that help CFL learners to understand semantics of Chinese language and apply those words in making sentences.

3   Results

3.1   Results of Chinese Word Segmentation

The average length of the sample videos is 90 minutes, and the standard deviation is 0. The number of the average segmented sentences in each video is 255.5, and the standard deviation is 145.66. The total number of the average words in the subtitles of the each video is 5786, and the standard deviation is 760.85. The randomly selected two videos that introduce Taiwan are intellectual videos which contain professional terminology used in subtitles that result in unknown words after Chinese word segmentation. The subtitles of the two videos are segmented according to the corpus that contains the top 800 high frequency words. The statistical results show that 37.7% of the subtitles in each video are segmented, and the standard deviation is 0.04; the average percentage of the unchanged sentences in each video is 62.3%, and the standard deviation is 0.04. The results indicate that using the top 800 high frequency words to conduct the word segmentation is not effective and significant.

Further, the subtitles of the two videos are segmented based on the corpus that contains the top 1600 high frequency words. The statistical results show that 61.55% of the subtitles are segmented in each video, and the standard deviation is 0.09;

the percentage of the unchanged sentences is 38.45%, and the standard deviation is 0.09; the average percentage of the segmented sentences is 61.55% which indicates that 60% of the subtitles can be effectively segmented, and one of the video has 67.58% of the segmented subtitles. In comparison with the top 800 high frequency words, the accuracy of the segmented subtitles of the two videos increase after using the top 1600 high frequency words to conduct word segmentation. The intellectual videos contain professional terminology that results in numerous unknown words. Moreover, active phrases, idioms, and short phrases in Chinese subtitles may lead to the difficulty in word segmentation and the segmentation errors. Therefore, the study should expand the developed corpus to effectively conduct word segmentation.

3.2   Word Segmentation Results of the Subtitles in the Videos

The study found that the length of the segmented subtitles in the two videos displayed on the screen becomes longer than the original ones based on the corpus that contains the top 800 and 1600 high frequency words because of adding segmentation boundaries (See Figure 2 and 3). The statistical results show that the number of the unknown words is more than the number of the properly segmented words in the subtitles which cannot enhance and increase learners' ability to recognize and identify the words because intellectual videos contains numerous professional terminology used in subtitles.

Fig. 2. The original subtitle (see left) and the segmented subtitle based on the corpus that contains the 800 high frequency words (see right)

Fig. 3. The subtitle (see right) based on the corpus that contains the 1600 high frequency words and the subtitle (see right) segmented by CKIP

3.3   Ambiguity Analysis

Mostly word segmentation is referred to the corpus which may not contain all the words so that the segmentation result may not be correct and cause ambiguity problems that usually happen to an unsegmented string of words which can be segmented into different ways based on the semantic structure of an article. For example, the string of words, "我們可以感受到樹幹裏流動的樹液", are segmented as "我們/可以/感/受到/樹幹裏流動的樹液" referred to the corpus. However, the composition ambiguity leads to the misinterpretation of the text; the correct word segmentation is "我們/可以/感受/到/樹幹裏流動的樹液".

4   Conclusion and Implication

The study adopts the forward maximum matching approach to conduct Chinese word segmentation. The system cannot accurately conduct Chinese subtitle segmentation and is unable to precisely identify and recognize Chinese subtitles. The statistical results show that most Chinese subtitles still remain unsegmented (62.3%) which means the Chinese subtitles in the videos are not appropriately segmented based on the corpus that contains the top 800 high frequency words. However, with the integration of the top 1600 high frequency words in the corpus, approximately 60% of the subtitles in each video are effectively segmented, and numerous unknown words still remain. Active phrases, idioms, and short phrases in Chinese subtitles may lead to the difficulty in word segmentation; moreover, the result of using high frequency words to conduct word segmentation is not significant.

It is anticipated to integrate other word segmentation models or algorithms to increase the accuracy rate of the word segmentation; it is worthy to expand the corpus to improve the word segmentation rate. Moreover, combining both forward and backward maximum matching methods is an alternative to discover the segmentation ambiguity and increase learning effectiveness.

The future study will integrate the top 3500 high frequency words in the corpus to increase the accuracy rate of the word segmentation and improve the word segmentation rate. Moreover, the corpus can be expanded by adding specialized terms to reduce the unknown word recognition, increase the rate of indentifying terminology, and enhance the proportion of word segmentation so that CFL learners can easily understand the contents of the videos and learn Chinese. The word segmentation of the current system may yield ambiguity errors that result in misplacement of segmentation boundaries in the subtitles. Therefore, it is necessary to integrate other word segmentation systems in the study to eliminate segmentation ambiguities.

Acknowledgement. The research reported in this paper has been supported by the National Science Council in Taiwan under the research project number NSC 100-2631-S-001-001, NSC 100-2628-S-024-001-MY3, and NSC 101-2511-S-024-007-MY2.

References

1. Chun, D.M., Plass, J.L.: Research on text comprehension in multimedia environments. Language Learning & Technology 1(1), 1–35 (1997)
2. Plass, J.L., Chun, D.M., Mayer, R.E., Leutner, D.: Supporting visual and verbal learning preferences in a second language multimedia learning environment. Journal of Educational Psychology 90(1), 25–36 (1998)
3. Danan, M.: Reversed subtitling and dual coding theory: New directions for foreign language instruction. Language Learning 42(4), 497–527 (1992)
4. Borras, I., Lafayette, R.: Effects of multimedia courseware subtitling on the speaking performance of college students of French. The Modern Language Journal 78(1), 61–75 (1994)
5. Danan, M.: Captioning and subtitling: Undervalued language learning strategies. Meta 49(1), 67–77 (2004)
6. Garza, T.J.: Evaluating the use of captioned video materials in advanced foreign language learning. Foreign Language Annals 24(3), 239–258 (1991)
7. Markham, P.L., Peter, L.: The influence of English language and Spanish language captions on foreign language listening/reading comprehension. Journal of Educational Technology Systems 31(3), 331–341 (2003)
8. Doughty, C.J.: Effect of instruction on learning a second language: A critique of instructed SLA research. In: VanPatten, B., Williams, J., Rott, S. (eds.) Form-Meaning Connections in Second Language Acquisition, pp. 181–202. Lawrence Erlbaum Associates, Mahwah (2004)
9. Burger, G.: Are TV programs with video subtitles suitable for teaching listening comprehension? Zielsprache Deutsch 20(4), 10–13 (1989)
10. Froehlich, J.: German videos with German subtitles: A new approach to listening comprehension development. Die Unterrichtspraxis/Teaching German 21(2), 199–203 (1988)
11. Grimmer, C.: Supertext English language subtitles: A boon for English language learners. EA Journal 10(1), 66–75 (1992)
12. Vanderplank, R.: The value of teletext sub-titles in language learning. English Language Teaching Journal 42(4), 272–281 (1988)
13. Baltova, I.: Multisensory language teaching in a multidimensional curriculum: The use of authentic bimodal video in core French. The Canadian Modern Language Review 56(1), 32–48 (1999)
14. Markham, P.L.: Captioned television videotapes: Effects of visual support on second language comprehension. Journal of Educational Technology Systems 21(3), 183–191 (1993)
15. Markham, P.L.: Captioned videotapes and second-language listening word recognition. Foreign Language Annals 32(3), 321–328 (1999)
16. Neuman, S.B., Koskinen, P.: Captioned television as comprehensible input: Effects of incidental word learning from context for language minority students. Reading Research Quarterly 27, 94–106 (1992)
17. Chenoweth, N.A., Murday, K.: Measuring student learning in an online French course. CALICO Journal 20(2), 285–314 (2003)
18. Chenoweth, N.A., Ushida, E., Murday, K.: Student learning in hybrid French and Spanish courses: An overview of Language Online. CALICO Journal 24(1), 285–314 (2006)
19. Sanders, R.F.: Redesigning introductory Spanish: Increased enrollment, online management, cost reduction, and effects on student learning. Foreign Language Annals 38(4), 523–532 (2005)

20. Scida, E.E., Saury, R.E.: Hybrid courses and their impact on student and classroom performance: A case study at the University of Virginia. CALICO Journal 23(3), 517–531 (2006)
21. Chen, L.F.: From file appreciation to the curriculum design and experiment of teaching Chinese. National Taiwan Normal Unversity Mandarin Training Center, Taipei (2007)
22. Fang, S.L.: Segmentation and pronunciation annotation in Mandarin Chinese. Master thesis. National Tsing Huan University, Taiwan (2008)
23. Tang, J.H.: A Chinese speech synthesis system improved by a word segmentation method. Master thesis. National Tsing Huan University, Taiwan (2010)
24. Cheng, C.C.: Word-focused extensive reading with guidance. In: Thirteenth International Symposium on English Teaching, pp. 24–32. Crane Publishing Co., Taipei (2004)
25. Cheng, C.C.: From Digital Archives to Digital Learning: Determining Sentence Readability. In: Bi-Jiaoda Conference on Corpus Linguistics and English Testing, Shanghai, June 13 (2005)

Young Egyptians Use of Social Networks
and the January 2011 Revolution

Ghada R. El Said

Future University in Egypt (FUE)
90th street, Fifth settlement, New Cairo
Ghada.refaat@fue.edu.eg,
Ghadarefaat_04@hotmail.com

Abstract. The 2011 Egyptian protests began on Tuesday 25 January in Tahrir, one of Cairo's biggest squares. On January 25 and 26, the Egyptian government blocked Twitter in Egypt and later Face book was blocked as well.[1] Most observers of the Egyptian scene at that time, claimed that the responsible governmental authorities did this, in an attempt to stop mobilization for anti-government protests.[2]

A report in March 2011[3] highlights a significant increase in the use of the Internet in Egypt in the wake of the January 25 protests. "*A large increase in the number of web surfers and users of social networking sites reported to change the pattern of use and the interests of the of the Internet contents*". According to the report, the number of Internet users in Egypt prior to January 25 was 21.2 million users, increased by almost 9% after this date to reach 23.1 million in two months. The time Egyptian users spent online was doubled from 900 to 1800 minutes per months after 25 January 2011. Still, Egypt's Internet penetration rate is less than 25%.

This paper investigates cultural issues in human computer interaction. The paper explores the specific experiences of young Egyptian Internet users and their interaction through social media during and after the Egyptian protest in 25 January 2011. The paper aims to reveal some the cultural characteristics of this user group in interacting with the Internet.

Keywords: Internet Social Network, User preference, Culture, language.

1 Introduction

In November/ December 2012, the author conducted series of interviews with 45 of young Egyptian Internet users about their experiences with the Internet in general and social media tools in specific. In Egypt, the youth represents 60% of the overall population, representing the highest majority of Internet users in the country, compared to other age groups. [3]

This paper goes beyond a particular channel to look more broadly at the social network tools use for a group of Egyptians Internet Users, namely during and after the Egyptian protest in 25 January 2011. The paper is examining in what circumstances,

A. Marcus (Ed.): DUXU/HCII 2013, Part II, LNCS 8013, pp. 38–43, 2013.

and why, this group uses social network tools in their computer-mediated communication. In the remainder of this paper, the author will first provide some background information on Internet use in Egypt, then introduce and discuss the study, and finally analyze the results.

1.1   Technology Context

It is important here to point a main factor framing this study which is the use of Internet in Egypt. The Internet was first introduced to Egypt in 1993, with a university network. Three years later, the business Internet use began in Egypt with government support through the Information Decision Support Cabinet (IDSC) government entity. Since its start, the Egyptian government placed great emphasis on the Information and Communication technologies (ICT), namely in terms if affordability, availability, and infrastructure and where Egypt is said to have one the fastest growing ICT markets in the world [4].

In 2010, the total number of Internet users in Egypt reached 21.2 million in a population of almost 87 million. This number of users increased by almost 9% after 25 January 2011 to reach 23.1 million in two months. The time Egyptian users spent online was doubled from 900 to 1800 minutes per months after 25 January 2011. Still, Egypt's Internet penetration rate is less than 25% [3]. On the other hand, those who are already connected represent the economic middle class and elite, so their influence extends far beyond their somewhat limited numbers, especially in major population centers such as Cairo and Alexandria, the second biggest city in Egypt.

With this context as a background, the exploratory study was conducted with a group of young Internet users in Egypt, namely in Cairo and Alexandria.

2   Method

The current research employs semi-structured interviews as an exploratory tool; Interviews are useful for acquiring a wide, yet detailed, picture of a respondent's beliefs about a particular phenomenon. The interviews aimed to find out what the Internet's social network is being used for and what problems, if any, the users experienced, while trying to link the findings with the 2011 Egyptian protests, knowing to be a Face Book revolution. As the Arabic society has been classified as an oral dominant society [5], therefore, the interview was preferred as an appropriate tool for exploratory data collection in this early stage of the research, enabling the researcher to diverge as appropriate from the prepared questions to explore the interesting points that came up. It is planned, on a later stage of the research, to conduct a survey to include more participants.

2.1   Participants

The study was carried out among 45 young learners and professionals in Cairo and Alexandria known to be Social Network Internet users. The participants in this study are of course not representative of the overall Egyptian population, but they do include among them sample of the protesters who participated in the Egyptian protest in 25 January 2011, known to be "An Egyptian Youth Revolution"[3].

The sample of the study was selected based on convenience sampling through personal contacts of the researcher. The participants were between the ages of 20 and 40 engaged in under-graduate or post-graduate education, and introductory or middle level professional and management positions. All of the participants in the sample uses both Arabic and English languages in online communication. The sample was fairly evenly balanced for gender, with 23young-men and 22 young-women, and teenager. A total of 25 of the people in the sample studied and worked in the information technology field. The remaining 20 studied and worked in a variety of fields such as literature, environmental, and business administration. All of the participants received or currently receiving their education in Egypt, with half of them are studying or studied in English Language.

2.2   Instrument

Series of semi-structured interview were conducted in different locations in Cairo and Alexandria, during the months of November/ December 2012. The interviews include one question acquiring demographic data (e.g., what is your field of education/ profession?), two general questions about social network tools use (e.g., what is your favorite social network tools, and for how long have you been using it before and after January 2011?), one question about language use online (e.g., what language(s) do you use in online "real-time" posting and chatting with Egyptians and other nationalities?), one question about topic discussed online (e.g., what topic(s) do you discuss online with Egyptians and other nationalities?), two questions about the perceived effect of social network tools in recent social and political changes in Egypt (e.g., do you think that social network tools contributed in any way in recent social and political changes in Egypt, and how?). The interview questions was first pilot tested among three individuals who were not in the in the final interviews, and then finalized and administrated with 45 participants.

The interviews were conducted face-to-face using semi-structured approach, that is, a set of interview questions were planned ahead of time, but the interviews diverged as appropriate to explore interesting points that came up. Each interview session lasted from 60 to 75 minutes and was tape recorded with the consent of the participants.

2.3   Data Analysis

The interviews were transcribed and analyzed through textual analysis and the written transcripts were examined by an individual judge, to identify patterns. Textual analysis involves coding participants' answers, and classifying words under main groups. The frequency of the answers helped to identify patterns and relationships and to distinguish differences and similarities within responses.

3   Results

The analysis of the interview data reveals some interesting findings about the way in which Egyptian users interact with the Internet's social network in general, and before and after January 2011 specifically.

The first general finding is that English is the language with which all interview's participants reported they interact online. This suggests a change in the language used on line for the Egyptians, contradicting with previous research, monitoring the Egyptians use of Internet over the last decade. In 1999, an early investigation of the adaption of Internet in Egypt suggested that language is one of the main barriers to the adoption of Internet in Egypt [6]. In 2001, another exploratory study recommended that Egyptians, in social communication online, use either Arabic or what is known as 'Romanized Arabic', here Latin characters are used to approximate Arabic words, in social Internet communication [7].

The second result is related to the change of Internet usage context and tools, for the target sample, before and after January 2011. The early investigational studies on online activities for Internet users in Egypt, conducted in the years 2000 and 2001 [6,7] reported that social communication and entertainment are the most popular use context of the Internet in Egypt. It seems that this was the case until early 2011!

The highest majority (90%) of the interviews' participants in the current study reported that before January 2011, they mainly used Face book for social communications with friends. After the Egyptian revolution in January 2011, and with the political fast changes happening in the country to date, they became Political News Seekers on Twitter and U-Tube. While the highest majority of the interviews' participants reported that they on daily basis seek political opinions and explanations from Egyptians political faces twits; they also cited that they regularly watch political talk-shows on U-Tube. ".....I use to use Face book for chat with friends before the revolution. Now me and most of my friends, we are daily users of Twitter and U-Tube, as it is faster, we seek political opinions and explanation from political leaders we trust, either by following politicians on Twitter, or by watching political talk-shows on U-Tube...." as expressed one of the interviewees. "The revolutions is still ongoing, things move fast in Egypt, many events are not comprehensive to youth like us.... we continuously seek explanation of what is happening from political faces who are now all on Twitter", as cited by Amr Mansour, a 21 years-old Egyptian graduate who was never interested in political issues prior 2011, but now is involved of political news and updates on the Internet.

The third result is related to the preference of text-based interpersonal communication. Previous social and cultural studies on preferences of Arab communication patterns, conducted in 1995 [5] reported that, due to their oral dominant culture, Arabic computer users may find text-based interfaces lacking when it comes to interpersonal communication. It seems that this might not be the case anymore.

The highest majority (87%) of the interviews' participants in the current study reported their preference for Internet text-based communication through social networks. "It is faster, affordable, and more practical", as cite by most of the interviewees. "During the old regime, Egyptians were unable to know the reality and express themselves freely because the media was controlled. Social networks helped to exchange opinions on what was happening and to mobilize people through face book pages such as Khaled Said and 6 April Movement... people exchange written comments, articles and published news" , as expressed by one interviewee.

4   Discussion

The preliminary analysis of interviews suggests a difference in the online behavior of Egyptians users in 2011 as they were before that date.

Firstly concerning use of language online: While all participants at the current exploratory study reported use of English language in all of their Internet communication, this is contradicting results of previous studies investigated language choice on line for Egyptian users in 1999 and 2001[6,7], and suggested that Arabic is dominant in communication on line for this cultural group. This suggested change in online behavior was anticipated by a study which was conducted in Egypt in 2007 and looked at language choice online in light of globalization and identity issues [9] . The study predicted that in Egypt, as in many other parts of the world, Internet will be having a great impact on language use; with a global use of English on line to such degree that other languages would be crowded out.

It worth mention that although English has been always the principal foreign language of the general population in Egypt and it is the only mandatory foreign language taught in schools in Egypt. It is only in 2004, English started to be mandatory taught in primary public schools, with obligatory instruction starting in first grade.

Secondly concerning the context of use of the Internet: According to the highest majority of interviewees, prior the Egyptian revolution, they were more interested in entertainment, but after the revolution they are now more interested in searching for credible news and finding sources for live political updates and follow-up. Though only a fraction of Egyptians have Internet access, "Through blogs, Twitter and Face book, the Web has become a haven for a young, educated class yearning to express its worries and anxieties" as expressed by a number of interviewees.

Thirdly concerning text-based interpersonal communication: According to the highest majority of interviewees, text-based interpersonal communication through the Internet is now preferable over oral communication through mobiles and phones. This finding is contradicting with what is known about Arabic society which has been classified as an oral dominant society. Previous studies looking at cultural preferences of Arab communication patterns [5] suggested that oral messages are more valued than written messages for their affective power in interpersonal association between communicators.

5   Conclusion

The social network tools are bound to have an important long-term effect on users' communication, empowering, and language use –which is the most salient cultural variable. The trends discussed in this paper can suggest that social change can be caused by Internet media. As some research [9] pointed out, the major social dynamic shaping international media and communication is the contradiction between global networks and local identities. In that light, it is worthwhile to investigate in more depth whether the online use of English and the shift from oral to text communication by this small group of young Egyptians might reflect broader and long-term social and cultural shifts.

6   Limitation

It is important to point out the limitation of this study. The sample size is relatively small and was selected through convenient sampling through personal contact of the researchers, and is thus non-random. The fact that the participants were known by the researcher may have affected people's answers. The interview items were explored for patterns and illustrative examples rather than systematically coded. No validity or reliability tests were done for the interviews items. Therefore, the results of the study cannot be generalizable to other populations beyond this group of participants. On the other hand, this study would be considered an exploratory investigation that had the goal of identifying possible issue and trends for further research.

References

1. Twitter blocked in EgyptAmidst Rising Protests. TechCrunch (January 25, 2011),
   http://techcrunch.com/2011/01/25/twitter-blocked-egypt/
2. Egypt severs internet connection amid growing unrest. BBC News (January 28, 2011),
   http://www.bbc.co.uk/news/technology-12306041
3. A significant increase in the number of Internet users in Egypt after the January Uprising. Reuters (March 19, 2011), http://mymobimobi.com/en-lang/viewNews/62
4. IT in Egypt, Cairo American Chamber of Commerce in Egypt (1998)
5. Zaharna, R.: Understanding Cultural Preferences of Arab Communication Patterns. Public Relations Review 21(3), 241–255 (1995)
6. El Nawawy, M.: Profiling Internet Users in Egypt: Understanding the Primary Deterrent against Their Growth in Number. In: The Tenth Internet Society (ISOC) Annual Conference: INET 2000 CD Proceedings, Yokohama, Japan, July 18-21 (2000)
7. El Said, G.R., Hone, K.S.: Use of Card Sorting for Cultural Web-Preferences Data Elicitation: The Case of Egyptian Internet Users. In: Stephanidis, C. (ed.) Universal Access in HCI: Inclusive Design in the Information Society, June 22-27. The Tenth International Conference on Human-Computer Interaction, HCI International' 2003 Proceedings, vol. 4. Lawrence Erlbaum Associates Publishers (2003) ISBN: 0-8058-4933-5
8. Warschauer, M., El Said, G.R., Zohry, A.: Language Choice Online: Globalization and Identity in Egypt. In: Danet, B., Herring, S. (eds.) The Multilingual Internet: Language, Culture and Communication Online, pp. 303–318. Oxford University Press (2007) ISBN: 978-0-19-530479-4
9. Friedman, T.: The sociolinguistic market of Cairo: Gender, class, and education. Kegan Paul International, London (1999)

Designing for a Thumb: An Ideal Mobile Touchscreen Interface for Chinese Users

Qian Fei

Taobao (China) software Co., Ltd Hangzhou, China
xiaoqian@taobao.com

Abstract. This paper focuses on designing for cross-cultural users; specifically, it describes a study conducted to determine the "Comfort Zone" and optimal touch target size for one-handed thumb use. Similar studies have provided general measurements for touch targets, but they are not applicable to all the slots on a touchscreen, nor are they consistent with the actual physiological measurements (i.e., the size of hands and fingers) of Chinese users. The study used repeated measures in a within-subject design of 16 (slots) × 5 (target sizes) × 10 (repetitions). The results indicated the Comfort Zone for the right thumb of Chinese users is significantly different at 0.01 level, and falls on a fan-shaped area located on the inclined left side of the screen. Different locations were required for different optimal touch target sizes.

Keywords: Design/evaluation for cross-cultural users, One-handed, mobile devices, touchscreens, touch target size.

1 Introduction

As the market share for smartphones grows, multi-point touch technology is increasing in popularity. In the design of touchscreen-based devices, the small interface is unique and is the interface for finger touch interaction, which differs from traditional interaction design. Direct thumb interaction on a small touchscreen raises several issues. On mobile devices, the human fingers – and particularly the thumb – replace traditional methods of small-screen interaction, such as the keyboard and stylus. It also raises several issues:

1. Not all the slots of a small-screen are suitable for finger touch interaction, particularly for thumb interaction. The morphology of the hand and particularly the thumb makes it difficult to reach the corners of the screen.
2. The problem of accuracy is recurrent because of the narrowness of the screen with thick information patterns, and this problem is exacerbated if the user is moving.
3. Standard touchscreen interface design guidelines give general guidance but do not account for users from non-western cultures. Differences in physiological measurements (such as the size of hands and fingers) between Chinese and westerners challenge the standard design guidelines.

A. Marcus (Ed.): DUXU/HCII 2013, Part II, LNCS 8013, pp. 44–53, 2013.

The objective of this study is to describe the shape and location of the "Comfort Zone" and the "Inaccessible Zone" for the right thumb of Chinese users. On the basis of this study, different slots of the screen were proposed for the minimum size of touch targets. We expect guidelines derived from these experimental results will help inform future cross-cultural research on smartphone interfaces designed to support the one-handed use of small touchscreen-based mobile devices.

2   Related Works

The beginning of touchscreen research occurred somewhat recently. Designing for the touchscreen is still at an early stage, whether in China or in the West; it dates back only to 1999, when touchscreen technology was first applied to mobile phones (MOTOROLA A6188). The design philosophy of the finger touch interaction area underwent a revolutionary change in 2007 with the advent of the iPhone and multi-point touch technology. Research on thumb interaction with touchscreen-based devices is a relatively new field, but the issues of reaching far targets, accuracy and cross-cultural users have not yet been resolved.

2.1   Target Accessibility

The borders of the screen are more difficult to reach [1], particularly with the thumb because the morphology of the hand constrains thumb movement. This will degrade interaction in the screen areas that are farthest from the natural extension of the thumb. In addition, thumb movements may also be hampered near the borders of the screen because of the thickness of the device's edges around the screen [2]. Thus, there should be a Comfort Zone and an Inaccessible Zone in the touchscreen for the thumb. In "Tapworthy-Designing Great iPhone Apps", Josh Clark discusses the design guidelines of iPhone apps; in particular, he discusses how right thumb interaction impacts app interface design, "Rule of Thumb: The comfort zone for the right thumb falls on the opposite side of screen, at the left edge and bottom of the screen. (The top right and bottom right corners are the toughest thumb zone for right-handed users.)[3]"

Fig. 1. Rule of Thumb and Magic Number 44

2.2   Accuracy

Direct thumb tapping is intuitive, it requires attentiveness and the following mistakes are easily made: a) Mis-Tapping（tap failed), and b) Missed Tapping (the tap was omitted because the target flashed). For users, the former more commonly happens with the vast majority of small-screen interface designs. Thus, our experiment was designed for the first case.

Smaller touch targets are more difficult for users to tap than larger ones. However, it is unclear exactly how large touch targets must be to offer the best ease of use for the majority of users. There is information from the industry about the minimum target size for touch interfaces. Apple's iPhone Human Interface Guidelines recommend a minimum target size of 44 pixels wide and 44 pixels tall [4]. Microsoft's Windows Phone UI Design and Interaction Guide suggests a touch-target size of 34 px with a minimum touch target size of 26 px [5]. Nokia's developer guidelines suggest that the target size should be no smaller than 1 cm x 1 cm or 28 x 28 pixels [6]. In ergonomics, smartphone predecessors had defined the minimum size for targets with the correct rate of operation. These definitions stated that 7 mm is the minimum size for targets to be easily accessible with the index finger and 9 mm for the thumb. Another study [7] has shown that 9.2 mm is the minimum size for targets to be easily accessible with the thumb. An MIT Touch Lab study of human fingertips with the objective of investigating the mechanics of tactile sense found that the average width of the index finger is 1.6 to 2 cm (16 – 20 mm) for most adults [8]. This converts to 45 – 57 pixels, which is wider than what most mobile phone guidelines suggest.

2.3   Summary

Josh Clark has not clearly explained the argument for or quoted sources delineating the comfort zone. We can neither distinguish an experimental result from a designer's empiricism nor know if it is consistent with actual physiological measurements (such as the size of hands and fingers) of Chinese users. We also note that guidelines are neither consistent with one another nor are they applicable to all slots on a touchscreen, although they do provide a general measurement for touch targets. In addition, walking is the most common activity of users when using their phones in daily life; this tendency will likely continue in the future. Do the guidelines specify measurements for moving?

3   Method

The study used a 16 (slots) ×5 (target sizes) × 10 (repetitions) repeated measures in its within-subject design, such that a total of 19,200 (16×5×10×24) units of experimental data were collected.

3.1   Independent Variable

Slots (16). The 16 target slots were defined by dividing the display into a 4×4 grid of cells (Fig. 2). Each slot was named by a combination of letter and number (e.g., A1).

Four rows were named A/B/C/D from top to bottom, and four columns were named 1/2/3/4 from left to right. Additionally, the 16 slots were not displayed on the front page. Participants were unable to detect the slots and were told that there were 16 slots. For each trial, the target was located in a random position in one of the 16 slots. Any part of the target could not be beyond the limit of the slot where it was displayed. As shown in Fig. 3, the location of the target center was random but was set by condition.

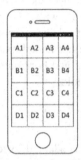

Fig. 2. Sixteen Slots of the Touchscreen

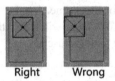

Right   Wrong

Fig. 3. The Regulation of Target Location

Target Sizes (5). Target sizes were set at 7, 8, 9, 10 and 11 mm on each side by the method of constant stimuli. We performed pilot studies to determine the appropriate target sizes for the study. Pilot studies indicated that performance ratios leveled off for target sizes greater than 11 mm; therefore, this represented the largest recommended practical size for singular targets. In accordance with the five groups of target sizes, the study was divided into five sessions, which were researched consecutively by the Latin square design. In each session, the same size target was randomly displayed one after another on all 16 slots. Each target size was repeated 10 times in every slot (16) for a total of 160 (10×16) trials in a session. Red-squares were designed as the target in this study.

3.2   Dependent Variables

Accuracy Ratio. Accuracy Ratio = (Successful Tapping trials / Total Displayed trials) × 100%. All the accuracy dates of each slot were recorded automatically by an experimental program in the phone. In each trial, a red-square was displayed randomly and disappeared after a successful tapping.

Comfort Zone. The mean Accuracy Ratio of the Comfort Zone is significantly higher than that of the other part of screen ($P < 0.01$).

Minimum Size of Touch Target. The minimum size of the touch target for each slot may be defined as when its mean Accuracy Ratio reaches 95%. This value may not be measured directly, but can be obtained indirectly by linear interpolation. Linear interpolation is used to draw a curve with "Target Size" as the abscissa and the "Mean Accuracy Ratio" as the vertical axis; from 95% of the longitudinal axis, a straight line is drawn parallel to the horizontal axis to intersect the curve at point a. From point a to the abscissa, vertical and horizontal axes are drawn perpendicular at the intersection to arrive at the threshold.

3.3   Participants

The within-subject design method was adapted. A total of 24 Chinese participants (12 male and 12 female) were recruited via online announcement, such as through email and campus BBS – the only restriction was that participants must be right-handed. The age of the participants varied between 20 and 37 years, with a mean of 24.5 years. Participants received $5 for their time. On the basis of GB10000-88 [9], "Human Dimensions of Chinese Adult", hand width and thumb length were recorded for each participant to choose typical Chinese users.

3.4   Equipment

The experiment was performed on an iPhone4 that measured 115.2×58.6×9.3 mm, with an 88.9 mm screen, as measured diagonally. The display resolution was 640×960 pixels with approximately 13 pixels per millimeter. The study interface and control program were developed specifically for this study, at:
http://www.taobao.com/go/chn/mobile/uedresearch.php

3.5   Task

The participant's task for each target trial was to tap the target. All tasks were performed walking and one-handed, using only the right-hand thumb for interacting with the touchscreen. The participants were instructed to perform the tasks intuitively without thought. They were also told that capability and reaction time would not be measured in this study and that there was enough time to finish the task. The walking speed of the participants was limited to 1-1.5 m/s, which is normal speed for Chinese adults. Their walking distance was limited to an indoor environment measuring 4 m×4 m.

3.6   Procedures

The researcher greeted the participants and provided them with a brief overview of the study. Before the experimental task, there was a practice session; targets were presented once at each size in each slot, for a total of 80 trials. After the practice session, users completed the experimental task. Researchers were responsible for logging in the website (http://www.taobao.com/go/chn/mobile/uedresearch.php) for every participant.

On the front page, there were several parameters that were required to be filled in by the researchers, including target size, participants' name and the type of finger (index finger and thumb could both be measured on this website, but only the thumb results will be shown and discussed in this paper). Then, the researcher pressed the OK button. When the experimental phone was transferred to the participant, the task began. At the end of every session, participants were sent a pop-up dialog: "Congratulations. All finished." Sixteen accuracy dates from Slot A1 to Slot D4 were displayed on the following page after pressing the OK button. Researchers were responsible for saving screen shots as JPG files in the iPhone Photo Library. After this, the session was over. The participant was allowed to rest for 3 minutes before the next session until all 5 sessions were completed.

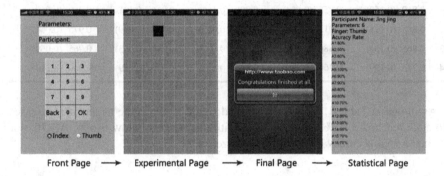

Front Page ⟶ Experimental Page ⟶ Final Page ⟶ Statistical Page

Fig. 4. Procedures of Study: Four phase of Each Session

4   Results

4.1   Accuracy Ratio

All the screen shots were collected and the dates were analyzed by SPSS. The Accuracy Ratio was analyzed using a 5×16 repeated measures analysis of variance with factors of target size (7, 8, 9, 10 and 11 mm) and location (16 slots derived from a 4×4 division of the screen). Erroneous trials were eliminated from the data set and the mean accuracy ratio of the remaining trials was computed. Repeated measures analysis of variance showed that the order of presentation of the techniques had no significant effect on accuracy ratio.

Table 1. Accuracy Ratio of Sixteen Slots in Each Session

Slots	Size=7 mm		Size=8 mm		Size=9 mm		Size=10 mm		Size=11 mm	
	Mean	(Standard Deviation)	Mean	(Standard Deviation)	Mean	(Standard Deviation)	Mean	(Standard Deviation)	Mean	(Standard Deviation)
A1	0.865	(0.114)	0.900	(0.119)	0.910	(0.117)	0.935	(0.135)	0.975	(0.044)
A2	0.870	(0.138)	0.920	(0.076)	0.930	(0.103)	0.965	(0.075)	0.995	(0.022)
A3	0.860	(0.127)	0.895	(0.110)	0.900	(0.108)	0.960	(0.082)	0.975	(0.055)
A4	0.770	(0.205)	0.855	(0.139)	0.915	(0.099)	0.935	(0.109)	0.960	(0.052)
B1	0.870	(0.142)	0.895	(0.139)	0.920	(0.149)	0.960	(0.069)	0.960	(0.050)
B2	0.935	(0.088)	0.920	(0.089)	0.935	(0.118)	0.975	(0.044)	0.975	(0.055)
B3	0.870	(0.145)	0.870	(0.108)	0.925	(0.079)	0.945	(0.076)	0.975	(0.044)
B4	0.750	(0.201)	0.890	(0.091)	0.925	(0.097)	0.950	(0.069)	0.965	(0.075)
C1	0.840	(0.167)	0.870	(0.126)	0.960	(0.068)	0.975	(0.044)	0.980	(0.052)
C2	0.845	(0.154)	0.910	(0.097)	0.960	(0.060)	0.975	(0.055)	0.965	(0.059)
C3	0.820	(0.161)	0.855	(0.170)	0.905	(0.143)	0.930	(0.086)	0.985	(0.049)
C4	0.750	(0.176)	0.830	(0.138)	0.915	(0.093)	0.930	(0.098)	0.985	(0.037)
D1	0.810	(0.152)	0.855	(0.154)	0.900	(0.165)	0.915	(0.131)	0.960	(0.060)
D2	0.885	(0.114)	0.915	(0.093)	0.930	(0.073)	0.955	(0.069)	0.975	(0.064)
D3	0.865	(0.104)	0.880	(0.120)	0.900	(0.097)	0.945	(0.093)	0.965	(0.059)
D4	0.745	(0.199)	0.760	(0.239)	0.840	(0.143)	0.935	(0.089)	0.960	(0.114)

As shown in Table 1, accuracy improved significantly as the target size increased. No slots reached a 95% accuracy level with target sizes below 9 mm. All 16 slots reached a 95% accuracy level with target sizes of 11.

4.2   Comfort Zone and Accessible Zone

Rule of Thumb. To verify whether the Rule of Thumb applies to Chinese users, we selected 9 slots (B1+B2+B3+C1+C2+C3+D1+D2+D3) as the approximate area that suggested by Josh Clark. These 9 slots formed the test area named Suggested Comfort Zone, whereas the other area of the screen was named Suggested Accessible Zone. To verify significant differences between the two areas of the screen, the differences in the measurement data were compared with a paired t-test. If this division also applies to Chinese users, significant differences in accuracy ratio would be found between the two areas (Suggested Comfort Zone v. Suggested Accessible Zone) in all 5 sizes in the experiments. This would mean that the accuracy ratio of the Suggested Comfort Zone would be significantly higher than that of the Accessible Zone, for any target size.

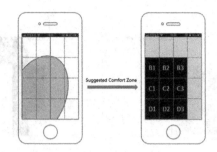

Fig. 5. Suggested Accessible Zone

However, the paired t-test analysis showed that there was no significant difference in the accuracy ratio when aiming for the 8, 9, 10, and 11 mm targets (Suggested Comfort Zone v. Suggested Accessible Zone: 8 mm targets, $t(19) = 0.99$, $p = 0.34$; 9 mm, $t(19) = 1.83$, $p = 0.08$; 10 mm targets, $t(19) = 0.86$, $p = 0.40$; 11 mm targets, $t(19) = -0.91$, $p = 0.37$). When the target was 7 mm, the two areas showed significant difference in the accuracy ratio (Suggested Comfort Zone v. Suggested Accessible Zone: 7 mm targets, $t(19) = 3.17$, $p = 0.01$). As shown in Figure 6, the accuracy ratio improves significantly as targets grow from 8 mm to 11 mm in both areas, whereas the significant difference between the two areas was disappeared. This division maybe suitable for Westerners, but this presents problems for Chinese users.

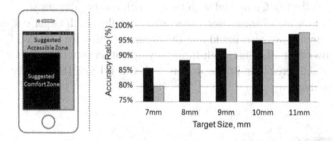

Fig. 6. Paired t-test results of the Suggested Comfort Zone and Suggested Accessible Zone

Comfort Zone for Chinese User. The Comfort Zone might be related to the natural extension of the thumb. As shown in Fig. 7, we located a fan-shaped area located on the inclined left side of the screen by observing the movements of the right thumb. Thus, we have another hypothesis for the Comfort Zone. We selected 7 particular slots (A2+A3+B1+B2+C1+C2+C3+D2) as the approximate fan-shaped area. These 7 slots formed the test area named the "Groping Comfort Zone", while the other area of the screen was named the "Groping Accessible Zone". Similarly, if the new division applies to Chinese users, significant differences in accuracy ratios would be found between the two areas (Groping Comfort Zone v. Groping Accessible Zone) in all 5 sizes of the experiments.

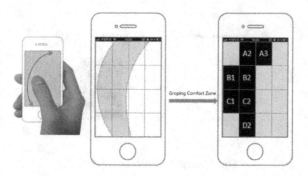

Fig. 7. Groping Comfort Zone

The paired t-test analysis showed that the accuracy ratio for the two areas (Groping Comfort Zone v. Groping Accessible Zone) differed significantly from one another when aiming for the 7, 8, 9 and10 mm targets, and the accuracy ratios of the Groping Comfort Zone were significantly higher than the Groping Accessible Zone (Groping Comfort Zone v. Groping Accessible Zone: 7 mm targets, $t(19) = 3.73$, $p = 0.001$; 8 mm targets, $t(19) = 3.57$, $p = 0.002$; 9 mm targets, $t(19) = 2.89$, $p = 0.009$; 10 mm targets, $t(19) = 3.10$, $p = 0.006$). When the target size increased to 11 mm, it was easier to aim and tap the target, and the significant difference disappeared between the two areas (Groping Comfort Zone v. Groping Accessible Zone: 11 mm targets, $t(19) = 0.46$, $p = 0.650$). Compared with the Rule of Thumb, the fan-shaped area was more reasonable for the Chinese user, especially when the touch target size was below 11 mm. Additionally, we also found that the accuracy ratios for Slot A4, C4, D1 and D4 were the lowest of all. Thus, high-frequency operation should be located in a reasonable area of the screen, and these 4 slots (A4, C4, D1 and D4) should be avoided as much as possible.

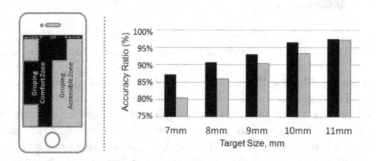

Fig. 7. Paired t-test results of the Groping Comfort Zone and Groping Accessible Zone

4.3   Minimum Size of Touch Target

The minimum sizes of touch target were obtained by linear interpolation. The results showed that the different locations required different minimum touch target sizes. More than half of the screen required a touch target size larger than 10 mm. The minimum touch target sizes were obtained as follows: A1=10.4 mm, A2=9.6 mm, A3=9.8 mm, A4=10.7 mm, B1=9.8 mm, B2=9.4 mm, B3=10.2 mm, B4=10.0 mm, C1=8.9 mm, C2=8.8 mm, C3=10.4 mm, C4=10.5 mm, D1=10.8 mm, D2=9.8 mm, D3=10.3 mm, and D4=10.6 mm.

5   Conclusion

In an effort to determine the Comfort Zone and minimum target sizes for Chinese users with one-handed thumb use of mobile devices, we examined the interaction between target size and target locations in detail. Based on our findings, we recommend a fan-shaped area located on the inclined left side of the screen as the Comfort Zone for the right thumb; in addition, the minimum size of the touch target was different in different locations of the screen. More than half of the screen required a touch target size larger than 10 mm.

References

1. Karlson, A.K., Bederson, B.B.: ThumbSpace: Generalized One-Handed Input for Touchscreen-Based Mobile Devices. In: Baranauskas, C., Abascal, J., Barbosa, S.D.J. (eds.) INTERACT 2007. LNCS, vol. 4662, pp. 324–338. Springer, Heidelberg (2007)
2. Roudaut, A., Huot, S., Lecolinet, E.: TapTap and MagStick: Improving One-Handed Target Acquisition on Small Touch-screens. In: AVI 2008, pp. 146–153 (2008)
3. Clark, J.: Tapworthy-Designing Great iPhone Apps, pp. 58–60 (2010)
4. https://developer.apple.com/library/ios/navigation/
5. http://msdn.microsoft.com/en-us/library/hh202915v=VS.92.aspx
6. http://library.developer.nokia.com/index.jsp?topic=/
   S60_5th_Edition_Cpp_Developers_Library/GUID-5486EFD3-
   4660-4C19-A007-286DE48F6EEF.html
7. Parhi, P., Karlson, A., Bederson, B.: Target Size Study for One-Handed Thumb Use on Small Touchscreen Devices. In: Proc. MobileHCI 2006, pp. 203–210 (2006)
8. Dandekar, K., Raju, B.I., Srinivasan, M.A.: 3-D Finite-Element Models of Human and Monkey Fingertips to Investigate the Mechanics of Tactile Sense. Journal of Biomechanical Engineering, 685 (2003)
9. http://wenku.baidu.com/view/4e23160a79563c1ec5da719c.html

Examining Interdisciplinary Prototyping
in the Context of Cultural Communication

Michael Heidt

Chemnitz University of Technology, Research Training Group crossWorlds, Thüringer
Weg 5, Chemnitz 09126, Germany
michael.heidt@informatik.tu-chemnitz.de
http://crossworlds.info/mitglieder/kollegiaten/michael-heidt/

Abstract. Designers typically have to operate in the environment of
highly interdisciplinary teams. However, at the same time mindsets of
project participants frequently remain framed within disciplinary and
professional boundaries. We argue that interdisciplinary communication
processes can be improved upon by further theorising the differences
between disciplinary cultures. Prototyping offers unique opportunities
concerning these situational configurations. It allows to make differences
productive on the level of practice whose incommensurabilities often preclude integration within the realm of theory and conviction. We thus provide a tentative set of communicative and methodological tools aimed
at improving the communicative process in these scenarios. Instead of
trying to establish a common language or common toolset, we try to
render the dynamic friction between disparate perspectives productive.
Our positions are illustrated by discussing them in the context of a case
study in the domain of cultural education.

Keywords: prototyping, interdisciplinarity, cultural informatics, critical technical practice.

1 Introduction

Interdisciplinarity is heavily promoted throughout the scientific world while already being commonplace within professional settings. Despite this operational
ubiquity, teams in the field tasked with design projects frequently find themselves confronted with a startling lack of methods explicitly accounting for
interdisciplinary perspectives.

We will outline how far reaching differences in individual and disciplinary perspectives can be rendered productive on the level of practice. The device used
to accomplish this goal is a prototyping approach informed by Value-Sensitive-
Design, Critical Technical Practice and Embodied Interaction. Our efforts are
aimed at providing conceptual and methodological building blocks towards enabling multiperspectivity on the levels of artefact production and artefact usage
alike. To this end, a case study in the field of cultural education is discussed. The
discussion will highlight both problems encountered as well as communicative devices employed to address these challenges. The development project described

A. Marcus (Ed.): DUXU/HCII 2013, Part II, LNCS 8013, pp. 54–61, 2013.
© Springer-Verlag Berlin Heidelberg 2013

was conducted as part of the interdisciplinary research training group cross-Worlds, combining perspectives from the fields of computer-science, philosophy, psychology, social-science, design, rhetoric and engineering.

In accounting for interdisciplinarity the text finds itself confronted with a fundamental difficulty. While it has to tell a coherent story, its subject, the multitude of perspectives, presents itself as inhomogeneous and non-linearisable. This of course is a situation every designer is familiar with - she must deal with the messiness of a chaotic world, hoping to make strife productive by embodying it into design and artefact.

2   Prototyping Approach

2.1   Examined Prototyping - Project Inception

The respective subproject was initiated by a participant with a strong background in philosophy. Initially, concepts were to be grounded within Jürgen Habermas' theory of communicative action [8]. This enterprise however soon proved to be too ambitious, since his ideas turned out not to be accessible enough to those without prior training in philosophy or social sciences. At this point first discussions erupted concerning the worth of the philosophical perspective, as well as a perceived incomprehensibility of philosophical discourse in general. Subsequently, ideas from ancient greek philosophy were introduced into the discussion process.

Since the early stages of the design process centered on identifying tacit assumptions guiding individual perspectives, the character of Socrates was used as an illustrative device. Following his famous adage stating that the unexamined life is not worth living (Apology, 38a), the approach to prototyping was dubbed *Examined Prototyping*. Philosophy served as a constant reminder throughout the project that untested assumptions should be identified and articulated.

3   Cultural Prototyping

After initial discussions had focussed on the general approach, in a subsequent step relevant sites for artefact deployment were examined.

3.1   Analysis of Museum Context

Analysis of museums creates unique challenges with respect to prototyping. Technological artefacts within museums neither are consumer products, nor are they part of a workplace and thus immediately accessible to criteria such as productivity. Rather, their function within the domain of analysis is notoriously hard to identify. In order to address these uncertainties our inquiries commenced by examining the historical dimension of the problem. We thus tried to retrace developments and frictions of user conceptions within HCI literature.

Traditionally in the field of technology design, museums were conceived as places of learning. Following cognitive science, the function of information arte-facts frequently was described as facilitating informational flow. Accordingly, their function was described as improving mnemonic performance of technology users. Within recent publications the focus has shifted from aspects of learning to that of user experience. Users are seen as demanding perceptually engaging media-installations.

With these developments in mind, our own explorations into the museum domain were informed by the concept of the *Blended Museum*, developed by Klinkhammer and Reiterer [13] at University of Konstanz. Highlighting both user experience as well as visitors' informational needs, Blended Museum focusses on the integration of medial effects between real exhibits and media installations.

3.2   Weak Spots

Following the predominantly conceptually oriented initial stage, the project moved on to integrate observations made in the field. Drawing both on afore-mentioned literature and observation alike our analysis highlights four key areas where traditional museums fall short:

1. Interactive possibilities remain severely limited. When they are presented at all, they usually take the form of 'special offers' and are typically poorly integrated with the immersive material museum experiences. Mobile tech-nologies make for especially efficient remedies in this respect, since they allow for continuous interactive possibilities.
2. Visitors often harbour diffuse informational needs , calling for informa-tional incentives. These typically remain unanswered in the museum en-vironment. The system is designed to address these using a communicative reconceptualisation of recommender engines.
3. Museums frequently fail to provide ample communicative incentives. The challenge is met in the course of a restrained approach towards technological implements. Not machine-user interactions are facilitated, instead the system only provides incentives, relying on users to produce actual communication.
4. Users crave take-away-experiences which traditional museums frequently fail to provide [11]. Traditional take-away items like guides, books and souvenirs do not incorporate a specific user's experience or past communications. The problem is addressed by allowing users to incorporate digital communications with fellow visitors and system interactions into their digital self. To this end, presentation devices ranging from social networks, timelines, narratives and suitable diagrams are proposed.

4   Prototyping Process

In its initial form, the system was conceived as a traditional recommender sys-tem. The system was targeted at exhibit centered recommendation, providing its users with additional information to exhibits encountered or pointing to potentially interesting exhibits within the museum.

Low fidelity prototypes were developed, showing how smartphones could be used to diseminate exhibit centered recommendations. Goals in this state of the project were to highlight the importance of exhibits while trying to render technological presentation transparent.

Within the following phase the prototypes were interrogated towards the implicit conceptions they embody. The following notions were identified:

1. Museums are spaces similar to online-bookstores or warehouses.
2. Museums can be conceived as learning environments.
3. Users are seen as consumers of information items.
4. Exhibits provide information.
5. Knowledge is transformed from documents into users in the form of information.

At this point in the design process, the problem of meaning was discussed explicitly. Participants with backgrounds in psychology were engaged in heated debates with social-scientists. Consequently, representationalist conceptions of meaning were called into question. In order to generate a theoretically sound foundation for the discussion, project participants adopted the paradigm *Embodied Interaction*, developed by Paul Dourish [4]. Drawing on a varied set of methods informed by phenomenology, ethnomethodology and anthropology, Dourish argues for a conception of meaning as a situational effect. As a consequence, a new stance towards meaning was adopted:

1. Meaning is a situated phenomenon.
2. Knowledge is constituted by discursive practice.

At this point of the discussion another tacit assumption presented itself:

1. Users can sensibly be addressed as individuals.

Its identification proved to be important with respect to later stages of the design process.

It has to be stressed that insights obtained from cognitive psychology were not dropped or refuted, rather they were recontextualised. Statements concerning the restrictions of the human physiology for processing large amounts of input still inform presentation strategies. For example Miller's classical discoveries concerning internal information processing are embodied in UI designs [10]. However, the museum experience is no longer conceived as a problem of information transferral.

4.1   Visual Communication

Visual communications devices such as diagrams proved to be especially valuable tools while trying to articulate differing perspectives on the design process. Due to the fluidity of the process itself, most of the devices detailed are exploratory in nature. They are described here in order to provide the discussion of the project with intelligibility as well as inviting others to adopt and improve on them. In order to facilitate detailed discussion of differences, project participants were encouraged to generate simple visualizations of their notions and theories. These were subsequently reworked into semi-formal versions. Within the diagrams produced, the key concept or notion is denoted by drawing a dashed ellipse around it. Furthermore, concepts that appeared in discussions but were found missing from perspectives were subsequently drawn into a box at the lower right of the diagram.

We will give a short overview of perspectives articulated:

The *representational perspective* as detailed above is outlined in figure 1. It centers on the role of mobile appliances as mediators between data stores and the user. It consequently conceives users as information sinks and databases as information sources.

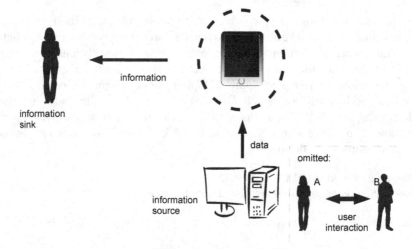

Fig. 1. Conception oriented towards informational flow

The *interactional perspective* as outlined in figure 2 focusses on the communicative-interactive relationship between visitors. Consistent with Embodied Interaction, knowledge is treated as constructed in an interactional and situated context. Technical appliances as well as the exhibits themselves were initially omitted from this discussion.

Both perspectives induced further discussions and led to a pragmatical reconceptualisation. The interactional effects of traditional recommender systems were depicted graphically as seen in figure 3. Contrasted with the interactional perspective, they were found to displace the intended communicative dynamics. Subsequent reframings gave rise to a second perspective, detailed on the right side of the diagram. Still bound to the recommender paradigm, recommendations are now routed through users. These reframings were facilitated by adoption of a systems centered view. The perspectives of representation and interaction could be integrated on the level of practice.

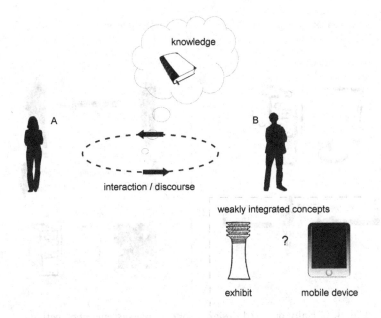

Fig. 2. Knowledge as interactional and situated phenomenon

5   Related Work

Embodied Interaction developed by Paul Dourish [4] proposes a blend of methods from social-sciences and humanities. Building upon a phenomenological under-standing of the world around us, a processual conception of reality as well as a situational conception of meaning constitute key concepts.

Participatory Design aims at communicative integration of all stakeholders potentially affected by an artefact [12]. It centers on democratic discussion and deliberative processes. Our approach is informed by Participatory Design, while highlighting our own intrinsic motives.

Value-Sensitive Design [6,7] describes itself as an alternative paradigm to participatory approaches. Whereas Participatory Design highlights the need for valuing every participants opinion, here adhering to human values is given pref-erence. Value Sensitive approaches emphasise the need to acknowledge tradeoffs between conflicting values. Consequently, the design process is aimed at enabling reasonable ethically informed decisions, while stating that these must remain publicly accountable.

User-centered-design is aimed at identifying the needs of end users, thus en-abling successful product deployment [9,14]. It tries to overcome preoccupations with technology, while differing from the other approaches in refraining from ethical grounding or socio-cultural intervention.

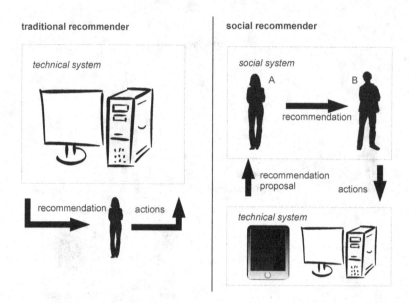

Fig. 3. Socially oriented design - contrastive systems perspective

Critical Technical Practice as initially put forward by Phil Agre constituted itself as an effort to reform the field of Artificial Intelligence [3,2,1]. Within these works, Agre argues for a situational approach towards AI problems, trying to highlight shortcoming of the idea of universal cognition.

Critical Technical Practice has since informed a multitude of concepts within the field of HCI. One of these influences is Reflective HCI [5], a joint effort of theorists affiliated with Embodied Interaction, AI centered Critical Technical Practice and other paradigms within the HCI community.

6   Conclusion

We have described how profoundly differing disciplinary perspectives can be integrated on the level of prototyping practice. Our ideas were demonstrated in the context of the development of a recommendation engine in the domain of cultural education. We observed that communicative processes should not be optimised towards erasing or bridging differences in perspective but rather should aim at rendering those differences productive and articulate. To this end, visual aids and semi-formal diagrams were identified as especially promising communicative resources. We see further potential in extensive dialogue between the disciplines and consequently invite scholars to collaborative develop a more extensive methods package.

References

1. Agre, P.E.: The Soul Gained and Lost: Artificial Intelligence as a Philosophical Project. Stanford Humanities Review 4(2), 1–19 (1995)
2. Agre, P.E.: Computation and Human Experience. Cambridge University Press (1997)
3. Agre, P.E.: Toward a Critical Technical Practice: Lessons Learned in Trying to Reform Al. Social science, technical systems, and cooperative work: Beyond the Great Divide (1997)
4. Dourish, P.: Where the Action is: the Foundations of Embodied Interaction. MIT press (2004)
5. Dourish, P., Finlay, J., Sengers, P., Wright, P.: Reflective HCI: Towards a Critical Technical Practice. In: CHI 2004 Extended Abstracts on Human Factors in Computing Systems, pp. 1727–1728. ACM (2004)
6. Friedman, B.: Value-Sensitive Design. Interactions 3(6), 16–23 (1996)
7. Friedman, B., Howe, D.C., Felten, E.: Informed Consent in the Mozilla Browser: Implementing Value-Sensitive Design. In: Proceedings of the 35th Annual Hawaii International Conference on System Sciences, HICSS, 10 p. IEEE (2002)
8. Habermas, J., Mccarthy, T.: The Theory of Communicative Action. Reason and the Rationalization of Society, vol. 1. Beacon Press (1985)
9. International Standards Organization: ISO 13407:1999, Human-Centred Design Processes for Interactive Systems
10. Miller, G.A.: The Magical Number Seven, Plus or Minus Two: Some Limits on our Capacity for Processing Information. Psychological Review 101(2), 343–352 (1994)
11. Mulholland, P., Collins, T., Zdrahal, Z.: Bletchley Park Text: Using Mobile and Semantic Web Technologies to Support the Post-Visit Use of Online Museum Resources. Journal of Interactive Media in Education 2005(2) (2005)
12. Muller, M.J., Kuhn, S.: Participatory Design. Communications of the ACM 36(6), 24–28 (1993)
13. Rdle, R., Heilig, M., Reiterer, H.: Interactive Reading: Serendipity in the Context of the Blended Library. In: Proceedings of the 1st International Workshop on Encouraging Serendipity in Interactive Systems, 13th IFIP TC13 Conference on Human-Computer Interaction, pp. 24–26. Springer (September 2011)
14. Rubin, J.: Handbook of Usability Testing: How to Plan, Design, and Conduct Effective Tests. John Wiley & Sons, Inc., New York (1994)

Intercultural User Interface Design –
Culture-Centered HCI Design –
Cross-Cultural User Interface Design:
Different Terminology or Different Approaches?

Rüdiger Heimgärtner

Intercultural User Interface Consulting (IUIC)
Lindenstraße 9, 93152 Undorf, Germany
ruediger.heimgaertner@iuic.de

Abstract. This paper presents the terminology containing several relevant concepts used in intercultural user interface design as well as the results of an analytic study of literature in the area of culture-centered human-computer interaction (HCI) design. Their meaning and application context is analyzed and implications are discussed. Some reviewed examples of related work helped to clarify the issues and to establish a conceptual basis to elucidate the different research approaches in the area of intercultural user interface design.

Keywords: Approach, Terminology, Research Paradigm, Culture, HCI, Cross-Cultural, Design, Intercultural, Culture-Centered, Methods, Tools, Standards, Overview, User Interface Design, User Interface, Human Computer Interaction.

1 Publications in the Field of "HCI and Culture"

"Intercultural research in Information Systems is a relatively new research area that has gained increasing importance over the last few years [..]" ([1]: 17). Publications compiled by the author within the field of research connecting culture and HCI support this and serve to determine the current state of research in this area and to categorize the main research topics in culture-centered human-computer interaction (HCI) design. Using the key words "cross-cultural HCI" when searching the ACM digital library reveals an exponential rise of publications in this area since the year 2000 (cf. [2]). There are several papers in the literature review concerning the usage of information systems in their cultural context. Two of the first important books regarding internationalization of HCI are *Designing User Interfaces for International Use* by [3] and *International User Interfaces* by [4]. Another introduction to the study of cross-cultural of HCI is [5] reviewing the research methodology, the technology transfer and the diffusion of innovation to shed light on the cross-cultural study of human-computer interaction. Another overview of culture and its effects on HCI is given by [6]. [7] reviews cultural information systems research to postulate a shift to a theory of information technology culture conflict. [8] illuminates the relationship between

A. Marcus (Ed.): DUXU/HCII 2013, Part II, LNCS 8013, pp. 62–71, 2013.
© Springer-Verlag Berlin Heidelberg 2013

culture and computers by a review of the concept of culture and implications for intercultural collaborative online learning. [9] provides an overview of a decade of journal publications about culture and HCI. From this survey several "hypes" can be identified in this area. The first one happened in the early 1990's. The next one was around 2000 and since about 2010 research in intercultural HCI design has steadily increased. In these "hypes" the number of publications is high indicating high research interests and rising effort.

2   Analysis of Concept Usage and Research Approaches

After clarifying the relevant terminology, it will be investigated, whether the same concepts are used differently or whether different concepts are used similarly as well as which concepts are used correctly in the related work. Then the question will be analyzed whether there are different research approaches and paradigms in the area of "HCI and culture."

2.1   Terminology

In scientific context, the interaction, at which information is exchanged between a user and some system via a user interface (UI), is called "human-machine interaction" (HMI) or "human-computer interaction" (HCI) (cf. [10]). The user initiates tasks with the system and the system responds with the results to the user and vice versa.[1] Hence, HCI design need not be used synonymously with UI design. However, in the industrial design context, the meaning of HMI is often defined as "human-machine interface" equaling the concept of "user interface". Similarly, even in the scientific context, the concepts "intercultural", "cross-cultural", "culture-centered" and "culture-oriented" are used intermingled with further related concepts such as globalization, localization, glocalization, internationalization, iconization and culturalization (cf. [11]). In addition, different concepts are applied in the same contents to express the relationship of user interfaces with culture. For instance, the content of the following papers is very similar even if the concepts in the titles are different: "globalization of user-interface design" ([12]), "global and intercultural user-interface design" ([13]), "cross-cultural user-interface design" ([14]), "international and intercultural user interfaces" ([15]), "globalization, localization and cross-cultural communication in user-interface design" ([16]) and "Cross-cultural user-experience design" ([17]).[2] To put it in a nutshell, when relating HCI and culture, the relevant terminology is not used coherently at all times.

---

[1] The system can be a machine or a computer. The concept of HMI is used so that it subsumes HCI because computers are special machines. Even if there is a difference between HCI and HMI, it is often wrongly confused.

[2] This is also supported by the fact that the content of these papers was created by the same author.

2.2   Concepts

At least the following concepts are used in the area of HCI / user interface design and culture:

- Cross-cultural HCI / user interface design ([14], [18]),
- Culture-oriented HCI / user interface design ([19]),
- Intercultural HCI / user interface design ([20], [21], [22]),
- Culture-centered HCI / (user) interface design ([11]).

Supported by the analysis in section 2.1 above, it can be assumed that these concepts are also similarly used to express similar meanings, i.e., taking cultural aspects into account in HCI design.

However, their connotations are different inclining the concepts to be applied differently in diverse contexts. Intercultural HCI design means the process of HCI design in the cultural context (cf. [23]: 42-43). According to [19], intercultural HCI design describes the user and culture oriented design of interactive systems and products taking the cultural context of the user into account with respect to the respective tasks and product usage ([24]: 87). [23] presented the steps of this process called "intercultural usability engineering" (cf. [23]: 60 et seq.). This approach has grown in academic literature from 1990 to 2000 and has emerged from the processes of globalization, internationalization, and localization of products. In addition, [14] required that cross-cultural HCI design should account for dimensions of cultures (cf. [14]). [11] introduced the culture-centered HCI design process based on research on cross-cultural interface design (cf. [14], [19]) and cross-cultural user experience design (cf. [25]) applying iterative analysis to take the target users and their cultural needs into account.

In addition, there are differences in meaning between the concepts "intercultural" and "cross-cultural" as explained by [26]. "Intercultural" variables represent knowledge that can be obtained only by observing at least two cultures and their differences, i.e. doing intercultural research (cf. [26]) to obtain relevant knowledge for the internationalization of software and system platforms. However, they can simply also be called "cultural" variables, because the values of those variables represent knowledge for a specific culture (relevant for system and software localization).

2.3   Approaches

[27] "developed an HCI cross-cultural design approach [called Meaning in Mediated Action (MMA)] which focuses specifically on how representations and meaning mediate action" ([27], p. 307) dealing with *cultural diversity* and differentiating between systems targeted for particular cultures and systems intended to be shared by culturally diverse users, because "existing approaches are inadequate for dealing with this issue." ([27], p. 287). This approach was referenced by several of the approaches that followed in the area of "HCI and culture". [24]: 108 developed an approach for the design of intercultural human-machine systems using the "method of culture-oriented design" (MCD). The MCD integrates factors from established concepts of

culture-oriented design into existing concepts of HMI design. Knowledge about cultural differences is thereby integrated into existing methods. [28] found out that the global software development life cycle works efficiently for multicultural societies such as Malaysia in contrast to the Western driven usability assessment techniques. [29] developed a cross-cultural interface design strategy with four phases:

1. Investigation: determination of user behavior, identification of social and cultural factors and assessment of different indigenous user attitudes,
2. Translation: generation of a consistent cultural model based on the output of the investigation phase to identify and illuminate similarities and differences of the user groups,
3. Implementation: utilization of the cultural model to create internationalized/localized prototypes to perform usability tests with indigenous user groups,
4. Evaluation: analyzing results, optimizing the prototype using iterative loops in order to reach the final product.

The authors emphasized the insights from [20], [30] and [31] as vital and based their work on them along with others such as [4], [28], [32], [33], [34] and [35] and, in fact, their approach resembles the MCD-approach of [24]. [36] provided an overview on the theory and methodology as well as the user interaction paradigms and technologies in the area under discussion (entitled "Cross-Cultural Design"). The authors wandered in this overview from cross-cultural psychology, physical ergonomics and anthropometry to graphical user interfaces, web and hyper media as well as mobile computing and presented the related methods. They elucidated all these areas in the light of culture and described the activities there. Therefore, "Cross-Cultural Design" as used by [36] is rather more a "headline" than an approach: the activities and methods used in this area were summarized and labeled by "cross-cultural design". [36] identified the following authors providing first milestones in cross-cultural HCI design: [31] and [37]. [14], [15] extrapolated user interface design guidelines from the classic works of Hofstede (cf. [38]) and Hall (cf. [39], [40], [41]). "A less explored direction of cross-cultural design research has focused on cultural differences in cognition." ([36], p. 183). [42] and [43] worked on cultural differences in user interface information structures and in cognitive styles respectively.

[11] "addresses culturally rooted factors within user interface design. The design implications of globalization are discussed, together with the related processes of internationalization, localization, 'globalization', ionization and culturalization in order to establish a basis for a new approach to HCI design. The potential for a more diverse culture-centred, design-based system —'Culture-Centered Design' (CCD) is introduced, and a CCD process developed. A redesigned computer interface, incorporating a consistent and culturally rooted metaphor for a Chinese user target group is discussed. A culturally specific 'garden' metaphor is developed and applied as an alternative to the current global 'office' or 'desktop' metaphor. A working demonstration of the interface is piloted with a group of Chinese users to assess its success in terms of interactivity, usability and cultural significance. The overall results of the first two evaluation phases have shown very positive outcomes for the use of the CCD system and Chinese garden metaphor." ([11], p. 1).

Within this approach, [11] focuses on culture-centered interface metaphors (e.g., [44]) as well as on iterative analysis taking into account Nielsen's usability engineering lifecycle model and Apple computer HCI guidelines as well as guidelines from ISO and W3C in order to cover the value of the user's cultural context. However, the simplified CCD process is similar to the standard usability process defined in ISO 9421-210 (cf. [45]) focusing on social and cultural aspects and does not differ significantly from the other approaches called intercultural design, culture-oriented design or cross-cultural design because [11] based their approach called "Culture-Centered Design" on the work of [12], [19] and others, who refer to cross-cultural interface design as the authors themselves admit: "The authors hereby introduce a new culturally oriented system, namely, Culture-Centred Design, whose development was based on existing literature and research by Marcus, Röse and others, who refer to cross-cultural interface design (Aykin, 2005)." ([11], p. 9). Even if, the CCD approach is a holistic one, i.e. a complementary view to existing design methodologies such as a task-centered design process considering research on target user group related to cognition and usability taking into account the end user's as well as the designer's view by appropriate "filters", i.e. lenses, it is very similar to the approaches of [23] and [24], who also emphasized the minimal gap in the socio-cultural background between user and designer. Therefore, the contrasts between the previous approaches that served as basis for CCD (cf. [24] and [23]) are not so different from CCD.[3]

Hence, in sum, there are no really different approaches related to the different concepts discussed in section 2.2 above. However, surveying literature in the area under discussion revealed that there are approaches used for the same purposes in the area which, however, are named totally differently from the concepts discussed before. For instance, one such approach is semiotic engineering. Semiotic engineering was suggested by [46] for user interface languages and by [47] for HCI. Since then, the group of De Souza worked on this approach to make it useful for HCI design and suggested 2012 metaphors for guiding the design of cross-cultural interactive systems. Semiotic engineering is considered to be a valuable approach to HCI (interface) design and a relevant and promising framework in the intercultural field (cf. [48]), because it can be combined with culture and HCI to take into account cultural aspects in HCI design (cf. [49]). In semiotic engineering, HCI is seen "as a two-tiered communicative process: one is the designer-to-user communication and the other is the user-system interaction. [..] HCI can only be achieved if both levels of communication are successfully achieved." ([47]: 55). [50] developed the communicability evaluation method taking into account "that interactive systems are metacommunication artifacts, by telling designers, in a number of ways, how well their message is getting across." ([47]: 56, cf. also [23]). The semiotic engineering approach complements cognitive and social theories useful for intercultural HCI design by providing new perceptions on the process and products in HCI design.

---

[3] Nevertheless, the application of CCD on the analysis of the desktop metaphor for the Chinese context led to the insight that the garden metaphor is more appropriate for Chinese users, which could cause a shift to the use garden metaphors for Chinese user interfaces in the future.

3   Discussion

It is important to consider fundamental cultural differences when dealing with members of cultures interacting with machines. Hence, the most important step is still to bridge the gap between cultural aspects and HMI design by determining relevant cultural parameters for intercultural user interface design using analytical research and empirical tests. Hence, it is necessary to perform research in this area by using existing, or introducing new, methods such as analyzing critical interaction situations between humans and computers or machines. Good opportunities for the transmission of intercultural competence are "critical incidents" (cf. [51]). Analyzing critical interaction situations between humans is a well-known method to find differences among cultures (cf. [52]). In addition, it is reasonable to apply the fundamental process, stated by "Grounded Theory" (cf. [53]) for research areas, which are still not completely analyzed in detail such as intercultural HMI design with its gaps in research until today. Furthermore, grounded theory constitutes an iterative scientific process similar to iterative software development cycles. Both, grounded theory and iterative software development can be underlying methods for all approaches in intercultural user interface design. Moreover, there are several research communities all over the world concerned with culture-centered HCI design applying different concepts and similar approaches for intercultural user interface design (IUID). These communities are centered on the people who strongly push the research towards culture-centered HCI design. Even if, there are several links between these communities by expert networks or personal meetings at conferences such as INTERACT, IWIPS, CHI or HCII or workshops such as "Re-framing HCI through Local and Indigenous Perspectives" (cf. [54]), most approaches settle on older ones without being completely new or establishing a new research paradigm.

4   Recommendations

As shown above, there is no systematic holistic approach integrating the benefits of all approaches to yield synergy effects and resulting in the universal basic approach that could be used by all researchers for intercultural user interface design. Therefore, the author suggests bundling the efforts of the research community to establish a general framework and approach to profit from it in (applied) research as well as in industrial design in the future. Furthermore, one of the most important objectives in intercultural HMI design is still to show developers of international products a way to develop their products such that they can be offered successfully in the global market. One of the most important tasks thereby is to explore the intercultural differences (e.g., different color meanings or cognitive styles) and then to consider the implications of the identified differences in designing intercultural HMI (e.g., different operation state colors, browsing style). Relevant cultural variables for intercultural HMI design have to be determined and specified by literature review and requirements analysis. The values of cultural variables show culture-dependent variations that can be exploited for intercultural user interface design. They can be found on all levels of HMI localization (surface, functionality, interaction) (cf. [24]). Here, also cultural universals [55] and universal design [56] should be taken into account in order to yield aspects for universal design and to reduce overall research efforts: the more universal aspects independently of culture can be applied the less cultural differences must be determined empirically. Finally, the empirical qualitative and quantitative analyses of the values of the cultural variables need to integrate the results into cross-cultural HMI. In addition, the author recommends that "intercultural variables" are to be preferred in cases where the intercultural research character for obtaining the values of the variables is meant and "cultural variables", when mainly the usage of the values of the variables themselves (concerning a specific culture) is important. For instance, "Intercultural" usability engineering is a method for designing products of good usability for users from different cultures ([23]). "Intercultural" in this context refers to the special methods that are necessary to do usability engineering for different cultures (cf. [26]). The term "intercultural usability engineering" is commonly used by German usability engineers (cf. [21]) whereas outside Germany researches often use the concept of "cross-cultural usability testing" (cf. [57]) that must be conducted in order to yield good "cultural usability" (cf. [57]).

5   Conclusions

The analysis of the different concepts in the field of "HCI and culture" revealed that there is no basic concept permitting consensus among researchers in order to generate a sound terminological framework in this area. The extension of the concept of "user interface design" contains "HMI design" as well as "HCI design". The author suggests using the concept of *Intercultural* User Interface Design (IUID)" instead of the manifold combinations of the concepts analyzed in this paper in order:

- (i) to express the relationship between user interfaces and culture,
- (ii) to avoid fruitless discussions concerning HMI and HCI as well as
- (iii) to emphasize the necessity to consider at least two cultures (that of the designer and that of the end-user) connected by the word "intercultural".[4]

In addition, the analysis of some of the most relevant approaches in the area of "HCI and culture" indicated that there are no different research paradigms but rather different concepts for the same research paradigms even though it is not easy to determine the differences within these approaches because most of them are not systematic enough. Instead the investigated approaches are (i) related to each other and (ii) use several methods and techniques which (iii) are not systemized within one general approach. Further comprehensive analysis of the state of research must show if these conclusions can be generalized.

---

[4] Even in the broadest sense of the meaning of the concept it would be also reasonable to say "design for cultural contexts" or "culture-centered design".

References

1. Kralisch, A.: The Impact of Culture and Language on the Use of the Internet Empirical Analyses of Behaviour and Attitudes, Berlin (2006)
2. Heimgärtner, R.: Intercultural User Interface Design. In: Blashki, K., Isaias, P. (eds.) Emerging Research and Trends in Interactivity and the Human-Computer Interface (2013)
3. Nielsen, J.: Designing user interfaces for international use. Elsevier, Amsterdam (1990)
4. Del Galdo, E.M., Nielsen, J.: International user interfaces. Wiley, New York (1996)
5. Day, D.L.: The Cross-Cultural Study of Human-Computer Interaction: A Review of Research Methodology, Technology Transfer, and the Diffusion of Innovation (1991)
6. Cagiltay, K.: Culture and its Effects on Human-Computer-Interaction. In: Proceedings of World Conference on Educational Multimedia, Hypermedia and Telecommunications 1999, p. 1626 (1999)
7. Leidner, D.E., Kayworth, T.: Review: a review of culture in information systems research: toward a theory of information technology culture conflict. MIS Q. 30, 357–399 (2006)
8. Vatrapu, R., Suthers, D.: Culture and Computers: A review of the concept of culture and implications for intercultural collaborative online learning. In: Ishida, T., R. Fussell, S., T. J. M. Vossen, P. (eds.) IWIC 2007. LNCS, vol. 4568, pp. 260–275. Springer, Heidelberg (2007)
9. Clemmensen, T., Roese, K., Clemmensen, T., Roese, K.: An Overview of a Decade of Journal Publications about Culture and Human-Computer Interaction (HCI) (2010)
10. Jacko, J.A., Sears, A.: The human-computer interaction handbook: Fundamentals, evolving technologies and emerging applications. Erlbaum, Mahwah (2003)
11. Shen, S.-T., Woolley, M., Prior, S.: Towards culture-centred design. Interact. Comput. 18, 820–852 (2006)
12. Marcus, A.: Globalization of User-Interface Design for the Web. In: Prabhu, G., Delgaldo, E.M. (eds.) 1st Intern. Conference on Internationalization of Products and Systems (IWIPS), Backhouse Press, Rochester (1999)
13. Marcus, A.: Global and Intercultural User Interface Design. The human-computer interaction handbook: Fundamentals, evolving technologies and emerging applications (2003)
14. Marcus, A.: Cross-Cultural User-Interface Design. In: Smith, M.J.S.G. (ed.) Proceedings of the Human-Computer Interface Internat. (HCII), vol. 2, pp. 502–505. Lawrence Erlbaum Associates, Mahwah (2001)
15. Marcus, A.: International and intercultural user interfaces. In: Stephanidis, C. (ed.) User Interfaces for All: Concepts, Methods, and Tools, pp. 47–63. Lawrence Erlbaum, Mahwah (2001)
16. Marcus, A.: Globalization, Localization, and Cross-Cultural Communication in User-Interface Design. In: Jacko, J., Spears, A. (eds.) Handbook of Human-Computer Interaction, ch. 23, pp. 441–463. Lawrence Erlbaum Publishers, New York (2002)
17. Marcus, A.: Cross-Cultural User-Experience Design. In: Barker-Plummer, D., Cox, R., Swoboda, N. (eds.) Diagrams 2006. LNCS (LNAI), vol. 4045, pp. 16–24. Springer, Heidelberg (2006)
18. Rau, P.-L.P., Plocher, T.A., et al.: Cross-cultural design for IT products and services. Taylor & Francis, Boca Raton (2012)
19. Röse, K., Zühlke, D.: Culture-Oriented Design: Developers' Knowledge Gaps in this Area. In: 8th IFAC/IFIPS/IFORS/IEA Symposium on Analysis, Design, and Evaluation of Human-Machine Systems, September 18-20, pp. 11–16. Pergamon (2001)

20. Honold, P.: Intercultural Usability Engineering: Barriers and Challenges from a German point of view. In: Day, D., Galdo, E.D., Prabhu, G.V. (eds.) Designing for Global Markets 2. Second International Workshop on Internationalisation of Products and Systems, pp. 137–147 (2000)

21. Zühlke, D.: Useware-Systeme für internationale Märkte. Useware-Engineering für technische Systeme, pp. 142–164. Springer, Heidelberg (2004)

22. Heimgärtner, R.: Cultural Differences in Human-Computer Interaction. Oldenbourg Verlag (2012)

23. Honold, P.: Interkulturelles usability engineering: Eine Untersuchung zu kulturellen Einflüssen auf die Gestaltung und Nutzung technischer Produkte. VDI Verl., Düsseldorf (2000)

24. Röse, K.: Methodik zur Gestaltung interkultureller Mensch-Maschine-Systeme in der Produktionstechnik. Univ., Kaiserslautern (2002)

25. Marcus, A.: Cross-Cultural User-Experience Design. In: Barker-Plummer, D., Cox, R., Swoboda, N. (eds.) Diagrams 2006. LNCS (LNAI), vol. 4045, pp. 16–24. Springer, Heidelberg (2006)

26. Honold, P.: "Cross-cultural" or "intercultural" - some findings on international usability testing. In: Prabhu, G.V., Del Galdo, E.M. (eds.) Designing for Global Markets 1, First International Workshop on Internationalisation of Products and Systems, IWIPS 1999, pp. 107–122. Backhouse Press, Rochester (1999)

27. Bourges-Waldegg, P., Scrivener, S.A.R.: Meaning, the central issue in cross-cultural HCI design. Interacting with Computers: the Interdisciplinary Journal of Human-Computer Interaction 9, 287–309 (1998)

28. Yeo, A.W.: Global-software development lifecycle: an exploratory study. In: Proceedings of the SIGCHI Conference on Human Factors in Computing Systems, pp. 104–111. ACM, Seattle (2001)

29. Jagne, J., Smith-Atakan, A.: Cross-cultural interface design strategy. Universal Access in the Information Society 5, 299–305 (2006)

30. Evers, V., Kukulska-Hulme, A., Jones, A.: Cross-Cultural Understanding of Interface Design: A Cross-Cultural Analysis of Icon Recognition, pp. 173–182 (1999)

31. Fernandes, T.: Global interface design (a guide to designing international user interfaces). AP Professional, Chestnut Hill (1995)

32. Hofstede, G.H., Hofstede, G.J., Minkov, M.: Cultures and organizations: software of the mind. McGraw-Hill, Maidenhead (2010)

33. Marcus, A., Gould, E.W.: Cultural dimensions and global web user-interface design: What? So What? Now What? (2000)

34. Nielsen, J.: Designing web usability. New Riders, Berkeley (2006)

35. Zahedi, F., Bansal, G.: Cultural Signifiers of Web Site Images. J. Manage. Inf. Syst. 28, 147–200 (2011)

36. Plocher, T., Patrick Rau, P.-L., Choong, Y.-Y.: Cross-Cultural Design. In: Handbook of Human Factors and Ergonomics, pp. 162–191. John Wiley & Sons, Inc. (2012)

37. Prabhu, G., Harel, D.: GUI Design Preference Validation for Japan and China - A Case for KANSEI Engineering? In: Proceedings of HCI International (the 8th International Conference on Human-Computer Interaction) on Human-Computer Interaction: Ergonomics and User Interfaces, vol. I, pp. 521–525. L. Erlbaum Associates Inc (1999)

38. Hofstede, G.H.: Cultures and organizations: Software of the mind. McGraw-Hill, London (1991)

39. Hall, E.T.: The Silent Language. Doubleday, New York (1959)

40. Hall, E.T.: Beyond Culture. Anchor Books, New York (1976)

41. Hall, E.T., Hall, M.R.: Understanding cultural differences. Intercultural Press, Yarmouth (1990)
42. Choong, Y.-Y., Salvendy, G.: Design of Icons for Use by Chinese in Mainland China. Interacting with Computers 9, 417–430 (1998)
43. Nisbett, R.E.: The geography of thought: How Asians and Westerners think differently... and why. Free Press, New York (2003)
44. Evers, V.: Cross-cultural understanding of metaphors in interface design. In: Ess, C., Sudweeks, F. (eds.) Attitudes toward Technology and Communication (Proceedings CATAC 1998), Australia, August 1-3 (1998)
45. DIN: DIN EN ISO 9241-210 Ergonomische Anforderungen der Mensch-System-Interaktion Teil 210: Prozess zur Gestaltung gebrauchstauglicher Systeme. BeuthVerlag, Berlin (2010)
46. De Souza, C.S.: The semiotic engineering of user interface languages. International Journal Man-Machine Studies 39, 753–773 (1993)
47. De Souza, C.S., Barbosa, S.D.J., Prates, R.O.: A Semiotic Engineering Approach to HCI. In: CHI 2001 (2001)
48. de Castro Salgado, L.C., Leitão, C.F., de Souza, C.S.: A Journey Through Cultures: Metaphors for Guiding the Design of Cross-Cultural Interactive Systems. Springer Publishing Company, Incorporated (2012)
49. de Castro Salgado, L.C., Leitão, C.F., de Souza, C.S.: Semiotic Engineering and Culture, pp. 19–42. Springer, London (2013)
50. Prates, R.O., de Souza, C.S., Barbosa, S.D.J.: Methods and tools: a method for evaluating the communicability of user interfaces. Interactions 7, 31–38 (2000)
51. Brislin, R.W., Yoshida, T.: Intercultural communication training: An introduction. SAGE Publications, Thousand Oaks (1994)
52. Thomas, A., Kinast, E.-U., Schroll-Machl, S.: Handbook of intercultural communication and cooperation. Basics and areas of application. Vandenhoeck & Ruprecht, Göttingen (2010)
53. Vollhardt, J.K., Migacheva, K., Tropp, L.R.: Social Cohesion and Tolerance for Group Differences. In: Handbook on Building Cultures of Peace, pp. 139–152. Springer, New York (2008)
54. Abdelnour-Nocera, J., et al.: Re-framing HCI through Local and Indigenous Perspectives. In: Campos, P., Graham, N., Jorge, J., Nunes, N., Palanque, P., Winckler, M. (eds.) INTERACT 2011, Part IV. LNCS, vol. 6949, pp. 738–739. Springer, Heidelberg (2011)
55. Schwartz, S.H.: Mapping and interpreting cultural differences around the world. In: Vinken, H., Soeters, J., Ester, P. (eds.) Comparing Cultures, Dimensions of Culture in a Comparative Perspective, pp. 43–73. Brill, Leiden (2004)
56. Stephanidis, C.: Universal Access in the Information Society, vol. 8 (2009)
57. Clemmensen, T., Goyal, S., Clemmensen, T., Goyal, S.: Cross cultural usability testing. The relationship between evaluator and test user, København (2005)

User-Experience and Science-Fiction in Chinese, Indian, and Japanese Films

Aaron Marcus

Aaron Marcus and Associates, Inc.,
1196 Euclid Avenue, Suite 1F, Berkeley, CA, 94708, USA
Aaron.Marcus@AMandA.com

Abstract. Chinese, Indian, and Japanese science-fiction films offer different and interesting views of user-experience that can inform user-experience researchers, designers, analysts, and evaluators. The author reviews Asian contributions to science-fiction media.

Keywords: China, culture, design, India, Japan, movies, science-fiction, user interface, user experience.

1 Introduction

The study of user-experience design in relation to science-fiction movies, television, comic books, animation, and other popular media is becoming more active worldwide. The popularity of science-fiction media, especially under the influence of Hollywood productions like *Avatar* and *Prometheus* unavoidably sets up a bias towards Western media. One should not forget Asian sci-fi film-makers who have been inspired by some of the classic Western novels/films as well as their own literature traditions. They have produced films that reflect their unique cultural heritages, such as Bollywood films that combine traditional storytelling with music and dance quite unlike most of the products of Hollywood.

The study of Chinese, Indian, and Japanese approaches to metaphors, mental models, navigation, interaction, and appearance, where it is not a derivative copy of Western approaches but more revealing creations based on different cultures, will be worth much further study. Research studies may reveal cross-cultural influences of one genre upon the other, e.g., the Hollywood influence on Indian sci-fi, a Bollywood influence on Hollywood sci-fi, or Hong Kong action-films' influence on Hollywood sci-fi. With the rise of multiple film production centers, for example, a new animation center being started in Shanghai under the auspices of Robin King, a Master of the De Tao Masters Academy of Beijing (King), it is possible that the influences may run in multiple directions in the decades ahead. Already, India has shown a desire to produce comic books featuring Hindu deities as super-heros and heroines instead of the classic Western Superman and other characters. Unfortunately, it is not always easy to locate examples of films that show UX interaction and appearance. At the very least, I cite some of the films (from Wikipedia) and urge readers to investigate further. The selections below are excerpted from my ebook: The Past 100 Years of the Future: HCI in Sci-Fi Movies and Television (Marcus).

A. Marcus (Ed.): DUXU/HCII 2013, Part II, LNCS 8013, pp. 72–78, 2013.

2   Chinese Sci-Fi Films

Chinese sci-fi film making seems to have started earlier than Indian. Jules Verne stories were imported intoChina during the late nineteenth and early twentieth centuries. Yueqiu Zhimindi Xiaoshuo (*Lunar Colony*), 1904, seems to be the earliest original Chinese Sci-Fi writing. Zheng Wenguang, father of modern Chinese science-fiction literature, wrote in 50s, 70s, e.g., Flying to the Centaur. Among other sci-fi films are the following (citations taken from Wikipedia, with apologies to academia):

Death Ray on Coral Island, 1980. Tong Enzheng wrote "Death Ray on a Coral Island," which was made into China's first sci-fi movie. A blogger comments on the film (Pickles): Death Ray: a good-hearted team of Chinese scientists, based in what appears to be San Francisco, finally succeed in completing their fabulous futuristic invention. That is, until the sinister back-stabbing Americans, played with Bond-villainous glee by Chinese actors in whiteface and prosthetic noses, decide to steal the invention for their evil plots. They use sabotage, death-ray guns, murder, and even cocktails, to get what they want. The head scientist, shortly after being gunned down with a ...laser and left for dead, hands off the circuit board to his brave son-in-law. "Take this, and flee!" But those lousy Americans don't give up... they shoot down the kid's plane over shark-infested, death-ray-filled waters, and he ends up on a mysterious Dr Moreau island.

Tong authored a textbook about cultural anthropology and specialized in early southwest China. In science-fiction, he wrote the short story "Death Ray on a Coral Island", which won an award for China's best short story in 1978 and which was later adapted to film. He died in the US after fleeing China following the government's crackdown on protests at Tiananmen Square.

Figures: Scenes from *Death Ray on a Coral Island* (1980).

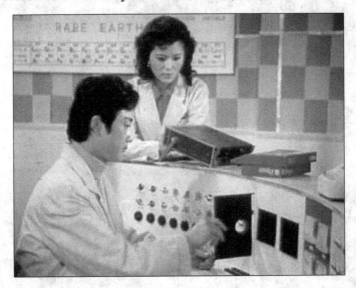

Fig. 1. Scene from Death Ray on a Coral Island (1980). Image source acknowledgment for this and other figures: `http://asiaobscura.com/2011/02/chinas-first-sci-fi-movie-death-ray-on-coral-island-1980.html`.

In this scene, modern-looking white-coated technicians use the latest current technology. The color scheme features the typical white, blue, gray, and black of modern high-tech interiors. Note the use of what seems to be a wall-chart of something like the Periodic Table of the Elements in the background to lend an authoritative scientifc aura to the scene.

Fig. 2. Scene from Death Ray on a Coral Island (1980)

Fig. 3. Scene *from Death Ray on a Coral Island (1980)*

The scientists/technologists stare intently at multiple screen displays in a scene similar to that depicted in many other Western sci-fi movies. The movie seemingly wishes to convey massive technology and massive data. Note the use of a conventional office desk phone on top of the control panel rather than individual head-sets. Perhaps in an emergency all might dive for the one phone to contact others. The use of a single phone was typical of corporate Japanese office groups in the 1980s.

As in other Western sci-fi films of the time, large-scale wall video displays help to convey advanced technology.

3   Indian Sci-Fi Films

Indian sci-fi films since 1952 are produced in many languages. India itself has about 22 national languages, which means production houses must translate films and/or provide subtitles in dozens of languages even for India's domestic market. Indian sci-fi film makers have even produced several Bollywood-style science-fiction movies like Robot (Enthiran), in Tamil, not Hindi (and thus what is called by some Kollywood, not Bollywood, based on an area near Chennai, not Mumbai), directed by S.Shankar in 2010. Such films feature music and dancing, unlike almost any sci-fi media in the West.

Action Replayy (sic, formerly *Action Replay*), Hindi, 2010. This Indian sci-fi romantic comedy film was based on the 1985 Hollywood blockbuster *Back to the Future*.

Kalai Arasi, c. 1960, Tamil. Aliens kidnap an Earth girl to teach them the arts; a hero rescues her.

Aditya 369, Tulugu.
Bharathan, Malayam.

Karutha Rathrikal, 1967, Malayam. A doctor takes revenge on his uncle's death with medicine he invented that creates a split personality. This is the first Malayam sci-fi film.

Dasavathaaram, Tamil. The third-highest-grossing Indian film. The story features a USA virus that threatens Earth.

Koi... Mil Gaya, 2003, Bollywood, perhaps the most famous Bollywood sci-fi film. An alien visits the earth, similar to ET. The film is a kind of Indian Alien.

Enthiran (*Robot*), Tamil, 2010. A scientist makes a robot, lives with it, and adds emotions. Alas, the robot falls in love with the scientist's girlfirend. The film was the most expensive India film made and the highest grossing film.

Krrish, Hindi. 2006. A super-hero film.

Love Story 2050. 2008. The setting is a future Mumbai.

Jaithra Yaathra, 1987, Malayalam. A scientist invents a locket to make himself invisible and battles a villain.

Mr. India, Hindi, 1987. A super-hero film, with super-hero Indian stars.
Patalghar, Bengali. An alien visits India.

Kaadu (The Jungle), 1952, Tamil-American. The first sci-fi film in Tamil Nadu tells of expedition finding the cause of strange behavior of animals. The film features an invasion of woolly mammoths.

Rudraksh, 2004, Hindi. An action-adventure, the film was based on Ramayana classical literature

The Alien, late 1960s, canceled. Alien Mr. Ang visits a Bengali urbanite.

4   Japanese Science Fiction

The many movies Japanese film-makers created over decades are too numerous to mention in detail. Their relations with Japanese Manga and *animé* films has yet to be explored in detail. To give an idea of the content yet to be examined and published in the West, I list Japanese science-fiction films noted on the Internet:

1,778 Stories of Me and My Wife
20th Century Boys
964 Pinocchio
A.LI.CE
Akira (film)
Alien vs Ninja
Andromedia
Appleseed (film)
Appleseed Ex Machina
Arcadia of My Youth
Assault Girls
Avalon (2001 film)
Battle in Outer Space
Be Forever Yamato
Casshern (film)
Cowboy Bebop: The Movie
Cyclops (1987 film)
Daijōbu, My Friend
Darkside Blues
Dead Leaves
Dead or Alive: Final
Death Powder
Dirty Pair: Project Eden
Electric Dragon 80.000 V
The End of Evangelion

The 6 Ultra Brothers vs. the Monster Army
Godzilla vs. *Megalon*
Godzilla and Mothra: The Battle for Earth
Godzilla vs. *SpaceGodzilla*
Godzilla, Mothra and King Ghidorah: Giant Monsters All-Out Attack
Godzilla: Tokyo S.O.S.
Goke, Body Snatcher from Hell
Gunhed (film)
Invasion of Astro-Monster
Meatball Machine
Memories (film)
Message from Space
Metropolis (animé)
Mirai Ninja
Neo Tokyo (film)
Paprika (2006 film)
Patlabor 2: The Movie
Patlabor: The Movie
Planzet
Prophecies of Nostradamus
Pyrokinesis (film)
Redline (2009 film)

Evangelion: 3.0 You Can (Not) Redo
The Face of Another (film)
Farewell to Space Battleship Yamato
Final Fantasy VII: Advent Children
Final Yamato
Full Metal Yakuza
G.I. Samurai
Gamera 2: Attack of Legion
Gamera 3: Awakening of Irys
Gamera vs. Zigra
Gamera: Guardian of the Universe
Gantz (live action films)
Ghost in the Shell (film)
Ghost in the Shell 2: Innocence
Godzilla 2000
Godzilla Against Mechagodzilla
Godzilla vs. Biollante
Godzilla vs. Destoroyah
Godzilla vs. Gigan
Godzilla vs. Hedorah
Godzilla vs. Mechagodzilla
Godzilla vs. Mechagodzilla II
Teito Monogatari Gaiden
Terror of Mechagodzilla
Tetsuo II: Body Hammer
Tetsuo: The Bullet Man
Time Traveller: The Girl Who Leapt Through Time
Toki o Kakeru Shōjo (1997 film)
Toki o Kakeru Shōjo (1983 film)
Tokyo: The Last War
Venus Wars

The Return of Godzilla
Returner
RoboGeisha
Rubber's Lover
Sayonara Jupiter (film)
Screamers (1995 film)
Seth et Holth
The Sky Crawlers (film)
Solar Crisis (film)
Sonic the Hedgehog: The Movie
Space Amoeba
Space Battleship Yamato (2010 film)
Space Battleship Yamato: Resurrection
Space Brothers (manga)
Specter (film)
Starship Troopers: Invasion
Steamboy
StrayDog: Kerberos Panzer Cops
Summer Time Machine Blues
Taitei no Ken
Tamala 2010: A Punk Cat in Space
Vexille
Virus (1980 film)
The War in Space
The War of the Gargantuas
Wicked City (film)
WXIII: Patlabor the Movie 3
Yakuza Weapon
Yamato: The New Voyage
Zeiram

5   Conclusion

This brief survey provides a place to start looking for cross-cultural similarities and differences, and innovation in approaches to UX design. What we find there may be quite valuable to UX researchers, designers, analysts, and evaluators. Already a colleague in India suggested several decades ago that the Microsoft Windows user interface was unsuited to India because its metaphors relied on assumptions that everyone in India knows about desktops. They didn't. In 1992, the Japanese Mininisty of International Trade and Industry released a report about the Friend 21 project, multiple-years of research into advanced concepts of future high-technology systems, which featured innovative metaphor-switching software and a distinctly Japanese approach to usability: providing things before the user realizes that he/she needs them. About a decade ago, I reviewed a paper from Chinese authors proposing graphical user-interfaces based on the concept of Chinese gardens, which seemed to be at the time quite unusual. Two years ago, a colleague in China proposed that there might be unique Chinese solutions to user-interface deign that the West had not yet discovered.

In a multi-polar world of user-experience innovation, one may not be able to predict from where the next big change in UX design may arise. Looking at sci-fi movies (and videos) provides a unique perspective on future user personas and use scenarios, as well as details of context, functionality, and content. We should take a longer look at this largely unexplored territory. The investigation may inform our understanding about the future of UX design.

Acknowledgements. The author thanks Ms. Theresa Schieder and Ms. Megan Chiou, AM+A Designer/Analysts, for their assistance with research and editing portions of this text, which is based on (Marcus).

References

1. King: De Tao Masters Academy, Studio Description (2013),
   http://107.22.197.5/studio/home/234 (accessed February 14, 2013)
2. Marcus, A.: The Past 100 Years of the Future: HCI in Science-Fiction Movies and Television. eBook published by Aaron Marcus and Associates, Inc. (2012),
   http://www.amanda.com/wp-content/uploads/2012/10/AM+A.SciFI+HCI.eBook_.LM10Oct12.pdf (accessed February 14, 2013)
3. Pickles, D.: Blog about Death Ray on Coral Island (2011),
   http://outthereasia.blogspot.com/search/label/movies?max-results=20 (accessed February 14, 2013)

Two Solitudes Revisited: A Cross-Cultural Exploration of Online Image Searcher's Behaviors

Elaine Ménard, Nouf Khashman, and Jonathan Dorey

School of Information Studies, McGill University
3661 Peel, Montreal, QC. H3A 1X1, Canada
elaine.menard@mcgill.ca, nouf.khashman@mail.mcgill.ca,
jonathan.dorey@mailmcgill.ca

Abstract. This paper presents and discusses the results of the second phase of the project that aims to investigate the roles and usefulness of search characteristics and functionalities used for image retrieval in a bilingual context, from the user's point of view. The difficulties encountered by image searchers are described. Finally, suggestions to be integrated in a search interface model are presented. This exploratory study provides an understanding of how users with different linguistic and cultural background search for images.

Keywords: Digital images, search interface, image retrieval, cross-language information retrieval, multilingual information.

1   Introduction

The image retrieval process supposes that users must search a database that contains many thousands, even millions of images. Ideally, the search interface must be hospitable and support query formulation with as little effort and frustration as possible for the user. It should also allow users to retrieve images from all origins, including images indexed in a language that does not match the query language.

However, many factors can overwhelm the image searcher, including functionalities that are well-designed but not particularly adapted to the retrieval of images indexed in an unknown language. The results of our previous study [13] on image searchers' behaviours of four different linguistic communities revealed significant differences in the searching process. These differences must be taken into consideration when developing any search interface used for image retrieval.

Despite the fact that some search engines already offer sophisticated search mechanisms and features, much remains to be done to ensure universal access to many textual or non-textual documents. The general goal of our research project proposes to develop an interface model for image retrieval in a bilingual (English and French) context, that is, when the query language differs from the indexing language. In particular, this study addresses the following three objectives:

A. Marcus (Ed.): DUXU/HCII 2013, Part II, LNCS 8013, pp. 79–88, 2013.
© Springer-Verlag Berlin Heidelberg 2013

1. To identify the characteristics and functionalities of existing search interfaces and similar tools available for image retrieval.
2. To investigate the roles and usefulness of these search characteristics and functionalities for image retrieval in a bilingual context.
3. To design and develop an interface model that allows image retrieval in a bilingual context.

This paper presents the second phase of the project aiming to investigate the roles and usefulness of the search characteristics and functionalities for the image search process in a bilingual context, from the user's point of view. Image searchers are viewed as informants who can help Web designers fill gaps with their knowledge.

2   Related Works

2.1   Content-Based Image Retrieval

The main focus of image retrieval research has been on how people search for and describe images. However, despite widespread studies on image searchers' behaviour or performance when searching for images, little is known about the image search functionalities that individuals actually use for image retrieval.

Image retrieval can be performed using the "Content-Based Image Retrieval" (CBIR) techniques. CBIR systems take advantage of the physical characteristics of the image [17] and do not involve the use of metadata, such as keywords, tags or any textual descriptions associated with the image at any stage. Images are indexed and eventually retrieved with the values associated with certain parameters, such as colour, texture and shape [2]. These low-level characteristics are generally automatically extracted from image files, as opposed to the so-called "high-level" indexing terms assigned following the analysis of the image by a human indexer.

With some CBIR systems, the users can submit an image or a drawing and the engine will retrieve images similar to these visual queries. It is also possible to search with a dominant colour. This feature is already offered by several search engines, therefore allowing the search to be conducted through millions of images using this technology based on colour histograms. Some CBIR devices have been expressly designed to help filter and identify skin tones and shapes that could indicate the presence of sensitive content, such as nudity.

Regardless of some weaknesses such as relevance of results, speed of execution of retrieval tasks and overall user satisfaction, the retrieval systems that use low-level characteristics are already offering interesting searching features and are advantageous in the case of browsing, that is, when image searchers do not have a very clear idea of what they are looking for [11]. Nevertheless, CBIR systems still present a number of imperfections and remain at the experimental stage [8], [5].

The future of these systems depends very much on the technological progress that will occur and the interest they will generate. Further, the usability of these systems, in terms of effectiveness, efficiency and satisfaction, will probably be a key element in the decision of the everyday image searchers to adopt them or not.

2.2   Text-Based Image Retrieval

Most search engines allow the users to look for images with the usual textual queries. With the "Text-Based Image Retrieval" (TBIR), the search engines will try to match the query words with the indexing terms associated with the image. In most cases, queries remain very short and less than developed. In 2010, Choi and Hsieh-Yee, [3], revealed that the average number of terms used in an image query was 3.12 terms. This finding is similar to that of previous studies on Web image queries [7], [9], [12]. Short queries such as "Kate Middleton", "Olympic games", "iPhone5", will be generally successful since most search engines use the text surrounding the image for describing and indexing the content of an image.

The use of the adjacent text allows fast and rather accurate indexing of billions of images. Nevertheless, two significant weaknesses tend to appear with this mass automatic indexing process. On the one hand, the surrounding words are often unconnected to the image or ambiguous. On the other hand, image retrieval will be unsuccessful if different languages are used in the description of the images, since it is difficult to map semantically equivalent words across different languages [10]. To these difficulties, we must add that the text-based approach may greatly limit the possibilities in terms of semantic interpretations of the image content. Consequently, the amount of resulting images will often be overwhelming, discouraging, even frustrating sometimes.

Research results from the field of image retrieval tends to indicate that a combination of the two types of retrieval systems (CBIR and TBIR) could overcome most difficulties of each individual approach [14].

2.3   User-Centered Techniques in Image Retrieval

Over the years, several studies were realized on text-based retrieval activity. For example, Fidel (1997) [6] suggested that image needs among users range from two extremes, the Data Pole (images as information, i.e., x-rays, maps) and the Object Pole (images as illustration, i.e., aesthetic objects), with the majority of cases falling at some point in between the two poles. Several studies ([7], [9], [16]) revealed a transformation in the way queries are formulated in the image retrieval process. Most recently, Wetsman et al. [18] stated that task type influences the use of query modes. Chung and Yoon [4] examined how the image need context impacted the kinds of attributes used in image seeking. This change leads to a reassessment of the way in which the image must be searched and whether the search tools traditionally employed for image searching and browsing are well-suited to all types of images.

The focus of these projects did not reveal much about the search functionalities use by image searcher. In fact, little is known about the interactions that take place between the image searchers and the retrieval system. The examination of Web image searcher's behaviour, therefore, seems crucial in order to improve retrieval systems. In the same way, it is crucial to continue the study of retrieval strategies of image searchers in order to establish better search tools that will be more appropriate to the needs and behaviours of image searchers.

3   Objectives

For the first phase of the study, a best practices review was performed in order to acquire knowledge of the existing search functionalities, and to assess how they can be integrated in the development of a bilingual search interface dedicated specifically to images. However, this review only provided a list of functionalities available to search for images. We can speculate if differences exist according to the linguistic preferences of the image searchers in terms of query types and the use of some search functionalities since this exploration is taking place within the very unique cultural context of Québec, a Canadian province with a predominantly French-speaking population and the only one whose sole official language is French at the provincial level.

To gain valuable information on the usefulness of these search functionalities, the next logical step was to talk to real users and analyze their behaviours and needs when searching for online images. There has been little research on investigating the characteristics and functionalities necessary to support image retrieval in a bilingual context and to integrate these characteristics and functionalities into a comprehensive yet flexible interface model. This project proposes to fill this gap and answer the following research questions:

1. What types of queries are used by individuals during the image search process?
2. Which functionalities are currently used for the image search process?
3. Which functionalities are considered to be useful to the image search process?
4. To what extent are there differences in the image search process between two groups of individuals with different languages?

4   Methodology

For this study, we used the methodology identified and described by Behesthi, Large and Clement [1] of "Informant Design," where participants' input is required at various stages of the design process [15]. Participants are viewed as a major source of information that can help researchers fill their knowledge gaps.

For the first step of our data collection a bilingual (English and French) questionnaire containing closed and open questions was developed and administered to two groups of participants: 20 English-speaking and 20 French-speaking respondents. The quantitative data was analyzed according to statistical methods while the content of the open-ended questions was analyzed and coded to identify emergent themes.

For the second phase, data was collected with semi-structured interviews conducted in two languages: English and French. The semi-structured interviews aimed to gather participants' knowledge and understanding of their perceptions for the image retrieval process. They also allowed users to articulate and express their experiences as image searchers. Two interview guides (English and French) were developed to assist in collecting the data. Five English-speaking and five French-speaking respondents accepted to be interviewed.

During the interviews, the participants were asked to identify and discuss the features and functionalities they usually employ to search for images. The answers received from participants were expected to help us understand the behaviours and needs of people who are frequently searching for online images and to identify cross-cultural difficulties. Some interview questions, as well as the topics explored during the interviews, depended on the direction in which the participant led the discussion. This approach was taken in order to determine how the participants experienced image searching which was directly related to their experience and search goals. As much as possible we asked respondents to express their thoughts and experiences without forcing them to answer in a formal manner.

The data from the ten interviews (approximately 45-60 minutes each) was audio-recorded and transcribed. Interviews have been analyzed and coded to determine emergent themes that could enrich our understanding of the image searcher's perspective. All text has been coded by at least two evaluators. An intercoder reliability test was conducted to ensure coding consistency. Participants' responses and related issues that arose during the interview process were grouped and analyzed as complete quotations and filed according to topic or issue. Responses have been analyzed thematically with emergent themes ranked by frequency and subsequently categorized.

5   Results

5.1   Type of Queries

Among French-speaking searchers, image retrieval is characterized typically by a two stage process: a short, general keyword search is first performed in the search box, followed by browsing of the results. French Participant 1 (FP1) states: "Mais je vais écrire peu importe – je vais décrire ce que je cherche dans une – dans la façon la plus simple possible sans utiliser trop de mots, parce que plus t'en mets, plus tu sors de trucs qui ont des fois pas rapport." [*But I will write whatever – I will describe what I'm looking for in a – in the simplest possible way without using too many words because the more words you use, the more stuff you get and it doesn't match.*] FP3 and FP5 also emphasize the importance of being specific when inputting a query. All five participants start a search with a minimal number of keywords, typically between one and three. FP2 usually launches a search with a single keyword, while FP3 adds that they rarely need more than two or three because they usually find what they are looking for with that number of keywords. Boolean operators are typically not used for images. FP1 states using them for textual searches, but only implicitly for images: "Je fais ma recherche sur le même principe, même si j'utilise pas le mot «AND» puis «OR» ." [*I do my search following the same principle, even though I don't use the word 'AND' or 'OR'.*]

Among the French-speaking participants, the intent behind the search reflected a mix of personal, work or school related needs. The preferred image browser was Google Images, but other tools were also used: JSTOR (FP1) and ARTStores (FP4) as well as Yahoo and Bing images, museum websites, and Wikipedia. The main arguments for relying on Google Images to perform their search is simplicity, ease of use and familiarity. When asked why they did not search on other websites, FP1 stated "C'est pas un réflexe." [*It's not a reflex.*] FP2 and FP3 mentioned returning to the website for future searches: "Oui, pour qu'on y revienne souvent." [*Yes, so that you return to it often.*] and "Ou parce qu'on l'a juste utilisé beaucoup, donc c'est devenu [habituel]." [*Or because you used it a lot, so it became natural.*] FP4 explains their lack of use of Flick as an image retrieval tool because they did not put any effort in trying to understand how it works: "J'ai pas encore fait l'effort de comprendre comment ça fonctionne."

The use of other websites to get more background information about a search was also common among French-speaking participants. FP2, FP3 and FP4 all gave the example of paintings and using Wikipedia as a source of information to learn more about a painter, the title of a work, the date, or the period. This information would help them to formulate more specific queries. FP5 added online forums to Wikipedia as a source for background information. The purpose of searching for background information is to build a specific vocabulary that would allow them to target known-items in their search: "Dans le sens que si jamais je connais pas le nom de la toile, tu sais." [FP3] [*In the sense that is ever you don't know the title of a painting, you know?*]

Among English-speaking participants, the image retrieval process is also based on a general keyword search followed by browsing the results. For all these five participants, the search query consists of very few keywords without having to use phrases or advanced searching options such as Boolean operators demonstrated by examples they gave for their search such as "Jennifer Aniston hair" (EP1), "rag weed" (EP4), and "heart disease" (EP5). Some of these participants indicated that they tend to refine their queries based on the results that they get from their search. English participant 2 (EP2) stated that: "I usually start with the best terms that I can come up with, and if that works then great but if it doesn't then I try narrow my search or broadening it and come up with better search terms"

Similar to the French-speaking participants, English-speaking participants search for images either for personal use or for school projects, only EP4 indicated searching for images for job related needs. All five participants indicated that they almost always start with Google to search for images, but Flickr/Flickr creative comments (EP2), Tumbler (EP3), and Bing (EP5) were also mentioned as secondary searching systems. The reasons for relying heavily on Google ranged from it offering free images (EP5), simplicity (EP1-5), to offering the basic [information] needs (EP4). When some participants were asked why they do not use other systems such as Flickr, they noted that because it requires them to create accounts which in turn hinder their accessibility to the site (EP3-4) and also requires them to identify themselves (EP4). EP3 states: "I could use Flickr but I'm just, don't even want to go there I feel like I have to sign up".

But unlike French-speaking participants, English-speaking participants did not rely on other websites to get background information about a search, except for EP2 who uses Wikipedia to validate search terms in Russian. Nonetheless, EP2 and EP5 indicated using other websites such as Flickr for browsing their friends' images without actually using it to search for images, as can be seen in EP5 statement: "like a couple of my friends have a Flickr account so I look at their photos but I don't use it specifically for an image search".

5.2   Functionalities Currently Used

None of the five French-speaking participants said they use advanced search functions when looking for images. At the most, they use the size and/or resolution of an image as selection criteria when browsing the search results. FP1 uses size, shapes and colours as a way to select and refine the results: "Généralement je vais juste comme vraiment faire un scan visuel de chaque page." [*Generally, all I will end up doing is a visual scan of each page.*] Searching by colour is seen as useful in the context of work-related searching, as stated by FP2: "Dans tous ces métiers-là où souvent ils recherchent des formes, des images, la couleur." [*In all these professions, where they often search shapes, images, colour.*]

English-speaking participants also indicated that they rarely, if ever, use advanced search functions such as colour, shape, and texture when looking for images. Nonetheless, all five participants said they would use the size function to select a desired image from the search results, usually after visually browsing what they retrieved. EP1 indicated the familiarity with other functionalities, but not using them in the search process: "the features that I use...choosing the size, but other than that I know that the features are there and I know if I need to refine it more".

5.3   Functionalities Considered Useful

When asked about the usefulness of various functionalities, French-speaking participants all recognized that while they may not use a specific function, there may be cases where it would be important to have it. FP1 says that it is important that searching by size and colour exists – "Je trouve que c'est important que ça existe." – but later admits to not usually using them. There was also a lack of knowledge regarding the possibility of searching by similar image, or searching by drawing, as offered in some systems. Both functionalities were viewed as potentially interesting. FP4 had just recently discovered the possibility of searching with a similar image and said: "Je viens juste de découvrir cette fonction qu'a Google, là, où on peut mettre l'image et qui donne des images semblables. Je l'ai découvert il y a, genre, deux, trois jours, puis ça a changé ma vie." [*I just discovered that function in Google, where you can put the image and it returns similar images. I discovered it about two, three days ago and it changed my life.*] FP4 later explained that they used this function to identify various paintings they had saved on their hard drive without any information about the title or the painter.

One functionality French-speaking searchers deemed useful, which English-speaking searchers did not appear to value, is the automatic translation of queries. All five participants recognized the usefulness and often the requirement of having to search in languages other than French, with English being the most important language. They all, however, cautioned on the quality of automatic translation, fearing the results for anything longer than a couple of words. FP2 stated her lack of confidence in automatic translation more strongly than the others: "Aucune confiance" [*No confidence*]. FP2 preferred to rely on dictionaries and self-translation for higher quality search terms.

The issue of automation also came up with various searchers regarding the development of a taxonomy to help index saved images. FP1 would like to have a combination of automatic suggestions and their own keywords: "Je pense qu'un mix des deux: pouvoir utiliser tes mots-clés, comme ça si tu trouves ce que tu veux, tant mieux." [*I think a mix of both: using our own keywords and that way if you find what you want, even better.*] FP5 would prefer to use their own keywords: "Bon, c'est assez fendant, mais oui, je préfère utiliser mes mots." [*Look, it's a little pretentious, but yes, I prefer to use my own words.*] FP4 tied automatic translation and the suggested taxonomy: "Si je pouvais définir mon propre et ensuite qu'il fasse la traduction." [*If I could define my own terms and have it translate them.*]

While searching for images using other images sounded "fun" (EP2), "cool" (EP3) and "helpful" (EP5) for English-speaking participants, the consensus indicated that it is just an "extra perk" (EP3) and not as important as other features such as accessibility (EP1). Searching for images by drawing also seemed "fun" (EP2), but four participants indicated that they probably will not use such functionality because they lack drawing skills (EP1,2) and it requires a lot of time. EP3 states that: "based on what I could draw and like the way I draw it and the size or shape or the texture I don't think that would be very helpful to me personally, and I think that even in general I think you will get a lot of [ambiguity in the] results".

As stated earlier, English-speaking participants do not rely on automated translation tools mainly for two reasons: first, they do not usually perform bilingual/multilingual search, except for EP2 who searches in multiple languages including Spanish and Russian very frequently. Second, they acknowledge the availability of whatever they look for in English since it is the dominant language on the internet (EP1,4). Even for those participants who indicated using Google translate in some occasions, translation quality offered by those tools was an issue for not relying on them as indicated by EP2: "[because] often I'm little skeptical whether or not that really is the proper translation".

On the other hand, other functionalities were suggested by those participants that they considered useful to search for images online, including a tool to adjust the images on the spot while retrieving images (EP1), automatic spell check (EP2), a tool that would enable them to insert special characters like accented letters in French (EP4), a toolbar to enhance the accessibility to the search tool (EP5), and the ability to tag images with accurate descriptors (EP2,4).

5.4   Differences in the Image Search Process between the Two Language Groups

As can be seen from the results of interviews both for French and English speaking participants, keyword searching seems to be the main approach for searching images online, without relying on advanced techniques such using Boolean operators or searching using similar images or having the ability to search by drawing. The search keywords are very few and descriptive as much as possible in order to enhance the accuracy and relevancy of the results. Unlike English-speaking participants, French-speaking participants occasionally use other features such as shapes and colours to refine a search, but most importantly they indicated the importance of having a bilingual search tool that could help them search in their secondary language, which is English.

6   Discussion and Conclusion

The main contribution of this phase of our research project is to help understand the difficulties encountered by image searchers when conducting simple image retrieval activities. It also highlights several interesting suggestions that could eventually be in a search interface model in order to ease the search process. Findings from this study have provided us with directions that lead us to the initial organization of the search interface model. The initial structure will be based on: (1) the potential characteristics and functionalities extracted from the existing interfaces review; (2) the results of the survey and interviews; and (3) the results of previous studies on search behaviours of image users and the comments received from the participants.

Above all, the results of this exploration of the image searchers' perspective intended to bridge a gap for unilingual individuals. The bilingual search interface we propose to develop in the ultimate phase of our research project will constitute a definite benefit for image searchers unfamiliar with more than one language, by giving them user-friendly bilingual access to visual resources, such as works of art, architecture, material culture, archival materials or visual surrogates.

References

1. Beheshti, J., Large, A., Clement, I.: Exploring Methodologies for Designing a Virtual Reality Library for Children. Paper Presented at the ACSI/CAIS, 36e Congrès Annuel de l'Association Canadienne des Sciences de l'information, Vancouver, B.C (2008), http://www.cais-acsi.ca/proceedings/2008/beheshti_2008.pdf (retrieved June 8, 2012)
2. Boudry, C., Agostini, C.: Étude comparative des fonctionnalités des moteurs de recherche d'images sur Internet. Documentaliste – Science de l'information 41(2), 96–105 (2004)
3. Choi, Y., Hsieh-Yee, I.: Finding images on an OPAC: Analysis of user queries, subject headings, and description notes. Canadian Journal of Information and Library Science 34(3), 271–296 (2010)
4. Chung, E.K., Yoon, J.W.: Categorical and specificity differences between user-supplied tags and search query terms for images. An analysis of Flickr tags and Web image search queries. Information Research 14(3) (2009), http://informationr.net/ir/14-3/paper408.html (retrieved June 8, 2012)
5. Datta, R., et al.: Image Retrieval: Ideas, influences, and trends of the New Age. ACM Computing Surveys 40(5), 1–60 (2008)
6. Fidel, R.: The image retrieval task: implications for the design and evaluation of image databases. The New Review of Hypermedia and Multimedia 3, 181–199 (1997)
7. Goodrum, A.A., Spink, A.: Image searching on the Excite Web search engine. Information Processing & Management 37(2), 295–311 (2001)
8. Jörgensen, C.: Image retrieval – theory and research. Scarecrow Press, Lanham (2003)
9. Jörgensen, C., Jörgensen, P.: Image querying by image professionals. Journal of the American Society for Information Science and Technology 56(12), 1346–1359 (2005)
10. Kherfi, M.L., Ziou, D., Bernardi, A.: Image retrieval from the World Wide Web: issues, techniques, and systems. ACM Computing Surveys 36(1), 35–67 (2004)
11. Markkula, M., Sormunen, E.: End-user searching challenges indexing practices in the digital newspaper photo archive. Information Retrieval 1(4), 259–285 (2000)

12. Ménard, E.: Étude sur l'influence du vocabulaire utilisé pour l'indexation des images en contexte de repérage multilingue. Doctoral Dissertation, Montréal, Université de Montréal (2008), https://papyrus.bib.umontreal.ca/jspui/bitstream/1866/ 2611/1/menard-e-these-indexation-reperage-images.pdf (retrieved June 8, 2012)
13. Ménard, E.: Méthodes et défis du repérage d'images sur le Web: Jean et John cherchent-ils de la même manière? Partnership: the Canadian Journal of Library and Information Practice and Research 7(1) (2012), http://journal.lib.uoguelph.ca/index.php/perj/article/view/ 1863 (retrieved June 8, 2012)
14. Müller, H., Ruch, P., Geissbuhler, A.: Enriching content-based retrieval with multilingual serach terms. Swiss Medical Informatics 54, 6–11 (2005)
15. Scaife, M., Rogers, Y.: Kids as informants: Telling us what we didn't know or confirming what we knew already. In: Druin, A. (ed.) The Design of Children's Technology, pp. 27–50. Kaufmann, San Francisco (1999)
16. Tjondronegoro, D., Spink, A.: Web search engine multimedia functionality. Information Processing & Management 44(1), 340–357 (2008)
17. Tsai, C.-F.: Stacked generalisation: a novel solution to bridge the semantic gap for content-based image retrieval. Online Information Review 27(6), 442–445 (2003)
18. Westman, S., Oittinen, P.: Image retrieval by end-users and intermediaries in a journalistic work context. In: Proceedings of the 1st International Conference on Information Interaction in Context, Copenhagen, Danemark (2006), http://tinyurl.com/2wcc55 (retrieved June 8, 2012)

Usability Assessment in the Multicultural Approach

Maria Lúcia L.R. Okimoto[1], Cristina Olaverri Monreal[2], and Klaus-Josef Bengler[2]

[1] Departament of Mechanical Engineering, Federal University of Paraná, Brazil
[2] Faculty of Mechanical Engineering, Technische Universität München , Germany
lucia.demec@ufpr.br,
{olaverri,bengler}@lfe.mw.tum.de

Abstract. In order for products to be marketed successfully, product designs should accommodate users' cultural differences. Considering these aspects, various authors have already pointed out the need for studies in cultural usability. The main objective of this paper is to identify culture usability elements for product design. First, we have selected associate usability studies with culture, specifically for cases applied to product design. The next step is to identify variables and methods used in a cultural and usability context. We characterize the usability research into practical elements, in order to then apply summative and formative usability methods. Next, we differentiate the type of knowledge involved in the variables: explicit or tacit knowledge. Finally, we discuss a possible preview of the system variables culture and usability within the concept of a complex system.

Keywords: usability, culture, usability test.

1 Introduction

In recent years, the Brazilian economy has grown significantly, and international partnerships in areas like education, energy, transfer of technology, are increasing, especially with Germany. Culture plays an increasing role in the interaction, acceptance and learnability, especially of digital products. The trend is the rise of digital products in several applications mainly that require input from the user. In order for products to be successfully marketed, product designs should accommodate users' cultural differences. Considering these aspects, various authors pointed out the need for studies in cultural usability [4], [5], [7], [8], [9], [12]. The importance of cultural usability is growing with the increasing numbers of different national and ethnic groups that use information technology on a daily basis. Confirming the importance of culture is given on the concepts. In the ease operation of everyday products, the cultural factor is described as an important element established [6].

Culture is understood as a complex concept that can be both a structure and a process [5]. From this perspective, we can consider that usability, in a cultural context, is derived from a complex system. As a result, these cultural variables should be treated as elements of a complex system [2]. In a complex system, understood according to the General System Theory (GST), the user (as a living organism), is in

A. Marcus (Ed.): DUXU/HCII 2013, Part II, LNCS 8013, pp. 89–94, 2013.
© Springer-Verlag Berlin Heidelberg 2013

constant transformation in the universe, changing and altering the environment and itself [2]. We can observe various elements concerning a complex system [1], [3], [13] using previous culture and usability studies. The most important elements used to describe this complex system are cognition and perception. Cognition and perception vary between different cultures, and cultural practices encourage and sustain certain kinds of cognitive processes, which then perpetuate cultural practices. Following GST [2], it is correct to say that a user's cognitive process can, at the same time perpetuates and turns continuously. When seeing culture and usability as a complex system, we need to look for all elements, as TGS is a general science of wholeness. The main objective of this paper is to identify culture usability elements for product design, considering it as a complex system. In the present context, this work is contributing to the studies of usability under cultural approaches in the use of comparable products in two different contexts (Brazil and Germany).

2   Steps of the Development Study

First, we discuss the following question: which variables are relevant to understanding the cultural aspects relative to usability context? To answer this question, we have collected associated studies on culture and usability that have been published in scientific congresses or journals in the past 15 years. Our goal is to provide selected usability studies associated with cultures from differently languages, especially those cases applied to product design. In the next step, variables and methods previously used to assess culture and usability context were identified. After reading the articles, we characterized the usability research into practical elements in order to classify them in a certain design group with suitable characteristics. We consider two types of usability evaluation, summative and formative [14]. The formative usability test is used to identify or to diagnose the conceptual design (project phases), while the summative usability test is applied to check the finished product or part of them (prototype or product in market).

3   Development of the Study

Firstly, it is important to clarify how the term "culture" is understood for researches in a usability context. Culture is defined as a phenomenon which is essentially dynamic and intimately linked to the process of social and economic development of a society [12]. According to another viewpoint, researchers believe that there is a causal chain running from social structure to social practice to attention and perception to cognition. This concept is being applied within the Nisbett's Theory, based on logics vs. dialectics and a cognitive perception [4], [9]. Cultural Models of Use (CM-U theory) as opposed to psycho-physiological approaches were proposed centered on social-cognitive approaches to usability by the authors in [3], [10], [13]. Hofstede's Cultural Model [1], can help identify some main elements for the structural analysis of a cultural context through his parameters: PD- Power distance / CI Collectivism X individualism/ F/M- Feminine x Masculine UA Uncertainty X avoidance and

CO- confusion X orientation. Elements of this model can also be used separately, for example, the power distance was used to evaluate the cultural effect on structured interviews [15]. Another method used is the Culturability Inspection Method (CIM), in which Identifying Cultural Markers are applied to software's summative usability [9]. Cultural diversity in industrial design has been identified by symbolical, practical and technical products requirements [12]. Another conceptual model proposed is based on design preferences and interface acceptance: "Modified Technology Acceptance Model" [13]. Table 1 shows an overview of the cited studies, including main characteristics and possible applications of the method / technique to acquire knowledge about intercultural aspects on usability. The concepts of three studies are most appropriate for summative usability, another three for formative usability. Another four studies have concepts that which can be applied to both formative and summative usability tests.

Table 1. Research aspects on cultural usability research

Author	Characteristics	Type usability test
Barber & Badre, 1998. [1]	-Inspection / Collect remote information.	Summative usability
Ono, 2006. [12]	-Inspection / Interviews with industrial designer.	Formative usability
Nisbett & Masuda,2003 [9]	-Theory / Discussion -Cultural differences in attention and perception.	Summative usability
Chu et all, 2005. [4]	-Experimental.	Summative usability / Learnability
Clemmensen, 2009.[3]	-Theoretical / Conceptual / Structural model-usability.	Theoretical basis (Formative and Summative Usability)
Tholacius,et all , 2009.[10]	-Research perception / Satisfaction Questionnaire.	Formative usability
Evers & Day,1997. [5]	-Perception of the design elements with usability elements.	Formative and Summative Usability
Q Shi & Clemmensen,2007 [13]	-Subjective aspects preparation / definition of usability testing.	Structural elements (Summative/Formative)
Vatrapu; Quiñones,2006. [15]	-Experimental / subjective aspects involved in usability testing.	Formative and Summative
Olaverri-Monreal; Bengler, 2011. [11]	-Tools to implement cultural factors in the Design.	Formative Usability / HTA

The knowledge theory divides knowledge into two separate parts: tacit and explicit knowledge, [16]. Tacit knowledge is described as acquired knowledge, for example, when someone bases a decision, they cannot describe why and what they did. Contrarily, explicit knowledge can easily be written down and transferred to other persons.

Identifying the type of knowledge involved in the variables is very helpful to executing an intercultural usability test. Table 2 shows grouped variables founded in the literature and shown in Table 1. We define visible variable's elements which can be easily represented in formal language as explicit knowledge in cultural usability studies. Table 1 identifies two variables that can be easily shared with explicit knowledge: cultural marks knowledge and task elements.

Tacit knowledge is better suited for three types of variables that are not observable in formal languages such as: feeling elements, social-cognitive process and structural elements of usability tests. Tacit and explicit variables can also be found together. These variables have not been discriminate by the authors, because the main objective of this study was to collect and characterize the cultural variables.

Table 2. - Researchers' variables found on culture and usability context

Explicit knowledge	Tacit knowledge
Cultural marks knowledge Metaphors /Specific Icons/ Specific Colors/ Grouping/ Language/ Geography/ Orientation/ Sound/ Font/ Links/ Regional/ Shapes/ Architecture/ Cultural diversity in industrial design, in relation to symbolical, practical and technical requirements of products/ accuracy rates from the object-recognition phase **Task elements** Data come from analysis: Tasks and instructions, number the usability problems found/ performance/ time of information's display, number of mouse moves or clicks/eye-movement patterns/ effectiveness	**Feelings elements** Perception usability : visual appearance of a System / weight; frustration, fun, and usefulness of systems; and ease of use. **Socio-cognitive process** Uncertainty/ avoidance;-need for significant others; parallel versus sequential actions; diffuse versus specific; particularism versus universalism; collectivism versus individualism; high context versus low context; transference; complex spatial area on the visual scene; Focal object information X contextual Information/ Attention to the Field (background) Affordances'' in the Environment/ Esthetics. **Structural elements/ usability test** Overall relationship between user and evaluator in Task analysis. Considerations about characteristic's evaluator. Evaluator's cultural background: foreign evaluator and local evaluator. The communication patterns of local pairs and distance pairs. Cultural profile of the interviewer.

4   Discussion

It is a challenge to introduce usability parameters for products in the global market. When considering the wholeness of the culture in terms of a usability system to make decisions about a feedback loop in a design process, we look at it as a complex system.

We need to consider too the distinct design phases (conception, development and prototype) and finally the user contact phase, where we could include all information, perceptions and knowledge about the product. These phases have different needs on information feedback loops. The process of developing innovative products require methods of formative usability mainly if it has demands for globalization markets, and the cultural elements can affect directly or indirectly a product usability. The surveys analyzed contribute for formative usability in both phases of knowledge, for example; [10] tacit knowledge (feelings elements in perception/satisfaction questionnaire; [11] explicit knowledge (task elements); and [12] explicit knowledge (cultural marks). The classical frame of knowledge, the "iceberg", show us of the top the explicit knowledge and of the bottom the tacit knowledge, but culture is not static like iceberg, is dynamic and changes. The dynamic and the real complexity of the system can be observed in the table 2, where the variables were treated and grouped by similarity but the comprisement of variables is huge. The cultural usability system includes variables such as feelings, socio-cognitive process, and also objective and subjective structural elements on usability test. This allowed us to identify the level of complexity on intercultural usability. We envision further studies with a larger number of the surveys of others authors.

Acknowledgements. This study was financially supported by the Brazilian National Council for Scientific and Technological Development – CNPq-Brazil, throughout the CsF - Science without Borders. We would also like to thank Univ.-Prof. Dr. phil. Klaus Bengler, from the Lehrstuhl für Ergonomie (LfE) at the Technische Universität München for the opportunity to be involved as a visiting researcher at the LfE.

References

1. Barber, W., Badre: Culturability: The Merger of Culture and Usability. In: Proceedings - 4th Conferences on Human Factors & the Web, USA, (1998)
2. von Bertalanffy, L.: General System Theory: Foundations, Development, Applications, New York (1976)
3. Clemmensen, T.: Towards a Theory of Cultural Usability: A Comparison of ADA and CM-U Theory. In: Proceedings of the 1st International Conference on Human Centered Design: Held as Part of HCI International 2009, San Diego, CA, July 19-24 (2009)
4. Chua, H.F., Boland, J.E., Nisbett, R.E.: Cultural Variation in Eye Movements during Scene Perception. Proceedings of the National Academy of Sciences of the United States of America 102(35), 12,629–12,633 (2005)
5. Evers, Day: The Role of Culture in Interface Acceptance. In: Howard, S., Hammond, J., Lindegaard, G. (eds.) Human Computer Interaction, Interact 1997. Chapman and Hall, London (1997)
6. DIN/ ISO 20282-1 – BSI/ ISO 20282-1:2006 Ease of operation of everyday products – Part 1: Design requirements for context of use and user characteristics (2006)
7. Guan, Z., et al.: The Validity of the Stimulated Retrospective Think-Aloud Method as Measured by Eye Tracking. In: CHI (2003)

8. Marcus, A., Baumgartner, V.-J.: User-Interface Design vs. Culture. In: Proceedings of International Conference on Internationalization of Products and Services (IWIPS 2003), Berlin, Germany, pp. 67–78 (July 2003)
9. Nisbett, R.E., Masuda, T.: Culture and point of view. Proceedings of the National Academy of Sciences of the United States of America 100, 11163–11175 (2003)
10. Frandsen-Thorlacius, O., Hertzum, Clemmersen: Non-Universal Usability? A Survey of How Usability is Understood by Chinese and Danish Users. In: CHI 2009. Designing for Other Cultures, Boston, MA, USA, April 6 (2009)
11. Olaverri Monreal, C., Bengler, K.: Impact of Cultural Diversity on the Dialog Design of Driver Information Systems. In: IEEE Intelligent Vehicles Symposium (IV 2011), Baden Baden, Germany, pp. 107–112 (2011)
12. Ono, M.M.: Cultural diversity as a strategic source for designing pleasurable and competitive products, within the globalisation context. Journal of Design Research 5, 3 (2006)
13. Shi, Q., Clemmensen, T.: Relationship model in cultural usability testing. In: Aykin, N. (ed.) HCII 2007. LNCS, vol. 4559, pp. 422–431. Springer, Heidelberg (2007)
14. Tullis, T., Albert, W.: Measuring the user experience: collecting, analyzing, and presenting usability metrics. Morgan Kaufman, Burlington (2008)
15. Vatrapu, R., Pérez-Quiñones, M.A.: Culture and Usability Evaluation: The Effects of Culture in Structured Interviews JUS. Journal of Usability 1(4), 156–170 (2006)
16. Nonaka, T.: The Knowledge Creating Company: How Japanese Companies Create the Dynamics of Innovation. Oxford University Press (1995)

Lessons from Intercultural Project Management
for the Intercultural HCI Design Process

Yvonne Schoper[1] and Rüdiger Heimgärtner[2]

[1] University of Applied Sciences Mannheim, 68163 Mannheim, Germany
[2] Intercultural User Interface Consulting (IUIC), Lindenstraße 9, 93152 Undorf, Germany
y.schoper@hs-mannheim.de, ruediger.heimgaertner@iuic.de

Abstract. Global competition requires that new technical products are launched at the same time in all relevant global markets. Therefore the Human Computer Interface (HCI) product designers need to know all requirements of all global customer groups before starting the global development process of user interfaces (UI), which takes normally place in dispersed intercultural mixed UI designer teams. Therefore the user-centered design process from ISO 9241-210 is analyzed concerning the requirements of intercultural management and particularly of intercultural project management. On this basis, an agile intercultural HCI design management process is developed. The resulting UI design approach empowered by cultural aspects makes sure that new systems are designed right from the beginning for the cultural diverse user markets in a time and cost efficient and effective way.

Keywords: User-Centered Design, ISO 9241-210, Agile Methods, Agile Project Management, Culture, HCI, Model, Approach, Process, Structure, Intercultural, Intercultural Project Management, Intercultural User Interface Design, Management Process.

1   Introduction

In times where new technical products like cars, mobile phones or digital cameras are launched at the same time in the global markets of America, Europe, Asia and Arabia, the product engineers must today consider from the very beginning of the product development process that there is not just one single user or user group for the future product. In comparison to earlier times when a technical product was first developed for one homogeneous target group (in most cases for the home market) and then adopted to other markets by simply translating the relevant user interfaces into the language of the export country, it is of critical importance for a successful new product today to know the requirements of all global customer groups first before starting the global development process. The usability of technical devices controlled by a user interface (UI) which were developed in the cultural context of the designer (e.g. mid Europe) for another culture (e.g. East Asia or India) is hardly possible as usability mainly depends on the application in the cultural context (age, sex, language, education, knowledge, experience, religion, self-conception, dealing with power) and environmental factors (such as politics, wealth, income, infrastructure) (cf. [1], [2], [3]). In this paper, the Human Computer Interface (HCI) Design Process defined in ISO 9241-210 is analyzed

A. Marcus (Ed.): DUXU/HCII 2013, Part II, LNCS 8013, pp. 95–104, 2013.
© Springer-Verlag Berlin Heidelberg 2013

in section 3 concerning the requirements of culturally different target groups demonstrated using a practical example presented in the next section. In section 4, an agile intercultural HCI design management process is proposed to cope with the problems caused by applying the standard HCI design process in the cultural context.

2   Case Study: Navigation System

Today, GPS based navigation systems can be found as a standard option in nearly all cars, as stand-alone equipment and as software for Personal Computers, PDA´s and smart phones. The users of these navigation systems are all car drivers all over the world, as fast and safe navigation is a requirement of all user groups. From the perspective of the navigation system designer one could imagine that the only difference between the different national customer groups is the language they speak and the map they use. Therefore, by translating the software into the different user languages and adapting the maps to the individual countries it should be possible to offer localized navigation systems to all relevant user groups worldwide. For example, from the European perception a navigation system should contain the features such as display in North/ South direction, display in driving direction, perspective of display in 2D or 3D, order of input data (e.g. in USA: Country, City, Zip Code, House Number, Street vs. in Germany: City, Street, House Number) as well as input via keyboard or via voice input. But the intercultural reality looks different: Let us take a look at the following real case examples from Japan, Nicaragua and the Arabian world. Following Motohiko Takayanagi, General Manager at Pioneer, the market leader for navigation systems in Japan, most streets in Tokyo have no name. The block of houses, the streets and the houses are indicated by numbers. In addition the house numbers are counted in the sequence of their construction in the district. Therefore the driver needs precise landmarks for orientation such as "leave the 20 floor high grey building on the right and the four floor high brown hall on your left". For better orientation the navigation system offers the Japanese driver two perspectives in 2D and in 3D at the same time on the same display (cf. Figure 1, source: URL= http://www.technewsdaily.com/5764-gps-navigation-displays-front-windshield.html, last access 3|15|13). As many streets and highways in the big cities in Japan (and also in China) are built over one another the other, the navigation systems in the cars have a height measuring sensor, which lets the driver know exactly where his current position is and which next street to go to. Figure 2 shows the height measuring function.

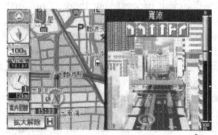

Fig. 1. 2D and 3D screenshot from Japanese navigation system display in windshield

Fig. 2. Height measuring sensors show the driver his position exactly, picture by: Alpine

In addition the Japanese customer expects that the navigation system acts as a planning guideline: it calculates current traffic congestion and calls the driver on his mobile phone to suggest that he should take off earlier than normal. But the Japanese drivers expect even more: with the menu "Date Planer" for example the system is supposed to find the most romantic route nearby and an appropriate restaurant with the telephone number for reservation and even includes recommendations for pleasant sightseeing. Now we sail over the Pacific Ocean to the capital of Nicaragua, Managua. In Managua there are no addresses at all. Only a few big axis, some through streets and ring roads have names or at least designations such as "Highway to Granada", "Diagonal of the Martyrs" or "Course of the Municipality". A typical turn-by-turn direction would be: „drive from the Hotel 'Princess' one street to the south, and then twenty five meters down on the left hand side". The system is based on points of interest (landmarks), if they still exist: "there, where the old cinema Cabrera was". "Up" and „down" do not mean upwards or downwards with respect to a hill, but to the orbit of the sun, therefore East and West, and West means "down", where the cemeteries are. Finally, we go to the Arabian world: for Islamic people it is of high importance to have a Mecca compass in their navigation system in order to know at any time in which direction the user must look and pray at the five praying times per day. Particularly for Islamic people on road this is a very important feature today. Therefore all application designers offer Mecca compasses for all types of smart phones. Figure 3 shows one Mecca compass example.

Fig. 3. Mecca Compass for iPhone Navigation system (source: URL=http://appfinder. lisisoft.com/ipad-iphone-apps/mecca-compass.html, last access 03|15|13)

These three examples show that a deep detailed cultural knowledge of the specific user habits is necessary for a designer of a navigation system in order to develop a new system that fits all customer requirements and can therefore be sold and implemented in different countries. But as the three examples show, it is impossible that one UI designer has all this specific information from all relevant user groups wordwide. He will, however, have a profound knowledge of the circumstances in his own cultural environment in order to be sensitive for relevant aspects in other cultures (cf. [4]). This is the basis for intercultural mixed UI designer teams (cf. [5]).

3   Analysis of the User-Centered Design Process

Today only few complete methodologies exist that are able to support UI designers while developing user interfaces in a systematic, structured and guided way in order to create better systems faster. Among these methods there is no systematic approach so far which embeds intercultural UI design. Therefore the standard HCI development process ISO 9241-210 will be analyzed concerning its ability to integrate intercultural management aspects (cf. [6]). Figure 4 shows an overview of the user-centered UI process. The ISO 9241-210 User-Centered Design Process (UCDP) consists of six steps which will be analyzed in the following chapters concerning their ability to integrate intercultural management aspects. First the weaknesses in every process are examined and recommendations for implementing an intercultural UCD process are then defined.

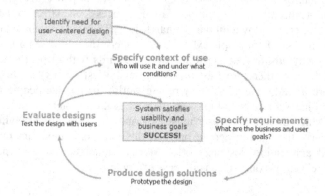

Fig. 4. User-Centered Design Process following ISO 9241-210

3.1 Identify the Need for User-Centered Design

It is the aim of this first process step to realize the necessity for the attractiveness and the market success of a new product, regardless of whether it is a technical device, an electronic product or new software, that it takes the user into the focus of the new design being developed. The analysis of the current ISO 9241-210 UCDP concerning the aspects of intercultural management and particularly intercultural project management shows that these aspects are missing in the UCD process, especially in the important early project phase. The following weaknesses in the current process can be stated thusly: There is no focus on a well-managed project start by an experienced project leader. A product development team of a worldwide successful future product should consist of representatives from the most important market. The first task of a UI design (UID) development team should be to acquire a deep understanding of the complexity of the task and its requirements. Therefore the authors recommend implementing the following intercultural project management elements in this first process step of an intercultural user-centered design process: Build a diverse team with representatives from all relevant user groups e.g. Japan, China, India, Latin America, North America, Arabia, Sub-Saharan Africa and Europe. Such a cross-cultural team has the potential to be far more effective and innovative than a mono-cultural one if it is managed well. Furthermore, to become a high performance team the team needs an experienced team leader who knows the different team development process phases and is able to moderate the team through them. Analyse the current market situation concerning existing products, main competitors, environmental factors like politics, new legislation, economic trends, sociologic and technological developments worldwide (i.e. doing the so called "PEST" analysis – Political, Economic, Social and Technological analysis which describes a framework of macro-environmental factors used in strategic management) as well as existing user groups worldwide and the new user groups.

3.2 Specify Context of Use

The usability of a system strongly depends on how the user can cope with the system (cf. [7]). This knowledge can be obtained, for example by observing and asking the user during his interactions with the system (cf. [8] and [9]). In this case the user articulates his desires and hence his needs regarding the usability of the system. Unfortunately, this method is applied far too little in industrial HCI design even today. This is critical because, if that knowledge is missing in the final product, it will not be wanted by the user. The user cannot apply it appropriately because important features are missing or it takes too long to do a certain task because of bad design caused by lacking or wrong user requirements. The analysis of the UCDP concerning the aspects of intercultural management and intercultural project management shows that these aspects are missing in the standard UCD process concerning the context of use in the cultural context because there is not sufficient focus on the profound analysis of the cultural aspects and their influences represented by HCI dimensions, UI characteristics, intercultural variables and cultural dimensions. HCI dimensions describe the style of human machine interaction expressed by information frequency and density and order as well as interaction frequency and speed. User interface characteristics capture the most relevant attributes of user interfaces containing metaphors, presentation, navigation, interaction and mental models ([10]. Intercultural variables cover the localization levels function, interaction and presentation ([11]). Direct intercultural variables concern HCI directly such as color, icons, language and layout as well as interaction speed and frequency. Indirect intercultural variables embrace HCI margins such as service manual or packaging. Cultural dimensions serve to describe the behavior and values of members of certain cultures like uncertainty avoidance, individualism or collectivism or power distance ([12]). [13] defined cultural dimensions that are related to human interaction such as universalism, neutrality, specificness, seriality and control. They can be related to HMI dimensions to establish a link between the cultural imprint of users to their HCI style ([14]). Hence, to specify the individual cultural context of use in the relevant usage situations it is important to develop a profound understanding of the individual culture specific needs of the users (as mentioned in the examples at the beginning of the article), to use methods to gather the deep understanding of the user requirements that are quantitative and even more the qualitative market research techniques, to consider international requirement clusters, e.g. in the case of navigation systems it could be that business managers word-wide have similar requirements to implement functions like receiving Emails, getting a regular news updates, whereas taxi drivers, in comparison need a precise forecast of the traffic congestions, to practice detailed observation of the users on-site in their typical usage behavior situations (following the principles of the method "design thinking": for instance, when, where, how, how long, does the user enter data in the navigation system?) as well as to describe on this analytical basis the HCI dimensions, UI characteristics, intercultural variables and cultural dimensions for the context of use.

3.3   Specify Requirements

The objective of this process step is to collect all needs, interests, expectations and behaviors patterns of the different user groups. In international context, it is important to determine that there is not one homogeneous user group but that there are thousands or even millions of individual users worldwide as in the case of a consumer product like a mobile phone. To better handle the complexity of this fact these users can be condensed to fictitious user groups, so-called "Personas". The fictitious, specific and concrete representation of target users help the product teams to better understand the users and thus to improve their products (cf. [15] and [16]). The intercultural UID process requires not one, but several personas that represent the culturally different user groups. The analysis of the standard UIDP in ISO 9241-210 shows that the current process does not fulfill these demands completely. If these requirements are not completely understood at the very beginning of the UIDP, there is the risk that it will not be possible to develop one single general platform that can then be localized to the cultural specific requirements. The specification of all the different requirements from all the stakeholder groups necessitates that all requirements from the previous process steps identification and specification of the requirements are collected regardless of their origin, the requirements are compared with the strategic goals of the company and those requirements that do not fit the corporate strategy are deleted, all conflicts of interests between the requirements are worked out (e.g. small display vs. large display, touch screen vs. keyboard), all conflicts of interests are solved, the remaining requirements are the product targets of the project and the targets are checked for following the SMART principle: specific, measurable, attainable, realistic and timely. It is important to note that they should not describe the solution of the existing problem as targets are supposed to be free of solution.

3.4   Produce Design Solution

In this process step the culturally diverse UI design team has the task to generate new innovative design solutions. Research shows that the more diverse the team members are concerning their age, sex, cultural background and education, the larger the chance for innovative new ideas (cf. [17] and [18]). Hence, the following topics are to be considered in intercultural UID teams: Intercultural product design team processes are much more complex to manage than mono-cultural teams. Problems during the planning of time and budget, managing the project, escalation of problems, conflict management, risk management or a different understanding of quality in the design phase will occur daily (cf. [19] and [20]). Because of the different cultural imprint and underlying assumptions of the team members, processes such as team development will take longer than in mono-cultural teams. Communication is a challenge in diverse teams: misunderstandings caused by talking the same language which is, however, not the mother tongue for most of the team members will happen frequently and can lead to anger and frustration. All these potential problems require an inter-culturally experienced professional team leader to cope with and manage these potential obstacles in a professional way.

3.5   Evaluate Design

The better and more precise the product targets are defined at the beginning of the development project, the easier it is to compare them with the current state of design. These target performance comparisons are to be carried out continuously to make sure that the resulting design solutions correspond to the objectives defined. In intercultural context, it is important to evaluate the design status from the perspectives of the different cultural user groups defined to ensure that the design fits to the different and sometimes even contradictory requirements of all stakeholders.

3.6   System Satisfies Usability and Business Goals

The continuous control mechanism of (i) testing the current design by all relevant cultural lead target group testers that know the environmental factors and local user requirements and conditions in detail and (ii) reworking the design on the basis of this feedback is the basis to fulfill the diverse requirements and objectives of all cultural target groups with the new product. In the case of severe conflicts of interests which cannot be solved in one product solution, but where the fulfillment of the requirements is of highest priority for the market success of the product (e.g. incompatible legal prescriptions for the display size of navigations systems) and where it is not possible to reconcile these requirements, another option must be found. In the worst case the requirements cannot be fulfilled by one user interface design and the management must specify how to proceed. Introducing agile methods in the UIDP can help to speed up this process of entangling the manifold and fast changing interests from stakeholders from different cultures.

4   Proposal of an Agile Intercultural HCI Design Process

As most user-centered design projects are IT or software projects and agile methods are already used in international development projects (cf. [21]), the authors suggest applying the methods of *agile project management* in intercultural user interface design projects. Agile Project Management (APM) is a project management method which was developed in the software industry (cf. [22]). It is an iterative method in engineering and information technology development projects to create innovative new products by using fast feedback-loops. By quickly producing rough prototypes and giving them to the customer it is the aim of the method to receive their fast direct feedback and to continuously optimize the product on the basis of the customer/user feedback (cf. [23]). The most dominant effect of this project development approach is that the team can be more effective in responding to change. In addition they can dramatically reduce the time between making a decision and seeing the consequences of that decision (cf. [24]). These benefits fit exactly to the demands of innovative intercultural user interface design (IUID) projects that require fast feedback loops. In addition, international product development teams are spread all over the world. Agile methods are a way to best use the alleged disadvantage of the time difference. By dividing the design work e.g. into the programming of the software (which could be carried out e.g. in Eastern Europe) and into the testing of the software (which could be done e.g. in Mexico or California by using the time difference of 7 to 9 hours), the software programmer could receive a feedback to his daily programming work over night and optimize it on the next day on the basis of the evaluation. This procedure can lead to a reduction of the development times by 50%. Moreover, the designers would receive feedback from software testers that derive from different cultures than the programmers and therefore know the specific requirement of the customers in their individual markets. Finally, with such a globally dispersed development process it can be ensured that the key relevant customer/user requirements are continuously controlled. Figure 5 shows the concept of the overall intercultural HCI design management process by using the methodology of Agile Project Management (APM).

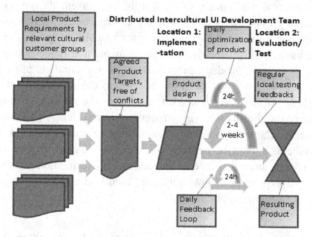

Fig. 5. Agile Intercultural HCI Design Management Process

This agile intercultural HCI design management process represents a new approach by combining the best practices of the current HCI design process with the elements of intercultural management. Living this process, the UI designers better accommodate the diverse global user requirements and respond faster to change. In addition, the approach reduces the development time dramatically by fast feedback loops.

5   Summary

In earlier times technical consumer electronic products with a user interface were first developed for the designers' home market and then exported to other countries by translating the user interface into other languages. The users realized quickly that the product does not fit their user needs and do not buy it. An alternative would be to develop country-specific products that correspond to the user requirements of the specific target user group. But that would mean that a company must develop several different product user interface designs to correspond to the cultural requirements of the most important key markets worldwide. Furthermore, with this procedure companies are not successful any more in this fast changing globalized world. Therefore, along internationalization additional procedures are needed to reconcile the partly contradictory requirements from the culturally different user groups in one user interface which fits all relevant user cultures. On the basis of the existing HCI development process defined in ISO 9241-210 an agile intercultural HCI design management process combining the best practices of the current HCI design process with the elements of intercultural management has been suggested. Thereby, the resulting user interface design method complemented by cultural aspects ensures that new systems can be designed right from the beginning for one or more cultures while designers better accommodate the diverse global user requirements and respond faster to change. In addition, the approach reduces the development time dramatically by fast feedback. The next step is to apply the proposed intercultural modifications to the user-centered design process in several practical intercultural user-centered design projects in order to prove the suggested lean process to be successful.

References

1. Honold, P.: Intercultural Usability Engineering: Barriers and Challenges from a German point of view. In: Day, del Galdo, E.D., Prabhu, G.V. (eds.) Designing for Global Markets 2. Second International Workshop on Internationalisation of Products and Systems, pp. 137–147 (2000)
2. Röse, K.: Methodik zur Gestaltung interkultureller Mensch-Maschine-Systeme in der Produktionstechnik. Univ., Kaiserslautern (2002)
3. Heimgärtner, R.: Cultural Differences in Human-Computer Interaction. Oldenbourg Verlag (2012)
4. Thomas, A., Kinast, E.-U., Schroll-Machl, S.: Handbook of intercultural communication and cooperation. Basics and areas of application. Vandenhoeck & Ruprecht, Göttingen (2010)
5. Heimgärtner, R., Tiede, L.-W., Windl, H.: Empathy as Key Factor for Successful Intercultural HCI Design. In: Marcus, A. (ed.) HCII 2011 and DUXU 2011, Part II. LNCS, vol. 6770, pp. 557–566. Springer, Heidelberg (2011)
6. DIN: DIN EN ISO 9241-210 Ergonomische Anforderungen der Mensch-System-Interaktion Teil 210: Prozess zur Gestaltung gebrauchstauglicher Systeme. BeuthVerlag, Berlin (2010)
7. DIN: DIN EN ISO 9241-110 Ergonomics of humans-system interaction Part 110: Dialogue principles. Beuth (2006)
8. Nielsen, J., Molich, R.: Heuristic evaluation of user interfaces. In: Proceedings of the SIGCHI Conference on Human Factors in Computing Systems, pp. 249–256. ACM, Seattle (1990)

9. Nielsen, J.: Designing user interfaces for international use. Elsevier, Amsterdam (1990)
10. Marcus, A., Baumgartner, V.-J.: Mapping User-Interface Design Components vs. Culture Dimensions in Corporate Websites. Visible Language Journal 38, 1–65 (2004)
11. Röse, K., Zühlke, D.: Culture-Oriented Design: Developers' Knowledge Gaps in this Area. In: 8th IFAC/IFIPS/IFORS/IEA Symposium on Analysis, Design, and Evaluation of Human-Machine Systems, September 18-20, pp. 11–16. Pergamon (2001)
12. Hofstede, G.H., Hofstede, G.J., Minkov, M.: Cultures and organizations: software of the mind. McGraw-Hill, Maidenhead (2010)
13. Trompenaars, F., Hampden-Turner, C.: Riding the waves of culture: understanding diversity in business. Nicholas Brealey Publ., London (2012)
14. Heimgärtner, R.: Reflections on a Model of Culturally Influenced Human Computer Interaction to Cover Cultural Contexts in HCI Design. International Journal of Human-Computer Interaction (2013)
15. Cooper, A.: The Inmates Are Running the Asylum. Macmillan Publishing Co., Inc. (1999)
16. Cooper, A., Reimann, R., Cronin, D.: About Face 3: The Essentials of Interaction Design. Wiley (2007)
17. Kochan, T., Bezrukova, K., Ely, R., Jackson, S., Joshi, A., Jehn, K., Leonard, J., Levine, D., Thomas, D.: The effects of diversity on business performance: Report of the diversity research network. Human Resource Management 42, 3–21 (2003)
18. Sethi, R., Smith, D.C., Park, C.W.: Cross-Functional Product Development Teams, Creativity, and the Innovativeness of New Consumer Products. Journal of Marketing Research 38, 73–85 (2001)
19. Hoffmann, H.-E., Schoper, Y.-G., Fitzsimons, C.-J.: Internationales Projektmanagement: Interkulturelle Zusammenarbeit in der Praxis. Dt. Taschenbuch-Verl, München (2004)
20. Binder, J.: Global Project Management: Communication, Collaboration and Management Across Borders. Gower (2007)
21. Ressin, M., Abdelnour-Nocera, J., Smith, A.: Defects and agility: Localization issues in agile development projects. In: Sillitti, A., Hazzan, O., Bache, E., Albaladejo, X. (eds.) XP 2011. LNBIP, vol. 77, pp. 316–317. Springer, Heidelberg (2011)
22. Highsmith, J., Cockburn, A.: Agile Software Development: The Business of Innovation. Computer 34, 120–122 (2001)
23. Gundelsweiler, F., Memmel, T., Reiterer, H.: Agile Usability Engineering. In: Keil-Slawik, R., Selke, H., Szwillus, G. (eds.) Mensch & Computer 2004: Allgegenwärtige Interaktion, pp. 33–42. Oldenbourg Verlag, München (2004)
24. Cockburn, A., Highsmith, J.: Agile Software Development: The People Factor. Computer 34, 131–133 (2001)

Localization beyond National Characteristics:
The Impact of Language on Users' Performance
with Different Menu Structures

Christian Sturm[1], Gerhard Strube[2], and Sara Gouda[3]

[1] Hamm-Lippstadt University of Applied Sciences, Germany
christian.sturm@hshl.de
[2] University of Freiburg, Germany
strube@cognition.uni-freiburg.de
[3] The German University in Cairo, Egypt
saragouda.91@gmail.com

Abstract. The consideration of cognitive differences between user groups in the field of human-computer interaction is still in its infancy. The present paper presents two explorative studies looking at the impact of the users' native language on their performance with different menu structures for mobile phones. Object- and verb-oriented menus with different levels of hierarchy were tested with users in Mexico and Germany. A follow-up study looked at the performance with verb- and object oriented menus by Arabic native speakers in Egypt. The results suggest that flat hierarchies are to be preferred independent from any cultural impact. While the first study did not yield a significant difference between Spanish and German native speakers using verb- and object-oriented menus, Arabic users performed significantly better with verb-oriented menus.

Keywords: internationalization, localization, cross-cultural usability, information architecture, user-centered design.

1   Introduction

Since the worldwide diffusion of information and communication technology (ICT) is increasing, so is the diversity of users and their characteristics. As a consequence, the efforts to internationalize and localize products and systems made their arrival into the field of human-computer interaction (HCI). While internationalization (i18n) refers to the removal of sensitive elements, localization (l10n) describes the process of adaptation by adding local components that are specific to a certain context of use [1]. These components and elements can be classified into four categories [2]: technology, language, culture and cognition. Technological adaptations refer for instance to different character sets, date and time formats as well as legal frameworks. In a broader sense, the technical aspects include furthermore areas like mobile network standards (GSM, TDMA etc.), electrical conditions, plugs, video standards and technical

A. Marcus (Ed.): DUXU/HCII 2013, Part II, LNCS 8013, pp. 105–114, 2013.

infrastructures in general that differ between countries. Language, the second category, describes the translation of text used in manuals and throughout the user interface. More often than not, cultural aspects are often not included. Spanish, for instance, allows through an international, a universal, a mid-Atlantic and a neutral version to translate any text for a worldwide audience without considering local characteristics [3] [1]. The meaning of color, icons, symbols, sounds, functionality and social aspects of technology add up to the cultural category. Central elements of ICT like menu trees, interaction principals or interactive sequences are related to the last category, cognition. Research on cognitive differences between user groups relevant to the HCI community is still in its infancy, while technological, linguistic and cultural factors for i18n and l10n have been investigated intensively during the last decades [4], [5], [6], [7], [8], [9], [10]. Therefore, we address these aspects reporting two exploratory studies that focus on the relationship of menus with the native language spoken by the user.

2   First Study

2.1   Derivation of Hypotheses

From literature review as well as from a preceding field study on the cultural differences of mobile phone usage in Mexico and Germany, two characteristics of menu structures were identified to function as independent variables: verb-object vs. object-verb orientation and the maximum number of hierarchical levels used for the menu.

Verb-Object vs. Object-Verb. Spanish can be considered a verb-first language due to the pre-dominant word order "subject-verb-object" (SVO) [11]. In German, however, SVO exists in the main clause only, while the subordinate clause is predominated by the word order "subject-object-verb". Koster [12] argues that the underlying structure of both Dutch and German has to be seen as SOV. Furthermore, German can be categorized as a "verb-second language" [13]. This supports its object-oriented character. Hereby, the only possible translation of the German predicate "die Freundin anrufen" (object-verb order, "call the girlfriend") into Spanish is "llamar a la amiga" (verb-object order). The same observation can be made using compound verbs expressing events of the past in both languages.

Command-line interfaces like MS-DOS or the UNIX shell are verb-oriented [14]. Hereby, the verb is specified first and then the object the action will be applied to. In order to delete a text file named "text.txt" the command "del text.txt" has to be chosen. In contrast, windows-based interfaces like MS Windows follow an object-oriented approach. The objects are chosen first and then the verb (action). In order to delete all files in a folder, the user needs to select all files (objects) first and then to choose the action (delete) [14].

Generally, this leads to the question of whether the dominant grammatical structure of a user's native language has an impact on the user's performance with verb- and object-oriented menus respectively.

Maximum Levels of Hierarchy. Chen and Macredie [15] found a correlation between the degree of field-dependency (FD) as a cognitive style and the navigational behavior in information spaces. The concept of FD used here is based on Witkin et al. [16]. People with a high level of FD tend to describe objects through their relationships with other objects in space, whereas people with a low FD-index separate objects from their context while perceiving them. According to Sherry and Macredie, high-FD is followed by a rather linear and serial navigation style. This could be supported by a rather flat hierarchy of a possible menu. In contrast, a low FD-index that results in a more non-linear and non-serial navigational style could be supported in a better way by a stronger hierarchy of a menu with more levels.

Several research projects demonstrated furthermore an impact of cultural differences on the FD-index. According to Holtzmann et al. [17], Mexicans tend towards field-dependency, whereas people in the U.S. show a stronger tendency towards field-independency. Based on the characteristics stated by Nisbett for explaining cultural differences in cognition [18], it is assumed that these results for the U.S. can be transferred to German participants. Holtzmann et al. [17] showed as well that the age of the participants tested influenced the results. The older they were, the more they tended towards field-independency. Halpern [19] states that men tend to be field-independent, while women show a stronger tendency towards field-dependency.

Hypotheses. The above discussion leads to the derivation of the following (partly opposing) hypotheses using both orientation (verb, object) and hierarchy as independent variables:

1. Spanish-speaking participants tend to show a better performance with verb-oriented menus based on the verb-orientation of the Spanish language
2. German-speaking participants tend to show a better performance with object-oriented menus due to the object-orientation of the German language.
3. Based on the expected differences in the FD-index it is predicted that German participants will show a better performance with menus of a stronger hierarchy while Mexican participants will show a better performance with flat hierarchies.
4. Based on the existing recommendations for the maximum level of hierarchies it is predicted that both Mexican and German participants will show a better performance navigating within low hierarchical menus than using menus with a stronger hierarchy.
5. Prior exposure to and experience with object-oriented user interfaces will lead to a better performance with object-oriented menus as well as to a decreasing performance with verb-oriented menus.

2.2   Menus

Two variables with two parameter values each allow the construction of 4 different menu versions: object-oriented with a strong hierarchy (oi), object-oriented with a low hierarchy (od), verb-oriented with a strong hierarchy (vi), verb-oriented with a low hierarchy (vd).

The different menus have been developed based on the standard original menu of the Siemens S55 mobile phone, which was classified as "object-oriented with strong hierarchy". The "object-oriented, low hierarchy"-version was developed through a re-ordering of the complete functions in a maximum of 2 instead of 4 menu-levels. The verb-orientation was constructed using the standard original menu in three steps: First, the corresponding verbs were derived from each noun (object). Second, this new list of verbs (actions) was clustered into one shorter list of 11 verbs covering all the functions. Third, this shorter list became the first menu level.

To take the connection to the Internet with the mobile phone as an example, the respective function can be found in the original standard menu by selecting "Surf & Fun" at the first menu level and "Internet" at the second menu level. The verb-oriented menu provides this function by selecting first "connect" at the first and "Internet" at the second level.

2.3   Method

Experimental Design. In order to test the hypotheses mentioned above a mixed across-and-within-subject design was chosen (3 groups of Ss $\times$ 2 hierarchy levels $\times$ 2 verb/object-oriented menus). Each participant was asked to find 4 functions in each of the 4 (= 2×2) different menu versions. The experiment was conducted with 3 groups (1 in Germany, 2 with low/high educational background in Mexico). This provided the opportunity to integrate language, computer literacy and formal education as possible factors. Each participant was assigned randomly to one of 24 (= 4!) conditions, where each condition represented a different order of the 4 different menu versions. Therefore, each of the 3 groups group consisted of 24 participants.

Test Procedure. Each test run started with an opening semi-structured interview of about 20 minutes to collect demographic data, level of education, attitudes to technology, technical experiences and cultural issues. The second step included a test of the level of FD with the test of Witkin et al. [20]. The third part consisted of the main task, i.e., finding 4 functions in each menu version on the mobile phone: dialed calls, volume of ringtone, alarm clock and SMS inbox followed by a short questionnaire to rate each menu individually. In a closing debriefing interview each participant was asked to provide an overall rating of the menus while mentioning the main positive and negative issues found.

Participants. As mentioned above, the sample consisted of 3 groups. Each group had been balanced concerning career, gender, age and native language (see table 1).

Table 1. Demographics of participants

Demographic	Group 1 (MX 1)	Group 2 (MX 2)	Group 3 (D)
Location	Mexico	Mexico	Germany
Recruiting	Craftspeople, vocational school students	University students	University students
Age	17-25	18-25	18-25
Mobilephone ownership (years)	0.26	0.09	0.30
Computer experience (years)	0.82	6.25	11.25
Formal education (years)	9.25	13.58	15.42

2.4   Results

Data Collection and Conditioning. The following objective measurements were extracted from the log file of the prototype: time in milliseconds for each task and menu version, errors for each task (an error was defined as a selection of a wrong function), number of steps for each tasks, navigation path and selections (not covered in this paper)

The following subjective measurements were collected during the semi-structured interviews that took place between each menu version as well as at the end of the test: rating of preference for each menu (position 1-4), easiness of task completion (scale 1-5), speed of task completion (scale 1-5), clearness of task completion and menu (scale 1-5), level of satisfaction with menus (scale 1-7).

Due to the different positions of the same function in each menu the measured times for the completion of the tasks would not be comparable. This is because a different amount of steps is needed to reach the function in each menu and it would overlay the effects that were planned to be measured (hierarchy and verb-object vs. object-verb orientation). Therefore the times for finding the functionality have been normalized with a GOMS model.

Data Analysis. A first analysis of the data shows an overall significant interaction of group membership with menu versions ($F_g = 29.51$, p<.01). Both hierarchy levels and verb/object-orientation presented separately as well a significant interaction with group membership ($F_{ov}=132.79$, p<.01, $F_h=132.79$, p<.01). No significant interaction of group membership with the levels object- and verb-orientation was found, while the levels flat and strong hierarchy showed a significant interaction with group membership.

Hypothesis 1 stated that Spanish-speaking participants tend to show a better performance with verb-oriented menus. This hypothesis has to be rejected as participants of both Spanish-speaking groups needed significantly more time for the task completion using the verb-oriented menus.

Hypothesis 2 argued that German-speaking participants tend to show a better performance with object-oriented menus due to the object-orientation of the German language. It has to be partly accepted. The German participants showed a significant better performance with the object-oriented menu versions. However, the results of the Spanish-speaking groups showing as well a better performance with object-oriented menus does not allow to conclude that the language might have an impact on the preferences for the menu structure.

In hypothesis 3 it was said that German participants will show better performance with menus of a stronger hierarchy while Mexican participants will show a better performance with flat hierarchies. This hypothesis needs to be rejected as all groups showed a significant better performance with flat hierarchies.

Hypothesis 4 claimed that both Mexican and German participants will show better performance navigating within low hierarchical menus than using menus with a stronger hierarchy. This hypothesis is accepted as all groups showed a significant better performance with flat menus.

Hypothesis 5 forecasts that prior exposure to and experience with object-oriented user interfaces will lead to a better performance with object-oriented menus as well as to a decreasing performance with verb-oriented menus. Both menu versions showed a strong and significant correlation with prior computer experience. This result, however, does not allow the conclusion that prior computer experience leads to a better performance with object-oriented menus and a decreasing performance with verb-oriented menus. Therefore, this hypothesis has to be rejected.

2.5   Discussion

The results presented in the previous section seem to provide a clear picture: Generally, flat hierarchies were preferred independently from any cultural factor. Similarly, all participants seem to perform significantly better with object-oriented menus in contrast to verb-oriented menus. A closer look at the quantitative and qualitative data, however, reveals that both Mexican groups showed an increased error rate with each task. In addition, it was observed that the strategy for solving the tasks changed from a structured one to a trial and error approach. Exploring the data further shows a significant interaction between object-oriented and verb-oriented on the one hand and group membership on the other hand ($F=4.97$, $p=.01$). Group MX1 shows a strong tendency towards a better performance with the verb-oriented menus ($F=3.66$, $p=.068$), whereas group D shows a strong tendency to perform better with object-oriented menus ($F=3.44$, $p=.076$).

The better performance with verb-oriented menus of group MX1 while showing a higher error rate compared to object-oriented menus and a lower number of correct first choices leads to the assumption that the time to recover from errors tends to be substantially less compared to object oriented menus. This way, the first hypothesis seems to be confirmed. However, it cannot be claimed that linguistic factors are causing this difference in performance because group MX2 does not show any significant difference. Therefore, it can be assumed that both computer experience and formal schooling might have a considerable greater impact on the performance of the participants. A stepwise regression of both factors for the verb-oriented menus does not exclude either of them. However, the significant result for the factor computer experience ($T = - 2.64$, p<.05) compared to the factor formal schooling ($T = - 1.63$, p<.20) suggests the tendency that computer experience can be used with more confidence as a predictor.

A possible explanation for this result might be that in order to achieve a goal using an object-oriented menu, the user needs to have a greater prior knowledge of the objects that the system offers to complete a task. The user needs to know in advance, which object of the system corresponds and implements the process to reach her goal. Thus, choosing the right object right at the beginning of a task is crucial to be able to complete it. The concept of the implemented objects is an additional aspect that has to be learned. On the other hand, verb-oriented menus seem to offer a smaller step in the beginning of the series of choices that the user has to make for completing a task or to search a function. Prior knowledge is not needed to the same amount, while simplicity is offered right from the beginning. The following example observed a lot at the group MX1 illustrates this possible explanation:

The first problem of the main task was to look up a number the user had already dialed before in the list of the dialed numbers. The object-oriented menu with a strong hierarchy required two steps selecting first the menu item "call records" (Spanish: "Lista de llamadas") and second the item "dialed numbers" (Spanish: "Números marcardos"). The verb-oriented menu with a strong hierarchy required three steps instead: "lock up" (Spanish: "consultar"), "call records" (Spanish: "Lista de llamadas") and "dialed numbers" (Spanish: "Números marcardos"). In spite of the fact that the verb-oriented menu required one step more, users found the respective function with an average of 20% faster.

2.6   Conclusion

Within the scope of this study, three different questions have been investigated.

The first question, deals with the impact of the user's native language on the preferences of menu structures. Both object- and verb-oriented menus as well as Spanish as a verb-oriented language and German as an object-oriented language have been tested. The results suggest that there is no direct influence of the mother tongue on the preferences of menus structures as both hypothesis one and two were rejected.

While answering the second question about the influence of prior computer experience and formal schooling on the preferences of menu structures, it could be shown that concrete prior experiences with object-oriented graphical user interfaces can be taken as a predictor for the performance with verb and object-oriented menus as hypothesis four and five were confirmed. The results suggest that verb-oriented menus lead to a significant increase of a system's usability, especially as far as novice users are concerned.

The participants showed, independently from any cultural or contextual factor, a significantly better performance with flat hierarchies (2 levels maximum), while menus with a strong hierarchy (4 levels maximum) led to a significant slower interaction.

3   Second Study

The second study follows up on the first hypothesis mentioned above: Speakers of a verb-oriented language would show better performance with verb-oriented menus. The results of the first study suggest that prior experience with information technology seems to be the decisive factor for the performance with menus instead of the word order given by the native language of the test subjects.

In order to verify this result, a similar test has been conducted with a group of Arabic native speakers in Egypt. Both "subject-verb-object" (SVO) and "verb-subject-object" (VSO) are the predominant word orders in the Arabic language according to Dahlgren [21]. Therefore, Arabic can be classified as a verb-oriented language.

Participants. The group's demographics corresponded to both Mexican groups of the previous study. 24 University students with extensive prior experience using ICT formed the first half of the group. The second half consisted of 24 subjects without any prior experience using ICT.

Procedure. The test subjects have been asked as well to find 4 different functionalities in a mobile phone menu, similar to the first study. This time, the device has been a smart phone while the menus were implemented as HTML pages. Interestingly, it was not possible to find enough Arabic native speakers in Egypt that would use their mobile phones in Arabic instead of English. Therefore, the respective menus presented were English translations of the menus used in the first study. Since English is a verb-first language (SVO) as well, there is no conflict between both languages with respect to effects of word order.

Results. Overall, it took the 48 test subjects significantly longer ($p<.001$) to find the given functionalities in the object oriented menu (8.87s) in comparison to the verb-oriented menu (6.49s). This effect was even more prominent within the subgroup of subjects with extensive prior experience using ICT. They found the functionalities in the object-oriented menu in 12.09s, while it took them 7.41s with the verb-oriented menu ($p<0.001$). The subgroup with no prior experience using ICT, however, did not show a significant difference ($p>0.4$) between the object-oriented version (5.69s) and the verb-oriented version (5.59s).

Discussion and Limitations. The results suggest rather clearly that the word order of the language spoken by the participants has an effect on the performance with verb- and object-oriented menu structures. The prior experience with ICT did have an impact resulting in a better performance with verb-oriented menus. Prior experience with existing menu structures could have had as well an impact on the results. In addition, the users were able to see 9 entries of the menu at a time instead of 3 in the first study. This aspect provided the participants with a better overview of the different options available.

4   Conclusion and Future Work

The work presented here covers two important aspects when designing menus for ICT: the levels of hierarchy and the criteria for sorting of functionalities. It has been shown that flat menus with a maximum depth of two levels are to be preferred independent from any cultural context. In contrast, the impact of the users' native language on the performance with verb- and object oriented menus respectively did not present such a clear picture. The first study focusing on Spanish (verb-oriented) and German (object-oriented) native speakers suggest that the prior experience with ICT can be seen as a determining factor while the language can be excluded. The second study looking at Arabic (verb-oriented) native speakers showed opposite results: the overall results show a significant better performance with verb-oriented menus while this effect is even stronger for the tech-savvy users.

The comparability between both studies is limited due to the methodological differences mentioned before. Therefore, there is no concluding answer to be given regarding the linguistic aspect of menu design. It is recommended to redesign the study while extending it to other languages. German is considered an object-oriented language even though both SVO and SOV sword orders are present. There are, however, other more prominent object-oriented languages such as Hindi and Korean that should be included. Both Spanish and Arabic are clearly verb-oriented languages and should be present in follow-up studies as well.

The first study accounted for the factor of prior experience with mobile phones with subjects that did not own a mobile phone before. The second study recruited participants with a uniform level of prior mobile phone usage. In order to account for this factor in a better way it is recommended to design a menu for an application that is not yet known to the participants. This could be a TV program guide on television or an app for a smart phone with a novel service not known to the users.

Finally the menu for the tested application should be translated into the local language completely. The challenge of participants being used to a user interface in English can be solved by adapting the content of the application to local customs. The native language would be more acceptable for instance in applications that deal with locally rooted traditions such as cooking.

References

1. LISA Glossary Project,
   http://www.lisa.org/term/termdefinitions/index.html
2. Sturm, C.: TLCC – Towards a framework for systematic and successful product internationalization. In: IWIPS 2002: Proceedings of the 4th Annual International Workshop on Internationalization of Products and Systems, Austin/Texas, USA (2002)
3. Piaggio, C.: Localization for the Spanish-speaking World, Multilingual (#67 Supplement), vol. 15 (2004)
4. Hoft, N.: International Technical Communication. How to Export Information about High Technology. John Wiley & Sons, New York (1995)
5. del Galdo, E.M., Nielsen, J.: International User Interfaces. John Wiley & Sons, Inc., New York (1996)
6. Dray, S., Mrazek, D.: A Day In the Life: Studying Context across Cultures. In: del Galdo, E.M., Nielsen, J. (eds.) International User Interfaces. John Wiley & Sons, Inc., New York (1996)
7. Marcus, A.: Human communication issues in advanced UIs. Communicatus of the ACM 36(4), 101–109 (1993)

8. Honold, P.: Cross-cultural Usability Engineering: Its development and state of the art. In: Bullinger, H.-J., Ziegler, J. (eds.) Human-Computer Interaction: Ergonomics and User Interfaces. Proceedings of the 8th International Conference on Human-Computer Interaction, HCI 1999, Munich (1999)

9. Honold, P.: Culture and Context: An Empirical Study for the Development of a Framework for the Elicitation of Cultural Influence in Product Usage. International Journal of Human-Computer Interaction 12(3&4), 327–345 (2001)

10. Röse, K.: Methodik zur Gestaltung interkultureller Mensch-Maschine-Systeme in der Produktionstechnik. Verlag Universität Kaiserslautern (2002)

11. Dunn, M., Greenhill, S., Levinson, S., Gray, R.: Evolved structure of language shows lineage-specific trends in word-order universals. Nature 473, 79–82 (2011)

12. Koster, J.: Dutch as an SOV Language. Linguistic Analysis 1, 111–136 (1975)

13. Haider, H., Prinzhorn, M.: Verb second phenomena in Germanic languages, Publications in Language Sciences, vol. 21. Foris, Dordrecht (1986)

14. Cooper, A., Reimann, R.: About Face 2.0 – The Essentials of Interaction Design. Wiley Publishing, Indianapolis (2003)

15. Chen, S.Y., Macredie, R.D.: Cognitive styles and hypermedia navigation: Development of a Learning model. Journal of the American Society for Information Science and Technology 53(1), 3–15 (2002)

16. Witkin, H.A., Dyk, R.B., Faterson, H.F., Goodenough, D.R., Karp, S.A.: Psychological differentiation. Lawrence Erlbaum Associates, Potomac (1974)

17. Holtzmann, W.H., Diaz-Guerrero, R., Swartz, J.D.: El desarrollo de la personalidad en dos culturas: México y Estados Unidos, Trillas, México (1975)

18. Nisbett, R.E., Norenzayan, A.: Culture and cognition. In: Medin, D., Pashler, H. (eds.) Stevens' Handbook of Experimental Psychology, 3rd edn. Memory and Cognitive Processes, vol. 2. John Wiley & Sons, New York (2002)

19. Halpern, D.F.: Sex differences in cognitive abilities. Lawrence Erlbaum, Mahwah (2000)

20. Witkin, H.A., Oltman, P.K., Raskin, E., Karp, S.A.: A manual for the Embedded Figures Test. Consulting Psychologists Press, Palo Alto (1971)

21. Dahlgren, S.: Word order in Arabic. Acta Universitatis Gothoburgensis, Göteborg, Sweden (1998)

Tracing Technology Diffusion of Social Media with Culturally Localized User Experience Approach

Huatong Sun

Interdisciplinary Arts & Sciences, University of Washington Tacoma
Tacoma, WA 98402, U.S.A
huatongs@gmail.com

Abstract. This paper examines two recent technology diffusion cases of social media in a global context, Facebook Japan and Sina Weibo. By tracing the local development of two social media technologies and probing into the deeper issues behind their peculiar use patterns, it presents a new framework—Culturally Localized User Experience (CLUE) for culturally sensitive design and argues the integration of action and meaning in design is key to the success of global social media.

Keywords: social media, culturally localized user experience, culturally sensitive design, postcolonial, SNS, microblog, Facebook, Weibo.

1 Introduction

For the past decade, social media technologies have acclaimed global successes and altered local cultures. However, the overt instrumentality of a social media technology is often lauded over its implicit values and sociocultural meanings during local uses, and people tend to apply an overly techno-utopian view to interpret the changes it has caused. This type of naïve responses contests and exemplifies a common problem in cross-cultural technology design, the disconnect of action and meaning [19]. As a result, the designed technology is usable, but local users do not relate to it or even resist it.

Cross-cultural studies indicate that those local social media use practices usually develop different communication patterns while responding to local cultural and rhetorical traditions and then take on different use trajectories in various locales [4, 10, 18, 19]. As Ito [9] suggests, we should regard those local uses "as a heterogeneous set of pathways through diverse sociotechnical ecologies" rather than "a single trajectory toward a universal good" (p. 6). However, those studies tend to focus on comparing and contrasting local differences without linking them to the impact of globalization and its accompanying power relationships. Indeed various local uses of social media technologies are profoundly complicated by the issues of value, identity, power, and hegemony in the postcolonial conditions [8].

In this paper I examine two recent technology diffusion cases of social media in a global context, Facebook Japan and Sina Weibo. By tracing the local development of

A. Marcus (Ed.): DUXU/HCII 2013, Part II, LNCS 8013, pp. 115–120, 2013.

two social media technologies, i.e., Social Network Service (SNS) and microblogging, and probing into the deeper issues behind their peculiar use patterns, I present a new framework—Culturally Localized User Experience (CLUE) [19] for culturally sensitive design and argue the integration of action and meaning in design is key to the success of global social media.

2   Local Development of Two Social Media Technologies

Originating from the U.S., social media technologies such as Facebook (SNS) and Twitter (microblogging) have been diffusing rapidly across the globe through themselves and through their copycats. The diffusion processes and the cross-cultural use patterns generated provide a lot of food for thoughts for cross-cultural design practices.

In the first case, the U.S.-based Facebook had a difficult five-year battle to take the Japanese market. As the Facebook has rapidly risen as the world's SNS website with a billion users [20], many local SNS websites were kicked out of the game [3]. However, Facebook might have never expected that it could take so long to win Japanese users. Why were Japanese users reluctant to accept Facebook, which has garnered one victory after another in other places throughout the world rapidly?

Facebook asks its users to use real names and photos for profiles. This distinctive feature that has made Facebook a huge success in American culture where it originated, conflicts with Japanese Internet culture. Japanese users prefer to use pseudonyms to interact with each other either for bonding with old friends or for bridging for new connections, with a different conceptualization of privacy. Over 75% of Japanese social media users chose to use pseudonyms around the time of 2009 [15], as supported by the top Japanese SNS website Mixi at that time. Consequently Facebook's penetration rate had been stagnating at 3% for a long time until fall 2011, long after a Japanese version was released in 2008 and after a Facebook office was opened in Tokyo in September 2010.

Facing such strong resistance from local users, the global IT giant determined to conquer this strategically important online market with bold localization initiatives while sticking to their real-name policy. Efforts include promoting the site with missions game, designing a customized mobile interface, allowing users to syndicate Facebook posts on Mixi, and introducing a job search application for college students. It eventually acclaimed victory in September 2012 after morphing into a professional networking site for Japanese users [5], similar to LinkedIn, where local users are more comfortable to use their real names for professional networking.

In the second case, a Chinese copycat of Twitter, Sina Weibo, outperforms Twitter behind the great Firewall of China. Sina Weibo was launched in August 2009 to fill the void after Twitter was blocked by the Chinese government since the Ürümqi riots that July. Here "Weibo" is the Chinese word for "microblogging". With more than 500 million registered users and 46.2 million daily active users as of February 2013, it is ranked as the No. 2 active social network in China [11, 14].

Starting as a copycat, Sina Weibo has adopted many successful features from American SNS websites such as Facebook, Foursquare, Pinterest, and many others. But what really distinguishes Sina Weibo from many other Chinese copycats and makes it a big success should be contributed to its own distinctive features originating from Chinese Internet culture, such as rich media, threaded comment, private chat, microgroup, microevent, and so on. As a matter of fact, it would be highly doubtful whether Twitter would succeed similarly on the Chinese market if not banned.

For example, it is interesting to see how different discursive relationships are built on Sina Weibo and Twitter by comparing how a response and the original author of a reposted message are presented differently on the interfaces of the two. The response to a Weibo message is set up as a threaded comment, under a lower level from the original Weibo, similar to an original post and its responses on a bulletin board system—bulletin board system has been popular in China. In contrast, all the responses on the Twitter are set up on the same level as the original one. In the case of original author of a reposted message, Twitter displays both the reposted message (i.e., retweet) and its original author in the timeline with a fine print noted as "retweeted by" a person one follows. In comparison, what is displayed in the timeline of Sina Weibo is still the user name of the person one follows, and the reposted message is presented as a sublevel message.

In both cases, there is a clear hierarchy of messages in the timeline of Sina Weibo and therefore a hierarchical discursive relationship forms. However, there is not such implied power relationship suggested on the interface of Twitter, and all the messages are treated as an equal contribution in a conversation. Such a difference could be explained with the difference between a collectivist culture like China and an individualist culture like the U.S.: In a collectivist culture, the originality of a microblog message is not necessarily noted in a collaborative discourse.

3   Integrating Action and Meaning with CLUE

These two cases above illustrate how important it is to integrate action and meaning in cross-cultural social media design. One common problem in cross-cultural design is the disconnect between action and meaning: Concrete user activities are frequently missing in design practices, and usually only static, out-of-context meanings are transferred through design. As a result, the designed technology is usable, but not meaningful to local users.

To tackle this problem, I developed a design philosophy and methodology Culturally Localized User Experience (CLUE) to create culturally sensitive design for local users [19]. In the CLUE framework, I regard local culture as the dynamic nexus of contextual interactions that manifests numerous articulations of practices and meanings, and advocate a holistic, integrated vision of user experience that takes user experience as both situated action and constructed meaning. Therefore, the CLUE methodology proposes a dialogical, cyclical design process to integrate action and meaning in order to make a technology both usable and meaningful to local users.

This dialogical, cyclical design process is important and valuable at this stage of glocalization. Glocalization is the third stage of contemporary international communication process after *cultural imperialism* and *globalization* [12]. Cultural imperialism is the time when one-way information flow and intentional cultural domination took place. Globalization stresses cultural synchronization and world homogenization and fails to see the dialogicality and complexity of contemporary international cultural relations. Thereby it implies a technology determinist view about development, ignoring local conditions and knowledge [17]. Glocalization recognizes the tension between the global and the local, encourages the interaction of both, and thus theoretically captures "receding center-periphery international arrangements and emerging decentralized, fragmented, and multifaceted patterns" [12, pp. 39-40].

Clearly the Facebook Japan case shows cultural imperialism is still pervasive everywhere, including in an affluent country with self-sufficient Internet culture such as Japan. With the mindset of cultural imperialism, static meanings out of context, influenced by a transmission model of communication [16], are often transferred in cross-cultural design, neglecting local cultural preferences and use habits [19]. Meanwhile, the simplistic transmission process and the static meanings transferred are intensified in the postcolonial conditions as both the cultural hybridity and the accompanying power relationships are "unavoidable" [13]. The singularity promoted in the Facebook Japan case—only one social networking mode is honored in this global village—is more alarming and disturbing than similar cases occurring in other developing countries: A local social network service is doomed before this global juggernaut no matter how hard local users fight. It also conflicts with the design goal of "pluralism" we would like to advocate in HCI research and design practices [1, 2, 7]. As Bardzell [1] warns, this type of singularity often "quietly and usually unintentionally imposes—without transparent or rational justification—Western technological norms and practices" (p. 1305).

On the other hand, the Sina Weibo case suggests the potential of a dialogic design cycle could bring to culturally sensitive design even for a technology with a humble start, i.e., a copycat. It illustrates how new meanings are generated in a technology localization process and how the same technology could bring up different discursive relationships with different interface features. I call the local instances of a globally-diffusing-technology as local *uptakes*, which is part of the glocalization, informed by Freadman's "uptake" from genre theory [6]. Local uptake is a peculiar phenomenon of this era of glocalization. They represent the pulling forces that re-assert local agency against the pushing force of globalizing trends towards homogeneity and synchronization in contemporary postcolonial conditions.

4   Conclusion

Integrating action and meaning is key to the success of global social media. To integrate action and meaning and to design meaningful interactions, the multi-voiced, dialogic approach CLUE argues for dialogic interactions between technology and its surrounding conditions, between action and meaning, between local and global, between instrumental and social affordances, and between designers and users. It is dialogism that integrates key concepts of the CLUE framework into a coherent structure, which makes it possible to connect action and meaning in technology design.

References

1. Bardzell, S.: Feminist HCI: Taking stock and outlining an agenda for design. In: Proc. of CHI 2010: World Conference on Human Factors in Computing Systems, pp. 1301–1310. ACM, New York (2010)
2. Bødker, S.: When second wave HCI meets third wave challenges. In: Proc. of NordiCHI 2006. ACM Press (2006)
3. Cosenza, V.: World map of social networks (December 2012), http://vincos.it/world-map-of-social-networks/
4. Donner, J.: The Rules of Beeping: Exchanging Messages Via Intentional "Missed Calls" on Mobile Phones. Journal of Computer-Mediated Communication 13(1) (2007), http://jcmc.indiana.edu/vol13/issue1/donner.html
5. Espinosa, J.: Facebook overtakes Japanese social network Mixi in Japan (September 13, 2012), http://www.insidefacebook.com/2012/09/13/facebook-overtakes-japanese-social-network-mixi-in-japan/
6. Freadman, A.: Uptake. In: Coe, R., Lingard, L., Teslenko, T. (eds.) The Rhetoric and Ideology of Genre: Strategies for Stability and Change, pp. 39–53. Hampton Press, Cresskill (2002)
7. Harrison, S., Tatar, D., Sengers, P.: The three paradigms of HCI. In: Ext. Abstracts CHI. ACM Press (2007)
8. Irani, L., Vertesi, J., Dourish, P., Philip, K., Grinter, R.: Postcolonial Computing: A Lens on Design and Development. In: Proceedings of Conference on Human Factors in Computing Systems (CHI 2010), pp. 1311–1320. ACM, New York (2010)
9. Ito, M.: Introduction: Personal, Portable, Pedestrian. In: Ito, M., Okabe, D., Matsuda, M. (eds.) Personal, Portable, Pedestrian Mobile Phones in Japanese Life, pp. 1–16. MIT Press, Cambridge (2006)
10. Ito, M., Okabe, D., Matsuda, M. (eds.): Personal, Portable, Pedestrian Mobile Phones in Japanese Life. MIT Press, Cambridge (2006)
11. Kemp, S.: Social, Digital, Mobile China (January 17, 2013), http://wearesocial.sg/blog/2013/01/social-digital-mobile-china-jan-2013/
12. Kraidy, M.: From Imperialism to Glocalization: A theoretical framework for the Information Age. In: Ebo, B.L. (ed.) Cyberimperialism? Global Relations in the New Electronic Frontier, pp. 27–42. Greenwood Publishing, Westport (2001)
13. Merritt, S., Stolterman, E.: Cultural hybridity and participatory design. In: PDC 2012, Denmark, pp. 73–76 (2012)
14. Ong, J.: China's Sina Weibo grew 73% in 2012, passing 500 million registered accounts (February 21, 2013), http://thenextweb.com/asia/2013/02/21/chinas-sina-weibo-grew-73-in-2012-passing-500-million-registered-accounts/

15. Orita, A., Hada, H.: Is that really you?: an approach to assure identity without revealing real-name online. In: Proceedings of the 5th ACM Workshop on Digital Identity Management, pp. 17–20. ACM, New York (2009)
16. Slack, J.: The theory and method of articulation in cultural studies. In: Morley, D., Chen, K.-H. (eds.) Stuart Hall: Critical Dialogues in Cultural Studies, pp. 112–127. Routledge, New York (1996)
17. Slack, J.D., Wise, J.M.: Culture + Technology: A primer. Peter Lang, New York (2005)
18. Sun, H.: Towards a rhetoric of locale: Localizing mobile messaging technology into everyday life. Journal of Technical Writing and Communication 39(2), 245–261 (2009)
19. Sun, H.: Cross-cultural technology design: Creating culture-sensitive technology for local users. Oxford University Press, New York (2012)
20. Zuckerberg, M.: This morning, there are more than one billion people... (October 4, 2012), http://www.facebook.com/zuck/posts/10100518568346671

The Interactive Media between Human and the Sacred

An Example for Taiwanese Spiritual Practice

Pi-Fen Wang

Lecturer, Dept. of Interior Design, Shu-Te University, Kaohsiung, Taiwan
fineland@ms27.hinet.net

Abstract. The aim of this study is to provide an understanding of interconnectedness between human, sacred and the attachment to sacred spaces. Further aim is to elevate the new architectural and interior design value. The method of this study includes the interview and case study from spiritual practitioner. The results from this study conclude several finding in the followings. First, the interactive media between human and the sacred usually includes some aspects such as the time, the behaviors, spaces, and the sacred objects. Second, the sacred behaviors include pray, meditation, rite, citing and educational course. They prayed to the gods, and meditated with their inner spirits. Third, sacred objects, symbolized the protection, power and the sacred. They are comprised with god sculptures, god pictures, Buddha bead, the sutra, the sacred pictures from the video, sacred incense and sacred light with sacred words. Forth, sacred communications from the small group of spiritual practitioners become very significant ways to sense the sacred. Fifth, they communicated each other anytime with computer website. Computer screen could present many changeable sacred images. The "Three Pins Group" for spiritual practice is an active group to enhance their spirits.

Keywords: sacred space, spiritual practice, rite, symbol.

1 Introduction

According to the high transitionary life, we usually feel the secular pressures in daily life. How to balance human's body and spirit becomes the significant issue. To sense the sacred can promote the spirit and feel their rebirth.

However, as society has diversified, spirituality has gradually turned from organized religion to personal spiritual life [1]. Creating sacred space in daily life is therefore an important topic and need.

1.1 Purpose

The aim of this study is to provide an understanding of interconnectedness between human, sacred and the attachment to sacred spaces. Further aim is to elevate the new architectural and interior design value.

A. Marcus (Ed.): DUXU/HCII 2013, Part II, LNCS 8013, pp. 121–128, 2013.

1.2   Method

The method of this study includes the interview and case study from spiritual practitioner. The study selected one group of modern spiritual seeker with 3 spiritual practitioners' house in Taiwan. The interviews were followed with case studies (Ye house, Chen house and Ho house).

2   Literature Review

2.1   The Content of Sacred Space

As Eliade (1987: 11-12) stated: "Man becomes aware of the sacred because it manifests itself, shows itself, we have proposed the term hierophany,…the sacred is equivalent to a power, … to reality. Sacred power means reality and at the same time enduringness and efficacy [2]. The sacred space provides two main functions: a place for spiritual enlightenment [3], and a symbolic location for family and group culture. The home is an important source of sacred space, since it provides a place for worshipping deity, ancestors, and other sacred beings [4]. Ritual atmospheres are often distinct from everyday spiritual space experiences, particularly in seasonal rituals, living ceremonies, or special celebrations [5]. Ritual purification symbolizes the "rebirth" of minds, allowing the spirits to return to their original states [2]. The complex rituals performed by Daoism priests in Taiwan involve ritual spaces modeled on sacred fields, symbolizing the arrival of numerous saints [6]. Eliade asserted that (1987: 20): "There is then, a sacred space, and hence a strong, significant space; …that is sacred the only real and really existing space and… For religious man, space is not homogeneous; he experiences interruptions, breaks in it. Sacred space refers to the "being space" formed by sacred beings [7]. Lin (2003: 44) noted that, "Deities are gods, primordial spirits are gods; the Han refer to the hearts and souls of people as primordial spirits [8]." The divinity and holiness of the sacred are interlinked; holiness is the nature of deity [9]. Li: "According to the sacred/profane dichotomy provided by M. Eliade, society is composed of the sacred and profane worlds. In other words, there is a clear division between the times and spaces of the "extraordinary" sacred and the "ordinary" profane." [10]

3   Results and Discussion

According to 3 case studies and several interviews, the important results and discussion would be listed below. Their concepts were focused on different sacred activities in daily life.

3.1   The Idea of "Three Pines Group"

The main idea of "Three Pins Group" modern spiritual practitioners (TPMSP) is to pursue the perfect life and the balance of body, mind and spirit. Jen-Mine Ye is the teacher of the small group (Three Pines Group). In ten years, the members are over 40members. The ways of their spiritual practices are combined to some Taiwanese traditional religions and create the new approach (Fig. 1).

Fig. 1. "Three Pines Group" at Youth Park

3.2   The Sacred Activities of "Three Pines Group" (TPG)

Table 1. The activities of   "Three Pines Group" modern spiritual practitioners (TPMSP)

Time Activity	personal Weekday	Group practice Fri.	Sat .& Sun.
Pray	Private home		Youth Park
Chi	Private home		Youth Park
Citing	Private home	Ye house (teacher)	
meditation	Private home	Ye house	Youth Park
Sutra education	Private home	Ye house	Youth Park
Communication on web	Private home		
Rite on festivals	Daily rite was held in private home	Important festivals were held in Ye house and Chen house	Chen house

The ways of their spiritual practices for TPG include 2stages. The sacred activities of TPG practice with some contents (Table 1.) in daily life. The first stage is to enforce Chi either at home or at Youth Park. To practice Chi is related to breathe. In order to get the fresh air, it is better to practice outside. The second stage is to modify and enlighten the spirituality. In this stage, the sacred activities include meditation, citing the sutra education, the rites on special festivals and communication on the website. Meditation would be done personally at private home (Fig. 2) during the weekday, and also become one of group practice during the rite. In order to meditate with safe feeling, teacher Ye like to site in the front of wall or the altar.

Fig. 2. Meditation in front of altar

Citing the sutra is held at Ye house on Friday night (Fig. 3). The sutra education course is held at Youth Park on Saturday and Sunday. It's one way to reflect the recent problem. It could be promoted through the teaching by teacher (Ye) and the other members' communication.

Fig. 3. Citing sutra on Friday night

By using the computer system, there are two types of interactions. One is to open to the public on website with some common information about the spiritual practice. The other type is only connected among the members of TPG. They try to keep some privacy for encouraging some personal inner spiritual world. The rites of important festivals usually were held in Ye house. Due to the member of participants participated to the rite in July (Chinese calendar). So there were two main altars in the altar room (Fig. 4-5), and the temperate altar is with simple offerings in the living room. Incense pot is situated at the middle of the altar. The temperate altar presented the changeable Buddha pictures and ancestors' lists on the wall in the video. Three members could communicate with the gods, and performed one by one. When sitting on the floor, pray, meditation and citing the sutra were usually combined together. Sometimes, the sound of sacred instruments was followed with citing the sutra.

Fig. 4. Temperate altar- simple offerings

Fig. 5. Some members could communicate with the god

3.3   The Interviews (Table 2.)

According to the interviews, some member of TPG agreed that "Through the practice could promote my own spirit, balance the body, mind and spirit". Good feelings "I felt the energy and power". "I also felt peaceful, stable, relax, pleasure and real". The other feeling about is to "connect to the universe". The sacred space of the atmosphere of the altar is "sublime". One of three houses with small garden was full of fresh and pure atmosphere. It's better to citing the sutra in the interior.

Table 2. The content of the interviews

	Content and cultural identity
motivation & Concept	◆ promote the spirit ◆ find back the original Buddhahood ◆ balance the body , mind and spirit
Sacred behavior	Meditation / citing / pray / sutra education / communication on web dedication/ chant incantations
Feeling	◆ feel the energy and power ◆ peace / stable / relax / pleasure /real ◆ connect to the universe
Sacred space	◆ altar-sublime atmosphere ◆ garden and park-natural and pure atmosphere ◆ citing in the interior

3.4   Spatial Comparisons of Case Studies (Table 3.)

Three case studies in different locations of Taipei have their own unique spatial cha-racteristics. Ye house is with sublime atmosphere, human scale and good view to Youth Park, maintain and river. The altar is situated in the center of book shelf along the wall. The symbolic god sculpture and pictures become the obvious focal point in the upper level (Fig. 6).

Fig. 6. Sacred altar- god sculpture and changeable picture

Chen house is with some artistic feeling. The altar is designed by the owner. The lighting is modern and fashion. Ho house is situated at roof floor with garden. The atmosphere is natural and quiet. Due to the tiny scale, sacred space is not clear. Even though case study has diverse space, they have common cultural identities including the incense, god pictures and god symbols.

Table 3. Comparisons with three Case Studies

Spatial	Ye house (12F)	Chen (11F)	Ho (4F) (Roof garden)
Atmosphere	◆ Sublime ◆ Human scale ◆ Good view	◆ Artistic feeling	◆ Nature ◆ Quiet ◆ Sunlight
Territory& define	◆ Single room with wooden floor ◆ Defined by flexible Japanese paper door	◆ Half of living room ◆ Defined by furniture	◆ Part of living room ◆ Defined by closet and desk
Centrality & focus	◆ Focal point in the center of book shelf	◆ Weak focus ◆ Sitting area is close to the altar	◆ Scale is small ◆ Focus is not clear
Elements	◆ Natural light ◆ Water and tea ◆ Symbols-incense/god sculpture and pictures/sutra/Buddha bead	◆ Water and tea ◆ Sacred light designed by owner ◆ incense	◆ crystal ◆ Incense ◆ Tiny god sculpture

4   Conclusion

Base on the previous research, this study conclude several finding in the followings. First, the interactive media between human and the sacred usually includes some aspects such as the time, the behaviors, spaces, and the sacred objects. Second, new ways of thinking everyday spiritual practice are different from Taiwanese traditional religion. There are more flexible, simple and diverse. Third, in addition to the festivals, the selections of the sacred time, is adapted to individual convenience and group's common gathering. Forth, the sacred behaviors include pray, meditation, rite, citing and educational course. They prayed to the gods, and meditated with their inner spirits. They also are citing together on Friday night, participates the educational and communicated course on weekend, and hold the rites during the traditional festivals. Fifth, sacred spaces include their own houses and outdoor park. The altar, the main sacred space at home, usually put in the middle of the book shelf in the altar room. There are some sacred objects arranged to the different levels in the book shelf. The atmosphere of the altar is sublime and closed to human scale. The altar room provides everyday pray and meditation, and citing the sutra. Semi-outdoor terrace and outdoor lawn in the park provide the educational and communicative course about the spiritual practice. Sixth, sacred objects, symbolized the protection, power and the sacred. They are comprised with god sculptures, god pictures, Buddha bead, the sutra, the sacred pictures from the video, sacred incense and sacred light with sacred words. God sculptures and god pictures are the most significant symbols. Facing the sacred objects, spiritual practitioner can feel the sacred peace and pleasure. Seventh, the rites of the festivals are the significant media to communicate with gods and sacred beings. The process of the rite usually includes pray with the offerings by using the incense, cite the sutra, listen to the musical instruments, and meditate at the same time. Eighth, meditation is another popular sacred behavior. Spiritual practitioners sitting on the floor, meditate in the front of the small altar or the still corners in the other quiet rooms. They usually sense the sacred from their inner spirits. Ninth, sacred communications from the small group of spiritual practitioners become very significant ways to sense the sacred. This paper has provided the preliminary model for the interactive media between human and the sacred from some spiritual practitioners.

References

1. Gilliat-Ray, S.: Sacralising' sacred space in public institutions: A case study of the prayer space at the Millennium Dome. Journal of Contemporary Religion 20(3), 357–372 (2005)
2. Eliade, M.: The sacred and the profane: The nature of religion, pp. 10–26. Harcourt Inc., New York (1987) Trask, W.R. (Trans.) (original work published: 1957)
3. Holloway, J.: Make-believe: Spiritual practice, embodiment, and sacred space. Environment and Planning A 35, 1961–1974 (2003)
4. Mazumdar, S., Mazumdar, S.: Sacred space and place attachment. Journal of Environmental Psychology 3, 231–242 (1993)
5. Li, F.M.: The ordinary and the extraordinary: Mad culture in Chinese festivals. Chung Way Literary Monthly 22(3), 116–154 (1993)
6. Li, F.: Solemnity and play: Ritual structure from the "year's end sacrifice" to the rite of "summoning the elders". Bulletin of the Institute of Ethnology Academia Silica 88, 135–172 (1999)
7. Pan, C.Y.: Spirit, space, and environment– geographic musings of humanism. Wu-nan Culture Enterprise, Taipei (2005)
8. Lin, M.-R.: An analysis of the construction of sacredness using traditional sacred literature. In: Lu, S.-X., Chen, D.-G., Lin, C.-K. (eds.) Religious Sacredness: Phenomena and Explanation, pp. 21–49. Wu-nan Culture Enterprise, Taipei (2003)
9. Chen, D.-G.: "The sole holy"," the duo holy"," the ultimate holy"–A Dialogue between Biblical Views of the Sacred and Religious Studies. In: Religious Sacredness: Phenomena and Explanation, pp. 295–327. Wu-Nan Culture Enterprise, Taipei (2003)
10. Li, F.-M.: The Ordinary and the Extraordinary: Mad Culture in Chinese Festivals. Chung Wai Literary Monthly 22(3), 116–154 (1993)

Banner Evaluation Predicted by Eye Tracking Performance and the Median Thinking Style

Man-Ying Wang[1], Da-Lung Tang[2], Chih-Tung Kao[1], and Vincent C. Sun[3]

[1] Department of Psychology, Soochow University, Taipei, Taiwan
mywang@scu.edu.tw, {athena1011,daluntang}@gmail.com
[2] Department of Mass Communication, Tam Kang University, Taipei, Taiwan
[3] Department of Mass Communication, Chinese Culture University, Taipei, Taiwan
csun@faculty.pccu.edu.tw

Abstract. The current study examined whether and how the Chinese culture rooted median thinking style may affect banner ad viewing and evaluation. Eye tracking performance was recorded as participants viewed banner ads of different information complexity. High median thinking participants were characterized by a flexible perceptual processing style. Their eye tracking performance showed that they responded to information complexity of the banner ads and attempted to integrate information spatially for low complexity banners. Less effortful (and more fluent) eye tracking performance was associated with more positive banner evaluation and the relationship was mediated by experienced fluency in high median thinkers. Information complexity also guided eye tracking. These findings demonstrated the potential of eye tracking measures in predicting effects of culture (and design) related factors on banner evaluation.

Keywords: banner advertisements, eye tracking, median thinking, ZhongYong, information complexity.

1 Introduction

It is well known that banner ads are typically ignored by viewers of a webpage (i.e., "banner blindness" as dubbed by[1])[2], [3]. However, other studies showed evidence of banner viewing or that some very general information could be captured by the viewer in a brief glance of the ad [4], [5]. Task goal of the user could be an important moderator of how attention is directed towards specific banner ad and search behavior in general [6], [7]. As a result, it is probably less fruitful to search for an optimal banner design than to understand the effect of user characteristics on the design of banner ads [7], [8]. An important aspect of user characteristic that has received less attention is on how culturally related individual differences in visual information processing may affect viewer's intention to click on the ad, given the brief processing time or limited processing resources allocated to the banner ad.

A culturally cultivated thinking style – median thinking (also known as ZhongYong, doctrine of the mean or midway thinking) (see [9], for a review) was the focus of this study. Median thinking is historically rooted in the Chinese philosophy of life that guides the deliberation, selection, and execution of action in daily life. It emphasized

A. Marcus (Ed.): DUXU/HCII 2013, Part II, LNCS 8013, pp. 129–138, 2013.

that one should "….consider things carefully from different perspectives, avoid going to extremes, behave in situationally appropriate ways, and maintain interpersonal harmony…." [10] (p 158).

Median thinking entails concrete cognitive and perceptual strategies to support the fulfillment of the above interpersonal goals. The wait-and-see cognitive processing style is conducive to the thorough examination of the situation before making any actions as well as the holding back of extreme emotions [9]. In a study using the Posner cuing paradigm, participants of high median thinking were less affected by the emotionality of cues than low median thinking participants regardless of the validity of the cue [11]. These findings suggested that high-median thinking participants tend to withhold the processing of emotional information and consider the nature of the situation first. High median thinking is also characterized by a global-yet-flexible perceptual style. Relative to low median thinkers, they preferred global to local processing and showed higher flexibility in the switch between global and local processing modes, especially at the presence of emotional primes [12]. As such, the viewer could quickly derive the gist of the visual scene (from global processing) based on which to determine the need to proceed with local processing or to remain at the global level of analysis.

The current study was focused on the global-yet-flexible processing style of median thinkers and its relationships with banner ad complexity and evaluation. Previous studies of visual scene processing demonstrated an increase in fixation duration and a decrease in saccade amplitude as viewing proceeded. They were also considered to be the hallmarks of global-to-local processing [13], [14]. Shorter fixations and larger saccades dominate during earlier global processing (first 2 s.) when the gist of a scene is captured. Object-centered analysis or local processing is performed later that is characterized by longer fixations and smaller saccades [14]. Since the gist of a banner ads is quickly available to the viewer (i.e., in the first 100 ms) [5], it is expected that visual behavior during early viewing of a banner could predict the viewer's evaluation or the intention to click through the ad. To reveal the relationship between viewing behavior and banner ad attitude, eye tracking performance of the viewer was recorded as they viewed each banner ad after which they gave evaluative responses towards whether the banner ad appeared clear and simple, was rich in information and whether the viewer would like to click on it.

High median thinking viewers who exhibited a global-yet-flexible perceptual style were expected to recognize the gist of a banner using global processing and switch to the detailed or local processing of product information more efficiently than low median thinkers. Their global/local processing was also expected to be more responsive than low median thinkers to information complexity manipulation since global and local processors are likely to also accommodate with the variation in complexity. For example, global processing could be sufficient to deal with needs to comprehend low complexity banner ads while local processing predominates in a high complexity ad in order to process the large number of details. Specifically, faster global-to-local switch (characterized by the increase in fixation duration and the decrease in saccade amplitude into viewing) [13], [14], was expected for high median thinking participants. Information complexity measured by the entropy measure in information theory [15] was expected to also affect the efficiency of global-local switch so that the switch was faster as complexity increased, especially for high median thinking participants.

2   Method

2.1   Participants

Participants were forty-nine female undergraduate students who were compensated NT$ 100 for their time.

2.2   Design and Materials

The design was a median thinking (2) x banner complexity (3) mixed design with median thinking serving as a between-subject factor and banner complexity being within-subjects.

Participants filled out the ZhongYong Belief-Value Scale [16] to evaluate their propensity to median thinking. Each banner ad subtended approximately 31°in width and 14° in height and the fixation cross subtended approximately 0.8° x 0.8° on the computer screen. Twenty-four banner ads of female apparels were collected from the internet that were divided into three levels of information complexity according to the computed information entropy measure (see [17] for detailed descriptions of information entropy calculation). Using seven-point scales, three evaluative responses were probed for each banner, i.e., "The layout in the ad is clear", "Product information in the banner ad is rich", "I would like to click on the ad".

2.3   Procedure

The experiment was conducted in a sound attenuated, softly lighted room. Participants were seated 60 cm in front of an HP-L1706 monitor. The experiment was controlled by a Visual Basic program run on a Core2 Duo E7400 (2.8 GHz) personal computer. Eye movements were recorded by the SR Research EyeLink 1000 System at the sampling rate of 500 Hz. The tracking was monocular and conducted in the remote mode. Fixations, saccades and eye blinks were determined using the default definition of the EyeLink System. A nine-point calibration procedure was conducted and the calibration was validated and repeated when necessary until the optimal calibration criterion was met.

Participants were asked to evaluate a series of ads when their eye movements were recorded. The experiment stared after 4 practice trials (repeated if necessary) and the calibration procedure. Each trial began with a fixation cross presented at the center of the screen. Participants moved the mouse cursor to the center location of the cross in order to start the presentation of the banner ad. Each banner was presented for five seconds followed by the three rating questions. The question was presented on the top and the seven-point rating scale was presented at the bottom. Participants indicated their responses by moving the cursor to the location of the corresponding digit. They were given 9 seconds to respond to each question.

3   Results

Fixation durations that were less than 90 ms or greater than 1500 ms were excluded from the analysis. Participants who scored at the top one third on their ZhongYong scores were treated as high in median thinking and those at the bottom one third were treated as low in median thinking (the cutoffs were 36 and 43 respectively).

3.1   Banner Ratings

Each of the three banner ratings were submitted to median thinking (2) x information complexity ANOVAs. For all three ratings, information complexity was the only significant effect (Clarity: $F(2,66) = 13.24$, $p < .0001$; Richness: $F(2,66) = 65.70$, $p < .0001$; Clicking: $F(2,66) = 9.76$, $p < .0005$). Clarity rating: low > high, medium > high (both $ps < .0005$), medium = low. Richness rating: high > medium > low (all $ps < .0001$). Willingness to click: medium > low ($p < .005$), high > low ($p < .001$), medium = high (see Table 1).

Table 1. The effect of information complexity on ratings of clarity, information richness and the willingness to click. Means and standard deviations are listed.

Information complexity	Clarity		Richness		Clicking	
low	4.93	.87	3.27	.78	3.85	.91
medium	4.90	.65	4.17	.68	4.44	.59
high	4.39	.80	4.83	.83	4.47	1.08

3.2   Eye Tracking Parameters

Mean fixation duration, mean saccade amplitude, mean fixation number, total fixation duration and total scan path were separately submitted to median thinking (2) x information complexity (3) ANOVA. The only significant effect involving median thinking was the interaction between median thinking and complexity for total scan path ($F(2,66)=3.68$, $p < .05$) (see Table 2). Total scan path was larger in high than low median thinking participants for low complexity banners ($p < .0005$) but the difference was not significant for medium or high complexity banners ($ps = .68, .75$). For all eye tracking measures analyzed, the effect of information complexity was significant (see Table 3): mean fixation duration ($F(2,66) = 73.92$, $p < .0001$), medium > low > high; mean saccade amplitude ($F(2,66) = 18.13$, $p < .0001$), low > medium = high; number of fixations ($F(2,66) = 90.73$, $p < .0001$), high > low > medium; total fixation duration ($F(2,66) = 5.81$, $p < .005$), high=medium > low; total scan path ($F(2,66) = 49.37$, $p < .0001$), low = high > medium.

Table 2. The effect of median thinking and information complexity on the total scan path (in degrees of visual angle). Means and standard deviations are listed.

Median thinking	Information complexity					
	low		medium		high	
low	77.3	11.5	70.6	12.8	83.0	14.8
high	86.1	13.1	73.3	12.7	85.6	14.0

Table 3. The effect of informaiton complexity on eye tracking parameters. Means and standard deviations are listed.

Eye tracking parameters	Information complexity					
	low		medium		high	
mean fixation duration	252.0	32.5	262.4	29.8	228.1	24.2
mean saccade amplitude	4.77	.56	4.34	.63	4.45	.53
number of fixations	16.9	1.7	16.5	1.5	18.7	1.6
total fixation duarion	4071.2	186.8	4150.7	190.6	4112.0	172.7
total scan path	82.1	13.0	72.0	12.6	84.4	14.2

Table 4. The quadratic model fit for fixation duration as the function of banner complexity, median thinking and the viewing period

Condition	time	Linear		Quadratic		Intercept		R^2
		Est	SE	Est	SE	Est	SE	
low complexity								
low median thinking	1s	152.4	153.2	-86.9	125.3	172.7*	40.2	.53
	2s	86.1	41.4	-22.4	18.3	185.6***	19.8	.61
	5s	45.9***	10.9	-7.8**	2.2	204.0***	11.3	.71
high median thinking	1s	349.7*	64.8	-224.4*	52.9	109.5*	17.0	.97
	2s	152.2**	28.9	-54.2**	12.8	153.5***	13.8	.86
	5s	45.3***	10.9	-7.5**	2.2	197.0***	11.3	.55
medium complexity								
low median thinking	1s	197.4	96.5	-105.0	78.9	175*	25.3	.89
	2s	128.8*	40.8	-46.9*	18.5	190.0***	20.0	.66
	5s	38.4**	12.9	-6.8*	2.6	226.8***	13.5	.34
high median thinking	1s	238.3	75.0	-89.0	61.3	130.5*	19.7	.98
	2s	192.9***	23.9	-64.0***	10.6	144.2***	11.4	.95
	5s	50.8**	16.4	-8.6*	3.3	209.7***	17.1	.38
high complexity								
low median thinking	1s	147.7	60.0	-94.4	49.0	166.0**	15.8	.86
	2s	32.4	21.7	-4.2	9.6	194.2***	10.4	.76
	5s	22.9**	6.9	-3.2*	1.4	201.2***	7.2	.55
high median thinking	1s	97.5	31.6	-47.7	25.9	178.9**	8.3	.96
	2s	75.5**	20.5	-26.4	9.1	182.9***	9.8	.76
	5s	27.6**	7.4	-4.9***	1.5	201.7***	7.8	.44

A quadratic regression model was used to fit the mean fixation duration on time of viewing. Table 4 listed all fitted parameters for time periods of 1, 2, and 5 seconds. The parameter for the linear component indicated the speed of increase in fixation duration over viewing time. For the 5 s. fit, this parameter was positive and significant for high and low median thinker at all complexity levels. However, for high median thinking participants, the linear parameter was significant at all of the time period examined when banner complexity was low, significant at 2 s and 5 s when banner

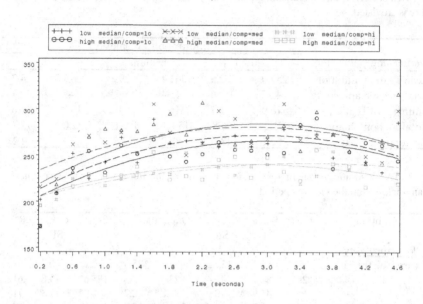

Fig. 1. The scatter plot of fixation duration as the function of information complexity and median thinking overlaid with the fitted quadratic function

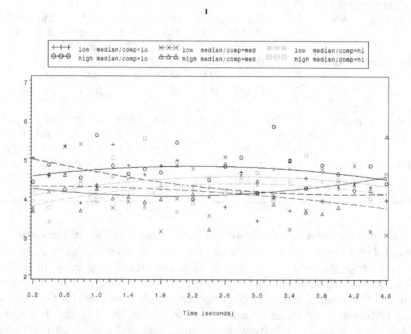

Fig. 2. The scatter plot of saccade amplitude as the function of information complexity and median thinking overlaid with the fitted quadratic function

complexity was medium and significant at 5s of viewing period when banner complexity was high (see Table 4 and Fig. 1). For high-median thinking participants, the global-to-local switch appeared to be earlier the lower the complexity of the banner ad was. The lack of similar pattern for low median thinking participants suggested that high median thinkers were more sensitive and responded to banner complexity by modifying the time of global-to-local switch.

As seen in Fig 2, there apparently lacks any clear quadratic trend or linear trend for saccade amplitude data. None of the linear (or quadratic) parameters was significant regardless of the level of information complexity and median thinking (see Table 5).

Table 5. The quadratic model fit for saccade amplitude as the function of banner complexity, median thinking and the viewing period

Condition	time	Linear		Quadratic		Intercept		R^2
		Est	SE	Est	SE	Est	SE	
low complexity								
low median thinking	1s	-.19	5.48	-.70	4.48	5.03	1.44	.33
	2s	-.75	1.23	.36	.55	5.02***	.59	.06
	5s	-.49	.30	.06	.06	5.08***	.32	.30
high median thinking	1s	-3.77	3.72	4.01	3.04	5.21*	.98	.66
	2s	.32	1.09	-.01	.48	4.43***	.52	.18
	5s	.28	.31	-.06	.06	4.49***	.32	.05
medium complexity								
low median thinking	1s	9.95	3.76	-7.35	3.07	1.82	.99	.80
	2s	1.13	1.61	-.75	.71	4.04**	.77	.32
	5s	.02	.45	-.03	.09	4.28***	.47	.07
high median thinking	1s	3.62	4.78	-2.94	3.91	3.26	1.25	.22
	2s	-.66	1.08	.35	.48	4.33***	.51	.10
	5s	-.25	.36	.07	.07	4.27***	.38	.07
high complexity								
low median thinking	1s	4.89	4.41	-3.44	3.60	2.56	1.16	.46
	2s	2.08	.99	-.90	.44	3.16***	.48	.39
	5s	.47	.28	-.08	.06	3.70***	.29	.14
high median thinking	1s	1.58	2.02	-.98	1.25	3.51*	.53	.42
	2s	1.39	1.11	-.35	.49	3.43***	.53	.50
	5s	.41	.30	-.06	.06	3.97***	.32	.09

3.3   Correlation between Eye Tracking Measures and Banner Evaluation

The correlation pattern in Table 6 (based on data from all participants) showed that the total scan path correlated negatively with participants' ratings of how willing they were to click on the ad. Willingness to click also correlated positively with mean fixation duration, negatively with the mean number of fixation and mean saccade amplitude. In other words, shorter total scan path and mean saccade amplitude, small-er number of fixations as well as longer mean fixation durations were consistent with higher willingness ratings of banner ad clicking.

A mediation analysis was performed to examine whether the relationship between the total scan path and the willingness to click was mediated by processing fluency [18]. Data from all participants were used in the analysis. The Sobel tests were separately performed on high and low median thinking participants (based on a median split) using clarity rating as the measure of processing fluency. For high median thinkers, processing fluency mediated the relationship between total scan path and willingness to click no matter the analysis was based on one or five seconds of viewing behavior (ps = .003, .004). For low median thinking participants, however, processing fluency did not mediate the relationship.

Table 6. Correlations among eye tracking measures and banner evaluative responses (*$p < .05$, ** $p < .01$, ***$p < .001$)

	Clarity	Richness	Clicking	mean fix. dur.	mean sacc. amp.	no. of fix.	total fix. dur.	total scan path	Zhong Yong
Clarity									
Richness	.48***	1.00							
Clicking	.44**	.69***	1.00						
mean fix. dur.	.27	.24	.29*	1.00					
mean sacc. amp.	.22	-.34*	-.23	-.27	1.00				
no. of fix.	-.25	-.24	-.27	-.93***	.34**	1.00			
total fix. dur.	.01	.10	.14	.67***	-.27	-.45***	1.00		
total scan path	-.27	-.39**	-.30*	-.67***	.81***	.66***	-.43**	1.00	
ZhongYong	-.05	-.03	.02	.06	.09	.03	.18	.08	1.00

4   Discussion

The current study examined and found evidence of differences in banner visual processing for high and low median thinking viewers. High median thinking viewers exhibited sensitivity to banner complexity. Their time of global-to-local processing switch appeared to earlier for lower complexity banner ads. They also exhibited larger total scan path than low median thinkers when the complexity was low. These findings suggested that, as high median thinking viewers quickly switched from banner gist to the processing of local details for low complexity banners, the scattered distribution of information in the ad made it necessary to integrate information across spatial regions. It could be this integration effort that resulted in the large total scan path. Low median thinkers' were either late at the global-to-local switch or they were less prone to integrate information in the face of scattered information distribution in low complexity banner ads.

For banner ads of medium and high information complexity, information gained from local analysis effectively helped comprehension and the need of spatial integration was low. The high mean fixation duration for banner ads of intermediate complexity (see Table 3 and Fig.1) suggested deeper processing (and better understanding) [19] was achieved for these banners. In contrast, the mean fixation duration was the lowest for high complexity banners, suggesting fast and shallow processing of each information source. It should be noted that the medium complexity banners not only enjoyed the longer mean fixation duration, they also had the lowest number of fixations and the smallest total scan paths. These banners appeared to require the least amount of efforts in eye tracking or, in other words, were high in perceptual fluency. As such, they were rated to be as clear as the low complexity ones. Medium complexity ads also received deeper processing to achieve reasonable level of ad comprehension. They were similarly liked (in terms of willingness to click) as the high complexity banners. Information complexity in the banner ads served to guide viewers' eye tracking behavior.

The willingness to click on the ad was associated with small total scan path, small numbers of fixation and long mean fixation duration. Since the direction of these eye tracking measures were suggestive of low efforts, or high fluency, in eye tracking, a mediation analysis was performed to examine if fluency mediated the relationship. It was interesting to see that the analysis indeed reveal a mediating role of fluency but the mediation was significant only for high, not low, median thinkers. This and other finding about the effect of median thinking suggested that high median thinking viewers are characteristic of flexible perceptual processing that was responsive to information complexity of the banner ads. They integrate information across spatial regions when necessary. Eye tracking parameters could be used to predict their banner evaluation as they relied on the experienced fluency in eye tracking for banner evaluation. These findings on the viewing behavior of high median thinkers are consistent with the general framework of median thinking [9] in that they help support flexible, situationally appropriate manner of information processing.

A practical implication of current finding is that, for Chinese users that exhibited an overall greater extent of median thinking, banner ads are better designed to decrease the total scan path and the number of fixation as well as to increase mean fixation duration since high median thinkers tend to rely on the experienced eye tracking fluency for ad evaluation. It is worthwhile for future research to direct efforts in uncovering visual design elements that are associated with these patterns of eye tracking performance. It is also of interest to see if web page design that increased experienced processing fluency may also contribute to positive banner evaluation. As a final note at a more general level, current findings also demonstrated the potentials of eye tracking measures in predicting user's evaluation of the banner ad.

References

1. Benway, J.P.: Banner Blindness: The Irony of Attention Grabbing on the World Wide Web. Proceedings of the Human Factors and Ergonomics Society Annual Meeting 42(5), 463–467 (1998), doi:10.1177/154193129804200504
2. Burke, M., Gorman, N., Nilsen, E., Hornof, A.: Banner ads hinder visual search and are forgotten. Paper Presented at the CHI 2004 Extended Abstracts on Human Factors in Computing Systems, Vienna, Austria (2004)
3. Nielsen, J., Pernice, K.: Eyetracking web usability. New Riders Pub. (2010)
4. Dreze, X., Hussherr, F.X.: Internet advertising: Is anybody watching? Journal of Interactive Marketing 17(4), 8–23 (2003)
5. Pieters, R., Wedel, M.: Ad Gist: Ad Communication in a Single Eye Fixation. Marketing Science 31(1), 59–73 (2012), doi:10.1287/mksc.1110.0673

6. Janiszewski, C.: The influence of display characteristics on visual exploratory search behavior. Journal of Consumer Research 25(3), 290–301 (1998)
7. Pagendarm, M., Schaumburg, H.: Why are users banner-blind? The impact of navigation style on the perception of web banners. Journal of Digital Information 2(1) (2006)
8. Hai, L., Zhao, L., Nagurney, A.: An integrated framework for the design of optimal web banners. Netnomics 11(1), 69–83 (2010)
9. Yang, C.F.: Multiplicity of Zhong Yong studies. Indigenous Psychological Research in Chinese Societies 34, 3–96 (2010)
10. Ji, L.J., Lee, A., Guo, T.: The thinking styles of Chinese people. In: Bond, M. (ed.) The Handbook of Chinese Psychology, 2nd edn., pp. 155–167. Oxford University Press (2010)
11. Lin, S.C., Wang, M.Y.: ZongYong affects the attention and memory performance for emotional stimuli. Paper Presented at the 7th Chinese Psychologist Conference, Taipei, Taiwan (2011)
12. Huang, C.L., Lin, Y.C., Chung, Y.C.: The relationship between ZhongYong thinking and the flexibility of attentioanl switch between global and local processing (2009) (Unpublished manuscript)
13. Castelhano, M.S., Mack, M.L., Henderson, J.M.: Viewing task influences eye movement control during active scene perception. Journal of Vision 9(3), 1–15 (2009)
14. Mills, M., Hollingworth, A., Van der Stigchel, S., Hoffman, L., Dodd, M.D.: Examining the influence of task set on eye movements and fixations. Journal of Vision 11(8), 1–15 (2011)
15. Shannon, C.E.: A mathematical theory of communication. . Bell System Technical Journal 27(4), 379–423, 27(4), 623–656 (1948)
16. Huang, C.-L., Lin, Y.-C., Yang, C.-F.: Revision of the ZhongYong Belief-Value Scale. Indigenous Psychological Research in Chinese Societies 38, 3–41 (2012)
17. Kao, C.T., Wang, M.Y.: The right level of complexity in a banner ad: Roles of construal level and fluency. Paper to be Presented at the 15th International Conference on Human-Computer Interaction, Las Vegas, USA (2013)
18. Tsai, C., Thomas, M.J.: When do feelings of fluency matter? How abstract and concrete thinking influence fluency effects. Psychological Science 22(3), 348–354 (2011)
19. Cowen, L., Ball, L.J., Delin, J.: An eye-movement analysis of web-page usability. In: Proceedings of Human Computer Interaction 2002, pp. 317–335 (2002)

Intercultural Design for Use –
Extending Usage-Centered Design by Cultural Aspects

Helmut Windl[1] and Rüdiger Heimgärtner[2]

[1] Continental AG
Siemensstraße 10, 93047 Regensburg, Germany
helmut.windl@continental-corporation.com
[2] Intercultural User Interface Consulting (IUIC)
Lindenstraße 9, 93152 Undorf, Germany
ruediger.heimgaertner@iuic.de

Abstract. In this paper the Usage-Centered Design approach is suggested as structured process for Intercultural HCI Design. Usage-Centered Design is extended by cultural models to take into account the cultural aspects in HCI design. The extensions cover as well common cultural aspects as system specific cultural aspects of the system to be designed. This approach makes it possible to track and trace the culture specific requirements and design decisions for internationalized user interfaces.

Keywords: Usage-Centered Design, U-CD, Culture, HCI, Model, Approach, Process, Structure, Intercultural, User Interface, Design for Use, Cross-Cultural User Interface.

1   Motivation and Goal: Structured Process for Intercultural HCI Design

Today in general there are just few complete methodologies helping user interface (UI) designers to design user interfaces. Amongst these there is no approach which embeds intercultural UI design. A UI design method helps designers

- starting the design process (what needs to be done and in which order),
- having guidance from requirements to the specification,
- creating better systems.

A UI design method empowered by cultural aspects enables the results from above for systems designed for one or more cultures. Using the proven and successful approach Usage-Centered Design (U-CD) as a starting point to integrate the aspects of intercultural user interface design, results in an intercultural Usage-Centered Design process that is provides the advantages listed above for intercultural user interface design. It provides clear guidance through the whole design process of an cross-cultural user interface and delivers an alternative to the trial and error approach of

A. Marcus (Ed.): DUXU/HCII 2013, Part II, LNCS 8013, pp. 139–148, 2013.
© Springer-Verlag Berlin Heidelberg 2013

trying to fix a bad design by iterations of testing and repairing found defects and problems.

2   Cultural Aspects to Be Included in the HCI Design Process

The cultural influences on the design process are represented by HCI dimensions, UI characteristics, intercultural variables, and cultural dimensions. HCI dimensions describe the style of human machine interaction expressed by information frequency and density and order as well as interaction frequency and speed ([1]). User interface characteristics capture the most relevant attributes of user interfaces containing metaphors, presentation, navigation, interaction and mental model ([2]). Intercultural variables cover the localization levels function, interaction and presentation ([3]). Direct intercultural variables concern HCI directly such as color, icons, language, layout as well as interaction speed and frequency. Indirect intercultural variables embrace HCI margins such as service manual or packaging. Cultural dimensions serve to describe the behavior of members of certain cultures ([4]). They can be related to HMI dimensions to get a link between the cultural imprint of users to their HCI style ([1]).

3   Usage-Centered Design (U-CD) in a Nutshell

Usage-Centered Design ([5]) is a systematic process using abstract models to design user interfaces for software systems fully and directly supporting all the tasks users need to accomplish. The user interfaces derive directly and systematically from a series of interconnected core-models. Center of the process is the robust, fine-grained task model comprising from user perspective the system's functionality expressed in use cases in essential form. Usage-Centered Design has a clear focus on user performance. Systems designed using this approach enable users to accomplish their tasks more accurate and reliable in less time (cf. [6]). First developed in the early 1990s, it is a proven, industrial-strength approach that has been used to design everything from industrial automation systems (cf. [7]) and consumer electronics to banking and automotive infotainment applications (cf. [8]). Because it is a streamlined process driven by simple models, it scales readily and has been used on projects ranging from a few person months to a 5 designers, 30 developers, 23 month project that produced the sophisticated integrated development and award winning environment "STEP 7 Lite" from Siemens AG ([5], [9]).

4   Analyzing U-CD

4.1   Process Overview

The U-CD process (Figure 1) can be split in analysis phase and design phase. Role model and task model are the results of a user and task analysis. The content models together with the implementation model are the results of the design phase.

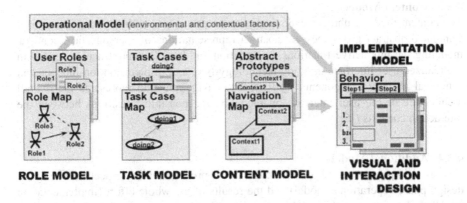

Fig. 1. Main Constituents of the Usage-Centred Design Process

4.2   Core Models

UC-D is built around three simple core models that represent the relations between users and system (role model), the work to be accomplished by the users (task model), and the contents and structure of the user interface (content model). The content model derives directly from the task model which is derived from the role model. All models consist each of two parts representing each its description and an additional model representing the relationship between the descriptions (role map, task case map and navigation map).

4.2.1 Role Model
The role model consists of the user roles and the user role map. User roles are abstract collections of needs, interests, expectations, behaviors, and responsibilities characterizing a relationship between a class or kind of users and a system ([5]). The user role map is a representation of the interrelationships and dependencies between the user roles.

4.2.2 Task Model
The task model combines task cases and the task case map. Task cases are structured narratives, expressed in the language of the domain and of users, comprising a simplified, generalized, abstract, technology-free, and implementation-independent description of one task or interaction that is complete, meaningful, and well-defined from the point of the users in some role or roles in relation to a system and that embodies the purpose or intentions underlying in the interaction ([5]).The task case map is a representation of the interrelationships and dependencies between the task cases.

4.2.3 Content Model

The content model embraces canonical abstract prototypes with the navigation map. Canonical abstract prototypes are abstract representations of user interface contexts modeling the interactive functions, information and basic layout structure needed in the realized user interface utilizing technology-free, and implementation-independent canonical abstract components ([10],). The navigation map represents the overall architecture of the user interface by modeling the possible transitions between the interaction contexts ([5]).

4.2.4 Additional Models

Two more important models complete the U-CD process holding aspects affecting the design phase (operational model) and the results of the whole effort (implementation model). The operational model comprises the aspects needed to adapt the user interface design to the conditions and constraints of the operational contexts. The implementation model poses a blueprint and construction plan for the final system describing all aspects of interaction and visual design for the implementers realizing the system.

5   Detailed Analysis

When looking at the cultural aspects we find a diversity of different aspects.

5.1   Common Aspects for Intercultural UI Design

Intercultural variables ([3]), user interface characteristics ([2]), and HCI dimensions ([1]) are all sets of culture specific rules and guidelines with more or less overlap that affect the visual and interaction design of a system. Since they are static (i.e. independent of the purpose of the system) and apply almost for all systems they are not specific for a certain system.

5.2   System Specific Cultural Aspects

This type of cultural aspects is genuine to the system to be designed. The aspects are usually a result of the user and task analysis and can affect user roles as well as task cases. For instance, one user role has different salient backgrounds in different countries and therefore requires different task structures in different countries. Another example would be that one and the same task has a radically different flow in different countries. An example for the latter one would be address input into a GPS navigation system in US and in China. In China the usual strategy to find a location is not to use the postal address but either a street intersection or using a point of interest nearby the desired location. Which method is used is even dependent on the part of China where the navigation system is used. Besides the different kinds of cultural aspects it is important to consider localization as well as internationalization within an intercultural UI design process.

6   Integration of Cultural Aspects in U-CD

To integrate the cultural aspects and the internationalization requirements in U-CD it is necessary to extend and adapt the existing process at different places.

6.1   Cultural Model

The common aspects for intercultural UI design will be included in a cultural model similar to the existing "operational model" (Figure 2).

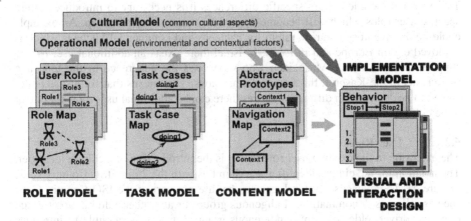

Fig. 2. Extended Usage-Centred Design Process by a Cultural Model

Since the content in the cultural model affects the visual and interaction design, this new model will affect the transitions from the task model to the content model and also from the content model to the implementation model. The cultural model captures the common rules for cultures the system will be designed for. For each culture one cultural model is used. Figure 3 shows the qualitative content of an cultural model.

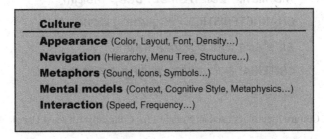

Fig. 3. Content of the Cultural Model

The content of the cultural model is mainly based on user interface characteristics (cf. [11]) and HCI dimensions (cf. [1]) describing a user interface at abstract level filled with the special values for the desired cultures.

6.2   System Specific Cultural Aspects

The system specific cultural aspects affect the role model and the task model. For the role model and task model in localized systems it is not necessary to have explicit cultural extensions. However in internationalized systems to be deployed in different cultures it is necessary to implement different cultures on the level of the role model and task model. There can be culture dependent versions of the same user role and also of the task cases.

6.2.1   Role Model

The user role model is composed of user roles plus the user role map (see chapter 4). To cover and include culture specific differences it is necessary to introduce culture specific user roles which will become part of a common user role map. An example could be an inventory control system for canteens and commercial kitchens which is deployed e.g. in Europe and in Israel. In Israel there exists an additional user role to support the tasks of the Mashgiach who supervises the adherence of the food and ingredients to the Kashrut, the Jewish dietary laws. This means that for a system designed to be deployed in different cultures there can be additional user roles for one or more cultures.

6.2.1.1   User Roles

The extension to the existing user role model is the introduction of a culture identifier. The notation for the culture identifier is a rhombus with the 2 digit ISO Country Code (Figure 4). To cover also cultural aspects that are not part of the ISO Country Code such as religious denominations, indigenous groups or any other cultural target group (e.g., car driver, elderly people, indigenous groups, etc.), it is possible to introduce project specific culture identifiers.

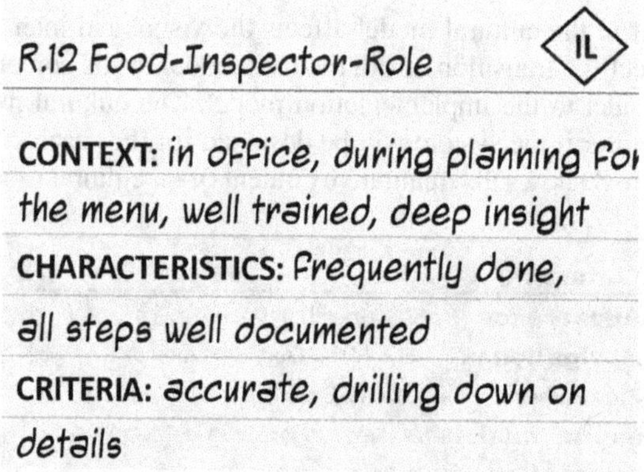

R.12 Food-Inspector-Role   〈IL〉

CONTEXT: in office, during planning for
the menu, well trained, deep insight
CHARACTERISTICS: frequently done,
all steps well documented
CRITERIA: accurate, drilling down on
details

Fig. 4. Culture Identifiers used as Notation for Culturally Affected User Roles

The culture identifier is added according to the following rules:

- In its simplest form user roles are described by the context within they are played, the characteristic of performance, and the criteria for support. A culture identifier in the upper right corner complements this description.

- If applicable it is possible that one role is shared between two or more cultures. In this case the role gets multiple culture identifiers.
- User roles that are common to all cultures remain without culture identifier.

It is useful to introduce an inverse culture identifier to be able to exclude certain culture groups from one user role. An example would be a "Facebook Poster" role that does not exist in China due to legal restrictions. The invers/not culture identifier is shown by adding a circle to the left corner of the rhombus (Figure 5).

Fig. 5. Notation for a Culture Identifier Expressing Validity for All Cultures except China

6.2.1.2   User Role Map
The user role map in general remains unchanged. There is still one user role map for one system; otherwise at this point the design process would split in the design of several different cultures specific systems. Nevertheless the culture specific roles keep the culture identifier and thus still can be identified.

6.2.2   Task Model

6.2.2.1   Task Cases
Task cases in their basic form are defined by a structured narrative in user's and domain language as two-column abstract dialog representing the user intention and the system responsibility (Figure 6, cf. [5]).

withdraw money from bancomat	
user intention	**system responsibility**
	request identification
identify myself	
	verify identification
	offer choices
choose	
	give cash
take cash	

Fig. 6. Basic Form of Task Cases

In this basic form culture dependency is already included in the abstract dialog, which itself expresses the abstract interaction specifically for a specific culture group. The only change is again the addition of a cultural identifier to be able to track, structure, and organize the task cases according to the following rules (cf. Figure 7):

- Task cases are derived from the user roles, therefore tasks derived from a culture specific role are also culture specific and inherit the same culture identifier as the user role from which they are derived.
- From one user role may different culture specific task cases be derived. These task cases get their culture identifier when they are created.
- It is also possible that a task case can be shared between user roles from different cultures and being marked with multiple culture identifiers.
- Task cases common to all cultures remain without culture identifier.
- Task cases, which are common but exclude one or more culture groups, get the inverse culture identifier for the affected culture(s).

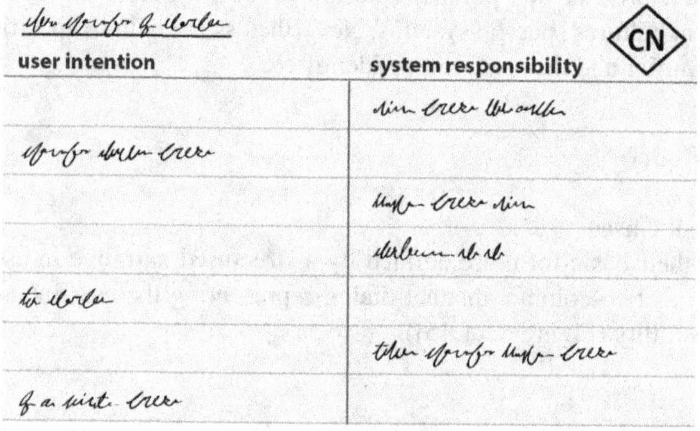

Fig. 7. Basic Form of Task Cases Indexed by a "Cultural Identifier"

6.2.2.2   Task Case Map

The task case map depicts the relationship between task cases in a system to guide content organization in the user interface. Thus all task cases including the culture dependent ones are shown in the task case map together, although some of them may be mutually exclusive due to a cultural setting.

In the task case map the task cases are shown by their name plus none, one or more culture identifiers (cf. Figure 8).

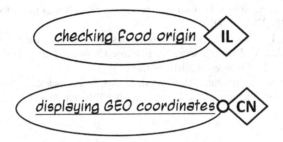

Fig. 8. Task Cases with Different "Cultural Identifiers"

6.2.3 Content Model

For consistency, completeness, and traceability it is possible but not necessary to use the cultural identifier also in the abstract prototypes and the navigation map. In both depictions the cultural identifier is used to mark up the contexts for specific cultures.

7   Conclusion

We suggest Intercultural Usage-Centered Design (IU-CD) as a method for designing cross-cultural user interfaces. This approach helps designers of cross-cultural user interfaces to get started, it provides structured guidance throughout the design process, it helps to retain insights in reusable models and thus to create better localized and internationalized systems.

References

1. Heimgärtner, R.: Cultural Differences in Human-Computer Interaction. Oldenbourg Verlag (2012)
2. Marcus, A.: Cross-Cultural User-Interface Design. In: Smith, M.J.S.G. (ed.) Proceedings of the Human-Computer Interface Internat (HCII), vol. 2, pp. 502–505. Lawrence Erlbaum Associates, Mahwah (2001)
3. Röse, K., Zühlke, D.: Culture-Oriented Design: Developers' Knowledge Gaps in this Area. In: 8th IFAC/IFIPS/IFORS/IEA Symposium on Analysis, Design, and Evaluation of Human-Machine Systems, September 18-20, pp. 11–16. Pergamon (2001)
4. Hofstede, G.H., Hofstede, G.J., Minkov, M.: Cultures and organizations: software of the mind. McGraw-Hill, Maidenhead (2010)
5. Constantine, L.L., Lockwood, L.A.D.: Software for use: A practical guide to the models and methods of usage-centered design. Addison-Wesley, Reading (1999)
6. Constantine, L.: Beyond user-centered design and user experience: Designing for user performance. Cutter IT Journal 17, 16–25 (2004)
7. Windl, H.: Designing a Winner. In: forUSE 2002 1st International Conference on Usage-Centered Design. Ampersand Press, Rowley (2002)
8. Constantine, L., Windl, H.: Safety, speed, and style: interaction design of an in-vehicle user interface. In: CHI 2009 Extended Abstracts on Human Factors in Computing Systems, pp. 2675–2678. ACM, Boston (2009)

9. Ferr, X., Juristo, N., Windl, H., Constantine, L.: Usability Basics for Software Developers. IEEE Softw. 18, 22–29 (2001)
10. Constantine, L.L.: Canonical Abstract Prototypes for Abstract Visual and Interaction Design. In: Jorge, J.A., Jardim Nunes, N., Falcão e Cunha, J. (eds.) DSV-IS 2003. LNCS, vol. 2844, pp. 1–15. Springer, Heidelberg (2003)
11. Marcus, A.: Global/Intercultural User-Interface Design. In: Jacko, J., Spears, A. (eds.) The Human-Computer Interaction Handbook. Lawrence Erlbaum Associates, Mahwah (2007)

A Usability Testing of Chinese Character Writing System for Foreign Learners

Manlai You and Yu-Jie Xu

123 University Road, Section 3, Douliu, Yunlin 64002, Taiwan
{youm,g9930807}@ yuntech.edu.tw

Abstract. Currently, the study of Chinese has become increasingly popular in the world. However, not every non-native Chinese speaker learning Chinese can have formal guidance from qualified instructors. Xi-Zi-e-Bi-Tong (習字e筆通) is one of the systems for writing Chinese characters and is used by the Ministry of Education's E-innovation School and E-bag Experimental Teaching Program in Taiwan. It was developed for native Chinese speaking elementary school students. However, foreign learners come from a variety of cultural backgrounds and ages, so this study looks at the efficacy of this system for these types of students. As a case study, this research performed a usability testing with this system in order to identify what typical usability problems may exist in off-the-shelf products for foreign learners. The usability testing is with thinking aloud, in order to avoid the frustration of participants during tasks, the combination of coaching method to provide help appropriately. The subjects for this research were six foreign students, they came from different cultural backgrounds and all were unfamiliar with Chinese. It was hoped that testing this level of learners would make it easier to ascertain the usability problems of the system. Each was given six tasks associated with system manipulation that was related to the research purpose, and the tasks were designed in accordance with the instructions. When they had completed all the tasks, in order to measure the satisfaction of the system, they were asked to immediately fill out a questionnaire on user interaction satisfaction (QUIS). The problems they encountered in the test can be categorized, in accordance to the interactive design principles and concepts, into: mental models, visibility, feedback, and control. This study can be used as a reference for the redesigning of a program to teach the writing of Chinese characters.

Keywords: Chinese Characters, Interactive Interface, Chinese Learning, usability testing.

1   Introduction

Currently, the study of Chinese has become increasingly popular in the world. However, not every non-native Chinese speaker learning Chinese can have formal guidance from qualified instructors. Thanks to the rise of learning technology, this deficiency can now be partially resolved by well-designed interactive interfaces. The role of Chinese characters is very important in Chinese history. But it is a very

A. Marcus (Ed.): DUXU/HCII 2013, Part II, LNCS 8013, pp. 149–157, 2013.

arduous task to learn how to write Chinese characters for foreign learners. Xi-Zi-e-Bi-Tong (習字e筆通) is one of the systems for writing Chinese characters and is used by the counseling program of Taiwan's E-innovation School and by the E-bag Experimental Teaching program. It was developed for native Chinese speaking elementary school students. Since foreign learners come from a variety of cultural backgrounds and ages, this study looks at the efficacy of this system for these types of students.

Chinese characters are not only communication symbols but also a form of art in China—calligraphy. Presently, though, most modern people are likely to use computers to write Chinese characters rather and writing them by hand.   However, according to some research, writing Chinese characters by hand is helpful (Li, 2009; Tan et al., 2005).   The reason is that the motor function of the hand is connected with the brain and research shows this is cognitively helpful for beginning learners (Mangen & Velay, 2010; Tan et al., 2005). With the current trend for digital learning have come many products for Chinese learning—most are found on the internet. A lot of detail should be considerate of Chinese characters writing learning system design, those include interactive design between the user and the system not only using feel about it but also the system target - learning writing character.

Usability testing can help researchers to understand the real conditions of the product that is being used, and it can also discern how easy the product is to use and how effective it is in teaching the target language. Rogers, Sharp & Preece (2011) have pointed out that the goals of usability include effectiveness, efficiency, safety, utility, learnability and memorability. The principle of design mix from several fundamental knowledge of theories, experience and common sense. It is important for researchers to understand how users of this interactive technology feel about the process and what they are seeing. The design principles that are most used include visibility, feedback, limitation, mapping, mental models, consistency and affordance (Rogers, Sharp & Preece 2011; Norman, 1988).

This study evaluates the typical work that users learn with the system, and both the thinking aloud method and the coaching method are selected. Thinking aloud demands that the user speak aloud what they are thinking and what they want to do when they operate the task. Thus, by the recordings and notes, we can analyze the operation and the voice records after the usability testing, which can help the researcher understand the user's problems and their thoughts (Nielsen, 1993). The coaching method guides the user through problems during the processing of doing tasks (Mack & Burdett, 1992).

2   Method

This study includes two parts, first is the task design for the Chinese character writing system. Second is the usability testing with thinking aloud and coaching, and after the experiment is finished, participants will fill out a QUIS Questionnaire to assess the user interface. The Questionnaire for User Interaction Satisfaction (QUIS) is a tool developed by a multi-disciplinary team of researchers in the Human-Computer Interaction Lab (HCIL) at the University of Maryland at College Park.

2.1   Task Design

Xi-Zi-e-Bi-Tong was selected as a case study. This system is composed of lesson selections, writing character learning, writing character exercises and writing character tests (Fig. 1). Users can select the default content, which provides both strokes and radical indexing for selection to help users input by themself on the lesson selection. The writing character learning part provides writing demonstrations, and users can follow the demonstration to practice writing. The system evaluates the writing results and provides the right stroke order and neat writing, and then gives a score. The writing character exercise is similar to ones found in a traditional Chinese writing book, and users can continue to practice writing Chinese characters, and each writing results will be graded and recorded. The writing character test will quiz learners on the learning content in order to confirm the learner's acquisition outcomes. The usability of writing character learning section is evaluated in this study.

The tasks were designed in accordance with the instructions of writing character learning, and each task contains operation actions for several function keys. They are described as follows:

1. Please play the pronunciation of each character, and find out if it is a polyphone or not. This mission evaluates how the vocabulary table, pronunciation playing and polyphone detecting ability are used.
2. Please play the writing demonstration of the steps of the strokes for each character, and then speak out the last stroke. This task evaluates the stroke tracing function for the writing demonstration that shows the steps of the character's strokes.
3. Please play the writing demonstration showing the continuous steps for writing each character, and then pause after the fourth stroke, and then again continue. This task evaluates the play and the pause functions of the system's writing demonstration.
4. Please write each character once with and without using the grid individually, and then evaluate and speak out the results. This task evaluates the functions for the grid, the evaluation and the erasing.
5. Turn on the character tracing function, and then select tracing with each stroke and write each character once individually. Then, evaluate the results and speak them aloud. This task evaluates how the user performs the functions for the stroke tracing steps, evaluation and turn off.
6. Turn on the character tracing function, then select tracing for whole characters and write each character once individually. Then, evaluate the results and speak them aloud. This task evaluates how the user performs the functions for the continuous strike tracing option, evaluation and turn off.

Participants were asked to sequentially perform pre-set tasks in this study to evaluate Xi-Zi-e-Bi-Tong's usability testing with the think aloud and coaching options. The entire process was designed to help the researchers understand the errors users made while operating the interface. After the experiment, the QUIS questionnaire with a 5-point scale was used to evaluate whether the users found the system satisfactory.

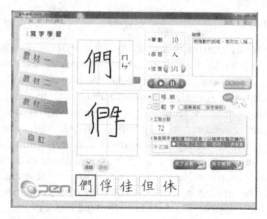

Fig. 1. Writing character learning of Xi-Zi-e-Bi-Tong

Table 1. The basic information of subjects

	S1	S2	S3	S4	S5
Age	8	8	8	9	8
Sex	F	M	F	F	F
Similar systems experience	No	No	No	No	No
Computer experience	No	Yes	Yes	Yes	Yes

2.2   Subjects

This study focused on usability testing of the interface design for a Chinese characters writing system. Presently, most systems are designed for beginning students learning Chinese characters. The subjects for this research were six foreign students studying basic Chinese at National Taichung University of Education's Language Center, and each of them performed six pre-designed tasks. The number of subjects is admittedly small. However, our findings using usability testing showed that 75% of problems could be ascertained (Rogers, Sharp & Preece, 2011; Nielsen, 1993). The beginners came from different cultural backgrounds and all were unfamiliar with Chinese. It was hoped that testing this level of students would make it easier to ascertain the usability problems with the system.Before the start of the experiment, participants finished reading the notice of informed consent and then were given oral instructions and finally gave their signatures.

2.3   Device and Process

Lenovo X220t Tablet PC with stylus served as the test tool, and it provided a similar feeling to using a real pen and paper, so that the eyesight of participants could look the pen tip in the process of writing, and avoid the problems of using a traditional handwriting Tablet which splits the visual and writing space leading to visual gap problems. During the experiment, a webcam was set up above the tablet PC, the recording of the screen and the area for the user's hands.

The experiment was described and explained prior to starting the experiment and the subject then gave their consent to participate in the experiments. An observer sat on the side of the participants to observe and record observations, and also provided help when the participants had difficulties. Participants explored the system for about 10 minutes, and then they started the tasks which took 30 minutes. When they had completed all the tasks, in order to measure the satisfaction of the system, they were asked to immediately fill out a questionnaire on user interaction satisfaction (QUIS). This questionnaire was developed to assess the user's responses with the user interface by the Computer Interaction Laboratory at the University of Maryland. This was then followed by unstructured interviews, which were used in order to understand the subjective feelings of the participants about the system in actual use.

3   Result and Discussion

3.1   Performance Evaluation

The performance evaluation methods for this study included the following: 1) the time to complete all the tasks, 2) the time to perform a task and its error rate, and 3) a recording of the scores of the writing characters tasks. The calculation of time to complete the task continued until it was completed, and when the participants wanted to tap a function but failed, then this counted as one error, and the same error would be calculated cumulatively.

Analysis of experiment's results showed that the error times for the control tasks (Task1 – Task 3) were higher than they were for the writing tasks (Task 4 – Task 6). The results of one-way ANOVA showed that there were no significant differences between the two groups. The writing method is divided into non-tracing (Grid, and Non-Grid) and tracing (Tracing Stroke, and Tracing Whole Characters) groups, and it was ascertained that there was a significant difference between the two group with ANOVA, and the scores of written results with tracing were better than with non-tracing. Because tracing is a writing guidelines in the process for participants. The task processing performances are affected by the previous tasks, and the Latin grid was not introduced to avoid any relative affects.   The reason for this is that each task was designed to be an independent event. However, possibly trial and error could have had some impact following the pre-learning tasks.

3.2   Questionnaire Analysis

The QUIS questionnaire was used by this study. It is a modified user interactive satisfaction questionnaire from the Human-Computer Interaction Lab (HCIL) at the University of Maryland at College Park. The study extracted past experiences, overall user reactions, screen, learning, on-line tutorials and multimedia from the original QUIS questionnaire. The researchers changed some items on the questionnaire to

Table 2. Performance evaluation

	Task 1		Task 2		Task 3		Task 4		Task 5		Task 6	
	CT*	NE**	CT*	NE**	CT*	NE**	CT*	NE**	CT*	NE**	CT*	NE**
S1	6'19"	27	6'21"	33	2'16"	0	3'30'	7	1'59"	7	1"11"	0
S2	6'10"	5	9"54"	3	6'30"	5	5'50"	2	3'24"	6	2'14"	0
S3	1'53"	3	2'53"	0	2'59"	1	8'36"	0	5'09"	12	3'09"	4
S4	1'37"	2	3'45"	0	2'29"	0	3'53"	2	2'18"	0	1'48"	1
S5	2'30"	0	3'35"	1	5'20"	3	9'18"	1	3'53"	0	3'58"	0
S6	3'25"	10	3'07"	2	2'41"	1	4'12"	5	2'50"	1	3'19"	13
Mean		7.8		6.5		1.7		2.8		4.3		3.0
SD		9.99		13.03		1.97		2.64		4.84		5.14

* CT (Completion time)   **NE (The number of errors)

Table 3. Writing score

	Grid	Non-Grid	Tracing stroke	Tracing whole character
S1	84.3	86.5	96.5	97.3
S2	81.5	84.8	98.3	98.3
S3	81.5	61.8	99.0	98.8
S4	83.0	93.3	98.3	96.5
S5	84.0	86.8	97.3	98.8
S6	74.5	76.3	94.0	98.0
Mean	81.4	81.6	97.2	98.0
SD	3.61	11.12	1.81	0.91

meet the specific needs of this research. For example, the nine-point scale was revised to five-point scale. The participants showed positive satisfaction with this system, so just low average grades are described for reference.

The system flexibility relative assessment, with an average score of 3.5; adequacy of the amount of information on the screen, with an average score of 3.7; through attempts to explore the new features, the average score was 3.7; information succinct and pointed out that the focus, the average score was 3.5. The average scores for these items are low on the questionnaire. Possibly this indicates that participants felt that the learning system still presented a certain degree of difficulty for them.

The participants' feedback comments as follows: 1) participants expected the system to be able to provide more learning information, for example, the pinyin, words, sentences, and so on to help them remember the Chinese character information; 2) the direction of the strokes for writing Chinese characters should not only provide a writing demonstration, but should also provide practice writing; 3) the speed of the writing demonstration should be adjustable; and 4) English explanations should be provided.

3.3   Analysis of the Interviews

After the participants finish the QUIS, they are immediately asked three questions. The first is the general feeling about the system's usability. Most gave a positive response. They felt the system was able to tutor them to write Chinese characters. Moreover, the scoring system seemed to motivate them to practice in order to achieve better results.

The second is which kind of practice ways were helpful to learn writing Chinese characters, and all participants agreed that the tracing stroke by stroke was the best for learning to write.   One of the participants hoped that a future system could combine tracing stroke by stroke with whole character tracing.   The participant felt this would be better.

The third are suggestions for future systems, and most of the participants expected different language interfaces and explanations, as well as more information that could help them remember how to write the Chinese characters.

3.4   The Description of Usability

Through the video record analysis of the system's operation, the researcher discovered and explored several usability problems. These problems as well as suggestions for their improvement are described below.

Pronunciation problems:

1. The left and right arrow buttons for polyphones caused confusion with the steps for writing strokes. Fig. 2 (labels 1 vs. 2) (s1, s2, and s4) shows that the buttons violate both the visibility and response principles. The buttons and responses should be located next to each other with precise labels explaining their functions.

2. The left and right arrow buttons are always present, and it does not matter whether or not the vocabulary word is a polyphone or not (Fig. 2, label 1). Even when the user pushes both buttons to repeat the action, it only responds verbally when the character is a real polyphone (s1, s2, s3, s4, and s6). This violates the response principle. We suggest canceling the polyphone or presenting the polyphone button when it is a real polyphone.

There are problems in the writing demonstration too.   Participants confused the button for the writing demonstration function with the one for continuous steps for the strokes (Fig. 2, label 2 vs. 3) (s1, s2, and s4). This violates both the visibility and mapping principles and the labels for the function should be more precise, or possibly an icon could be provided for the button which would be more intuitive.

There are several problems in the writing practice:

1. The hierarchy relation in the tracing function (tracing with each stroke and tracing with a whole character) (Fig. 2, label 6) has a problem, in other words, participants must turn on the tracing function first and then select tracing with each stroke or tracing with whole character presentation, but they cannot select the needed function directly. This can cause some confusion (s1, s2, s3, and s6) which violates

the visibility principle. We suggest canceling the tracing function hierarchy setup and letting the users select which function they need directly.

2. There is confusion when there is no response to the request to change the tracing or grid options (s1, s2, s3, and s6). This is caused by the masking that occurs when users are writing characters in a certain area (see Fig. 2, labels 4 vs. 5 and 4 vs. 6). It is a problem with the response design. We suggest having a separate function setup area which apart from the main area. It would give immediate responses when the users prompt the function setup.

3. The presenting of unclear evaluation results (see Fig. 2, label 7) (s1, and s5) violates the visibility principle. One suggestion is to provide a detailed explore button, or present the evaluation results in a more visible way.

4. During the tracing practice, sometimes an incorrect operation will occur because of a touch or broken strokes. The system cannot accurately judge of the stroke is complete or not, and thus, it shows the next tracing stroke resulting in user confusion.   This is the program problem due to the visibility and feedback.

Further problems include (a) function button sometimes misses being touched or misses the correct location (s2, s5, and s6), which violates the visibility principle. One suggestion is to resize the button to a more appropriate size, and arrange proper gaps between buttons. (b) after miss touching the button during writing practice (Fig. 2, label 8) the user cannot go back to the writing lesson where the entry writing practice began (s1, and s4). This violates the visibility principle. (c) Participants try to push the button for the writing character exercises and writing character tests (Fig. 2, label 8) (s1, s2, s4, and s5) when they find the function, and this violates the response principle. For both of the above problems, we suggest locating buttons nearby each other when the functions are close to decrease users accidentally touching the wrong one.

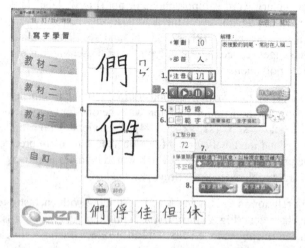

Fig. 2. The usability problems of writing character learning

4   Conclusion

This study used the Xi-Zi-e-Bi-Tong for its research case, which was to detect the foreign learner typical learning barriers when they are using the Chinese characters writing system. Although participants could interact with system, still some barriers existed. After analyzing the results, we hope to propose some suggestions for improving or redesigning the system.

Acknowledgements. We would like to thank the National Science Council of the Republic of China (Taiwan) for financial support of this research under contract numbers NSC 101-2410-H-224 -019 -MY2.

References

1. Li, C.Y.: The Cognitive and Neural Basis for Learning to Read Chinese. Journal of Basic Education 18(2), 63–85 (2009) (in Chinese)
2. Mack, R.L., Burdett, J.M.: When novices elicit knowledge: Question-asking in designing, evaluating and learning to use software. In: The Psychology of Expertise: Cognitive Research and Empirical AI, pp. 245–268. Springer, New York (1992)
3. Mangen, A., Velay, J.L.: Digitizing Literacy: Reflections on the Haptics of Writing. In: Zadeh, M.H. (ed.) Advances in Haptics. InTech (2010) ISBN: 978-953-307-093-3
4. Nielsen, J.: Usability Engineering, United Kingdom edition publish by Academic Press Ltd. (1993)
5. Norman, D.A.: The psychology of everyday things. Basic Books, New York (1988)
6. Preece, J., Rogers, Y., Sharp, H.: Interaction Design: Beyond Human-Computer Interaction. Wiley, New York (2002)
7. Tan, L.H., Spinks, J.A., Eden, G.F., Perfetti, C.A., Siok, W.T.: Reading depends on writing. PNAS 102(24), 8781–8785 (2005) (in Chinese)
8. The Questionnaire for User Interaction Satisfaction, http://lap.umd.edu/quis/

Part II

Designing for the Learning and Culture Experience

A Cross-Cultural Evaluation of HCI Student Performance – Reflections for the Curriculum

José Abdelnour-Nocera, Ann Austin, Mario Michaelides, and Sunila Modi

Sociotechnical Centre for Internationalisation and User Experience
University of West London, Ealing, W55RF, 69121 United Kingdom
{jose.abdelnour-nocera,ann.austin,mario.michaelides,
sunila.modi}@uwl.ac.uk

Abstract. Human-computer interaction has become a subject taught across universities around the world, outside of the cultures where it originated. However, the implications of its assimilation into the syllabus of courses offered by universities around the world remain under-researched. Our research project provides insights on these implications by studying the performance of HCI students in universities in UK, India, Namibia, Mexico and China engaged in a similar design and evaluation set of tasks. It is argued that the predominant cognitive styles and cultural attitudes of students located in different types of institutions and countries will shape their learning of HCI concepts and tools. This paper in particular reports the analysis of cognitive styles and cultural dimensions of students engaged in a heuristic evaluation of a science education portal. An emergent pattern between adaptive cognitive styles and high uncertainty avoidance is identified in the assessment of the richness of students' heuristics exercise completion.

Keywords: HCI education, culture, cognitive style, design, evaluation.

1   Introduction

Human-Computer Interaction (HCI) is a well-established and important subject in computing, technology and design in universities across the world. HCI is taught in order to explore, understand and aid in improving the usability and user experience of interactive systems and products. Though similar methodologies and frameworks are taught in this subject, little is known of the student experience and how local perspectives could influence their content and approach to teaching. Therefore, a current challenge for this discipline is making visible the possible tensions created between local cultures and predominant cognitive styles and the assumptions, priorities and values embedded in HCI concepts and methods mainly developed under particular paradigms.

In pursuing the above challenge, we studied how undergraduate students of HCI engaged and performed in similar design and evaluation tasks in institutions in China, Namibia, India, Mexico and the United Kingdom. By doing this, we hope to provide insights on the nature of HCI education as an intercultural encounter and the

A. Marcus (Ed.): DUXU/HCII 2013, Part II, LNCS 8013, pp. 161–170, 2013.
© Springer-Verlag Berlin Heidelberg 2013

opportunities this can bring to locally validate, question and enrich some its curriculum and associated delivery. Including these insights into an international HCI curriculum will make it more sensitive to different types of students, which in turn will be better prepared to engage in tasks requiring different types of skills. This paper describes this study and initial findings about cognitive styles and cultural attitudes for HCI students located in the aforementioned countries.

The paper first defines our key working concepts for culture and cognitive styles. This is followed for a brief overview of research in HCI education and culture. The methodological strategy and the nature of workshops done with students are then presented. We then go on to report initial findings in terms of cognitive styles, culture and student performance in a heuristic evaluation task. The paper closes by highlighting main contributions and take-aways for developing a stronger HCI curriculum more sensitive to different types of students.

2   Culture and Cognition

Western HCI tools and techniques might not be effective in developing countries and that some degree of localization or adaptation are required [1]. An objective of this project is to look into this in a HCI education context, and to make sense of variations, convergences and emergences from a student centred perspective. In this section we introduce the main cultural theories underpinning this objective.

Researchers in the fields of both culture and cognitive styles have identified a correlation between cultural characteristics and the holistic or intuitive versus analytical dimensions of cognitive style [2,3].

Nisbett & Norenzayan [2] explored the relationship between culture and cognition by looking at cultural differences between East Asians and people from the Western world. They discussed how an inclination towards holistic or analytic reasoning is influenced by cultural identities. Nisbett differentiates between holistic and analytic reasoning, defining holistic thought as 'an orientation to the context or field as a whole' and analytic thought as 'detachment of the object from its context' [2, p.19].

Hayes and Allinson [3] tested the hypothesis that culture would account for differences in learning style in a study involving managers from East Africa, India and the United Kingdom. Using Hofstede's [4] four national culture dimensions and Honey and Mumford's Learning Style models, Hayes and Allinson identified two dimensions of learning style, Analysis and Action [2]. Further work in this area resulted in Allinson and Hayes' Cognitive Style Index (CSI) designed to test whether individuals tends more towards an intuitivist (right brain dominant) or analyst (left brain dominant) approach.

3   HCI Education in Different Countries

Though there are numerous articles on HCI education and a few in relation to a country's delivery of the subject, there is no substantial body of literature which offers a thorough investigation into the influence that culture and cognitive styles have on learning HCI concepts and tools in comparison with other countries/cultures. There are however a number of studies that discuss HCI education delivery in certain countries such as New Zealand [5], Sweden [6], South Africa [7], Brazil [8] and Costa Rica [9].

These studies offer a brief view into HCI education. Sharkey & Paynter [5] investigated the need and coverage of HCI in relation to their educational courses in New Zealand. Their research came to the conclusion that the use of design tools was the most common topic followed by task analysis. This contrast with Sweden [6] where design principles, processes and cognitive psychology are the two subjects deemed to be the most important. Both countries had different approaches in their decisions but it would be interesting to investigate this factor especially regarding the time elapsed since these papers were published. Also, students in Costa Rica [9] offered their view that HCI should include more graphical design and heuristic evaluations, which the institution amended to accommodate. In Brazil, de Souza [8] confirms semiotics has had a stronger influence, unlike traditions in Europe and North America, and that along with social inclusion are the two key areas that define Brazilian attitudes towards HCI.

This literature shows that despite the fact that largely the same concepts and tools in HCI are included in the curriculum of universities around the world, their delivery, in terms of what aspects are emphasized and most valued by teachers, tend to change. This existing body of research plus already available teaching materials in universities can be used as starting point to study how the teaching of HCI differs as a consequence of local academic and professional cultures. However, it is much harder to visualize cultural and learning preferences in the case of students because their work is usually more private and inaccessible. Our research contributes toward addressing that visibility gap.

4   Methodological Strategy

The case study in each country included a visit to a university where a group of around 15 - 20 undergraduate HCI students were asked to engage in a workshop, which included evaluation and design tasks for a science education portal. The activity given to students acted as a 'cultural probe' [10] as it contains elements with different cultural affordances, e.g. heuristic evaluation as stimulating analytic thinking and prototype sketching as stimulating holistic thinking. The performance of students in the workshop is analyzed and correlated with the findings for cultural dimensions and cognitive style profiles. In this paper, we only discuss the overall student performance for the heuristic analysis part of the assigned task. We quantified the richness of observations in each student's heuristic assessment using the scale of Table 1.

Quantitative data on culture for each student group was collected using Hofstede's VSM instrument [4], and Hayes and Allinson's CSI survey [3] was used to situate each student in an intuitive-holistic scale. We acknowledge the limitations of Hofstede's model on national culture [10] and are very careful not to make stereotypical interpretations or generalizations from the data collected. We were not expecting students to match the national culture scores 'predictions' for their country.

Table 1. Scale used to code the level of richness for each heuristic assessment done by students

3= clear example reference to a concrete aspect of the design of planetseed.com
2= reference to the website but only a general comment, description is provided. It is not possible to identify reference to a concrete aspect of the site.
1= general comment about the heuristic without clearly referring to website
0= no meaningful comment or no comment provided but a Yes, NO or NA was recorded for each question about the design.

The fact that they are in different countries makes them more likely to be contrasting. However, we found it useful to find out the mean scores for each group on each cultural dimension, e.g. power distance, masculinity and collectivism, to enrich our comparative analysis of quantitative and qualitative data. Qualitative data will be analyzed for manifestations of national culture dimensions [4] and cognitive styles [2]. While these different cultural models give us a top-down framework for analysis, a bottom up analysis of this data will also be developed. In this case the aim will be to uncover cultural patterns, themes and dimensions exclusively emerging from the HCI education domain. A full qualitative analysis for cultural differences is still being developed and is not included in this paper.

4.1   Workshops

Workshops were conducted at the Polytechnic of Namibia (PN), the Instituto Tecnológico Autónomo de México (ITAM), the Indian Institute of Technology Guwahati (IITG) and the Dalian Maritime University in China (DMU) and University of West London (UWL). All 5 institutions are well known within their country. Within these institutions, HCI was a core subject in PN and UWL, an option in ITAM, embedded within the whole curriculum in IITG and a core subject in the last semesters in DMU's Computer Science course. The visit also included meetings and interviews with lecturers and staff in charge of curriculum design.

The workshop involved the student in evaluating a learning node in the SEED science portal (www.planetseed.com). The target audience of this portal is schoolchildren aged between 10 and 18, and the HCI students were required to evaluate the node in this context. The SEED portal supports a number of different language options, allowing students who do not have English as their first language to use their preferred language option and concentrate on the task in question.

These activities included a heuristic evaluation of a learning task in the portal to determine whether the design satisfied certain predefined characteristics, which requires an analytical approach. In addition, the students were asked to analyze and comment on the case study scenario. The next tasks required a more holistic and intuitive approach: the students were required to develop the persona of both a student and her teacher, and to redesign the portal in view of their findings from the heuristic evaluation. The final tasks related to analyzing their redesign in relation to standard

HCI theory and concepts. As indicated above, in this paper we are only focusing on the analysis of the heuristics task.

5   Findings

In this section we report some of our findings in relation to the cognitive styles and culture surveys with the student groups in these five countries. We also report on their performance on one of the tasks given at the workshop, namely the richness of their heuristic evaluations on the science education portal.

5.1   Cognitive Styles of HCI students

HCI practitioners act as an interface between the developer and the users during the development of computer application or website. In terms of cognitive styles this means they need analytical skills to understand the functionality of the website or application, but at the same time, they need to be able to see the 'whole picture' and put themselves in the shoes of the user. Some HCI evaluation techniques such as heuristic evaluations require an analytical approach. Others, such as the production of a persona need a more intuitive approach. In addition, whilst the developer may be more concerned with the functionality of the application, the HCI practitioner also needs to balance the need for the interface to be user friendly, and the layout, appearance and aesthetics of the interface will contribute to this. Given this, we would expect the most typical styles to be found in successful HCI students to be more balanced, ranging from quasi intuitive and intuitive to quasi analytic.

With the above expectation, the CSI was administered to a total of 109 HCI students in Namibia (n=21), Mexico (n=25), India (n=23), China (n=20) and UK (n=20). Of these, 9 surveys had missing responses and were disregarded. Of these remaining 100 students, 79% were found to fall in the category of Quasi Intuitive (n=28), Adaptive (n=25) and Quasi Analyst (n=26). The remaining 21% were split between Intuitive (n=6) and Analyst (n=15). However, what is particularly interesting is the difference between the 5 cohorts. Namibia, Mexico, China and the UK have 78%, 73%, 70% and 79% respectively falling in the categories of quasi-intuitive, adaptive and quasi analyst; however, in the case of the Indian students, 95% fell into this range.

One possible reason for the difference in profile could be due to the unique nature of the programme at the IITG in India. The IITG has both a Department of Computer Science and Engineering and a Department of Design, and the students who took part in these workshops were Design students. Cohorts from Namibia and Mexico originate in engineering faculties. This correlates with the fact that their student packs were the most detailed of the different country groups. For the UK students, this is a core module for most of the computing degree courses, with the students ranging from those with a business specialism to those on more programming focused programs, which may explain the more even spread of the profile.

Cloninger [11] differentiates between usability (the masculine, the left side of the brain, rational, and logical action) and design (the feminine, the right side of the brain, emotional, and intuitive action), and with these particular cohorts we would expect to see both dimensions represented, which goes some way to explaining the unusual CSI profile where 95% of Indian students demonstrate styles around 'adaptive' middle point. After all, they are scientists with an aptitude for design.

5.2   Cultural Dimensions Found in Student Groups in Each University

The VSM data gave us interesting findings in terms of cultural dimensions for the student groups we studied. We do not claim in any way the scores are a reflection on national culture, but mainly use the scores obtained as top-level indicators of students' attitudinal trends in particular dimensions such as power distance and collectivism. The groups of students who completed the survey were nationals of the same country, except in Namibia where we had two Angolans and one South African, and the UK, where 10 different nationalities or cultural backgrounds were represented, reflecting the cosmopolitan character of the university.

For the cohort in the Polytechnic of Namibia (N=21), the mean scores for the VSM94 survey indicate the group is individualistic with very low power distance. This is in contrast with Hofstede's scores for most of sub-Saharan Africa indicating collectivistic societies with a tendency to a high power distance. They seem to be consistent with South Africa's scores but the latter represent respondents with British or Dutch background, whereas the Namibian cohort is fundamentally African. This might be a reflection of the culture of Namibian universities founded and developed by Europeans.

For students in ITAM (Mexico) (N=24), IITG (India) (N=27), DMU (China) (N=31), and UWL (UK) (N=21) VSM 08 was used. The decision to move to a more recent instrument was based on the fact that it offered more flexibility in establishing baseline scores for comparison of the groups. This means, however, we cannot make a direct score comparison with the students in Namibia. Figure 1 presents the results for these countries and there are some contrasts worth noting.

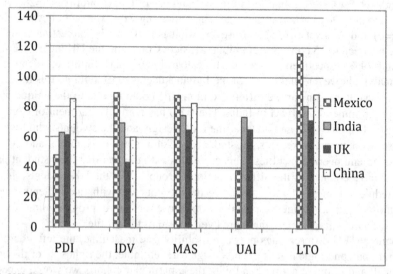

Fig. 1. VSM98 cultural dimension scores for student groups from Mexico, India, UK and China

The Power Distance (PDI) dimension was evident particularly in the relationship between the students and their professor or ourselves as researchers. The behavior of students in China, India and Mexico during the workshops reflects the difference indicated by the survey: Chinese students were the most complying ones in relation to instructions given by us and followed instructions without any question (PDI=85), Indian (PDI=62) students were more respectful and distant while Mexican (PDI=47) students were slightly more relaxed. This has a direct effect on the reflective learning process required in concepts and methods in HCI where the student is required to approach users and stakeholders with different levels of authority.

Original Hofstede's scores for Mexico and India indicate that the former is less individualistic than the latter. In our survey we have found the opposite (IDV: Mexico=89; India=69). This can be a reflection of the university culture in ITAM, where a lot of emphasis on individual success is evident in terms of financial awards in the form of fee waivers for the best performing students. While attempting the tasks, Mexican students displayed more independence and less interaction between peers than in India. Chinese students were clearly the most collectivist ones in terms of their group behavior during the exercise and this is echoed in the comparative score (IDV=60). They would be very careful of individual comments while in the group and were attentive of keeping the same pace as that of the group. UWL students in the UK scored an even lower figure (IDV=43), but given the mixed ethnic and cultural background, it could be argued that the presence of Asian students in the group affected the scores as can be seen in the individual responses.

Uncertainty avoidance was particularly evident in the difference in the style of teaching between ITAM (UAI= 38) and IITG (UAI= 73). During the workshop in IITG, certain elements of the theory were revisited prior to the activity taken place. These were delivered by us in the same style that they are delivered to UK students, which was to explain the theory and explain the task in relation to the theory. Feedback from the faculty staff indicated that this would not have been sufficiently structured for Indian students, who would expect a framework of theory, some examples, followed by a worked case study example. In contrast, Students in ITAM and DMU completed the activity independently at their own pace after a common induction and required minimum assistance to get them started. Low UAI score for Chinese students in this study (UAI=0) reflects also the same independence as ITAM students. Again a high uncertainty avoidance score for UWL (UAI=65) reflects the strong influence of the cultural expectations of students of Asian background (i.e. Pakistan, Sri Lanka, Nepal and India) in this group. During the session, these students at UWL required extra instructions as compared those from other backgrounds.

5.3   Analysis of Performance in Heuristic Task

At the time of writing this paper, we have analyzed heuristics richness for each student and all groups except for Mexico, which is still to be analyzed. Each student's response for each heuristic used to assess planteseed.com was coded using the scale presented in Table 1. The richness average for each institution is as follows: IITG (India)= 2.53, DMU (China)=2.23, PN (Namibia)=1.96, and UWL (UK)=1.83.

A pattern is emerging when noting the highest score for assessment richness belongs to the Indian student group. This group was the most balanced group in terms of cognitive styles, i.e. largely adaptive, which theoretically suggests they are better prepared to design usability with a balance of analytic and intuitive skills. Students from IITG also scored high in uncertainty avoidance (UAI=73), which is also in line with their effort of being less equivocal and more detailed in their assessment of each heuristic for the science education portal.

To validate the significance of group differences in evaluation richness an analysis of variance (ANOVA) was run by comparing the student performance means for each group. The results in Table 2 show a significant difference (p<0.004).

Table 2. Analysis of Variance Comparing Heuristic Richness Performance Between Groups

ANOVA

Richness

	Sum of Squares	df	Mean Square	F	Sig.
Between Groups	4.050	3	1.350	5.005	.004
Within Groups	15.644	58	.270		
Total	19.694	61			

The Tukey HSD Post-Hoc Test was applied to examine differences on a per group basis (Table 3). It can be seen the Indian group differed significantly from Namibian and UK results. This further supports our observation about the unique nature of IITG cohort and their ability to engage with tasks central to the HCI curriculum.

Table 3. Multiple Comparisons Test confirming significant difference of Indian group

Multiple Comparisons

Richness
Tukey HSD

(I) C2	(J) C2	Mean Difference (I–J)	Std. Error	Sig.	95% Confidence Interval	
					Lower Bound	Upper Bound
China	India	-.29857	.18098	.359	-.7773	.1801
	Namibia	.26929	.18098	.451	-.2094	.7480
	uk	.39786	.18098	.136	-.0809	.8766
India	China	.29857	.18098	.359	-.1801	.7773
	Namibia	.56786*	.19630	.027	.0486	1.0871
	uk	.69643*	.19630	.004	.1772	1.2157
Namibia	China	-.26929	.18098	.451	-.7480	.2094
	India	-.56786*	.19630	.027	-1.0871	-.0486
	uk	.12857	.19630	.913	-.3907	.6478
uk	China	-.39786	.18098	.136	-.8766	.0809
	India	-.69643*	.19630	.004	-1.2157	-.1772
	Namibia	-.12857	.19630	.913	-.6478	.3907

*. The mean difference is significant at the 0.05 level.

6   Conclusion

This project is aimed at finding opportunities and challenges for the dissemination and enrichment of this discipline through eliciting and assessing the importance of students' cognitive styles and local cultures. It does so by exploring the context, performance and views of stakeholders involved in learning HCI. The preliminary findings presented here make visible the values and assumptions potentially shaping the learning of HCI and the preparation of better interaction designers.

While Hofstede's dimensions have been heavily criticized as valid indicators of national culture, we believe that their use at group level can introduce HCI educators to an initial reflection on the implications for students of the values, relations and interactions scripted in the content and delivery of HCI concepts and methods. In addition, our initial analysis of cognitive styles indicates an interesting tension between HCI as design subject and as an engineering subject. This leads us to another observation: the entry exams for some schools like ITAM or DMU will filter a particular type of student who will tend to be more of an engineer than a designer, therefore reducing the number of potentially 'ideal' HCI professionals.

The initial analysis of student performance for the assigned heuristic evaluation task indicates an emergent pattern linked to particular types of cognitive style and cultural dimension.

Once the qualitative phase of the analysis of student work begins, we hope to obtain richer insights that connect their outputs with the cultural and cognitive profiles presented in this paper. This project provides a unique opportunity to systematically compare and analyze data obtained from students in four continents. We are aware that it stands in different epistemological positions as it looks, on one hand, at performance and, on the other hand, at meanings used to represent and experience HCI. However, we see this as an opportunity for triangulation, co-validation and enhanced understanding of HCI education in a multicultural context.

References

1. Smith, A., Joshi, A., Liu, Z., Bannon, L., Gulliksen, J., Baranauskas, C.: Embedding HCI in Developing Countries: Localizing Content, Institutionalizing Education and Practice. In: Baranauskas, C., Abascal, J., Barbosa, S.D.J. (eds.) INTERACT 2007. LNCS, vol. 4663, pp. 698–699. Springer, Heidelberg (2007)
2. Nisbett, R.E., Miyamoto, Y.: The Influence of Culture: Holistic Versus Analytic Perception. Trends in Cognitive Sciences 9(10), 467–473 (2005)
3. Hayes, J., Allinson, C.W.: Cultural Differences in the Learning Styles of Managers. Management International Review, 75–80 (1988)
4. Hofstede, G.: Cultures and Organizations: Software of the Mind. McGraw-Hill, Berkshire (1991)
5. Sharkey, E., Paynter, J.: CHI education in New Zealand. Bulletin of Applied Computing and Information Technology 2(3) (2004), http://citrenz.ac.nz/bacit/0203/2004Sharkey_CHINZ.htm (retrieved February 28, 2013)

6. Gullisksen, J., Oestreicher, L.: HCI Education in Sweden. SIGCHI Bull. 31(2) (1999)
7. Kotzé, P.: Directions in HCI education, research, and practice in Southern Africa. In: CHI 2002 Extended Abstracts on Human Factors in Computing Systems (CHI EA 2002), pp. 524–525. ACM, New York (2002)
8. de Souza, M., Baranauskas, C., Oliveira, R., Pimenta, M.: HCI in Brazil: lessons learned and new perspectives. In: Proceedings of the VIII Brazilian Symposium on Human Factors in Computing Systems (IHC 2008). Sociedade Brasileira de Computação, Porto Alegre, Brazil, pp. 358–359 (2008)
9. Calderon, M.: Teaching Human Computer Interaction: First Experiences. CLEI Electronic Journal 12(1) (2009)
10. McSweeney, B.: Hofstede's model of national cultural differences and their consequences: A triumph of faith - A failure of analysis. Human Relations 55(1), 89–118 (2002)
11. Cloninger, C.: Usability experts are from Mars, graphic designers are from Venus. A list Apart (74) (2000), http://alistapart.com/article/marsvenus (retrieved February 28, 2013)

Desirability of a Teaching and Learning Tool for Thai Dance Body Motion

Worawat Choensawat[1], Kingkarn Sookhanaphibarn[1], Chommanad Kijkhun[2], and Kozaburo Hachimura[3]

[1] School of Science and Technology, Bangkok University, Thailand
{worawat.c,kingkarn.s}@bu.ac.th
http://mit.science.bu.ac.th
[2] Suan Sunandha Rajabhat University, Thailand
[3] School of Science and Engineering, Ritsumeikan University, Japan
hachimura@media.ritsumei.ac.jp

Abstract. This paper investigates the desirability of using a teaching and learning tool for Thai dance in the context of higher education. Unlike the Western dances where dance notation have been widely used for recording the dance body movement, students in Thai dance classes have to memorize a series of body movements by observation from their teachers. In Thai dance communities, dance notation is very new, and few of professional people in Thai dance understand and use it to record the Thai dance body movement. In this paper, we demonstrate the adaption of a notation system to describe Thai dance and introduce a learning tool for facilitate students to understand the notation. Our presented tool for teaching and learning Thai dance is as a result from a collaboration research between researchers from performing arts and computer science. We measure the desirability of our tool with four Thai dance schools dispersedly located in the north and middle of Thailand, and we receive a promising feedback from them.

Keywords: Desirability Methodology, User Evaluation, Dance notation, Labanotation, LabanEditor, Multimedia Tool, Dance Animation.

1 Introduction

Thai dance, like many forms of traditional Asian dance, can be divided into two major categories that correspond roughly to the high art (royal dance) and low art (folk dance) distinction [9]. In this study, we are interested in the high art or performing art. One of famous high arts is called *Khon*, which is a traditional most sophisticated form of Thai masked drama which combines gracefulness with masculinity in its dancing and singing. Unlike tangible cultural assets like paints and archaeological site, dances are intangible cultural property [6]. The challenge with intangible heritage is that it is not preserving an object, but a process to pass it on to the next generation. Textbooks for teaching Thai dance are literately written with the context of drawing and photography material

A. Marcus (Ed.): DUXU/HCII 2013, Part II, LNCS 8013, pp. 171–179, 2013.

Fig. 1. Textbook used for Thai dance

to illustrate a movement of dancers as shown in Fig. 1. However, the rhythm cannot be expressed. Therefore, the knowledge of Thai dance has been taught to students by observation and imitation of body movements.

It is widely acceptable that Labanotation is a useful tool for human movement recording, choreography and dance training [7]. Labanotation is one of the most common movement notation systems. From unique characteristic of Thai dance, most people understand that it would be difficult to handle this kind of stylized traditional movement with Labanotation. Even though it is possible, a resulting notation would become very complicated.

Because of the complexity of Labanotation, it is not an easy task to introduce this new learning method based on the notation scheme to the dance community in Thailand. To overcome the barrier, one of the solution is to use a computer-aided tool to help new learner in understanding the Labanotation. We have been developing a system for preparing Labanotation scores and displaying 3D animation associated with the score [2,3,4]. In this paper, we measure the desirability of the tool for describing and reproducing Thai dance. The survey experiment was conducted on over 200 students and 17 teachers in four well-known schools in Thai dances.

2   Teaching and Learning Tools in Dance Communities

For anyone who can read music, reading a musical score is much more straight-forward than trying to pick out the sounds of all the instruments by ear, and to figure out the composer's intention from an audio recording alone. The same is true for dance notation. Dance notation captures the choreographer's creative idea, just as music notation captures the composer's creative idea. Dance notation can be thought analogous to presenting dance that is an output of what the choreographer wants and what the dancer actually does. Several dance notations were devised and have been used for recording and educating dance. The most commonly adopted notation systems are Labanotation [7] and Benesh Notation [1]. Among them Labanotation is most popular.

2.1   Labanotation

Labanotation is the system of recording human movement devised in the 1920's. Labanotation scores are similar to musical scores that record the human body movement by using graphical symbols. Labanotation score is drawn in a form of vertical staffs where each column represents the motion of a body part as shown in Fig. 2 (a). The symbols are placed on the vertical staff; the horizontal dimension of the staff represents the parts of the body, and the vertical dimension time. The center line of the staff represents the center line of the body; symbols on the right represent the right side of the body, symbols on the left, and the left side. Fig. 2 (b) shows the basic arrangement of columns in the staff.

The direction of movements are identified by a set of direction signs as shown in Fig. 3 . The shape of symbol represents the direction of horizontal motion. A shade of direction sign shows the level of a movement. The motion of each body part is expressed by a sequence of symbols placed in the corresponding column.

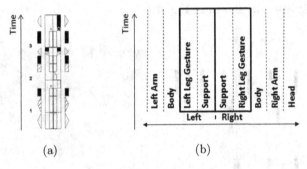

(a)   (b)

Fig. 2. Labanotation score: (a) Example of Labanotation score, (b) Definition of staffs in each column

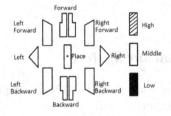

Fig. 3. Symbols for direction signs

2.2 LabanEditor

LabanEditor was introduced by Hachimura and his research team [2,8] as an interactive graphical editor for writing and editing Labanotation scores. By using LabanEditor, a user can input/edit dance movement and replay the animation of human body motion corresponding to the Labanotation score via 3D computer graphics. There are also other software, for example LabanWriter [5] is the most widely used Labanotation editor. LabanWriter is only for preparing Labanotation scores and recording them in digital form. It does not provide a function for displaying character animations corresponding to the notation. LabanDancer (developed by Wilke et al. [10]) is a LabanWriter scores to 3D animation translation tool, LabanDancer does not have function for preparing Labanotation scores.

At present, LabanEditor can serve the needs of dance community because its full feature of description and reproduction. Fig. 4 shows a user interface of LabanEditor. While displaying the CG animation of the score, we can observe the animation as well as the red horizontal line cursor, moving upward as the animation progresses, as shown in Fig. 4 (a).

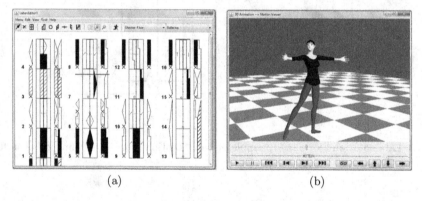

(a)   (b)

Fig. 4. User interface of LabanEditor: (a) Main editing window of LabanEditor, (b) CG animation display window

3 Thai Dance Notation System

Labanotation is able to describe very detail of movement such as a finger movement; however, the combination of symbols becomes too complex to understand. It would be very difficult for introducing this kind of complex language to Thai dance communities. To solve the problem, we develop a set of new symbols that can describe all movements of the fundamental Thai dance. As a rule of thumb, we have the design decision in terms of efficiency, comprehensibility, and advantage of this new notation system. It is called *Thai dance notation system*. For example, such a hand pose in Fig. 5 (a) can be written with our symbols as

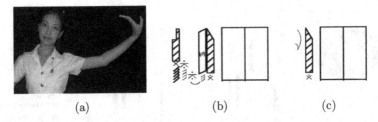

Fig. 5. Thai notation for hand gesture (*Wong*): (a) Hand gesture, (b) Standard Labanotation, and (c) Thai notation

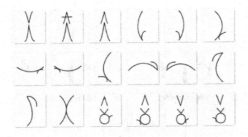

Fig. 6. New symbols for describing Thai dance

shown in Fig. 5 (c). For the Thai dance notation system, most of new symbols (Fig. 6) can represent all basic hand gesture, and the others try to describe a detail of foot movement that are very special and important of Thai dance (Fig. 7). Essentially, these symbols can picture the specific posture of classical Thai dance, such *Jiib*, *Wong* and *foot lifting*. To make the Thai dance notation system compatible with standard Labanotation, we also write the definition of all new symbols with a group of standard symbol of Labanotation.

4 Measuring Desirability

4.1 Participants

In context of higher education, we selected four Thai dance schools that are well-known in the north and middle of Thailand. The amount of students and teachers involving in our study is 202 and 17, respectively. All of participants have already had a basic skill of Thai dance, but none of them know Labanotation before. This is because most of Thai dance schools do not have a class of Western dances, where students will learn Labanotation.

4.2 Tools

The questionnaire has three parts: personal information, selecting words, and writing comments/ suggestions. There are totally Thai 24 words for both positive and

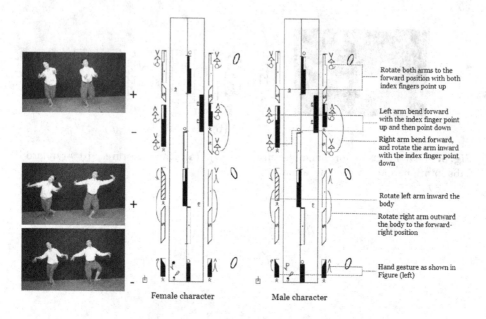

Fig. 7. Example of scores produced from Thai dance notation system

negative words in fairly balance (Translation into English is shown in Table. 1). For selecting words, subjects have to choose any words (subjects can choose more than one) that can explain the software.

Table 1. Choose word(s) for suitably describing our tool

☐ appealing	☐ creative	☐ fun	☐ time-saving
☐ attractive	☐ desirable	☐ high quality	☐ too technical
☐ boring	☐ difficult to use	☐ inefficient	☐ unconventional
☐ common	☐ easy to use	☐ low quality	☐ undesirable
☐ complex	☐ effective	☐ not valuable	☐ usable
☐ confusing	☐ frustrating	☐ time-consuming	☐ valuable

4.3   Procedure

For each school, we gave them a tutorial and demonstration of the teaching and learning tool for Thai dance. The procedure was divided into three sessions: i) tutorial of Labanotation, ii) introducing Thai dance notation system, iii) demonstrating LabanEditor with examples of ballet and Noh. Total time of a whole procedure was approximately 3 hours. After presentation, we conducted the survey experiment by using a questionnaire that subjects had about a few minute for this task. In addition, subjects were allowed to write any feedback about the teaching and learning tool for Thai dance.

The first and second sessions were conducted by Kijkhun who is a professional in Thai dance and a specialist of Labanotation teaching. The aim of the first session was to give the subjects an impression how the notation looks like and how to read the basic notation score. All participants had to practice with the fundamental symbols by reading the score and trying to move their body. In the second session, we demonstrated how to utilize the Labanotation for Thai dance and introduced Thai notation system to the subjects. For the last session, we demonstrated a computer-aided tool to accelerate them about memorizing all notation, and we also presented a case study of Ballet and Noh dance.

5   Results and Discussion

Fig. 8 shows the desirability of the software for describing and reproducing Thai dance body motion. Since Thai dance has not been described in a unified approach. For standardization, we have investigated to adopt the Labanotation for describing Thai dance. Since the notation has been never used for Thai dance, the understanding the notation is very difficult, and it will be a barrier for learning Thai dance. One solution is to investigate a computer-aided tool such as LabanEditor. LabanEditor is an interactive system for inputting/ editing Labanotation scores and displaying 3D CG character animation associated with the scores.

In this paper, we measure the desirability of this tool for describing and reproducing Thai dance. The survey experiment was conducted on over 200 students and teachers in four well-known schools in Thai dances. The results show that about 70% of subjects think that the software has usability, desirability, creativity, and fun. Feedbacks from subjects who are teachers in Thai dance shows more desirable to use the tool than those from students, and less than 5% of the subjects are unwilling to use the tool.

From the results, the barrier of using the technology is slightly found with the chosen words like *frastrating, unconventional, confusing*. However, the percentage is about 12-15% that is under expectation from our experience in art and humanity area. Moreover, there are some subjects who selected two conflicting words such as (*too technical* and *easy to use*), (*complex* and *time-saving*). The reasons are about the subject give their opinion on both Labanotation and the software that the notation is complex and too technical, but the software is easy to use and time-saving.

In the future work, we will create a content that includes both the score in Thai dance notation system and the corresponding animation. After completing the content, we will promote our tools in Thai dance schools and conduct the user evaluation.

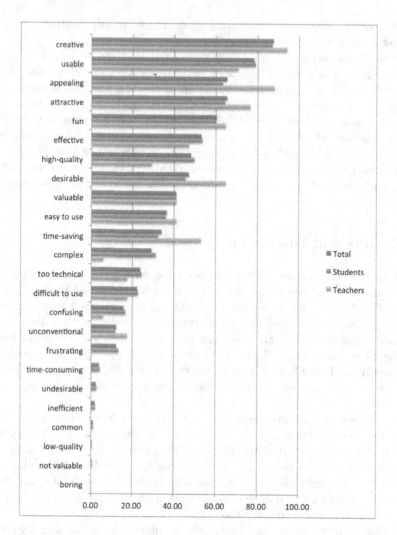

Fig. 8. Chart of chosen words which can explain the tool where number of teachers and students is 17 and 202, respectively

References

1. Benesh, R., Benesh, J.: Reading Dance: The Birth of Choreology. McGraw-Hill Book (1983)
2. Choensawat, W., Takahashi, S., Nakamura, M., Choi, W., Hachimura, K.: Description and reproduction of stylized traditional dance body motion by using labanotation. Transactions of the Virtual Reality Society of Japan 15(3), 379–388 (2010)

3. Choensawat, W., Takahashi, S., Nakamura, M., Hachimura, K.: The use of labanotation for choreographing a noh-play. In: 2011 Second International Conference on Culture and Computing (Culture Computing), pp. 167–168. IEEE (2011)
4. Choensawat, W., Takahashi, S., Nakamura, M., Hachimura, K.: Labanohtation: Laban meets noh. In: ACM SIGGRAPH 2012 Posters, p. 5. ACM (2012)
5. Fox, I., Ryman, R., Calvert, T.: Documenting dance for the 21st century: A translation interface between labanwriter and life forms. In: Twenty-Second Biennial Conference of the International Council of Kinetography Laban, July 26-August 2, vol. 26, pp. 193–205 (2001)
6. Hachimura, K.: Digital archiving of dancing. Review of the National Center for Digitization (Online Journal) 8, 51–66 (2006)
7. Hutchinson, A.: Labanotation. Dance Books (1996)
8. Kojima, K., Hachimura, K., Nakamura, M.: Labaneditor: Graphical editor for dance notation. In: Proceedings of the 11th IEEE International Workshop on Robot and Human Interactive Communication, pp. 59–64. IEEE (2002)
9. Rutnin, M.: Dance, Drama, and Theatre in Thailand: The Process of Development and Modernization. Silkworm Books (1996)
10. Wilke, L., Calvert, T., Ryman, R., Fox, I.: From dance notation to human animation: The labandancer project. Computer Animation and Virtual Worlds 16(3-4), 201–211 (2005)

Improving User Experience in e-Learning, the Case of the Open University of Catalonia

Eva de Lera[1], Magí Almirall[2], Llorenç Valverde[2], and Mercè Gisbert[1]

[1] Universitat Rovira i Virgili, Escorxador s/n, Tarragona, 43003, Spain
[2] Universitat Oberta de Catalunya, Av. Tibidabo 39, Barcelona, 08035, Spain
eva.delera@estudiants.urv.cat, {malmirall,lvalverdeg}@uoc.edu,
merce.gisbert@urv.cat

Abstract. E-Learning, or online learning, seems to have been stalled in the past. As we look at the different learning management systems used by educational institutions worldwide, it becomes obvious that the designs of the learning interfaces look more like instruction booklets and manuals and less like interactive and exciting environments through which to foster learning. The following paper presents the work being carried out by the Universitat Oberta de Catalunya, UOC (a.k.a. Open University of Catalonia), in their commitment to radically change the way the internet is used for learning in higher educational institutions. In order to go along with students' practices and realities, and taking full advantage of what the web offers. The UOC is working toward creating new online spaces where students can encounter richer and more engaging and emotionally fulfilling experiences.

Keywords: e-learning, user-experience, human-computer interaction, usability, emotions, user-centered design, informal learning, personal learning environments.

1 Introduction

Founded in 1994, the UOC was born as a fully online learning University, an institution where the whole learning system and its services allowed students to learn beyond the boundaries of time and space, as it offered an asynchronous pedagogical model. It currently serves more than 60.000 students pursuing undergraduate, graduate and PhD degree programs. It's important to note that all offices, campuses, community spaces and classrooms are online, all institutional interaction is done online (with the exception of proctored exams). The UOC has had to, alone for the early years of the internet, lead the way in online learning via experimenting, creating and innovating in education in the digital era.

Since its inception, the leadership team at UOC was aware that learner's interactive experience with the online platform, tools and services would be a critical aspect for student's to achieve their learning objectives through a highly positive experience and satisfaction. In this regard, the UOC captured a top team of expert and visionary faculty, pedagogs and technologists, to help build what is now known as the UOC's

A. Marcus (Ed.): DUXU/HCII 2013, Part II, LNCS 8013, pp. 180–188, 2013.

Virtual Campus, an environment which has received several international awards for its work in creating and designing rich online learning experiences. This innovation led the UOC team to collaborate with institutions such as MIT and UC Berkeley, amongst many others, and their work has been presented in most renowned conferences around the world. Designing engaging online learning experiences is UOC's priority and, in consequence, the UOC contributes and adds value to the fields of User Experience, Human Computer Interaction, Affective Design and many other emotion, interaction and experience design related areas.

Most human computer interaction professionals are focused in basically achieving three objectives when designing and evaluating online interactions: efficacy (ensuring that the user can achieve the desired goal), efficiency (the quickest and easiest way possible) and satisfaction (prompting a positive emotional and engaging response to the interaction). There are many well known and demonstrated effective user-centered design methodologies to help evaluate both efficacy and efficiency (usability inspection methods, usability testing, qualitative questionnaires and survey methods, etc.). Some of the most recognized work being that of Jakob Nielsen's Usability Engineering book published in 1993 [10]. Since, the methods have been expanded to include new technologies as well as new design methodologies such as rapid prototyping, participatory design and more. However, measuring, evaluating and designing for user satisfaction remains a challenge.

The Office of Learning Technologies at UOC, responsible for the design of this University's learning environment, began applying user-centered design methodologies in 2001 and incorporated all of the above mentioned methodologies to each of their design projects. The team included designers, psychologists and a broader and more diverse group of experts to help tackle the "experience challenge". However, the results of many of the evaluations carried out by UOC's user experience team questioned the methods being used for measuring satisfaction, as these were perceived as partial and often unreliable. UOC then committed part of its efforts to work toward finding new methods that could help evaluate this emotional dimension better.

Focus groups were then considered useful to generate brainstorm activity and the feedback and discussions were not reflecting individual emotional or experience-related responses. In consequence, the user experience team believed that group dynamics, as well as the settings and moderation were variables that may have been interfering with the information needed to extract the necessary data to help evaluate emotional responses and levels of engagement with the designed learning environments or spaces.

In conclusion, and after several years of implementing every methodology available (including objective measures such as capturing galvanic skin response from the users), the group created a list of challenges that they would focus in resolving, to help integrate the emotional dimension into their designs:

- **subjective measures were not reliable enough to measure satisfaction:** using user feedback surveys or questionnaires, and asking people about their experiences with the system, was providing unreliable data.

- ⅄ **focus groups were not effective to evaluate satisfaction:** certainly a great methodology for exploring ideas, concepts, encourage discussion and exchange experiences, users often could not provide information about what was missing or what they would do, nor were aware about their needs (as concepts, ideas or experiences are evaluated in relationship with what they now know and have, and usually is hard for them to envision what the future may bring and how this would affect their use of this particular learning environment).
- ⅄ **Test observations were not optimized:** regular test observations allowed the "testers" to listen to and observe the person as they interacted with the test environment, were able to contextualize and extract more information than that gathered through recording systems such as Morae [9], yet more methodologies were needed to extract better and more accurate emotional-related data.

While there are several objective data collection techniques for evaluating websites and other online learning environment's efficacy and efficiency, finding objective techniques for evaluating satisfaction is still a challenge. The user experience team at UOC began tackling this challenge by demonstrating, in a controlled test environment, that the subjective methodologies being used were unreliable, and that there was a need for proposing a new method that would begin to gather objective satisfaction measures. The result of this first effort generated the 10 Emotion Heuristics [4].

2   The 10 Emotion Heuristics

The 10 Emotion Heuristics were UOC's first approach for trying to gather objective measures to evaluate satisfaction and engagement. The heuristics are a set of guidelines for user experience experts to help evaluate, besides the traditional data gathered in user testing, a set of expressions a user may demonstrate while interacting with a system. The ten measures, which include frowning, compressing the lips, and leaning back on the chair, are easy to detect during a user evaluation (either recorded with a front camera, or observed). Analyzed in conjunction with other data gathered through the more traditional methods, these cues are considered as signs for detecting user frustration, deception, confusion, etc. Each of these measures was assigned a specific measure for positive, neutral, and negative value, and they were primarily aimed at evaluating the frustration emotional state [12]. For example, frowning is related to obstacles while the movement of the cheeks is related to pleasantness [11].

The tests analysis considered the three dimensions. The cognitive dimension was analyzed through the number of clicks, the time needed to accomplish the task, and the number of errors. The user's emotional perception was gathered through the feedback questionnaire. The affective dimension was observed through the ten emotional cues and users' expressions and comments were noted to support the test results. The tests were observed by a multidisciplinary team; one user experience director, one psychologist and one graphic designer.

The observers' analysis of both the interactions and observations recorded concluded that user feedback gathered through questionnaires completed at the end of the test was, in most instances, inconsistent with the emotional cues observed. These affective signals were recorded and suggested that participants were frustrated or anxious due to errors and the amount of time the task was taking, but these emotions were not mentioned in the users' feedback questionnaire that users filled out.

The analysis of these signals, or emotional cues, also showed consistency of emotional state throughout all participants as they all expressed frustration in similar ways. However, these cues were harder to identify as participants did not display facial or bodily expressions in the same way (and wearing eyeglasses was also an obstacle, and that data discarded).

In summary, measuring the affective dimension in conjunction with the other data provided a better and more in-depth understanding of the user's experience. At the same time, it is important to note that not all emotions can be identified through facial or bodily movements, so the team understood that the information was still limited yet a step forward, as they were not be able to evaluate all moments of frustration, anxiety, or satisfaction. Further research should be conducted in evaluating emotions when these occur without expression [2].

This study validated that evaluating the emotional cues provides additional information that contributed to understanding the user's emotion while interacting with a particular system. Moreover, it provided a clear set of guidelines for usability and user experience designers and practitioners interested in adding this dimension in the evaluation of user interfaces.

The 10 Emotion Heuristics led the way to what was going to be its second next step toward improving the user experience in an online learning environment. The user experience team began collaborating with UOC's stakeholders responsible for understanding user profiles (mainly marketing and communication staff, and faculty) to help create yet a new set of heuristic design recommendations to also be used in the new designs and developments, elements that would help incorporate more aspects of the emotional dimension of the students' in their overall learning experience. The result was the creation of the Enjoy Guidelines [3].

3   The Enjoy Guidelines

The Enjoy Guidelines was UOC's second major step toward incorporating the emotional and psychological dimension of the students to the design of the learning environment. These guidelines were generated from the information that had been gathered throughout the years from several user analysis, as well as all quantitative and qualitative data provided by institutional stakeholders (specially the faculty and the marketing and communications professionals). The key aspects identified during this major data gathering phase were then "translated" into design guidelines or principals, in a way that those professionals taking part in designing the online learning environment would understand and be able to easily apply. The Enjoy Guidelines were used in conjunction with the other and more traditional user centered design

(UCD) methodologies carried out to design virtual campuses [6]. Compared to UCD methodologies always aiming at ensuring the efficiency, efficacy and satisfaction at a very functional basic level, this newly proposed methodology aimed at introducing emotions through psychographic data to help increase satisfaction, motivation and overall engagement.

The Enjoy (design) Guidelines generated were:

1. **Personalization** – *"They know who I am, I'm not just another student"* - encouraging the development of a "closer" relationship with the student as opposed to focusing on the system interaction and the specific necessary tasks. This means revising the communication style to be more personal (one-on-one), increase the use of common language and other strategies to help the student develop a closer and more trustful relationship with the people "behind" the University.
2. **Identity** – *"It's MY University"* - enforcing the institutional values through which students could easily and constantly relate, to increase a sense of community and belonging. It encourages the use of photographs and images portraying the values, dreams and believes (as images can be more impacting than text on the screen).
3. **Brand** – *"I LOVE UOC"* - reinforcing the relationship between the student and the institution in which he/she is now a part of. This meant increasing branding elements, yet not being abusive of these (finding a balance), but ensuring the student feels a part of the institution. Some may include "I love UOC" stickers for cars, iphones and others.
4. **Community** – *"We started a running club"* - encouraging the "we" by increasing the options to communicate, relate and participate. Making them visible and easily accessible. Even though UOC prides in offering asynchronous learning, synchronous opportunities favor and promote the collaboration and networking amongst colleagues and peers.
5. **Surprise** – *"I did not expect it"* - introducing positive surprise elements or special events in the initial entry pages or in strategic locations to make the students feel that they are part of a creative, different and dynamic community. Breaking with the routine offers an opportunity to generate engagement in new ways.
6. **Innovation** – *"It's an amazing experience"* - making students feel as they're in an innovative environment, the kind that will lead them to excellence in whatever their purpose for learning is. By integrating innovating elements in the virtual environment, those that they may begin hearing or reading about in the media and other trend environments.
7. **Zen** – *"It just flows"* - offering an environment that does not saturate them with overload of information. Avoiding unnecessary text and information, increase the use of white spaces, as well as photographic or graphic elements that helps the screen "breathe" and provide a more "relaxed" environment for the student, therefore avoiding unnecessary noise.
8. **Search** – *"Wait, it'll just take a sec"* - time is at essence, and providing shortcuts offers a quicker access to students that have little time.
9. **Clarity** – *"I can see it's going to be tomorrow"* - ensuring visibility lively and bright colors to facilitate interaction, reading and information visualization.

10. **Situation** – *"Hmmm... there it is!"*- ensuring that the student quickly recognizes the structure or map of the environment in a glimpse, without needing to scroll.

11. **Aesthetics** – *"Its easy to follow all my courses"*- ensuring a consistent aesthetic throughout, to help guide the student through his or her tasks and objectives (aesthetics as an obstacle remover *facilitating* the online learning experience).

12. **Recognition** – *"I'm not a techie but can easily use all the latest technologies used at the UOC Virtual Campus!"*- utilizing standard icons, symbols, tools and more common styles of interactions can help to easily and quickly understand how the system works without requiring a learning curve.

This integration of psychographics, marketing communications and ethnography to the more traditional user-centered designed methodologies allowed the creation of the above Enjoy Guidelines, a quick and simple 12-step methodology for designers to try and incorporate each dimension into their work. Its objective was to help create an engaging learning experience.

Advances in technology contributed to two major changes that would greatly influence and add value to the work being done by UOC's user experience group:

- **personalization through customization**: the possibility for students (and the UOC community at large) to participate in de design and look-and-feel, and have more control over their learning environment. Some of these elements were:
  - changing background colors (or images)
  - selecting the information visible to them
  - from 1 design for 60.000 students to 60.000 designs, one personalized design for each student.
- **flexibility through interoperability**: the possibility to customize and personalize the information that is available to them.
  - integration of external elements (i.e. twitter or facebook) into their learning environment.
  - removal of institutional elements that may not be of interest to them (due to time restrictions or interest in general, amongst others).
  - Integration of tools and services from other learning platforms and environments.

The above technological innovations were able to add value to the global user experience for all learners at UOC. At all times, the new previously described methodologies were integrated, in conjunction with the more traditional UCD methods.

4   GUX, Re-Designing the e-learner's Experience

These methodological additions helped UOC advance toward defining yet a new opportunity for taking this "experience" concept into a higher level, and created the GUX concept. GUX, or Global User Experience, is aimed at addressing the affective dimension more holistically (a 360° dimension), and beyond the online learning environment.

By taking a holistic approach to the design of UOC's online learning spaces, the Office of Learning Technologies proposed expanding its work, the findings and possibilities of these new methods, to the overall experience of the learner as it interacted with UOC's spaces, from the moment a potential student first receives information about the Institution, all the way until the student graduates, becomes an alumni, stays as an active and participatory part of the community and, hopefully, desires to become a life-long learner.

To assess its potential impact, the Office followed one student's step by step interaction with UOC's online space, from her first click until she completed her first course. The team observed that the student's "passage" through UOC was inconsistent in the different online learning environments that she encountered (registration, library, classrooms, etc.). These inconsistencies were perceived as a frustration by the student, an obstacle and problem, and it was suggested that all elements with which students interact should be "experientially" consistent, promoting the inspirational environment through which their goals can be achieved, from start to finish.

With the collaboration of a diverse and interdisciplinary group of experts (marketers, communicators, sociologists, linguists, psychologists and many other), the UOC tries to bring this more holistic approach to design for motivation and engagement in online learning spaces.

5   Conclusions and Next Steps

Emotion is a key aspect in user experience since measuring emotions helps us understand the user's engagement and motivation and understand their overall experience as this is how they are challenged, excited or interested [7]. Accounting for emotional and experiential cues during user evaluations provides user experience and learning technologists practitioners with key valuable information. As measuring emotion is both difficult and costly [1, 8], most interface evaluation efforts had been focused on cognitive aspects while neglecting this so necessary affective dimension, but UOC believes that unifying all user data.....

In comparison to how traditional UCD methods had been used to design e-learning environments, the UOC has demonstrated through these initial steps that there is a need for integrating the emotional and more "human" dimension to the design of learning environments. It believes that aiming at a truly holistic affective approach will contribute to:

- increasing overall satisfaction
- reducing abandonment

    ⅄   attracting new students (and maintain current ones satisfied)
    ⅄   increasing the joy of the learning
    ⅄   improving the learning experiences
    ⅄   improving the learning spaces
    ⅄   innovating in education

In conclusion, the UOC continues its work toward designing rich and engaging learning experiences by defining and implementing GUX in a way that can have a higher and more stronger effect in learner's achievements, satisfaction, motivation and engagement. It also hopes to build a stronger relationship between the University and the community it serves, to help learners achieve their objectives, and dreams.

The following is a short list of basic recommendations for user experience evangelists and advocates for carrying such a holistic methodology in their institutions, as they pursue the joy of learning [4]:

    ⅄   share all the information related to who the learners are (their needs, skills, believes, expectations, preferences, who they are in and outside the institution, what they care about, what motivates them, etc.)
    ⅄   define the vision, the Joy of Learning
    ⅄   create the necessary steps to define GUX, Global User Experience, as a transversal practice across the University.
    ⅄   work together to ensure that all of UOC's interaction with the learners is consistent in delivering and promoting the desired global user experience.
    ⅄   Collaborate within the institution, and beyond, for continuous innovation.

References

1. Chin, J.P., Diehl, V.A., Norman, K.L.: Development of an instrument measuring user satisfaction of the human-computer interface. In: CHI 1988 Conference Proceedings: Human Factors in Computing Systems, pp. 213–218. Association for Computing Machinery, New York (1988)
2. Dalgleish, T., Power, M.: Handbook of Cognition and Emotion, ch. 3. John Wiley & Sons, Ltd., Paul Ekman, Sussex, U.K. (1999)
3. De Lera, E., Almirall, M.: ENJOY: guidelines for designing engaging eLearning environments. Proceedings iLearning Forum (2008)
4. De Lera, E., Garreta-Domingo, M.: Ten emotion heuristics: guidelines for assessing the user's affective dimension easily and cost-effectively. In: Proceedings of the 21st British HCI Group Annual Conference on People and Computers: HCI... but not as we know it (2007)
5. De Lera, E., Mor, E.: The joy of e-learning: redesigning the e-learning experience. In: Proc. of HCI 2007 Workshop: Design, Use and Experience of e-learning Systems (2007)
6. Gabbard, J.L., Hix, D., Swan, J.E.I.: User-centered design and evaluation of virtual environments. IEEE Computer Graphics and Applications 19(6), 51–59 (1999)
7. Helander, M.G., Tham, M.P.: Hedonics-affective human factors design. Special Issue in Ergonomics 46(13-14) (2003)

8. Ives, B., Olson, M.H., Baroudi, J.J.: The measurement of user information satisfaction. Communications of the ACM 26, 785–793 (1983)
9. Morae: Usability Testing for Software and Websites, http://www.techsmith.com/morae.asp
10. Nielsen, J.: Usability Engineering. Academic Press, Boston (1993)
11. Pope, L.K., Smith, C.A.: On the distinct meanings of smiles and frowns. Cognition and Emotion 8, 65–72 (1994)
12. Scherer, K., Wallbot, H.G., Summerfield, A.: Experiencing Emotion. A cross-cultural study. Cambridge University Press, Cambridge (1986)

Math Fluency through Game Design

Wanda Eugene[1], Tiffany Barnes[2], and Jennifer Wilson[3]

[1] School of Computing, Human-Centered Computing Division,, Clemson University, Clemson,
SC, 29634, USA
[2] Department of Computer Science, North Carolina State University, Raleigh,
NC, 27695, USA
[3] Department of Communications Studies, University of North Carolina-Charlotte, Charlotte,
NC, 28223, USA
weugene@clemson.edu, tmbarnes@ncsu.edu, jwils200@uncc.edu

Abstract. Our goal in this research is to create a comprehensive framework establishing guidelines for the design of math fluency games for adult learners. Our user-centered design approach consisted of focus groups with students, faculty, and administrators from a two-year and a four-year institution to probe more deeply into the ways students perceive the value of math in everyday activities. Using our comprehensive focus group protocol, we evaluated users' perception and understanding of culture-based mathematics to determine value-laden game designs that will promote math fluency among developmental math students. During these sessions, we collected quantitative and qualitative data in the form of survey data, play-test data, and field notes. The data speak to various issues such as games as a learning tool, interests and mismatches between designers and the target audience. Moving forward, our research will provide future directions for defining holistic usability by integrating user-centered design and game design.

Keywords: Game Design, User Centered Design.

1   Introduction

People who are math literate have knowledge or competence of basic math skills, while people who are math fluent having the ability to unconsciously and smoothly demonstrate mastery. Even though math is integrated into many aspects of everyday life, many people are math literate, but not math fluent [1]. The majority of our society is capable of appropriating math in terms of telling time, adding single digit numbers, etc. However, many struggle with applying mathematical foundations, principles, and theories such as balancing a checkbook, or calculating a tip. According to Ginsburg et al. [2], 58.6% of U.S. adults were below level 3, the minimum level for coping with today's math skill demands. This may seem trivial in this technological age where everyone has immediate access to calculators or other technological devices. However, lacking in these skills can be extremely problematic when those same skill sets become the barrier to successfully meeting goals in life.

A. Marcus (Ed.): DUXU/HCII 2013, Part II, LNCS 8013, pp. 189–198, 2013.

2   Background

In order to strengthen scientific competitiveness in the U.S., there has been a rapid societal shift from a need for laborers to a need for knowledge workers [3]. In parallel with this shift, the recession is forcing many adults (ages 25-54) to return to higher education, such as trade schools and community colleges, in order to develop their skill sets and expand their career options. For many of these learners, however, a lack of math skills, necessary for most entry-level community college curricula, will prevent them from progressing toward their goals. In fact, while sixty percent of all community college students are required to take at least one developmental math course to matriculate, only thirty-percent pass the developmental math courses they need [4]. This means that forty-two percent of all community college students are failing to pass the math they need for their coursework. This lack of preparation in basic math skills, paired with the hierarchical nature of math, results in hindered comprehension of more advanced mathematical skills [5]. To address this issue, building math fluency -- the ability to perform a behavior correctly, quickly, and with minimal effort [6]-- is key. Math fluency contributes to learning outcomes of performing a skill or recall knowledge independently, maintain performance levels, and effectively reappropriate that same skill and knowledge [7]. Educational games are one approach for building math fluency because of what they offer in terms of engagement, repetitive actions, immersion, and exposure time [8]. While games might not immediately seem like a viable approach for adult learners, a recent Pew Internet survey [9] found that 53% of American adults participate in digital games through mobile applications, video games, or electronic games. Though games are a popular medium, not all types of games are popular with all audiences. For example, women tend to be drawn more towards cooperative types of games [10] versus competitive games and older adults prefer games on the computer as opposed to console and mobile games [9]. As with any software, a keen understanding of the target audience is needed to build effective math fluency games for adult learners. However, there are few guidelines for designing math educational games targeted towards this unique subset of users. We propose to use user-centered design [11] techniques to create a design framework that establishes guidelines and criteria for math fluency games for adult learners. To do so, we must build an explicit understanding of users, tasks, and environments; and this knowledge must be iteratively refined during the design and development process [12].

3   Method

The overall project's goal is to improve performance in developmental mathematics courses by building games that help students develop the number sense required to succeed in mathematical problem solving. To improve our designs for this specific audience, we evaluated students' perception of their learning of math and how they think about learning math from game environments. This study was conducted in three parts. Each part of the study focused on a different aspect of the design to better understand the target audience. Part I was an online pre-questionnaire/survey on basic demographic information. Part II was a focus group discussion where participants describe and identify math in their everyday activities. The focus group protocol used was an adaption of the Family Math Protocol created by the Family Math Project [13], with questions designed to solicit narratives about math usage in everyday activities. Part III consisted of play-testing one or two math-centered educational games, where students played games and provided their feedback. After each game they completed an evaluation and provided their own ideas of what an ideal math learning game would entail. The data of part III is beyond the scope of this paper as we are focusing primarily on students' perception of their learning process.

3.1 Participants

We recruited participants from the STARS Computing Corps program at Central Piedmont Community College (CPCC), and the Fall 2013 developmental math courses at University of North Carolina-Charlotte (UNCC) through in-class announcements. The STARS Computing Corps seeks to increase the participation of women, underrepresented minorities, and persons with disabilities in computing disciplines through multi-faceted interventions that lead to computing careers. These STARS students at CPCC had already completed higher-level math and computing courses, and participated in projects where they applied these skills. As such, the CPCC students are considered to have high math fluency (HMF). Conversely, we consider the UNCC students to have low math fluency (LMF) because they were recruited from the lower level developmental courses.

3.2 Procedure

At the start of the study, participants were asked to read and sign the consent form. Then, participants completed the pre-questionnaire on demographic information and prior education. The questionnaire gives the researcher a better feel of the group in preparation for the focus group. Discussion occurred in four sessions. During the discussion participants were asked to think and respond to each question as the moderator asks them. The discussions lasted for about 30-45 minutes. Studies took place on the students' respective campus, in Charlotte, North Carolina. Participants were compensated with gift cards for participating in the study.

4 Results

In total, 17 participants participated in the entire study with a gender breakdown of (n=7) male participants and (n=10) female. Students were majoring in both Science-related fields (n=11) and the Liberal Arts (n=6). Table 1 further describes the demographics of the participants. We provide this level of detail since a thorough understanding of the user is fundamental to user-centered design.

Table 1. Description of Participants in Study, with numbers (and percentages) given for each group

Demographics	n(%)	
	CPCC	UNCC
Gender		
Male	8 (88.9)	1(10.0)
Female	1(11.1)	9(90.0)
Highest Education completed		
High school diploma (including equivalency)	1(11.1)	4(40.0)
Some college, no degree	7(77.8)	6(660.0)
Associate degree	1(11.1)	
Age		
18-24 years	4 (44.4)	10(100)
25-34 years	4(44.4)	
35-44 years	1(11.1)	
Ethnicity		
White or Caucasian	4 (44.4)	3(30.0)
Black or African American	3(33.3)	3(30.0)
Hispanic or Latino	1(11.1)	
Asian	1(11.1)	
Multiracial/ Other (please specify		4(40.0)

4.1   High Math Fluency - STARS students at CPCC

The HMF focus group consisted of (7) males and (1) female. Majors were primarily computer science-related (7 of 9 participants). Most reported having a high math fluency (HMF) and had positive historical experience with math learning and activities. The most common hobbies reported were going to the gym/exercising, programming, and reading. Most participants reported a moderate-to-high interest in play videogames and one participant had experience with programming rudimentary games. Most participants expressed a comfortable working knowledge of math or even an appreciation of using math; "for me personally, I love puzzles and that's essentially what math is; it's...just concrete evidence and just proof and facts and it just like is everything of what math is... I wouldn't believe anything without...." (HMF, P2) "...Proof." (P4) "Right, exactly" (P2). When participants described how math could be seen in everyday life, the most common responses were angles, force and trajectory in sports such as basketball, swimming, billiards and soccer. Participants agreed that in order to achieve a high level of play, it was necessary to consider the math involved in athletic competition, "...in basketball, if you don't see the angles you're not going to be good." (HMF, P4). Another participant used the recent Olympics as an example, "with the Olympics this past year...they had swimmers putting...sensors on their bodies so they could see how...the drag...in the water [could] be reduced" (HMF, P5). Although they acknowledged this need for math in sports, participants in this group unanimously agreed that focusing too much on the math involved would have a negative impact on the level of fun. "When you break it down to it's mathematical form you've removed all passion out of it. Who's gonna sit there and think while they're playing a little game about the physics of it?" (HMF, P1) Though several participants in this group said they enjoy playing video games, most were skeptical about the value of games as an educational tool for adult learners such as themselves: "For me it was learning by touching and doing. It wasn't learning by playing. Not everything can be fun, and that's something that also needs to be learned" (HMF, P5).

4.2   Low Math Fluency –Developmental Math students at UNCC

The LMF groups consisted of a focus group with (7) participants and (2) in-depth interviews with (1) participant in each interview. All participants from LMF were female and majors were split almost even with (4) students from Science-related fields and (5) from Liberal Arts fields. The most common hobbies reported were reading, listening to music, watching TV/movies, religious activities and playing sports. The most frequently mentioned use of math in everyday life was budgeting/financial management. The second most common was time management. "I use math when I'm deciding on what time I should wake up in the morning...I set my alarm clock to the last possible minute. I get ready in like twenty minutes." (LMF, P7) Overall, the LMF participants made more references to friends and family when discussing hobbies, learning and playing games. "I'm beating my mom [at Words with Friends]...I have like 230, she has like 170, and I think I'm beating my other friend by maybe 20 points..." (LMF, P9) Overall, participants spoke extensively of low math fluency (LMF), claiming to have inferior math skills or possess a strong dislike for math in general with (19) negative references and only (4) positive references in regard to their thoughts on math. Two participants mentioned being capable with math, "*I was naturally good at math, but with Physics I was actually able to see how it works*" (LMF, P6), but others in this group spoke negatively of their math skills and admitted to struggling with the subject, "*math is...my weakness and it has always been*" (LMF, P3). Their opinion of the subject seemed directly influenced by the perception of their abilities, "*I don't like math, like simple math is okay, but I don't do well a whole lot of math.... If I'm good at something, I like it. If I'm bad at something, I don't like it.*" (LMF, P1).

Having problems broken down seemed key to understanding for some participants, "*...the easiest way to learn it would be to have it... broken down...*" (LMF, P2). Participants also stressed their need for step-by-step instructions; "*I probably learn the best when the steps are in detail. So, like, 'step one is this, step two is this, and then three and then four', however many...that really helps me, to go step-by-step.*" (LMF, P8).

Nearly all participants from the LMF group spoke of getting frustrated when teachers or others would falsely assume the participant understood a particular concept; *"'I never learned this. Can you explain this formula to me?' and they're just like, 'you should have learned this two years ago. It'll be okay'"* (LMF, P5). *"I feel like a lot of the teachers I have... they think that you should know it, so they just keep on going and they don't stop"* (LMF, P1). When participants in this group did not have their needs addressed when learning math, they spoke of withdrawing completely, *"I'm just like 'I don't know', and...I get frustrated...I'll just be like 'forget it'"*(UNCC, P7) or giving up on trying to learn, *"I just got to the point where... I just couldn't study it because... I was like, I don't know this so what's the point of me studying it. I'm not going to get it...I turn all the way off. I shut down. I start ignoring it."* (LMF, P3). Instead of seeking assistance, participants spoke of internalizing their failure, *"If I don't know what I'm doing it's, it's really hard for me to ask for help 'cause I feel stupid"* (LMF, P1). Participants spoke positively about previous math education games played in Elementary and Middle School, for example, The Lemonade Stand game, but had mixed opinions of games being used in their current math courses, *"I can't honestly...really picture it. I think it'd be too juvenile...I can't picture...a math game with the math we're doing now. I feel like I'd just get bored with it."* (LMF, P6) Half of the participants believed the addition of games would be beneficial and said they would be open to the idea, *"I think the math games would work, because I think one thing why math is so unpopular is because you actually have to put time into understanding things and I think games provides it in like a fun way...like you're not dragging on..."* (LMF, P7) *"...doing homework problems out of a textbook for two and a half hours..."* (LMF, P5) . The other participants said games would not be effective for them, citing concerns such as the inability to ask questions, the idea that games might be "too juvenile", and having to stop and do problems with pen-and-paper would be similar to homework and therefore detract from the level of fun, *"...you'd be like, 'okay, this is gonna be awesome and then you'd get to the actual mini games and it's like, this sucks, this is just school all over again'"* (LMF, P2). One participant did not comment on the topic.

4.3   Cross-Group

When asked, "How often do you play digital games (online, on your phone, on the computer, console, etc)", about half of the participants overall reported playing some type of digital game often. The two groups differed, however, in the types of games they played. The HMF students primarily played console and first person shooter games, while the LMF students primarily described games played on the mobile games, cooperative games, etc. For example, one student from HMF mentioned Black Ops and one student from LMF mentioned the Sims 3. Participants in both groups expressed an interest in the repetition of fundamental skills, with an HMF participant admitting love of math started at an early age: *"I remember when I was younger, my father would do drills with me (laughs) and he would make me do drills over and over..."*(HMF, P3) One LMF participant remembers slowly building confidence, *"once I get it right, I'll repeat it over and over and over again. and then...that's when*

I'll kind of start trying to figure out the shortcuts and then I repeat it and that's kinda how I build... I'll use a bunch of little math and I know it takes longer, but once I get that, that's when I kind of build off it, but it's mostly repetition for me." (LMF, P1)

5   Analysis

5.1   High Math Fluency - STARS Students at CPCC

The HMF students saw math as ubiquitous. As they described how one would come to excel in some of their hobbies and activities, they would often discuss it in terms of the higher-level math it entailed; for example, algorithms in video games and angles in basketball, billiards, etc. When asked about how they approached math, the HMF students frequently responded, "we just do it." This casual sentiment displays fluency, their ability to smoothly navigate through much of their day-to-day math skills without much thought.   In addition, the average age of the HMF students was older than the LMF students, which could impact their opinion on games used as learning tools. Many spoke of learning math fundamentals prior to the heavy use of technology, such as calculators, in the classroom. Additionally, the types of games participants cited were typically complex, high graphic console games such as Black Ops, etc. This could impact their opinion of games as a learning tool as their expectation of the constitution of games would be more than simple 2D graphics.

5.2   Low Math Fluency –Developmental Math Students at UNCC

The LMF students often lack the confidence in their ability to fully grasp the math used in everyday activities independently, for example calculating discounts while shopping. They identified simple direct math existing in various activities such as tipping, measuring, and counting. However, they often do not possess the comprehensive understanding behind tasks that call for more complex math. For example, one participant described ice-skating and using trial and error to effectively make turns rather than explaining the force, trajectory, and angles that are inherent in the process.

Participants involved in the study seemed to value community as participants made more references to friends and family when discussing hobbies and more reference to one another - even at times finishing each other's sentences. Most hobbies included descriptions of other people in addition to the participant - for example: cooking with family, team sports, traveling with friends/family, and playing games with friends/family. When responding to questions, LMF used more high-context style descriptions than participants in the HMF group. The types of games played primarily consisted of simple, community or collaborative-style games such as Words with Friends and The Sims 3. Participants in the study also seemed highly influenced by external perceptions by describing situations in which the teachers' attitude negatively impacted the students' perceptions of their abilities. The negative perceptions of their ability to learn math may make them both less likely to seek help when unable to understand, and quicker to lose interest. Essentially for these LMF students, poor performance in math becomes a self-fulfilling prophecy. When learning a new concept, or reviewing previous concepts, participants in this group preferred to have problems broken down into step-by-step instructions or easily-digestible components. The LMF students frequently emphasized the need to visualize and understand the entire problem-solving process as it is developing. This step-by-step method was seen as a means to providing building blocks and build confidence and competence with math skills. When imagining math learning games, some of these students seem to feel that they would be superficial and juvenile exercises that required students to do math outside the game in order to play.

5.3   Cross-Group

About half of all of the participants played digital games regularly. While their perception of how they engaged in the games differed greatly, both groups were opposed to learning that impeded the fun-factor in the realm of playing games. Participants equated this to parents hiding vegetables in food - they can get away with it when children are young, but after a certain age, we all know they are there. One of the most important themes pulled from this research was that individuals learn math at different speeds and through different methods. Some participants preferred visual tactics while others emphasized learning by doing, but everyone enjoyed the positive feeling that came from understanding and feeling successful. Participants stated the need for repetition of fundamentals/basics in order to move on to a higher level or more complex math. Participants across both groups described using math every day through activities such as time management and budgeting. As all participants are current students, time management concerns revolved around balancing schoolwork and course schedules with extracurricular activities, hobbies, and sleeping. Financial management consisted of budgeting; the primary budgeting mentioned involved food and shopping in general.

6   Recommendation

Due to the variety and depth of information gathered, we feel valuable considerations may be drawn for future game design research. When designing developmental games for the audience of LMF students, the following should be taken into consideration:

- Due to the variety and depth of information gathered, we feel valuable considerations may be drawn for future game design research. When designing developmental games for the audience of LMF students, the following should be taken into consideration:
- The design of the game should include options for several learning styles, e.g., auditory, visual, and kinesthetic.
- Games should allow players to set their own pace or should adapt to each individual's pace of learning.

- Players are more likely to disengage faster when they don't understand the math or how to play.
- Players may be less likely to seek help or assistance when they feel they possess inadequate math skills. Therefore, the game should scaffold problem solving with built-in step-by-step instructions. This may downplay the negative perception of needing assistance.
- Design for multi-player and/or collaborative game experiences..
- Do not try to hide the math. Instead, incorporate high-context scenarios that are applicable to the target audience outside of the game.
- Provide positive, reinforcing feedback that allows students to perceive incremental improvements to build confidence.
- Embed the math within the game as the core game mechanic, so students don't have to work problems on paper outside of the game environment, or feel that the game is superfluous to learning.
- Explicit connection should be made between the game, the skill, and the context it will be applied in outside the game as LMF students do not see how games would facilitate practice of the skills they need in everyday life.

7   Conclusion

The aim of this paper is to better inform the design of games targeted to increase the math fluency of developmental math collegiate students. This was accomplished by exploring how developmental math students perceive learning math overall and how they think about learning math from gaming environments. Using focus groups and in-depth interviews, we attempted to probe more deeply into the ways students perceive the value of math in their everyday activities and connect these experiences to their learning of math. The main findings from this research emphasized that, while participants have different needs when it comes to learning math, most emphasized the need for step-by-step instructions. With this, low math fluency students feel that fully understanding basic math is essential before adding a higher level or more complex math. Repetition of the fundamentals is the best way to gain this comprehensive understanding for these participants. Additionally, multi-player collaborative games can prove quite beneficial to low math fluency learners as it depicts their preferred learning and gaming environment of being part of a community. Based upon this information, we presented several recommendations for designing educational games to help adults build math fluency. Respecting the needs and perspectives of adults within the designs of these games is critical for their potential adoption. Games designed without sufficient scaffolding or instruction can leave this audience frustrated and uninterested. Instead of being tricked to develop math skills in abstract game contexts, these low math fluency adults want to know specifically how and when they will use the skill they are developing.

References

1. Fischer, G.: Computational Literacy and Fluency: Being Independent of High-Tech Scribes. In: Engel, J., Vogel, R., Wessolowski, S. (eds.) Strukturieren - Modellieren - Kommunizieren. Leitbild mathematischer und informatischer Aktivitäten, Franzbecker, Hildesheim, pp. 217–230 (2005), `http://l3d.cs.colorado.edu/~gerhard/papers/hightechscribes-05.pdf`
2. Ginsburg, L., Manly, M., Schmitt, M.J.: The Components of Numeracy. NCSALL Occasional Paper. National Center for the Study of Adult Learning and Literacy, NCSALL (2006), `http://www.ncsall.net/fileadmin/resources/research/op_numeracy.pdf`
3. Eugene, W., Gilbert, J.E.: C-PAL: Cultural-Based Programming for Adult Learners. In: ACM Southeast Conference (ACMSE), Auburn, AL, March 28-29 (2008)
4. Attewell, P., Lavin, D., Domina, T., Levey, T.: New evidence on college remediation. Journal of Higher Education 77, 886–924 (2006)
5. Codding, R.S., Eckert, T.L., Fanning, E., Shiyko, M., Solomon, E.: Comparing mathematics interventions: The effects of cover-copy-compare alone and combined with performance feedback on digits correct and incorrect. Journal of Behavioral Education 16(2), 125–141 (2007)
6. Cates, G.L., Rhymer, K.N.: Examining the relationship between mathematics anxiety and mathematics performance: A learning hierarchy perspective. Journal of Behavioral Education 12, 23–34 (2003)
7. Binder, C., Haughton, E., Bateman, B.: Fluency: Achieving true mastery in the learning process, University of Virginia, Curry School of Education (2002), `http://special.edschool.virginia.edu/papers/Binder-et-al_Fluency.pdf` (retrieved October 15, 2012)
8. Farmer, L.S.: Gaming in Adult Education. In: Gaming and Simulations: Concepts, Methodologies, Tools and Applications, p. 194 (2010)
9. Lenhart, A., Jones, S., Macgill, A.: Adults and Video Games (2008), `http://www.pewinternet.org/Reports/2008/Adultsand-Video-Games.aspx` (retrieved October 15, 2012)
10. Procci, K., Bohnsack, J., Bowers, C.: Patterns of gaming preferences and serious game effectiveness. In: Shumaker, R. (ed.) Virtual and Mixed Reality, Part II, HCII 2011. LNCS, vol. 6774, pp. 37–43. Springer, Heidelberg (2011)
11. Usability Professionals' Association (UPA) (1991), `http://www.usabilityprofessionals.org/usability_resources/about_usability/what_is_ucd.html` (retrieved on: September 21, 2011)
12. ISO 9241-210:2010 - Ergonomics of human-system interaction – Part 210: Human centered design for interactive systems, `http://www.iso.org/iso/catalogue_detail.htm?csnumber=52075` (retrieved October 29, 2012)
13. Martin, L.M., Goldman, S., Jiménez, O.: The tanda: A practice at the intersection of mathematics, culture, and financial goals. Mind, Culture and Activity 16(4), 338–352 (2009)

Musical Experience Development Model
Based on Service Design Thinking

Sunyoung Kim and Eui-Chul Jung

Human Environment and Design, Yonsei University, Seoul, Korea
kim_sunyoung@outlook.com, jech@yonsei.ac.kr

Abstract. After 2012, the number of Korean musical audience grew larger than 5 million, which is the starting point of popularization. Considering new-coming audiences and changing market environment, overall analysis of musical art management and customer-centered approach is needed. Performance experience process and details of musical service will be analyzed based on 5 principles of service design thinking. This paper will study purchase stages from musical perspective, analyze flow experience structure model and the relationship between different musical contents. This paper has the characteristic of basic study to enhance musical experience and suggest planning direction.

Keywords: Musical Experience, Service Design Thinking.

1 Introduction

Starting from Phantom of the Opera performed at LG Art Center in 2001, blockbuster musicals based on major halls made a huge success. Since then, domestic musical market has been led by producers with license. The resulting increase in the production cost raised ticket price, which led consumers of musicals to become multi-layered based on social class(Choi, 2006). This phenomenon shows that at that time musical was recognized as high culture, and was not easy for most people to experience.

The number of musical audience grew from 300 thousand in 2001 to 3 million in 2010, and at the same time, the market size expanded to 200 billion won from 10 billion won. Currently, in 2012, it is estimated that there are 7million consumers and the market worth 250 to 300 billion won(Interpark, 2012). Current point of musical audience larger than 5 million can be seen as the starting point of popularization.

When performance market environment changes and develops, market participation of government, pubic organization, arts organization, performance planning agency, theater, company, audience, media and others will increase. This will change and complicate interests within those concerned. Substantial changes of each sectors will require further realization and understanding of such changes (Lee, 2002). Since the ratio of consumers who are not familiar with musicals is increasing, measures must be taken to answer their wants and needs as well as explaining to them the existing musical culture.

A. Marcus (Ed.): DUXU/HCII 2013, Part II, LNCS 8013, pp. 199–208, 2013.

Performance has the characteristics of different elements such as art products, expected products, and value-added products, various functions. That is why performance's match different product characteristics must be taken into consideration(Jang, 2007). Art products are closer to service than products, and both have intangibility, heterogeneity, inseparability and perishability. Due to intangibility, performance exists as a sound source or DVD as well as performance itself. Because performance exists at the moment when it is performed, each performance is not the same product, and because of this, production and consumption happen at the same time which enables various interactions with consumers during the consuming process. Moreover, after the performance starts, the economic value disappears(Lee, 2001; Yong, 2010). Expected products has the characteristic of first purchasing and later consuming, and value-added products has the characteristic of providing various services other than performance in order to maximize consumer satisfaction.

Performance also has the characteristic of experience goods, which elicit stable and continuous consumption when repeatedly experienced and emotional taste is formed(Lee, 2009). This means performance experience forms conscious and unconscious structure that connects to coming performances, instead of ending as separate projects for each performance. Musical experience at the theater can be the basis for musical culture formation because it enhances recognition toward musical as well as increasing individual value creation.

Art management was founded in 60s to enhance marketability of nonprofit arts organizations and arts creation due to their shortage of financial resources in America. Moreover, it was meant to play the role of a medium between divisions as arts was divided into different division and the role of medium grew larger compared to previous individual-centered production system. The role of arts manager as a medium that adjusts creation process to deliver art works clearly to the audience, and interprets the works became important(Yong, 2010).

Currently, Arts & Cultural Management is recognized as a development from the previous fundraising method. It was to realize artistic qualities, publicity, and financial independency as the center of proper growth and management of institution, and fundamentally vitalize arts organizations and institutions, and contribute to independent consumer culture formation(Park, 2008).

As can be observed, approach to performance is changing from product-centered to sale-centered to consumer-centered. This trend is similar to service dominant logic, which recognizes product as the medium or means to provide fundamental service. Products and service differ only in materiality and immateriality, and form one bundle for the customer's value creation, not separate elements(Kim, 2009). Among service-related sectors, service design, unlike existing service-related sectors, takes Manifestation independent approach and understands customer's emotions and actions in integrated perspective and embodies this into service(Service Design Council).

In the changing environment of musical market, service design has fitting characteristic for art management. Service design recognizes audience's emotions, behavior and service process in integrated perspective. Considering the feature of musical, the work of arranging tacit information of audience's experience formation process on performance and performance related services into explicit information is such a work.

This study will analyze performance experience formation process and variables within overall musical service. This paper is basic study which means to enhance musical experience and suggest planning direction using service design principles.

This study is comprised of following procedure in table 1.

Table 1. Research Phases

Phase 1	literature study and preceding studies	studying service design thinking, audience, and the theory of flow experience
Phase 2	extracting musical experience formation process and specific elements	extracting musical flow model extracting specific variables that affect the flow
Phase 3	structure formation	developing structure of experience formation and elements
Phase 4	application direction suggestion	suggesting possibility of expansion

First, this paper will study the overall service design thinking, audience, and the theory of flow experience. Second, based on the previously analyzed theory, it will extract specific elements of musical experience formation process. These elements all act as the variables in the experience formation process. Third, the structure of specific elements and basic theory will be formed and visualized. Fourth, possibility of expansion will be suggested considering the formed structure.

2 Theoretical Background

2.1 Service Design

Service Design Council suggests that service design is the methodology and a field of study that enhances effective and attractive service experience of customer and service supplier by first, finding potential needs of interested parties by utilizing customer-centered contextual research method toward all material and immaterial elements(people, objects, action, emotion, place, communication, diagram, etc) that the customer experiences through the service and all routes(process, system, interaction, emotion road map), and then embodying them in a creative and interdisciplinary and cooperative design method. Stickdorn(2011) argues that service design is interdisciplinary rather than a new independent 'study field', and explains service design with five basic principles of service design thinking.

— **User-centered.** understanding customer and using appropriate language according to their situation,
— **Co-creative.** Enabling participation of various interested people including customer in service design process and enhancing the interaction between service and interested people,
— **Sequencing.** Arranging service flow in a way that best delivers the service,
— **Evidencing.** Visualizing service that can be immaterial experience,
— **Holistic.** Understanding the broad context of all process of the service.

2.2   Audience

Customer understanding in service design is closer to real-time communication on all processes of performance with the audience than merely providing appropriate service. Performance experience formation process leads to individual value creation of musical experience, and forms the basis for musical culture formation.

Abercrombie and Longhurst(1998; Kolb, 2000) divided consumers of performance arts to 5 categories according to voluntary community type and media participation as can be seen in table 2; consumer, fan, cultist, enthusiast, and petty producer. These 5 types each have different views on performance. Majority of consumers are those who are not willing to learn musicals (Kolb, 2004).

Table 2. Medium use model

	Consumer	Fan	Cultist	Enthusiast	Petty Producer
	average customer		professional customer		amateur producer
Emotion	fun			serious interest	
Frequency	low frequency		high frequency		
Approach method	choose freely	choose based on experience		approach as a form of art. enjoy most types.	
Choice criteria	Accessibility, cost	Star, program			
Community			social activity	organizational activity	occupation
Probing action and Knowledge level		bear additional cost and inconvenience	researching star and publication visiting related historical sites	high level of contents and producer knowledge	

Domestically, research on musical audiences has been done in the perspective of lifestyle, audience division, and consuming tendency(Kang and Lee, 2001: Ko and Park, 2008: Hyun and Kang, 2012).

3   Musical Experience Formation Model Structure

3.1   Purchase Stages

There are five stages in purchase: problem recognition, information search, evaluation of alternative products, product purchase, post-purchase product evaluation(Lamb, Hair, and McDaniel, 1999). Table 3 shows details about musical experience based on these five stages. In the problem recognition stage, the reason for enjoying a performance, what is to be achieve from watching the performance, and what the audience wants is to be perceived. They pursue mental satisfaction, want to enjoy cultural life, and refresh themselves(Kang and Lee, 2001).

Audiences search for events that can satisfy their needs in information search. They have access to information such as summary, contents, commentary, cast, synopsis, making story, reservation and contact number from various promotion, media, broadcast and internet(Jeon, 1999). When sufficient information is gathered, the audience chooses performances by evaluating alternatives according to their preferred standards, and purchases the products through reservation. This process exists also after the reservation is done. This level ends after enjoying the performance and evaluating the product.

Table 3. Stages of purchase about booking musical ticket

Problem recognition	What is to be done? Reason for consumption_ leisure, entertainment, custom, self-improvement Convenience_ mental satisfaction, cultural life, refreshing			
Information search		**Alternative evaluation**	**Product purchase**	**On the spot**
product characteristic	information source	standard	booking_	receiving ticket_
original work, history, background content_ theme, sub topic Song_ OST, features	poster leaflet ticket pamphlet	format content level quality	reservation by phone on the spot reservation group reservation reserved ticket invitation	receiving on the spot mail delivery storage
producer_ writer, director, lyricist, composer, choreographer cast_ actor, ensemble	banner footbridge signboard vehicle AD electronic display	production cast venue location		related purchase_ program book OST promotion products
scale	newspaper, magazine TV, Radio	seat		opera glasses rent
location characteristic				
venue, location theater structure seat arrangement parking lot additional facilities	official homepage Social Media affinity society fanclub personal blog	service prior knowledge expert evaluation		
schedule	rumor			
additional service				
Product Evaluation	Was the performance experience in consistent with the expected benefit? Did it satisfy the expectation?			

The standard for alternative evaluation is similar to the contents of information search, and table 4 shows the standard applied in previous studies.

Table 4. standard for alternative evaluation in previous studies

Author	Object	Standard
Kang and Lee (2001)	musical audience	cast, contents, summary, reputation of the work, nationality of the work, production and planning, admission fee, recommendation, venue, expert evaluation, sponsor
Kim, S., Kim, Y. and Kwak (2003)	audience	performance genre, characteristic of the work, selling point, additional service, venue, ticket price
Kolb (2004)	consumer	cost, value, satisfaction
Ko and Park (2008)	Musical performance audiences in online community	venue, seat, cast and director, performance genre and type, contents, previous knowledge on the performance, quality of the performance, ticket price, venue surroundings, customer service and management
Hyun and Kang (2012)	culture consumer	applying marketing 7P mix strategy price(admission fee, discount), promotion(convenient access to tickets, ADs), distribution(location accessibility), product(degree of completion, easy to understand, famous, creative), people(production crew, staff, actor), physical evidence(comfort of the seat, resting place, lighting, sound system, parking, performance facilities), process(program)

3.2   Flow Experience

Csikszentmihalyi(1975) first introduced the concept of flow, which is the mental state of operation in which a person performing an activity is fully immersed in a feeling of energized focus, full involvement, and enjoyment in the process of the activity.

Jee and Kim(2009) suggested a study model that broadly applies the background variables of flow, antecedent variables, and dependent variables of musical based on study done by Novak, Hoffman and Yung(2000), which is recognized as the key study model.

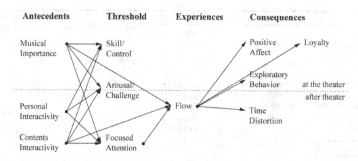

Fig. 1. Structural Model of Musical Audience's Flow Experience(Source: Jee and Kim, p. 107)

As the result, the model was tested holding musical involvement/importance, personal(audience) interactivity, contents interactivity as antecedents, skill/control, arousal/challenge, focused attention as threshold, and positive affect, exploratory behavior, time distortion as consequences. The flow in performance has impact on time distortion, positive affect, exploratory behavior and loyalty, and is affected by the importance, contents interactivity and focused attention. Contents interactivity is related to the connection between the audience and each elements of the musical which are script, lyrics, music, dance, direction, actor, and acting. In order to facilitate contents interactivity during the performance, the audience must be able to choose musicals matched their desired contents.

Because musical has high price level than other alternatives such as plays and movies, it is important that the audiences watch musicals that match their personal taste in order to for a pleasant experience of musical. Consumers usually watch musicals for pleasure and their standard for musical choice is convenience and cost, not professional knowledge. However, musical is an integrated stage art, and a lot of professional knowledge is needed to choose an appropriate musical for oneself, because the overall type of musical changes depending on the forms of musical elements such as script, lyric, music, dance, and direction. This makes it difficult for the each audience to choose the best musical experience that he or she prefers.

Moreover, consumer, fan, and those above cultists all have different eyes for a musical while all of these form characteristics of musical. Therefore, musical information is needed to find out what kind of people placed more importance on which characteristics, and to learn what their standards were.

3.3 The relationship between Musical Contents

Musical knowledge is divided according to different levels described below in table 5.

Table 5. Product Knowledge Level on Musical

Product Class	Product Form	Brand	Model/ Features	
Musical	Live	Producer	Book Show	Writer
	Live recording	Drama company	Concept musical	Composer
	Live concert	Concert hall	Dramacal	Lyricist
	Concert recording		Jukebox Musical	Director
	Musical movie		Moviecal	Choreographer
			Nonverbal performance	Actor
			Novelcal	Program
			Small theater musical	

Because musical has heterogeneity, same performance can give different impression depending on the actors. And different contents can give similar impressions when watching performances by same composer or actors. Thus, connections can be created in the process of forming musical experience from one musical to another. In other words, depending on the type of musical information contents, various relationships are possible between musicals and between contents.

For example, in 2012 Tom Hooper's Les Miserables was released in the Korean market. Before its release, the figure skating champion Kim Yuna used the song edited from the musical Les Miserables in her performance, which introduced Les Miserables to a large number of people. When the movie was released, the popularity of the premiere Korean musical Les Miserable which started before the release, increased. At the same time, the novel Les Miserables and its author Victor Hugo drew attention. Interest toward the musical numbers of Les Miserables increased, and numerous parodies were created, the most famous one being the Les Militaribles produced by air force band and media video team which hit 4 million views on Youtube.

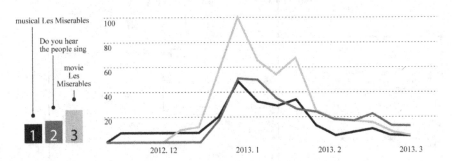

Fig. 2. Google Trend Search (musical, musical number, movie)

This can be observed in google trend search which helps comparing proportions of search words as well. This graph shows the ratio of search keywords in Korean google. Black(1) shows the musical Les Miserables, dark gray(2) represents famous one of the Les Miserables' musical number, and light gray(3) is the movie Les

Miserables. The frequency of searching the musical Les Miserables increased after the performance started in November. The movie Les Miserables was released on December 18th, and the frequency of searching for the movie increased in December, reaching its peak one week after the release. Although there was no significant change regarding the musical Les Miserables in the last week of December, the frequency for searching for it increased with the release of the movie. 'Do You Hear the People Sing' received the same level of attention as the musical Les Miserables during the same period. The middle of January, which is the second peak, is the time when Les Miserables OST won the first place in the weekly Billboard chart.

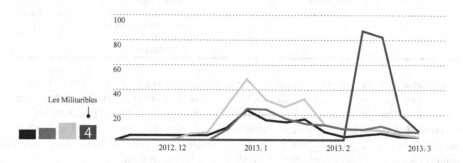

Fig. 3. Google Trend Search (musical, musical number, movie, parody)

Forth one represents Les Militaribles. The graph shows that after Les Militaribles was uploaded on Youtube, the frequency of the search for the musical, 'Do You Hear the People Sing', and the movie all increased. This shows that musical Les Miserables and its various contents were recognized in relation to each other. Thus musical information is more efficiently utilized when arranged together with structure.

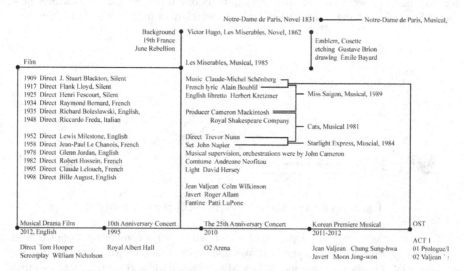

Fig. 4. Contents Map for Musical Les Miserables

As can be seen in figure 4, the musical Les Miserables is connected to premiere musical, Victor Hugo's original novel, OST, musical live concert video, Korean premiere musical and musical movie with same contents. The premiere musical Les Miserables is one of the big 4 which is comprised of Miss Saigon, Cats, and Phantom of the Opera, and can be connected to Miss Saigon by composer and lyricist, Cats and Starlight Express by stage and director. The original author Victor Hugo can be reached by three different types of translation in domestic market, and another dramatized work of his is Notre-dame de Paris. There are two types of the musical concert Les Miserables: the 10th anniversary and the 25th anniversary version. The movie Les Miserables can be compared to other movies that were previously filmed.

Accordingly, people who are interested in the musical Les Miserables can broaden their understanding of it or expand their interest to other works by taking those routes mentioned above. Figure 4 shows twice contents expansions from the elements of the original musical Les Miserables as the base. Because the standards are the musical elements, this data shows the audience's expansion of knowledge on the musical. If the producer was the standard and the contents expansion is progressed without setting limits, the information structure of the relationship between musicals of different producers can be found. Depending on the standards, the contents expansion can happen not only between musicals but also novels, movies, concert videos, OST, historical backgrounds, and etc.

4   Conclusion

This study defined and arranged elements that affect musical experience formation model and musical experience in various perspectives. It started from the effort to understand the experience of the audience by arranging them in the perspective of service design thinking. Then, it found the context existing in the relationship between purchase level, flow experience process, and contents relationship of the musical experience service, and visualized them in material form after arranging them. This expands the range of service design thinking to musical experience which is a form of popular arts, and can be used as basis for finding directions in understanding musical art management in design perspective through expansion of integrated thinking.

This study has two limitations. Although elements of musical experience were analyzed, whether each elements have meaningful effect on consumer experience formation when such relationship was formed, or whether there are meaningful or meaningless elements depending on the type of the consumer are not verified through experiments. Therefore, additional study on the definition and application of elements is needed.

Moreover, although this data was compiled by applying service design perspective, only surface levels are dealt with, without considering the psychology of the audience toward each situations or background to each experience situation. Thus, only basic parts of the study for applying service design to art management.

References

1. Choi, S.Y.: A Study on Aspects of the Performance of Musical Theatre in Korea from 1990 to 2000. Journal of Korean Theater Studies Association 29, 263–291 (2006)
2. Hyun, J., Kang, S.K.: Market Segmentation for Culture Facilities According to Culture Consumption Pattern and Lifestyle. Review of Cultural Economics 15(20), 79–101 (2012)
3. Jee, J.E., Kim, S.Y.: A Study on the Structural Model of Flow Experience Among Musical Audience 2(12), 87–114 (2009)
4. Kang, G.D., Lee, J.H.: An Exploratory Study on the Life-style of Audience for Culture and Art Performance. Korean Management Review 30(4), 1143–1167 (2001)
5. Kim, S.Y., Kim, Y.J., Kwak, Y.S.: Marketing Segmentation by Mixture Model for Cultural & Art Institutions. The Korean Journal of Advertising 14(5), 49–74 (2003)
6. Kim, Y.J.: Service Innovation, Way to dominate the Market. Dong-A Business Review 28, 66–69 (2009)
7. Ko, J.M., Park, S.Y.: Analysis in Community Activities and Watching Behavior of Musical Performance Audiences in Online Community. Review of Cultural Economics 11(1), 33–59 (2008)
8. Lee, S.Y.: A Study on Role Adjustment and Combination in Korean Performing Arts. Review of Cultural Economics 5(2), 23–45 (2002)
9. Park, S.E.: Arts & Cultural Management, Prospective View in 21st Century of Theoretical Basis and Practice. Journal of Arts and Cultural Management 1, 205–214 (2008)
10. Abercrombie, N., Longhurst, B.: Audiences: A Sociological Theory of Performance and Imagination. Sage, London (1998)
11. Csikszentmihalyi, M.: Beyond Boredom and Anxiety: Experiencing Flow in Work and Play. Jossey-Bass, San Francisco (1975)
12. Jang, H.J.: Performance Planning. In: Lee, G.S., Lee, S.H. (eds.) Performing Art. Geulnuri, Daejeon (2007)
13. Jeon, S.H.: Performance Planning Handbook. Jeyoung Communications, Seoul (1999)
14. Kolb, B.M.: Marketing Cultural Organizations, Oak Tree, Cork (2000)
15. Lamb, C., Hair, J., McDaniel, C.: Essentials of Marketing. Southwestern College Publishing (1999)
16. Lee, I.G.: Management of Performing Arts. Adbooks, Seoul (2009)
17. Stickdorn, M., Schneider, J. (eds.): This is Service Design Thinking. BIS, Amsterdam (2011)
18. Yong, H.S.: Arts Management. Gimmyoung, Paju (2010)
19. Google Trend, http://www.google.com/trends/explore?hl=ko#q=%EB%AE%A4%EC%A7%80%EC%BB%AC%20%EB%A0%88%EB%AF%B8%EC%A0%9C%EB%9D%BC%EB%B8%94%2C%20do%20you%20hear%20the%20people%20sing%2C%20%EC%98%81%ED%99%94%20%EB%A0%88%EB%AF%B8%EC%A0%9C%EB%9D%BC%EB%B8%94&geo=KR&date=11%2F2012%205m&cmpt=q
20. Interpark Performance Settlement of Accounts, http://incorp.interpark.com/communication/PressNewsListMgt.do?_method=list
21. Service Design Council, http://www.servicedesign.or.kr

Investigation of Interaction Modalities Designed for Immersive Visualizations Using Commodity Devices in the Classroom

Kira Lawrence[1], Alisa Maas[2], Neera Pradhan[1], Treschiel Ford[3],
Jacqueline Shinker[1], and Amy Ulinski Banic[1]

[1] University of Wyoming, Dept. 3315, 1000 E. University Ave, Laramie WY, 82071
[2] Wheaton College, 501 College Ave Wheaton, IL 60187
[3] Alabama A&M University, 4900 Meridian Street North, Huntsville, AL 35810-1015
{klawren2,jshinker,abanic}@uwyo.edu, npradhan0603@gmail.com,
Alisa.Maas@my.wheaton.edu, treschielford@live.com

Abstract. In this paper we present initial research of the investigation in the design collaborative interaction modalities for classroom-based immersive visualizations of 3D spatial data, with an initial implementation for geo-spatial applications. Additionally we allowed some pilot testing to gain a sense of our design decisions and where user error might occur. Valuable feedback will allow us to redesign and refine implementation for a much more formal long-term evaluation of the system. Initial results give indications that our interaction modalities may facilitate teaching and learning, but the use of devices should be different for user type.

Keywords: Immersive Visualization, 3D User Interfaces, Collaborative Interaction, Classroom, Geospatial data, and GeoWALL.

1 Introduction and Motivation

The field of Visualization was described as transferring the symbolic into the geometric, enabling researchers to observe their simulations and computations [6]. The goal of visualization is to leverage existing scientific methods by providing new scientific insight through visual methods. Visualizations have been and are continuing to be developed for many different fields and purposes, such as medical research and procedure assistance, biological research, physical sciences, engineering, geosciences, security, business, and education. For education purposes, visualizations offer insight, many visualization applications are being used for discovery and learning in the classroom. Additionally, it has been shown that immersive visualizations provide facilitate discovery and allow for better workflow [8,10]. Immersive 3D visualization has been promoted by geoscientists to understand the physical world because of its positive impact on understanding the phenomenon for geoscientists as well as any novice user with minimal information [12]. One example of an immersive visualization for educational purposes is the use of a GeoWall, a large polarization-based passive, or not

A. Marcus (Ed.): DUXU/HCII 2013, Part II, LNCS 8013, pp. 209–218, 2013.

head-tracked, dual projector-based stereoscopic or immersive display, for the pur-
posed of teaching geographical concepts, with interactivity of real-time data exploration being a crucial aspect [5]. A Geowall is a stereoscopic display system built by
collaboration between computer science and geoscience to help in understanding the
spatial relationships in the study of earth sciences.

One possible issue with this system is that there are particular limitations in interaction with this display. Typically these systems are used by one user, usually the
instructor. This creates a problem if the instructor wishes to allow the students to explore the visualizations for themselves rather than driven by the instructor. The other
issue is that some devices and interaction may cause reduced usage due to the complexity of 3D interaction. As a result more investigation is needed for solving similar
collaboration issues in interaction. Additionally, once allowing for collaboration in
interaction, other issues present themselves, such as cost of multiple devices, interaction techniques that facilitate collaboration, how to mitigate turn taking or should
simultaneous interaction be permitted. Several researches have shown that similar
immersive display technologies are better utilized depending on interaction techniques [7, 14]. Also, according to the NIH/NSF visualization research challenges
report in 2006, designing effective visualizations is a complex process that requires a
sophisticated understanding of human information processing capabilities, outlining
interaction as one of the main areas where visualization research needs to focus [6].
There is a need then for the development and evaluation of general interaction techniques that can be applied to broader categories of visualization applications. In this
research, we will focus mainly on collaborative interaction for scientific visualizations, using climate visualizations as a test case, for classroom usage. In this paper,
we propose initial designs of interaction modalities, such as multiple views, independent navigation and selection tasks, and multiple cursors, for the use of immersive
visualizations in learning environments such as learning geo-spatial concepts on
the GeoWall. We additionally present some insights gathered while pilot testing our
initial prototype implementation.

2   Background and Related Work

2.1   GeoWall

In 2001, the GeoWall project found that the building GeoWalls in university classrooms aided introductory students with understanding new concepts [5]. Students
displayed 3D immersive models both in class and for projects. The GeoWalls were
also found to be incredibly helpful for demonstrating complex processes to the
general public. A GeoWall is comprised of a large silver screen that faces two projectors. The projectors are aligned so that both images pass through a polarized filter and
then overlap on the screen. This filtering matches polarized glasses to filter out images from either the right or left eye, similar to the passive, stereoscopic setup used in
commercial movies and amusement park attractions.

Fig. 1. a) View of GeoWall configuration at WyGISC at the University of Wyoming. b) View of students wearing polarized glasses in the classroom to be able to see the images on GeoWall.

2.2   3D Input

GeoWall has been proven successful at other universities and has proven itself an important tool for viewing 3D data [5], and there have been an extensive number of studies done on suitable input devices for 3D environments [1, 9, 15, 16]. Devices with six degrees of freedom such as 3D mice, wands, and gloves have been tested in a variety of computer applications for their ability to navigate and manipulate a 3D scene. However, no single device has been shown to be superior for 3D applications[3]. Considering low-cost robust options for our system, we investigated a Nintendo Wii Remote as input devices for classroom use with the immersive display. Nintendo Wii Remote, or Wiimote, is one input device that has been growing in popularity to be used. Wii Remotes have been implemented as computer mice before [13]. Additionally they have been studied by many as input for interaction with 3D and immersive environments [4, 9, 13, 15]. Research showed that using Wiimote as a mouse to operate is viable approach and supports multiple interactions. It is cheap, affordable and offers as reliable hardware for input interaction. Other research has shown that 2D devices can perform adequately in a 3D environment when using them with a limited scope of options and navigation [11].

3   System Framework

For our system, we chose a Nintendo Wii Remote as our input device. We used the remote as a 2D mouse, with button-mapped tasks that were specific for use in ArcScene. Furthermore, 3D tasks could be mapped to the accerometer input from the device. Our implementation utilized both the Wii Remote and the Nunchuk as a single asymmetric bimanual device. Since we wanted interaction to be able to be utilized in a standard way across multiple applications, we used an input emulator rather than handling all of the Wii Remote events directly. By using an emulator, we could easily adapt our existing code for more applications, allowing more departments to use our interface within their programs with little to no consultation.

Fig. 2. An example view of visualization of 3D geo-spatial data

3.1   Software

The GeoWall at the University of Wyoming makes use of ArcGIS Desktop 10.0 geographical information software to view the data. In particular, our case study focused on the use of ArcScene, since it is capable of creating and processing 3D visualization data and was used heavily in one of the classes for visualization examples, where in the future we could likely conduct an evaluation in this type of class.

ArcScene is a program that is heavily dependent on mouse input. We decided to use the Nunchuk joystick to control the cursor rather than the Wii Remote's motion sensing capabilities, and rather reserve that for other tasks. This made the implementation similar to the mouse and cursor setup that faculty would be accustomed to while optimizing the button layout for the program. By using the joystick, we also eliminated the repetitive wrist movements from constantly clicking and dragging an object in ArcScene, and can cause discomfort and fatigue.

3.2   Input Devices

Selecting a suitable input device was an important factor in this project because it needed to be robust, flexible, cheap, and duplicable for use in the classroom setting. It was also critical that our device was both as accessible to faculty as possible while still functioning within ArcScene. We took the environment in consideration as well, examining the range, portability, and extensibility the device had for multiple users. Based on these criteria, we determined that a gesture recognition device, such as a Kinect, may not have been the best solution for this particular case study. In a classroom setting where number of students can be large and only a limited open space may be available within the classroom, gesture recognition may become less accurate as we engage multiple students to interact. Such a device requires exaggerated body movements from the user, and becomes tiring after long periods of use. Since typical classroom usage could require anywhere from fifty minutes to two and a half hours, we determined this type of device would be unsuitable for this purpose. In some cases, a device of this nature may require the user to be interacting in a limited line-of-sight range directly in front of it. Also, a user may unconsciously gesture when using the GeoWall, causing the device to read extraneous input and alter the scene without the user's intent. An example is that an instructor may use hand gestures while lecturing which may causes recognition errors or require mechanisms to switch modes. Also, since we wanted users to use devices efficiently without much training, we found a gesture-based input device problematic in this setting for the following reasons: 1) Users would not be aware of which gestures could be interpreted as commands. 2) Therefore, users would more likely to require extensive training and a manual to understand the controls. This may make the system appear more, not less, complicated.

Another category of input device we investigated but decided it also would not be sufficient for our needs was a standard game controller. A typical device of this category has more buttons and control options than needed for this case study, and appeared complex to novice users based on initial pilot testing. As a result, we believed faculty might feel overwhelmed by this controller and have difficulty remembering where functions were mapped. These issues may increase cognitive load, and therefore decrease insight and learning, which is counterproductive to the purpose of the GeoWall. Ultimately, we selected the Nintendo Wii Remote to serve as the input device for the GeoWall in this context. The Wii Remote had fewer buttons and joysticks, making the setup easier for the users to understand and remember. The Wii Remote does not confine lecturing faculty to specific regions of the classroom, and does not require extreme gestures as input.

Another category we considered were natural user interface based controllers, such as a Nintendo Wii Remote. It is a low cost, easy to use, hand held device that can be used and well-suited for an immersive environment [13]. This device may be more suited for classroom use, because of small localized area of control, intuitiveness, affordability, and flexibility in control. However, a Wiimote sensor was not accurate to use as mouse cursor movements because of its sensitivity and error. For user convenience, we found that Nunchuk works more effective as mouse. Then, we decided to choose Nunchuk to emulate mouse buttons because it was easier to map the cursor movement with joystick and we could do it with more accuracy than with Wiimote sensor movement.

3.3   Input Mapping

We used Glove Programmable Input Emulator (GlovePIE) for mapping button presses and other actions to keyboard keys, mouse input or joystick buttons. A Targus Bluetooth dongle was used to enable a wireless connection between the device and the system to be used throughout the classroom. This Bluetooth device is capable of locating and connecting to up to four Nintendo Wii Remotes at a time. With ArcScene open, an image could be panned up, down, left, and right by pressing the corresponding direction on the Wii Remote's directional pad. Additionally, the accelerometer could be used for more generalized gross changes in orientation, while the buttons could be used for more precise navigation.

Initially, we implemented the mapping for Wiimote buttons A and B as mouse left and right click respectively. However, we decided this setup was unintuitive after several pilot trials and user feedback. As a result, we then mapped Nunchuk Z and C as mouse left click and right click respectively, as it is convenient for users to have mouse click buttons on the same device. The plus and minus buttons on either side of the remote changed cursor sensitivity, while the "A" button re-centered, resized, and repositioned the scene back to its default view. The "Home" button in the center of the Wii Remote created two new window views of the scene. The new viewers were quickly set to stereo display, sized, and positioned across both monitors so that the screen holds two separate 3D views of an image that can be manipulated separately. The following provides an overview of the subset of commands in ArcScene that were implemented with Wiimote buttons:

Wiimote A	*= reset image*
Nunchuk C + Nunchuk Joystick	*= zooming*
Nunchuk Z + Nunchuk Joystick	*= rotation*
Wiimote Home	*= setting window viewers*
Wiimote 1	*= Exit Program*
Wiimote DPad	*= panning (Single Wiimote)*
Nunchuk Joystick	*= mouse*

When doing pilot testing, we did not discuss the mappings, but rather let the user investigate and learn the tasks in relation to the performed action.

Fig. 3. Image of user with input device while interacting with multiple views of the immersive visualization

4   Collaborative Interaction

Our goal was to facilitate collaborative interaction with a GeoWall for the classroom use. We first needed to address the need for multiple camera projections of the same data to facilitate independent exploration. We therefore designed and implemented our interaction techniques to activate multiple windows in ArcScence with Wiimote Home button. We made use of Desktop's multiple viewers to make this possible.

We set up the Home button on the Wii Remote to open two viewers, position and size them ideally for 3D, and set the viewing mode in stereo. This way the instructor would be capable of opening and positioning the viewers for multiple students instantly, rather than being required to manually set them up. Our intention is doing this is to provide the instructor with a way of involving the students more directly in the learning process.

Next, we needed to address the problem of users' input competing for mouse pointer usage, where in these applications many of the tasks were dependent on. GlovePIE makes it possible to add FakeCursors, which look and behave, for the most part, like regular cursors. Using Glovepie, we created an imitation cursor that can move and work independent of the real cursor. As a result, multiple windows using two Wiimotes could be interactively updated simultaneously. With multiple cursors and windows, instructors can interact in a window to explain one concept while a group of students can interact with another window freely to explore the visualization, with the potential of "just-in-time" active learning. There were no conflicts between two Wiimotes for any button press except for panning. For some reason, panning did not work as smooth as with the mouse and the images appear to flicker and sometimes disappear from the screen. Our reasoning behind this was that input from multiple cursors was taken into account and the ArcScene used both inputs to get the median value to position the graphics which caused a few registration errors. Another challenge was that since the software was not equipped to manage multiple sources of input at once, some functionality had to be removed from the second user. We intended the secondary capabilities to be used with the instructor as primary controller, while students had a sub-set of actions they could perform, though sufficient for exploration.

5   Initial Pilot Testing

In pilot testing, we asked several instructors and students involved with the project to try out our interaction modalities: three instructors and six students provided feedback. For instructors, we wanted to gauge the usability of the system we created. We adapted questions from the System Usability Scale (SUS) and tailored them to fit with our system characteristics [2]. As they used the system, we allowed participants in the evaluation to hold the Wii Remote in any hand they were comfortable with. We noticed those familiar with the Wii Remote tended to hold the Nunchuk in the non-dominant hand, as is typical in Wii games; and those unfamiliar with the console preferred to hold the Nunchuk in the dominant hand. We provided participants with a sheet that provided the information for what each button did. After the participants were comfortable for using buttons, we gave them break 5 to 10 minutes. Then, we brought them back into Geowall room to explore use of interaction modalities without the information sheet. When they felt they had used all the buttons possible, we asked them to fill out a post evaluation form. We also conducted an open interview with them to get more detailed answers to word questions. Responses to each statement were given on a likert-type scale of one to seven, with one indicating strong disagreement, and seven indicating strong agreement. Four was a neutral response. These responses were then categorized and averaged across respondents to obtain a rating for each usability criterion.

Table 1. Pilot Testing Results on subjective rating scales from 1 to 7, with higher ratings reflecting a more positive response

	Instructors	Students
Efficiency	4.00+/-0.82	4.05+/-1.36
Ease of Use	3.82+/-1.85	4.68+/-1.16
Learnability	3.88+/-1.72	3.87+/-1.50
Errors/Problems	6.33+/-0.47	4.25+/-1.79

5.1   Discussion

The initial results from instructors' feedback are presented in Table 1. Instructor ratings were much lower than we had expected. We believe the instructor scores were lower for several reasons. 1) 2 out of the 3 faculty member participants had never seen a Wii Remote before. Therefore, they were unfamiliar where the buttons were located. Instructors had difficulty understanding and remembering where the buttons were located. This would lead to lower scores in Ease of Use, Learnability, and User Comfort. 2) Due to time constraints, we were only able to find 3 faculty participants, meaning the scores are not a good representation of other faculty members. 3) Also at times there was some interference with Bluetooth, so as a result we may need to implement a more robust solution for the connectivity. Overall, we were able to conclude that efficiency, ease of use, comfort, and learnability scores were neutral for instructors. Instructors thought the use of multiple views and control for the students were a good idea, so as to describe concepts while the students could see multiple aspects of the visualization at one time. Geo-spatial concepts could particularly benefit from this type of exploration since not all components when explaining a particular concept can be seen in one static view.

The initial results from students' feedback are presented in Table 1. We found higher results of usability for students. We believe that results for ease of use, learnability and user comfort were higher due to familiarity with Wiimotes. Students welcomed the idea of not only using 3D visualizations on this type of display more often, but thought the idea of having additional control over what they were seeing could be beneficial for learning. However, there was some concern over if they would need to take turns with other groups.

6   Conclusion

In conclusion, we present initial research in the investigation of collaborative interaction modalities for classroom-based immersive visualizations of 3D spatial data, with an initial implementation for geo-spatial applications. Additionally we allowed some pilot testing to gain a sense of our design decisions and where user error might occur.

Valuable feedback will allow us to redesign and refine implementation for a much more formal long-term evaluation of the system. In conclusion, faculty had difficulty with the devices, but valued the interaction capabilities for multiple users. Students have less difficulty, possibly due to familiarity with the system. Students also were concerned about having to take turns to control the visualization. Use of the Wiimote facilitates students' engagement but lead to frustration for instructors, so there is a possibility of using focused devices for the user type.

7   Future Work

An immediate step would be to revise the interaction mappings according to the feedback provided, such as adjustments to zooming and panning. Additionally, we shall refine the collaborative techniques and conduct a long term user study with actual usage in a classroom that typically utilizes these types of visualizations in an immersive environment. Since the Bluetooth used only supports up to four input devices and the visual display is limited in the number of separate views we can provide, we will investigate groups of student users. Also, we could compare with other input devices in order to provide a usability benchmark. We can evaluate whether any enhanced learning occurs as the result of our interaction system. Long term we plan to investigate interaction techniques and other hardware solutions which will allow multi-user collaboration without multiple divided views.

Acknowledgements. This work was supported in part by, the CRA-W Distributed Research Experiences for Undergraduates (DREU) and the University of Wyoming EPSCoR Research Experiences for Undergraduates (REU) programs. Also, a special thanks to the University of Wyoming Geographic Information Science Center (Wy-GISC) for permitting usage of their GeoWall facility and providing valuable initial feedback on our system.

References

1. Ardito, C., Buono, P., Costabile, M.F., Lanzilotti, R., Simeone, A.L.: Comparing low cost input devices for interacting with 3D Virtual Environments. In: 2nd Conference on Human System Interactions, HSI 2009., May 21-23, pp. 292–297 (2009)
2. Brooke, J.: SUS: a "quick and dirty" usability scale. In: Jordan, P.W., Thomas, B., Weerdmeester, B.A., McClelland, A.L. (eds.) Usability Evaluation in Industry. Taylor and Francis, London (1996)
3. Frohlich, B., Hochstrate, J., Kulik, A., Huckauf, A.: On 3D input devices. IEEE Computer Graphics and Applications 26(2), 15–19 (2006)
4. Gallo, L., Ciampi, M.: Wii Remote-enhanced Hand-Computer interaction for 3D medical image analysis. In: 2009 International Conference on the Current Trends in Information Technology (CTIT), December 15-16, pp. 1–6 (2009)
5. Johnson, A., Leigh, J., Morin, P., Van Keken, P.: Geowall: Stereoscopic Visualization for Geoscience Research and Education. IEEE Computer Graphics and Applications 26(6), 10–14 (2006)

6. Johnson, C., Moorhead, R., Munzner, T., Pfister, H., Rheingans, P., Yoo, T.S.: NIH/NSF Visualization Research Challenges Report. IEEE Press (2006)
7. Marcio, S., Pinho, D.A.: Bowman, and Carla M.D.S. Freitas. 2002. Cooperative object manipulation in immersive virtual environments: framework and techniques. In: Proceedings of the ACM Symposium on Virtual Reality Software and Technology (VRST 2002), pp. 171–178. ACM, New York (2002)
8. Prabhat, A.F., Katzourin, M., Wharton, K., Slater, M.: A Comparative Study of Desktop, Fishtank, and Cave Systems for the Exploration of Volume Rendered Confocal Data Sets. IEEE Transactions on Visualization and Computer Graphics 14(3), 551–563 (2008)
9. Santos, B.S., Prada, B., Ribeiro, H., Dias, P., Silva, S., Ferreira, C.: Wiimote as an Input Device in Google Earth Visualization and Navigation: A User Study Comparing Two Alternatives. In: 2010 14th International Conference on Information Visualisation (IV), July 26-29, pp. 473–478 (2010)
10. Sherman, W.R., O'Leary, P., Kreylos, O., Brady, R.: IEEE Visualization 2008 Conference Workshop on Scientific Workflow with Immersive Interfaces for Visualization, Columbus, OH, October 19-24 (2008); DVD
11. Teather, R.J., Stuerzlinger, W.: Assessing the Effects of Orientation and Device on 3D Positioning. In: IEEE Virtual Reality Conference, VR 2008, March 8-12, pp. 293–294 (2008)
12. Terrington, R., Napier, B., Howard, A., Ford, J., Hatton, W.: Why 3D? The Need for Solution Based Modeling in a National Geoscience Organization, May 7. AIP Conference Proceedings (serial online), vol. 1009(1), pp. 103–112 (2008)
13. Yang, Y., Li, L.: Turn a Nintendo Wiimote into a Handheld Computer Mouse. IEEE Potentials 30(1), 12–16 (2011)
14. Kitamura, Y., Konishi, T., Yamamoto, S., Kishino, F.: Interactive stereoscopic display for three or more users. In: Proceedings of the 28th Annual Conference on Computer Graphics and Interactive Techniques (SIGGRAPH 2001), pp. 231–240. ACM, New York (2001)
15. Wingrave, C.A., Williamson, B., Varcholik, P.D., Rose, J., Miller, A., Charbonneau, E., Bott, J., LaViola Jr., J.J.: The Wiimote and Beyond: Spatially Convenient Devices for 3D User Interfaces. IEEE Computer Graphics and Applications 30(2), 71–85 (2010)
16. Zhang, S., Overholt, M., Gerard, J., Striegel, A.: WiiDoRF: Decision and recording framework for educational labs centered on the Nintendo Wiimote. In: 2010 IEEE Frontiers in Education Conference (FIE), October 27-30, pp. S1F-1–S1F-6 (2010)

Legibility in Children's Reading:
The Methodological Development of an Experiment
for Reading Printed and Digital Texts

Daniel Lourenço[1] and Solange Coutinho[2]

[1] IFPB, Design Dept. João Pessoa-PB, Brazil
[2] UFPE, Design Dept. Recife-PE, Brazil
lourencodesign@yahoo.com.br, solangecoutinho@globo.com

Abstract. The aim of the present article is to address a number of essential questions regarding children reading printed and digital texts. The objective is to develop a methodological procedure with children in the 3rd year of the 1st Cycle in Municipal Schools in the city of João Pessoa, in Paraíba, Brazil. The experiments have been produced to be implemented in schools. In Brazil, the subject of digital artifacts is still regarded as being precarious; however, the children surveyed have experience with digital artifacts and digital reading.

Keywords: legibility, children's reading, experiment for reading.

1 Introduction

The present article presents part of an ongoing research project, which with experimental activities, sets out to assess the manner in which children read printed and digital textbooks.

The general aim of the research is to: develop an experimental methodology for children in the 3rd year of the 1st Educational Cycle in Brazilian state schools, in order to analyse the legibility of printed and digital texts (especially the use of infant fonts and of cursive style calligraphy) so that in the future, with the obtained results, this may contribute to the creation of favourable conditions for reading children's textbooks.

Although there are few studies regarding legibility in children's printed books, for Brazilian readers, this study has elected to focus on two types of reading (printed and digital). The main reason for this particular choice is that the Brazilian state school education authorities are increasingly adopting digital media, however printed artifacts will continue in use for a long time to come.

According to the Ministry of Education (MEC), with the aim of enabling all students to access technology, in 2012 the Federal Government distributed 600 thousand tablets to 58 thousand high schools, which were part of the Proinfo programme [8]. Moreover, according to government sources, once teachers and students have signed a liability waiver, they will be allowed to take their tablets home.

A. Marcus (Ed.): DUXU/HCII 2013, Part II, LNCS 8013, pp. 219–228, 2013.

Therefore, there is strong evidence to suggest that the use of digital artifacts in Brazilian classrooms is becoming a reality. Thus, research on legibility involving both children and digital books has become indispensable, in order to discover the real needs of children with regard to reading texts in these types of media.

2   Some Questions

A number of questions warrant special attention and should serve to support the development of this study (Figure 1): **If children are becoming increasingly familiar with digital texts, does this signify that the use of infant fonts (Figure 1) will no longer assist in improving children's reading skills?**

Fig. 1. Adult and infant fonts. (Source: Author)

With the frequent use of digital reading both in schools and in the everyday lives of those learning to read, would it be correct to state that cursive style calligraphy is no longer favourable to reading? Especially since, in the first cycle (1st to 3rd years) of Brazilian state schools, children still learn to read and write with the cursive style (Figure 2).

Fig. 2. Cursive style fonts. (Source: Authors)

3   Typography for Children

The main issue raised by researchers [15], [16] is that, decisions regarding parameters for children are made by adults, whether educators, with no particular knowledge concerning the design of letters, or designers, who tend to focus on aesthetic issues rather than the perception and interests of children.

There are a number of studies related to the specific development of types for children's learning, such as regular fonts that accompany the natural forms of the letters. [5]

Miranda & Vasconcelos, in their research of collecting and analysing textbooks, indicated that two problems were observed regarding the typography adopted for textbooks, such as: the use of different types, with or without serifs, as well as many variations of upper and lowercase, italics, amongst others. [9]

3.1   Legibility

This study has adopted the consensus that the term legibility refers both to the form of the letters, i.e., to recognising an individual font, as much as to the spacing between the lines, the letters and the words, which is related to the empty spaces between the lines, the letters and the words. There is also a relationship with the speed of reading, environmental factors, such as tiredness of the reader, as well as cultural aspects and the reader's skills and experience [17], [6], [3], [2], [12].

When the target is children, more specific features become involved, such as wider spacing, larger sizes of typographic font, and other determinations. It is recommended that the different needs of children and word spacing should be taken into account and a justified text should only be employed if it is absolutely necessary. In research with young readers the importance of consistent spacing is extremely relevant[16].

4   Digital Reading

Reading e-books is far more dynamic than reading printed books. The e-book may contain several layers, arranged in a pyramid. Readers can either read superficially or may explore the content more extensively. [4]

The relationship that a digital book proposes, even if virtual, promotes learning, as it allows the reader to act on the content, thus enabling a dialogue with the text [13].

However, other aspects should be considered when reading on the web. Inappropriate reading through hypertexts may cause the hyperreader to lose concentration, since it is possible to become lost in the midst of so many nodes and links, which may then cause the reader to become distressed and therefore abandon the text. [18].

It may be perceived that there is a greater freedom in reading digital artifacts. However, Xavier indicates that this freedom is not ideal, since it is the e-text producer who decides whether to make links with other hypertexts available or not (XAVIER, 2002: 173). [19]

Certain disagreements exist among researchers regarding the legibility of text in digital artifacts. Some authors (ALMEIDA,[1]; ROUET[14]; NIELSEN [11]) emphasize that reading digital artifacts may be considered more tiring, and results in lower levels of comprehension. Others (VENKITESHWAR M. SUBBARAM [18]; Muter & MARUTTO [10] on the whole, do not confirm that reading on a screen is necessarily slower or more tiring than reading printed material.

5   Methodological Development

Specifications for the implementation of the experiment were prepared from visits to four municipal schools in the city of João Pessoa, in the state of Paraíba, Brazil.

The expectation was to encounter children who were just beginning to read. However, the ideal situation would involve children who were already able to read whole words and not syllable by syllable. According to the teachers surveyed, this stage of reading would be expected in the 3rd year of the 1st Cycle (In Brazil, the State School

Education system is divided into Cycles. In the first cycle, which is the research object of this study, pupils are not allowed to fail. Thus, in any same year it is possible to encounter pupils from different levels attempting to achieve reading.) in Brazilian state schools, with children aged eight years. Below is a brief description on each school visited:

- **1st School: Colégio Frei Albino (Municipal school from 1st to 5th year)**

At this school, the average number of pupils per class is 25. The mean age in the third year is between 7/8 years and in the 4th year is 9 years. However, it is important to highlight that age differences can exist in the same year, and it would be essential to triage in order to conduct the legibility study, so that no discrepancies appear in the results.

One important aspect cited by the teachers, is that textbooks are supplied by a number of different publishers across the country, and it is left to the teachers to select books for the children from a government provided list. Teachers may select books from different publishers for the same year.

It should be emphasized that photographs were taken of various books from several different publishers in order to assess the relationship of the text on the pages of the different publications, as well as to decide if there are any major differences between one publisher and another with regard to layout. Below is an example (Figure 3):

Fig. 3. Example of a page from a 2nd year book. (Source: Author)

With regard to the picture below, it is important to mention the views put forward by teachers, and which were unanimous. In the 1st year, children learn to write in uppercase and soon after begin to develop the act of reading and writing with cursive letters. However, soon into the 2nd year, books feature lowercase typography. Teachers reported that pupils encounter great difficulties in reading and writing with this type of letter, since they are accustomed to uppercase, cursive letters. One further highlighted aspect was the whiteboard on which teachers write in the classrooms, and that directly influences the manner in which the children read and write. As in the example below (Figure 4):

Fig. 4. Example of a whiteboard for a 2nd year class where the teacher is using cursive writing. (Source: Author)

With respect to digital reading, teachers have reported that the Government has not yet supplied the tablets. However, according to teachers, students have daily experience with computers in the computer lab at school, with many different activities, and all students have access to computers at home, therefore illustrating the facility with which pupils have contact with the digital artifact.

- **2nd School: Escola Municipal de Ensino Fundamental Nazinha Barbosa**

At the second school, the average number of pupils was the same as the first, 25 per class. The teachers surveyed reported that second year students tend to read syllable-by-syllable and with no fluency. This fluency then appears during the 3rd year, when they are able to read short lines with little difficulty. Many of the aspects cited were very similar to those of the previous school.

During the 2nd year, lowercase typography begins to appear, and is one of the teachers' most common complaints. However, by the third year, lowercase typography has become more familiar to the young readers.

- **3rd School: Escola Estadual Dona Alice Carneiro**

Until this point, visits to collect data had taken place at municipal schools. However, in order to verify the reading conditions of schools under the state authority of Paraíba, a visit was undertaken to Escola Estadual Dona Alice Carneiro.

Once again, teachers reported similar conditions to those working in the municipal schools: an average of 20/25 pupils per class; difficulties during the 2nd year with lowercase; computer lab facilities provided by the school and that children have experience with computers and digital reading both in school and at home and the manner in which the teacher writes on the whiteboard has significant influence on how children learn to read and write.

However, teachers reported that the schools run by the state government receive less financial support, which was the justification for the shortage of textbooks in the school.

- **4th School: Escola Municipal Silvana Oliveira Pontes**

This school is located in the district of Cabedelo, in the metropolitan region of João Pessoa.

This school also presents some of the previous occurrences encountered in other schools: teachers are permitted to select textbook publishers, therefore, in any one year there may be books from different publishers. The average number of pupils per class is 20. Teachers reported difficulties encountered by 2nd year pupils in relation to lowercase, and that from the 3rd year these children manage to stop reading syllable by syllable. In the 3rd year, children present a mean age of 8 years, which refers to the research object of this study. This school does not have a computer lab on its premises.

6   The Digital Textbook

Although most of the schools surveyed do not have digital textbooks, it is perceived, based on the opinions of teachers, that children interact with computers both at school and at home.

In Brazil, a number of publishers already offer digital textbooks. The aspect of the page in a digital book has continued the same as in the printed book. There has merely been a shift from one medium to another. Therefore, both the font and page layout have remained similar to printed books. Hence, when conducting the reading study with children, the tests will be the same, and the only change will be from one medium to another (from printed medium to digital). Below is a sample page from a digital textbook for the 2nd year of the 1st cycle (Figure 5).

Fig. 5. Detail of text from a 2nd-year digital textbook. (Source: Author)

7   Methodology

At the schools visited (4 in total) the average number of pupils per class is 20/25. Therefore, it was decided that the number of participants for each variable would be 25 pupils. There is a total of 2 variables: infant fonts and cursive style calligraphy.

The study groups have been divided as follows: Group 1: Digital text with infant fonts, Group 2: Printed text with infant fonts; Group 3: Digital text without infant texts; Group 4: Printed text without infant texts; Group 5: Digital text with cursive style calligraphy; Group 6: Printed text with cursive style calligraphy; Group 7: Digital text without cursive style calligraphy and Group 8: Printed text printed without cursive style calligraphy.

The assessment methods selected for the experiment are: quantity of work, errors and the opinions of readers. Below is a brief explanation of each methodological tool:

Quantity of Work: This technique may be summarized as the measurement of a reading performance through the amount of text read in a given time. Following this, questions are posed in order to assess comprehension of the text. From all tests involving legibility, this comes closest to what could be considered ideal, by demonstrating greater validity, assessing the effect of typographical aspects in real situations. [7]

Errors: Counting and analyzing the errors are also assessment criteria used in studies that seek to measure legibility [15].The number of errors is important in methodological development to reveal where and when children experience most difficulty in reading. **Opinion of the readers:** Generally, in qualitative research, the opinion of the research participant is sought through interviews or questionnaires [15]

The texts for the tests were created from the textbooks used in schools. The layout of the texts will be taken into consideration and maintained, so that they remain very similar to blocks of text in the books. All the following variables will be maintained: (a) line and body size; (b) spacing, (c) the text-figure relationship, and (d) word complexity. Below is an example of text that each group will receive during the tests. Each group will receive a reading card. The printed text reading groups will receive the text printed in black on A4 paper, and the digital screen reading groups will receive a slide with black text on a white background.

Group 1: Digital Text with Infant Fonts: The typography chosen for this first reading card was Primary Infant Sassoon. This is a typography created specifically for children, with infant fonts (Figure 6).

Sabe-se que, no primeiro dia marcado para o evento, houve um imprevisto. Uma forte chuva desabou sobre Olímpia, limitando as competições a, apenas, uma corrida pelo estádio. Assim, surgiu o primeiro campeão Olímpico, o cozinheiro-atleta Coroebus de Elis, que venceu uma corrida de, aproximadamente,192 metros.

Fig. 6. Example of the reading card for Group 1. (Source: Authors)

Group 2: Digital Text without Infant Fonts: The typography chosen was Times New Roman, in many children's books, as well as the internet and digital books, this font is often used for reading (Figure 7).

Sabe-se que, no primeiro dia marcado para o evento, houve um emprevisto. Uma forte chuva desabou sobre Olímpia, limitando as competições a, apenas, uma corrida pelo estádio. Assim, surgiu o primeiro campeão Olímpico, o cozinheiro-atleta Coroebus de Elis, que venceu uma corrida de, aproximadamente,192 metros.

Fig. 7. Example of the reading card for Group 2. (Source: Authors)

Group 3: Printed Text with Infant Fonts: Group 3 has the same reading card as Group 1. The only change will be from the digital medium to the printed, as undertaken with the analysed books.

Group 4: Printed Text without Infant Fonts: Group 4 has the same reading card as Group 2.

Group 5: Digital Text with Cursive Style Calligraphy. The font chosen for the calligraphy style was Cursive Standard. This font is very similar to the teachers' handwriting and is the same as that which the children learn in the first phase of the 1st Cycle in Brazilian state schools (Figure 8).

Sabe-se que, no primeiro dia marcado para o evento, houve um emprevisto. Uma forte chuva desabou sobre Olímpia, limitando as competições a, apenas, uma corrida pelo estádio. Assim, surgiu o primeiro campeão Olímpico, o cozinheiro-atleta Coroebus de Elis, que venceu uma corrida de, aproximadamente, 192 metros.

Fig. 8. Example of a reading card for Group 5. (Source: Authors)

Group 6: Digital Text without Cursive style calligraphy. The chosen font was Arial. This is one of the most used fonts in books and on the internet. Arial is most commonly used in children's textbooks. This typography does not present infant fonts (Figure 9).

Sabe-se que, no primeiro dia marcado para o evento, houve um emprevisto. Uma forte chuva desabou sobre Olímpia, limitando as competições a, apenas, uma corrida pelo estádio. Assim, surgiu o primeiro campeão Olímpico, o cozinheiro-atleta Coroebus de Elis, que venceu uma corrida de, aproximadamente,192 metros.

Fig. 8. Example of a reading card for Group 6. (Source: Authors)

Group 7: Printed Text with Cursive Style Calligraphy. The font used is the same as in Group 5. The only change will from the digital medium to the printed.

Group 8: Printed Text without Cursive Style Calligraphy. The font used is the same as in Group 6. The only change will from the digital medium to the printed.

Digital reading will be carried out in the school's computer lab on desktop computers. The most appropriate manner would be to conduct the experiment with tablets, however, the government has not yet provided them to schools in João Pessoa.

8   Conclusions and Final Considerations

In Brazil, many aspects in the education system are different from other countries, such as the UK, where most experiments involving children and legibility are conducted. It was perceived from the school visits, that a number of difficulties must be addressed in order to obtain satisfactory results from the studies involving legibility. Among these difficulties are: choosing schools with favorable testing conditions, such as classrooms with children of the same age; finding schools that have books for all pupils in the same classroom and schools that have good computer labs in order to perform the tests with digital reading.

With reading on digital artifacts, some authors have highlighted that legibility decreases. Tests with digital reading may prove whether this is true or not. **Is the experience of children with computers and consequently with digital reading, a way of indicating that there is no difference between reading printed or digital texts?**

With regard to the questions raised at the beginning of this article, only an experiment with children may indicate whether the use of infant fonts or cursive style calligraphy presents any difference in children's reading performance, and therefore if it is liable to affect their learning process in relation to the texts.

References

1. de Almeida, R.Q.: O leitor-navegador II. In: da Silva, E.T (Coord.), 2nd edn. Cortez, São Paulo (2008)
2. Baines, P., Andrew, H.: Type & Typography, 2nd edn. Laurence King Publishing, London (2005)
3. Bringhurst, R.: Elementos do estilo tipográfico, 3rd edn. Tradução de André Stolarski. Cosacnaify, São Paulo (2005)
4. Danton, R.: A questão dos livros: passado, presente e futuro. Companhia das letras, São Paulo (2010)
5. Heitlinger, P.: Escolar: uma fonte contemporânea para aprender a escrever e a ler. Cadernos de tipografia e design, Portugal, vol. (14) (2009)
6. Lund, O.: Knowledge construction in Typography: the case of legibility rsearch na the legibility of sans serif typefaces. Tese de doutorado do Department of Typography & Graphic Communicatioon (1999)
7. Martins, R.: Análise Gráfica de Receitas Médicas. Dissertação de mestrado em Design na UFPR. Curitiba, Paraná. Ano (2009)

8. Brasil, MEC - Ministério da Educação. Portal do MEC: Ministério da Educação: http://portal.mec.gov.br/index.php (acesso em: Janeiro 12, 2013)
9. Miranda, M., Souza, S., Vanconcellos, L.: O livro didático infantil na escola pública: Análise gráfica para um bom projeto gráfico. Anais do 4° Congresso Internacional de Design da Informação/ 3° InfoDesign Brasil. Rio de Janeiro (2009)
10. Muter, P., Maurutto, P.: Reading and skimming from computer screens and books: the paperless office revisited? Behavior & Information Technology 10(4), 257–266 (1991)
11. Nielsen, J.: Designing Web Usability. The practice of Simplicity, 420 p., pp. 100–130. New Riders, Indianapolis (2000)
12. Niemeyer, L.: Tipografia: Uma apresentação. 3ª Edição. Editora 2AB, Rio de Janeiro (2003)
13. Paulino, S.F.: livro tradicional x livro eletrônico: a revolução do livro ou uma ruptura definitiva? Hipertextus: Revista Digital, N° 3, Junho (2009)
14. Rouet, M.M.: Legibilidade de revistas eletrônicas. Inf. Brasília 32(3), 103–112 (2003)
15. Rumjanek, L.: Tipografia para crianças: um estudo de legibilidade. Dissertação de Mestrado em Design da UERJ (2009)
16. Sassoon, R., Williams, A.: Why sassoon? (2000)
17. Strunck, G.: Viver de Design. 2AB, Rio de Janeiro (1999)
18. Subbaram, V.M.: Effect of display and text parameters on reading performance. Dissertação, Ohio State University (2004)
19. Xavier, A.C.: O hipertexto na sociedade da informação: a constituição do modo de enunciação digital. Tese (Doutorado) – Unicamp, Campinas (2002)

PALMA: Usability Testing of an Application for Adult Literacy in Brazil

Francimar Rodrigues Maciel

Designer, Nokia Institute of Technology, Manaus, Amazonas, Brazil
francimar.maciel@indt.org.br

Abstract. Currently in Brazil, a large number of illiterate adults want to learn to read, but few of them are being provided with opportunities to learn. They are a large audience with social barriers and limited knowledge about the usage of technology. From this scenario, studies about how to conduct evaluation to understand the user experience can contribute to design and get opportunities for creating and improving interactive learning environments. This paper seeks to present the usability testing of a mobile application for adult literacy conducted in Brazil. The Methodologies and issues for further research on M-Learning will also be indicated.

Keywords: mobile learning, usability testing, adult literacy.

1 Introduction

The era of mobility makes it easy to get information and communication in real time anywhere. At school, at home or at work, the diversity of mobile devices and the variety of prices allow the access to mobile technology for all economic classes in different age groups.

This scenario admits the development of applications for different subjects, including education. The usage of mobile devices in the teaching process, called Mobile Learning or M-Learning, presents itself as a way to complement the activities in the classroom and improve the performance of students in the learning process. That service provides a new way of learning to 10 million people around the world [1]. While mobile technology is not and will never be an educational panacea, it is a powerful and often overlooked tool – a repertoire of other tools – that can support education in ways not possible before [5].

In Brazil, the scenario of M-Learning applications is still small. In some discussions that theme is only related to Online Learning or Online Education. Most researches of this field are either experimental or limited to academic access [10].

Aiming to contribute to adult literacy through the resources offered by mobile technology in 2011, the PALMA project was created by IES2 company in Brazil – Programa de Alfabetização da Língua Materna (originally in Portuguese). This paper aims to present the description of usability testing of PALMA application performed in Manaus for one month with 10 participants.

A. Marcus (Ed.): DUXU/HCII 2013, Part II, LNCS 8013, pp. 229–237, 2013.

2   Mobile Learning

2.1   Definition

Mobile Learning involves the use of mobile technology, either alone or in combination with other communication technology, to enable learning at anytime and anywhere [5].

Mobile Learning consists of a series of adaptations of technology for the learning strategy of distance education (Fig.1). Therefore, m-learning is a natural evolution of technology's adaptations applied to the concept of d-learning and e-learning) [7].

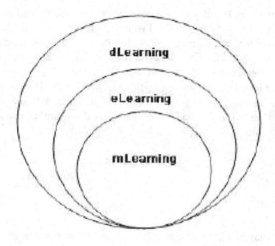

Fig. 1. The place of mobile learning as part of e-learning [7], [8]

Core characteristics can define mobile learning: spontaneous, private, portable, situated, informal, bite sized, light-weight, context aware; and perhaps soon it will be: connected, personalized and interactive [6]. PDA, Pocket PC, E-book, handheld game console, handheld audio and multimedia guides, tablet, mobile phone and smartphones are examples of mobile learning devices.

The technology presents an unique opportunity for creating, sharing, and improving quality of life. Students, teachers, people with disabilities, communities positioned in far places, a large diversity of contexts, and users can take it as a way to access educational content. Some factors must be identified and regarded with focus on the success of mobile learning [3]:

- Access to technology: the successful project make mobile technology available where and when it is needed, either by developing for users own devices such as phones and media players, or by providing learners with devices that they can use at home and on the go.

- Ownership: it is important that learners are able to either own the technology, or to treat it as if they own it. Using the technology for entertainment and socializing does not appear to reduce its value as a tool for learning, but rather helps to bridge the gap between institutional and personal learning.
- Connectivity: many successful mobile learning projects have been based on wireless or mobile phone connectivity, to provide access to learning resources, to link people across contexts, and to allow students to capture material that can sent to a personal media space and then shared or presented.
- Integration: successful mobile learning projects are integrated into the curriculum, the student experience, daily life, or a combination of all of these. One way to achieve this integration is to extend a successful form of learning onto mobile devices, such as frequently asked question, or audio/Powerpoint recordings of lectures.
- Institutional support: successful projects also need strong institutional support, including the design of relevant resources in mobile format, staff training and technical support.

Concerned in stimulating the development for mobile learning, the UNESCO researchers created in 2012 policy guidelines for helping institutions, national government and educators to think about how to use mobile technologies for education. The latest version was updated in early 2013 and recommends:

- Create or update policies related to mobile learning;
- Train teachers to advance learning through mobile technologies;
- Provide support and training to teachers through mobile technologies;
- Create and optimize educational content for use on mobile devices;
- Ensure gender equality for mobile students;
- Expand and improve connectivity options while ensuring equity;
- Develop strategies to provide equal access for all;
- Promote the safe, responsible and healthy use of mobile technologies;
- Use mobile technology to improve communication and education management;
- Raise awareness of mobile learning through advocacy, leadership and dialogue.

2.2   The Context and Environment Relevance

Knowing the environment and its elements is a fundamental process to develop projects, comprehend the specificities about how people use mobile technology to learn (and if they do not, why) and evaluate the users main needs. It makes it possible to know and have access to all stakeholders, teachers, coordinators and assistants, everybody is important in the learning process. Those components present cultures, values and thoughts, essential points to create contextual tools and tasks to promote engagement through the study of their own conditions.

According to Saccol et al. [2], Sharples et al. [3], these different types of contextual mobility can be understood through:

- Learners' physical mobility: people are constantly moving and they can find spare time to learn;
- Technology mobility: many mobile devices can be carried around as the learner is moving around, and they can be interchangeable, depending of the context and needs;
- Mobility in conceptual space: learning topics and themes compete for each learner. Themes should be created and changed according To the students' life experiences
- Social/interaction mobility: people learn at different levels and in a diversity of social groups like family, workplace, social events, at school;
- Temporal mobility: a learning process means that a large number of experiences will be connected between a large variety of experiences, temporal and informal.

Another attributes must also be considered to improve a good mobile learning experience [1]:

- Ubiquity: how widely available is the application that will be required for the viewer to see the content on the device display?
- Access: how widely available is the wireless network that will distribute the mobile learning content?
- Richness: do pages load quickly?
- Efficiency: How intensely the cliente will make use of a particular media?
- Flexibility: will the application be viewable on a variety of devices?
- Security: is the interactive mobile device protected from worms and viruses? Is the shared content protected from being intercepted by unintended recipients?
- Reliability: will content be displayed in a consistent manner;
- Interactivity: does the application allow users to interact freely with other learners?
- Collaboration: is it easy to collaborate on knowledge creation?

3   Application PALMA

The PALMA is a literacy tool created to develop ability to read, write, comprehend texts and solve elementary problems in the math and science fields for young and adult people through mobile devices and Web systems. An interdisciplinary team developed it: teachers, engineers, psychologists and developers of IES2 in São Paulo, Brazil. The application is based on synthetic approach using the Phonic and Alphabetical methodology (combining sounds and letters) for elaborating the content of the app.

The application content is splited into 5 levels, correlating time and complexity, from Vowels (level 1) to Reading Comprehension (level 5). Each levels is divided into five sub-levels. For this experiment only the level 1, Vowels, trough Nokia X5 device, was evaluated.

4   Methodology

4.1   Participants Profile

A qualitative approach was defined for evaluating the difficulties and easiness of application usage with emphasis in verifying the PALMA icons, voice guidance and the navigation flow. 10 participants were selected to participle of the evaluation, 9 female, 1 male, adults in literacy, with age between 23 and 59 years old. All of them Literacy Program for Youths and Adults students, a Brazilian Federal government's project.

The participants were indicated by their professors following the recommendation of being in basic level of learning, with instructions in Portuguese. When asked about the services they used most in their mobile devices, the participants commented the following answers: voice calls and contact list. When asked about how they used these services they showed the mental model through the access memorizing ways through their mobile devices' keys. They explained that they were instructed by their familiars about how to access these services. According to them these two services, voice calls and contact list are essential, because they allow to request help and notify familiars in urgency situations. During the beginning of evaluation the most part of participants did not know what the letters or signs on the keys meant, but they were sure about to access or find voice calls and contact list on their mobile phones.

4.2   The Study Description – Phase 1

The study was conducted in three phases: in a first moment, the participants received a visual guide (Fig.2) and oral instructions during the first contact with the app. An apart module of Palm app was used for the training, the level 'Avaliação Diagnostica' is used for training and measuring the level of knowledge of each participant through the tasks similar to the level 1, Vowels. After completing the training module each participant was instructed to press the navigator key and send the results of the evaluation to the online server. From this first moment, it was possible to observe the first contact and initial barriers of users, the level and speed of each one and the first points of improvements on user interface. Each participant received a Nokia X5, with prepaid SIM card of R$30,00 charge (local money) for using the PALM app during one month. For providing more confortable and familiarization to all the participants, the training was conducted in the same school where the participants perform their literacy classes.

In the end of the training, the next steps and proceedings were explained to the participants, and they were told they would be contacted via their phones, after 8 days of application usage to schedule the next meeting. They were asked to use and complete all the tasks related to the level 1, Vowels, according to their availability. They were instructed to call the researcher at anytime in case of doubts or questions. A printed card with a number to contact the researcher was delivered to each participant, professors and educators of the school.

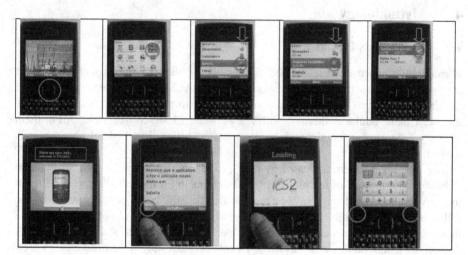

Fig. 2. Visual guide used for the first contact with the PALMA application. Basic shapes in red were used to highlight the steps and sequence as a way to facilitate the user comprehension.

A group interview was conducted to verify the participants' first impressions.

4.3   The Study Description – Phase 2

In the second phase the participants were asked do an individual interview after 8 days of application usage. All interviews were conducted in non-controlled environment, according to the availability of each participant. All the participants preferred to be interviewed at home. Two participants preferred being interviewed in pairs. They commented that they felt uncomfortable to talk alone because some doubts could be described well by a friend or by a familiar who gave support to them during the usage. From this feedback, it was perceived how important is to provide training to familiars and friends which are asked frequently to solve problems related to devices and appliances at home, daily.

At each 5 days, voice calls were made as a way to help and clarify the participants' doubts.

4.4   The Study Description – Phase 3

In the third phase, a group interview at school, was conducted to verify the final perception, the comprehension of the PALMA features after one month of usage and others positives and negatives points. After finishing the evaluation, each participant received a gift card of $40.00 (local currency).

5   Results

At their first contact with the app, it was observed that the most part of the users tried to access the application over three times. They commented that the amount of steps is confusing. The unfamiliarity with the icons was one of the reasons responsible for that low performance. The participants searched for the researcher to solve doubts after 5 days of usage. According to them, they initially had doubts after the first day of usage but their friends and familiars helped them.

The participants showed interest for the innovation characteristics of mobile learning. On the other hand they commented that the app was very limited because it was available only in one specific model of Nokia device.

The navigation key was described by 1 participant as a barrier because sometimes is confusing to know when "go forward" or "go backward".

The size of the keys was highlighted by two participants as something uncomfortable. According to them, the number of keys could be reduced to make possible increase the size of the essential keys (without diacritical signs).

Some participants, after listening to the voice instructions were confused about which button or command should be selected to continue the task. About the volume, two participants commented that it was very confusing increasing the sound of Nokia Device. They sad it was very difficult to comprehend the voice instructions and consequently they had difficulty in completing the task.

After the first week of usage, 3 participants forgot how to access the application, during the trials they accidentally uninstalled the application. 5 participants completed all tasks after that period.

The most part of the participants completed all the tasks in 15 days. After that period they continued to use the application, they started all the tasks again. Upon returning the devices, all participants commented that they would like to continue studying through the app.

They really liked the app voice guide, all of them commented that it seems like the mobile device is really a friend. It was observed that this feature made the interface more human to their perception. They suggested that the voice could be customized, man voice for female students and woman voice for male students.

The number of steps to access the application was highlighted as confusing, mainly during the first week of usage. On the other hand, it was observed that at the end of evaluation, all the participants were familiarized with the steps to access. A suggestion to improvement the access, reducing the steps or creating a shortcut, was strongly recommended in the usability report.

It was possible to observe that teachers must be trained to advance teaching and learning through mobile technologies. All the professors commented that those applications offer opportunities to share content, to clarify doubts and mainly to personalize the content in a way to improve the pedagogy in their classroom. on the other hand, they got afraid before the possibility of having to solve problems in case something went wrong during use, because of their lack of technical knowledge.

6   Final Thoughts

All the participants felt confortable to explore others services/applications available in the devices after completing the tasks of the app. It was possible to evaluate the aspects defined during the initial planning. Thoughts about needs and accessibility were identified during the evaluation process.

Social and economic aspects, the lack of standards between devices and operating systems, the insufficient Internet infrastructure, the individual barriers to adopt a new technology are the main challenges for providing news ways of learning.

We must consider all the contexts and grades of education, high and middle school must have access to services like PALMA and similars. PALMA is an pioneer initiative in Brazil.

The initial training also must be provided for parents and friends, they have a very important role in all performance and usability testing. They also can contribute for implementing features and proposing improvements to the app.

Contextual evaluation has some risks about the use of equipment and devices. One mobile phone was stolen. The SIM card number and the device IMEI are essentials information for locking all the access.

Today in Brazil, a large number of people in the literacy process are over 50 years old. People over this age have to vision and hearing issues due to the natural aging process. These limitations must be considered during the development of interfaces for learning environments regardless the device, mobile or portable.

References

1. Lisboa, R.: While I Live, I Learn: Mobile Learning Project Summary. Editora: Instituto Nokia de Tecnologia, Brazil (2008)
2. Saccol, A.Z., Reinhard, N., Schlemmer, E., Barbosa, J.L.V.: M-Learning (Mobile Learning) in practice: a training experience with it professionals. FEA-USP: Journal of Information System and Technology Management 7(2), 2 (2010)
3. Sharples, M., Sánchez, I.A., Milrad, M., Vayoula, G.: Mobile Learning: Small devices, Big issues. In: Balacheff, N., Ludvigsen, S., Jong, T., Lazonder, A., Barnes, S., Montandon, L. (eds.) Technology Enhanced Learning: Principles and Products, pp. 233–249. Springer, Berlin (2009)
4. PALMA, official website (2012)
   http://ies2.exbr.com/php/palma.php?valor=1#
5. Policy Guidelines for Mobile Learning. United Nations Educational, Scientific and Cultural Organization, Paris, France (2013)
6. Traxler, J.: Defining Mobile Learning. In: Proceedings International Conference Mobile Learning, pp. 261–266. IADIS, Qawra (2005)
7. Moura, A., Carvalho, A.A.: Mobile Learning: Two Experiments on Teaching and Learning with Mobile Phones. In: Hijon-Neira, R. (ed.) Advanced Learning, pp. 90–103. In-Tech, Vukovar (2009)
8. Georgiev, T., Georgieva, E., Smrikarov, A.: M-Learning – A new stage of E-Learning. In: Proceedings International Conference on Computer Systems and Technologies, CompSysTech IV, pp. 1–5 (2004)

9. Jhoanna, R.: Mobile Devices for learning, what you need to know. Getting kids engaged with learning, focused on working smarter, and ready for the future. In Edutopia.org (2012),
http://www.edutopia.org/mobile-devices-learning-resource-guide

10. Fernandes, K.T., Trindade, G.O., Rêgo, A.H.G., Miranda, L.C., Lucena, M.J.N.R., Gomes, A.V.: E-Learning via dispositivos móveis no Brasil: Estado da Arte e desafios à luz do acesso participativo e universal do cidadão brasileiro ao conhecimento. In: Proceedings 32° Congresso da Sociedade Brasileira da Computação. Desafie! Workshop de Desafios da Computação aplicada à Educação (2012)

Setting Conditions for Learning: Mediated Play and Socio-material Dialogue

Emanuela Marchetti[1] and Eva Petersson Brooks[2]

[1] Centre for Design, Learning and Innovation, Department of Learning and Philosophy,
Aalborg University Esbjerg, Niels Bohrs Vej 8, 6700 Esbjerg, Denmark
[2] Centre for Design, Learning and Innovation, Department of Architecture and Media
Technology, Aalborg University Esbjerg, Niels Bohrs Vej 8, 6700 Esbjerg, Denmark
{ema,ep}@create.aau.dk

Abstract. This study discusses how mediated play support learners' under-standing of abstract concepts, through ownership and expression of self. The studies, Design-Learn-Innovate and MicroCulture, are targeted to primary and high school pupils, and are respectively set in a secondary school and in an ar-chaeological museum. The impact of a dialogic setting for learning, based upon mediated play and design activities, on pupils' understanding of abstract con-cepts as well as active participation to learning are investigated. Results from both studies show that mediated play and design based tasks can contribute to learning in formal and non-formal contexts by setting conditions for children to take possession of their learning process and of the concepts, exploring them through their senses and social interaction. As a result, children can achieve complex forms of understanding, which can be useful in future learning experiences.

Keywords: design based learning, playful learning, mediated play, facilitation.

1   Introduction

This paper proposes a meta-level reflection, based upon data from two empirical stud-ies, investigating how introduction of mediated play and sociomaterial forms of dia-logue affects learning practices in formal and non-formal contexts. Both studies aimed at exploring how mediated play could allow learners to gain ownership over their own learning process, communicating with their teachers on a peer basis, and to achieve deep forms of understanding.

The first study is called Design-Learn-Innovate and it focuses on investigating playful approaches, so as to support primary school pupils to learn from project or-ganised design activities, representing conditions for non-formal (playful) learning, supported by hands-on projects. The project was conducted in cooperation with a secondary school in Southern Denmark, and it involved pupils between 15-20 years of age, teachers (facilitators), and domain experts. The second is a doctoral project, aimed at enriching the practice of guided tours, in particular regarding learning of historical processes. The target group is primary school children, in between 9-12

A. Marcus (Ed.): DUXU/HCII 2013, Part II, LNCS 8013, pp. 238–246, 2013.

years old, for whom guided tours may represent their first experience of museums. Play is seen in this project as form of multimodal language, allowing children to break the ice with guides and sharing with them control the learning activity.

The issue tackled in both studies is the static form of interaction emerging between learners and teachers in formal as well as in non-formal contexts of learning. Hence in both cases, learning practice tend to converge towards lectures, in which children act as receiver of the message sent to them by the teachers, resulting into lack of engagement and difficulties for teachers to support the children in gaining new knowledge.

Results gathered from both studies suggest that forms of mediated play elicit an articulated sociomaterial dialogue [3, 26] between teachers and learners. Moreover, it seems to allow learners to make individual statements on themselves and their own interests in learning. In this way, learning is characterized as an emergent experience, for which teachers have to set conditions for, without steering it completely.

In the next section (2) related work is discussed in combination with details that are provided from the two empirical studies; Design-Learn-Innovate and MicroCulture. A critical discussion on the data is conducted in section three, and then, section 4, outlines the conclusions.

2   Design-Based Learning

The two projects, on which this reflection is conducted, aimed at enrich learning condition for the learners, so that they could gain a rich understanding of complex concepts in a hands-on way, so as not to oversimplify them and, at the same time, allowing them to gain ownership of their own learning process.

The target group includes primary school pupils between 9-20 years of age, but the two projects were set in different contexts of inquiry. The investigation conducted for Design-Learn-Innovate took place in a secondary school, which means that it focused on a formal context for learning, in which teachers acted as facilitators and the classroom was the main space for learning practice.

On the contrary, MicroCulture was conducted into two settings, the Viking Museum in Ribe and an afterschool facility in a local school, in Oksboel, Denmark. The museum represents the main focus for the project and an unfamiliar learning context, involving new spaces, objects, such as archaeological findings and reconstructions, and new people, the guides, who are supposed to facilitate their learning. On the contrary, the afterschool facility constitutes a familiar environment, such as the school for Design-Learn-innovate, for everyday playful activities. The design workshops for MicroCulture were conducted in the afterschool facility, as it allowed the researchers to establish a relationship with the children in an environment in which they are confident, it also allowed to see how children relate to play. It was also used as a design collaboratorium [6], in which the children and the researchers had regular sessions including cooperative inquiry based on creative tasks [9], so as the process of making and their artefacts provided probes for reflections, and also testing and co-prototyping sessions.

Both projects were conducted through qualitative methods inspired by design methodologies, involving ethnographic observations, situated interviews and prototyping.

Design is a central aspect to both projects, as they explore the application of design tasks into learning practices. Within the Design-Learn-Innovate project, the students participating in the project were asked to develop prototypes of innovative solutions for specific problems, using different materials and based on lectures, given by specialists from relevant fields. The students had to put into practice the content of the lectures they attended, elaborating it in a creative way and taking decisions on their own. In this way, the concept of design thinking as an approach to learning was introduced, targeting a transformation of the learning environment to a creative and innovative practice. Our definition of design thinking is process oriented emphasising design actions [21]. In this way, we consider the classroom setting as a design-like practice, which, in line with [21], is learnable but not teachable (p. 157).

In the case of MicroCulture instead, participatory design was adopted, in order to involve the children as co-designers and gather insights about their interests and needs regarding play, learning of history, and museum experience. During the design workshops, children expressed interest for creating their own tools and toys for themselves or to share with their playmates, also when playing with a low-fidelity prototype, engaging in a form of playful play [23]. The same designerly form of play supported individual as well as social play, according to children's preferences. Individual players preferred to focus on creative exploration of new items and their use, not communicating with other players very much. Some of them explicitly made items for other players and simply placed them close to them. On the other hand, social players engaged in a competitive form of play, challenging and teasing each other [17]. This interaction form was concretised through the creation of weapons or military ships, and other similar artefacts.

Data from the projects were gathered through ethnographic observations, field notes, and video recordings from the observations conducted during the process and the final evaluations, and from interviews with children/students and teachers or guides. In the following subsections, results from the empirical studies are discussed in details in relation to how mediated play affected learning in the different contexts, focusing on the emergent dialogue.

2.1   Design-Learn-Innovate

The main focus of the Design-Learn-Innovate project is to apply design thinking as a resource for non-formal learning by implementing project-organised design activities in order for the students to learn from specific project themes. The students select the themes themselves, for example: "Future green transportation"; "How to improve the everyday life for people with disabilities"; and "Human-Computer Interaction". This is to create conditions for ownership, creativity and innovation in learning situations that normally have a formal lecture format [2].

Learning in secondary school is not just about acquiring knowledge, but also about the way students handle that knowledge through a sequence of activities; the learning process. Dewey [8] addressed this question by stating that education should offer a generic understanding of how knowledge is created. Through hands-on activities students are offered opportunities to create generic skills possible to transfer to different conditions and situations. Dewey [8] is aware that there is always a danger when teaching remotes from everyday life and thereby becoming technical and artificial.

Besides contextual attributes related to the physical setting, this project takes into account students' prior knowledge, enjoyment, and interest. This is to reinforce non-formal-based experiences and achievements; a process which we have termed non-formal learning [18, 21, 1]. Having enjoyable experiences means being engaged and that the individual is offered possible choices of action. This kind of interest can be characterised as persuasive and associated with increased knowledge and desire to learn more [15]. Dewey [7] emphasises the importance of individual interest in learning situations characterised by having high personal meaning.

Starting from these theories and methods, we defined a learning scenario for secondary school students. The intervention took place over three days and was based on the model of an iterative design cycle, specifically focusing on the phases of discover, design, sketch and prototype, and thoughtful reflection [21, 16]. The primary tools for the design thinking approach were expert presentations related to the chosen project theme, brainstorms, sketches, and low-fi prototypes. The students' choice of project theme was based on their interest, which constituted the base for the creation of project groups. This means that the groups were mixed in terms of age and education line. Each group was designated two facilitators to facilitate the process (Figure 1). The task for each group was to create a concept idea of a product, service or process related to their specific project theme.

Fig. 1. Dialogue between facilitator and student

Empirically this specific study was based on a field study including 116 students (89 females and 27 males) between 15 and 20 years of age. The students were divided into 12 groups of various size (between four and twelve participants in each group), where the data collection was based on video observations, interviews, follow-up questionnaires to students, photos and sketches from the learning situations. The results from the Design-Learn-Innovate project showed that design thinking is a way to create conditions for creativity and innovation in the form of participatory in-action learning. However, these conditions are dependent on idiosynchratic tendencies. The question of how to use and overcome such possible constraints is a crucial facilitator consideration.

2.2   MicroCulture

The main focus of MicroCulture was to explore how to transpose historical processes in to playful interactions, so as to elicit an understanding of history from a sociocultural perspective, at the same time allowing children engaging on a dialogue with the guides, so that they could gain more ownership over their learning process.

The outcome of the design process is a tabletop digital game, illustrating how kings affected urban development, through placement and maintenance of infrastructures. The set up includes a flat TV screen, a laptop, a webcam, and a set of paper tangibles, with which the children are supposed to play. The system is implemented in Python and ReacTIVision [14], an open-source software application that allows to create tangible user interface, exploiting tracking of a set of predefined markers through a regular webcam (Fig. 1). The children play with a set of tangibles, representing each a different infrastructure: bridge, wooden paved street, market place, and defensive rampart. The screen displays a simulation of a village and its population, the players are supposed to develop the settlement into a town, by placing infrastructures, which allows the inhabitants growing in number, establishing new households, and overcome natural obstacles (Fig. 2 and 3).

Fig. 2. Children playing during final evaluation in the museum

The project focuses on introducing mediated play as a communication resources, so to turn guided tours a typical museum learning practice, which has been little studied [6], into a playful apprenticeship in thinking. The theoretical framework is based upon the studies conducted by Rogoff [20], which refer to the theory of play formulated by [24], and [4]. According to Rogoff [20], children learn new skills and

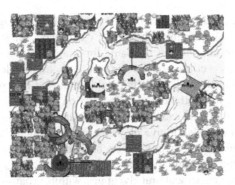

Fig. 3. Strategic use of ramparts and bridges

knowledge, by engaging in goal directed activities with fellow adults, who already master the given activity. The role of adults is fundamental, as they provide support, adjusting the activity according to the needs of the children, when they reach their zone of proximal development, defined as the boundary between what they already know and what they can learn, according to their developmental stage [20, 24]. In this learning scenario, that is called by Rogoff [20] "apprenticeship in thinking", children are supported by adults, in the coordination of the shared activity, but are active participants to their own learning process. Moreover, play is vital for the development of abstract thinking in young children, who playing with toys learn to reflect upon the implications of their actions projected upon a fantasy world.

Furthermore, play is also seen as a state of mind, allowing the participants to explore possibilities in a self-motivated way [23] and also to become more daring in relation to normal social rules. In this sense, play is used as a mean to allow the children to explore abstract knowledge through mediated manipulation, at the same time forgetting about the hierarchical relationships they with teachers and guides, so as to become able to ask questions to the guides.

Final evaluations with a working prototype of MicroCulture, show that through mediated play, children were able to acquire a playful state of mind, expressing themselves ours, verbally and non-verbally, in a more playful and spontaneous fashion, than observed during regular guided tours [17]. Moreover, it was noticed that presence of an interactive game elicited a need for information in the children, so that they asked questions, regarding playing modalities and meaning of the items represented, which could be used by the guides to provide individually meaningful information, grounded on play.

Four different stages were identified, in the way the children inrected with the guides during the final evaluation:

1. Technical.
2. Collaborative play.
3. Role-play.
4. Competitive play.

During the first stage children's main interest is to explore the digital solution offered to them, so that they ask questions on how they can play. For instance they asked if they could place more tangibles at the same time or what specific items were. The emergence of questions is considered a main result, as children do not ask direct questions to the guides. Shortly afterwards the children moved towards the second stage, Collaborative play, in which the children focused on the game and its narrative elements, so that their talk dealt with the settlement and their actions in relation to its development. A form of collaborative play emerged, in which they focused on a particular area of the landscape (screen) and exchanged tangibles, in order to help each other in developing the different areas. At this stage, the guides can start to use MicroCulture to talk about sociocultural dynamics within urban development, linking them to the features of the game and to the children's actions. Collaborative play quickly evolved into Role play, expressed through utterances, such as: "We need more streets for our settlement!" or "We have to set up a bridge here for our people!" However, some children did not join these forms of social play, exploring possible configurations for their territory on an individual basis. The children developed an attachment to the portion of the landscape they played with; in so doing they acted as kings reflecting upon the impact of their actions on the territory and its population. This is an interesting result, as it shows that MicroCutlure allows children to understanding through play, the dilemmas landlords faced in engaging in urban development. Finally only one group engaged in Competitive Play, which represent an evolution of the stage of collaborative play. Some children started to tease each other, for instance a girl placed a series of circular rampart, so as to block the characters populating the land a boy close to her was playing with. She directly addressed the boy saying: "You are stuck!" and as an answer the boy acted angry in an exaggerated way and joined a series of bridges in order to allow the character to pass anyway. In the other groups, this stage was mostly represented by laughs and expressions of teasing in relation to unsuccessful placement of infrastructure, for instance: difficulty in placing bridges, which require a specific orientation for the character to cross the rivers.

In terms of learning, playing with MicroCulture allows the children imagining how it could have been to be a king in the past and having to deal with the development of rural areas. Furthermore, through play the children were able to engage in a polyphonic dialogue [4] with the guides, in which the multiple voices of the participants could express themselves freely, and not simple by non-verbal implicit cues. In this way the children were able to participate in steering the discourse emerging during the guided tour, as by addressing questions the guides had the opportunity disclose information that the individual children found interesting. On the other hand, the game was also adjusted according to the guides suggestions, so that sociocultural elements they assign priority were represented in the game.

In conclusion, it is possible to conclude that playful design activity can significantly contribute to learning in non-formal context, so as to allow learners participating actively and gaining more ownership over their learning process, through free, creative exploration supported by both play and design.

3   Discussion

Results from both studies showed that mediated play and design based tasks can contribute to learning in formal and non-formal settings, allowing children/students to gain ownership of their learning process and of their knowledge, through independent exploration and play. In this way, the children/students took possession of the concepts and formulated questions that derived from in-action reflections. In this way, the participants in the both projects explored abstract concepts through participation, creative expressions, their senses and social interaction.

Results from the MicroCulture project emphasized the emergence of questions and interaction with the guides; the guide as king or as nobleman advisor; children's understanding of strategic use of infrastructure in warfare in collaborative and competitive play

A major concern in the Design-Learn-Innovate project was the experienced gap between the creative (open-ended and chaotic-like) character of the design thinking based learning situation and students' expectations on a more lecture-format-like structure of teaching and learning. Many of the students experienced that the situation was unstructured, chaotic, and sometimes too challenging. Schön [21] underlines that students learn to fill this gap by engaging in such a design activity. This is to say, that the experienced lack of structure does not necessarily emerge from misunderstandings or from an imprecise introduction to the learning activity, but from the creativity inherent in the design thinking actions and interactions. This, according to Schön [21], cannot be taught but has to be learnt. We argue that the facilitation as a reflective design practice might improve learning conditions generally applicable to several kinds of learning situations. Cross-disciplinary and age-mixed groups where interest was the unifying factor, elicited experiences of ludic engagement and collaborative learning.

4   Conclusion

In conclusion, we claim that introducing design thinking to encourage innovation can turn learning situations into creative action and participatory based opportunities to generic skills and competencies. This participative way of learning and create was in many ways based on dialogues between peers and individuals/peers and facilitators/guides. Halliday [13] terms such turntaking activities as speech acts and emphasizes:

An 'act' of speaking /..../ might more appropriately be called an 'interact': it is an exchange in which giving implies receiving, and demanding implies giving in response. [13]

References

1. Aderklou, C., Fritzdorf, L., Petersson, E.: Pl@yground: Pedagogical Innovation and Play Products Created to Expand Self-development through Child Collaboration through Computer-Mediated-Communication (CMC). Socrates, Leonardo & Youth, Project No.: 91893-CP-1-2001-1-SE-MINERVA-M. Halmstad University, Sweden (2001)
2. Arminen, I.: Institutional Interaction. Studies of Talk at Work. Ashgate, Farnham (2005)
3. Bakhtin, M.M.: Speech Genres and Other Late Essays. University of Texas Press, Austin (1986) (Trans. by McGee, V.W.)

4. Bakhtin, M.M.: Discourse in the novel. In: Bakhtin, M.M. (ed.) Dialogic imagination. Four Essays, 1st edn. (1981), 10th edn. (1996). University of Texas Press, Austin (1981)
5. Best, K.: Making Museums Tours Better: Understanding What a Guided Tour Really is and What a Guided Tour Really Does. In: Museum Management and Curatorship, vol. 27(2), pp. 35–52. Routledge, London (2012)
6. Bødker, S., Buur, J.: The Design Collaboratorium—a Place for Usability Design. Proceedings of ACM Transactions on Computer-Human Interaction 9(2), 152–169 (2002)
7. Dewey, J.: Interest and Effort in Education. Riverside Press, Boston (1913)
8. Dewey, J.: Democracy and Education: an Introduction to the Philosophy of Education. Cosimo Classics, New York (1916/2005)
9. Druin, A.: Cooperative Inquiry: Developing New Technologies for Children with Children. In: Proceedings of CHI 1999, Pittsburgh, USA, pp. 595–599 (1999)
10. Dysthe, O., Bernhardt, N., Esbjørn, L.: Dialogbaseret Undervisning. Kunstmuseet som læringsrum. Skoletjeneste (2012)
11. Ewenstein, B., Whyte, J.K.: Knowledge Practices in Design: The Role of Visual Representations as 'epistemic objects'. In: Proceedings of EGOS 2005, Unlocking Organizations, Berlin, Germany (2005)
12. Fallman, D.: Design-Oriented - Human Computer Interaction. In: Proceedings of CHI 2003, Human Factors in Computing Systems, Fort Lauderdale, Florida (2003)
13. Halliday, M.A.K.: An Introduction to Functional Grammar. Edward Arnold, London (1985)
14. Kaltenbrunner, M., Bencina, R.: reacTIVision: a Computer-Vision Framework for Table-Based Tangible Interaction. In: Proceedings of TEI 2007 the First International Conference on Tangible and Embodied Interaction. ACM (2007)
15. Krapp, A., Hidi, S., Renninger, K.A.: Intrest, Learning and Development. In: Renninger, K.A., Hidi, S., Krapp, A. (eds.) The Role of Interest in Learning and Development. Erlbaum, Hillsdale (1992)
16. Löwgren, J., Stolterman, E.: Thoughtful Interaction Design. A Design Perspective on Information Technology. The MIT Press, Cambridge (2004)
17. Marchetti, E., Petersson Brooks, E.: Playfulness and Openness: Reflections on the Design of Learning Technologies. In: Brooks, A.L. (ed.) ArtsIT 2011. LNICST, vol. 101, pp. 38–45. Springer, Heidelberg (2012)
18. Petersson, E.: Non-Formal Learning
19. Petersson, E.: Ludic Engagement Designs for All. Digital Creativity 19(3), 141–144 (2008)
20. Rogoff, B.: Apprenticeship in Thinking. Cognitive Develoment in Social Context. Oxford University Press, Oxford (1990)
21. Schön, D.A.: Educating the Reflective Practitioner. Jossey-Bass. A. Wiley Imprint, San Francisco (1987)
22. Star, S.L., Griesemer, J.R.: Institutional Ecology, 'Translations' and Boundary Objects: Amateurs and Professionals in Berkeley's Museum of Vertebrate Zoology 1907-39. Social Studies of Science 19(3), 387–420 (1989)
23. Sutton-Smith, B.: The Ambiguity of Play. Harvard University Press (1987)
24. Vygotsky, L.S.: Mind in Society. The Development of Higher Psychological Processes. Harvard University Press, Cambridge (1978)
25. Vygotsky, L.S.: Play and its role in the mental development of the child. Voprosy Psikhologii 2, 62–76 (1966)
26. Wertsch, J.V.: Voices of the Mind. A Sociocultural Approach to Mediated Action. Harvester Wheatsheaf, London (1991)

The Learning Machine: Mobile UX Design
That Combines Information Design with Persuasion Design

Aaron Marcus, Yuan Peng, and Nicola Lecca

Aaron Marcus and Associates, Inc., 1196 Euclid Avenue, Suite 1F, Berkeley, CA, 94708, USA
Aaron.Marcus@AMandA.com, tristapy@gmail.com,
grouchomarx87@yahoo.it

Abstract. In an era of increasing need for educated workers, higher costs of education, and emergence of virtual universities appealing to worldwide markets, new tablet-based online learning solutions are inevitable. The Learning Machine project of 2012 combines information design with persuasion design and seeks to change learning behavior in the short- and in the long-term. This paper explains the development of its user interface.

Keywords: courses, culture, dashboard, design, development, education, incentives, information, learning, mobile, persuasion, social networks, tablet, user interface, user experience, virtual university.

1 Introduction

Many schools around the world are in crisis. Especially for the U.S., current education systems are failing. Dropout rates are particularly high among minority children in urban schools. Approximately 7,000 students drop out of U.S. high schools each school day [Alliance for Excellent Education (2010), as cited in "High School Dropouts in America"] The U.S. now ranks 31st world-wide in math, 23rd in science, and 17th in literacy among 65 participating nations in the latest survey [Juan Williams (2012)]. Deep changes are needed in the attitude toward teaching and learning. Digital learning gives young minds a chance at educational excellence. With digital learning being used by schools, "our teachers are better informed, our parents are better informed, and our students are understanding what they're doing and why they're doing it," notes Mr. Mark Edwards, [Juan Williams (2012), as cited in "A High-Tech Fix for Broken Schools"]. The *Wall Street Journal* indicates the competition between newly increasing online courses and name-brand schools: "revolutionaries outside the ivy walls are hammering their way not onto campus but straight into class" [Holly Finn, March 23, 2012]. Besides the new attitude toward learning, it is also essential to apply scientific methods of learning to a new model. According to learning theories, learning is not compulsory, it is contextual. Learning does not happen all at once, but builds upon and is shaped by what people already know. To that end, learning may be viewed as a process, rather than a collection of factual and procedural knowledge. Thus, understanding how to harness and improve the learning process is vital to improve a student's behavior and to achieve successful results.

A. Marcus (Ed.): DUXU/HCII 2013, Part II, LNCS 8013, pp. 247–256, 2013.
© Springer-Verlag Berlin Heidelberg 2013

Responding to these challenges, the authors' firm created the Learning Machine, which aims to lead the nation, even the world in a different way: by using digital technology combining with learning theories, user-experience design, information-design, and persuasion design, to improve education. As a tablet concept-prototype design, the Learning Machine is intended to demonstrate how users can be guided through the learning process more efficiently and effectively, with greater usability, usefulness, and appeal. The Learning Machine is a suite of functions and data, tools and content, best practices and templates, that are tailored to help users obtain necessary resources, manage knowledge and track progress, connect to peers and experts, find tips and advice regarding the learning process, and to seek out and enjoy appropriate incentives to behavior change. Within this virtual space, users can easily search for necessary books, articles, resources, or topics via the Internet, a Bookstore and a Discussion area. Within this virtual space, learning communities develop within and among universities, teachers, and students, in which people can discuss, share, and exchange knowledge more frequently than ever before.

Current applications and services tend to be specialized and seldom address all aspects of the learning process. Moreover, after reviewing existing mobile applications, the authors found opportunities for further adaptations and improvements to serve users' needs better. Finally, some existing products seem not engaging enough and do not provide an overall "persuasion path" to change users' short-term and long-term behavior. Such a path is essential for leading users to improved learning habits. The Learning Machine is intended for use by people from any university/college, country, and culture. It is intended to assist in the complete learning process, from joining in/participating in learning, to evaluating the results of learning. The Learning Machine will be a platform that facilitates open discussion about knowledge among students and teachers all over the world. The Learning Machine's primary objectives are the following: Combine information design/visualization with persuasion design; persuade users to adapt their behavior and lifestyles to include better understanding of engagement, exploration, explanation, extension, and evaluation in the learning process; and apply user-centered design along with persuasive techniques to make the Learning Machine highly usable, useful, and appealing, thereby increasing the efficiency and effectiveness of users' efforts of knowledge-acquisition and retention behaviors.

This paper describes the development of the Learning Machine, a protototype mobile tablet application that seeks to change a student's behavior. The Learning Machine combines information-design and persuasion/motivation theory, based on the works of Maslow (2006) and Fogg's captology theory (Fogg, 2003), thereby distinguishing it from the majority of mobile online learning apps that limit themselves to registration functions or to the mere provision of information and location-based services (LBS). This approach has been realized in previous AM+A projects: (Marcus and Jean, 2010; Marcus, 2011a, b; 2012). All of these Machine projects, including the current one, rely on using user-centered user-experience (UX) design (UCD) in the development process. "User experience" can be defined as the "totality of the [...] effects felt by a user as a result of interaction with, and the usage context of, a system, device, or product, including the influence of usability, usefulness, and emotional impact during interaction, and savoring the memory after interaction" [Hartson/Pyla, 2012]. UX goes well beyond usability issues, entailing also social and cultural interaction, value-sensitive design, emotional impact, fun, and aesthetics [Hartson/Pyla, 2012].

2   Learning Theory

Learning refers to "acquiring new, or modifying existing knowledge, behaviors, skills, values, or preferences and may involve synthesizing different types of information." [Wikipedia, "Learning", 2012] To be more specific, human learning may occur as part of education, personal development, schooling, or training. Learning may be goal-oriented and may be aided by motivation; it may occur consciously or without conscious awareness. To describe how information is absorbed, processed, and retained during learning, AM+A studied conceptual frameworks, i.e., learning theories, which mainly include three domains: behaviorism, cognitivism, and constructivism. According to those theories, a majority of scholars believes learning is shaped by what people already know and should be viewed as a process [Kolb, D.A., 1984)]. Kolb's Learning Cycle involves concrete experience, reflective observation, abstract conceptualization, and active experiementation. People believe learning is influenced by not only internal factors but also by external factors. The Learning Machine planned to infuse these philosophies in a tablet application to help students, teachers, and administrators learn more successfully and understand learning better by using a structured learning process combining internal and external resources.

Learning Models. AM+A explored two popular models of learning, Neil Fleming's "VARK model" [Finn, 2012] and "Learning Pyramid" [Fleming, 1987]. The first learning model is now one of the most common and widely-used categorizations of the types of learning styles. This model, which expanded upon earlier neuro-linguistic programming models, was developed by Neil Fleming, who theorized that combinations of different communication characteristics determine five learning styles: Visual, Aural/Auditory, Read/Write, Kinesthetic, Multimodals (VARK). In the VARK model, Fleming proposes that individuals learn in different ways with a predilection for certain methods. The theory states that there are five distinct learning styles and self-knowledge of one's preferred communication characteristics is an effective way to improves learning. This model focuses on how people learn and indicates the importance of internal influence. Another model, the Learning Pyramid, which was developed by National Training Laboratories, shows an important learning principle that is supported by extensive research: people learn best when they are actively involved in the learning process. This learning retention is achieved through *discussion groups, practice-by-doing, sharing ideas, and teaching others*, all of which contribute to significant effectiveness in achieving a deep understanding and transformational learning. In addition, based on the results of marketing surveys, students' primary concern about on-line education is the interaction with teacher and students. Therefore, the Learning Pyramid illustrates the fact that interaction is crucial in one's learning process as one of the external influences. The VARK model and the Learning Pyramid model build together a philosophy that the learning process is influenced by both internal and external factors. Both effective learning methods and active collaboration between people are imperative for learning. The Learning Machine planned to utilize these ideas by creating a collaborative learning community with rich resources. As a result, people of different learning styles can study individually in an efficient way, and can share, validate, and discuss knowledge more frequently than ever before.

E-Learning Theory. From the didactical point of view, there are numerous approaches to learning, such as learning by observation, learning by enquiry and investigation, learning by doing, learning individually, learning face-to-face with individuals and in groups, learning by experiment learning by evaluation, and learning by reflection. E-learning includes all forms of electronically supported learning and teaching. Whether networked or not, the information and communication systems serve as specific media to implement the learning process. E-learning environments that exploit interactive multimedia are of special interest. Interactivity fosters active learning; the sensory-rich nature of technology facilitates the engagement of additional powerful cognitive processes, and integration of assessment tools into the environment can provide students with feedback, encouragement, *etc.* However, society still lacks information and communications technology (ICT) use in schools throughout the world, despite the possible educational benefits and social learning opportunities they promote. Though several factors are important in the lack of e-learning, for example, technical constraints, integration into the teaching process, innovation of teaching methods, general acceptance, *etc.*, one of the most important reasons is the attitude toward e-learning. With regard to e-learning, people are still afraid of lacking "social presence", which is defined as "the degree of awareness of another person in an interaction and the consequent appreciation of an interpersonal relationship." [Walther, 1992]

Social presence in a computer-mediated communication environment refers to the user's degree of feeling, perception, or reaction being connected to another personal and intellectual entity [Tu and McIsaac, 2002], which involves a subjective quality of the communication medium related to the concepts of intimacy and immediacy. Earlier research has shown that effective management of the social presence in user-interface design can improve user engagement and motivation. Enhancing social presence in an e-learning environment seems to instill the learner with an impression of a quality learning experience. One benefit is to induce and sustain the learners' motivation. The enhancement of social presence can create a successful learning experience in situations involving learners and instructors in online environments. Besides, computers could also be perceived as a social actor to improve involvement and motivation while a single learner participates in computer learning activity with no instructor involved. [Text adapted from "Designing Social Presence in e-Learning Environments: Testing the effect of interactivity on children", Kathryn's Blog, 2012)]

In conclusion, learning is a social activity that requires a close connection to achieve better quality. The social connection is important in an online environment due to the more likely isolated nature of the instructional settings. Thus, attention must be paid to the social demand of the users in the design of computerized learning.

Creating a social interface for an e-learning environment can help counterbalance the negative effects that the lifeless computer environment may have on users.

Learning Process. AM+A's research of various models of learning show that learning is related to both internal and external factors. Alternately, both people and environment are capable of contributing to learning process. We wanted to present a learning process that was clear and comprehensive, suitable for users of varying backgrounds and expertise. One compelling approach was "5E's Learning Cycle Model", an instructional model for constructivism (educatonal constructivism, not art historical constructivism) developed by The Biological Science Curriculum Study (BSCS), a team led by Principal Investigator Roger Bybee. [Bybee, 1989]

As mentioned before, learning is not compulsory, it is contextual. Learning does not happen all at once, but builds upon and is shaped by what people already know. To that end, learning may be viewed as a process, rather than a collection of factual and procedural knowledge. This learning cycle rests on learning or educational "constructivism," which is "a dynamic and interactive model of how humans learn" [Bybee, 1989, p. 176]. Numerous studies have shown that the learning cycle as a model of instruction is far superior to transmission models in which students are passive receivers of knowledge from their teacher In this model, learning is divided into five stages: Engagement, Exploration, Explanation, Elaboration (Extension), and Evaluation. In studying this cycle model, AM+A utilized these different approaches to create a process that contains these five aspects in learning, which are reflected in the Learning Machine's information architecture described below.

3   Persuasion Theory

Regarding the science of persuasion, Cialdini [2001a, 2001b] concentrates particularly on the psychological dimensions concerned in the act of persuasion: What makes an individual comply with another's request? What makes someone change or adapt new attitudes or actions? Cialdini distinguishes six basic phenomena in human behavior, which are supposed to favor positive reactions to persuasive messages of others: reciprocation, consistency, social validation, liking, authority and scarcity. These tendencies of human nature seem to be valid across national boundaries; although cultural forces can impact the relative weight of each of the six factors.

Fogg's persuasion theory[Fogg 2003; Fogg/Eckles, 2007] has defined five key processes to achieve behavioral change. Each step provides requirements for the Learning Machine's functions and data: increase frequency of using application, motivate changing some learning habits, teach how to change learning habits, persuade users to change learning habits (short-term change), and persuade users to change general approach to learning (long-term, or life-style change). We also drew on Maslow's Theory of Human Motivation [Maslow, 1943], which he based on his analysis of fundamental human needs. We adapted these to the Learning Machine context: safety and security needs being met by the assistance of educational advisors and by the provision of curriculum-related information and tips; belonging and love needs expressed through friends, family, and social sharing and support; esteem needs being satisfied by educational comparisons that display progress and acquired expertise, as well as by self-challenges that are suggested by the educational advisors that display goal accomplishment processes; and self-actualization needs being fulfilled by being able to follow and retrace the continuous educational progress and advancement in a personal learning diary.

Each persuasion step impacts the informaton architecture (IA) of the Learning Machine, that is, the metaphors, mental models, and navigation described below,

4   Market Research

In order to have a clearer vision of the target market for the Learning Machine, AM+A conducted market research with potential customers, in collaboration with marketing students of the University of California at Berkeley (UC/B), International Diploma Program (IDP), under the direction of Prof. Bob Steiner. One research objective was to find out about students' willingness to use online learning applications as a way of studying, graduating, and obtaining certification, instead of real-time, face-to-face education. A second objective was to get a better understanding of their learning behavior and their attitude toward online education.

The research process included an exploratory part and an active part. First secondary research was carried out in order to find greater understanding about the topic and summarizing existing knowledge, theory and practical examples. The secondary research also included an exploratory interview of typical users, which, together with the findings of the data research, led to a guideline for the qualitative part of the research project. As qualitative research, the marketing research team conducted six in-depth interviews, including techniques such as probing, storytelling, word association and photo association. The findings of the in-depth interviews led to the construction of a questionnaire, accessed online via SurveyMonkey, which included 10 questions posted in a Facebook group of 130 UC/Berkeley IDP students. The survey had 43 respondents; the main results can be summarized as follows:

Qualitative Research. The in-depth interviews were carried out with 6 participants, 3 male and 3 female, who were aged between 18 and 32. The interviews particularly focused on students' learning behavior, expectations of the Learning Machine and the attitude toward online education. Some primary findings from the interviews are the following:

— **Learning behavior:** Interviewees explained they have similar learning habits, such as studying from books, highlighting most important phrases, listening to teachers, and interacting with other students.
— **Attitude toward online education:** Most did not have experience with online learning. People can imagine taking an online course. Their answers and attitude towards online education was more positive than negative. Social interaction in classroom with students/teachers is highly valued. Interviewees feared body language and enthusiasm a good professor can deliver would be missing in online

education. More respondents felt online education doesn't have the same quality as face-to-face.

— **Expectation of online education:** Downloadable content and live lectures were mentioned to be extremely necessary for a possible online learning tool. People would prefer using a desktop or portable PC rather than a tablet for an online learning tool. Most people think the price of an online course should be less than half of a face-to-face education.

The marketing research showed that students emphasized interaction with other students and that teachers (body language), and the social interaction is highly appreciated in the classroom. Thus, to develop the Learning Machine, we need to design active social interaction for users to communicate with others.

Quantitative Research. In order to enrich the market research with quantitative data, AM+A prepared a questionnaire that was distributed among 43 UC/Berkeley Extension IDP students, most of them are undergraduates or graduates aged between 18 and 34 years. The questionnaire can be found in the appendices of the present document.

More than half of the respondents (29 out of 43) claimed that they have a tablet or want to buy one. Only a small number of the respondents (12 out of 43) disagred with the statement that they can imagine attending an online course using a tablet. Quite interestingly nearly half of the respondents who own a tablet were neutral on this question. This result may be due to the lack of good learning-related applications in the current market. According to the survey results, the main concern about online education is the course content. However, most of the learning applications that already exist in the market lack resources or seldom update their content. Regarding the students' primary need in education, these products seem likely not to be able to satisfy users. That situation might also explain why nearly half of the respondents (26/43) have not taken an online course before. The marketing research that AM+A conducted via UC/B Extension, IDP, offered interesting findings about students' attitudes towards traditional, face-to-face education and new forms of online education. The findings of the research were useful to AM+A in developing the Learning Machine and led to better development of the application suite's functions.

Competitive Analysis. Before undertaking conceptual and perceptual (visual) design of prototype screens, AM+A studied approximately seven online-education Websites and learning-related tablet applications. Through screen comparison analysis and customer-review analysis, AM+A determined major benefits and drawbacks. This in-depth analysis helped further to develop ideas about detailed functions, data, information architecture (metaphors, mental model, and navigation) and look and feel (appearance and interaction). Products/services analyzed included learning applications:,BlackBoard, Khan Academy, MIT Open Course Ware (OCW), TED (Technology, Entertainment, and Design), Together Learn (Net Power and Light, Inc.), and Shufflr (social video app); and online education Websites: Schoolloop and Coursera.

5 Metaphors, Mental Model, Navigation: Information Architecture

In designing the Information Architecture (IA) for the Learning Machine, AM+A began by examining the IA for past Machines, including the Green Machine, the Health Machine, and the Money Machine. We discovered an overarching model for the IA that permeated throughout each of the past Machines. In this model, there are five primary 'modules', or branches of the IA, each of which is described below. While we altered slightly the details of each module to fit the needs and requirements of each respective Machine, a generalized model was still evident. These modules are described below.

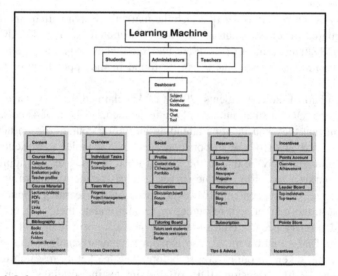

Fig. 1. Information Architecture of the Learning Machine. Image credit: AM+A.

— **Dashboard:** The Dashboard module is similar to a landing page for its respective Machine. The Dashboard is an overview into the status of the user's behavior change. Here, the user gets a view of his/her goals and where s/he stands in achieving them.

— **Process:** The Process View module is an overview/roadmap in which the user sees a high-level view of the process and more details regarding each objective and goal. The user sees progress being made, as well as next steps in achieving a goals.

— **Social Network**: The Social Network module is an integral part of behavior change in modern software. Users engage in focused, subject-matter-based connections with friends, family, and/or like-minded people that either share similar goals or wish to support others in achieving behavior-change objectives.

— **Tips/Advice**: The Tips/Advice module provides focused just-in-time knowledge about a given topic to give users insight into the habits they wish to change.

— **Incentives**: The Incentives module presents users with enjoyable and engaging ways to change their behavior, including competitions, awards, rewards, momentos, trophies, leader boards, and specific games. Gamification has proven to be a powerful tool in encouraging users to try an application, even with virtual incentives, although in some cases, real incentives may be provided. A leaderboard allows a user to compare his/her progress with others, tapping in the competitive nature of the human mind to create behavior change.

6   Screen Design (Look-and-Feel)

Based on all of the preceding, AM+A designed the initial and revised portions of the Learning Machine's screens, which show layouts, contents, widgets, and implied interaction. Images shows are revised versions of initial screen designs

Fig. 2. Prototype revised screens show typical key steps in navigation. The first screen shows the main "dashboard" of the Learning Machine.

7   Evaluation, Next Steps, and Conclusions

AM+A presented initial screens to an internal AM+A group. There was consensus that the concepts seemed novel, but the screen designs seemed too complicated and insufficiently visual. AM+A sought to make the revised screens more visual. AM+A plans to continue improving the Learning Machine, which will require additional time and outside funding. Tasks include: revise personas and use scenarios, conduct user evaluations, revise/complete the information architecture and look-and-feel; build initial working prototype (e.g., for iPad or other tablets); redesign, if appropriate, the Learning Machine for different corporate and country cultures; evaluate the Learning Machine across different corporate and country cultures; develop the Learning Machine for enterprise use as well as personal use; and research and develop improved information visualizations.

AM+A sought to incorporate information design and persuasion design for behavior change into a tablet application. This self-funded Learning Machine project is current, ongoing, and incomplete, but demonstrates the direction and process for such innovation in online education.

Acknowledgements. The first author thanks Peter Rinzler, AM+A Designer/Analyst, for his assistance with imagery for this paper, and Prof. Bob Steiner and his students at the University of California at Berkeley's Extension Program's International Diploma Program.

References *

1. Berman, D.K.: In the Future, Who Will Need Teachers? Wall Street Jour., B1 (October 2012)
2. Bybee, R.W., et al.: The 5 E Learning Cycle Model (1989), http://faculty.mwsu.edu/west/maryann.coe/coe/inquire/inquiry.htm
3. Cialdini, R.: The Science of Persuasion. Sci. American 284, 76–81 (2001a)
4. Cialdini, R.: Influence: Science and Practice, 4th edn. Allyn, Bacon, Boston (2001b)
5. Finn, H.: Watching the Ivory Tower Topple. Wall Street Journal (March 25, 2012)
6. Fleming, N.: VARK: a guide to learning style, http://business.vark-learn.com/about-vark/introduction/ (retrieved October 3, 2012)
7. Fogg, B.J.: Persuasive technology: Using computers to change what we think and do. Morgan Kaufmann, Amsterdam (2003)
8. Fogg, B.J., Eckles, D.: Mobile persuasion: 20 perspectives on the future of behavior change. Persuasive Technology Lab, Stanford University, Palo Alto (2007)
9. Hartson, R., Pyla, P.S.: The UX Book. Process and guidelines for ensuring a quality user experience. Elsevier, Waltham (2012)
10. Kathryn's Blog (2012), http://npf551kathryn.wordpress.com/2012/12/15/the-future-of-interactivity-and-education/
11. Kolb, D.A.: Experiential learning: experience as the source of learning and development. Prentice Hall, Englewood Cliffs (1984)
12. Marcus, A.: The Health Machine. Infor. Design Jour. 10(1), 69–89 (2011a)
13. Marcus, A.: The MoneyMachine. User Experience 11(2), 24–27 (2011b) (Second Quarter 2012)
14. Marcus, A.: The Story Machine. Workshop on Legacy Design. In: Proc. ACM SIGCHI, CHI 2012 Conference, May 1-7, CDROM, Austin (2012)
15. Marcus, A., Jean, J.: Going Green at Home: The Green Machine. Information Design Journal 17(3), 233–243 (2010) (First Quarter 201)
16. Maslow, A.H.: A theory of human motivation. Psychological Review 50, 370–396 (1943)
17. Polovina, S.: The Learning Pyramid (November 16, 2011), http://homepages.gold.ac.uk/polovina/learnpyramid/about.htm (retrieved October 3, 2012)
18. Tu, C.H., McIssac, M.: The relationship of social presence and interaction in online classes. The American Journal of Distance Education 16(3), 131–150 (2002)
19. Walther, J.B.: Interpersonal effects in computer-mediated interaction: A relational perspective. Communication Research 19(1), 52–90 (1992)
20. Wikipedia. E-learning, http://en.wikipedia.org/wiki/E-learning (retrieved October 3, 2012)
21. Wikipedia. Learning, http://en.wikipedia.org/wiki/Learning (retrieved October 3, 2012)
22. Williams, J.: A High-Tech Fix for Broken Schools. Wall Street Journal, A11 (August 14, 2012)

---

* All URL citations are 1 August 2012 unless otherwise stated.

Information Accessibility in Museums with a Focus on Technology and Cognitive Process

Laura B. Martins and Felipe Gabriele

Federal University of Pernambuco, Design Department, Recife, Brazil
{laurabm@folha.rec.br, felipegabriele@hotmail.com}

Abstract. The present article is part of a more broaden study regarding the integrated systems of information. The focus of this research is the informational accessibility in museums under the perspective of the universal design and the ergonomic information and cognition. Its objective is to report the research regarding new information and communication technologies, based on bibliographic researches and synchronic analysis in Brazilian and European museums. This work was carried out under the intention to gather data about the state of the art in the area, aiming to understand it enough to find more proper solutions to be applied in the object of study – the Kahal Zur Israel synagogue.

Keywords: Information design, Information ergonomics, Universal design.

1 Introduction

One of the main objectives of a system of information is to communicate for the user. The way this information is transmitted will dictate the quality and effectiveness of the system and, to do so, must take into account the fact that there are specific technologies to facilitate the process of assimilation and access.

In Brazil, according to the Census made in 2010[1], there was an increase of 86% in relation to the Census of 2000, in the quantity of people who declared to have some sort of disability. From around twenty four million habitants, this number jumped to more than forty and five million. At the same time, the Brazilian population had a 12.3% increase. The inclusion of this population in the several sectors of the everyday life, rather in the social, labor, educational, leisure or others sectors, have been widely discussed and encouraged in the federal, state and municipal scopes through several laws and decrees. However, it is noted that the current legislation doesn't guarantee the inclusion of people with disabilities, turning this into a tough task that has been finding some difficulties, such as the architectonical, informational, educational and organizational barriers.

Considering the human-computer interaction (as *human-information* interaction), we conceive that, depending on the system, this interaction may have problems of effectiveness. "The problems originate with different people: the end-users who directly experience the consequences of poorly designed systems; the developers who make decisions about system interfaces; the engineers concerned with formulating

A. Marcus (Ed.): DUXU/HCII 2013, Part II, LNCS 8013, pp. 257–265, 2013.

principles, methods and tools for system developers; and the scientists interested in explaining and predicting the behavior of human-computer systems"[2]. Such problems should be anticipated and avoided or, once detected after system application, sought to be repaired the best way possible for the end-users.

Based on this purposes, the universal design is inserted, as affirmed by Soares & Martins[3], as a way to direct the processes of design towards the comprehensiveness of all the potential users. According to Mace[4], one can define universal design as the project of products and environments able to be used by the largest number of people without the need to be adapted nor of a specialized project. Ergonomics is an important tool, once it enables products, environments and systems of information to be suited to all users, including those with some sort of disability, becoming indispensable for adjusting demands to the specific needs of this population.

In this context, the objective of the present article is to report the gathering of data made regarding new technologies of information and communication to be applied in the museum Kahal Zur Israel Synagogue – as part of the research, current being developed, about information accessibility in museums – through the principles and methods of Ergonomics. Kahal Zur Israel Synagogue is located in Recife, capital of the State of Pernambuco, Brazil.

First synagogue of the America, Kahal Kadosh Zur Israel (Rock of Israel Holy Community) was created during the Dutch domain in the city of Recife, between 1640 and 1641. The original building was demolished in the early 20th century and, thanks to archeological and cartographic studies, the exact place of the synagogue was discovered. Entirely rebuilt, it was reopened in 2001. Currently it hosts, besides the synagogue, the Jewish Cultural Center of Pernambuco and the Jewish Memorial Museum, where is displayed the history of Jewish communities in Brazil.

Such research gains importance as it focus in quality of life, proposing the strategic development of accessibility to environments and systems of information, to make them compatible with the needs, potentialities and limitations with the performance of all users.

2   Methods and Techniques

Thus, it's necessary to deepen into investigations regarding technologies that enable the implementation of systems of information related to accessibility in museums, considering the principles of the universal design. Through the bibliographic researches in brazilian and international articles published in periodicals and conferences alike, besides the survey on the reality of interactive museums and exhibitions in Brazil – Museu da Língua Portuguesa and Museu do Futebol (Portuguese Language Museum and Soccer Museum); England – Tate Modern; Spain – Reina Sofia (Queen Sofia); Italy – a tour through the historical part of Milan; and Museo Virtuale della Memoria Collettiva (Virtual Museum of the Collective Memory) and France – Louvre, a survey was made to know the condition of the art of information and communication technologies, thus aiming at an efficient communication between the information offered and the user.

For the bibliographic research, means of publication that had relevance in the academic scenario were sought. To do so, initial parameters were determined for periodicals search. Initially, publications with a good rate of impact factor or Qualis A qualification were researched; besides a broad indexing basis, as the Directory of Open Access Journals – DOAJ – and the Capes basis (Coordination for the Improvement of Higher Education Personnel), Brazilian federal department responsible for the academic organization. Besides periodicals, publications of conferences and some essays that had similarities with the subject were analyzed.

3 Outcomes and Discussions

Through the issue: how to enable, with the support of the Information and Communication Technologies – ICT, the development of accessibility strategies towards museums – in this case, the Kahal Zur Israel Synagogue – for the access and use of spaces of historical and cultural character to the wide range of population? And, through the survey made, the analyzed technologies are presented.

3.1 Touchscreens

Allow a better interaction with the user through an intuitive interface, enhancing the capture of information. There are four types of touchscreen technology: resistive, capacitive, acoustic wave and optical imaging systems. The current most used are the capacitive, which are equipped in the large variety of smartphones and tablets available in the market. Those kind of screens are used, for example, in the Portuguese Language Museum, in São Paulo, Brazil (Fig. 1), through an educational and ludic manner, aiding the user to form words and sentences.

3.2 Internet

The world wide web of computers is becoming an ally in disseminating information with an increasingly higher quantity of potential the receptors. May be used to create virtual museums, where the user can access it from anywhere in the world and explore its rooms and expositions. Usually two forms of creation are used. One is the virtually created environment similar to the original, with practically infinite capacities of use and possibilities; while the other one is with the use of images or videos in 360 degrees, where the user may meet all the rooms and works exhibited as he were in the museum itself. Louvre, in Paris, France, is one of the examples of museums which use this technology.

3.3 Virtual Reality

An advanced interface technology between a user and a computerized system, with the purpose to create a parallel reality, where the user may interact and have sensations as similar to reality as possible.

Fig. 1. Portuguese Language Museum. São Paulo, Brazil.

After the creation of a specific virtual environment, to fulfill the proposal, the user access through specific glasses or a helmet, where he is immersed in that environment by his senses, such as vision and hearing. Through the use of special gloves, is also possible to have tactile feeling.

May be used in the creation of fictional settings, as in the technique called Virtual Heritage, used to recreate historical settings and explore them.

3.4   Audio Guide

Using a specific device (Fig. 2) or the smartphone itself, the user may listen to explanations about the museum or about the exhibitions.

With the development of a specific applicative or with the recording of a guiding visit through the area to be explored – considering the use by a person with visual impairment – the audio guide is made by introduction stops, welcoming and explanations of use; first level stops, where the main information is given; and second and third level stops, where any other information is given.

The audio guide is used not only in museums but also in historical tours, as for example in Milan, Italy, where the tourist takes a tour while listening to the explanations regarding the places visited through the audio guide. Great European museums, such as the Louvre, allow the user to download for free an application with audio guide direct to their cellphones; the Tate Modern, in London, however, has guided visits where, besides the audio guide, it's also allowed interaction by touch with the exhibited works.

Fig. 2. Example of audio guide

3.5   Tactile Map

A map containing relevant information accessible to visual impaired people through embossed elements and writings in Braille (Fig. 3). The same goes to plates written in Braille, used for informational guidance.

The map reproduces bidimensionally the environment, which it is representing with traces, and symbols that represent places and/or embossed obstacles, in a way that may allow the visual impaired to read it with his hands, getting a visual guidance of the environment. There are written information with embossed letters and in braille, making the offered information more easily comprehensible. Tactile map is complemented with other types of inclusive technologies, like the tactile floors.

3.6   Tactile Floors

Tactile floors (Fig. 4) are also known as podotactile, which means the sensation through the feet. They serve to assist people with visual impairment to walk, guiding and marking their routes, or alerting them for possible gaps and barriers. As coatings for the floors, they don't work alone, rather with a composition of pieces for a safe walk with autonomy.

In Brazil there are two types of tactile floors, which are described by NBR 9050[5] (Brazilian Norm who defines the edification accessibility) as (a) directional or guiding floor, with the function to guide the user through a pre-defined route; and (b)

Fig. 3. Example of tactile map

Fig. 4. Example of tactile floor

awareness floor, with the function to alarm the user about dangers, obstacles, bumps and route changes.

3.7   Considerations about the ICT

As affirmed by Muchacho[6], "the ICT are precious instruments in the process of communication between the museum and its audience. Its utilization as a complement of an exhibition comes to facilitate the transmission of the intended message and to gain the attention of the visitant, enabling a new vision of the museology object".

Because it is a subject rarely addressed in the field of information ergonomics, the analysis of positive experiences with the ICT becomes relevant in the research of informational accessibility in museums while it makes possible for an analysis of the rights and wrongs of pre-established informational systems, helping in the future implementation of the Synagogue system of information.

3.8   Considerations about the Cognitive Process

Mankind is seen, according to the approach of information processing [1], as a system that receives, processes, transmits, stores and uses information. This approach has emerged since the 1970s, with the aim of investigating the responsibility of basic internal mechanisms in the production of movement and behavior modification in the individual [2]. Over the years the human race begins to acquire a gradual knowledge in the engine process of your body in the same way that, according to Tani *et al* [2], this whole movement is also essential for cognitive development. We may conclude with these thoughts that the cognitive and motor skills are closely linked in their learning process and progress along the maturity of the individual. In other words, according to Schmidt [3], no matter how cognitive ability may seem, it requires at least one motor feedback, while all motor skill also requires at least a decision prior to your move.

When analyzing motor learning among individuals with a physical disability, you must also take into consideration their cognitive abilities during the process. A difficulty to learn certain movement can be explained by the type of disability and the level of commitment of the same, so some specific methods and approaches should be used to might work around this impasse in the best way possible. The way that an individual who has some physical disability has, inherently, difficult to perform motor tasks, it is necessary that the corresponding and dependent information on some level to such action is as clearly, accurately and objectively as possible, reducing thus, the response time of the reaction and contributing to the overall effectiveness of the system. Taking into account the visual disability, for example, where the user has at his disposal tactile guides that help him to move around independently – or touch screens that allow editing of the information, so text can become enlarged readable for a user with low vision (according to Brazilian law – Law No. 10,098, of December 19, 2000 –, a user with low vision have visual acuity between 0.3 and 0.05 in the better eye with best correction optics, or the sum of the measured visual field in both eyes equal or less than 60°)[10]. Or even a user with physical disabilities, which takes an environment previously thought to have no architectural barriers or a readily movable movement and escape in an emergency. These scenarios are possible thanks to an information system thought to have the full accessibility that preaches universal design.

Cognitive science seeks choose the leveling descriptive of behavior, sign interpretations and observations and inferences about mental processes to reconstruct the processes of the tasks imposed implementation[4]. The cognitive effectiveness, in this case, search the informational efficiency as a catalyst for actions planned and programmed or until the unplanned and emergency actions and what, specifically in this case, can be a vital ally to the security and survival of the individual. The informational ergonomics, as scientific discipline that deals with the relationship and their peculiarities between man and communicational environment where information is inserted, combined with the concepts of universal design and ICT, ensures the concern for transmitting the information efficiently and effectively to any type of user, with or without disabilities, with the commitment of the correct perception of information in the shortest time.

4   Final Considerations

The current study is justified by its contribution with the union of ergonomics, cognition and technologies of information and communication as a way to attend the principles of the universal design to the development of accessible projects. The study regarding interactive museums, cognitive processes and ICT enables a variety of possibilities to be considered in the development of accessibility strategies for settings and informational systems, adjusting compatibilities to the needs and limitations of all users, with or without disabilities, thereby improving the *human-information* interaction. In the Kahal Zur Israel Synagogue, object of this research, the use of a great part of the technologies researched will be defended as facilitators and inclusive tools for the full and unrestricted access to settings and information.

The purpose of this article is not to end discussions about the information system, but collect data that may serve as an incentive for further research. It is intended, mainly, to make clear the importance of participation by ergonomics and design professionals from the stage at which the "museum" design project itself starts. By focusing projectuals guidelines under the lens of universal design, to have a project that, since their beginning, serves the public to the fullest.

It is also necessary to make a deep discussion of the subject with other professionals and researchers of the fields involved and alike, with the intention to evaluate the purpose and the paths taken in this research in favor of a more effective analysis. It was noticed during the bibliographic research a certain shortage of publications in the field, raising even more the importance of similar studies.

References

1. IBGE: Censo 2010. Instituto Brasileiro de Geografia e Estatística (2011)
2. Long, J., Whitefiled, A.: Cognitive Ergonomics and Human-Computer Interaction. Cambridge University, Cambridge (1989)

3. Soares, M.M., Martins, L.B.: Design universal e Ergonomia: uma parceria que garante acessibilidade para todos. In: Almeida, A.T., Souza, F.M.C. (eds.) Produção e Competitividade: Aplicações e Inovações, pp. 127–156. Editora UFPE, Recife (2000)
4. Mace, R.L., Story, M.F., Mueller, J.L.: The Universal design File: designing for people of all ages and abilities. North Carolina State University School of Design, Raleigh (1988)
5. NBR 9050: Acessibilidade em edificações, mobiliário, espaços e equipamentos urbanos. Rio de Janeiro, Associação Brasileira de Normas Técnicas
6. Muchacho, R.: O Museu Virtual: as novas tecnologias e a reivenção do espaço museológico. Actas do III SOPCOM, VI LUSOCOM e II IBÉRICO, vol. I, Covilhã, Universidade da Beira Interior (2005)
7. Connel, R.: Processo Cognitivo e Comportamento Motor. In: Rodrigues, D (org.): Métodos e Estratégias em Educação Especial – Antologia de Textos, Lisboa, Faculdade de Motricidade Humana (1991)
8. Tani, G., et al.: Educação Física Escolar: fundamentos de uma abordagem desenvolvimentista. EPU, São Paulo (1998)
9. Schmidt, R.A.: Aprendizagem e Perfomance Motora. Movimento Ltda, São Paulo (1992)
10. Brasil: Decreto nº 5296, de 02 de dezembro de 2004. In: Diário Oficial da União, n. 232 (2004)
11. Silva, E.R.G., et al.: Processamento cognitivo da informação para tomada de decisão. In: Perspectivas em Gestão & Conhecimento, João Pessoa, Brasil, vol. 1, pp. 25–39 (2011)

Luz, Câmera, Libras!: How a Mobile Game Can Improve the Learning of Sign Languages

Guilherme Moura, Luis Arthur Vasconcelos, Aline Cavalcanti, Felipe Breyer,
Daliton da Silva, João Marcelo Teixeira, Crystian Leão, and Judith Kelner

Virtual Reality and Multimedia Research Group, Computer Science Center,
Federal University of Pernambuco, Recife, Pernambuco, Brazil
{gsm,lalv,asc3,fbb3,ds2,jmxnt,cwml,jk}@cin.ufpe.br

Abstract. There is a natural communication barrier between hearing and non-hearing people, and one of the reasons is the lack of knowledge about sign languages. This paper presents a study about a mobile application for learning and practicing the Brazilian sign language (Libras). The application consists of a guessing game in which two players must guess each other's signs. For two months, the data collected from the game server and from the user gaming experience was analyzed with regard to the user interaction, engagement, fun and learning. The obtained results indicate that due to the mobile nature of the application, the drop rate was higher than expected. However, the user information demonstrated that learning tools can benefit from the mobile and ubiquitous nature of such devices. Despite the many drawbacks found, users confirmed the game was fun and effective for learning a sign language.

Keywords: Mobile, Sign Language, User Experience, Games.

1 Introduction

Deafness, or hearing loss, is defined by the IDEA (Individuals with Disabilities Education Act) as a hearing impairment so severe that the person is unable to process linguistic information through hearing. According to the World Health Organization, in 2004, 275 million people had moderate-to-profound hearing impairment.

Although deafness does not affect a person's intellectual capacity or ability to learn, it directly affects how a person interacts with the world and can lead to difficult challenges in some situations, including learning. The communication gap between hearing and non-hearing people is aggravated by the fact that the major percentage of the population does not know any kind of sign language. In this scenario, every deaf person would need an interpreter in order to communicate without issues.

Concerning the Brazilian context, there are about two million people with moderate-to-profound hearing impairment, according to the 2010 census. In 1857, within the first Brazilian School for Deaf People, a sign language was developed in order to ease communication between hearing-impaired people. The Brazilian Sign Language (Libras) is derived from the French Sign Language.

A. Marcus (Ed.): DUXU/HCII 2013, Part II, LNCS 8013, pp. 266–275, 2013.

However, nowadays only a small percentage of the Brazilian population actually knows Libras. In addition, the Brazilian Federation for Education and Integration of Deaf People (Prodeaf) estimates that only 7% of the deaf population in the country are capable of properly understanding Portuguese written language, because they were not alphabetized [1].

Observing this communication barrier, it is clear that a better understanding of sign languages can facilitate the interaction between hearing and deaf people. But learning Libras requires as much effort as any spoken language, and unless the students have a strong motivation or objective, they tend to give up along the way. One method to engage students in the learning process is to create a ludic tool that keeps their attention while it continuously presents the signs and vocabulary contents.

The recent growth on the use of smartphones and other mobile devices has made it an interesting field to tackle some of these communication issues. A game called Luz, Câmera, Libras! (LCL) was developed for iOS and Android devices with the objective of creating an interaction between the users, using sign language to communicate. The LCL is a turn-based guessing game, which main objective is to create on the players some interest about sign languages and diminish the existing communication barrier.

In such way, this work presents an alternative for learning and practicing sign languages, and intends to help the interpersonal interaction mediated by digital devices. At the same time, this paper aims to analyze the LCL gaming experience, by examining the user engagement with the game, the users' interaction during gameplay and the application's ability to teach basic Libras vocabulary.

2   Digital Interfaces and Tools for Learning Aid

Along with the advances in electronic computing, the digital revolution has affected several human activities. For instance, education is facing many changes due to the new technologies. Digital learning environments afford dynamicity and flexibility to the act of acquiring information, updating content and adopting specific practices according to each one's needs. However, easy to reach content and digital tools do not guarantee one of the most important education factors: motivation. When applied to the educational context, digital games have proven to be quite efficient in approaching this issue. In sequence, a few digital tools or games for aiding education are presented.

The LVILibras [10] is a digital tool for teaching Libras, developed for both Android and iOS platforms. The process is based on videos, animations and images in which general Libras concepts are presented. This tool does not present any innovation regarding didactics, since its focus is to bring digital resources into a traditional class procedure.

The AutoVerbal Talking Soundboard [14] (Figure 1A) is an application designed for Apple mobile devices, which purpose is to help a deaf or mute person communicate with other people that do not know a sign language. The system has several images by default for which user can assign words individually. This way, whenever that icon is touched, the word is reproduced aloud. The program has a Text-to-Speech feature as well, which verbalizes any written text typed.

The Ldn Access [17] was designed for multiple purposes. It stores routes, obstacles, ramps and several adapted toilets throughout the city of London. The system is based on GPS for a more accurate guidance. Users can also filter establishments by category, like when looking for Indian food. According to the developers, the application was made simple for users with deficient motor skills. Thus, instead of typing long words, such users may simply touch icons on screen (Figure 1B). It does not depend on internet, which guarantees autonomy for most of the system features.

Fig. 1. A: AutoVerbal Pro screen (iPhone version); B: London Access screen

Also, some analogic games have adapted versions for teaching sign languages, commonly meant for children [3]. Figure 2 shows two different games. The first one is a lotto-like game, in which alphabet letters are drawn and the user must fulfill cards with the correspondent Libras letter. The second follows a dominoes mechanics. Each piece has both an object picture and a letter from the Libras alphabet. Users must match the Libras letter with the first letter of the object.

Fig. 2. Libras adapted Board games

3   Ludic Learning

The use of ludic approaches for learning is not a new phenomenon, especially regarding children's education. From the early decades of the twentieth century, teaching methods like the Montessori [13] use, among other resources, ludic activities in order to teach children basic concepts such as mathematical operations, reading and writing abilities. More recently, there is a wide range of digital games designed to be used as additional pedagogic material in classroom environments.

The idea of using games for learning purposes fits well with the constructivist approach to the process of acquiring knowledge. The widely accepted theory, proposed by Jean Piaget in the 60's, applies the concepts of cognitivism – a field of Psychology that focuses on mental processes such as perception, problem-solving and decision-making – to learning processes. The basic premise of constructivism is the idea that an individual is capable of building his own knowledge by gathering information and resources provided by the environment and/or a facilitator, whose role is assumed by a teacher, in the most traditional learning contexts. [8]

Leont'ev [9] added a social component to the constructivist learning dynamics. He states that the cognitive development cannot be held apart from the social and cultural context in which it happens. Being so, the superior mental processes (thought, language and willful behavior), are originated by social interactions, through activities that take place in specific environments, and are mediated by instruments. Such instruments can be as diverse as a notebook and pencil, a movie, an electronic device, or even a game.

Being the game an environment, as well as a mediating tool, part of the information that will become knowledge on the subject's mind already exists; ready to be combined with the player's experiences and mental connections.

One of the concepts bounded to games is the idea of flow, defined by Csíkszentmihályi [2] as "the satisfying, exhilarating feeling of creative accomplishment and heightened functioning." It happens when an individual is completely focused on the task being performed, and there is a good balance between the challenges, the player's skills and the rewards from doing the task. A person can experience flow in various activities, but playing a well-designed game has proved to be one of the quickest ways of achieving it.

The major objective in the realm of educational games is to introduce flow into learning activities, thus engaging the players/learners into a pleasing task that has embedded in it the content that is expected to be learned.

The LCL game helps learning and practicing sign languages by adopting game characteristics, as well as a constructivist knowledge-acquiring approach. This way, it creates an environment for learning sign languages that aims to attract and motivate players to improve their abilities in game and, consequently, to increase their sign language abilities.

4   Usability, Accessibility and Interaction in Games

Usability is a measure composed by three metrics: effectiveness, efficiency and user satisfaction, where each of these can assume different measures as desirable system's properties. However, the LCL has hybrid characteristics since it aims to teach sign language as a distance learning tool, besides entertaining by incorporating competitive elements from games. Thus, it becomes a challenge to define a design methodology capable of covering both characteristics. As explained by [7], user-centered design methods, usually applied to production software, can be adapted for evaluating certain aspects of games. Among usability methods, the ones that focus on user satisfaction evaluation become more suitable for evaluating games thus enable the extrapolation of this feature to achieve answers about how fun the game actually is, thereby obtaining a more reliable overview of user experience.

Some researches approach usability of systems for people with disabilities such as the ones performed by [16], who employed the Think Aloud Protocol for individuals who are deaf or [18], who worked on the development of an educational game for deaf and hearing children. There are efforts in adapting traditional methods of usability evaluation for games, as it is observed in [12], the RITE method; an adaptation of Usability Testing. Similarly, [6] analyzes the contribution of inspection methods with experts. However, it could not be found any research focused on developing a game to teach sign language to normal people and its respective usability evaluation.

Starting from these concepts, we must select from among several usability evaluation methods those that will be able to extract better qualitative information from users. We can find in HCI literature various evaluation methods that can be used in different scenarios. In turn, [5] describes the Self Reporting Log method as a diary in which the volunteer can make notes about his/her interactions with the system. It is recommended applying Self Reporting Log when the user is at distance, factor that favors the LCL's evaluation because it is a mobile application, and therefore cannot set a specific location for its use. In addition to this method, the Server Log was also analyzed in order to gather information about the rate of voluntary use and some patterns in usage behavior. After the testing period, the users had also answered a survey about their experiences with the game, which will be presented further along.

5   The Luz, Câmera, Libras! Application

The game was built around the guessing word mechanics, (e.g. Pictionary [4], Draw Something [15]). The main goal of the game is to create a learning session between two players, where basic sign language gestures can be assimilated during the leisure activity. One of the main attractions for the user engagement is the limitation to play only among the user's Facebook friends. The familiarity with the other player creates an additional layer of entertainment which relies on watching your friends mimic a sign language gesture in front of the camera, which is funnier than watching a strange person in the same situation.

The application was developed for the iOS platform, being available for iPhones, iPods and iPads. An Android version was also developed alongside the iOS version, but for the current evaluation, only the iOS version was used. In addition to the client application being executed in the players' device, a server application was created to receive the players' responses, coordinate the matches and store the game statistics.

5.1   Game Mechanics

Currently, each match is playable by exactly two people, but the players can hold many concurrent matches. At each round the player must watch a video recorded by his friend and guess which word was signed. Next, the player must record his own video, based on three given options. Then, the recorded video is sent to the server, the round restarts, and the other player receives a notification to guess the new word.

When asked to choose between the three options, in fact three videos are shown, and the user can play them repeatedly as many times as wanted, until he feels comfortable to mimic the sign in front of the camera (Figure 3A). In the next step, the chosen video is still available to be played again, while the player is recording his own version. This way, the learning by repetition process takes place while the player tries to memorize the sequence of gestures that must be reproduced.

The words available for choosing were manually classified in three difficulty levels by the development team. Using this criterion, it was possible to initiate beginner users in the sign language, by showing them some signs that they might have used before, and then presenting some other options that required more memory effort.

In the first version of the application, the player had to choose the correct answer among four options presented on the screen. However, after initial tests, this implementation was considered inadequate for the gameplay for it was too easy to rule out the incorrect. Thus, the guessing mechanics was changed into a modified keyboard, containing a random set of possible letters mixed with the correct set of letters for the given word (Figure 3B and 3C).

The keyboard was designed to allow the user freedom to experiment with different possible answers. There is no penalty in wrong attempts, as the only way to fail this stage is to give up. In addition to manually rearranging the letters, the possibility to shuffle them is also given. To aid the user in the guessing stage there is a 'Help' feature, which puts some word letters in their right place, giving a glimpse of what the answer might be.

Once the whole gameplay is asynchronous, the two players do not have to be using the application at the same time. A normal play session would involve a player recording multiple videos for different rounds and guessing words for others. When the player is done, he/she should be comfortable to leave the application without having to wait for answers from other players. This comfortably fits the mobile nature of the platform, where players do not always have time to wait for other people's answers.

Fig. 3. A: The reference video to be memorized and mimicked; B and C: The evolution of the word guessing mechanics

6   Analyzing the Luz, Câmera, Libras! Experience

The LCL evaluation process is described next. After a testing and debugging stage, the beta version of the game was made available online (through Apple Store). The release was shared in Facebook for its quick spreading, reach and ease of regular instant updates. The user evaluation period comprehends the months of December of 2012 and January of 2013. The game was hosted on a cloud application platform, so it was possible to analyze both server and user information. Server data may provide user engagement information, whereas user answers deal with the playing experience.

6.1   Server Data Analysis

A total of 230 players were registered in the game server starting from December the 10th, from which 47 people did not play any match afterwards. From the actual 183 players, 12 of them were regular players (group A) and 30 played between 1 and 10 days (group B). The other 141 players had just about 24 hours of gaming experience (group C), which represents a rejection rate of about 77%.

During the evaluation time, 479 matches were created and 827 rounds were played. It represents approximately 1.7 rounds per match. Players from group A had a total of 139 matches they created or joined, whereas the number of rounds played was 304. As the duration of the gaming experience decreases, the number of rounds per matches behaves accordingly. Group B had 78 matches in which they played 142 rounds and group C – the larger group – had 262 matches to 381 rounds.

Regarding the number of correct answers, the longer the players kept on playing the higher was their accuracy rate. The players from the group A correctly guessed their partner's sign 56 times against 21 mistakes, which represents approximately a ratio of 2.6 for correct/incorrect answers. On the other hand, both groups B and C presented a much higher error rate than correct answers.

6.2 User Data Analysis

During the testing period, the users were asked to maintain a Self Reporting Log in order to keep track of any strange behavior the application could present, as well as ideas to improve the player experience by criticizing the game interface. This information is condensed and further explained in Figure 4A and 4B.

After the testing period, the users were asked to answer an online survey so they could provide feedback as regards several aspects, such as the interaction with the application, in game interaction, and learning and practicing issues.

About 15 users were actual respondents on the evaluation phase. Although the server data provided all user information, such as name, email or Facebook account, it was decided to do not ask for any personal information on the survey, so users could answer completely anonymously, therefore avoiding any influence on the answers.

Again, to reinforce the information gathered with the Self Reporting Log results, the users were asked to comment any problem found on the application functioning (Figure 4A), as well as interface issues (Figure 4B).

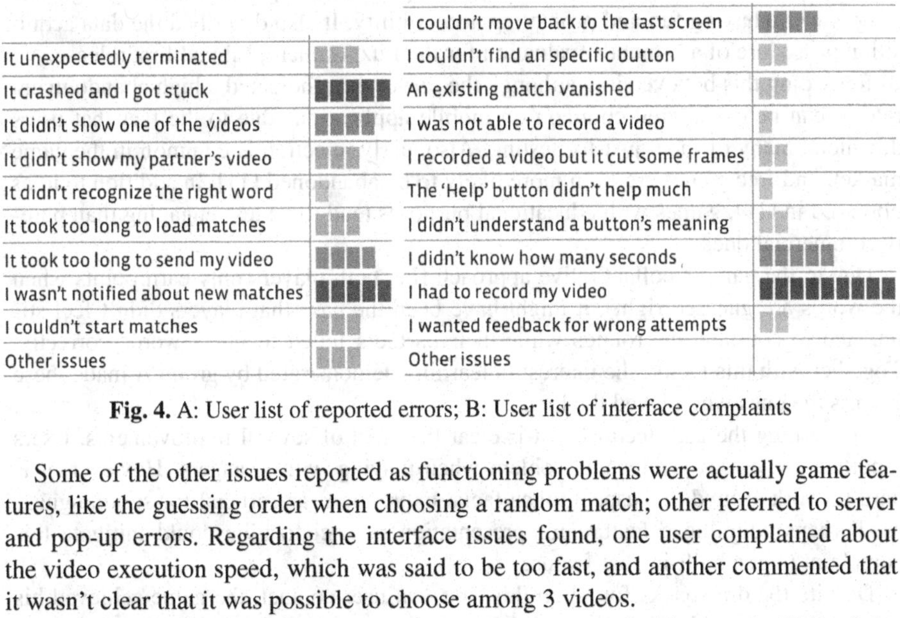

		I couldn't move back to the last screen	▮▮▮▮
It unexpectedly terminated	▮▮▮	I couldn't find an specific button	▮▮
It crashed and I got stuck	▮▮▮▮▮	An existing match vanished	▮▮
It didn't show one of the videos	▮▮▮▮	I was not able to record a video	▮
It didn't show my partner's video	▮▮▮	I recorded a video but it cut some frames	▮▮
It didn't recognize the right word	▮	The 'Help' button didn't help much	▮
It took too long to load matches	▮▮▮	I didn't understand a button's meaning	▮▮
It took too long to send my video	▮▮▮▮	I didn't know how many seconds	▮▮▮▮▮
I wasn't notified about new matches	▮▮▮▮▮	I had to record my video	▮▮▮▮▮▮▮▮▮
I couldn't start matches	▮▮▮	I wanted feedback for wrong attempts	▮▮
Other issues	▮▮▮	Other issues	

Fig. 4. A: User list of reported errors; B: User list of interface complaints

Some of the other issues reported as functioning problems were actually game features, like the guessing order when choosing a random match; other referred to server and pop-up errors. Regarding the interface issues found, one user complained about the video execution speed, which was said to be too fast, and another commented that it wasn't clear that it was possible to choose among 3 videos.

When asked if they faced difficulties in order to record videos, only 27% of the players answered negatively. About 13% reported high difficulty, 33% medium, and 27% said it was somewhat difficult. These results probably reflect the need of using both hands and face to perform some signs.

The game was randomly published at one time, aiming to replicate a real market context. In such way, only 27% of the players answered they found enough friends with whom they could play. However, it did not prevent people from playing the game. About half of the players informed they mostly interacted with unknown people.

It is important to notice that, while similar games like Draw Something also encourage the interaction with strangers, the LCL game requires users to show themselves when recording the videos. It was expected that players could feel uncomfortable or shy when playing with unknown people, which could be confirmed by 33% of the respondents. Moreover, 40% of the players reported feeling ashamed to play in public environments and 13% indicated inconvenience or intrusion in some situations.

Finally, despite the drawbacks discussed previously, 87% of the respondents said they enjoyed playing the game and had fun. Concerning the sign practice, 93% of the players indicated the game helped they learn Libras (60% reported some help and 33% said it was very helpful). In order to reinforce these results, 27% of the users informed they remembered ten or more words in Libras, 40% said they remembered around 6 words, and 20% answered about 2 words. Only 13% admitted that they did not remember a single word.

7   Conclusions and Future Work

This work introduced an innovative opportunity for learning and practicing sign languages while having fun and promoting accessibility. It also described the data acquisition procedure of a 2-month evaluation for the Luz, Câmera, Libras! first release.

Regarding this beta version, although the server data indicated a high abandonment rate, it can be considered common on mobile applications due to the fact that users download many of them just for testing. Also, early rejection is common in the game market, and free games are even more likely to be abandoned [11]. In addition to it, as observed in [19], games with educational purposes tend to be less engaging than purely commercial ones.

Due to the game's collaborative approach (i.e. both players only earn points when the words are guessed right), it might have been the case that players didn't feel stimulated to continue the rounds while their partners failed to guess words correctly. Together with this factor, the interest in learning demonstrated by group A made these players the ones who played the longest.

Concerning the user feedback, it is clear the need of several improvements. Users reported shyness as a relevant problem when playing with strangers. However, it is hard to work around this aspect, once facial expressions are crucial for sign languages. Perhaps adopting a feature for presentation or socialization could mitigate this complaint (e.g. a built-in chat feature).

Despite the drawbacks found on this first real user contact, the game achieved his main objectives: it has proven to be fun, and people also confirmed that it helped learning Libras, being possible to make use of language databases of other countries in order to develop a multilanguage solution.

As future work, the application must be continuously developed and improved to fix the many problems reported by the users and to implement some new features to promote more engagement. More than using only Libras, other sign languages are already being integrated into the system. Finally, the Android version of the game was recently finalized, so it can be integrated and distributed alongside with the iOS version, reaching a wider public this way.

References

1. Amara, F.T.: Bilingüísmo e surdez. In: Anais I Congresso Brasileiro de Linguística Aplicada, Federal University of Campinas (1983)
2. Csíkszentmihályi, M.: Flow: The Psychology of Optimal Experience. Harper Perennial (1991)
3. DMGA Brinquelibras: DomiLIBRAS Digital (2013), http://www.brinquelibras.com.br
4. Hasbro: PICTIONARY (2013), http://www.hasbro.com/shop/details.cfm?R=96C13CEE-19B9-F369-D9E8-73D9C5517F50:en_US
5. Hom, J.: The Usability Methods Toolbox Handbook, http://www.idemployee.id.tue.nl/g.w.m.rauterberg/lecturenotes/UsabilityMethodsToolboxHandbook.pdf (retrieved March 2012)
6. Laitinen, S.: Do usability expert evaluation and test provide novel and useful data for game development. Journal of Usability Studies (2), 64–75 (2006)
7. Lazzaro, N., Keeker, K.: What's my method?: a game show on games. In: CHI 2004 Extended Abstracts on Human Factors in Computing Systems (CHI EA 2004), pp. 1093–1094. ACM, New York (2004), doi:10.1145/985921.985922
8. Leonard, D.: Learning Theories: A to Z. Greenwood, 1st edn. (2002)
9. Leont'ev, A.N.: The problem of activity in Psychology. In: Wertsch, J. (ed.) The Concept of Activity in Soviet Psychology, pp. 37–69. M. E. Sharpe, New York (1979)
10. Linha Verde Interativa: Lvi LIBRAS - Curso de Língua Brasileira de Sinais (2013), http://www.linhaverdeinterativa.com.br
11. Luban, P.: The Megatrends of Game Design, Part 2, http://www.gamasutra.com/view/feature/132236/the_megatrends_of_game_design_.php?pprin=1 (retrieved March 2013)
12. Medlock, M.C., Wixon, D., Terrano, M., Romero, R., Fulton, B.: Using the RITE Method to improve products: a definition and a case study. Usability Professionals Association (UPA), Orlando (2002)
13. Montessori, M.: The Montessori Method (Translated by George, A.E.). Frederick A. Stokes Co. (1912), http://digital.library.upenn.edu/women/montessori/method/method.html
14. No Tie Software: AutoVerbal Pro Talking Soundboard (2013), http://www.autoverbal.com/
15. OMGPOP: Draw Something (2013), http://omgpop.com/drawsomething
16. Roberts, V.L., Fels, D.I.: Methods for inclusion: Employing think aloud protocols in software usability studies with individuals who are deaf. International Journal of Human-Computer Studies 64(6), 489–501 (2006) ISSN 1071-5919
17. The App Studio: Ldn Access (2013), https://itunes.apple.com/br/app/ldn-access/id496845113?mt=8
18. Villani, N.A., Wright, K.: SMILE: an immersive learning game for deaf and hearing children. In: ACM SIGGRAPH 2007 Educators Program, Article 17. ACM, New York (2007), doi:10.1145/1282040.1282058
19. Virvou, M., Katsionis, G.: On the usability and likeability of virtual reality games for education: The case of VR-ENGAGE. Computers & Education 50, 154–178 (2008)

Toward Social Media Based Writing

John Sadauskas, Daragh Byrne, and Robert K. Atkinson

Arizona State University, Tempe, AZ - 85281
{john.sadauskas,daragh.byrne,robert.atkinson}@asu.edu

Abstract. Although text-based digital communication (e.g. email, text messaging) is the new norm, American teens continue to fall short of writing standards, claiming school writing is too challenging and that they have nothing interesting to share. However, teens constantly and enthusiastically immerse themselves in social media, through which they regularly document their life stories and voluntarily share them with peers who deliver feedback (comments, "likes," etc.) which has been demonstrated to impact self-esteem. While such activities are, in fact, writing, research indicates that teens instead view them as simply "communication" or "being social." Accordingly, through a review of relevant literature, interviews with teachers, and focus groups with students, this research offers recommendations for designing technology that infuses school writing with the aspects of social media that teens find so engaging—including multi-platform access to personal informatics, guided prewriting tools, and structured peer feedback—with the ultimate goal of improving student writing.

Keywords: storytelling, usability methods and tools, social media, writing, education, educational technology, instruction, design.

1 Introduction and Background

Human beings crave stories, and in this digital age where viral videos can exceed 100 million views in under a week, crowdsourcing can fund a music album in under an hour, and self-published authors can sell several hundred thousand books in under a month, well-told stories—whether factual and fictional—can profoundly impact the world. Furthermore, as digital connectivity becomes increasingly pervasive and text-based digital communication is the norm in both professional and personal settings, writing effectively is arguably a more important skill than ever.

Yet, American students—adolescents in particular—continue to fall short of national writing standards [1], a deficiency further exacerbated by a national emphasis on reading and STEM education [2], leaving little room for the instructional time required for developing the complex cognitive processes associated with writing [3]. Self-beliefs profoundly impact one's actions [4], and because adolescents tend to believe their academic abilities are fixed rather than malleable [5, 6], those who struggle with writing often find themselves in a difficult cycle to break, as low writing confidence produces low-quality work, further reinforcing low confidence in future writing, and so on.

A. Marcus (Ed.): DUXU/HCII 2013, Part II, LNCS 8013, pp. 276–285, 2013.

The Writer's Workshop, a vastly popular writing instruction model, has shown some promise in motivating writing improvement. Its intent is to engage students by letting them choose writing topics they care about—their lives, interests, family, friends, etc.—thus intrinsically motivating them to craft stories thoughtfully and carefully [7]. These stories are then shared with peers who offer positive feedback, reinforcing the authors' efforts and ultimately improving skills and confidence in all writing genres [8, 9]. Teens themselves support this methodology, as *"they are motivated to write when they can select topics that are relevant to their lives and interests, and report greater enjoyment of school writing when they have the opportunity to write creatively...Teens also report writing for an audience motivates them to write and write well"* [10].

Unfortunately, this approach's caveat is its dependence on student self-perception. While effective with confident students, it is difficult to put into practice with struggling writers, who believe they lack the natural abilities required to write effectively [5, 6, 11] and that they have nothing interesting to say about themselves, and thus fear embarrassment in sharing writing with peers [12]. However, without realizing it, teens do have these abilities. They regularly document their lives and thoughts via social media, smartphones, and digital media [10, 13]—essentially "authoring" stories every day—and voluntarily share these stories with a "real" peer audience who deliver feedback via comments, "likes," etc. [14–16]. Teens welcome this feedback, as social acceptance is deeply important to them, and unsurprisingly, research demonstrates that feedback received via social media impacts the self-esteem of adolescents and young adults [17–19]. Interestingly, research also indicates that although such digital activities are, in fact, writing, teens do not see them as such, instead viewing them as simply "communication" or "being social" [10].

Thus, since adolescents are already immersed in practices found to improve writing outside of the classroom through social media (which, in turn, boosts self-esteem), it stands to reason that incorporating social media into the classroom will illuminate students' natural abilities as storytellers, positively affect their writing self-confidence, and ultimately motivate them to improve their writing. Accordingly, through a review of relevant literature and probative interviews and focus groups with English teachers and high school students, this research investigates opportunities for integrating social media into a writing curriculum and, based on these findings, offers recommendations for designing technology to support social media based writing.

2   Research Questions and Purpose

Because in-class writing instruction time is limited and the act of writing itself is time-intensive, a logical remedy is computer-mediated solutions supporting students both in and out of the classroom (even without a teacher present). Consequently, researchers have explored numerous computational writing intervention applications, a vast majority of which use natural language processing to support revising [20]. However, although prewriting exercises positively impact writing quality [21], few computational interventions approach writing from the content perspective [20]—i.e.

supporting personally relevant idea generation. This is largely because it is easier to have computers analyze language patterns than to mimic creative human thought. Yet, lifelogs and social media data have proven effective in seeding narratives [22, 23], and as teens regularly create digital content about themselves via social media, using these digital extensions of themselves as a browsable dataset for brainstorming would inject that missing human element into a computational framework. With this in mind, one aim of this research is to investigate such possibilities:

RQ1: In what ways might students' social media data be used for generating personally relevant writing ideas and planning a first draft?

Additionally, critiquing exemplars and work by peers is a powerful educational practice fostering self-regulation within the writing process [21, 24], allowing students to learn about form, process, and good/bad practices. In response to Web 2.0's popularity, much educational research has explored the effects of computer-mediated interaction, employing participatory web modalities through message boards, blogs, wikis, etc. for peer evaluation [14–16], particularly because students are already familiar with and voluntarily engage in such interactions. Although research implies that online interactions can influence adolescents' self-views [17–19, 25], few computational writing interventions exist that leverage these findings [20], and little to no literature formally evaluates this digital peer feedback's impact on writing quality and motivation. Hence, a second intent of this research is to explore such opportunities:

RQ2: What aspects of social media and modern digital literacy would be desirable in a peer feedback system for sharing student writing?

With the intent of compiling a set of design guidelines for social media based writing technology, these questions guided a series of explorative interviews and focus groups with teachers and students, the technology's intended users.

3   Methodology

This probative study consisted of interviews with 6 middle/high school English teachers and focus groups with 14 high school students. All sessions were audio-recorded, then transcribed, iteratively coded, and conceptualized using Grounded Theory [26].

Teacher interviews were conducted and analyzed before any student focus groups and discussed: 1) the needs, expectations and challenges in teaching writing; 2) best practices for engaging students in writing and eliciting quality work; 3) how each teacher utilizes technology in writing instruction; and 4) opportunities for integrating social media into a writing curriculum. The 6 participants (4 female, 2 male) all work as English teachers in the American Southwest, but vary in age (31-54 years), current teaching assignment (grades 6-12), and years of teaching experience (4-28).

Student focus groups were held in single, two-hour sessions, with discussion topics including: 1) students' experiences and challenges with writing; 2) their technology/social media habits and preferences; and 3) participatory design sessions for applications melding social media and classroom writing. A total of three focus groups were conducted and included 3-6 students per session. The 14 student participants (4 female, 10 male) ranged from ages 13-18 and from grades 9-12. Students were recruited from two American Southwestern high schools, both of which place particular emphasis on integrating technology into their curricula.

4   Results

General findings provided further justification for a social media based writing approach and are as follows.

4.1   Student Self-Confidence is a Major Challenge in Teaching Writing

Teacher interviews confirmed the overall reluctance adolescents have toward writing, perceiving it as beyond their skill sets [5, 6, 11, 12, 27]. In fact, when asked about their challenges in teaching writing, a majority of teachers cited student self-confidence. One said: *"I think the [greatest challenge is the] preconceived notion that "I can' t write. I'm bad at writing." I think lots of kids come into middle school saying "I am a bad writer," and they don't have confidence in their writing...They come in and they have just made a decision that reading is boring and writing is too hard."* Additionally, when asked to rate their own writing abilities, 10 out of 14 students ranked themselves as *"okay"* or even *"bad"* writers. Interestingly, these self-rated *"okay/bad"* writers included not only students enrolled in regular-level English, but even students in AP/Honors English, suggesting that the issue of writing self-confidence transcends students' actual abilities.

4.2   Personally Relevant Topics Ease Students into Writing

Supported by writing instruction literature discussed above [7–10], to ease students into writing, all interviewed teachers attempt to pique students' interest by asking them to write about topics they find relevant and meaningful. One teacher reported: *"I try to make it personal, so that writing isn't scary and this big overpowering thing."* Another added: *"I encourage students to write about things personally relevant to them 100% of the time, because no matter what, if it's relevant to them and they're revealing a little bit about themselves, it's going to be more interesting."* Unsurprisingly, students also agreed that writing is less intimidating when they are able to choose topics that interest them. One student shared: *"When you're able to choose your topics, it's much easier, I think, for me to write about because I'm interested in it."* Teens appreciate creative choice in writing, allowing them to *"branch out and do something different"* and *"play to their strengths,"* particularly enjoying the *"personal reflection"* and *"epiphanies"* afforded by writing about their experiences.

4.3   Writing for a Real Audience of Peers Increases Student Efforts

Students consistently described sharing writing with an audience beyond just one teacher as *"exciting."* In reflecting on a project where students created a public blog as a class that received local media attention, one student shared that having a wider audience is *"better than just the teacher...because I [can] produce something that could make a difference and someone could look at it and look at my ideas—someone outside of school, someone I don't even know...that was interesting, that I could do that through technology."* Additionally, students expressed that they *"like"* receiving peer feedback on their writing, describing it as *"helpful"* and *"worth it."* One student in a regular-level English class who feels he is not a strong writer even seeks peer feedback outside of his class, from friends in Honors English: *"I do have a lot of friends in [Honors English] so I'll say, 'Oh, look this over,' and then I'll get multiple opinions...and that's probably why [lately] I've been getting A/B papers."* Although teachers all agreed that peer feedback is beneficial, many felt it *"takes time,"* often more than their schedules allow. However, similar to [14–16], 3 of 6 teachers found success in extending the classroom to the digital realm, having students participate in class activities via blogs. One teacher posted weekly questions on a class blog, offering students extra credit for responding with comments: *"It was actually really effective. Students would look forward to the Sunday question and it sort of framed the week that was coming up...students and parents really liked it. Students connected to content that way a lot better than just [asking them in a class discussion] 'Well, what do you think about this?'"* Teachers also found that eliciting digital responses encouraged students who are usually *"shy"* in class to share thoughtful ideas that would not be voiced otherwise. Similarly, a student added: *"Behind the computer screen it's so much easier to talk to the person"* as there are *"not other people around"* listening.

4.4   Teens Are "Defined by" Social Media

Students and teachers alike confirmed teens' constant engagement in text-based digital communication [10], afforded primarily by smartphones, which students admit to *"always"* and *"constantly"* using and keeping within reach, even late at night: *"Mine's normally on my nightstand or if I just end up falling asleep [using it] it'd be under my pillow."* Adolescents also report their social media activity as a deliberate, carefully-maintained extension of themselves allowing them to shape their *"public"* identities (similar to [28]), often used as a venue for social affirmation. When asked how involved his students are in social media, one teacher laughed: *"I wouldn't say [students are] involved in social media. I'd say they're <u>defined</u> by social media. Looking at when I was in high school and comparing it to now, a lot of the socializing we'd do in person is now done through a mediated thing [Facebook]."* Teens appreciate the ability to share news about their lives with all of their friends at any moment and confessed their excitement when receiving notifications that a friend has "liked" or commented on one of their social media posts. One student described this feeling as *"Yay! Someone appreciates me!"* However, focus groups indicated that such behavior is more typical of younger students, and begins to wane with age. High school seniors joked about how only a year ago their social media mindsets were *"however many likes you got on a status determined how cool you were,"* but that they were now *"cleaning up"* and *"deleting dumb stuff"* on their profiles, as they looked toward more *"family-oriented"* use as adults, realizing once content is shared, *"it's all public"* and could have consequences on their futures.

5   Design Recommendations

Based on this study's conversations with students and teachers, we now offer the following design recommendations for creating technology to support social media based writing in the classroom.

5.1   Cloud-Based, Multi-platform Web Applications

As confirmed by both teachers and students, teens use multiple devices during the course of a day for school assignments. While many students indicated owning laptops and tablets at home, they rarely bring them to school because their schools provide access to *"computers and netbooks"* which they use *"every day,"* often with cloud storage to manage their files: *"I really don't need to worry about [my files] because I do a lot of stuff on Google Drive now, so I can pull it up anywhere, from any laptop."* Additionally, while teachers value student access to technology, they noted that *"having to install"* and *"set up"* new software can be frustrating and *"by the time you actually get started, you only have about twenty minutes and the class period's over,"* leaving little actual work time in class.

Teachers added that although many schools have *"policies against cell phone use,"* administrators support teachers having students use cell phones *"for instructional purposes."* As a result, teachers have found great success in allowing students to use their phones for class activities such as SMS text polls, which *"give the students and opportunity to use their phones because they WANT to use their phones. It's integrated—it is their lives. Their lives are integrated within their phones."*

With these considerations in mind, a first recommendation for social media based writing application design is a cloud-based framework, accessible on multiple devices (computers, tablets, and cell phones). Additionally, to minimize setup and eliminate the need for software installation, such applications ought to be web-based rather than local, making a web browser and Internet access the only two access requirements and thus affording students and teachers both flexible and ubiquitous use.

5.2   Scaffolded Writing Planning

Teachers agreed that, due to their resistance to writing, students often do not know where to begin with an assignment. Even given the option of choosing their own topic, students often claim they *"don't have anything interesting to write"* and even *"My life is boring."* Consistent with [21, 24], teachers unanimously cited *"scaffolding"* (walking students step-by-step through the entire writing process) as the most effective strategy for addressing this resistance. Of particular interest is how teachers guide students through prewriting, with structured questions and prompts for generating personally relevant ideas: *"I give them various questions based on experiences they've had in the past—relationships with family members, holidays, memories that are funny or things where they have a lot of emotion are really good to get them started."* Teachers encourage students to generate multiple ideas since their *"first ideas"* are typically less reflective (and thus less workable). Choosing the *"best"* from a large set of possible topics usually yields better results and encourages students that they do have *"interesting"* ideas after all: *"When they can map out all of their ideas in some way, whether through questioning or drawing, it really helps them to see that there's lots of ideas to choose for a story."* Some teachers even have students save their prewriting work as a bank of ideas to facilitate future writing topic choices.

Fittingly, in discussing social media based writing opportunities, students expressed excitement about the possibility of bringing their social media data together, *"all in one place"* as an explorable dataset of writing topic ideas, describing the idea as *"really cool"* and *"interesting"* (further detail in 5.3 below). Furthermore, teachers felt that *"using the social media as a bridge"* to a writing assignment *"would be very non-threatening"* and using this familiar, personal content to seed writing would particularly help struggling writers, as elaborating on the story behind a status update or wall photo would find them *"writing without really realizing that they're writing."*

Once a topic is chosen, teachers typically continue to guide students through *"narrowing [the topic] down"* to a usable story idea: *"you've got this huge monstrosity and you want to pick just a slice...I don't want to hear about your entire day at Disneyland...I want to hear about a moment in time."* Students appreciate when teachers facilitate this with a variety of *"mind maps," "graphic organizers,"* and *"outlines"* in order to flesh out and organize their ideas in preparation for a draft. One student who struggles with writing noted that *"lately my teacher...has been helping me with my outlines and from there, it's just—I've been getting A's and B's on my papers."*

Accordingly, a second suggestion for social media based writing technology is a scaffolded workflow with structured questions guiding students from 1) choosing an initial (social-media-inspired) idea to 2) a more focused, specific topic, and then to 3) a formal, organized plan to aid in writing a first draft.

5.3   Auto-updated Personal Informatics

Both teachers and students felt adolescent writers would benefit from sifting through their digital datasets to aid prewriting. Students in particular indicated interest in the personal informatics that a social media based writing system could afford, saying *"we never see all of our [online] activity all in one place,"* and that they could *"learn about themselves,"* and *"reflect"* on trends in their data through statistics such as *"most used words"* (visualized through word clouds), *"friends who tagged you the most,"* and common places they have "checked in" via location-based applications. As writing assignments often call for different types of topics, teachers and students felt a filtering option would be beneficial, allowing them to query specific dates or date ranges, call up *"only pictures"* or *"only status updates,"* and even *"key words you can type in"* to find data containing a search term of interest. For instance: *"if I wanted to write about Christmas, then I could go back and type in 'Christmas' and then all of the posts that I've ever posted about Christmas would show up."* Students also felt such an application ought to automatically update with any new social media activity, rather than continually importing data manually to keep it up to date: *"...it should automatically synchronize...just because you don't want to go back and drag [data] from different places. I think if it could automatically synchronize, like, anytime you post something on Facebook or Twitter or whatever, then they would automatically go to this one place. So you don't have to worry about it. It's just there."*

Therefore, a third social media based writing recommendation is for the technology to automatically synchronize with social media data, report personal informatics on this data, and provide options for filtering data based on attributes such as time, text content, and geographical location.

5.4   Prompt, Digitally-Mediated Feedback from a Peer Audience Based on Standards and Rubrics

As discussed in section 4.3, all participants felt that: 1) a peer audience increases student motivation, and 2) peer feedback is *"helpful."* While students value *"quick"* feedback [2], they often feel the quality of in-person peer review is reduced due to the time constraints of a class period. Because they must review several classmates' work in a short period of time, they often find peer reviews *"rushed,"* allowing little time for a reader to reflect. Accordingly, students especially expressed interest in using a digitally-mediated peer feedback system allowing reviewers to *"take their time."* Understanding that sometimes reviewers need to *"read [a writing piece] a few times to actually get what I'm talking about,"* students felt they would both give and receive better feedback with a turnaround time of *"within a few days"* rather than instantly.

Because students need to be trained to give quality feedback on writing [2], teachers often give students editing checklists or rubrics to facilitate the process, asking peer reviewers to look at specific aspects of the writing, such as content, organization, and punctuation. Students appreciate this guidance, and in discussing peer feedback technology possibilities, suggested the option for teachers to include *"a template online of how we should edit"* a peer's work. A particularly popular suggestion was to use the widely-adopted 6 Writing Trait rubrics[1], an assessment model asking students (and teachers) to consider and evaluate six particular aspects of writing: *"ideas/content, organization, word choice, sentence fluency, voice, and conventions."* As students have used this model in school for years, they felt it would be a suitable, universal guide for rating peers. Furthermore, students believed it would be beneficial for a peer feedback application to deliver informatics on past scored writing, reporting suggested writing traits with which the student typically struggles: *"If there was a way to—like after someone edited your paper—to rank your paper based on the 6 Traits of Writing, and then you could see over time if the comments based on these 6 Traits have changed...[For example,] if it's constantly [a low score in] word choice, then you know, 'I have to work on word choice.'"* Consequently, a fourth and final suggestion for social media based writing technology design is a system affording prompt, digitally-mediated peer feedback allowing teachers to embed standards

---

[1] http://educationnorthwest.org/traits

and/or rubrics for guiding students through a review, enabling them to deliver quality feedback.

6   Conclusion and Future Work

In response to the text-based nature of modern communication, low national adolescent writing proficiency, and shortage of in-class time for personally relevant and social components of writing instruction that are known to engage teens, this research aims to develop technology integrating social media elements into writing instruction.

Interviews with English teachers and focus groups with high school students confirmed this as an exciting approach to engage adolescent writers, and yielded four design recommendations for social media based writing: 1) cloud-based web applications that are accessible on multiple devices; 2) scaffolded, step-by-step tools for prewriting; 3) auto-updated informatics on personal data that are browsable and searchable; and 4) prompt digital feedback from peers based on standards and rubrics. The authors are currently developing applications based on these recommendations which will be piloted in high school classrooms, iteratively refined, and evaluated for both affective and academic implications. Ultimately, the goal of this work is to make available robust applications for students and teachers nationwide that will not only help students improve their writing, but also make the act of writing more enjoyable.

References

1. The Nation's Report Card: Writing, Washington, DC, USA (2011)
2. Cope, B., Kalantzis, M., McCarthey, S., Vojak, C., Kline, S.: Technology-Mediated Writing Assessments: Principles and Processes. Computers and Composition 28, 79–96 (2011)
3. Flower, L., Hayes, J.: The dynamics of composing: Making plans and juggling constraints. In: Gregg, L., Steinberg, E. (eds.) Cognitive Processes in Writing, pp. 31–50. Erlbaum, Hillsdale (1980)
4. Pajares, F.: Motivational Role of Self-Efficacy Beliefs in Self-Regulated Learning. In: Schunk, D.H., Zimmerman, B.J. (eds.) Motivation and Self-Regulated Learning: Theory, Research, and Applications, pp. 111–139. Routledge, New York (2008)
5. Anderman, E.M., Maehr, M.L.: Motivation and Schooling in the Middle Grades. Review of Educational Research 64, 287–309 (1994)
6. Dweck, C.S., Master, A.: Self-Theories Motivate Self-Regulated Learning. In: Schunk, D.H., Zimmerman, B.J. (eds.) Motivation and Self-Regulated Learning: Theory, Research, and Applications, pp. 31–51. Routledge, New York (2008)
7. Atwell, N.: In the Middle: New Understandings about Writing, Reading, and Learning. Heinemann, Portsmouth (1998)
8. Harrison, M.D.: Narrative Based Evaluation: Wording Toward the Light. Peter Lang, New York (2002)
9. Nelson, G.L.: Warriors with Words: Toward a Post-Columbine Writing Curriculum. The English Journal 89, 42–46 (2000)
10. Lenhart, A., Arafeh, S., Smith, A., Macgill, A.R.: Writing, Technology and Teens, Washington, DC, USA (2008)

11. Pajares, F.: Self-Efficacy Beliefs, Motivation, and Achievement in Writing: A Review of the Literature. Reading & Writing Quarterly 19, 139–159 (2003)
12. Furr, D.: Struggling Readers Get Hooked on Writing. The Reading Teacher 56, 518–525 (2003)
13. Lenhart, A., Purcell, K., Zickuhr, K.: Social Media & Mobile Internet Use Among Teens and Young Adults, Washington, DC, USA (2010)
14. Atkins, J.: Reading and Writing with Purpose: In and Out of School. The English Journal 101, 12–13 (2011)
15. Kitsis, S.M.: The Facebook Generation: Homework as Social Networking. The English Journal 98, 30–36 (2008)
16. Pascopella, A., Richardson, W.: The New Writing Pedagogy: Using social networking tools to keep up with student interests. District Administration 45, 44–50 (2009)
17. Ellison, N.B., Steinfield, C., Lampe, C.: The Benefits of Facebook "Friends:" Social Capital and College Students' Use of Online Social Network Sites. Journal of Computer-Mediated Communication 12, 1143–1168 (2007)
18. Gentile, B., Twenge, J.M., Freeman, E.C., Campbell, W.K.: The effect of social networking websites on positive self-views: An experimental investigation. Computers in Human Behavior 28, 1929–1933 (2012)
19. Valkenburg, P.M., Peter, J., Schouten, A.P.: Friend networking sites and their relationship to adolescents' well-being and social self-esteem. Cyberpsychology & Behavior: The Impact of the Internet, Multimedia and Virtual Reality on Behavior and Society 9, 584–590 (2006)
20. Vojak, C., Kline, S., Cope, B., McCarthey, S., Kalantzis, M.: New Spaces and Old Places: An Analysis of Writing Assessment Software. Computers and Composition 28, 97–111 (2011)
21. Graham, S., Perin, D.: A meta-analysis of writing instruction for adolescent students. Journal of Educational Psychology 99, 445–476 (2007)
22. Byrne, D., Kelliher, A., Jones, G.J.F.: Life Editing: Third-Party Perspectives on Lifelog Content. In: Proceedings of the 2011 Annual Conference on Human Factors in Computing Systems (CHI 2011), pp. 1501–1510. ACM, Vancouver (2011)
23. Appan, P., Sundaram, H., Birchfield, D.: Communicating everyday experiences. In: Proceedings of the 1st ACM Workshop on Story Representation, Mechanism and Context, SRMC 2004, p. 17. ACM Press, New York (2004)
24. De La Paz, S., Graham, S.: Explicitly teaching strategies, skills, and knowledge: Writing instruction in middle school classrooms. Journal of Educational Psychology 94, 687–698 (2002)
25. Steinfield, C., Ellison, N.B., Lampe, C.: Social capital, self-esteem, and use of online social network sites: A longitudinal analysis. Journal of Applied Developmental Psychology 29, 434–445 (2008)
26. Charmaz, K.: Grounded Theory. In: Smith, J.A. (ed.) Qualitative Psychology: A Practical Guide to Research Methods, pp. 81–110. Sage Publications, London (2003)
27. Tompkins, G.E.: Struggling Readers Are Struggling Writers, Too. Reading & Writing Quarterly: Overcoming Learning Difficulties 18, 37–41 (2002)
28. Goffman, E.: The Presentation of Self in Everyday Life. Doubleday, New York (1959)

Participatory Design for Mobile Application for Academic Management in a Brazilian University

José Guilherme Santa Rosa[1], Andrei Gurgel[2], and Marcel de Oliveira Passos[3]

[1] Ph.D. in Sciences and Health Education (UFRJ); MS in Design
(PUC-RIO) /LEXUS/UFRN, Brazil
[2] Attending Masters Degree in Design (UFRN); LEXUS/UFRN, Brazil
[3] Undergraduate in Design (UFRN); LEXUS/UFRN, Brazil
andreigurgel@gmail.com

Abstract. The object of this work is to report on the research process for the development of a mobile software application devised for academic management - SIGAA - at Rio Grande do Norte Federal University (UFRN), in Brazil. Using the methodology of Participatory Design (PD), Prototyping, and other participatory techniques, the application's interfaces were developed, and three types of prototypes for the registering and editing of student presence were tested. The implications inherent to each model, and usability recommendations for the formulation of usability guidelines for the academic information management applications project were also ascertained.

Keywords: Design, Participatory Design, Mobile.

1 Introduction

Students have increasingly been exchanging messages and searching for information by means of mobile phones and smartphones instead of using only microcomputers for these purposes. Faced with this trend, the Informatics Superintendency (SINFO) at Rio Grande do Norte Federal University (UFRN) chose to develop a mobile version of its Academic Activities Integrated Management System (SIGAA) and started a partnership with the Interface Ergodesign and Usability Experimentation Laboratory (LEXUS/UFRN) for the interface redesign, since after the development of several initial prototypes, several usability problems were found in unsystematic surveys.

SIGAA, an application originally devised for desktops, enables communication between professors and students by means of divulging student presence, evaluation grades, class plans, news, projects, message exchange, school library book collection consulting, student enrollment, among other functionalities related to academic activities.

It is important to state that the proposition for the mobile version of the application is not to replace or reproduce all functionalities found in the desktop application already deployed and consolidated at that University, but to adapt to the needs presented by new use contexts. To this end, the Participatory Design [1], [2], [3]

A. Marcus (Ed.): DUXU/HCII 2013, Part II, LNCS 8013, pp. 286–295, 2013.

approach was employed to: a) further the understanding about the user profiles (students and professors at the institution) and their needs and specificities; b) propose functionalities that are more appropriate to their ends and use contexts; c) propose more natural and effective interaction models and interface styles.

2   Methodology

In this research, the methodology adopted was the Participatory Design approach, where users are actively involved in all stages of the project, in the definition of the resources to be made available, and in the visual solutions to be implemented.

The research was carried out in two phases. 'Phase I - Survey and Problematization' was aimed at inquiring on values, beliefs, opinions, use patterns and use contexts of the users interacting with SIGAA, both in the desktop version and in the mobile version currently in initial development process by SINFO. In 'Phase II - Project and Prototyping', taking into consideration investigative aspects in 'Phase I', prototypes were developed with three different interfaces and interaction models for the functionality used by professors to include and maintain information regarding students' presence — which had been detected as one of the most troublesome during interaction.

2.1   Phase I - Survey and Problematization

In this phase of the research, studies based on ethnography were carried out involving professors (n=7) and students (n=10) from the institution. Below are the techniques employed in 'Phase I - Survey and Problematization' of this research:

Focus group [4], [5]: meeting of a representative group of the system's users, with different profiles, to enumerate needs and expectations towards the product — seven students took part, distributed in two sessions.

Contextual analysis [4]: in their work environment, the interviewees expose their difficulties and expectations when interacting with the application. Analysis was carried out with five professors who demonstrated their usage relations with the desktop version.

Cooperative evaluation [6], [5]: participants are solicited to interact with the system while conducting tasks defined by the research team. They are encouraged to verbalize their thoughts and opinions regarding usage of the system and elements of the graphical interface, exposing their impressions and expectations. Two professors and three students took part.

Regarding quantitative techniques to analyze reports and interaction logs, information from 26,219 students [7] and 1,896 professors at UFRN was considered [8]. It should be noted that the logs and reports analysis was useful to identify navigation patterns, behaviors and system functionalities more often used by the participants.

2.2 Phase II - Project and Prototyping

In 'Phase II - Project and Prototyping' of this research, prototypes were elaborated for the evaluation of three interaction models of the process wherein professors include and maintain information regarding student presence. Subsequently, a Usability Test was filled out. Below are defined the techniques employed in 'Phase II' of this research:

Prototyping [9], [10], [5]: the limited representation of a design, allowing users to interact with it and explore its conveniences. A communicational environment among members of the team, and an efficient way to test possibilities responding to matters that can effectively help the designers to choose one among several alternatives.

Usability Test [10], [4]: a source of information on how people use computers and which interaction problems they find when interacting with the interfaces being tested.

It is important to mention that, owing to the complexity of the interaction models involved in the resource being investigated, it was decided to use High Fidelity Prototyping, as it allows for greater interaction resemblance with the finished product. Santa Rosa & Moraes [5] further point out that paper prototyping brings along the difficulty of simulating the behavior of some interface elements, such as scrollbars, information conveyance through colors, execution of animations, and the fact that this type of methodology does not allow the detection of all types of usability problems.

Description of the proposed interaction models:

Model I. In 'Model I', interaction for launching and editing student presence is accomplished via a contextual menu that is presented at the moment when the user selects one of the students in the listing. Once selected, the option is positioned on the screen near the student's name (Fig. 1).

Fig. 1. Illustration for Model I interaction

Model II. Interaction in 'Model II' is closer to the version originally implemented by the programming team at SIGAA mobile, with the change of the presence status indicator happening by consecutive tapping gestures over the cell that contains the student's name onscreen. However, it should be noted that, should a user inadvertently select an unwanted option, they will need to cycle through all other options again until being able to select the desired status (Fig. 2).

Fig. 2. Illustration for Model II interaction

Model III. 'Model III' eschews the contextual menu or consecutive tapping gestures. Student presence is entered via a horizontal slide gesture over the cell that contains each student's name. Placed near the student's name, the student presence indicator cycles between the options (Fig. 3).

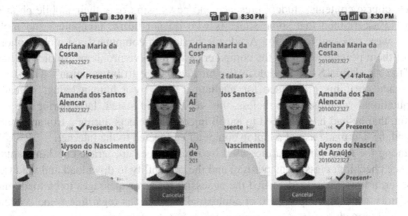

Fig. 3. Illustration for Model III interaction

Participants in the Usability Tests were professors from the Science and Technology area (n=3) and Design area (n=2).

Below are presented the main results obtained from the research, using the aforementioned methods.

3   Results

3.1   Results from Phase I (Survey and Problematization)

Focus Group. Two homogeneous group focus sessions were conducted, with three participants in the first one and four participants in the second. The first group was formed by students from the Arts field who did not own smartphones. The members of the second group, students at the Design course, were well acquainted with such devices.

To guide the focus group effectuation, questions were developed, aimed at gathering information regarding the usage of the SIGAA desktop application in students' everyday life, which system functionalities are considered more important, the locations from which the system is more often accessed, possible usage difficulties, behavior patterns for reading and communication, estimates of access session durations, participants' inclination towards using the Academic System's mobile version, and resources considered by participants as essential in the mobile application.

When asked about how their daily procedures would be without SIGAA, most participants remarked that it would be a retrogression, since the Academic System enables students to procure enrollment certificates and documents, renew book loans at the University library, and register enrollment. "I would not have as much free time as I currently do", one interviewee mentioned, referring to the time gained due to the ease to obtain class material, circumventing the old need to get in line to use a copying machine.

Altogether, it was found that the students were keen at the possibility of checking grades, course contents, student presence and news using only their mobile phones. I was also ascertained that some students who do not utilize computers and mobile phones were resistant to use the Academic System in computers and mobile phones. One of them pointed out that "the computer came to solve problems we did not have" and "the Academic System could make him a hostage to information". The student also made clear his preference for mediation done by a human being, instead of computational systems. Nevertheless, this very student stated, later during the same session, that he had had the need to enroll in course subjects during a trip and that, to this end, he had made use of a laptop computer connected to the internet.

Among the main functionalities used by interviewees are: grade checking, student presence checking, class plans perusal, and the possibility to download and read texts. However, a few students identified the necessity for error messages to be made more elucidatory, and for the presence of contextual instructions regarding some academic norms and procedures.

Some members from the second group recounted the experience of reading information in the mobile phone screen: "it's a tedious process because we keep needing to use zoom in and zoom out", in reference to readability problems. Everyone was in favor of the mobile application development, as it would become one more access medium to the aforementioned main functionalities, in addition to the new functionalities that mobile technology has to offer, such as: GPS system to locate designated sectors inside the campus, quick access to the library book locator, and the possibility of viewing urgent notices, for example last-minute changes in class times and locations, and in grades, among others.

Students also pointed out that both the desktop and mobile systems enable greater agility, time saving, and more autonomy in the ambit of the University. According to some of them, being able to monitor the course program and the class content, viewing messages sent by professors, and accessing files containing class material and notes submitted by professors, helps students to better comprehend each class program's role in the course. As stated by one of these students, from the frequency with which a professor submits educational material, it is possible to glean an idea on how much this professor is committed to the course program.

Contextual Analysis. The method was used to analyze the ways in which professors make use of the desktop SIGAA system. Contextual analysis is based upon four concepts: context, partnership, interpretation and focus. In cooperation with the user, the developer analyses the software tool in their own working environment, thus focusing on interpreting and solving problems pertaining to their own context [4], [3].

It was possible, by way of interviewing the five professors in their work environments, to achieve an understanding of the desktop system's usage in its actual context, thus enabling a more precise consideration on the resources needed and on what would be the most adequate interaction model for the mobile version. Although a prior procedure list had been prepared, a partnership relation with the interviewees was sought, encouraging them to recall difficult situations when using the system, always in the scope of the main tasks performed by them. One example were the frequent mentions of SIGAA's news system, which holds special value for most of the interviewees owing to its functioning as a formal register for events in case a student claims any particular activity has not been published, "a safeguard against unfounded accusations", one professor stated. Another professor participating in the research highlighted the need for the system to enable the sending of messages to specific groups of students, and not only to one student or to all students in a class. According to the participant, this would be especially useful in periods when students are turning in essays, when the professor needs to send or request specific information to and from a particular group of students.

All participants agree that the system furthers effective interaction between student and professor. Besides registering grades and student presence, professors regularly publish class material, news, tasks and polls. There were complaints about the system being at times bureaucratic, demanding that unnecessary fields in reports be filled out, and about a few individual usability problems — "tab usage and the 'back' button are not allowed". Everyone pointed out occasional occurrences of system downtime and instability causing the loss of inputted data in critical situations, for instance when filling out grades or student presence. The security factor was mentioned by one interviewee who showed concern regarding data privacy when the system is used on mobile equipment. Faced with this fact, the development team is implementing an approach using offline data input, which is later submitted when the device next connects to the network.

Due to being a complex system, it was found that the SIGAA desktop application is not yet utilized to its full potential — "I don't really 'get around' it that well", stated a professor, even though he has been trained on using the system. It is important to note that there is a resource for registering technical support issues built into the system, where the user can report errors, present questions or suggest modifications. In prior unsystematic surveys made with the professors, it was found that all those who had used this resource were contacted by the development team. According to some professors, this lends credibility to the system, evidencing it as an endeavor that is up to date and in constant expansion and refinement.

System usage via mobile phone application was approved by the majority of professors, even though some of them are not smartphone or tablet users. They were however favorable to using the mobile option when one wishes to check for brief information, send particular alerts to students or input student presence and grades.

Cooperative Evaluation. During Cooperative Evaluation, the user receives specific tasks and navigates through the system while in the presence of the researcher. The technique utilizes the 'think-aloud' protocol, where the researcher asks the user questions seeking to know what the user thinks, for example, when faced with a usability problem. This is an opportunity to obtain tangible answers and perform changes to the project [6]. By using Cooperative Evaluation, the development team can be immediately aware if people are understanding the interface as it is expected to be [5].

For the evaluation, a simulator of the Android operational system was used, running in computers and in smartphones. Also used was the Camtasia Studio software application, which makes it possible to simultaneously capture the screen's video and the user's image during interaction.

The majority of students had no problems carrying out most of the requested tasks, while pinpointing problems related to issues already detected in previous analyses — such as readability problems and issues with information recognition onscreen due to the fact that the current system does not have an adequate typographical deployment.

The absence of labels to identify the names and codes of course programs also contributed to usability flaws. When asked which course program he was currently accessing, an interviewee alleged not to recall.

Some interviewees saw the impossibility of sending messages directly to colleagues and professors as a usability flaw. Comparatively, professors encountered more difficulties when using the system — owing to the need to use a larger number of resources. Opinion diverged regarding the grade input process. One interviewee favored the opening of a panel every time one to four student absences were to be input. Others are comfortable with the system's standard procedure, which works by pressing the same button until four student absences are reached.

All interviewees had a hard time understanding the "delete" button's function — "delete the student here? I will not use it, it feels like I will delete the student from the list". Proximity of this button to the "cancel" option also caused ambiguous understanding — it was not clear to them if the button would undo the current operation or navigate back to the main screen.

Based upon the surveys and evaluations carried out, the screens for the new mobile version of SIGAA were prepared (Fig. 4). The observations raised also motivated 'Phase II' of this research, where prototypes were formulated for a more in depth investigation regarding the student presence registering resource in the mobile SIGAA system.

Fig. 4. Screens for News, Participants and Student Presence

3.2   Results from Phase II (Project and Prototyping)

In this research phase, the participants were professors from the Science and Technology course and from the Design course. The choice for these professor profiles allowed the research of different scenarios — while classes in the Science and Technology course usually count 150 students, in the Design course there are about 40 people.

Results from the Usability Test with the Prototypes. 'Model I' was considered the easiest to use. One participant stated that the contextual menu's presence conveyed a sensation of control. Another underscored the slow interaction with the model: "In a real life scenario, where professors from Science and Technology have very numerous classes, it would be impracticable to deploy this option". 'Model II' was considered the best alternative due to its agility and the possibility of selecting any point within a cell. And 'Model III', as one participant remarked, was initially seen as "counterintuitive": "what's the secret with this?". However, once acquainted to it, all participants considered the interaction model in this proposition as the most adequate to the context of numerous classes, due to the ease of entering consecutive registers of student presence — as users interact in a more natural way, moving a finger towards the person's photograph when attributing a presence mark to a particular student, and in the opposite direction when registering absences.

4   Recommendations (Usability Guidelines)

According to the surveys and evaluations carried out in the two phases of this research (Survey and Problematization I Project and Prototyping), procedures were devised in the form of usability guidelines that can advise the institution's designers and developers during the development of the application and of other modules that may be designed in the future.

D.1   Utilize minimalist design for the interface;

D.2   Always take into consideration using language that is natural to the user when presenting information, especially regarding dates and information about class times;

D.3   Always identify where the user is in the application in a clear manner, showing the selected option's title in an easily viewable area;

D.4   Consider a grid with enough spacing to create whitespace areas and content separators, making item selection easier and improving interaction;

D.5   Apply reduced chromatic variation;

D.6   Standardize the use of colors in order to highlight information that is urgent or very relevant to the user;

D.7   Present the most often used options above the screen "fold";

D.8   Avoid unnecessary elements in the design, such as headers and footers with decorative images or information irrelevant to interaction;

D.9   Opt for tap interaction. Where a screen slide is needed for interaction, it is necessary to signal this option in a clear and readable manner;

D.10   Typography should be compatible with platform specifications.

5   Conclusion

Although techniques such as usability testing and heuristic evaluation are known to be useful for interface assessments, the participatory approach, where users (students and professors) actively participated, proved helpful to gather more consistent information concerning usage contexts and users' characteristics and purposes. This enabled the design team to better comprehend not only the resources that should be included or left out of the application, but also the manners in which information is accessed and displayed in the interface. Therefore, taking the proposed system's users into consideration contributes both to the formulation of system and usability requirements and to the proposition of new functionalities and interaction models.

It is also noteworthy that, based on this research, guidelines were formulated which will assist developers in the deployment of new application modules, and, above all, inculcate the programming team with the importance, since initial project stages, of considering "user centered design" as a way to minimize usability problems and flaws and maximize chances of acceptance by the system.

Acknowledgements. To the team at Rio Grande do Norte Federal University Informatics Superintendency, and to Glaydson Lima and Gibeon Aquino. To the Research Pro-Rectory, to the Post-Graduation Rectory and to the Rio Grande do Norte Federal University Design Post-Graduation Program.

References

1. Muller, M., et al.: Participatory Practicies in the Software Lifecycle. In: Handbook of Human-Computer Interactions, 2nd edn. Elsevier Science B V, Amsterdam (1997)
2. Kensing, F., Blomberg, J.: Participatory Design: Issues and Concerns. Computer Supported Cooperative Work 7, 167–185 (1998)
3. Santa Rosa, J.G., Moraes, A.: Design Participativo – Técnicas para a inclusão de usuários no processo Ergodesign de Interfaces. 2ab, Rio de Janeiro (2012)
4. Cooper, A., Reimann, R., Cronin, D.: About Face 3 - The Essentials of Interaction Design. Wiley Publishing, Inc., Indianapolis (2007)
5. Santa Rosa, J.G., Moraes, A.: Avaliação e Projeto no Design de Interfaces. 2AB, Rio de Janeiro (2012b)
6. Monk, A., Wright, P., Haber, J., Davenport, L.: Improving your human-computer interface: A practical technique. Prentice-Hall, London (1993)
7. PROPLAN - UFRN em Números (2011), http://www.sistemas.ufrn.br/portalufrn/documentos/ufrn_em_numeros_2011.pdf
8. DAP - UFRN em Números (2011), http://www.sistemas.ufrn.br/portalufrn/documentos/ufrn_em_numeros_2011.pdf
9. Preece, J., Rogers, Y., Sharp, H.: Interaction Design – Beyond Human-Computer Interaction. Wiley, Chichester (2011)
10. Nielsen, J.: Usability Engineering. Morgan Kaufmann, San Francisco (1993)

YUSR: Speech Recognition Software for Dyslexics

Mounira Taileb, Reem Al-Saggaf, Amal Al-Ghamdi,
Maha Al-Zebaidi, and Sultana Al-Sahafi

Information Technology department, King Abdul Aziz University
P.O Box 42808, Jeddah 21551, Saudi Arabia
mtaileb@kau.edu.sa

Abstract. Learning disability is a classification including several disorders in which a person has difficulty learning in a typical manner. Reading disability or difficulties in reading is one of these disorders. Many researchers assert that there are different types of reading disabilities, of which dyslexia is one. Dyslexic children suffer from reading difficulties and face many challenges in their educational life. In this paper we propose an Arabic reading assistance solution for dyslexic children, it is an automatic speech recognition software based on analyzing phonetic isolated Arabic alphabet letters. The software application provides an environment for dyslexic children to develop and improve their skills of reading and spelling.

Keywords: Dyslexia, Speech Recognition, Usability.

1 Introduction

There are many learning disabilities that may impede the child's progress in learning and developing his capabilities, the most prevalent one is the disability in reading called dyslexia. One of the core problems of children suffering from dyslexia is the difficulty of learning how the printed word maps into spoken language [1]. Moreover, most dyslexic children have been found to have problems with identifying the separate speech sounds within a word and/or learning how letters represent those sounds. The causes of dyslexia are still not clear, but anatomical and brain imagery studies show differences in the way the brain of a dyslexic person develops and functions [2].

We are concerned that dyslexia is still not widely known in the Arab world; and academic researches on this specific condition in the region are extremely scarce. Some studies reported that dyslexia has analogous underlying causes in both English and Arabic and that there is potentially a common causal pathway for the phenomenon across different languages [3]. With regard to the prevalence of dyslexia in Arab populations, a nationwide study by the Kuwait Dyslexic Association reported a rate of 6% among Kuwaiti nationals [4]. A later study has identified a higher prevalence of 20% among young Kuwaiti offenders [5]. Internationally, the number of students with dyslexia entering higher education has been increasing steadily. Alarmingly, the overall incidence of dyslexia in English-speaking higher education institutions increased by almost 41% - 47% between 1994 and 1996 [6].

A. Marcus (Ed.): DUXU/HCII 2013, Part II, LNCS 8013, pp. 296–303, 2013.

With the aim of developing the skills of reading and spelling of dyslexic children and dealing with the increasing rate of dyslexic children in the Arab world, an automated speech recognition system called YUSR is proposed. It focuses on interface design and interaction and how to make them more supportive for the preferences and learning styles of dyslexics.

Developing software for dyslexic children is very useful since they are increasingly using computer technologies. It helps parents and teachers and facilitates their task to teach dyslexic children to read.

The rest of the paper is organized as follows. In section 2, a brief overview of related work is given, followed by the description of the proposed software application in section 3. Section 4 presents the discussion of the results obtained after using the application by dyslexic children. Finally, the section 5 concludes the paper.

2   Related Work

Many researches concentrate on the use of computer technologies to address the problem of dyslexia. In [7], speech recognition and eye tracking are used to adapt to readers' progress. And in [8], speech recognition and image recognition are used in AGENT-DYSL, which is an adaptive reading assistance system that allows dyslexic students to read arbitrary text documents. Speech recognition is also used in [9] to propose an automatic speech transcription for dyslexic children, it uses a speech recognition engine trained on lexical and language models specifically constructed based on their recorded readings. As example of commercial software applications there is Kurzweil 3000[1] and ReadOn[2]. Most of the software applications process the English language.

Regarding to Arabic reading applications for dyslexics, there are relatively few software applications that are targeting dyslexia and its specific problems.

3   YUSR Methodology

YUSR[3] is an Arabic software for dyslexic children. It is an automatic speech recognition (ASR) system based on analyzing phonetic isolated Arabic alphabet letters. YUSR is built to be an assistant software application for dyslexic children to learn Arabic letters pronunciation . This application aims to develop skills of reading and spelling, it provides an environment for dyslexics to use their senses in learning (vision – speech – hearing).

YUSR is an Arabic software dedicated to dyslexics of early ages depending on the discovering of the dyslexia. Target users are often of age between 5 and 10 years old.

---

[1] http://www.kurzweiledu.com
[2] http://www.readonsoftware.com
[3] In Arabic means to facilitate.

Research, questionnaire and interviews were conducted to understand the users' needs because this understanding is one of the most important factor to design user interface and ensure a high level of usability. The goal is to design and build the best suitable interface for dyslexics. As results, the following requirements were taken into account:

— Using large text and white space, this helps to make the text more readable[10].
— Considering the colors used in background and texts.
— Avoiding online classes entirely because of the reading requirements in them.
— Providing feedback about performance correctness [11].
— Providing easily clickable button size and using of meaningful icons instead of words.

YUSR is designed to provide two learning levels for users. Figure 1 illustrates the main interface of the software, it contains three buttons . The first button, represented by the cloud on the right side of the rainbow, leads to first level of the application where the user can learn the letters pronunciation. The second button, represented by the cloud on the left side of the rainbow, leads to the second level of the application. The word YUSR in Arabic is written on it. And the third button is the help button, it is in the left bottom side of the interface .

Fig. 1. YUSR's main interface

Learning the Arabic letters and their pronunciation is considered as the first stage to learn Arabic language. The first level of YUSR is dedicated to learn the dyslexic children the 28 Arabic alphabets, the first level interface is shown in figure 2. The main function of this level is providing the speech recognition of the Arabic letters; the child can record his pronunciation of the chosen letter, by clicking on the microphone icon, and get a feedback from the application. The feedback is displayed in window messages as shown in figure 3. If the pronunciation is accepted by the speech recognition system, the figure 3.a is displayed as a feedback to congratulate the child. Otherwise, the figure 3.b is displayed to ask the child to pronounce the letter again. By clicking on the headphone icon, the child can listen to the correct pronunciation of the letter with its three Harakat (short vowel marks). The pronunciation of each letter articulation is played by clicking on each of them. The pencil icon shows the child   an animation of   how to write the letter.   Also, in this window there is the letters' bar, in the left side of the figure 2, it contains all the Arabic letters as clickable icons to move between letters windows.

Fig. 2. YUSR first level interface

(a) Congratulation message   (b) Warning message

Fig. 3. Feedback messages

The second level of YUSR is about using the letter in words, as shown in figure 4. It allows the user to listen to the pronunciation of the chosen letter in three positions; at the beginning, in middle and at the last of the word. This level helps the dyslexic child to connect the knowledge of pronunciation learned in level one to the spelling and the utilization of the letter in words. Giving word examples with their associated figures supports learning and memorization.

Fig. 4. Level two of YUSR interface

The speech recognition is done by extracting the features of the sound using Mel-Frequency Cepstral Coefficients (MFCC). While The statistical model used in the recognition process is developed using Hidden Markov Model (HMM) and implemented in Hidden Markov Model toolkit (HTK toolkit). The application was trained by more than 500 samples of the Arabic alphabets with different volumes and different sounds of males and females to provide variety. The recognition rate achieved by the application is 82 % (recognition of 23 letters out of 28 Arabic letters).

By testing each letter individually, the system recognized the Arabic letters with different rates; results are shown in figure 5. Some of the letters have high rate of recognition (like the letters Jeem جيم and Ha'a حاء). However, there are some letters with a low rate of recognition (like the letters Dal دال and Seen سين) because of the confusion with similar letters (Thal ذال and Sheen شين).

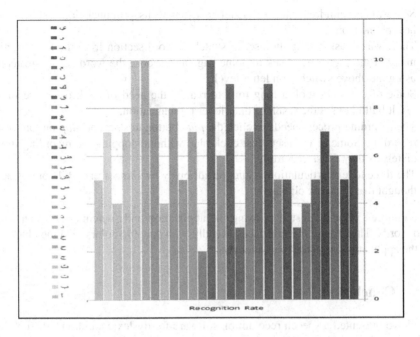

Fig. 5. Recognition rate of letters

4   Results and Discussion

Tests were conducted on seven children, three boys and four girls. The children ages are between 4 and 8 years old. The tests started by giving the children an overview about YUSR application, and then giving them tasks to perform. Testers observed tests and recorded information about time needed to perform each task and the number of correct clicks and wrong clicks. An interview is conducted with children about the software application and the problems they faced after using it.

The following are the tasks given to users:

1. Select the letters section from home.
2. Listen to letter pronunciation
3. Record your letter pronunciation
4. See how the letter is written
5. Move to another letter
6. Move to the words of the chosen letter
7. Back to the home window

After observation of the testing process, results showed that most of users did the tasks correctly. In the following, the problems that these children encountered while using the application are:

- Some of the children click the letter to listen to its pronunciation instead of the headphone icon.
- There was a task asking the user to switch to word section from the letter section. many of the users click back to home page and choose the word section instead of using the above switcher on letter level.
- Some of the users took a long time to realize the need of click on the recording result button to get the result of their letter pronunciation.
- The recording process needs to click the *play* button to start and *stop* button to stop recording. Some of the users just click play without stopping the recording immediately as they finish recording.
- The three letter's articulation is clicked curiously by some users while others never thought that there are clickable.

The children were interested in using the application and switching between letters and words. They found the interfaces friendly with suitable colors, and the characters of the application attracted their attention.

5   Conclusion

We have presented a speech recognition software for dyslexic children called YUSR. The aim is to provide an assistance to dyslexic children to improve their skill of reading. The proposed software application covers the 28 Arabic letters. For each letter, the application provides the letter pronunciation, how the letter is written and gives examples with words containing the letter at the beginning, in the middle and at the end of a word. After testing, results showed that he application reached its goal of providing a suitable and useful environment for the dyslexic child to use his/her senses in learning and encourage the interaction with the application.

For future work , we recommend to upgrade of the application by including the foundations of education for advanced cases of dyslexia, such as learning word pronunciation and assess these skills in speech recognition at the level of words. Also, add more activities to the application such as exercises with gaming functions to provide a test for the users' learning. It is also important to evaluate the application by involving more dyslexic children in the testing phase, this will help to adapt the application according to their assessed needs.

References

1. Barbra, R.: Preventing and Remediating Reading Difficulties, pp. 47–75. York Press, London (2003)
2. Klassen, R.M., Neufeld, P., Munro, F.: When IQ is Irrelevant to the Definition of Learning Disabilities. School Psychology International 26, 297–316 (2005)
3. Al Mannai, H., Everatt, J.: Phonological processing skills as predictors of literacy amongst Arabic speaking Bahraini school children. Dyslexia 11(4), 269–291 (2005), http://dx.doi.org/10.1002/dys.303

4. Kuwait Dyslexia Association: A survey study of dyslexia in Kuwait. Kuwait Dyslexia Association, Kuwait City (2002)
5. Elbeheri, G., Everatt, J., Al Malki, M.: The incidence of dyslexia among young offenders in Kuwait. Dyslexia 15(2), 86–104 (2008), http://dx.doi.org/10.1002/dys.361, doi:10.1002/dys.361
6. Dearing, R.: Higher Education in the Learning Society: Report of the Committee of Inquiry into Higher Education. Department for Education and Employment (DfEE), London
7. Amiri, H.: Reading Assistance Program for People with Dyslexia. PhD thesis, Clayton School of Information Technology, Monash University (1997, 2006)
8. Schmidt, A., Schneider, M.: Adaptive Reading Assistance for Dyslexic Students: Closing the Loop. In: Proceedings of the 15th Workshop on Adaptivity and User Modeling in Interactive Systems. FZI Research Center for Information Technologies, Karlsruhe, Germany (2007)
9. Husni, H.: Automatic transcription of dyslexic children's read speech. In: Proceedings of 2nd World Conference on Innovation and Computer Sciences 2012. School of Computing, University Utara Malaysia, Malaysia (2012)
10. Abdul Rahman, F., Mokhtar, F., Alias, N., Saleh, R.: Multimedia Elements as Instructions for Dyslexic Children. International Journal of Education and Information Technologies 6(2) (2012)
11. Dziorny, M.A.: Online course design elements to better meet the academic needs of students with dyslexia in higher education. Ph.D, University of North Texas, Texas (2012)

Measuring Usability of the Mobile Mathematics Curriculum-Based Measurement Application with Children

Mengping Tsuei, Hsin-Yin Chou, and Bo-Sheng Chen

Graduate School of Curriculum and Instructional Communications Technology
National Taipei University of Education, Taipei, Taiwan
{mptsuei,wwjdcmtc}@gmail.com, loveqoo0134@hotmail.com

Abstract. In this paper, we present the application software on mobile tablet device called mathematics curriculum-based measurement (iCBM). The iCBM was developed by various mobile technologies. Thirty-four fifth-grade elementary students participated in the study. The findings demonstrated that students had positive attitudes toward the iCBM system as well as taking math tests through mobile tablet devices. The observations of usability test on iCBM system indicated that children can use iCBM successfully. Suggestions are made about the interface design for children while using iCBM to solve math problems.

1 Introduction

As mobile devices become increasingly prominent in the lives of children, many educators are enthusiastic about the use of mobile devices for teaching and learning purposes. Children can use their fingers to surf the websites, type emails, write texts, read books, swipe photos, and switch between various applications (Apps). The mobile learning applications for children should be designed and developed in accord with their technological skills and learning capabilities.

The mobile tablet devices provide a more flexible environment for computer-based assessment than paper-and-pencil assessment. However, computer-based assessment comes in mathematics with challenges of its own because of the very nature of mathematical notations. It is not easy for children to use mathematical representatives by the keyboard. Moreover, most of the computer-based assessments in mathematics are based on the objective tests and closed-type items, like true-false and multiple choices. These assessment systems can't match the trend in mathematics education which emphasizes various dimensional aspects of students' math abilities [4]. The curriculum-based measurement (CBM) is a data-based and problem-solving model for indexing students' academic competence and progress through ongoing assessment [2][6]. This study argues that a mobile tablet environment can provide better user interface, where students can naturally write mathematical symbols for online mathematics assessment. The aim of this paper describes the design of mobile mathematic curriculum-based measurement application (iCBM) in mobile tablet device for elementary students. The initial usability measurement of iCBM was also conducted.

A. Marcus (Ed.): DUXU/HCII 2013, Part II, LNCS 8013, pp. 304–310, 2013.

2   The Curriculum-Based Measurement

Curriculum-based measurement is premised on several salient characteristics such as its focus on direct and repeated measurements of student performance in the curriculum [6]. The assessment and decision making of CBM are directly linked with local curriculum [2]. That is, a student's performance on a test should indicate the student's level of competence in the local school curriculum. In our pervious study, we have developed ECBM system to perform the mathematics CBM tests in elementary schools in Taiwan [7]. The ECBM system had the mathematics CBM item bank which included all questions on two versions of mathematics textbooks in Taiwan.

Another important characteristic of CBM is the concept of repeated measurements. The ECBM system provided each teacher with his/her own privilege to dynamically generate CBM probes through randomized-selected module. Therefore, teachers can frequently administer CBM tests in regular classrooms. The CBM probes generated from the ECBM comprised the mixed-type math questions. Each mixed-type math CBM probe included five concepts, three computations and two application questions.

The use of ECBM system helps teachers implement CBM not only by saving substantial time in collecting data, but also by analyzing ongoing assessment information in an effective way. The positive findings suggested that applying class-wide dynamic-growth modeling as well as the assessment of integrated mathematics competency in the instructional processes facilitated students' mathematics learning. However, there are two major issues need to be improved for implementing CBM tests. First, CBM probes generated from ECBM were administered in the paper-and-pencil settings. Second, teachers indicated that the digital scoring process was time consuming. Given the characteristic of mobile devices, especially their pervasive and ubiquitous nature, the unique interaction modalities (e.g., touch screens, stylus, fingers) are very suitable for children to input the mathematics notations. Therefore, in this study, we put great efforts to develop the iCBM application on a mobile tablet device for assessing children's math proficiency. In addition, we intend to measure the usability of iCBM in terms of appropriateness for children to manipulate CBM test.

3   The Usability of Mobile Tablet Device for Children

Different platforms require different user interface designs. What works for mouse-driven desktop design is not the same as for gesture-driven touch screen design. Badiu and Nielson [1] measured the usability of iPad apps and indicated that usability guidelines have to be studied about users' experience using touch screen apps. The results of the study showed that usability problems with iPad were threefold: the content was large enough to read but too small to tap, the touchable areas were too small, and the users disliked typing.

Moreover, the measurement of the usability of technology-supported learning systems is needed in order to know what the intended students think about the system. Isabwe [3] investigated the usability of a formative assessment system of mathematics on iPad. The study showed that using iPad in mathematics learning had added value. It enabled students to write using pens stylus-like to solve math problems.   However, the usability measurement of mobile tablet devices for children remains scarce. As the mobile tablet devices such as iPad and EeePad become popular in children's daily lives, research focusing on children's needs is important.

4   Method

4.1   The iCBM System

The iCBM was developed by Adobe Air and C# technology on the Android mobile platform. The EeePad mobile device was used to implement iCBM tests for elementary students. The iCBM system architecture was composed of the following two main modules:

1. The Online Measurement Module
Figure 1 presented the iCBM online testing interface. On the top of the screen were the math questions. On the left of the screen was the question number marked as written or not written. The blue background was the canvas area where students can write math expressions on the touch screen by hand. On the bottom screen of iCBM interface was the math keypad. Students can drag the math keypad to any spot on the screen. There were two math keypads provided by the iCBM. The basic math keypad included numbers (0-9), equation symbols (+,-,x,÷) , and deleting function. The dynamic keypad was shown according to the definitions in each question in the itembank, such as km, gram, degree, square centimeters, and Chinese numerical characters.

The interface designs for various math question-types were developed according to the specific rules defined in the itembank of ECBM system. There were nine question-types developed in the iCBM system.

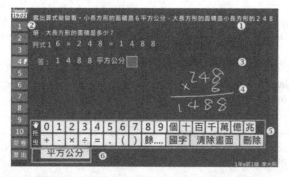

Fig. 1. The interface of iCBM (1) question area (2) question number (3) math sentences (4) drawing area (5) basic keypad (6) dynamic keypad

2. The Automated Digital Scoring Module

The scoring module of the iCBM system was developed according to the digital scoring rules of CBM model. For each question, we aggregated the correct digits of each part of a math question. For the question presented in the figure 2, students have to give answers in two parts. One is 10920 in the parentheses (5 digits), and the other is the multiplication in the records (17 digits). Then, students can get 22 digits for correct answers. For this question, the answer field defined in the itembank was [10920][##280, ###39, #2520, #840#, 10920]. The brackets were used to separate different part of answers and the "#" was defined as blank space.

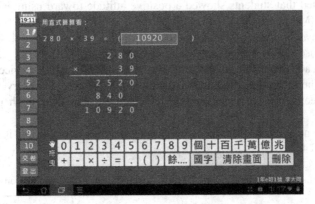

Fig. 2. The interface for question-type: Rewriting number sentences as records

4.2   Participants and Procedures

Thirty-four fifth-grade students (14 boys, 20 girls) in an elementary school in Taipei, Taiwan participated. First, they followed the researcher's instructions to complete the iCBM sample test. Then, all participants were required to take one iCBM test individually. After one week, they took another iCBM test.

For usability testing, twelve students were randomly selected for video recording on screen while they were performing the iCBM tests. The researcher made observation on how they manipulated the iCBM system.

All of the students were asked to complete a questionnaire concerning the extent of perceived usefulness and users' ease.

5   Results

5.1   Students' Performance on the iCBM Tests

The average time that students completed an iCBM test was 9.48 minutes (SD=2.12). Comparing to the previous study, the average time for completing paper-pencil CBM test was 7.5 minutes. Due to the online test on the touch screen, students took longer time to input their answers in the corresponding answer areas.

The average digital scores of students' performance on iCBM tests were 52.15 (maximum digital score=65, SD=11.37) and 57.55 (maximum digital score=70, SD=10.06). Apparently, the iCBM automatic scoring module performed correctly.

5.2   Students' Attitude toward Using the iCBM Application on EeePad

In terms of students' attitudes toward using iCBM application on EeePad, a questionnaire was implemented after the second week of iCBM test. Based on 1-5 point Likert scale, ranging from 1 ("Strongly disagree") to 5 ("Strongly agree"), the results of the survey indicated that students showed a positive attitude toward using iCBM system on math tests (M = 4.46, SD = 0.46) (Table1).

The system and interface design were easily for children to use (M=4.41,SD=0.51). They like to use iCBM system to take math tests (M=4.71,SD=0.39). They agreed with the efficacy of taking math tests by using mobile tablet devices (M=4.35, SD=0.56). The interesting finding was that children showed a conservative attitude about the effectiveness of using mobile tablet device and their math performance (question 14).

There was no gender differences on the perceptions about using iCBM system (t = -7.7, p = 0.46).

Table 1. Mean scores for the students' attitude toward using iCBM application on EeePad

	M	SD
Easy to use on iCBM	4.41	.51
Using iCBM for math test	4.71	.39
Efficacy of using EeePad on math learning	4.35	.56

5.3   Results of Usability Testing of iCBM System

It was observed that most participants took math tests on mobile devices successfully. We adopted five criteria for analyzing the videos of usability testing on the second iCBM test: the number of times that children login successfully, the number of times that children choose the test number correctly, the number of incorrect answer formats of math questions, the number of times that children drag the math keypad, and the number of times that children compute on the drawing area. The third to fifth demotions were analyzed by each question on iCBM test. The results of analysis were presented on the Table 2.

We used the numerical characters as the username and password for children to login the iCBM. The results indicated that all of students could login to iCBM successfully. Two of observed children could not choose the iCBM test correctly. The observation showed that these children forgot to choose the test number after login the system. Therefore, it was suggested that the interface design for choosing the iCBM test number has to be revised as the one-step task instead of two-step tasks.

Table 2. The usability measure of students' performance on the iCBM test (N=12)

Measures	Count
The number of times that children login successfully	12
The number of times that children choose the test number correctly	10
The number of incorrect answer formats of math questions	7
The number of times that children drag the math keypad	24
The number of time that children compute on the drawing area	54

All students indicated that the operations on iCBM system was easy to remember while taking math tests. Some of the students still needed help to change the numerical keypads to Chinese numerical characters on the math keypad. According to the results, most errors occurring during the manipulation on iCBM were to input answers in the wrong formats for specific math questions. We found that there were two math question-types deserving more attention. First, the interface of the question, "multiplication: computing 90x80 in rewriting number sentences as records", has three rows to be answered. However, some students ignored the rows for 0 multiplications. They wrote the answer directly on the bottom row (Fig. 3). Second, the inputted answers in the wrong formats occurred in the word-problem type questions. Figure 4 represented the question: "List one math sentence for the following question: Chi bought two pencils. Each costs 35 dollars. She paid 100 dollars. How much could she get back?" The interface presented one math sentence area for students to input answers. However, some students still use two sentences in one row. To avoid this problem, the interface should prevent children from using equal sign twice in one math sentence.

Fig. 3. The screenshot for input answers in the wrong formats for the multiplication question

Fig. 4. The screenshot for input answers in the wrong formats for the word problem

The results of observation indicated children drag the math keypad very often while manipulating iCBM tests. Due to limited space on mobile tablet screen, students need to drag the math keypad to the upper area to get more space for hand writing computing, especially for the word-problem questions. The other situation that children will drag the math keypad occurred when the figure underneath of the math keypad. They usually drag the math keypad to the upper place of the screen.

It was observed that children used hand-writing computation on the drawing area very often (n=54). We observed that low-achieving students used more hand-writing computation than high-achieving students did. This feature was very helpful for children while taking math assessment on mobile tablet device, especially for low-achieving students.

Based on these results, we will add the "hide/show" function to the math keypad for improving drawing area for hand-writing computation.

6   Conclusion and Future Work

Our results indicated students showed the positive attitudes toward using iCBM system. They also showed the positive attitudes toward using mobile tablet devices for math tests. In terms of interface design, most of children can perform iCBM system successfully. We found that every task performed on the iCBM has to be revised to the single-step manipulation, e. g. choosing the test number. To improve interface about inputting answer format for math questions, the interface design of two question-types were needed to be revised in the future study. We also found that the math keypad and drawing area were very essential features for mathematics assessment on the mobile tablet devices, especially for low-achieving students. A mobile tablet device assess to mathematics assessment could be another promising approach for future work in this domain.

References

1. Badiu, R., Nielson, J.: Usability of iPad Apps and Websites, 2nd edn. Nielson Normal Group. CA, http://www.nngroup.com/reports/mobile/ipad/
2. Deno, S.L.: Curriculum-based Measurement: The Emerging Alternative. Exceptional Children 52, 219–232 (1985)
3. Isabwe, G.M.N.: Investigating the Usability of iPad Mobile Tablet in Formative Assessment of a Mathematics Course. In: Proceedings of the International Conference on Information Society, pp. 39–44. IEEE (2012)
4. National Council of Teachers of Mathematics Principles and Standards for School Mathematics. Author, Reston, VA (2000)
5. Nielsen, J.: Usability Engineering. Morgan Kaufmann, San Francisco (1993)
6. Shinn, M.: Curriculum-based Measurement: Assessing Special Children. Guilford Press, New York (1996)
7. Tsuei, M.: A Web-based Curriculum-Based Measurement System for Class-wide Ongoing Assessment. Journal of Computer Assisted Learning 24, 47–60 (1998)

Teachers and Children Playing with Factorization: Putting Prime Slaughter to the Test

Andrea Valente[1] and Emanuela Marchetti[2]

[1] Department of Architecture, Design and Media Technology
[2] Department of Learning and Philosophy
Centre for Design Learning and Innovation, Aalborg University Esbjerg, Denmark
{av,ema@create.aau.dk}

Abstract. This study presents results from the evaluation of Prime Slaughter, a computer game aimed at supporting learning of factorization and prime numbers. The game was tested and re-conceptualized during a whole-day participatory workshop, involving two classes of pupils and their math teacher. As a result, it was possible to see that social play elicits fundamental questions about the nature of abstract concepts, in our case the operations involved in factorization and the relationship between natural numbers and primes, supporting sense making and reflections through verbal articulation. Moreover, new insights were gathered, in relation to enrich the game, taking inspiration from emergent meaning regarding the different forms of play allowed and the need to better support multi-player interaction.

Keywords: Playful learning, factorization, social interaction.

1 Introduction

Prime numbers and factorization are challenging and fundamental topics for mathematics and computer sciences, moreover, they are regarded as confusing and boring by pupils that have to understand and work with them for the first time. In order to facilitate learning of these topics Prime Slaughter was designed, a computer game aimed at representing factorization and primality in a playful and intuitive way. The scenario envisioned for Prime Slaughter (PS for short), was as a mediating tool for learning, to support sense making, so that a teacher could use the game as grounding for theoretical concepts and for their students to practice.

A one-day evaluation was conducted involving two classes and their math teacher, in which the participants had to play with Prime Slaughter and afterwards design low-fidelity prototypes for the game, with different materials, so to gain inspirations about how the game could be improved.

The design and gameplay of our current prototype is explained in section 2, together with related work. Section 3 presents our empirical study, focusing on methods, and the test setup. Section 4 discusses the results and user-feedback we obtained from the test, and section 5 concludes the paper.

A. Marcus (Ed.): DUXU/HCII 2013, Part II, LNCS 8013, pp. 311–320, 2013.

2   Prime Slaughter

The development of Prime Slaughter aimed at creating a mediating tool for learning, which could allow students approaching the concepts of prime numbers and factorization, to gain a multimodal grounding for the knowledge to be learnt.

Theoretically the creation of PS is based upon play, intended as a resource to foster conceptual thinking. Play mediated through tangible artefacts allows individuals to move towards an imaginary world, in which they can reflect upon their actions in play and their implications for the imaginary world (Vygotsky 1978). In this way, artefacts become tangible symbols eliciting what if questions, providing a grounding for exploration of meaning and conceptual thinking (Sutton-Smith 1987).

In the scenario we envisioned, Prime Slaughter is supposed to be used as a learning tool, to support communication between teachers and learners in a form of collaborative sense making. Hence, in our scenario, teachers may introduce factorization and prime numbers to their class and use the game to demonstrate meanings and dynamics, by playing, in a situation of apprenticeship in thinking (Rogoff 1990). In this way, the teachers can use Prime Slaughter to support their students to go beyond what they already know, supporting theoretical explanations with a multimodal and interactive representation of the concept. By multimodal representation, we intend a rich illustration of theoretical concepts, combining multiple sensory modalities (van Leeuwen 2005), specifically through audio-visual feedback in the game, and also social interaction and verbal communication among the players. Prime Slaughter is intended to provide an interactive representation of concepts, but it is not supposed to be self-explanatory, the use scenario is conceived so to rely upon teachers' experience to make it effective. When fully completed, teachers may also use the different levels of PS to perform distal arrangement (Rogoff 1990), defined as a segmentation of tasks, through which teachers adapt the content of learning and related activities to the level of mastery expressed by the students. In this sense, the teachers could assign initial or more advanced levels to the students, asking them to pay attention to different elements of the game, according to their individual needs.

Prime Slaughter is also supposed to be used independently by students as part of their homework, so that after being introduced to factorization, they can practice by themselves in order to develop their theoretical understanding through play. In this sense, it became a priority in the project to accommodate individual needs regarding play, which is also intended as a state of mind, in which learners can act in an internally motivated and exploratory way, in which they should be given the possibility to choose their course of actions (Sutton-Smith 1987, Apter 2007). Hence based upon empirical data gathered in a previous study (Marchetti and Petersson Brooks 2011), according to which different individuals tend to select among two different forms of play: a competitive and an exploratory one. It was observed that some children enjoyed play in a military form of play, in which the goal is to fight against an enemy or another player, eventually challenging and teasing each other through their play. On the contrary, other children may prefer to explore how can they modify and affect the game environment, without having to fight or to win (Marchetti and Petersson Brooks 2012).

2.1   The Prototype

The current prototype of Prime Slaughter has only one level, composed of 6 rooms, as visible in Fig. 1. In the game numbers to factorize are mapped into enemies, i.e. monsters, while division is mapped into slicing with a sword. To maintain the coherence with the source domain, swords are also numbers, but only prime numbers can be swords. In the game various clues are offered to the player, to make more sense of the source domain, for example the size of the monster-numbers depends on the number of factors. A 12-monster is therefore larger than a 6-monster, and prime monsters (e.g. 3-monsters) are the smallest. Since 1 is not a prime, 1-monsters are special and they vanish as soon as they are created. At the beginning the player only has a 2-sword, so only even monsters can be sliced in 2 halves, however, prime monsters can be captured and converted into swords, so the player can collect swords and engage larger and larger monsters.

Two different modalities of play are supported in Prime Slaughter: a classical adventure gameplay, in which a hero kills the jelly monsters, and an exploratory play style, in which players prune number-trees and collect number-fruits.

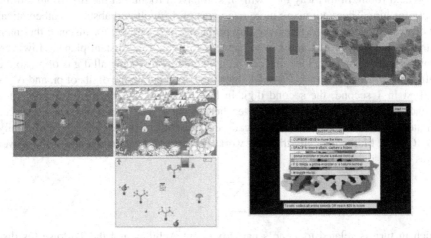

Fig. 1. Map of Prime Slaughter's first prototype. The first screen presented to the player shows instructions, then the player's character starts in the left-most room and explores all rooms. The lowest room is special: monsters cannot enter it, instead.

The number-trees are only present in the Bonsai Graveyard room (Fig. 1, lower room of the level), and since no monsters are present in the room, players can enter and leave the Graveyard to switch modality of play. Finally, testing whether a number is divisor of another is transposed into exploration of the rooms of the game, sword collection and slicing of number-monsters: in fact slicing a 3-monster with a 2-sword causes damage to the player, hence learning about divisibility provides an advantage in our game.

2.2   Related Work

In our previous study (Valente and Marchetti 2012) we surveyed math-related games, especially free online games, and found that they can be clustered in 3 groups: augmented exercises (the large majority), exploratory/manipulative environments, and very few genuine math games. We could not find any games about factorization, except computer-augmented exercises; however, if we consider fractions (a domain that makes use of factorization, for instance when adding 2 fractions) we have the IXL[1] website with augmented exercises, and the Refraction game[2], a rare and very good example of playful learning.

Considering other media, not only games as is our case, the novel *White Light* (Rucker 2001) offers an example of transposition of complex mathematical concepts into narrative. *White Light* is about Cantor's Continuum Problem, a complex mathematical problem related to the cardinality of infinite sets, and the baffling properties of infinity are a recurring theme in the book. The main character is a math teacher, who is somehow transported on a distant planet where he stays at a hotel with infinite rooms (in specific the hotel has $\aleph_0$ rooms, i.e. one room for every natural number), the Hilbert Hotel. The hotel is full, so the mathematician suggests moving every guest in the next room, in this way they will all still have a room, but the first room will be empty for him. There are many more examples of difficult and abstract mathematical concepts that become concrete everyday problems in the novel, for instance the main character wants to meet Cantor, who happens to live on the distant planet. However, Cantor's front door has a lock that can only be opened by typing all digits of pi, so the math teacher uses one of the classical algorithms to generate the digits of pi, and types the first in 1 second, the second digit in half a second, the third in a quarter of a second, and so forth. Luckily for the teacher, in the distant planet physics allows for infinite acceleration, so he can practically compose all of pi in 2 seconds and finally meet Cantor. Mathematically the trick works because of the convergence of the power series

$$\sum_{i=0}^{\infty} \frac{1}{2^i} = 2$$

which in turn is related to Zeno's paradox about Achilles and the Tortoise (as discussed also in Hofstadter 1999), the origins of calculus and Newtonian physics.

For us Rucker is very inspiring by the way he turns abstract puzzles into practical problems, and also because of the surreal and goliardic way he mixes serious topics with ordinary and often squalid situations. Making fun of (or at least having fun with) serious, tough concepts is quite close to our idea of modeling games after abstract math concepts, as it introduces a rebellious element in learning experience, linked to freedom and learners' ownership over their own learning process (Apter 2007).

---

[1]   See http://www.ixl.com/math/grade-2 at the *fraction* section.
[2]   Playable at
http://www.centerforgamescience.org/site/games/refraction

3   Evaluation and Method

A whole-day participatory workshop was set up in our university, with students from a local school in Bramming (Denmark), and their math teacher. The target group for the study is primary school and junior high school students, who are facing the topic of factorization and prime numbers for the first time, in the Danish school system it corresponds to kids 12-16 years old. All the students knew about prime numbers and factorization prior to the study (the youngest ones were introduced to the concept just the day before by their math teacher). The workshop itself was structured so that in the morning the children could test the game, alone or in pairs, and in the afternoon they could engage in a prototyping workshop in small groups.

The goal of the study was to evaluate if Prime Slaughter could support learning of factorization in a meaningful way, allowing the learners to reflect upon the represented concepts and be able to grasp their meaning. The study should also evaluate if the teachers could see learning potential in Prime Slaughter, also from the perspective of using it as a tool to demonstrate abstract concepts through the game.

During the morning the students were welcomed and introduced to Prime Slaughter by one of the authors, who also teaches math at the university, with their own teacher attending the session and assisting them in case of need. Then the students could test the game in a computer room, some of them preferred to sit alone while others were happy to share a computer with a classmate. During the session, the researchers conducted ethnographic observations and situated interviews (Pink 2006), observing the students' actions without interfering, unless some difficulty may emerge, the students called for assistance, or a particular event was spotted. The students were also filmed (with a mobile video camera in the morning and with fixed cameras in the afternoon participatory design workshop), to document their interaction and the discussions that the game elicited. An interview was also conducted with the math teacher, so that his perspective could be considered in the evaluation of the game.

In the afternoon the students were then invited to create new low-fidelity prototypes for a new version of the game, they were asked to split into groups of more or less four participants. A participatory design workshop, intended as a cooperative inquiry in which the pupils acted as design partners (Druin 2002), was run in one of the university's classroom. Each group was supposed to occupy a large table and was assigned a *design kit*, including colored cardboard, a few colored markers, a set of post-its, scissors, glue, and an envelope with screenshot prints from the different rooms of the PS game. The prints were supposed to be used as probes in the design phase (Preece et al. 2011), so that they could remember the different rooms and features of the game look like, their functionalities and their experience with them. Moreover, they could use the probes in designing their prototypes, in case they wanted. The workshop was also filmed and close-up shots of the artefacts created by each group were taken. The researchers also took field notes during the observation, so to register interesting occurrences and compare them later to the video material.

Data analysis, conducted after the workshop, involved the video material, field notes and artefacts. Visual ethnographic methods (Pink 2006) and the critical accident technique (Gremler 2004) were used as a framework to analyze video material and the artefacts created by the students. In this particular case, the critical incident technique was combined with visual ethnography (Pink 2006), so that the analysis focused on identifying meaningful incidents, during ethnographic observations, supported by situated interviews, so that the participants were interviewed while they played and while they were making prototypes, and while something interesting seemed to happen. The goal of the study was also to balance the design process of the game, which was initially decided by the authors, giving more ownership to potential users in this initial test.

Specific incidents were identified, in order to gather data about: interaction, in relation to specific features and their functionalities, signs of engagement or frustration, indicating the participants enjoyed playing our game, learning, in particular focusing on think aloud reasoning and performance in the game. These results are being used in redesigning a new prototype, which will be soon reevaluated with the same group; the results from the workshop are discussed in details in the next section.

4   Results and Discussion

In the whole-day workshop several insights were gathered, regarding how Prime Slaughter affects:

1. Learning and understanding of factorization, in relation to social play.
2. Playability and design suggestions for the creation of the next prototype.

These aspects are discussed in details in the following subsections.

4.1   Learning and Social Play

Interestingly the aspects of learning and social interaction through the game emerged as strictly interconnected. The game itself, in particular in the goal-directed activity of collecting prime-number swords in order to win, succeeded in eliciting critical questions regarding primality. Observing the students play, we noticed that individual players were sometimes talking also to other players, but in most cases called the researchers (their teacher was not present, and tested the game separately). Emerging questions opened up the possibilities to see how students relate to concept of prime numbers, what did they grasped or not from the introduction they received, such questions included: "What is the next prime number we need for our collection?", "How can we determine the next prime number?", "How can we define a prime number?". It was also noticed that doubts about the identification of the next prime numbers emerged especially for two digits numbers. Generally it seems that students expect odd numbers to be prime, as they have absorbed the notion that all the even numbers are divisible by 2, but confusion may emerge with odd numbers such as 9 and 15.

In the interview with the teacher, he expressed positive remarks on the game, stating that the students were very excited both before and after testing it, and suggesting that it may "support learning of a subject that is considered boring and hard to grasp".

These findings suggest that Prime Slaughter can also be used by the teacher as a teaching aid, to gain a clearer understanding of what the students have understood and what they find difficult, in order to support their individual needs. Considering the teacher's remarks and the students' questions, the game fits well the scenario of apprenticeship in thinking we originally had in mind, in which adults act as facilitators, supporting learners in acquiring new knowledge (Rogoff 1990).

Fig. 2. Pairs of girls and boys sharing the keyboard, one moves the hero while the other one kills and freezes monsters

The PS prototype was designed with individual players in mind, but many students played in pairs, and were able to find strategies to enjoy the game sharing one computer with a single keyboard. Some started taking turns, with one player actively playing while the other advised or commented; in other cases they shared the controls, with a player steering the character and the other killing and freezing the monsters (Fig. 2). They also expressed to each other their emotional state, talking, laughing and pointing at the screen to indicate a playmate that an action was required. Moreover, participants playing in pairs were able to support each other, discussing their questions together, hence they called for assistance only when in serious troubles. On the other hand, individual players were able to play and get in flow: some appeared very focused and quiet, others instead expressed lively their emotional state, verbally and non-verbally, for instance a girl who was eager to freeze a prime monster to gain a new sword was sitting in a tense attitude leaning towards the screen and shouted several times, but not too loud: "Freeze, freeze, freeze!" or "Bang, bang, bang!". These results suggest that PS provides adequate support for both individuals and pairs, but that social play can be a vital element in terms of user experience and learning. However, these results also suggest that the players are smartly adapting to the given interface, but that there might be other possibilities to explore, in order to support better social play and learning; for example provide a single-machine multiplayer mode and use classic Nintendo-style controllers.

4.2   Design Suggestions

Regarding possible improvements for the game, several girls suggested to introduce a distinctively feminine character, so that before starting the game, the players could choose if playing as male or female, similarly to Role Play Games. This request seems to introduce an identity aspect, which might relate to the reflective level of aesthetic experience (Norman 2004), dealing with identity and perception of self.

Moreover, several participants proposed that future levels would be shaped as mazes, with a more articulated layout and closed doors that could be opened with hidden keys (Fig. 4). These features already exist in classic games like the Legend of Zelda, which was a source of inspiration in first place, and may enrich the gameplay with new dynamics. Moreover, it could be interesting to explore how to map them into the factorization theme. For instance, the concept of a key relates both to doors and treasure chests, and to cryptography, where keys are often related to prime numbers and factorization plays a central role.

Fig. 3. Prototype of a maze level with doors and hidden keys, Lego and paper

The current PS prototype has a trap room called the "passage" (Fig. 1): the first time the player traverses it, the room appears empty, but at the next visit the room is full of 11-monsters. This trap room was highly appreciated by the students, for different reasons: some said that it was fun because of the challenge of killing so many monsters at once, on the other hand it is the only room in PS that resembles a maze, an interesting feature in itself for the test participants.

Many participants preferred the rooms with the monsters: a girl said it is fun to kill the monsters, and rarely played with the Bonsai Graveyard room (the special room where number-trees grow). However, most participants liked to shift from one room to the other and play both modalities. In some cases they realized they could strategically use the different areas to ease the collection of swords. For instance obtaining a 19 sword is quite difficult in our game. In PS monsters, trees and fruits range from 1 to 20, so 19 is the largest prime in the game. Moreover, monsters from 10 to 20 can only be found in the room called "plain" (Fig. 1), and in every room monsters spawn randomly. If the plain room does not contain any 19-monster, the player would have to kill all monsters to trigger the spawning of new (random) monsters, and eventually repeat this process until a 19-monster is eventually available, then freeze it. Hence, some of the players realizing the need a 19-sword to complete their collections, may go to the bonsai-tree room and prune trees until they get a 19 apple; in some cases this solution was suggested by the researchers. In the next prototype, it could be interesting to explore how to suggest this possibility through the game, so that it becomes an intuitive way of play.

Other improvements suggested by the children were a prize, such as a trophy, so as to allow players to gain an acknowledgement of their success and also more challenging monsters in the transition from one level to the next. Finally, several students completed the game, then decided to start playing again from the beginning; some even played the game multiple times during the test, which we interpret as a sign of appreciation. The observations, interviews and suggestions obtained in this study are the basis for the design of our next prototypes.

5   Conclusions and Future Work

The Prime Slaughter game was designed and implemented to enable primary and early secondary school students to play with prime numbers and factorization. The game design was informed by the results obtained in a 1 year field study exploring and assessing techniques for transposing dynamic and complex domain-specific knowledge into games. Empirical results from the field study suggested implementing different forms of play in the game: a competitive form of play, which was mapped into the 2D adventure game, and a designerly-creative play, which was mapped into a puzzle game (Valente and Marchetti 2011).

PS was later evaluated with a math teacher and two classes from a school from Bramming, Denmark. The participants, 12 to 16 years old, tested the game in pairs or individually and afterwards created low-fidelity prototypes with paper and Lego bricks, to give us suggestions for improvement. The players took advantage of the 2 modalities: they either tended to play with their preferred one (and the monsters rooms were the most popular), or interchanged between the two modalities, for fun or to collect swords easier. Interestingly while playing the participants asked themselves, their mates and the researchers, critical questions about primality, which prime to use to slice a particular monster, and how many primes are there between 1 and 20.

The main contribution of this work is to show how a computer game can effectively turn an abstract concept into a virtual artefact, that learners can then probe in a playful way, as well as study empirically, to explore alternative hypothesis circa its workings and verify them through experiments. This allows the learners to move from cognitive to more experiential reflection (Vygotsky 1978). The results from the test and participatory session are used as new requirements for the next PS prototype, and to reflect upon the value of social-mediated interaction in the classroom. Guidelines are also emerging from this study, that allow for a systematic analysis and design of knowledge transposition games for playful learning (Marchetti, Valente and Jensen 2013).

References

1. Apter, M.: Reversal Theory: The Dynamics of Motivation, Emotion, and Personality. Oneworld Publications, Oxford (2007)
2. Druin, A.: The Role of Children in Designing New Technology. Behaviour and Information Technology (BIT) 21(1), 1–25 (2002)
3. Hofstadter, D.R.: Gödel, Escher, Bach: An Eternal Golden Braid. Basic Books edition (1999)
4. Marchetti, E., Petersson Brooks, E.: From Lecturing to Apprenticeship: Introducing Play in Museum Learning Practice. In: The Fourth International Conference on Mobile, Hybrid, and On-line Learning: eL&mL, pp. 94–99 (2012)
5. Norman, D.: Emotional Design. Why we Love (or Hate) Everyday Things. Basic Books, New York (2004)
6. Pink, S.: Doing Visual Ethnography. Sage, London (2007)
7. Preece, J., Rogers, Y., Sharp, E.: Interaction Design. Beyond human-computer interaction. John Wiley and Sons (2011)
8. Rogoff, B.: Apprenticeship in Thinking. Cognitive Development in Social Context. Oxford University Press, New York (1990)
9. Rucker, R.: White Light, 4th edn. Four Walls Eight Windows (2001)
10. Sutton-Smith, B.: The Ambiguity of Play. Harvard University Press, Cambridge Massachusetts (2001)
11. Van Leeuwen, T.: Introducing Social Semiotics. Routledge, London (2005)
12. Vygotsky, L.S.: Mind in Society. The Development of Higher Psychological Processes. London. Harvard University Press, Cambridge Massachusetts (1978)
13. Valente, A., Marchetti, E.: Kill it or Grow it - Computer Game Design for Playful Math-Learning. In: DIGITEL 2012, pp. 17–24 (2012)
14. Marchetti, E., Valente, A., Jensen, K.: PlayDT: Transposition of Domain Knowledge into Educational Games. In: Accepted for publication in the 9th International Conference on Technology, Knowledge and Society. Common Ground Publishing Pty Ltd. (2013)

Towards a Common Implementation Framework for Online Virtual Museums

Katarzyna Wilkosinska, Andreas Aderhold, Holger Graf, and Yvonne Jung

Fraunhofer IGD, Darmstadt, Germany
kasia@wilkosinska.com, {aaderhol,hgraf,yjung}@igd.fraunhofer.de

Abstract. We present a prototypical solution to a common problem in the Cultural Heritage (CH) domain. After creation, 3D models of CH artifacts need to be processed to a format suitable for presentation on multiple platforms, e.g. in a Web Browser for online virtual museum applications, to target desktop computers and mobile devices alike. The constraints of an in-browser presentation give rise to a series of optimization and conversion concerns that need to be addressed to successfully display the CH objects in a Web application. Current 3D authoring tools do not readily support this kind of optimization and conversion required for CH domain scenarios. We therefore propose a web-based service framework, which solves the problem of pipelining 3D models for interactive Web presentations. We apply open-source technologies like X3DOM, Flask, Celery, and Redis to create a *Common Implementation Framework* (CIF) that allows content designers or researchers to optimize their 3D models for the Web through a simple one-step process.

Keywords: Web3D, Virtual Museums, Content Authoring, Cultural Heritage.

1 Introduction

Internet services like Google search or online shopping are getting more and more ubiquitous. Nevertheless, most Web applications are still 2-dimensional, though 3D graphics allows new applications, such as a Web shop, to present its products as 3D models. Likewise, interactively exploring Cultural Heritage (CH) artifacts in an online Virtual Museum based on HTML5 is possible today, even on a smart phone or the iPad [15]. Recently, with WebGL [14], real-time 3D graphics in the Browser became a reality. But since WebGL is a low-level API wrapping GPU functionality, it is not very accessible for the typical Web developer who is used to build Web applications using HTML, CSS, and scripting the DOM. Therefore, the JavaScript-based open-source framework X3DOM [3] provides declarative 3D in HTML5 while utilizing modern Web technologies like Ajax, CSS3, and WebGL.

However, the given 3D models first need to be converted into a representation suitable for the presentation on the Web. Moreover, for preview or to ease further application development, the 3D objects should be directly integrated into

A. Marcus (Ed.): DUXU/HCII 2013, Part II, LNCS 8013, pp. 321–330, 2013.

an HTML template. Finally, as the 3D visualization is part of a web page, high performance is required. Here, mesh optimization is of high importance. Essentially, Scopigno et al. [23] stated that historians, curators and other professionals are seeing more and more the need for 3D data to support their work, but that the greater challenge lies in creating new tools that use 3D models to assist CH research, to plan and document restoration, and so on.

Thus, in this paper we present an online platform that combines web-based tools and services to support the development of Virtual Museums with particular focus on presentation and visualization of Cultural Heritage assets in online virtual museums. Likewise, Berndt et al. [4] proposed a full workflow pipeline from data acquisition up to interactive web-based visualization in the Cultural Heritage domain. However, they primarily discussed 3D surface reconstruction and for presentation the authors embedded the 3D objects into a PDF document. Contrariwise, the main goal of our proposed "Common Implementation Framework" (CIF) is to provide to stakeholders and application developers alike, a useful Web platform with a harmonized pool of tools based on integrated Web technologies, to support and help them in the development of their projects.

2   The CIF Platform

The design of the CIF is based on an analysis of typical modeling workflows in the Cultural Heritage domain, starting from raw data, including the perceived limitations of current technologies, such as the deployment of 3D CH visualizations and their seamless combination with other media.

2.1   Workflows in the Cultural Heritage Domain

To prepare 3D models of artifacts for display, a multitude of operations are required, like creating a 3D model from a point-cloud, cleaning, healing and optimizing that model, converting between formats and make it suitable for display on networked devices. So, when creating a virtual museum, it is desirable to show 3D representations of CH artifacts and architectural structures on a variety of devices and operating systems to address the currently ongoing divergence of application platforms. Therefore, recently Rodriguez et al. [18] for instance presented a mixed client/server architecture, where an intelligent server prepares and delivers large point clouds in such a way that even a mobile client can display the data at interactive frame rates. However, besides their special render server, data compression along with encoding/decoding is still an intricate and time consuming process. Therefore, we focus on simpler optimization schemes (cp. e.g. [3] and [13] for more details).

It is also necessary to provide intuitive interaction possibilities tailored to a specific device – e.g., multi-touch on tablet vs. mouse on desktop. Additionally, showing or even adding meta data or annotations might be of benefit for experts [15], while the system should also provide means to navigate around and examine the object. Another very interesting application would create an entire immersive

3D world of a museum or an archeological excavation site, so that scientists, historians, etc. are able to get a better insight than it would be possible from photographs. Currently, there are several processes that need to be performed to achieve these goals. The first step is to scan the artifacts or historical sites to create digital 3D models. After scanning, the models need to be further refined using standard DCC tools like 3ds Max or Blender.

In order to present the models online, it is essential to have small file sizes and low memory footprints. This allows not only for faster download but also accounts for limited computing power of handheld devices and the constraints of Web applications running in a browser. Therefore, another process is usually model optimization that can be performed with a dedicated mesh optimization software such as MeshLab [5]. The output of this process, however, typically consists of another file in a standard 3D format like OBJ or PLY, which cannot be interpreted by a browser. Moreover, the mesh structure is not optimized for web-based rendering (e.g., for indexed rendering WebGL requires having geometry chunks of at most 2^{16} vertices). And finally, the optimized and converted models should be stored in a standardized format that will still be available in the future, why special proprietary WebGL-based 3D formats are obviously not useful. Otherwise, the underlying format should be declarative so that it can be easily integrated into a web service architecture. Here, using standardized Web techniques and services also enables an automated connection of existing data with related data to be visualized. In this context, [22] outline how to combine and link 3D data with other sources of information on the Web.

Therefore, we propose using X3DOM, a JavaScript-based framework for declarative 3D graphics in HTML5, that is based on the open ISO standard X3D [25] for describing the scene and runtime behavior. For data transcoding, the *aopt* tool from the InstantReality framework [8] can be used (see [12] for details). Thus, the model will be available for presentation in a HTML page. Though, using multiple command line tools chained together and applying styling and HTML markup by hand is possible for a few models and with appropriate knowledge, yet it is usually not a feasible approach for real-world scenarios. Thus, to achieve a more user friendly content preparation workflow esp. for non-experts, we have implemented a special web service as part of the Common Implementation Framework (CIF) proposed in this paper.

2.2 Proposed Methods and Components

For our prototype (cp. Figure 1), we have selected important visualization tools as well as optimization and transcoding services, which we will present within this paper, while also discussing possible guidelines for further design and development of the proposed architecture. The current CIF pipeline is basically as follows. First, the 3D model is uploaded. Then, a sequence of pre-processing steps is applied in order to optimize the model. Finally, the given model is transcoded into an X3DOM file and ready to be displayed on the Web.

In order to build a solid foundation of the CIF, it is mandatory to design a technology stack that is future proof. The technology and process choices have

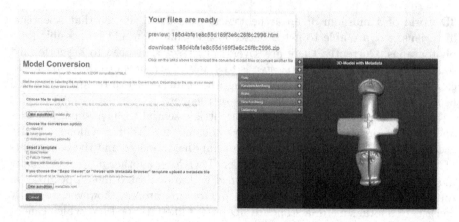

Fig. 1. Entry point for uploading and converting a 3D model (left). After the conversion is ready, a new page appears (top) with an option for online preview (right) and one for downloading a zipped package.

been taken to support ultimate flexibility, ease of integration of third party tools, and highest possible degree of maintainability, scalability and testability. In order to build a maintainable long-lasting system, it was paramount to select components and processes that are not owned by a corporation (hence are truly open source) and which are widely used in the HTML5 domain and unlikely to be vulnerable to the bus factor. Therefore, we decided to base the CIF on modern open source web application technologies with the following technology decisions. All components in this stack (compare Figure 2) are loosely coupled and thus replaceable at any time, should the need arise to exchange a specific component within the stack.

Python a stable general purpose programming language to create the web service and integrate other tools. It is a core system component of most Linux/ Unix-style operating systems and therefore already available.

Apache/mod_wsgi as web server front-end; Apache is a web server and mod_-wsgi a module to run Python application services from within Apache.

Celery as the task queue to make processing asynchronous.

Redis a key-value database for storing transient data, messages, and caching.

MeshLab to reduce and clean-up triangular meshes.

InstantReality transcoder to optimize large models for the Web.

X3DOM to present interactive 3D models in a Web browser.

Tools for 3D Rendering and Optimization. As mentioned, *X3DOM* (see http://www.x3dom.org) is an open source framework and runtime to integrate declarative 3D content directly into HTML5 by using a so-called "polyfill" layer to mimic native Web browser support. We use X3DOM [3,13] mainly for two reasons: on the one hand, the declarative data representation fits nicely with our

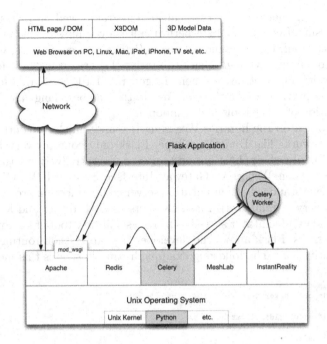

Fig. 2. The proposed CIF stack (green denotes Python-based components)

service architecture (cp. Figure 3), and on the other hand, various compressed binary formats are supported. Due to its seamless DOM integration X3DOM provides another advantage, since the application developer or content editor only needs to deal with interaction and presentation, whereas the graphics artist only needs to prepare the 3D models.

For data transcoding we have developed the *aopt* transcoder tool for optimizing 3D models with special focus on scene-graph data [12]. The transcoder is part of the *InstantReality* framework [8] that uses the X3D standard [25] as application description language. The CIF stack presented here uses aopt to convert the MeshLab optimized model into an HTML5 representation suitable for the presentation in X3DOM. The tool also allows to optimize large models for progressive loading through X3DOM (compare [3,13]). For more advanced healing and filtering processes like removing faces from non-manifolds or edge collapse mesh decimation, we use a service instance of *MeshLab* (called Mesh-LabServer), which is a portable open source system for processing and editing unstructured triangular 3D meshes [5].

Utilized Web Technologies. The core technology of our service platform is *Flask* [20], a Python-based micro framework designed for developing Web applications conforming to the Representational State Transfer (REST) paradigm [9,24]. For scalability, we furthermore use Celery [17], an asynchronous distributed task queue library that can be integrated well into Flask and uses message passing. Redis [21], a high-performance key-value store, suits as message broker. First of all, the dynamic nature of *Python* and ease of use, in combination with comprehensive high-quality libraries [11] creates a "best-for-fit" web application development environment in general [1,10] as well as for the CIF framework in particular. We therefore use Python as base language for the CIF and integration of other tools and components.

Flask is based on the libraries Werkzeug [19] and Jinja2. In contrast to fully fledged frameworks like Django or Zope, Flask only contains very basic functionality to build web applications and services. Essentially, it is a thin wrapper around the Python Webserver Gateway Interface Standard (WSGI) [7] – the Python specific standard of a application server communication protocol (similar to the Java Servlet Standard). Flask also acts as URL router and Model-View-Controller (MVC) facilitator as well as provides a library toolset for common web application tasks. Flask allows the developer to map Python routines to URLs in a declarative way. The following example listing illustrates this mechanism.

```
from flask import Flask
from flask import render_template

app = Flask("HelloWorldApplication")

@app.route("/hello")·
def hello():
    return render_template('hello.html')

app.run()
```

This example app contains a method to render a given HTML template. Once the script is executed, the application serves itself on a given port. The decorator @app.route is used to instruct the Flask kernel to call the hello method when the URL /hello is accessed in the browser. The render_template method then parses the given template and returns a string, which forms the HTTP response body that is sent back to the browser. This idiomatic approach gives the developer flexibility in library choices while removing the pain of doing error prone HTTP input/output work manually and in turn allows for easy creation of RESTful applications and APIs without hiding actual functionality. A clean separation of concerns is easily maintained but not enforced.

The *Apache HTTP server* is the de-facto standard of delivering web sites and applications today [16]. Apache listens for HTTP connections on a port and then delivers files within a HTTP response. It also automatically spawns, scales and restarts web application processes as required. In order to interface with programs like a C application, PHP, or our CIF, it needs a special extension (called module) which facilitates communication between the web server and the web application. *Mod_wsgi* [6] is such a module, which allows to run Python application servers behind the Apache HTTP server. It should be noted that the Apache HTTP server, while very useful and easy to configure, is not always a sensible choice in production environments that need to support performance and scalability with a low memory footprint. However, due to the modular design of the CIF stack, Apache can very easily be exchanged in favor of a more modern web server/ app server frontend (i.e., nginx/gunicorn).

Celery is a Python-based open source asynchronous task queue based on distributed message passing. It is easy to integrate in Python applications like Flask web apps or command line tools. Celery requires an additional component to send and receive messages, usually in form of an additional message broker service like RabbitMQ. The message broker can also be a database (e.g. Redis or CouchDB [2]) in order to retain task status information. We use Celery in order to make processing tasks in the pipeline asynchronous. Instead of letting the user wait on the processing, which could take up to minutes or even longer during high-load situations or for large models, the task is executed in the background. Once completed, the status is reported back to the web application which then lets the user download the converted model. This allows starting multiple conversion tasks simultaneously and checking the results at a later time. To find the tasks later on, a unique URL is created. At this URL the current status is displayed and, in case of successful conversion, download links are provided.

Redis is a high-performance key-value "no-SQL" Web 2.0 tool. In our technology stack, Redis is used by Celery for message passing and storing of tasks as well as status information. This allows appropriate feedback when a task fails. It may also be used to implement a rate-limit system or data caches. We thus also use Redis to implement a basic Denial of Service (DoS) attack vector counter measure called rate-limiting. In order to prevent abuse of the web application and bring down our servers, we limit the frequency of requests to the conversion pipeline for a specific user. To keep track of the IP addresses and requests already performed, Redis is used as well.

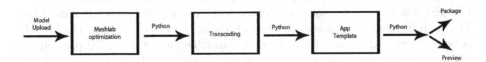

Fig. 3. The CIF workflow: a Python-based pipeline architecture for 3D model conversion and application generation

3 The Conversion Pipeline

Our proposed platform should provide the missing link between model creation and the presentation in a web browser and web services that automatically combine raw data and pre-prepared application templates into interactive 3D visualizations for the Web. The application templates define the desired application type, e.g. walk-through or standard 3D scene exploration, a user interface, etc. Our integrated online service platform thereby allows for enabling data transfer and automatic workflows for the creation and deployment of 3D Virtual Museum assets. This way, a simple method to integrate 3D visualizations into a Web application and to easily build prototypes is offered, while interactive elements can be easily added afterwards by the application developer or directly specified by providing appropriate application templates in advance.

As mentioned, the heart of the CIF is a Flask application (section 2.2), a lightweight Python component which orchestrates user input, processing, and output. It also performs mapping of URLs to Python routines – the so-called URL mapping. The first step is to upload the raw model into our application as seen in Figure 1 (left). This is achieved via a web form that is rendered by the flask application. At this point the user can also select which optimizations need to be performed on the model and which template he wants to select for the subsequent HTML presentation. After sending the form via the *Convert* button, the model file is uploaded to the web application and the conversion starts.

The entire conversion is handled by a Celery worker in the background, which allows the web app to continue while the processing happens. A unique URL is generated and sent back to the user, which informs about the current status of the process. This URL can also be used to come back later, if it should take too long to wait or the user wished to start another conversion. A Celery worker (Figure 2) performs the optimization of the model, converts it to X3DOM and creates a compressed package of the generated model data. In case of an error, the result page shows more details. Otherwise, a download link as well as a preview link are provided (see Figure 1, top) to allow downloading the whole package or directly viewing the results in the browser (Figure 1, right).

As shown in Figure 3, the CIF pipeline consists of several steps. First, the user logs in using an auth mechanism, which not only allows uploading models but also to mark them for conversion at a later time, re-process the model with different settings without uploading it again, or emailing the converted model to the user. After uploading the model, the mesh reduction and optimization starts (e.g., removal of duplicate faces, vertices or degenerate triangles). Depending on the selection of optimization parameters, a filter is created which is passed to MeshLab in a subsequent call. In case of a successful optimization, the model is being converted to an X3D/X3DOM compatible format using the previously discussed transcoder tool, where the input meshes are also further optimized and restructured if necessary. During this process, status updates of the current conversion progress are provided as feedback. Then the model is embedded into an HTML template. Currently, a basic and full-size viewer are integrated here as well as a viewer with additional meta-data browser. The final step is compressing everything to an easily downloadable zip package and generating a preview URL, which can be used to immediately view the results in the browser.

4   Conclusion and Future Work

The CIF presented here is available on GitHub (https://github.com/x3dom/pipeline) and provides a new way to rapidly develop online virtual museum applications using 3D technology. Moreover, through our proposed platform the application developer is able to quickly create small prototypes to find better solutions for larger projects. Therefore, it becomes a simple task to rapidly create a prototypical web application with embedded 3D graphics, which then can be extended with further interactive elements or just published on the web as-is. The user does not need to have deep knowledge of the tools involved, nor is it required to use all those tools manually to optimize a model.

The presented framework is still of prototypical nature but lays the foundation for further work. By choosing interchangeable open source components for building the technology stack, as well as architecting the software by standards like the MVC pattern and modularization of functionality, parts of the system can be extended, customized and refined further. Even if the need should arise to replace certain layers of the stack, this is entirely possible with minimal effort. There are many more areas in which the CIF can be improved. One such optimization is to provide the user with a broader variety of application template options that allow to choose much more different designs into which the converted model will be embedded. Alongside a greater selection of preset templates, the user should also be able to upload his own template files in order to fully customize the appearance of the optimized and HTML-ified 3D model.

At the moment the CIF only supports interaction via a web interface. This means that the user has to upload a 3D model and select optimization parameters, templates, etc. through an HTML-based interface. While this is a good way to work with less tech savvy content creators or editors or for quick tests and just a few models to be converted, it might pose a challenge to high-volume scenarios that demand a more automated workflow. One possible solution to this is accessing the conversion pipeline programmatically, through a standardized web services API. Such an API would allow automating the conversion processes through a scripting language or enables plugin writers to create e.g. a 3ds Max plugin to automatically convert and/or optimize a model through the pipeline via the exposed web service. It also allows exposing this service to other web applications, which can build upon the pipeline, like for example a web-based editing utility that allows to further edit the generated 3D app visually. Such an API would also allow integration or chaining of other, third party pipelines or provide batch processing solutions for a large collection of models.

Acknowledgements. The described work was carried out in the project *v-must*, which has received funding from the European Community's Seventh Framework Programme (FP7 2007/2013) under grant agreement 270404.

References

1. Python programming language – official website. Website, http://python.org/
2. Apache Software Foundation: The Apache CouchDB Project (2012), http://couchdb.apache.org/
3. Behr, J., Jung, Y., Franke, T., Sturm, T.: Using images and explicit binary container for efficient and incremental delivery of declarative 3d scenes on the web. In: Proceedings Web3D 2012, pp. 17–25. ACM, New York (2012)

4. Berndt, R., Buchgraber, G., Havemann, S., Settgast, V., Fellner, D.W.: A publishing workflow for cultural heritage artifacts from 3D-reconstruction to internet presentation. In: Ioannides, M., Fellner, D., Georgopoulos, A., Hadjimitsis, D.G. (eds.) EuroMed 2010. LNCS, vol. 6436, pp. 166–178. Springer, Heidelberg (2010)
5. Cignoni, P., Callieri, M., Corsini, M., Dellepiane, M., Ganovelli, F., Ranzuglia, G.: Meshlab: an open-source mesh processing tool. In: Sixth Eurographics Italian Chapter Conference. pp. 129–136 (2008)
6. Dumpelton, G.: Python wsgi adapter module for apache (2013), http://code.google.com/p/modwsgi
7. Eby, P.J.: Python web server gateway interface v1.0. Website (2003), http://python.org/dev/peps/pep-0020/
8. FhG: Instant Reality (2012), http://www.instantreality.org/
9. Fielding, R.T.: Architectural styles and the design of network-based software architectures. Ph.D. thesis (2000)
10. Foundation, P.: Python application domains (2012), http://www.python.org/about/apps/ (accessed October 18, 2012)
11. Hellmann, D.: The Python Standard Library by Example, 1st edn. Addison-Wesley Professional (2011)
12. Jung, Y., Behr, J., Graf, H.: X3dom as carrier of the virtual heritage. In: Remondino, F. (ed.) Intl. Society for Photogrammetry and Remote Sensing (ISPRS): Proceedings of the 4th ISPRS International Workshop 3D-ARCH 2011: 3D Virtual Reconstruction and Visualization of Complex Architectures (2011)
13. Jung, Y., Limper, H.P., Schwenk, K., Behr, J.: Fast and efficient vertex data representations for the web. In: Proceedings of the 4th Intl. Conf. on Information Visualization Theory and Applications, pp. 601–606. SciTePress (2013)
14. Marrin, C.: WebGL specification (2012), https://www.khronos.org/registry/webgl/specs/latest/
15. Michaelis, N., Jung, Y., Behr, J.: Virtual heritage to go. In: Proceedings Web3D 2012, pp. 113–116. ACM, New York (2012)
16. Netcraft.com: January 2013 web server survey (2013), http://news.netcraft.com/archives/2013/01/07/january-2013-web-server-survey-2.html
17. Rocco, M.: Celery Task Queue (2012), http://celeryproject.org
18. Rodriguez, M.B., Gobbetti, E., Marton, F., Pintus, R., Pintore, G., Tinti, A.: Interactive exploration of gigantic point clouds on mobile devices. In: The 14th Intl. Symposium on Virtual Reality, Archaeology and Cultural Heritage (2012)
19. Ronacher, A.: Werkzeug (python wsgi utlity library) (2011), http://werkzeug.pocoo.org/
20. Ronacher, A.: Flask (python microframework) (2012), http://flask.pocoo.org/
21. Sanfilipo, S.: Redis Remote Dictionary Server (2012), http://redis.io/
22. Schubotz, R., Harth, A.: Towards networked linked data-driven web3d applications. In: Dec3D. CEUR Workshop Proceedings, vol. 869. CEUR-WS.org (2012)
23. Scopigno, R., Callieri, M., Cignoni, P., Corsini, M., Dellepiane, M., Ponchio, F., Ranzuglia, G.: 3d models for cultural heritage: Beyond plain visualization. Computer 44(7), 48–55 (2011)
24. W3C: Relationship to the world wide web and rest architectures (2004), http://www.w3.org/TR/ws-arch/#relwwwrest
25. Web3D Consortium: Extensible 3d (X3D) (2011), http://www.web3d.org/x3d/specifications/

Part III

Designing for the Health and Quality of Life Experience

Towards an Arabic Language Augmentative and Alternative Communication Application for Autism

Bayan Al-Arifi, Arwa Al-Rubaian, Ghadah Al-Ofisan,
Norah Al-Romi, and Areej Al-Wabil

College of Computer and Information Sciences,
King Saud University, Riyadh, Saudi Arabia
{bayan.i.alarifi,gadah.oth,norah.r.it}@gmail.com,
{aalrubaian,aalwabil}@ksu.edu.sa

Abstract. In this paper we describe the development and evaluation of an iOS application designed as an augmentative and alternative communication (AAC) tool for individuals with speech and language impairments in Arabic-speaking populations. Formative evaluations carried out in different settings are described with insights obtained from involving users and domain experts in the User-Centered Design approach. Moreover, we summarize experts' reviews on the impact of using the developed application in special education classrooms.

1 Introduction

Verbal communication is essential for an individual's daily interactions with others, as it is the first tie to the world we live in. People with speech and language difficulties often experience barriers in understanding and using verbal language in communication. Speaking well-structured sentences and making themselves understood is a key challenge for them. Language impairments are linked to many disabilities such as Autism Spectrum Disorders and some cerebrovascular accidents such as strokes.

People with language impairments use augmentative and alternative communication (AAC) systems as assistive technology tools to help them in carrying out conversations in daily activities. AAC is a specialized area of the tools (high and low tech) that aim to develop techniques, aids and systems to improve the communication abilities of people with speech and language problems by the supplementation or replacement of natural speech [1].

This paper sheds light on user involvement in the design and development of AAC systems in general, and in the context of learning environments for children in particular. The system presented in this paper, called *'Touch-to-Speak*, is a novel contribution to the AAC domain, by offering a portable and configurable AAC application that supports different dialects in the Arabic language as well as Modern Standard Arabic (MSA),. This AAC application is envisioned as an assistive technology tool that can facilitate the integration of children with speech and language impairments in learning environments.

A. Marcus (Ed.): DUXU/HCII 2013, Part II, LNCS 8013, pp. 333–341, 2013.
© Springer-Verlag Berlin Heidelberg 2013

2   Background

Recent advances in mobile computing have facilitated rapid growth in AAC applications' design for tablets and mobile phones. Our research has concentrated on developing an Arabic computer-based application to enhance communication skills of people with autism spectrum disorders (ASD), with an emphasis on supporting verbal communication in local dialects as well as Modern Standard Arabic (MSA). Few AAC applications which support the Arabic language exist in the marketplace, and the ones that exist limit verbal communication to MSA despite the dominance of using local dialects in clinical settings for speech and language therapy as well as everyday communication in non-formal settings such as at home, leisure, and in most contexts in schools and at work. Consequently, the demand for AAC applications that support local dialects and have configurable settings for customizing the image-based communication and the spoken dialects has emerged. This is mainly to extend the therapy beyond the clinical settings and to facilitate communication in Arabic-speaking contexts. Anecdotal evidence together with publications in Arabic in the field of assistive technologies have highlighted the lack of AAC technologies supporting individuals with speech and language impairments, particularly in the Arabic language.

Applications for AAC are often Picture Exchange Communication (PECs) based interactive applications designed as communication solutions to help individuals whom experience difficulties in speaking to express their needs using pictures and/or typing coupled with automatically generated spoken dialog. Applications in this domain include Voice4u, TapToTalk, TouchChat, and Proloquo2Go [2]. Typical users for such applications are children or adults with ASD, Down Syndrome, Cerebral Palsy, Apraxia, Traumatic Brain Injury, ALS, Stroke (Aphasia) or other conditions that affect a person's ability to communicate effectively with natural speech.

Selecting the iPad platform for the initial proof-of concept phase for our application was based on the extensive body of research that has demonstrated how portable electronic devices (such as iPads) enhance the learning experience for children (e.g. [3], [4]). Moreover, evidence suggests that direct-manipulation interaction types that are inherent in touch screen interfaces are often easier to use for children in general and those with ASD in particular [5].

3   System Description

Inadequate support for Arabic-based AAC applications has motivated us to build Touch-to-Speak, an AAC application that is developed in the area of assistive technology to support people with communication difficulties. The target population varies in age groups and disabilities, as it includes children with autism and elders with stroke. Therefore, due to the different characteristics and needs of our target users, the application contains two separate interfaces. One interface is designed for children with ASD and is based on PECS adapted to the Arabic-speaking population.

The second interface is designed for individuals with aphasia resulting from stroke, and is based on communication boards used in clinical settings for communicating with stroke patients, which were adapted to the local context and dialects. Figure 1 illustrated the ASD interface.

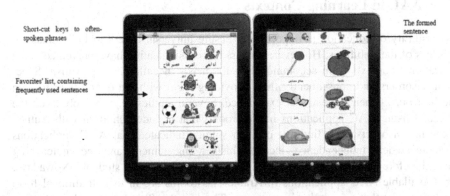

Fig. 1. Touch-to-Speak's interface for ASD

3.1   Context of Use

This application was designed as a tool to mediate communication between children and individuals in the educational context. Interaction with the AAC application takes place in the middle of conversations that involve a child with autism or an individual who has speech problems. *Touch-To-Speak* will act as a supervised translator that translates a series of pictures to well-structured sentences. When the child needs to say something he/she simply taps a picture and the application will form the sentence and read it out-loud.

The key contribution of *Touch-to-Speak* is providing augmentative and alternative communication for Arabic-speaking populations, which is not available in the market today. Moreover, it is the first Arabic AAC system that includes both local dialects and Modern Standard Arabic (MSA). This is particularly important for educational contexts in which MSA is used for the curriculum but local dialects are used for verbal communication with teachers and peers. As for our contribution to the Assistive Technology field in general, *Touch-to-Speak* adds to the existing research available covering this field. Aside to that, we have developed distinctive key features that are not available in other AAC systems that include:

- Enable creating several accounts to facilitate sharing the application on one iPad.
- Two types of images: photographic and boardmaker. This variation in image representation was included in response to bespoke design requests of speech and language therapists to address the needs of children with autism spectrum disorders who perceive these images differently.

- Customized favorite icon, where the user can choose -based on his personal preferences- one of the available icons as his/her favorite icon.
- Log report, that displays the time and date the user has used the application to facilitate progress tracking of children using these applications.

4   AAC in Learning Contexts

Accessibility of education is important to ensure universal access to individuals regardless of their abilities. However, barriers of communication have prevented some educational contexts from accommodating the needs of children with Autism Spectrum Disorders and consequently from providing them with the opportunity to gain the best out of their educational experience. Several studies (e.g. [6]) observed the effect of using AAC applications in classrooms that included children with Autism spectrum Disorders. The findings of such studies indicated that AAC applications promote student independence, increase his/her engagement, and reduce teaching time, therefore enhance and ease the education process for such students. Nowadays, most available AAC applications in Arabic classrooms are in their traditional form (picture cards) that are cumbersome to use. The fact that Touch-to-Speak is the first Arabic AAC iPad application gives it a potential role in enhancing and easing the education experience in Arabic classrooms.

5   Design Considerations

Touch-to-Speak was iteratively designed by adopting a user- centered design approach, where both Subject Matter Experts (SMEs) and children were involved in requirements' discovery phases as well as the review phases of design prototypes. Testing in design iterations of the system involved cognitive walkthroughs in which scenarios were presented with low-fidelity prototypes depicting the proposed system to SMEs; namely a speech pathologist experienced in working with children with autism and an autism specialist in special education. Feedback was solicited on the general design of the application, the structure, and the flow of the application. In later phases of the project, SMEs were involved in revising the images and spoken dialogue generated by the system. In the final stages of the project, both regular and autistic children where observed while using the application and some design elements were modified according to the problems faced by the majority of the sample.

Personas which are hypothetical characters resembling real people were created during the design process by observing the environment where the system will be applied to keep realistic analysis about its various potential users. These personas were used throughout the development of the application to enhance system's design, usability and functionality in order to meet the needs of the various end users [7].

Table 1 summarizes mapping user requirements to design elements in the application.

Table 1. Mapping user requirements to design elements

User Requirement	Design Element
The application shall to be used by users with unstable hand movement.	1. Spacing between images was measured to offer an optimal distance. 2. The image's audio description will be spoken only once (regardless of how many times it has been tapped).
The application should act as a conversation facilitator.	1. Providing categorized images, structured sentence forming, a favorite list, and quick reply buttons (e.g. thank you, yes and no) that appear on all interfaces. 2. While creating a sentence, each image's audio will be played out immediately after tapping it, without the need to finish structuring the whole sentence. 3. Providing both Modern Standard Arabic (MSA) and local dialects.
The application shall be designed to accommodate the needs of autistic children who have comorbid disorders such as ADHD.	The application provides a distraction-free environment containing static images and uses limited color schemes.
The application needs to be used by autistic children without the need of assistance.	1. Usability with a particular focus on learnability and memorability were key design considerations. 2. The navigation between interfaces was clearly designed and evaluated by SMEs.
The application should assist autistic children with various severity levels.	The system is fully customizable; it gives the user the choice between photographic and digital images.
The application should be understandable.	1. The application allows choosing a customizable favorite icon. 2. Each account is represented by the user's picture to recognize his/her account easily.

6   Formative Evaluations

Touch-to-Speak was examined as a prototype in iterative cycles with SMEs (speech and language therapists, special educational needs teachers and psychiatrists), intended target users, and caregivers of the intended target population. Various tests have indicated that Touch-to-Speak was precise in assisting verbal communication.

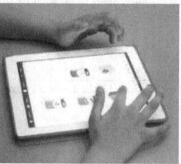

Fig. 2. Usability evaluation

The application was evaluated in terms of functionalities, task-based performance evaluations of users in using the application for communication and subjective satisfaction. User satisfaction was measured with the System Usability Scale (SUS) and resulted with 77.66 percent as an overall score across all SMEs involved in the usability sessions. In the user acceptance testing, the application's functionalities were split into two parts based on the intended users (child with ASD and the administrator) where each part was tested separately. Fourteen ASD SMEs, five typically developing children and two children with ASD were involved in the testing phase. Insights obtained from formative evaluations led to adding features and revising designs in prototypes. A summary is listed in Table 2.

Table 2. Formative evaluations

Participant (s)	Insights for Design
Autism SMEs (13) Three sessions; high fidelity prototypes	Understanding context of use; assessing the complexity of the navigation; suggestions for future work.
Speech Pathologist Two session; Requirements discovery and high fidelity prototype	Local dialect usage; configurable spoken dialog; including recorded clips to account for limitations in pronunciation in Arabic TTS engines; visual design features.

Table 2. *(Continued)*

Children with ASD High fidelity prototype and final version	Interaction modes; observations of repetitive clicking was addressed with added control of spoken dialog.

The testing process of *Touch-to-Speak* has been conducted from another viewpoint that includes enhancing the experience of communication and educational activities in learning contexts. Therefore, the team has visited one of the local intellectual education institutes to conduct interviews with speech pathologists, teachers and a psychiatrist, and test the application with some students with varying disabilities, educational levels and age groups. The following summarizes the points we have concluded from the interviews while the latter is still ongoing.

- The application was perceived by teachers working with children who have cognitive difficulties as a tool that can facilitate expression of thoughts visually for children who lack the ability to eloquently describe their needs verbally; thus it was perceived to offer an opportunity to address the gap between understanding and communicating this understanding in a classroom setting.
- It was perceived as a mediator to accelerate the communication process in an educational setting, which consequently can lead to more effective learning, especially after the student has acquired the basic skills of structuring sentences with the application.
- The application will help the teachers understand their students' needs and feelings, and therefore be able to respond to their needs.
- The time needed for training the student on using *Touch-to-Speak* depends on the student's educational level, severity of the disability and parents' cooperation in supporting the training and adoption process of this AAC application. It is estimated to range from one week to six months.
- Using *Touch-to-Speak* in education was perceived by teachers as facilitating the following:
  - Assessment of the students' understanding by whether or not s/he is participating (using the application).
  - Initial identification of the current educational level the student has reached; hence provide him/her with appropriate material.
  - Increase the chances of the student's participation in class as the application's sounds draws the teacher's attention to the student who has something to share, especially if the class includes children with no verbal communication problems, in that both groups have the chance to participate.
- The application was perceived as a tool to leverage the availability of direct-manipulation technologies that can reduce time, effort and expenses exerted in learning contexts.

- The application was perceived to assist children in different learning levels in both basic skills (e.g. learning colors and numbers) and social interaction (e.g. greeting others).

Among *Touch-to-Speak*'s spectrum of features, SMEs had a great deal of interest in the following features, where they sensed their valuable effect in education as illustrated in Table 3.

Table 3. Features contributing to the educational process

Feature	Effect On Education
Providing two types of images (Photographic and Boardmaker)	<ul><li>Supports both intermediate and advanced level students.</li><li>Understandable, clear and expressive images.</li></ul>
Localizing the images to the local culture.	Students would not find any contradiction between what s/he learns and what is in real life.
Playing back the created sentence	Playing back a sentence repeatedly helps students learn faster.
Log report	Helps teachers track and check the child's usage of the application, even outside the classroom without the need of continues observation.
The depth of the sentence (three layers maximum)	Allows a fast and an easy way to learn and form a complete correct sentence. The breadth vs. depth complexity issue was perceived as balanced given the constraints on working memory of children in the target user population.
Adding images by the built-in camera	Having images identical to real life objects facilitates easier recognition and allows students to learn more efficiently and effectively.
Speed of creating a sentence	Has the sufficient time needed for creating and learning a sentence as needed in real life.
Favorite list	Fast access to the sentences that the student should focus on.

7   Conclusion

This paper outlined the key design considerations for developing an AAC application, *Touch-to-Speak* for Arabic-speaking populations. The design process provided insights into requirements for integrating children with speech and language impairments in educational contexts. The application's features of facilitating communication in both Modern Standard Arabic (MSA) and local dialects addresses the communication needs at different levels in educational environments. Furthermore, providing two interfaces, customized accounts, dual-mode for pictures, and customized favorites' list, were key features that were perceived by practitioners and educators as means for improving the user experience in this application, and were derived from iterative cycles of design involving SMEs and intended user populations. *Touch-to-Speak* is envisioned to support the integration of children with speech and language difficulties in mainstream education and to support special education initiatives in Arab-speaking populations.

Acknowledgment. The authors extend their appreciation to the Deanship of Scientific Research at King Saud University for funding the work through grant RGP-VPP-157.

References

1. Car, E., Vuković, M., Vučak, L., Pibernik, J., Dolić, J.: A Platform Model for Symbol Based Communication Services. In: Proceedings of the 11th International Conference on Telecommunications ConTel 2011, Graze, pp. 141–147 (2011)
2. Autism Speaks (2008), http://www.autismspeaks.org/family-services/resource-library/assistive-technology (accessed June 29, 2012)
3. Frutos, M., Bustos, I., Zapirain, B.G., Zorrilla, A.M.: Computer Game to learn and enhance speech problems for Children with Autism. In: The 16th International Conference on Computer Games CGAMES 2011. IEEE (2011)
4. Reed, R.H., Berque, D.A., Pery, J.C.: The impact of tablet PCs and pen-based technology on education. Purdue University Press (2008)
5. Whalen, C., Liden, L., Ingersoll, B., Dallaire, E., Liden, S.: Behavioral improvements associated with computer-assisted instruction for children with developmental disabilities. Journal of Speech and Language Pathology - Applied Behavior Analysis 1(1), 11–26 (2006)
6. Cramer, M., Hirano, S.H., Tentori, M., Yeganya, M.T., Hayes, G.R.: Classroom-Based Assistive Technology: Collective Use of Interactive Visual Schedules by Students with Autism. Paper presented at CHI 2011, Vancouver (2011)
7. Henry, S.L., Martinson, M.L., Barnicle, K.: Beyond Video: Accessibility Profiles, Personas, and Scenarios Up Close and Personal. In: Proceedings of UPA 2003 (Usability Professionals' Association Annual Conference), Abridged (2003)

Improving Autistic Children's Social Skills Using Virtual Reality

Omaima Bamasak, Roa'a Braik, Hadeel Al-Tayari, Shatha Al-Harbi,
Ghadeer Al-Semairi, and Malak Abu-Hnaidi

Computer Science Department, College of Computing and Information Technology,
King AbdulAziz University, Jeddah, Saudi Arabia
obamasek@kau.edu.sa,
{computergirl_4,hadeel.mahamed,sha_magh,gadooorah}@yahoo.com
mabuhenidi@gmail.com

Abstract. This project presents an approach to improve autistic children's social and interactive behavior through involving them in an interactive virtual reality environment. The targeted group is in the age of 5 to 16 years. The environment to be simulated is a typical house. The autistic child will have the chance to move from one room to another and to engage in a series of activities related to each of these rooms. After each activity in each room, games will be presented to test the child's understanding and perception of the aforementioned activities. Using our developed software, the autistic children gaining improvement in their communication skills such as following commands, identifying vocabulary , linking the words to their meaning and eye contacts. They will also witness an improvement in learning the religious routines, daily habits, awareness of danger and awareness of surrounding environment.

Keywords: Autism, Autistic children, virtual reality, social skill, behavior, simulate, software.

1 Introduction

Children are invaluable assets, they are the men and women of the future who will lead the next generation. Autistic children are part of the community and of our families. "Education for All, Education for Excellence, Excellence for All", all mankind deserve this regardless of any obstacles that may impede their learning process, whether it is physical or mental, to give them the opportunities to shine and lead. This can be done by giving them the same attention and support that are given to the normal children to enhance their learning and understanding abilities.

Autism is a severe developmental disability that generally begins at birth or within the first three years of life. It is the result of a neurological disorder that changes the way the brain functions -- causing delays or problems in many different skills from infancy to adulthood. For example, both children and adults with autism usually exhibit difficulties in social interaction as well as in verbal and non-verbal communication. They also tend to be interested in odd, repetitive, or restricted activities. While

A. Marcus (Ed.): DUXU/HCII 2013, Part II, LNCS 8013, pp. 342–351, 2013.

the majority of autistic children look completely normal, they differ from other children by engaging in perplexing and distressing behaviors [1].

Statistics about autism have been particularly rare in the Middle East. One rough estimate is that the prevalence of autism in Saudi Arabia is 18 per 10,000, which is slightly higher than the 13 per 10,000 reported in the developed countries. Also, males are four times more likely to have ASD than females [2] .

Several methods have been developed over the past forty years to educate children with autism, including Applied Behavior Analysis, the TEACCH program, and sign training. These methods have proven successful to varying degrees, but come at a high cost, in terms of both time and money, due to their intensive nature. In addition, these successes are often dependent on prior student ability, working better for some subpopulation

Children with autism seem to learn best when the instructional material is presented in visual form. In this case it might be worthwhile to try different computer-based educational programs. For children, using a computer for learning is fun and attractive. The majority of educational programs are highly visual. Many of the games available involve storylines, plots, and realistic human behaviors.

Therefore, we have chosen the virtual reality concept to simulate a real home for the rehabilitation of autistic children in an attempt to improve their social and behavioral side. This choice was made because the main benefit identified for this type of disability is that the autistic children can engage in a range of activities in a simulator relatively free from the limitations imposed by their disability, and they can do so safely. Evidence that the knowledge and skills acquired by disabled individuals in simulated environments can transfer to the real world is presented. Hence, the focus of the project is not to diagnose the case, propose a treatment and then monitor the progress when applying the treatment. The remaining of the paper is organized as follows: Section 2 presents and analyzes related work in the filed, Section 3 outlined the requirements specification, Section 4 explains software architecture, Section 5 describes the implementation process, Section 6 presents the software testing results on sample of real users, and finally Section 7 concludes the paper and gives direction for future work.

2   Related Work

2.1   International Treatment Programs for Autism

Communication happens when one person sends a message to another either verbally or non-verbally. With Autistic children, communication is difficult because they are visual thinkers. For this reason, pictures are the first language they would be interested in and words are their second language. Therefore, most of international treatment program use pictures to help these children in communication. These programs have the same aim of children rehabilitating but using different approaches with a mutual goal of helping in children treatment via enhancing their communication skills.

There are several autism centers use international treatment programs and they may combine them according to a center's strategy. Most well known programs are summarized in the following.

1. ABA (Applied Behavior Analysis)

Applied Behavior Analysis (ABA) is the science of human behavior. It involves applying behavioral principles and techniques to improve socially significant behavior. ABA therapy is two-fold: interventions are used to increase behaviors that are not occurring at an appropriate rate (i.e. the individual has a skill deficit) or interventions are used to decrease behavior that is occurring too frequently (i.e. problem behavior.) [3] .

The goal is to determine what happens to trigger a behavior, and what happens after that behavior that seems to reinforce the behavior. The idea is to remove these triggers and reinforce from the child's environment. New reinforcement is then used to teach the child a different behavior in response to the same trigger. [4]

There is no cut-off age for ABA therapy as it helps individuals of all ages, including older adults. However, for the most effective therapy, early intervention is the key. Specialists recommend children in need of ABA therapy begin services before the age of 5 to have the best possible outcome. [3]

2. TEACCH (Treatment and Education of Autistic and related Communication handicapped Children)

TEACCH is a complete program of services for autistic people which makes use of various associated techniques depending upon the individual person's needs and emerging capabilities.

The main goal of TEACCH is to help autistic children grow up to their maximum ability by adult age. Advocates of TEACCH state that it aims for a 'whole life' approach in supporting children, adolescents, and adults with an Autistic Spectrum Disorder such as Autism or Asperger syndrome, through the help of visual information, structure and predictability. There is an emphasis on continuance care so where services are available, it is possible for an individual with an Autistic Spectrum Disorder to be supported from two years of age into adulthood. [5]

3. PECS (Picture Exchange Communication System)

PECS is a form of augmentative and alternative communication (AAC) that uses pictures instead of words to help children communicate. PECS was designed especially for children with autism who have delays in speech development. [6]

The main goal of PECS is to help autistic children begin to understand the usefulness of communication, then begin to use natural speech. The effective age of the youngest child was three years, and the oldest was twelve years [7]. It can be used in schools, homes and therapy setting .[6]

PECS may also help improving social interactions in autistic children. Because the child is in charge of approaching the communication partner, the child learns how to make the first move. For autistic children, approaching another person socially can be difficult. However, in this case, the child is not expected to speak, so the initial approach may be less intimidating.[8]

4. BHS (Boston Higashi School)

Boston Higashi School is a unique educational philosophy, developed by the late Dr. Kiyo Kitahara and Mr. Katsuhei Kitahara who were the founders of both the Musashino Higashi Gakuen School in Tokyo, Japan and the Boston Higashi School, in Randolph, MA. [9]

This school incorporates a broad and balanced curriculum including academics, art, music, physical education, computer technology and social education. Students take on challenges, learn to overcome obstacles and gain confidence from their own success. [9]

Boston Higashi School help children and young adults with Autism Spectrum Disorder to learn to reach their full potential through the application of the methodology of Daily Life Therapy , this process allows students to develop a love for learning so they may fully enjoy their family, community, and all that life has to offer. As students grows and learns, their personality and individual character matures allowing them to benefit from and, most importantly, contribute to society as adults. Its students are from 3 years old through 22 years old who do not suffer from severe mental retardation, uncontrolled seizures or physical disabilities. [9]

2.2   Software Solutions for Autism

Games for autistic children can provide many educational benefits. There are variety of single-player and multiple-player games that can improve important developmental and behavioral skills, for example

1. MouseTrial's Autism Software

MouseTrial's autism software is a collection of fun-filled exercises and games design for Autistic children. It is based on ABA treatment to develop the vocabulary and Communication in children with autism.[10]

The main goal of the MouseTrial is to help kids with autism on [11]

- Concentration: the ability to focus on an exercise for increasingly long periods.
- Cooperation willingness: to take part in activities when asked to.
- Vocabulary Acquisition and retention of new words and their meanings.
- Literacy Recognition of written words and letters (by switching pictures).

MouseTrial is used by children covering a very wide range of ages from toddlers to teenagers. You can adjust the level of difficulty to make sure that the player is successful most of the time while still making progress and encountering new challenges. [12]

2. ZAC Browser (Zone for Autistic Children)

It is the first browser for Autistic children that include games , stories , music and videos. It was designed to offer a pleasant, rewarding children sing, play and discover the best that the Internet has to offer with only a few clicks of the mouse. [13]

The main goal of ZAC is the zone that will permit the child to interact directly with a lot of games and activities (focused on many interests) that cater specifically to children who display the characteristics of autism spectrum disorders, like impairments in social interaction, impairments in communication, restricted interests and repetitive behavior. ZAC has been an effective tool for children and high functioning autism. . [13]

2.3   Related Work Analysis

In the following table, we compare the common treatment programs and software against the criteria that we specified for Autistic enhancement program .

Table 1. Evaluation of treatments and software programs

Criteria	Treatment Programs				Software Programs	
	TEACCH	PECS	ABA	Higashi	Mouse Trial	ZAC browser
1) Communication skills : 1-1 Follow commands	√	√	√	√	√	
1-2 Identify Vocabulary	√	√	√	√	√	√
1-3 Link words to their meaning	√	√	√	√	√	√
2) Sociability : 2-1 Eye contact	√	√	√	√	√	√
3) Awareness of environment	√	√	√	√	√	√
4) Structure teaching 4-1 Look at pictures	√	√	√	√	√	√
4-2 Define the main part s of the house	√	√		√	√	
4-3 Religious habits						
4-4 Daily habits	√	√	√	√	√	
4-5 Awareness of danger				√		

Table 1. (*Continued*)

5) Software features : 5-1 Interaction						√	√
5-2 User friendly						√	√
5-3 Freely available							√
5-4 Easy to download						√	√
5-5 Using 3D modals							√

As a result of the analysis presented above, we have determined the requirements of our virtual reality software by incorporating some features found in the treatment programs and others that are not available in the related software such as building up their religious habits, awareness of danger and the manners they need inside the house, which will improve their overall behavior.

3   Requirements Specification

We have determined the program's requirements based on the results concluded from the literature review of the International treatment programs, software and the collected data from the interview the specialists and questionnaire.

The project requirements are categorized in two groups: functional and non-functional.

3.1   Functional Requirements

This subsection represents the activities and behaviors that the program must provide for autistic children.

— Provide a welcome page that will contain description of the game.
— The house contains four rooms : bedroom, kitchen, living room and bathroom
— In the kitchen, the child will learn:
  ○ Decencies of eating.
  ○ Identifying the name of fruits, vegetables and kitchen tools.
  ○ Asking the child about the name of food and tools to make sure of his understanding.

• In bedroom, the child will learn:

  ○ Defining how to pray and asking the child about it.
  ○ Teaching the child the sleeping decencies.

• In bathroom, the child will learn:

  ○ Identifying the steps of ablution and asking the child about it.
  ○ Identifying the steps of brushing teeth and asking the child about it.

  o Identifying the tools of bathroom.
  o Identifying the bathroom decencies.

- In living room the child will learn :

  o Reading book to recognize the animals and colors.
  o Playing puzzle to improve his concerning ability.

3.2 Non Functional Requirements

This subsection represents the features, characteristics and constraints that provide a satisfactory program for autistic children.

— Colours and sounds must be appropriate.
— The graphics and animations in virtual reality will be simple, does not contain a lot of shapes that may disturb the child.
— Repeat the questions to child if he chooses wrong answers.

4 Software Architecture

The environment is a typical house consists of living room , kitchen , bedroom and bathroom . The scenario will be as follows:
The first interface will contain three buttons (Start –How to play – Exit), start button to start the game , how to play button contains general instruction as a guidelines to use the game and exit button to exit from the game . If the child selects start button , the animated character called Amjed ,who will guide the child with autism through the virtual reality, will introduce himself and name of te rooms to the child. Then a list of rooms will appear to the child to select which room he wants to play in .

- The child selecting the living room :

In the living room the child can read books of animals , colors and Amjed will utter the name of each animals , color to clarify and facilitate the understanding. Alternatively, the child can play a set of puzzles to increase his mental skills. Also he can go back to the list of rooms by selecting exit button .

- The child selecting the kitchen :

Amjed will teach the child eating decencies and introduce him to the name of kitchen tools and some fruits. Then, automatically a set of match games will appear containing fruits , vegetables and kitchen tools . The child must click on the appropriate picture depending on the matching words . If he select a wrong picture, three buttons will appear (help – try again – exit) . Help button will show the correct answer , try button will return the child back to the last correct answer then he can complete the game, while exit button will exit from the game to the list of rooms . If the child answers correctly, a winning window will appear with motivating song then he will directly go to the list of rooms .

- The child selecting the bedroom :

Amjed will teach the child sleeping decencies and the steps of pray with animation and sound . After that, a pray match game will appear , in which the child must select the appropriate picture depending on the order of pray's steps . If he select a wrong picture, three buttons will appear (help – try again – exit) . Help button will show the correct answer , try button will return the child back to the last right answer then he can complete the game, while exit button will exit from the game to the list of rooms . If the child answers correctly, a winning window will appear with motivating song then he will go directly to the list of rooms .

- The child select the bathroom :

There will be four buttons in the bathroom, (let's learn ablution – let's learn brushing teeth – let's learn bathroom tools – exit). If the child selects "let's learn ablution ", Amjed will teach him the ablution steps then ablution match game will appear in which the child must select appropriate picture depending on the order of ablution's steps. If the child selects " let's learn brushing teeth " , Amjed will teach the child the brushing teeth steps then brushing teeth match game will appear , in which the child selects appropriate picture depending on the order of brushing teeth's steps. If the child selects "let's learn bathroom tools ", Amjed will utter the name of bathrooms tools for the child to recognize. For each matching game, if the child selects a wrong picture, three buttons will appear (help – try again – exit) . Help button will show the correct answer, try button will return the child back to the last correct answer then he can complete the game, while exit button will exit from the game to the bathroom . If his answer is correct, then a winning window will appear with motivate song . When he finishes any game and returns back to the bathroom , he can select exit button to return back to the list of rooms .

5   Implementation

The tools that have been used to implement the virtual reality are Blender, Make human 1.0 alpha 5.1 , Python , Adobe Audition 3.0 , Format factory , Adobe Photoshop and Microsoft Office Visio 2007. The implementation process consists of four phases:

1. Modeling and Texturing.
2. Animation.
3. Game logics.
4. Direction.

We started building the house as plans, which was developed to form as a complete house structure, and then we built and textured each room individually. Afterwards, we built the character, named "Amjad" using Make Human software and we added some modification on it such as clothes , shoes and hair using Blender. This was followed by defining the game logics for each room including animation of the character and the activities. Finally, in direction phase, we modified the size of the camera and equality in all scenes so that the required parts are visible. These phases are shown in figures 1-3 for the living room as an example. The software was produced in executable format (.exe) , so that any user can easily download and run it.

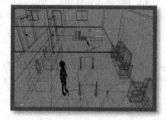

Fig. 1. Modeling phase of living room

Fig. 2. Texture phase of living room

Fig. 3. Complete living room

6   Results

We have tested the project on a sample of 10 autistic children in the specified age group. The test showed that the software was easy for them to use. The use of colors and sounds was suitable to their condition. The scores of the games following each activity showed that the children have gained benefit and that they learnt the presented behavior and skills successfully.

The project was presented to the specialists from Dubai Autism Center and Jeddah Autism Center for evaluation. They found that he buttons in home page are clear. They also found that the colors and furniture are appropriate and non-dispersive for the autistic children. The songs were found to be non-disturbing for most children. At the end, they concluded that the developed software is appropriate for autistic children as it covers several domains, i.e. Cognitive, Social, Self-care. The developed software has the advantage of implementing   visual stimuli which is a source of strength for autistic children.

7   Conclusion

Based on the recommendations of specialists and the results of tests we found that the idea of simulating the real home using the virtual reality helps the autistic children to get the acquired skills and learnt better to get other skills. Autistic child is like any normal child possesses the effective skills but need a special software to discover and develop those skills. The future work will be extending the software to include environment outside the house, i.e. streets, schools, supermarket, etc.

References

1. My child without limits,
   http://www.mychildwithoutlimits.org/?page=autism
2. Wikipedia, http://en.wikipedia.org/wiki/Epidemiology_of_autism
3. Autism Learning Felt, http://www.autismlearningfelt.com/2010/04/providing-aba-therapy-for-your-child.html
4. Healing Thresholds, http://autism.healingthresholds.com/therapy/applied-behavior-analysis-aba
5. Bright Tots, http://www.brighttots.com/TEACCH_Method_autism
6. Healing Thresholds, http://autism.healingthresholds.com/therapy/picture-exchange-communication-system-pecs
7. National Professional Development Center on Autism S spectrum Disorders,
   http://autismpdc.fpg.unc.edu/sites/autismpdc.fpg.unc.edu/files/PictureExchangeCommunication_Brief_0.pdf
8. Pedia Staff, http://www.pediastaff.com/resources-picture-exchange-communication-system-featured-october-13-2011
9. Boston Higashi School,
   http://www.bostonhigashi.org/about.php?id=7notused
10. Mouse Trial Autism Software, http://www.mousetrial.com/index.html
11. Mouse Trial Autism Software,
    http://www.mousetrial.com/home_benefits.html
12. Mouse Trial Autism Software,
    http://www.mousetrial.com/home_suitable.html
13. PC Win, http://pcwin.com/Home___Education/Kids___Parenting/Zac_Browser/screen.html

Lazy Eye Shooter: Making a Game Therapy for Visual Recovery in Adult Amblyopia Usable

Jessica D. Bayliss[1], Indu Vedamurthy[2], Mor Nahum[3],
Dennis Levi[3], and Daphne Bavelier[2]

[1] School of Interactive Games and Media , Rochester Institute of Technology, Rochester, USA
jdbics@rit.edu
[2] Department of Brain & Cognitive Sciences, University of Rochester, Rochester, USA
ivedamurthy@bcs.rochester.edu, daphne@cvs.rochester.edu
[3] School of Optometry, University of California, Berkeley, Berkeley, USA
mor.nahum@brainplasticity.com, dlevi@berkeley.edu

Abstract. As many as three quarters of a million preschoolers are at risk for amblyopia in the United States, so appropriate screening and accessible treatment are very important. Recent studies have shown that playing action video games results in a range of improved spatial and temporal visual functions, including visual acuity. Lazy Eye Shooter is a game treatment that takes advantage of these findings in that the software contains a dichoptic display in a First Person Shooter (FPS) action video game. FPS games are unfortunately among the most difficult games to learn for naïve subjects. Given that the treatment requires over 40 hours of playtime, we wanted to make sure that subjects were successful at the game from the very beginning. We describe several methods we have used to make the overall experiences of subjects more positive and discuss current preliminary results from the use of Lazy Eye Shooter.

Keywords: amblyopia treatment, video games for health, serious games, UT2004, lazy eye treatment, Unreal Tournament 2004, game treatment, game design.

1 Introduction

As many as three quarters of a million preschoolers are at risk for amblyopia (also known as 'lazy eye') in the United States, and roughly half of those may not be detected before school age [1]. Amblyopia is characterized by reduced vision in the amblyopic eye and the potential loss of stereo vision. Appropriate screening and accessible treatment for amblyopia are therefore very important. Recent studies with both normal subjects [3] and amblyopic adults [2,6] have shown that playing action video games result in a range of improved spatial and temporal visual functions, including visual acuity.

Lazy Eye Shooter is a game treatment that takes advantage of these findings. The software contains a dichoptic display in a first person shooter (FPS) action video game

A. Marcus (Ed.): DUXU/HCII 2013, Part II, LNCS 8013, pp. 352–360, 2013.

that requires player responses using their "bad" (amblyopic) eye. This is not the only game treatment for amblyopia. Thompson, Blum, et. al. [4] reported the release of an Apple iPod Touch game for treatment that uses an overlay lenticular lens in combination with a modified game of Tetris. It is unknown if this game will show the same broad range of visual improvements that action video games have shown [5].

FPS games are also among the most difficult games to learn for naïve subjects. Difficulties encountered by the new player range from control of their player avatar with the mouse to trouble against computerized opponents. Poor mouse control may commonly lead to nausea due to jerky and uncontrolled avatar movements. After becoming used to the video game controls, subjects still have potential difficulties as they play against computer-controlled opponents or "bots" that often have better skills than they have. Given that the treatment requires over 40 hours of playtime, we wanted to make sure that subjects were successful at the game from the very beginning. This took the form of both a training paradigm as well as several adaptations to the game to improve usability for new players.

Current preliminary results from the use of Lazy Eye Shooter show that all subjects tested had improved visual acuity, reported a dramatic reduction in switching between eyes with training, and were able to use their eyes simultaneously. A large sample clinical study is currently underway to further assess game efficacy.

2   Methods

Lazy Eye Shooter is a game modification or "mod" which uses Unreal Tournament 2004 (UT2004) in order to combine conventional anti-suppression therapy principles for amblyopia with the benefits rendered by action video games for visual recovery and binocularity. The new game type for UT2004 included the following features, most of which are shown in Figure 1:

- Display of two screens in a single game window with the same game view for display to each eye either with a stereoscope or through the use of video eyewear
- The ability to change the contrast dynamically in order to degrade whichever screen appears to the subject's "good" eye in a manner that is exclusive for each subject
- The ability to display an item (in our case a Gabor patch) to only the amblyopic eye within the game world and to have the player able to interact with it
- A calibration image to move the two screens in software in order to account for individual subject ocular deviation
- A network connection and interaction with an outside program that controls the dynamic difficulty adjustment for the player as well as records and saves all necessary data for an experimental session
- Movement of all user interface functionality to the dichoptic display with the ability to have some parts of the user interface split between the two eyes as a suppression check
- Training levels and a training paradigm for subjects inexperienced with games

- The ability for experimenters to change various parameters in the game from session to session as well as some of the parameters while the game is in play
- The ability to pause the game

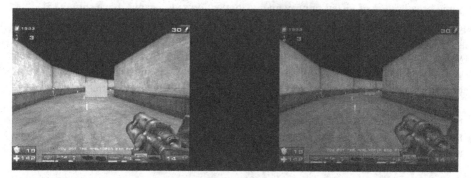

Fig. 1. Two game screens are shown. The good eye is shown the dimmed screen and the amblyopic eye is shown the screen with the extra object in it.

Players that are not used to digital video games commonly had problems learning how to play the game. The constant action and required movement accuracy in FPS games that makes them ideal candidates for visual acuity improvements also makes them harder to learn for new players. As we ran the first pilot subjects, we found the following common difficulties experienced by new game players:

- Mouse control difficulties: New players did not have the accurate mouse control skills required to play FPS games. This commonly caused nausea due to "spinning" the in-game camera too much when the player tried to move their player avatar. Additionally, new players tended to physically pick up the mouse and move it n order to try and move their character in the game.
- Learning the game: Many commercial FPS games assume that players are familiar with the game genre and do not include any tutorial or overall introduction to their game. Allowing new players to play without training them meant that they lose consistently against computerized opponents.
- Learning the treatment paradigm: Subjects not only have to learn the game, but they also need to concentrate on learning to respond to the patch object placed in view of their amblyopic eye at random intervals. They must not play the rest of the game at the expense of the treatment paradigm, but they also should not ignore the original gameplay either.

2.1   Addressing Mouse Control Problems

Mouse control problems can cause nausea in new players and would make our treatment paradigm meaningless if they could not be overcome. Our first idea was to train players to better use their mouse for control by slowing the game down. Unexpectedly, this did not work at all – the slowed down game was still too difficult for our pilot subject that tried it. We then tried several tactics to improve control and the combination worked very well. The list of changes we made to the game appears below:

- We trained naïve subjects on games that had less movement (or movement primarily in one direction) on the screen and simpler control schemes. These games took the form of 2D side scrolling games with primarily horizontal or vertical movements. The goal behind this was to just get our users "used to" playing games before moving them onto the more difficult FPS genre.
- We used a track ball rather than a mouse. After noticing that new players wanted to physically pick their mouse up and move it in order to move their in-game avatar, we decided to use a track ball for control. The track ball was a more natural fit for how naïve subjects wanted to move their game character.
- We removed all "busy" textures from the walls/floor and made the ceiling black for the training levels. We noticed that new players tended to move the in-game camera more often than players with some experience. This meant that normal game textures on the walls, floor, and ceiling could cause nausea due to how quickly new players were moving across them while playing. Removing the "business" from the textures helped solve this problem. A sense of direction was added to training levels via wall patterns to encourage movement. An example from the "Cylinder" level is shown in Figure 2.

2.2   Learning the Game

Unreal Tournament 2004 is one in a succession of several FPS games for the Unreal Tournament franchise and the game came with no real tutorial levels for beginning players. This made it difficult for new players to both orient themselves on the large, confusing game maps for the original game as well as to perform well on those maps. Additionally, our treatment paradigm for amblyopia involved subjects watching for an object to appear within view of their amblyopic eye and then responding to whether or not the object contained a Gabor patch at any one of several different frequencies. In order to keep the treatment as part of the game, players shoot objects containing a Gabor patch and ignore objects that do not have a patch (a "blank" patch) or they may be instructed to shoot a patch tilted in a particular direction and ignore anything tilted in another direction. They obtain a health or ammunition reward if they're correct and are punished with an extra non-player character known as a "Gabor monster" that will fight them if they are wrong. In this way, subjects must pay attention to the treatment paradigm as part of the game. Examples of a Gabor patch are shown in Figure 3.

In order to allow new players to learn the game as well as the treatment paradigm within the game, we created several training levels. These training levels were generally small and simple game maps composed of easily recognizable shapes such as a cylinder, a square, and a figure eight. This allowed players to easily orient themselves on the map. Additionally, these maps had areas where a player could "get away" from computerized opponents and the opponents commonly had only one spawn point where they would

Fig. 2. The left image shows an example from the Cylinder map with the original game's DM Rankin map on the right. The Cylinder map shows how textures were changed in terms of the black ceiling, simple textures on the walls and floor, and a sense of direction for movement shown through the use of horizontal lines on the walls. The textures from the DM Rankin map were "busy" and promoted nausea for players with poor mouse control. The image on the right shows a wood grained floor, horizontal grating on the left wall, a brick wall on the right wall, and lots of lights and piping on the ceiling.

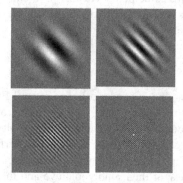

Fig. 3. Example Gabor images that could be shown in the game to the amblyopic eye. For treatment as part of the game, subjects are required to shoot patches with a Gabor and ignore patches without the Gabor.

start on the map. This made it easy to know where "opponent rich" areas of the game map were as well as "opponent poor" areas. Computerized opponents can have their difficulty set at the beginning of a game, so that those more used to playing can have more challenging opponents.

The difficulty level for subjects in terms of performance with their amblyopic eye was dynamically increased and decreased throughout playing the game within sessions. The Gabor patches shown to the amblyopic eye would become more difficult to see for those correctly identifying them and the Gabor patches would become easier to see for those having problems with correct identification.

This means that the treatment program is different for every subject as it depends on subject performance in order to dynamically adjust the treatment during play.

2.3   Handling Sophisticated Players

After playing the game for a few hours, subjects do not have problems orienting themselves and can take on more challenging opponents. At this point, players are moved to play on the original game maps such as DM Rankin and Asbestos. With more sophistication, players may also start to try and "game" the system. If computer opponents prefer certain areas of the map then players will adjust their playing accordingly. Luckily, the game itself comes with different "bot" difficulty settings that may be tweaked to make the game more challenging for these more sophisticated players.

The more problematic situations occur with the Gabor patch object that players must react to for treatment. So that players cannot run up to a patch to see whether it contains a Gabor or is blank, the patch object dynamically leads the player at a specific distance. Unfortunately, keeping the patch away from the player means that it can potentially hit walls and other obstacles. When this occurs, the patch is removed from the game and redisplayed when it would not appear in a wall or obstacle. This means that a smart player can purposefully run the patch object into a wall when they are not sure if it is a Gabor or blank patch. After all, it will then be redisplayed so they can try again.

In order to stop this potential exploitation of the system, there is a counter that keeps track of how many patches are run into a wall in a row. If this number is more than a certain amount, then a "Gabor monster" is automatically spawned as a player opponent. We find in practice that this is enough to keep players from taking advantage of the game in this fashion.

3   Pilot Test Results

Lazy Eye Shooter was piloted on four adult individuals with strabismic and or anisometropic amblyopia. Subjects were trained for 1-2 hours/day, 3-5 times per week, for a total of 40 hours.

Several outcome measures were used to assess training-induced changes. Figure 4 shows changes in visual acuity (VA) with training for four subjects (S1-S4) who completed the study, measured using a standard clinical test, the ETDRS chart. VA improved in all subjects. Stereo vision was assessed before and after training using the clinical Randot Stereo test. Subjects S1 and S2 had no stereo vision before and after treatment owing to large angle strabismus that was not corrected with the game. Subjects S3 and S4 had measurable stereo vision (200 and 70 arc seconds, respectively) before training, which improved to 25 and 20 arc seconds (respectively) following training. All subjects reported a dramatic reduction in switching between eyes after training, and were able to use both eyes simultaneously. This is evidenced by an increased tolerance to a high contrast image in the fellow eye.

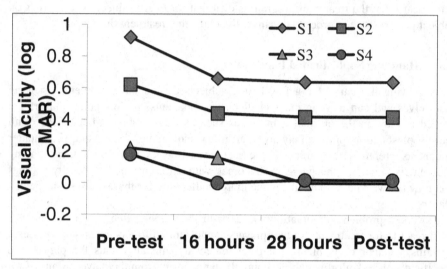

Fig. 4. Visual acuity (in logMAR units) of the amblyopic eye before (pre), during (at 16 & 28 hours of training), and immediately after training (post-test) obtained from four amblyopic patients

4   Discussion and Future Work

Unreal Tournament 2004 was used for the first version of a treatment game designed specifically to provide good compatibility through using the same game as with previous results on increases in visual acuity for action video games]. Unreal Tournament 2004 is known to show good improvements for normal subjects in terms of visual acuity [2,3,5].

The game has only been used with adult participants due to the violence found in the gameplay. We have been designing a newer version of the game using the Unreal Development Kit (UDK) that is not violent and may be used to treat amblyopia in children. The kids version of the LES game has no weapons that look like guns, has no blood or gore, and it does not include any human death animations (including the player). We have chosen to make the game more cartoon-like and there is a minimal amount of cartoon type violence in the new version. This version of the game is aimed at children that are aged 7 and older. Figures 5 and 6 show screenshots from the game that will be used to treat children.

While treatment with the game works, users playing the game for 40 hours usually become bored. There are several ways of varying gameplay that could help with this issue. Right now, Lazy Eye Shooter uses only the original Deathmatch type of gameplay. Modern first person shooters normally contain several types of games that expand on the initial concept of Deathmatch where players try to get the highest score in terms of number of kills through giving players a wider variety of goals such as holding control points for a specific amount of time (in the game type Domination)

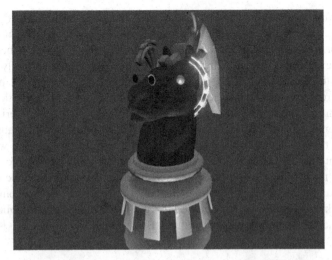

Fig. 5. The new "Gabor monster" that will appear when a mistake is made in reacting to the patch appearance in the game

Fig. 6. A more cartoon-like level with brightly lit paper lanterns

and capturing an object to bring it back to a home base (in the game type Capture the Flag). We would like to include these game types in a future release of the game. Using different game types would give players different goals and help to stave off boredom, without requiring expensive additional content creation for the game.

Cooperative multiplayer should additionally be considered as a way to make the game more interesting, especially for parents willing to participate in the treatment of their amblyopic child. We do not believe competitive gameplay should be considered as it can be discouraging for the people that lose. The game is not currently designed for multiplayer due to the extent of experimenter control needed in the game.

More work remains to be accomplished regarding the integration between the game and the treatment system within the game. The Gabor patch currently interrupts the flow of the game when it appears and it should be a more integral part of the game. The reasons for this particular implementation have to do with technical considerations for the scope of the project. For the future, we are considering putting the Gabor onto the uniform of a computer player and making the game so that enemies are those wearing the Gabor uniform. The main technical issue with this is the constraint that the Gabor uniform should only appear to the amblyopic eye. Since the game world is only a single place two screens are drawn of the same world and then changed after the world is drawn), this could prove difficult to accomplish. We are still working on other ways of increasing the involvement of the Gabor patches with the gameplay for future versions of Lazy Eye Shooter.

Acknowledgments. This work is supported by an Office of Naval Research grant (MURI Award 00140710937), National Eye Institute grants (EY020976 and EY16880), and the McDonnell Foundation.

References

1. Wu, C., Hunter, D.G.: Amblyopia: diagnostic and therapeutic options. Am J. Ophthalmol. 141, 175–184 (2006)
2. Li, R.W., Ngo, C., Nguyen, J., Lam, J., Nia, B., Ren, D., Levi, D.M.: Playing Video Game Improves Visual Acuity and Visual Attention in Adult Amblyopia - A Potentially Useful Tool for Amblyopia Treatment. Invest Ophthalmol. Vis. Sci. 49 (2008)
3. Li, R.W., Polat, U., Makous, W., Bavelier, D.: Enhancing the contrast sensitivity function through action video game training. Nature Neuroscience 12, 549–551 (2009)
4. Thompson, B., Blum, J.R., Maehara, G., Hess, R.F., Cooperstock, J.R.: A game platform for treatment of amblyopia. IEEE Trans. on Neural Systems and Rehabilitation Engineering 19(3), 280–289 (2011)
5. Green, C.S., Bavelier, D.: Action video game modifies visual selective attention. Nature 423(6939), 534–537 (2003)
6. Li, R.W., Ngo, C., Nguyen, J., Levi, D.M.: Video-Game Play Induces Plasticity in the Visual System of Adults with Amblyopia. PLoS Biol. 9(8), e1001135 (2011), doi:10.1371/journal.pbio.1001135

Designing Supportive Mobile Technology
for Stable Diabetes

Katherine S. Blondon[1] and Predrag Klasnja[2]

[1] Department of Health Services, School of public Health, University of Washington,
Seattle, U.S.A.
kblondon@uw.edu
[2] School of Information, University of Michigan, Ann Arbor, U.S.A.
klasnja@umich.edu

Abstract. Diabetes is a complex, evolving chronic disease, with an evolving need for self-management as the disease progresses. Through patient interviews and a focus group, we explored the changing need for technological support for diabetes self-management over the course of the disease, with a particular focus on insulin users. We propose a design for supportive technology aimed at the stabilization and progression stages of diabetes, which focuses on the creation of an individualized database of how new experiences with food, physical activities and travel affect one's glucose levels. Our design supports feedback and improvement for future similar experiences, while avoiding the burden of intensive tracking. We propose a mechanism to suggest insulin doses adapted to the user, and sharing data with peers according to individual privacy wishes. Future research could allow this innovative approach to benefit non-insulin users.

Keywords: Diabetes, self-management, mobile technology, health informatics.

1   Background

Diabetes is an evolving chronic disease, and its management involves many lifestyle changes. A large part of daily disease management is incumbent on the patient, and happens in the absence of the care-provider. Mobile technology can support diabetes self-management through educational resources, data collection, data visualization, sharing results with a provider, or through encouraging feedback.

Diabetes actually represents three types of populations, characterized by their self-management and insulin needs: (1) Individuals with type 1 diabetes (T1D), who are dependent on insulin because their bodies do not produce it; (2) individuals with type 2 diabetes (T2D) *with* insulin; and (3) individuals with T2D *without* insulin, who can use diet and oral medications to treat their disease. In T2D, the body produces insulin, but its effect is decreased. Earlier stages of T2D can be treated with medications to enhance the body's response to insulin, whereas later stages of T2D require supplementation with insulin to produce an adequate glucose metabolism. Self-management needs of individuals with diabetes who use insulin differ greatly from those who only use oral medications or diet. The use of insulin requires a closer control of glucose

A. Marcus (Ed.): DUXU/HCII 2013, Part II, LNCS 8013, pp. 361–370, 2013.

results, because insulin doses have to be carefully adjusted to avoid hypoglycemia. This more intense tracking of glucose results is particularly important for individuals with T1D, and has led to the development of continuous glucose monitors and insulin pumps. Individuals with T2D on insulin can control their glucose levels somewhat more leniently, as they may use a combination of oral medications and insulin to help their glycemic control. For individuals with T2D who do not use insulin, there is insufficient evidence to support routine self-monitoring of blood glucose.[4]

The most beneficial type of supportive technology for a given patient will depend on the type and stage of disease. Early in the disease, patients need to gain better understanding of the disease with the complex physiology related to glucose metabolism. For example, they need to learn how various factors such as diet and physical activity affect their glucose levels, as well as the meaning of measures such as glycated hemoglobin (HbA1c), which is commonly used to assess glucose control over the previous eight to twelve weeks.[9] Patients are also overwhelmed by all the new lifestyle behaviors they are supposed to adopt: adapting their diet, monitoring their glucose levels, and adjusting their physical activities and medications. Many mobile apps for patients with diabetes target user needs at this early stage of the disease.[2]

As they live with diabetes, patients begin to better understand their bodies' needs and responses. Patients typically learn how to make healthy choices about food, exercise and medications, which lead to better glucose control. As a result, self-tracking, which is common is early stages of the disease, is often significantly reduced. However, this stable phase is not without difficulties. As the Illness Trajectory framework notes, there are potential crises and acute episodes during the stable phase as well.[3] Some of them are caused by the patients' changing physiology, while others occur when patients attempt to change or expand their routines. Patients on insulin are particularly vulnerable to such crises, since inadequate insulin dosing can easily lead to hyper- or hypoglycemic events. In this paper, we discuss our formative work on the design of an application for self-management of stable diabetes with insulin aimed to help patients to more fully enjoy their lives by exploring new foods and activities while maintaining good glucose control and hopefully preventing acute hypoglycemic or hyperglycemic events. The application was designed based on interviews and a focus group with twelve diabetes patients. High-fidelity mockups of the application were presented to five T1D patients for feedback in an additional focus group. In what follows, we review the results from our formative study, the features of the application we designed based on those results, and the initial patient feedback on the design.

2   Related Work

Adoption of mobile technologies for health has grown rapidly over the past couple of years, and applications for diabetes and wellness have flourished. A recent review [2] has found that a majority of technologies for diabetes self-management have focused on tracking and data visualization, with a subset offering support for data sharing to facilitate social support from friends or care-providers. Meanwhile, educational applications have focused on diabetes literacy or insulin dose calculations. Such mobile technologies have shown promise in clinical trials, with a meta-analysis of 22 trials showing a reduction of HbA1c of 0.5 percent over a median of 6 months' follow-up.[8] A recent randomized controlled trial showed a reduction of HbA1c of 1.2 percent over one year using a combined mobile and web-based approach.[10]

Most of the technology tested in such clinical trials focuses on the support for early stages of diabetes. Given the shock of the diagnosis and the sheer amount patients have to learn early on, this is understandable. At the time of diagnosis, 85 percent of individuals report a high level of distress, including feelings of shock, guilt, anger, anxiety and helplessness.[5] Support at this stage is clearly needed. Yet, diabetes is a progressive, chronic disease, and the need for self-management remains in the later stages of the disease as well, albeit in a different form.[11] For instance, studies find that longer duration of disease is associated with lower adherence to self-care activities, and poorer glycemic control, even though patients have a better understanding of the disease and its management.[7] It is, therefore, important to develop supportive technologies for patients with longer duration of the disease to prevent or delay the consequences of poorer glycemic control. Such technologies are currently lacking. Our work begins to address this gap in supportive technologies for diabetes.

Long-term diabetes self-management is difficult due to the incessant need to make healthy choices and constrain daily routines over many years of the disease progression. A technology aimed to help patients with such a long-term condition thus faces a challenge: how to help patients stay engaged with the self-management technology over long periods of time? The Technology Acceptance Model demonstrates that initial engagement with technology is associated with perceived usefulness and usability, [6] and is reinforced by novelty. A technology for long-term diabetes management cannot rely on novelty for its continued use, but must carefully balance the value that users get from the technology with the effort needed to use it. Given that a fourth of smartphone applications are abandoned after just one use, [12] designing such a technology is a serious challenge. Our work attempts to address this challenge by supporting intermittent use, by providing immediate value through information obtained from validated and social network sources, and by increasing the value of the application to the user the longer she continues to use it.

3   Method

For the initial study, we recruited English-speaking participants with diabetes aged 18 to 64 years. We excluded individuals on dialysis, those with cognitive impairment, and those with gestational diabetes because of their closer contact with their care-providers, more severe disease, or impairments that may hinder the adoption and use of mobile technologies. Gestational diabetes is a different form of diabetes, which is generally limited in time and is associated with different motivations for self-management. All participants were recruited in the Seattle, WA metro area.

We conducted semi-structured interviews with the participants to explore how participants' diabetes and their self-management needs evolved over time, and to discuss their past or current use of mobile applications and Internet sites as supportive tools. We also held one focus group with four patients (three with T2D, one with T1D), three of whom also participated in individual interviews, to explore further what types of features the participants would like to see in supportive technologies. The interviews and focus group were audio-recorded, and then fully transcribed for subsequent analysis. In addition, we collected field notes of discussions with two participants (one with T1D, one with T2D) specifically about which features a technology for self-management during the stable stage should have. We analyzed the data through a modified grounded theory approach, using free codes and pre-established codes based on a literature-based conceptual model of the use of mobile technologies for diabetes self-management. Both authors coded the transcripts, then extracted themes and categories, focusing on the evolving needs for diabetes self-management over time.

Based on the results of our analyses, we created a high-fidelity mock-up of a smartphone application for unmet needs of insulin users with stable diabetes. To get feedback on the general concept and the initial design, we presented the mock-up to five patients with T1D in a two-hour focus group.

4   Results

4.1   Participant Characteristics

We recruited twelve adult individuals (>18 years old) with T1D (n=6) or T2D (n=6) for interviews and an initial focus group. We present participant characteristics in Table 1. The distribution of gender, age categories and insulin use reflects the characteristics of the disease in the population.[1] In spite of a difference in age, duration of disease was similar for both types of disease.

Table 1. Participant characteristics for the interviews and focus group

	Type 1	Type 2
n	6	6[1]
Female: male	5:1	2:4
Age range	18-34 yrs	35-64 yrs
Duration of disease	2-27 yrs	6 months to >20 years

To get feedback on the design of the application, we presented the mock-up to five women with T1D, two of whom had taken part in the initial interviews. The five participants were between 20-30 years of age. Four were insulin pump users, and the fifth one used multiple daily injections of insulin.

---

[1] One T2D individual on insulin.

4.2   Changing Self-Management Needs

At the time of diagnosis, participants describe the onset of disease as an intense learning experience. They needed to rapidly comprehend the essentials of disease management and apply their knowledge to their behaviors. For example, they had to learn which foods to choose and what quantities were appropriate:

Going back, early on, it's food. You know, you have to figure out what you can eat, and then it's exercise and then it's the combination of everything and then it's working it all in the lifestyle stuff too. You know, it doesn't mean just food and exercise, it's also plenty of rest. – FG, P7 (T2D)

Early in the disease, participants used a range of solutions to collect and organize data, from handwritten charts to websites, Excel spreadsheets, and mobile applications. They tracked glucose levels, carb consumption, diet, insulin or weight. They appreciated food diary apps for their large nutrition databases. Visualization of the data helped participants understand the relationships among the exercise, food and glucose results. They liked having reminders to test for blood glucose, and kept fixed schedules for meals and testing:

I became really, really religious about [tracking foods and glucose], really quite strict about what I was eating and almost too strict. – FG, P11 (T2D)

I was tracking down to individual ingredients I was putting into my recipes and just breaking it down to what I can. You know, we were measuring every two hours after a meal, doing exactly what they were telling us to do, wake up: check, after breakfast: check, two hours before lunch: check, two hours after lunch: check. So it was a whole routine for about the first month, two months – FG, P7

As participants gained control over their disease, they progressively decreased self-tracking, often supported by the improved health status. Tracking is effortful and time-consuming, and the perceived benefit at the point of stabilized disease was much smaller than during the initial phase. They did not want to track meticulously for the rest of their lives. As they often restricted their food choices to predefined amounts of selected diabetes-compatible foods to stay within a satisfactory range of glucose results, they did not find tracking to be necessary for their usual foods and routines. They also acquire skills in assessing what they ate and predicting insulin needs.

[I made] a master list of all the items that I could possibly eat and the glycemic load and the calories [...] For the first 60 days, [our glucose results] were always low because we knew exactly what we ate. So then after a while it was like it was the same thing we're eating every day, you know what it's going to be. So after that I just stopped [tracking]. – FG, P7 (T2D)

You know, I can usually look at things and [...] probably 70 - 75 % of the time I get at least in the ballpark. – Intv, P8 (T1D)

As they gained control of their diabetes, the participants' priorities changed. They discussed the importance of quality of life, and the desire to try new foods and have the freedom to change their routines. For these new behaviors, tracking retained its usefulness. As during the initial learning phase, tracking allowed adjustment and improvement for repeated behaviors. Rather than needing to do it constantly, though, participants in later stages only tracked intermittently, when a particular need arose:

I want to be able to eat food. Like I want to able to try food and not be really scared of everything I put in my mouth [...] I've had [diabetes for] almost 20 years now, it's crazy. But, I'm still learning every day just what I can and cannot eat - FG, P4 (T1D)

I don't really track much unless I am specifically looking for a pattern. – Intv, P4 (T1D)

Evolving disease and management led to evolving needs for supportive technology. After the initial stage of the disease, participants wanted to be able to test new foods while maintaining their health. To accomplish this, they wanted an individualized, continuously growing database of how foods, activities or events affected their health. As FG-P9 said, *"the most important is knowing the consequence on the glucose of whatever you're doing."* Available food diary apps lack data on ethnic and homemade foods. Trying out new foods or physical activities requires an estimation of physiological responses, taking many factors into consideration (amount and composition of food, physical activities, hydration, stress, etc.). Our participants wanted a customized diary with personal notes about the accuracy of their estimations for new foods or activities. They emphasized the importance of these narratives to interpret glucose results. They described how care-providers were sometimes quick to comment on abnormal results because they did not know the context behind the numbers:

The chart of all my blood sugars, it's, like, each number has a story behind it. And it's like, I remember, you know, that meal or I was sick or, you know, there's so much more than just numbers that goes into it. – Intv, P4 (T1D)

Furthermore, they wanted these notes to be easily retrievable to be able to remember, adjust and improve their estimation the next time they found themselves in a similar situation. Such an app would allow the creation of a highly personalized database of the effects of food, physical activities and insulin needs on the user's body.

Participants also found social support to be very useful for diabetes self-management. Most participants belonged to a peer network, either in person or online. They explained how different it was to receive advice from a peer, someone who "got it," than from a healthcare provider. They emphasized that sharing experiences with peers could fill gaps in the advice received from health professionals:

My friend actually was the one who told me to take my insulin earlier to offset like spikes and stuff. [...] She was the only person who said that to me, I guess. She's kind of clued me in - that's helped a lot. – Intv, P10 (T1D)

4.3   Designing IDiDit: Integrated Diary for Diabetes

Our results show how useful tracking and educational apps are, particularly early after diagnosis. But we also found a need for supportive technology for the more experienced individuals who have reached a point where intensive tracking is no longer perceived as useful. At this stage of stabilization, individuals have adopted routines for foods and activities, but they do not want to restrict themselves to these routines. They want to maintain a "high quality of life." By this, they mean that they would like to maintain good glycemic control while being able to have some degree of flexibility, to keep experiencing new foods and adventures. Although they have acquired sufficient diabetes self-management skills to get by many unexpected situations by performing additional glucose checks or by learning how to "eye-ball" the insulin requirements, supportive technology could help by suggesting individualized insulin doses, keeping track of these novel experiences, and providing feedback for future improvement in similar situations. Based on these results, we created a high-fidelity interactive mock-up of a diary application aimed at the needs of patients with stable diabetes. Key features of the application, Integrated Diary for Diabetes (IDiDit), are shown in Figure 1.

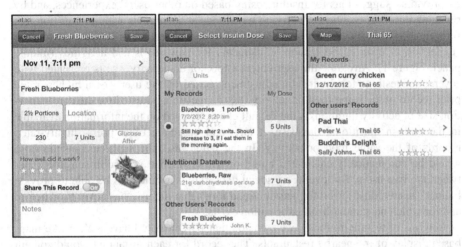

Fig. 1. Mock-ups of IDiDit: food entry; insulin selection based on user's previous records, a nutritional database, and records from other users; user's own and other users' records for a local restaurant.

We are designing IDiDit to be a personalized diary application intended to help diabetes patients who use insulin to explore new foods and activities while maintaining good glucose control. The application's basic function is to track how food, physical activity, and travel affect the user's glucose levels and the insulin adjustments that the user makes to compensate for those activities. When entering foods and physical activities, the user can record before and after glucose levels, insulin adjustment, and a rating of how well the adjustment worked to bring—or keep—glucose level in the normal range. The user can also enter any addition information, in the form of a free-text note, which can help make sense of the recorded glucose change. For example, the user might note that she substituted brown rice for white rice in a restaurant meal or that she had a mild fever (left panel, Figure 1). For travel, the user enters any time change and free-text notes about how glucose management was affected by the trip.

At the most basic level, then, IDiDit provides the user with a history of her glucose management around food, physical activity, and travel that can be searched whenever the user needs to make a similar food or activity choice. To make this functionality more robust, however, IDiDit is being designed to provide several unique features. First, all data in IDiDit is fully searchable, including any free-text comments. If a user searches for "fever," for example, she would get all results that contain the word "fever," enabling her to better understand how being sick affects her glucose metabolism. In this way, IDiDit is not only a repository of knowledge about foods and activities, but also about a variety of contextual factors that affect the user's glucose management. The richer the data that the user enters in the application—and the longer she uses it—the more IDiDit can support discovery of highly personal patterns.

Second, to leverage experience of other patients and to make IDiDit useful before the user has much data of her own in the system, IDiDit is being designed to have a robust social component. Social functionality enhances the application in two ways: by providing suggestions for insulin dosing based on other users' experiences, and by reducing uncertainty inherent in trying new foods at restaurants without nutrition fact information. In terms of insulin dosing, a fundamental feature of IDiDit is automatic suggestion of customized insulin adjustments for new foods and activities (middle panel, Figure 1). Any time the user enters a food or an activity, she is presented with several suggestions for the insulin adjustment: based on the user's own highest rated prior record of the same food or activity (this suggestion, adjusted for the correct portion size or activity duration, is the default choice); based on the information available in the built-in nutritional database, if any; and based on other users' highly-rated records of the same food or activity. In the latter case, the suggested insulin dose would be automatically calculated based on the difference in insulin sensitivity between the two users. By leveraging social data, IDiDit would thus be able to provide ballpark insulin doses even for activities and foods that the user has never tried before and for which no standardized information exists.

In terms of restaurant foods, we envision that IDiDit would have a Yelp-like map-based display of the nearby restaurants. The record for each restaurant would contain information about foods that are present either in the user's own diary or that have been logged by other IDiDit users (right panel, Figure 1). In this way, the user would get access to insulin dosing information that would help her make an informed insulin adjustment even for foods that the user might not be able to correctly eye-ball.

Finally, to make these functions to work well, IDiDit needs to have both robust privacy settings and sufficient information about users' insulin sensitivity to be able to automatically calculate insulin doses for different people. In regards to privacy, our initial plan was to make diary records private by default, but to enable users to override the sharing setting for any individual record either at creation time or later on.

4.4   Feedback on IDiDit

To get feedback on the concept and design of IDiDit, we presented an interactive, high-fidelity mock-up of the application in a focus group with five T1D patients. Their reactions on the concept were very positive, and they thought that an application like IDiDit could effectively support glucose management. More concretely, the participants had several insightful comments about IDiDit's functionality that are relevant not only to IDiDit but to other diabetes self-management applications as well.

To track food amounts, we proposed to log food in terms of "portions," which people seem to relate to easily based on their "eye-balling" skills. Participants expressed concern, however, about the uncertainty of what a portion meant from one person to the next, and how that could affect reliability of data entry and insulin dosing suggestions. They suggested that portion size be logged in terms different-sized balls, as participants did not commonly use units such as cup, tsp or Tbsp. They thought that a golf ball or tennis ball were better standardized units that most people could imagine.

This idea is intriguing but it is not without its own problems. While a tennis ball worth of rice or beans is easy to visualize, it is not clear that such units would work for all foods. For instance, measuring liquids such as soup in tennis balls seems rather unintuitive. This comment does point to the importance of a thoughtful choice of measures in applications like IDiDit, and that finding a right measure that works across a broad range of foods or activities can be difficult.

Also in relation to logging food, we envisioned that users would be able to take a picture of the food to better jog their memories. This functionality was perceived to be more important than we originally thought, however. Participants thought that pictures would be key for helping understand portion sizes or to have a better idea of the composition of the eaten meal in relation to the administered insulin dose. The use of pictures before and after a meal was suggested as a way to address the portion variability: participants all agreed that seeing a sequence of pictures would help make data from peers more helpful, allowing them to compare other users' data with their own usual estimations. Moreover, pictures could document substitutions (e.g., brown rice instead of white rice), and food combinations (e.g., avoiding starches). In addition to supporting before and after pictures to address these comments, we will be introducing structured prompts in the notes for substitutions for those who do not take pictures.

Privacy is an important issue to users when recording personal events, particularly when an application offers options for sharing this personal data with peers. Our study results revealed how easily our participants felt judged about their glucose results or other data. At the same time, our focus group participants clearly understood the value of data sharing in an application like IDiDit. To balance these two sentiments, they emphasized the importance of granular privacy settings. In addition to being able to override a global sharing setting, participants thought that what was needed was to allow control over which parts of the dataset are shared. For instance, they wanted to be able to share glucose results and insulin doses, while keeping private personal notes, or name and demographics. This is an important point but also one that does not have an easy solution. How exactly such settings should be implemented is not clear. Should there only be global settings that apply to all records in the same way? If per-record overrides are provided—as we originally intended—would these need to be granular as well or should they merely switch sharing of the current record on and off? Answers to such questions are not obvious but designing privacy settings correctly is an essential condition for acceptance of social applications such as IDiDit.

Feedback on IDiDit mock-ups reinforced the point that when it comes to patient technologies, design details matter hugely. How data entry or privacy is designed can make or break an application. Iteration and early feedback are thus invaluable.

5   Conclusion

As diabetes changes over time, so does the patients' need for technological support. Based on interviews and focus groups, we described features of one type of application that can support patients in stable stage of the disease: an individualized database for estimation of glucose trends or insulin needs personal history, commercial food datasets, and peer experiences. Such an application could enable patients to experiment with new foods and activities while maintaining health and living their lives to the fullest.

References

1. (ADA), A.D.A. Diabetes statistics (2012),
   http://www.diabetes.org/diabetes-basics/diabetes-statistics/
2. Chomutare, T., Fernandez-Luque, L., Arsand, E., et al.: Features of mobile diabetes applications: review of the literature and analysis of current applications compared against evidence-based guidelines. J. Med. Internet. Res. 13(3), e65 (2011)
3. Corbin, J.M., Strauss, A.: A nursing model for chronic illness management based upon the Trajectory Framework. Sch. Inq. Nurs. Pract. 5(3), 155–174 (1991)
4. Farmer, A., Wade, A., Goyder, E., et al.: Impact of self monitoring of blood glucose in the management of patients with non-insulin treated diabetes: open parallel group randomised trial. BMJ 335(7611), 132 (2007)
5. Funnell, M.: The Diabetes Attitudes, Wishes and Needs (DAWN) Study. Clinical Diabetes 24(4), 154–155 (2006)
6. Holden, R.J., Karsh, B.T.: The technology acceptance model: its past and its future in health care. J. Biomed. Inform. 43(1), 159–172 (2010)
7. Ko, S.H., Park, S.A., Cho, J.H., et al.: Influence of the duration of diabetes on the outcome of a diabetes self-management education program. Diabetes Metab. J. 36(3), 222–229 (2012)
8. Liang, X., Wang, Q., Yang, X., et al.: Effect of mobile phone intervention for diabetes on glycaemic control: a meta-analysis. Diabet. Med. 28(4), 455–463 (2011)
9. Nathan, D.M., Turgeon, H., Regan, S.: Relationship between glycated haemoglobin levels and mean glucose levels over time. Diabetologia 50(11), 2239–2244 (2007)
10. Quinn, C.C., Shardell, M.D., Terrin, M.L., et al.: Cluster-randomized trial of a mobile phone personalized behavioral intervention for blood glucose control. Diabetes care 34(9), 1934–1942 (2011)
11. Strauss, A.L.: Chronic illness and the quality of life. St. Louis, Mosby (1984)
12. Suthoff, B.: First Impressions Matter! 26% of Apps Downloaded in 2010 Were Used Just Once. Localytics (2011), http://www.localytics.com/blog/2011/first-impressions-matter-26-percent-of-apps-downloaded-used-just-once/

Application of Rhetorical Appeals in Interactive Design for Health

Sauman Chu[1] and G. Mauricio Mejia[2]

[1] University of Minnesota, 240 McNeal Hall, 1985 Buford Ave., St Paul MN 55108, USA
[2] University of Caldas and University of Minnesota
240 McNeal Hall, 1985 Buford Ave., St Paul MN 55108, USA
schu@umn.edu

Abstract. The theory of rhetoric could provide critical foundations for interactive design. One core idea of rhetoric is the rhetorical appeals, which include logos, pathos, and ethos. The authors report a research-based design project with reflections from the design process and usability evaluations. The project explored the application of the rhetorical appeals in the design of a mobile web application for childhood obesity prevention.

Keywords: Design and health, mobile app, child obesity, rhetorical appeals, interactive design.

1 Introduction

Designed interfaces need to present persuasive arguments to the users in order to allow effective interaction; hence, the theory of rhetoric could provide critical foundations for interactive design. Ancient rhetoric is the art of persuasive speech; in the field of design, rhetoric implies a deep concern for the audience. Design researchers have previously proposed using theory of rhetoric in the field with several objectives such as to aid visual concept development [1], to bridge art and science [2], or to cope with information complexity [3].

One core idea of rhetoric is the rhetorical appeals or modes of persuasion, which include logos, pathos, and ethos. Logos appeal concerns with rationality and formal structure of arguments, pathos relates to emotional aspects, and ethos refers to character and credibility of information in the communication process. In this paper, the authors report a research-based design project with reflections from the design process and usability evaluations. The project explored the application of the rhetorical appeals in the design of a mobile web application for childhood obesity prevention.

This paper also describes outcomes from the user research during the design process. The user research methodology consists of two data collection stages. First, interviews and usability tests (paper prototype) were conducted early in the process. The objectives were to improve the interaction design and visual rhetorical appeals in the application before developing the software. Second, interviews and usability tests

A. Marcus (Ed.): DUXU/HCII 2013, Part II, LNCS 8013, pp. 371–380, 2013.

(digital prototype) were conducted after the creation of the application. The objective was to identify any shortcomings and fix any possible issues before releasing the first version of the application.

2   Theory of Rhetoric

A theory of rhetoric has been discussed in the broad field of design and in the discipline of visual communication design. Such theory recognizes design objects and systems as language that contains persuasive arguments. Bonsiepe [3] argued that modern graphic design should incorporate rhetoric with a primary role. While this gives significant weight to aesthetics, it could help people dealing with information complexity. He added that this would help limited focus of usability on speed and cognition. This implies that all appeals (logos-reason, pathos-emotion, and ethos-character/credibility) may be used to create effective interaction and communication.

Kostelnick and Hassett [4] have a different view from the field of technical communication. They explained that designers adapt visual conventions according to rhetorical situations. They see these conventions as logical structures that appeal to reason (logos) and facilitate understanding. For them, appeals to emotion and credibility (pathos and ethos) affect conventions and reduce understanding.

This study is based on a theoretical model [5] that the authors developed connecting the theories of design, rhetoric, and functional literacy. This model shows that when the design problem accounts for the human needs, a central challenge is the configuration of the rhetorical appeals in the design object (a mobile web application for this project). In this study the authors experiment with the appeals aiming to understand visual rhetoric and communication efficacy.

Previous studies in design that use the theory of rhetoric are limited and mainly in analysis, which is not for production. For example, Van der Waarde [6] analyzed rhetorical components of information about prescription medicines in Europe, including the rhetorical appeals. The analysis using rhetorical elements elucidated interaction and communication issues of the information. Winn and Beck [7] also used rhetorical analysis to study persuasive arguments in a ecommerce web site focusing on the rhetorical appeals. They described how the site appealed to the subjects' reason, emotion, and credibility and they proposed an evaluation tool for designers based on the appeals.

3   Obesity and Health Communication

Obesity is a chronic condition with growing prevalence in the world and a major factor that causes chronic disease conditions. In the US, one out of five children are obese [8] with higher prevalence among low-income and minority families [9]. Latino children double the rate of obesity of non-Latino children and their parents are likely to have limited functional health literacy [10]. Functional health literacy is defined as the ability of self-care, following medical instructions, and understanding the health care system. Since verbal and oral directions (such as information from health professionals) are not an effective way of communicating the information to this population, this project takes a different approach to this issue by proposing a design solution on using Mobile/Web application that promotes interactivity on learning health information.

Health communication, including medication instructions, nutrition therapies, or risk decision-making, is often delivered in oral and written languages using primarily appeals to logos (reason). Visual language can be an additional complement to increase comprehension in health communication [11] [12]. Research reviews show that the use of graphics in health [13] usually focus on compositional elements that affect cognitive processing and perceptual accuracy and are delivered through simple formats such as brochures or leaflets. These are a few examples that address uses other rhetorical appeals other than logos.

4   Objective of the Mobile Web App

The objective of the mobile app is to provide a learning platform for parents to learn about nutrition and diet for developing children in a playful and engaging environment. The goal of the app is not to encourage weight loss dramatically. We aim to educate parents with limited functional health literacy about the balance of diets and physical exercise and their long-term effect based on their children's growth chart. Our goal is to encourage healthy weight management through a long-term and sustainable method. Therefore the program is created and designed to allow the audience to see the long-term impact on body weight changes from 1 month to 3 years.

5   Method

5.1   Instrument - The Mobile Web App

The mobile web application is called Lifecast. It is a tool that aids parents' understanding of core concepts related to childhood obesity and healthy behaviors; for instance, the effects of fruit and vegetables in the diet, physical activity, and processed foods. Parents are able to foresee effects of diet and exercise in children with different health conditions such as healthy, overweight, or obese (see figure 1). Changes of body shape was created based on dietary and exercise recommendations from the Institute of Medicine of the National Academies [14] and the growth charts published by the US Center of Disease Control and Prevention [15].

The app is not intended to be a game because it does not provide a challenge for the user or response with quantifiable outcome. Instead, the app allows users to navigate different dietary options and learn how these changes affect the weight of the characters. It could be used as a simulation tool that will enhance understanding. However, the tacit goal will be to keep all characters healthy, which is culturally desirable. Characters may probably relate to the parents' own children. We expect that these concepts in the app will foster healthy attitudes.

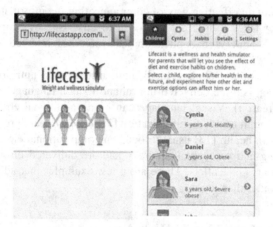

Fig. 1. Lifecast app screenshots in logos

The application is targeted to low-income Latino communities. It is specifically for adults whose children are in the transition from parental influence to independent diet and physical exercise decision-making.. The decision of designing for mobile media is justified because low-income and minority populations tend to have Smartphone and connect to the Internet with these devices [16].

To illustrate the concept of how the app works, let's use Cynthia, one of the characters, as an example. Cynthia is 6 years old and is at a healthy status. With her current diets and exercise, she might be staying with the healthy weight for another year. However, the same diets might not meet the demand of the body as she continues growth. She might be underweight when she reaches 8 years old. Therefore an alternative diet will be necessary and parents can look up the food items from the app to find out what would be helpful for Cynthia to intake in order to gain or maintain healthy weight. On the other hand, with someone who is overweight, the app can help the user to determine what diet would be helpful to lose weight gradually and sustain it in a long-term basis. Again, our goal is not to encourage dramatic or fast pace weight loss. Therefore one with an overweight status might not see the results until a year or more later.

5.2   Rhetorical Appeals

The exploration of the rhetorical appeals seeks to optimize the designed interface and to increase the persuasive arguments in the interaction, which is expected to improve the engagement of the audience by increasing their knowledge, changing their attitudes, and stimulating healthy behaviors.

Based on the profile and values of the cultural group of Latinos, we created three modes of use, each with a different configuration of the appeals. One mode was focused on a logos argument, which uses simplified and rational arguments built with verbal and visual elements. The other two modes also use a rational structure of arguments, but were enriched with pathos and ethos ((see figure 2). They are extensions of the logos argument that include emotional indices in pathos and credibility indices in ethos. For example, the ethos mode uses the University of Minnesota brand as an index of credibility. The pathos mode uses short personal stories for the characters as an index of emotion.

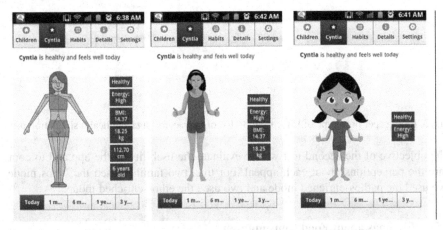

Fig. 2. Lifecast app screenshots in logo, pathos, and ethos

5.3   First User Research Participants

Five Latino families participated in the first user research session and six Latino families participated in the second session. All families were recruited in a low-income community. The number of children in each family ranged between two to six and each family has at least one child between the ages of 6 to 12 years old. Only the parents participated in the usability test. The researchers interviewed each family separately. One of the researchers can speak Spanish, therefore, all interviews were conducted and communicated in Spanish.

5.4   User Research Procedures

These sessions consisted of an interview about health habits and a usability test with a paper prototype. The objective of the first usability test was to improve the interaction design and visual rhetorical appeals in the application before developing the software. Parents were shown with the prototype in Spanish. The prototype contained 26 individual pages. Each page has its function and navigation (see figure 3). The pages include choices of settings, choices of characters (6 options), pages for individual characters, images of food items for different meals, and effects on the character's weight after certain diets or exercise options were selected.

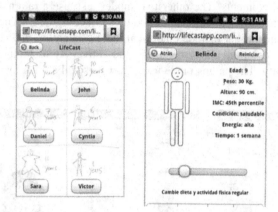

Fig. 3. Early paper prototype of Lifecast app - list of characters page and health simulation page

The objective of the second test was to evaluate the usability of the app and to compare the perceptions about each appeal. For this, two families used the logos mode, two used the pathos-enriched mode and two used the ethos-enriched mode.

5.5   Findings about Food Consumption

Findings about food consumption and nutrition were very helpful. Most children from these families have their lunches at schools. Their meals are very regular with breakfast, lunch, and dinner for weekdays and in a quite fixed schedule for each meal. The most common food items that are consumed by majority of the families for breakfast are eggs, pancakes, cereal, bread and with drinks such as 'jugo' (bottled orange juice) and milk. Food items for lunch quite vary since they depend on the school lunch. Food including pizza, sandwiches, chicken and veggie soup, spaghetti, and cheese are some common items. However, when it's the weekend, parents tend to provide their children with more ethnic food such as quesadillas and enchiladas with beans, rice, lettuce, tomato, and onion. Chicken tends to be a very common item for dinner with just different ways of preparation. Beef or veggie soup is also popular for dinner.

Most parents know that vegetables and fruits are good healthy food for their children but it seems that they need to force their children to eat these items. One parent even found a creative way by cooking the rice with celery and mixing the vegetable juice with the rice. Therefore, the issue is that children just do not like vegetables.

All of the parents think that processed food is canned food, food served in fast food restaurants, and microwave food. A couple parents think that frozen vegetables or meats are not good which is a common misperception. Although most of these children participate in regular exercise, some of them have weight issues and have been advised by doctors or dieticians on their diets. Findings from this discussion have helped us to design and create the menu in a more realistic way. We also worked on different ways in communicating the food items to reduce confusion.

5.6   Findings from the First Usability Testing

Task one was "Select a child and see what is his or her future weight." Participants did not realize the function of the slider in the health simulation page or understand that it was an interactive element. All of them failed to perform the task and the researcher needed to clarify and show them how the slider functioned since it was needed to perform the next task.

The second task was "Change the child's habits and see again the future weight of the child." It was expected that participants would click and look at the meals and/or exercise pages, change habits, and find out the changes on the character's weight through dragging the slider. Two participants successfully completed this task and others seemed to be lost and unsure about what to do. A couple participants commented that some icons were very confusing such as the plus icon and the only selectable option was the one link marked as current. One participant commented on the confusion of foot images.

The third task was "Find out the information details." Participants clicked on the information button. However, this finding may be useless because the task direction included the word of the name of the button.

Through the usability testing, it seems that most participants were confused by the function of the slider. The slider was an interactive timeline that allowed users to click and slide so that they could see the different stages of time (from 1 month to 3 years). But with the confusion, we have decided to develop an alternative solution.

5.7   Development of the Digital Mobile App

The application was developed based on the usability test outcome. Since the app is developed for the Latino population, we have decided to build in the bilingual feature. That means users can select the text to be displayed in either Spanish or English. This feature will benefit new immigrants or Hispanics with limited English proficiency. In addition, the app will help users learn the vocabularies in English (or in Spanish). Regarding the character styles based on the rhetorical appeals, users can decide which one they would like to see. Our hypothesis is that different cultural groups would have a different preference of the presentation of the image. This hypothesis will be tested in a future study.

Although we thought that the slider would be a great interactive feature to implement and to show the changes of time, based on the usability test, it has proven to not be an appropriate approach. Most participants did not understand the purpose of the slider. Therefore, to show the advancement of time, we have decided to use clickable buttons (see figures 1 and 2). For instance, as the user clicks on the 6 months button, the shape of the character will change based on the new input of the diet or exercise plan. In addition, since different countries or cultures implement and use different units for measurement, we decided to provide the options for this feature - centimeters vs. inches and kilograms vs. pounds.

We also decided to redesign the navigation by creating a persistent and simple top menu. This was expected to create a better sense of place for the users. We also created the habits page, which allows the user to see a brief of common weekly exercise and common daily meals.

Based on the inputs from the usability test about food intake, we have created the menu highly targeted to Latino families. That means food items shown on the menu are generally being consumed by this population. All of these food items can be updated/modified easily in the future if necessary. It is important to note that the food menu was created with the consultation of a dietitian from a local clinic.

5.8   Findings from the Second Usability Testing

Task one was "Select a child character and see what is his or her condition in 1 and 3 years." All of them were successful selecting a character but three of them failed to respond the correct conditions and one used the energy value. One of the reasons for this is that they were confused by the word "condition".

The second task was "Change the child character's exercise and see how that affects his or her condition in 3 years." The third task was the same, but it asked to change the common lunch meal. These tasks were not achieved correctly for any participant. While the majority of them actually changed exercise and meal habits, no one could see how it affected the character's condition in 3 years. The observation and the later debriefing showed that the participants did not understand that the app could do the projection. They thought that app was a passive source of information rather than an interactive tool. Additionally, the wording of the test instructions were not clear for them.

The fourth task was "Find details about what the child character should do regarding the proteins." Only one participant completed this task. The main reason for the failure was the lack of understanding of what the app could do. Additionally, no participants fully understood the concept of protein in food.

The fifth task was "Select another child character." Five participants completed this task. At this point they were familiar with the page structure and knew where to select another character.

6   Discussion and Future Direction

Navigation and information elements show good visibility and clarity. While there were more failures than expected in the second usability test, the app needs a few number of corrections to be finished. One of the actions that is needed is to create a promotional information video that briefly explains the possibilities of the app. Such videos are common in app marketplaces. We believe that once the users understand what can be done in the app, they will use it effectively.

Regarding the rhetorical modes, the second usability test showed limited results in difference of preference. The limited time that the app was used explains in part why there is no sufficient data. Additionally, first time users focus their attention in navigation and tasks, not in the information presented in the content. All of them were motivated to use the app more, which suggests that they might focus on the educational content in the later uses.

The next step in our research is to evaluate how users change health attitudes and increase knowledge, and to compare the performance of the rhetorical appeals. We will need to let them use the app more often in order to be able to obtain significant data. Based on the user research, our preliminary hypothesis is that Latinos will have a preference for the pathos-enriched graphics, but more fieldwork is needed. Additionally, our future goal is to create a second version of the application that allows individual to enter his/her own information in a personalized way. For instance, one can enter his/her own child height and weight and diet info based on cultural preference In addition, there will be options of diet selection based on different cultural populations and their food preferences.

References

1. Ehses, H.: Representing Macbeth: A Case Study in Visual Rhetoric. Design Issues 1, 53–63 (1984)
2. Buchanan, R.: Rhetoric, humanism, and design. In: Buchanan, R., Margolin, V. (eds.) Discovering design, pp. 23–66. The University of Chicago Press, Chicago (1995)
3. Bonsiepe, G.: Design as Tool for Cognitive Metabolism: From Knowledge Production to Knowledge Presentation. In: Bonsiepe, G. (ed.) Presented at the International Symposium on the Dimensions of Industrial Design Research Ricerca+Design, Politecnico di Milano, Milan, Italy (2000)
4. Kostelnick, C., Hassett, M.: Shaping Information: The Rhetoric of Visual Conventions. Southern Illinois University Press, Carbondale (2003)
5. Mejia, G.M., Chu, S.: A Model for Visual Communication Design: Connecting Theories of Rhetoric, Literacy, and Design. The Design Journal (in press)
6. Van der Waarde, K.: Visual Communication for Medicines: Malignant Assumptions and Benign design? Visible Language 22(1), 39–69 (2010)
7. Winn, W., Beck, K.: The Persuasive Power of Design Elements on an E-Commerce Web Site. Technical Communication 49(1), 17–35 (2002)
8. Center of Disease Control and Prevention. Childhood Obesity Facts, http://www.cdc.gov/healthyyouth/obesity/facts.htm
9. Ogden, C., Carroll, M.: Prevalence of Obesity Among Children and Adolescents: United States, Trends 1963-1965 Through 2007-2008. NCHS Health E-Stat, http://www.cdc.gov/nchs/data/hestat/obesity_child_07_08/obesity_child_07_08.htm
10. Huizinga, M.M., Pont, S., Rothman, R.L., Perrin, E., Sanders, L., Beech, B.: ABC's and 123's: Parental Literacy, Numeracy, and Childhood Obesity. Obesity management 4(3), 98–103 (2008), doi:10.1089/obe.2008.0163
11. Houts, P., Doak, C., Doak, L., Loscalzo, M.: The role of pictures in improving health communication: A review of research on attention, comprehension, recall, and adherence. Patient Education and Counseling 61, 173–190 (2006)
12. Katz, M., Kripalani, S., Weiss, B.: Use of pictorial aids in medication instructions: A review of the literature. American Journal of Health-System Pharmacists 63, 2391–2397 (2006)
13. Anker, J., Senathirajah, Y., Kukafka, R., Starren, J.: Design Features of Graphs in Health Risk Communication: A Systematic Review. Journal of the American Medical Informatics Association 13, 608–618 (2006)

14. Institute of Medicine of the National Academies. Dietary Reference Intakes for Energy, Carbohydrate, Fiber, Fat, Fatty Acids, Cholesterol, Protein, and Amino Acids (Macronutrients). National Academies Press, Washington, D.C, `http://www.nap.edu/openbook.php?record_id=1049`

15. Center of Disease Control and Prevention. Clinical Growth Charts (2009), `http://www.cdc.gov/growthcharts/clinical_charts.htm` (retrieved February 19, 2013)

16. Zickuhr, K., Smith, A.: Digital differences. Pew Research Center, `http://pewinternet.org/Reports/2012/Digital-differences.aspx`

Addressing Human Computer Interaction Issues of Electronic Health Record in Clinical Encounters

Martina A. Clarke[1], Linsey M. Steege[1,2], Joi L. Moore[1,3], Jeffery L. Belden[4], Richelle J. Koopman[4], and Min Soon Kim[1,5]

[1] University of Missouri Informatics Institute, University of Missouri
[2] School of Nursing, University of Wisconsin - Madison
[3] School of Information Science and Learning Technology, University of Missouri
[4] Department of Family and Community Medicine, University of Missouri
[5] Department of Health Management and Informatics, University of Missouri
mcyyf@mail.missouri.edu

1 Background

Electronic Health Records (EHRs) are known to reduce medical errors and store comprehensive patient information, and they also impact the physician-patient interaction during clinical encounters. This study reviewed the literature to (1) identify the most common challenges to patient-physician relations while using an EHR during a clinical visit, (2) discuss limitations of the research methodologies employed, and (3) suggest future research directions related to addressing human computer interaction issues when physicians use an EHR in clinical encounters.

2 Method

A literature review was conducted and the selection criteria for inclusion were abstracts written in English between the years 2000 and 2012. The chosen Medical Subject Heading (MeSH) terms were: electronic health records, computerized medical records, physician-patient relations, and user-computer interface. Other search terms included: human computer interaction (HCI), ergonomics, human factors, and usability. The searches in PubMed, CINAHL, SCOPUS, and OVID MEDLINE identified 121, 159, 569, and 233 citations, respectively. Hand-searching was also conducted through bibliography of relevant papers to identify any further studies that may have been overlooked by the database literature search. After examination of articles, 17 final articles (Table 1) were identified to be a part of the review.

3 Results

Four common areas of human computer interaction issues during clinical encounters were identified from the reviewed articles.

A. Marcus (Ed.): DUXU/HCII 2013, Part II, LNCS 8013, pp. 381–390, 2013.
© Springer-Verlag Berlin Heidelberg 2013

3.1   Poor Display of Information

Using a computer during a patient visit with poor display of information may not present all the necessary data or satisfy the information needs of physicians, which may frustrate the physician and cause a negative experience for the patient [1-7]. For example, poor information display can cause prescribing errors [8, 9].

3.2   Cognitive Overload

Physicians have to process a large amount of information that is readily available in the EHR during the patient visit, which may cause cognitive overload. Cognitive load theory assumes that the working memory has limited capacity when processing new information [10]. Cognitive overload is caused when the demand to process information exceed the capabilities of the cognitive system [11]. Processing text, analyzing images, and attempting to address problems being brought up by the patient simultaneously may cause errors such as analyzing lab results incorrectly and engaging patients less in conversation [2, 4, 12, 13].

3.3   Navigation Issues

Navigation issues make information difficult to find, which contributes to physicians spending more time looking at the screen, typing, and focusing more on filling out required fields than asking patients open-ended questions. Thus, the patient may feel that they are not being heard and physicians may lose visual observation of patients' emotions that may have a negative effect on patient satisfaction [2, 14-17].

3.4   Workflow Issues

Many EHRs do not integrate well with physician clinical workflow, which forces physicians to change their practice causing more time and effort from the user and delay in patient care, and ultimately resulting in limited user acceptance of the EHR [15, 18-24]. For example, physicians changing the way they interact with patients when inputting information into the EHR so that the physicians would not seem rude [22].

4   Discussion

Failing to consider usability issues when designing EHRs, results in potential human-computer interaction concerns that may contribute to loss of productivity and decreased quality of patient care. Employing human-centered design by including users' input into the EHR development process, could successfully create a user-friendly system and may assist in reducing the frustration that come with poor information display [25].

Designing displays in the EHR that capture the relevant information physicians need during clinic visits may reduce errors caused by cognitive overload [26]. A review by Khajouei and Jaspers also showed several studies reporting difficulty to find certain information in medication ordering systems because of poor screen displays[27].Improving EHR design based on clinician specific information needs in the electronic progress note by reducing unnecessary information included in the display, simplifying the information being presented, could address the human computer interaction issues presented in this study faced by users of the progress note [28].

Designing systems to use as few clicks as possible to get to pertinent information could reduce navigational issues and allow the physician to focus more on the patient than the screen. A literature review by Phansalkar et al, found that many basic human factors principles are not followed when designing clinical information systems [29]. A study of a diabetes dashboard showed that reducing clicks from 60 to three clicks to obtain all the relevant clinical data from one screen led to fewer errors. This paper illustrates not only how poor display and organization take time and cause errors, but how optimized display corrects these problems [7].

Many EHRs do not integrate well with physician clinical workflow. Multiple studies found decreased face to face interaction between physician and patients when using EHRs in a desktop computer during the office visit [1, 14, 15, 30]. Studies found that patients preferred being able to see the computer screen the physician was using [31, 32].The use of desktop computers could affect the positioning of physicians in the office. Positioning may become less of an issue when using portable devices such as tablets, because patients would not feel the physician was watching the screen more than communicating with them [33-35]. Studies comparing the desktop versus handheld devices should be conducted to verify how modality influences physicians' interaction with EHRs and its influence on clinical encounter.

The articles revealed a variety of research methodologies to investigate issues faced when physicians use an EHR during a clinical encounter; however there were limitations to these methodologies that warrant attention.

While the observational method was commonly used and is useful in viewing real time interaction among subjects, observational studies could produce the Hawthorne effect [36] wherein participant physicians and patients change their behaviors during a study because they are aware of being observed [14, 15, 37-39]. The patients, therefore, may not feel comfortable expressing all their concerns, which could shorten visit time [2]. Patient visit time has been shown to increase because of HCI issues in the use of EHR during the clinical encounter [15]. A study defined EHR usage as "any contact with the computer" [30]. The study, however, did not consider physicians' interactions with programs other than the EHR. This may be a concern because the physician may be researching educational materials to share with the patient, which would cause a higher EHR usage and can add bias to the results. Physician experience in making a diagnosis can also influence the length of EHR use; which factor warrants further research [30].

Table 1. Summary of studies selected to address human computer interaction issues (poor display, cognitive load, navigational issues, and workflow issues) of electronic health records in clinical encounters

Study & HCI Issue	Aim and Sample Population	Findings
Makoul et al., 2001. HCI issues: Navigational issues, workflow issues	Assess physician-patient communication patterns associated with use of an electronic medical record (EMR) system in an outpatient setting using exploratory, observational study involving analysis of videotaped 238 physician-patient encounters with six study physicians, questionnaires, and medical-record reviews in a general internal medicine practice at an urban, academic medical center in Chicago	An EMR system may enhance the ability of physicians to complete information-intensive tasks but can make it more difficult to focus attention on other aspects of patient communication. Further study involving a controlled, pre-/post-intervention design is justified.
Penrod and Gad, 2001 HCI issue: Navigational issues	Compare and contrast the attitudes of academic-based and community-based primary care physicians toward EMR use and investigate some of the factors influencing their attitudes toward the EMR implementation using surveys and interviews of physicians and patients from 6 practices of a large academic health system	Physicians in both an academic-based and community-based practice settings endorse improvements in quality and communication as well as concern over rapport with the patient and privacy issues.
Krall and Sittig, 2002 HCI issue: Workflow issues	Discerning the elements that determine alerts and the requirements of what makes a helpful alert or reminder by conducting three focus groups with 16 participants	Five usability themes emerged from participants: Efficiency, Usefulness, Information Content, User Interface, and Workflow
Wang et al., 2002 HCI issues: Workflow issues	Build a new module for our ambulatory electronic medical record system to automate "end of visit" (EOV) activities and improve provider workflow efficiency.	An EOV module must be carefully designed to incorporate the needs of multiple stakeholders.

Table 1. (*Continued*)

Study & HCI Issue	Aim and Sample Population	Findings
Ash et al., 2004 HCI issue: Poor display	Describe kinds of silent errors and interpret the nature of these errors through a literature review and qualitative research studies in the United States, The Netherlands, and Australia based on ethnographic observation in health care delivery settings and semi structured interviews with professionals.	The errors fall into two main categories: those in the process of entering and retrieving information, and those in the communication and coordination process that the PCIS is supposed to support. Informaticians can educate, design systems, implement, and conduct research in such a way that they might be able to avoid the unintended consequences of subtle silent errors.
Poon et al., 2004 HCI issue: Cognitive load	Identify problems in current test result management systems and possible ways to improve these systems by surveying 168 participants affiliated with 2 major academic medical centers and 1 integrated delivery network in Boston, MA.	Significant deficiencies in test result management exist in the ambulatory setting. The test result review system is still inefficient and may cause delays and loss to follow-up.
Garg et al., 2005 HCI issue: Workflow issues	Review of 100 controlled trial studies assessing the effects of computerized clinical decision support systems (CDSSs) and to identify study characteristics predicting benefit	Barriers to implementation include failure to use the CDSS, usability issues, poor integration into practitioner workflow, or practitioner non-acceptance of computer recommendations
Kushniruk et al., 2005 HCI issues: Poor display, cognitive load	Describes an innovative approach to the evaluation of a handheld prescription writing application with ten internal medicine physicians	It was found that certain types of usability problems were closely associated with the occurrence of specific types of errors in prescription of medications.
Rose et al., 2005 HCI issue: Poor display	Improve the usability of a results management module of a widely deployed web-based EMR. Sample: Observation of five primary care physicians and two nurses associated with Brigham & Women's Hospital (BWH) and Massachusetts General Hospital (MGH) and five focus group sessions	Findings raised issues with the amount and organization of information in the display, interference with workflow patterns of primary care physicians, and the availability of visual cues and feedback

Table 1. (*Continued*)

Study & HCI Issue	Aim and Sample Population	Findings
Linder et al., 2006 HCI issue: Workflow issues	Assess EHR use during ambulatory visits and determine barriers to such use utilizing a cross-sectional survey of 225 primary care clinicians.	Barriers to using the EHR during patient visits were loss of eye contact with patients (62%), falling behind schedule (52%), computers being too slow (49%), inability to type quickly enough (32%), feeling that using the computer in front of the patient is rude (31%), and preferring to write long prose notes (28%).
Margalit et al., 2006 HCI issue: Navigational issues	Examine the relationships between the extent of electronic medical record use and physician-patient communication in videotapes of 3 Israeli primary care physicians and 30 of their patients.	Physicians typically faced the desktop computer and patients did not have a view of the screen. On average, physicians spent close to one-quarter of the visit gazing at the computer screen, and in some cases it was as much as 42% of visit time.
Koppel et al., 2008 HCI issues: Poor display, workflow issues	Identify and quantify the role of CPOE in facilitating prescription error risks using qualitative and quantitative study of 261 house staff at a tertiary-care teaching hospital from 2002-2004 using surveys , 5 focus groups, and 32 interviews with house staff, information technology leaders, pharmacy leaders, attending physicians, and nurses; shadowed house staff and nurses; and observed them using CPOE.	This CPOE system often facilitated medication error risks, with many reported to occur frequently. Clinicians and hospitals must attend to errors that these systems cause in addition to errors that they prevent.
Rosenstand and Waldorf, 2008 HCI: Navigation issues	Describe how 253 Danish patients perceive and nine general practitioners (GPs) use of computers during consultation at five primary care clinics by completing complementary questionnaires.	More patients experienced discomfort with GPs computer use and did not get their problem solved. 28% of patient found their GP's computer use extensive.
Smith et al., 2008 HCI issues: Poor display, workflow issues	Present three case studies that highlight common e-prescribing problems involving diabetes patients.	Close attention is needed to the e-prescribing application features and level of clinical decision support to avoid clinical blind spots, including incomplete or inaccurate patient medication lists, and poor drop-down menu or

Table 1. (*Continued*)

Study & HCI Issue	Aim and Sample Population	Findings
Alsos et al., 2011 HCI issues: Poor display, cognitive load, navigational issues	Explore the effects of PDA usage on the physicians' prescription work, their concerns about using it in point-of-care situations, and the effects on the patient-physician dialog. Video recordings, semi-structured interviews, and focus group with 14 physicians simulating four ward rounds.	screen design. PDA usage at the point-of-care comes with the increased risk of distractions for physicians and can cause a negative patient experience. Designers of point-of-care systems need to be aware of, and address, the problems with handhelds and learn from the attributes and access capabilities of paper charts
Goh et al., 2011 HCI issue: Workflow issues	Gain an understanding of the interplay between technology and patterns of clinical work embodied in routines using a detailed field study of an HIT implementation in a large hospital	Implementation caused changes in rounding routines and in consulting routine. There was also loss of performance due to longer times to complete familiar tasks.
Koopman et al., 2011 HCI issue: Poor display	Compared 10 family physicians use of a new diabetes dashboard screen at the University of Missouri Health System (UMHS) to the conventional approach of viewing multiple electronic health record (EHR) screens to find data needed for ambulatory diabetes care	This paper illustrates not only how poor display and organization take time and cause errors, but how optimized display corrects these problems.

5   Conclusion

HCI issues in the design of EHRs can have negative impacts on physician-patient interaction in a clinical encounter. Future studies should consider the confounding factors of differences in patient diagnoses when assessing the length of consultation in relation to EHR use.

References

1. Hsu, J., et al.: Health information technology and physician-patient interactions: impact of computers on communication during outpatient primary care visits. J Am Med. Inform. Assoc. 12(4), 474–480 (2005)
2. Alsos, O.A., Dabelow, B., Faxvaag, A.: Doctors' concerns of PDAs in the ward round situation. Lessons from a formative simulation study. Methods Inf. Med. 50(2), 190–200 (2011)
3. Ash, J.S., Berg, M., Coiera, E.: Some unintended consequences of information technology in health care: the nature of patient care information system-related errors. J Am Med. Inform. Assoc. 11(2), 104–112 (2004)
4. Kushniruk, A.W., et al.: Technology induced error and usability: the relationship between usability problems and prescription errors when using a handheld application. Int. J. Med. Inform. 74(7-8), 519–526 (2005)
5. Rose, A.F., et al.: Using qualitative studies to improve the usability of an EMR. J. Biomed. Inform. 38(1), 51–60 (2005)
6. Van Vleck, T.T., et al.: Content and structure of clinical problem lists: a corpus analysis. In: AMIA Annu. Symp. Proc., pp. 753–757 (2008)
7. Koopman, R.J., et al.: A diabetes dashboard and physician efficiency and accuracy in accessing data needed for high-quality diabetes care. Ann Fam. Med. 9(5), 398–405 (2011)
8. Smith, M., Dang, D., Lee, J.: E-prescribing: clinical implications for patients with diabetes. J. Diabetes Sci. Technol. 3(5), 1215–1218 (2009)
9. Koppel, R., et al.: Role of computerized physician order entry systems in facilitating medication errors. JAMA, 2005 293(10), 1197–1203 (2005)
10. Van Merrienboer, J.J., Ayres, P.: Research on cognitive load theory and its design implications for e-learning. Educational Technology Research and Development 53(3), 5–13 (2005)
11. Mayer, R.E., Moreno, R.: Nine ways to reduce cognitive load in multimedia learning. Educational psychologist 38(1), 43–52 (2003)
12. Poon, E.G., et al.: "I wish I had seen this test result earlier!": Dissatisfaction with test result management systems in primary care. Arch Intern. Med. 164(20), 2223–2228 (2004)
13. Wipfli, R., Lovis, C.: Alerts in clinical information systems: building frameworks and prototypes. Stud. Health. Technol. 155, 163–169 (2010)
14. Margalit, R.S., et al.: Electronic medical record use and physician-patient communication: an observational study of Israeli primary care encounters. Patient Educ. Couns. 61(1), 134–141 (2006)
15. Makoul, G., Curry, R.H., Tang, P.C.: The use of electronic medical records: communication patterns in outpatient encounters. J. Am Med. Inform. Assoc. 8(6), 610–615 (2001)

16. Penrod, L.E., Gadd, C.S.: Attitudes of academic-based and community-based physicians regarding EMR use during outpatient encounters. In: Proc AMIA Symp., pp. 528–532 (2001)
17. Rosenstand, J., Waldorff, F.B.: Views of GPs and patients on use of computers during consultation. Ugeskr Laeger 170(17), 1449–1453 (2008)
18. Garg, A.X., et al.: Effects of computerized clinical decision support systems on practitioner performance and patient outcomes: a systematic review. JAMA 293(10), 1223–1238 (2005)
19. Goh, J.M., Gao, G., Agarwal, R.: Evolving Work Routines: Adaptive Routinization of Information Technology in Healthcare. Information Systems Research 22(3), 565–585 (2011)
20. Kawamoto, K., et al.: Improving clinical practice using clinical decision support systems: a systematic review of trials to identify features critical to success. BMJ 330(7494), 765 (2005)
21. Krall, M.A., Sittig, D.F.: Clinician's assessments of outpatient electronic medical record alert and reminder usability and usefulness requirements. In: Proc. AMIA Symp., pp. 400–404 (2002)
22. Linder, J.A., et al.: Barriers to electronic health record use during patient visits. In: AMIA Annu. Symp. Proc., pp. 499–503 (2006)
23. Tamblyn, R., et al.: The development and evaluation of an integrated electronic prescribing and drug management system for primary care. J. Am Med. Inform. Assoc. 13(2), 148–159 (2006)
24. Wang, S.J., et al.: End of visit: design considerations for an ambulatory order entry module. In: Proc. AMIA Symp., pp. 864–868 (2002)
25. Maguire, M.: Methods to support human-centred design. International Journal of Human-Computer Studies 55(4), 587–634 (2001)
26. Belden, J., Grayson, R., Barnes, J.: Defining and testing EMR usability: Principles and proposed methods of EMR usability evaluation and rating. Chicago (IL): Healthcare Information and Management Systems (2009)
27. Khajouei, R., Jaspers, M.W.: CPOE system design aspects and their qualitative effect on usability. Stud. Health. Technol. Inform. 136, 309–314 (2008)
28. Clarke, M., et al.: Creating a More Readable Electronic Health Record (EHR) Model: Analysis of Primary Care Physicians' Information Needs. In: AMIA 2012 (2012)
29. Phansalkar, S., et al.: A review of human factors principles for the design and implementation of medication safety alerts in clinical information systems. J. Am Med. Inform. Assoc. 17(5), 493–501 (2010)
30. Arar, N.H., Wang, C.P., Pugh, J.A.: Self-care communication during medical encounters: implications for future electronic medical records. Perspect Health Inf. Manag. 3, 3 (2006)
31. Als, A.B.: The desk-top computer as a magic box: patterns of behaviour connected with the desk-top computer; GPs' and patients' perceptions. Fam. Pract. 14(1), 17–23 (1997)
32. Ridsdale, L., Hudd, S.: Computers in the consultation: the patient's view. Br. J. Gen. Pract. 44(385), 367–369 (1994)
33. Houston, T.K., et al.: Patient perceptions of physician use of handheld computers. In: AMIA Annu. Symp. Proc., pp. 299–303 (2003)
34. Berner, E.S., et al.: Impact of patient feedback on residents' handheld computer use: a multi-site study. Stud. Health. Technol. Inform. 107(pt 1), 582–586 (2004)
35. Strayer, S.M., et al.: Patient attitudes toward physician use of tablet computers in the exam room. Fam. Med. 42(9), 643–647 (2010)

36. French, J.R.P.: Experiments in field settings. Research methods in the behavioral sciences, pp. 98–135 (1953)
37. Arar, N.H., et al.: Communicating about medications during primary care outpatient visits: the role of electronic medical records. Inform. Prim. Care 13(1), 13–22 (2005)
38. Ventres, W., et al.: Physicians, patients, and the electronic health record: An ethnographic analysis. Annals of Family Medicine 4(2), 124–131 (2006)
39. Booth, N., Robinson, P., Kohannejad, J.: Identification of high-quality consultation practice in primary care: The effects of computer use on doctor-patient rapport. Informatics in Primary Care 12(2), 75–83 (2004)

Designing Co-located Tabletop Interaction
for Rehabilitation of Brain Injury

Jonathan Duckworth[1], Patrick R. Thomas[2], David Shum[3], and Peter H. Wilson[4]

[1] School of Media and Communication, RMIT University, Melbourne, Australia
jonathan.duckworth@rmit.edu.au
[2] School of Education & Professional Studies, Griffith University, Brisbane, Australia
p.thomas@griffith.edu.au
[3] Behavioural Basis of Health, Griffith Health Institute and School of Applied Psychology,
Griffith University, Brisbane, Australia
d.shum@griffith.edu.au
[4] School of Psychology, Faculty of Arts and Sciences, Australian Catholic University,
Melbourne, Australia
peterh.wilson@acu.edu.au

Abstract. This paper surveys emerging design research on co-located group interaction with tabletop displays as an approach toward developing an upper-limb movement rehabilitation system for acquired brain injury (ABI). Traditional approaches and newer virtual reality interventions for physical therapy tend to focus on individuals interacting one-on-one with a therapist in a clinical space – this is both labor intensive and costly. Co-located tabletop environments have been shown to enhance the engagement of users, translating to skill acquisition. We describe the principles of group interaction that inform our understanding of motor rehabilitation using interactive media; explore four constructs from interactive tabletop research that may influence the design of co-located systems for rehabilitation: 1) physical space, 2) group awareness, 3) territoriality, and 4) interaction simultaneity; and consider how each construct can be expressed in particular design solutions for rehabilitation of ABI.

Keywords: Co-located, Group Interaction, Tabletop Display, Movement Rehabilitation, Acquired Brain Injury.

1 Introduction

Acquired brain injury (ABI) from stroke and traumatic brain injury (TBI) is a major global health issue [1]. Neurological trauma can lead to a variety of physical, cognitive, emotional and behavioral deficits that may have long-lasting and devastating consequences for the victims and their families. The capacity of health services to cater to large numbers of clients with differing needs is limited. Traditional approaches to physical therapy require intensive one-to-one work over an extended period using a variety of props, in relatively large workspaces [45]. Whilst time-on-task is a good predictor of recovery, a 1:1 therapist-client ratio is labor intensive and cost prohibitive.

A. Marcus (Ed.): DUXU/HCII 2013, Part II, LNCS 8013, pp. 391–400, 2013.

Accordingly, enhancing physical rehabilitative processes in the early stages following a brain injury is one of the great challenges facing therapists given the huge demands on the health system.

There is now strong evidence to support the use of group-based rehabilitation as a way of leveraging therapy and reducing health care costs [9]. For example, circuit class therapy has been shown to reap significant mobility outcomes for ABI in a group setting, regardless of the severity of injury and chronicity [49]. Indeed, studies have suggested that group-based therapy provides additional benefits through observational learning [44], and fostering peer support [11].

The way computers can mediate and support work in a group environment has become a research domain in Computer Supported Cooperative Work (CSCW), a sub-field of Human Computer Interaction (HCI). The advent of large-format interactive walls and tabletop displays heralded the potential of computers to facilitate the work practices of small teams co-located around the same physical interface [6], [48]. In particular, tabletop displays can support face-to-face multiuser interaction through the physical affordances of the horizontal interface or the users' mental models of working around traditional tables [42]. Tabletop displays can support a broad range of user interactions such as multifinger touch, hand gesture and simultaneous manipulation of physical objects [17], [47], [50], lead to collaborative learning in a group setting [22], [37], and foster multimodal communication between users [10]. For example, tabletop computer games have been shown to support social competence training for children with Autism Spectrum Disorder [13].

How group work using tabletop technology can enhance motor rehabilitation of ABI is relatively unexplored. Our research seeks to address this gap by exploring how social aspects of group interaction and physical affordances of tabletop displays may be exploited to enhance the design of environments for such rehabilitation. We consider design research on tabletop displays, social psychological literature on group-based interaction, concepts from ecological psychology, and work in CSCW to forge an integrated view of the possibilities of co-located interactive workspaces. In particular, we examine the advantages of tabletop interfaces based on our observation of patients from prior research [29] and identify areas of potential development.

2   Prior Work

2.1   Elements: A Single-User Tabletop Workspace

As reported elsewhere, our prior work called Elements is a single-user interactive tabletop environment used to enhance upper-limb rehabilitation for TBI patients [7]. The physical design of the environment is comprised of a tabletop graphics display, four soft graspable objects used by the patient (i.e. tangible user interfaces, TUIs), a computer vision camera to track the position of the TUIs, and a secondary display for the therapist to control the task parameters presented to the patient.

A suite of interactive software applications provides the patient with tasks geared toward reaching, grasping, lifting, moving, and placing the TUIs on the tabletop display. Real-time audiovisual feedback is designed to help the patient refine their movements over time. Patients can also manipulate the computer-generated feedback to create unique audiovisual outcomes. For example, in one environment the patient might feel pleasure from being able to mix and manipulate sound and colorful graphics in an aesthetically pleasing way. The overall system design provides tactility, texture, and audiovisual feedback to encourage patients to move in response to external cues or in a self-directed way. The various feedback mechanisms provided by the system assist patients and therapists monitor their progress and plan for improvement over time. Our preliminary findings suggest that performing tasks on the Elements system is a viable adjunct to conventional physical therapy in facilitating motor learning in patients with TBI [28-29].

2.2   The Advantages of Tabletop Interaction for Rehabilitation

Interactive tabletop displays offer several unique advantages for motor rehabilitation. Foremost, the tabletop display supports upper-limb interaction as the main form of user input. Approximately 85% of brain injured patients suffer acute impairment to their upper body, so a majority of patients rate the return of upper-limb function as a high priority [25]. The horizontal display and TUIs logically constrain user movement within a defined (planar) area above the table. The task constraints include the ways in which the TUIs can be held, moved, and stabilised in relation to the virtual environment projected on the tabletop display and the audiovisual feedback. By reducing the number of alternative actions that can be performed by the patient in the early phase of recovery we make explicit the functionality of the user interface to perform a certain task or function. Varying the task and environmental constraints is designed to increase the patient's ability to plan and initiate movements over time.

Secondly, tabletop environments support multimodal forms of communication between co-located users [33]. For example, the configuration of the Elements system enables a close visible relationship between the patient and the therapist. The therapist can supervise the patient's activities and provide feedback, encouragement and prompts. Patients can explore, learn and share how new movements can be performed and validate these actions in direct communication with the therapist.

Thirdly, tabletop interaction supports an embodied, first-person view of performance that capitalizes on our physical skills and our familiarity with real-world objects [8]. A key feature of tabletop displays is their capacity to integrate and support the manipulation of physical objects such as TUIs [20]. TUIs placed on the tabletop are used as the primary means for users to control the Elements interactive environment. The shape and physical weight of each TUI offers the patient varying perceptual motor cues for action [12].

3   Design Characteristics of Tabletop Interaction

In this section we focus on related work on tabletop interface design that supports co-located forms of user interaction. We identify the socio-physical characteristics of co-located workspaces that designers should consider when developing rehabilitation applications. We describe four main characteristics or factors – physical space, group awareness, territoriality, and interface simultaneity – and outline how they can be exploited in the design of therapeutic tasks in a group setting.

3.1 Physical Space

The physical space surrounding tabletop displays can influence the dynamics of collocated interaction. For example, the spatial orientation of users around tabletop displays has been shown to influence how individuals comprehend information, coordinate actions between one another, and communicate in a collaborative setting [23]. Tasks may support the arrangement of users sitting side by side; but other tasks may support users sitting opposite one another depending on the orientation of the information displayed. Other findings have shown user position affects the level of participation across a tabletop surface [36]. The level of participation is partially dependent on how well a participant is able to physically reach across the table [46]. As well there is a generalized preference for users to interact within the region of the display closest to their body [43]. This has basic implications for the design of tabletop interfaces that enhance group cohesion and provide space for collaboration. The software design will affect how groups of participants partition the tabletop display and whether this is scaled optimally to the physical ability of the users.

Other physical attributes such as the shape and width of the non-interactive edge surrounding the display can assist how interactivity is managed [27]. For example, the size of the rim around the tabletop display can enable users to rest their arms without interfering with the interactive area of the display. The rim can also influence how physical resources (e.g., papers, TUIs) are arranged and selected for use both on and off the display during performance [27].

The table must have sufficient height and size to comfortably accommodate the group. Users should be able to maneuver around the table and sit or stand comfortably facing toward the display for extended periods of time. Many current systems incorporate technology that may render one or more sides of the table unusable. For a detailed review of these systems see Muller-Tomfelde et al [26]. For easy access, active sides of the table should be free of encumbrances such as rear projection equipment or display attachments. Accessibility is a common issue for ABI patients who may have postural difficulty in sitting and standing. Physical obstructions may impact on their level of comfort and interfere with their interactions with others.

3.2 Group Awareness

Awareness is regarded as the first step in self-regulation and plays an important role in skill development [35]. Group awareness is the degree to which people perceive and understand others' existence and activities in a shared task [30]. The ability of interactive tabletops to support awareness of others' actions is often cited as one of the main benefits of collaborative face-to-face learning [37]. Participants can observe and learn from how others are directly manipulating objects. Awareness of what others in a group are thinking and doing is also essential in coordinating collaborative learning and achieving common goals around a shared tabletop. Such learning is effective when the tabletop is a shared resource, participants using gesture and moving icons to communicate their ideas and understanding to others [10].

Communication patterns in co-located groups, including the use of gesture have been examined in various ways [4], [14]. Both communication and participation increase when groups interact around a tabletop display [39]. Tabletop games have been used effectively to develop social skills and foster collaboration in children and adolescents, including those with Autism Spectrum Disorder [3], [31]. Providing shared access to physical and digital artifacts can help maintain group focus and facilitate group awareness [40]. Moreover, tabletop interfaces can be designed to enable more equitable participation and sharing among members of the group [2], [18], [24], [32], although sometimes groups work well together when one person dominates the action [37].

Differences in the way tabletop interactions are designed affect individual and group processes, and thus participants' experiences. Nacenta et al. considered three perspectives in the design of tabletop interactions [30]. The *action perspective* refers to whether local space or shared space is used to provide input for the technique and display the action's output. The *person perspective* differentiates physical and virtual embodiments for people in shared workspaces. The *group perspective* deals with policies and rules that govern interactions and provide support for those participating. The elements of these three design perspectives have differing effects on the criteria used to evaluate interaction techniques. Nacenta et al. found higher levels of awareness when input and output are in shared space, objects are manipulated through direct-input techniques such as touching, dragging, and lifting, and participants are represented by their physical body.

3.3   Territoriality

The notion of territoriality has its roots in both ethology and more recently in evolutionary psychology and ecological psychology. In essence it refers to the spatial area that an individual or group lays some claim to [15]. Related to this is the notion of peripersonal space, which is the perceived boundary within which personal actions are performed [34], as distinct from those of others. These spatial frameworks bias our behavior according to the location of objects in the environment relative to the self and their reward or resource value to the species. Put another way, territorial behavior is bound up with the notion of resource and its proximity.

These resources are traditionally environmental (like food sources or nesting sites), but can also be other valued commodities like a site where a valued object is situated (like a cache of money or jewels) [19]. Importantly, in advanced human behavior, resources can be purely symbolic (like a token that can be exchanged later for some reward). This capacity of the human mind enables resources and the experience of reward to be extended in time; that is, the physical object does not need to be physically present to elicit territorial behavior. However, the symbolic value of a resource can be highlighted by the use of salient physical cues.

Accordingly, a range of non-verbal factors influences territoriality and the notion and experience of personal space. Edward T. Hall delineated at least 6 such factors that influence how humans and non-humans position themselves in relation to each other: visual, touch, kinaesthetic, voice loudness, thermal, and olfactory [16]. This approach has some useful implications for interaction design insofar as some combination of these cues can be manipulated using the display and user interfaces to alter the performer's perception of personal space and territory.

In the sphere of virtual rehabilitation, for example, these non-verbal factors can be manipulated in strategic ways to compensate for the impaired processing capacities of the patient, post injury. For example, sound pitch and/or loudness might be used to signal a form of interaction with a tangible interface, perhaps inviting manipulation on the one hand, or signalling that an approach might infringe on the territory of another person. This scenario can also be imbedded within the context of a game where permitted actions are defined by both physical and symbolic cues.

Research also suggests that the physical size of the tabletop display can impact the social interaction and working strategies among groups of users [41]. For example, physical size may engender a particular style of interaction when there is a clear perception of personal and/or group territory [43]. The table size directly impacts the physical proximity between individuals around a display, which can change how they collaborate when performing individual and group tasks. A smaller table ensures all users can reach every part of the table, which may encourage them to negotiate and collaborate. By comparison, partitioning the display environment and orientating parts of the graphics to each user may support both personal and group spaces on the table and transitions between personal and group work [42].

Territoriality can be used as an organising principle in the design of rehabilitation tasks. The proximity of users should be considered carefully so that interactions within a person's intimate or peripersonal space do not feel socially awkward. The location of the patients and the scale of the workspace, considered together with rules of interaction and the number of resources, can define how a co-located space is utilised and explored in rehabilitation. Depending on the rules by which resources are collected and distributed, different modes of interaction may be afforded, some cooperative, some playful, and some competitive. Each mode of interaction may achieve slightly different therapeutic ends in the realm of motor rehabilitation. For example, competition for resources in a discrete space, under time pressure, may enhance the reward value for patients while also encouraging faster actions. Although little is known about how groups of ABI patients interact with each other in rehabilitation, tabletop displays may offer ways for patients to relearn social skills and sense of personal space which may be adversely affected as a result of their injury.

3.4   Interface Simultaneity

Unlike single user interfaces such as desktop computers, tabletop technology can support multiple interfaces for collaborative work. TUIs can be selected, passed around, manipulated and shared by groups of users [40]. With groups of users comes the possibility for individuals to interact simultaneously with others and the tabletop interface. Concurrent interaction among groups enables a wider variety of collaboration styles, including working in parallel, working sequentially in tightly coupled activities, working independently, and working in assumed roles [42]. Scott et al suggest concurrent interaction enables the user to focus on the task at hand rather than monitoring others in order to tell when the system is available. The Rogers et al. findings indicate that sharable interfaces promote more group participation, highly coordinated forms of collaboration and verbal communication when tabletops support multiple points of interaction. Importantly, they suggest more tangible and accessible interfaces may consequently encourage greater participation from people who normally find it difficult to communicate verbally or those who simply find contributing in a group setting socially challenging.

A key advantage of tabletop displays is that the technology supports tangible interaction using multiple physical input devices and multi-touch input [26]. Conventional interfaces like keyboard and mouse tend to neglect the intrinsic importance of body movement and tangible interaction [5] and limit opportunities for relearning movements among brain-injured patients. Physical input devices or TUIs, however, can exploit multiple human sensory channels otherwise neglected in conventional interfaces and can promote rich and dexterous interaction [21].

The development of these naturalistic interfaces for user interaction is essential to optimise performance and improve access for patients with cognitive and motor impairments [38]. The form factor of the interfaces should take into account the deficits experienced by patients. Brain injured patients frequently suffer perceptual difficulties in auditory and visual functions, perception of objects, impaired space and distance judgment, and difficulty with orientation. High contrast colors and simple graspable shapes for example, may be used in the design of TUIs to assist a visually impaired user individuate each interface and ease cognitive overload.

4   Conclusion and Future Work

We have identified and discussed four key characteristics that can be used to guide the design of multiuser rehabilitation applications using tabletop surfaces. What is both challenging and intriguing for the developer are ways of designing features that leverage the type of therapeutic interaction and efficacy. Such design considerations are particularly important in therapeutic environments where patients may initially be hesitant about working in a group of people they do not know and reluctant to reveal their level of disability. A shared physical space and resources can be structured in ways that assist a patient group to develop an alliance and shared agenda. For example, a simple tabletop game can be set up that requires the group to work together and compete against the computer to score points. For the practitioner, the ability to manipulate the physical workspace (or territories) can, in turn, cater to patients with different needs and skill levels. How patients will collaborate with each other and the possible consequences of participation are less predictable.

The conceptual issues discussed in this paper are a starting point for understanding how to design effective multiuser applications for rehabilitation using interactive tabletops. This presents an avenue for transcending a traditional reliance on single-user applications. By understanding the intrinsic characteristics of shared workspaces, we aim to develop therapeutic group applications using tabletop displays that can maximize patients' potential to "learn from others", to develop social skills and confidence, and to instill motivation to work harder through collaboration and competition with fellow patients. Our principled approach to interface design that supports groups of patients will hopefully make brain injured individuals more willing to persist in rehabilitation, ultimately speeding their recovery.

Acknowledgements. This work is supported by an Australian Research Council (ARC) Linkage Grant LP110200802, and Synapse Grant awarded by the Australian Council for the Arts.

References

1. Australian Institute of Health and Welfare.: Health Care Expenditure on Cardiovascular Diseases. Canberra (2009)
2. Arias, E., Eden, H., Fischer, G., Gorman, A., Scharff, E.: Transcending the individual human mind: Creating shared understanding through collaborative design. ACM Transactions on Computer-Human-Interaction (ToCHI) 7(1), 84–113 (2000)
3. Battochi, A., et al.: Collaborative puzzle game: A tabletop interactive game for fostering collaboration in children with Autism Spectrum Disorders (ASD). In: Proceedings of ITS 2009, pp. 197–204. ACM Press, New York (2009)
4. Beattie, G., Shovelton, H.: Do iconic hand gestures really contribute anything to the semantic information conveyed by speech? An experimental investigation. Semiotica 123(1-2), 1–30 (1999)
5. Djajadiningrat, T., Matthews, B., et al.: Easy doesn't do it: skill and expression in tangible aesthetics. Personal and Ubiquitous Computing 11, 657–676 (2007)
6. Dietz, P.H., Leigh, D.L.: DiamondTouch: A Multi-user Touch Technology. In: Proc. UIST 2001, pp. 219–226. ACM Press (2001)
7. Duckworth, J., Wilson, P.H.: Embodiment and play in designing an interactive art system for movement rehabilitation. Second Nature 2(1), 120–137 (2010)
8. Dourish, P.: Where the action is: The foundations of embodied interaction. MIT Press (2001)
9. English, C., Hillier, S.: Circuit class therapy for improving mobility after stroke. Cochrane Library 1 (2009)
10. Fleck, R., Rogers, Y., Yuill, N., Marshall, P., Carr, A., Rick, J., Bonnett, V.: Actions speak loudly with words: Unpacking collaboration around the table. In: Proceedings of ITS 2009, pp. 189–196. ACM Press, New York (2009)
11. Fraser, S.N., Spink, K.S.: Examining the Role of Social Support and Group Cohesion in Exercise Compliance. Journal of Behavioral Medicine 25(3), 233–249 (2002)
12. Gibson, J.J.: The ecological approach to visual perception. Houghton Mifflin, Boston (1979)
13. Giusti, L., Zancanaro, M., Gal, E., Weiss, P.: Dimensions of collaboration on a tabletop interface for children with autism spectrum disorder. In: Proc. CHI, pp. 3295–3304. ACM Press (2011)

14. Goldin-Meadow, S.: Hearing gesture: How our hands help us think. Harvard University Press (2003)
15. Hall, E.T.: The Hidden Dimension. Double Day, Garden City (1966)
16. Hall, E.T.: A System for the Notation of Proxemic Behavior. American Anthropologist 65(5), 1003–1026 (1963)
17. Han, J.F.: Low-cost multi-touch sensing through frustrated total internal reflection. In: Proc. UIST 2005, pp. 115–118. ACM Press (2005)
18. Harris, A., Rick, J., Bonnett, V., Yuill, N., Fleck, R., Marshall, P., Rogers, Y.: Around the table: Are multiple-touch surfaces better than single-touch for children's collaborative interactions? In: Proceedings of CSCL 2009, pp. 335–344. ISLS (2009)
19. Hinsch, M., Komdeur, J.: Defence, intrusion and the evolutionary stability of territoriality. Journal of Theoretical Biology 266, 606–613 (2010)
20. Ishii, H.: Tangible Bits: beyond Pixels. In: Proceedings TEI 2008, pp. xv–xxv. ACM Press, New York (2008)
21. Ishii, H., Ullmer, B.: Tangible bits: towards seamless interfaces between people, bits and atoms. In: Proceedings of the SIGCHI Conference on Human Factors in Computing Systems. ACM Press, Atlanta (1997)
22. Kharrufa, A., Leat, D., Olivier, P.: Digital Mysteries: Designing for Learning at the Tabletop. In Proc. ITS 2010, pp. 197-206, ACM Press (2010)
23. Kruger, R., Carpendale, S., Scott, S.D., Greenberg, S.: How People Use Orientation on Tables: Comprehension, Coordination and Communication. In: Proceedings of GROUP 2003, pp. 369–378. ACM Press (2003)
24. Marshall, P., Hornecker, E., Morris, R., Dalton, S., Rogers, Y.: When the fingers do the talking: A study of group participation with varying constraints to a tabletop interface. In: Proceedings of TABLETOP 2008, pp. 33–40. IEEE Computer Society, Washington, DC (2008)
25. McCrea, P.H., Eng, J.J., Hodgson, A.J.: Biomechanics of reaching: clinical implications for individuals with acquired brain injury. Disability and Rehabilitation 24(5), 780–791 (2002)
26. Muller-Tomfelde, C., Fjeld, M.: Introduction: A Short History of Tabletop Research, Technologies, and Products. In: Müller-Tomfelde, C. (ed.) Tabletops – horizontal interactive displays, pp. 1–24. Springer, London (2010)
27. Muller-Tomfelde, C., O'Hara, K.: Horizontal Interactive Surfaces in Distributed Assemblies. In: Müller-Tomfelde, C. (ed.) Tabletops – horizontal interactive displays, pp. 435–456. Springer, London (2010)
28. Mumford, N., Duckworth, J., Thomas, P.R., Shum, D., Williams, G., Wilson, P.H.: Upper limb virtual rehabilitation for traumatic brain injury: Initial evaluation of the Elements system. Brain Injury 24(5), 780–791 (2010)
29. Mumford, N., Duckworth, J., Thomas, P.R., Shum, P., Williams, G., Wilson, P.H.: Upper-limb virtual rehabilitation for traumatic brain injury: A preliminary within-group evaluation of the Elements system. Brain Injury 26(2), 166–176 (2012)
30. Nacenta, M.A., Pinelle, D., Gutwin, C., Mandryk, R.: Individual and group support in tabletop interaction techniques. In: Müller-Tomfelde, C. (ed.) Tabletops – horizontal interactive displays, pp. 303–333. Springer, London (2010)
31. Piper, A.M., O'Brien, E., Morris, M.R., Winograd, T.: SIDES: A cooperative tabletop computer game for social skills development. In: Proceedings of CSCW 2006, pp. 1–10. ACM Press, New York (2006)

32. Piper, A.M., Hollan, J.D.: Tabletop displays for small group study: Affordances of paper and digital materials. In: Proceedings of CHI 2009, pp. 1227–1236. ACM Press, New York (2009)

33. Piper, A., Hollan, J.D.: Analyzing Multimodal Communication around a Shared Tabletop Display. In: Proc. ECSCW 2009, pp. 283–302. Springer (2009)

34. Previc, F.H.: The neuropsychology of 3-D space. Psychological Bulletin 124, 123–164 (1998)

35. Ravizza, K.: Increasing awareness for sport performance. In: Williams, J.M. (ed.) Applied sport psychology: Personal growth to peak performance, 6th edn., pp. 189–200. McGraw-Hill, Boston (2010)

36. Rick, J., Harris, A., Marshall, P., Fleck, R., Yuill, N., Rogers, Y.: Children Designing together on a Multi-Touch Tabletop: An Analysis of Spatial Orientation and User Interactions. In: IDC 2009, pp. 106–114 (2009)

37. Rick, J., Marshall, P., Yuill, N.: Beyond one-size-fits-all: How interactive tabletops support collaborative learning. In: IDC 2011, Ann Arbor, USA, June 20-23 (2011)

38. Rizzo, A.A.: A SWOT Analysis of the Field of Virtual Reality Rehabilitation and Therapy. Presence 14(2), 119–146 (2005)

39. Rogers, Y., Lindley, S.: Collaborating around vertical and horizontal large interactive displays: Which way is best? Interacting with Computers 16, 1133–1152 (2004)

40. Rogers, Y., Lim, Y., Hazlewood, W.R., Marshall, P.: Equal Opportunities: Do Shareable Interfaces Promote More Group Participation Than Single User Displays? Human-Computer Interaction 24(1-2), 79–116 (2009)

41. Ryall, K., et al.: Exploring the effects of group size and table size on interactions with tabletop shared-display groupware. In: Proceedings of CSCW 2004, pp. 284–293. ACM, New York (2004)

42. Scott, S.D., Grant, K.D., Mandryk, R.L.: System Guidelines for Co-located Collaborative Work on a Tabletop Display. In: Proc. ECSCW 2003, pp. 159–178 (2003)

43. Scott, S.D., Carpendale, S.: Theory of Tabletop Territoriality. In: Müller-Tomfelde, C. (ed.) Tabletops – horizontal interactive displays, pp. 357–385. Springer, London (2010)

44. Shea, C.H., Wright, D.L., Wulf, G., Whitacre, C.: Physical and Observational Practice Afford Unique Learning Opportunities. Journal of Motor Behaviour 32(1), 27–36 (2000)

45. Shumway-Cook, A., Woolacott, M.H.: Motor control: Translating research into clinical practice. Lippincott Williams & Wilkins, New York (2011)

46. Toney, A., Thomas, B.H.: Considering Reach in Tangible and Table Top Design. In: Proceedings of the First IEEE International Workshop on Horizontal Interactive Human-Computer Systems (Tabletop 2006). IEEE Computer Society (2006)

47. Ullmer, B., Ishii, H.: The metaDESK: Models and prototypes for tangible user interfaces. In: Proc. UIST 1997, pp. 223–232. ACM Press (1997)

48. Wellner, P.: Interacting with paper on the Digital Desk. Communications of the ACM 36(7), 87–96 (1993)

49. Williams, G.P., Morris, M.E.: High-level mobility outcomes following acquired brain injury: A preliminary evaluation. Brain Injury 23(4), 307–312 (2009)

50. Wu, M., Balakrishnan, R.: Multi-finger and whole hand gestural interaction techniques for multi-user tabletop displays. In: Proc. UIST 2003, pp. 193–202. ACM Press (2003)

Paindroid: A Mobile Tool for Pain Visualization and Management

Tor-Morten Grønli[1], Gheorghita Ghinea[1,2], Fotios Spyridonis[2], and Jarle Hansen[1]

[1] The Norwegian School of Information Technology, Schweigaardsgt. 14, 0185 Oslo, Norway
[2] School of Information Systems, Computing and Mathematics, Brunel University, Uxbridge
UB8 3PH, London, United Kingdom
`tmg@nith.no`, `{george.ghinea,fotios.spyridonis}@brunel.ac.uk`,
`jarle@jarlehansen.net`

Abstract. This paper presents a tool that addresses self-management expression of pain, through an Android application based on multimodal and 3D. Our pilot evaluation highlighted a positive attitude towards the usability of PainDroid's novel functionality, as well as the potential of the application to open up new avenues of patient-clinician interaction with the use of an innovative user experience.

Keywords: Android, Pain Visualization, Tablet, HCI.

1 Introduction

Pain presents a significant challenge to citizens and the healthcare system of countries. Evidence from a pan-European consensus report [1], suggests that one in five Europeans is estimated to have some form of chronic pain. Efficient intervention seems to be limited in most cases, with studies indicating a partial success of current approaches in efficiently assessing the pain experience [2 - 6]. Typical intervention practices include the visualization of pain information by using a paper-based, 2-D representation of the human body. The "pain drawing", as this representation has been named, is considered to be a valuable and useful tool in describing certain aspects of pain, such as the pain location and sensation type [3, 4, 6, 7]. Nevertheless, the consensus of the pain literature seems to indicate that such studies rely on the 2-D representation of the pain drawing. Notwithstanding its advantages, the 2-D pain drawing has its limitations, as it does not capture the 3-D nature of the human body. Thus, patients are unable to visually express the pain that they are experiencing, as statements of the form —I have a pain on the inside of my thigh‖ are not easily captured in a 2-D pain drawing, and the accuracy of the reported information can be often questioned. To date, however, the majority of efforts in the development of 3D pain applications have been focused on the management of pain in a clinical setting (i.e. hospitals). There is also only scarce research investigating the employment of the pain drawing for pain assessment on a *mobile* platform. Motivated by this situation we propose PainDroid: a mobile application for improved pain assessment visualization, which has been designed to run on handheld devices (i.e. a smartphone/tablet). Employing the benefits of 3D technology, the PainDroid application can provide the

A. Marcus (Ed.): DUXU/HCII 2013, Part II, LNCS 8013, pp. 401–406, 2013.

user with a 3-D visualization of the human body which aims to enable a user to improve their user experience and ability to report pain through a more realistic and interactive manner at any possible moment and place in time. The aim of this study is to tackle the issue of the small screen interface that normally a mobile device has. It is proposed that a VR component that is included would augment the small screen interface. While it could be argued that the solution to this issue could be to use a mobile device with the largest screen possible or bring the device at a comfortable self-chosen best viewing distance, this cannot always be the case with disabled users, who, in some occasions, due to their e.g. arm mobility problem might not be able to hold or move around a device that is bigger or weighs more. We therefore further investigate how to enhance the modes of interaction with a mobile solution to improve the experience of users that have mobility difficulties. Evidence from the literature seems to support the employment of additional modalities for interaction, for instance gesture input to effectively interaction [10].

2   Application Design

The PainDroid application has been developed on the Android platform. On the screen (Figure 1), the user is presented with five different pain types; *numbness, stabbing, pins & needles* (or tingling), *burning, and stiffness* (or taut), which were respectively color-coded. These types were chosen carefully after consultation with clinical staff, and are well documented in the pain literature [2, 7, 8, 9].

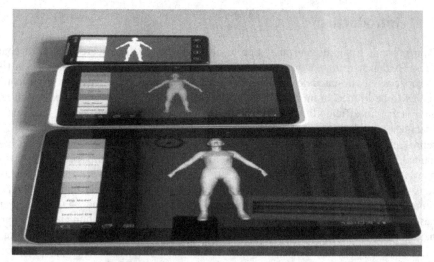

Fig. 1. PainDroid running on three different devices

In PainDroid user interaction is based both on direct touch and hand movement gesture input, in the anticipation that improving the interfacing modalities can make an important contribution to the interaction and usability of the relatively small-sized interface. As a result, touch gesture input in PainDroid is implemented as follows: first, the user selects an appropriate pain type by tapping on the predefined list presented on the left of the screen, and then the location of the pain is selected, again by tapping on the desired body part of the model. Each color represents a pain type and the model is colored at the selected location (Figure 2). To be able to see more details, pinch-to-zoom in/out, drag to move the model, and flipping of the model are implemented, so as to be able to position the model at an angle and zoom level suffi-cient for interaction. The data that are saved consist of information about the selected body part (s) and pain type (s), and a timestamp.

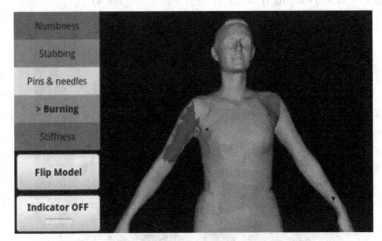

Fig. 2. Interaction with the 3-D PainDroid model using touch gesture input

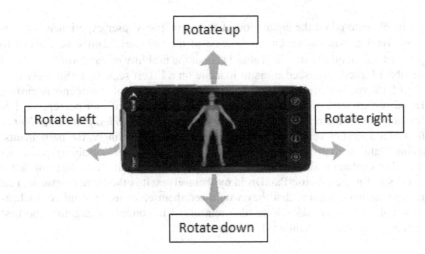

Fig. 3. Hand movement gestures

Specifically, the function between the data sampled by the accelerometer and the induced rotation of the 3-D model was implemented by directly mapping the an-gular deviation of the device from its initial position to the angular velocity at which the model is rotating. As such, the rotation of the 3-D model could stop by simply bringing the device back to its initial position.

3   Results & Discussion

The evaluation of PainDroid was performed with a group of seven wheelchair users (3 females; 4 males) ranging from 21 to 65 years old (Figure 4).

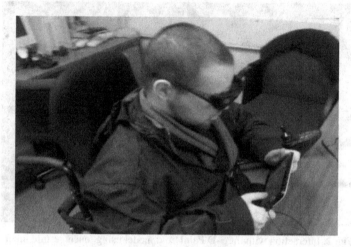

Fig. 4. User evaluation

The protocol centered on the evaluation of the participants' user experience and was examined via a questionnaire. On completion of the tasks, evaluators were asked to complete a 13-item questionnaire (Table 1) about the usability of PainDroid.

The first 13 questions asked users to indicate on a Likert scale of 1 (Strongly Disagree) to 5 (Strongly Agree) their (dis)agreement to a series of statements regarding PainDroid, which were grouped to four different dimensions of user perception. Reliability analysis of the responses received indicated a *Cronbach alpha coefficient of 0.890*, which underlies very good internal consistency. Accordingly, the participants' evaluation highlighted positive bias in respect of the application's usability and functionality. The evaluation demonstrated that participants generally felt confident that it would be easy for them to use PainDroid by themselves. It is therefore reassuring that participants further indicated that they would see themselves using PainDroid whenever available. These attitudes were also reinforced in comments targeting the best user perceived aspects of PainDroid, for instance:

"...the ease of use, the clarity of images and versatility of the program."

"...relatively intuitive and clear cut."

"...easy to use for people who have hard time writing by hand."

Table 1. User Evaluation of PainDroid

Dimension of User Perception	Question	Mean	SD
Ease of Use	Q1. I think that I would like to use this application frequently	3.85	1.46
	Q2. I felt very confident using the application	4.57	0.53
	Q3. I thought the application was easy to use	4	1
	Q4. I think that I would need the support of a technical person to be able to use this application	1.14	0.38
	Q5. I found the application very cumbersome to use	2.57	1.72
	Q6. I felt it difficult to recover after making a mistake	1.85	1.21
Consistency of Application	Q7. I found the various functions in this application were well integrated	4.29	0.49
	Q8. I thought there was too much inconsistency in this application	1.28	0.76
Required Learning	Q9. I would imagine that most people would learn to use this application very quickly	4.14	1.07
	Q10. I needed to learn a lot of things before I could get going with this application	1.14	0.38
Simplicity, clarity and helpfulness of UI	Q11. I found the application unnecessarily complex	2	1.15
	Q12. I liked using the interface of this application	3.85	1.07
	Q13. The information (e.g. menu) provided by the application was clear and helpful	4	1

Similar encouraging responses were finally received with regards to the simplicity, clarity and helpfulness of the PainDroid's user interface. Participants were generally satisfied with the level of simplicity that the application demonstrated, they thought that it was straightforward, and thus, they liked to use the functionality provided in the user interface.

4   Conclusion

There is a scarcity of tools that address self-expressed dimensions of pain. In this paper, we described PainDroid, a prototypical Android-based multimodal and 3D application for pain assessment. Our pilot evaluation highlighted a positive attitude towards the usability of PainDroid's novel functionality, as well as the potential of the application to open up new avenues of patient-clinician interaction through improved user interface design and user experience.

References

1. Baker, M., et al.: Improving the current and future management of chronic pain: A European Consensus Report,
http://www.mijnpijn.nl/pdf/PainProposalEuropeanReport.pdf
(accessed on: July 27, 2012)
2. Lee, S.J.: Pain measurement: Understanding existing tools and their application in the emergency department. Emerg. Med. 13, 279–287 (2001)
3. Mannion, A.F., Balague, F., Pellise, F., Cedraschi, C.: Pain measurement in patients with low back pain. Nat. Clin. Pract. Rheumatol. 3, 610–618 (2007)
4. Haefeli, M., Elfering, A.: Pain assessment. Eur. Spine. J. 15, 17–24 (2006)
5. Ohnmeiss, D.D.: Repeatability of Pain Drawings in a Low Back Pain Population. Spine 25, 980–988 (2000)
6. Jamison, R.N., Fanciullo, G.J., Baird, J.C.: Usefulness of Pain Drawings in Identifying Real or Imagined Pain: Accuracy of Pain Professionals, Non-professionals, and a Decision Model. J. Pain 5, 476–482 (2004)
7. Masferrer, R., Prendergast, V., Hagell, P.: Colored pain drawings: preliminary observations in neurosurgical practice. Eur. J. Pain. 7, 213–217 (2003)
8. Ohnmeiss, D.D., Vanharanta, H., Ekholm, J.: Relationship of pain drawings to invasive tests assessing intervertebral disc pathology. Europ. Spine. J. 8, 126–131 (1999)
9. Jacob, E., et al.: Usability Testing of a Smartphone for Accessing a Web-based e-Diary for Self-monitoring of Pain and Symptoms in Sickle Cell Disease. J. Pediatr. Hematol. Oncol. 34, 326–335 (2012)
10. Paggio, P., Jongejan, B.: Multimodal Communication in the Virtual Farm of the Staging Project. In: Proc. Int. Workshop Inf. Present Natural Multimod. Dialogue, Verona, pp. 41–45 (2001)

Usability Testing Medical Devices:
A Practical Guide to Minimizing Risk
and Maximizing Success

Chris Hass and Dan Berlin

Mad*Pow, Boston, MA
{chass,dberlin}@madpow.net

Abstract. This experience-based paper provides an introduction to U.S. regulations, example methodology documents, and practical advice for planning and executing medical device usability studies.

Keywords: Medical Device usability testing, procedures, practical guide, minimizing risk.

1   Introduction

Usability practitioners must be prepared to study not only websites and software but also physical devices and human interactions in a variety of settings. Rarely are the procedural and interaction stakes higher than when conducting usability research to envision, evaluate, or enhance a medical device. The safety risks for participants, the regulatory oversight, and often the scope of studies are magnified by the importance of and risks associated with medicinal delivery device interactions, populations who may have chronic or acquired medical conditions and/or diseases, and clients who view the approximations of usability research as a poor substitute for the precision of clinical trials.

Usability practitioners who are used to performing "discount" research techniques [2] may discover that these techniques are insufficient (or that client partners may deem them inappropriate) when human safety is in the balance. With this in mind, we have structured this paper to provide a practical, lessons-learned introduction to, and overview of, preparing for and conducting medical device usability testing. Our hope is that this information will inspire other practitioners and lower the learning curve associated with this important usability research arena.

2   A Meeting of the Minds

The process of conducting a successful medical device usability test begins by understanding the clients typically associated with medical device design and manufacturing. As a heavily regulated industry closely affiliated with the biological and medicinal sciences, medical device manufacturers, pharmaceutical companies, and healthcare institutions have a tendency to expect that any usability study involving a

A. Marcus (Ed.): DUXU/HCII 2013, Part II, LNCS 8013, pp. 407–416, 2013.

medical device will be conducted with exacting precision, scientific procedures, fine-ly defined decision making, and the execution associated with clinical trials. Clinical trials may take months or years to plan and execute, and are both minutely documented and tightly regulated. Moreover, a client with a medical device interest may have invested enormous sums of money in the product being evaluated. There is little room, in their minds, for approximation.

Usability work, however, is often rife with approximation. Studies are often more loosely defined, faster to execute, may be conducted without pre-defined moderators' guides or note taking, and typically involve small numbers of participants per activity. Usability studies often stress simulation (of device use, for example) rather than field deployment. Usability practitioners are often unable to determine medical efficacy or clinical impact, focusing rather on ergonomics, safety (according to highly precise definitions), ease of use, efficiency of use, and device appeal. Furthermore, usability practitioners are rarely qualified to handle or administer medicinal agents, so conduct-ing studies with active pharmaceutical agents can raise concerns.

It becomes contingent upon usability practitioners to recognize that some "typical" practices may seem to clients like casual or bad science - even when practitioners' experience indicates otherwise. Far from knocking the nature of usability work, when evaluating ergonomics, ease of use, efficiency, and device appeal (among other traits), usability techniques have much to offer and clients associated with medical device design and evaluation are well served to collaborate with usability practitioners.

2.1   Bridging the Usability Gap

In the United States, the U.S. Food and Drug Administration (FDA) regulates medical devices and determines whether or not a medical product or medicinal agent may be offered to the U.S. market. The FDA often requires proof of human factors/usability procedures in the development or (re)design of the medical devices it approves. In our experience, the relationship between medical device manufacturers and clients who "don't speak usability" can be at best confusing and at worst tempestuous.

As a result, practitioners are well advised, especially where regulatory bodies are concerned, to learn about the client's relationship to these governing bodies. It may be advantageous to ask:

- What are the relevant regulations governing this product?
- Who is the client's regulatory liaison?
- What is the client's relationship to regulating bodies (such as the FDA)?
- Has the client met with them? If so, when? What transpired?
- Have they received Comments (written feedback or directives)?
- What criteria will the regulators use to evaluate the usability study's validity and findings?
- Does the client understand usability research?
- Is it permissible to talk directly with the regulatory bodies?

There are other agencies that can help bridge the gap between usability research and clinical trials as well. Internal Review Boards (IRBs) can be invaluable (and sometimes required) resources to help practitioners and clients define regulation-appropriate methodologies and to select research best practices. IRB involvement can also boost confidence among clients that a usability team's seemingly "casual" approaches are valid and based on industry best practices. IRBs may be found within research organizations or hired on a consulting basis to provide document review, procedural oversight, and ultimately to certify that research conducted with human participants is carried out properly and humanely.

Generally, we have found within the U.S. that engaging an IRB to review documentation adds roughly $2,000-$5,000 in costs to a study. Practitioners may expect to add the IRB's review time to a project timeline, and should be cognizant of any non-disclosure agreements in place before sharing details of the study with external partners. IRBs typically require formal document versioning and use signature pages to ensure that all parties reviewing a document are identified. They may physically inspect your usability lab and study setup.

It is especially important to note that once an IRB has approved a document or series of documents (such as a Usability Specification, consent forms, etc.) they may NOT be amended or altered during the course of the study without the changed documents being re-reviewed and approved by the IRB. This can come as a surprise for practitioners who may be used to adjusting study methodologies during a study to streamline session time, improve procedural clarity, or adjust recruitment criteria. IRB-approved documents are often stamped to identify the final approved version.

3   Planning

Communicating the value of this collaboration may prove challenging. This communication happens not only in client discussions, but through the generation of precise documentation. In the planning stages of a medical device usability study we recommend the generation of "Usability Specification" documents that define and present, among other things:

- Study goals and methodologies
- Recruitment screener text and images
- Recruitment flyer text and images
- The moderator's guide including: tasks, their associated steps; what should be observed; questions to be asked of participants; observer ratings scales, tally methods.
- Consent and Assent forms for adults and children, respectively
- Safety concerns outlining potential risks associated with each study activity
- Steps to be taken to ameliorate or reduce risks
- Procedures for safeguarding participants in the event of accident or incident
- Procedures for identifying and reporting adverse events
- Device background detailing the purpose of the device to be evaluated including salient device features
- Device instructions for use (IFU) if they are to be included in the study
- Explanations of how the study will validate the device's usability including:

- o The rationale behind every quantitative metric used including ease of use ratings scales, instructions for use clarity, design, ergonomics, observed data such as usability, help needed, number of errors, *etc.* (see Fig. 1)
  - o Definitions of use errors, how they will be identified, noted, and prioritized
  - o Each question to be asked, metric to be used, how it will be tallied/captured, and how it will be analyzed, interpreted, and presented
  - o Detailed task breakdowns of each action associated with utilizing the device
  - o Detailed explanations of data NOT to be captured with exclusion rationales
- Notes grid(s) for consolidating data that include:
  - o Clear delineation of "micro tasks" involved in device use
  - o Each task step and question on its own spreadsheet row
  - o Clear identification of study sections (Introduction, Task 1, Task 2, etc.)
  - o Greyed out areas that may be ignored
  - o Identification of roles (*e.g.*, a moderator will focus on the participants' device use, a note taker will capture participant comments)

Rating	No Help Needed	Little Difficulty	Some Help	Much Help	Task Failure
Explanation	Completed with no help	1-2 small errors	3-5 errors	Moderator gets involved	Failure
Small errors:	Doesn't press green button Doesn't remove cap properly				

Fig. 1. Example Participant/Moderator Help Metric and Error Definition

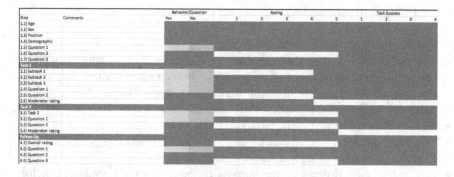

Fig. 2. Example Notes Grid

These documents are frequently required and are typically referred to as a "Usability Validation" (Risk assessment and amelioration) document and a "Usability Engineering File" or "Design Efficiency File" (Methods and procedural rationale).

Typically these documents are informed by Federal and international regulations related to the design and evaluation of medical devices. For US medical device studies the following documents are highly recommended:

- FDA Quality System Regulation (US FDA, 2011) [5]
- HE: 75 2009 (AAMI. 2009) [1]
- ISO/IEC 62366:2007 (ISO, 2007) [3]
- The Health Insurance Portability and Accountability Act of 1996 (HIPAA) (US H&HS, 1996) [6]

Both established and emerging standards are essential reading and clients will often expect a thorough understanding of them. Practitioners should expect that the drafting, review, and ratification of usability specification documents may be a significantly time-consuming process and involve many parties including: the client, regulators associated with the client's work, Internal Review Board(s), compliance personnel, Adverse Event personnel, other subcontractors, clinical personnel, subject matter experts, and legal teams.

However, given that these usability specification documents provide a precise roadmap for all pre-, intra-, and post-research activities, they are well worth the focus, collaboration, and foresight required to shape and execute a reliable, unbiased, and repeatable study. Identifying risks associated with the study, for example, is an invaluable activity, given that safety protocols may be exacting: even simulated product use may put participants at risk, target audiences may be physically or cognitively vulnerable, activity environments may be unusual for practitioners (a care clinic, a patient's home), discussions of patients' health may become personal or emotional – and defining appropriate safeguards may involve consultation with clients and medical care specialists.

When preparing for data analysis during the creation of the Usability Specification documents, it may be helpful to think in terms of a "micro task" scale: Every individual step of using the device should be observed and recorded. However, it's difficult to watch and report on every step of a complex interaction and to document it perfectly, especially when dealing with a device that participants are manipulating quickly. Tallying procedures need to be streamlined and specific, but also realistic. Pilot testing potential approaches will provide invaluable insights for practitioners and their clients to establish reasonable data capture, and therefore data analysis approaches.

When planning, it is also helpful to be mindful of capturing and organizing the most salient qualitative data. We recommend summarizing qualitative data immediately after a given study session, before the moderator and note taker's memory of the session fades.

4   Recruiting

Recruiting participants for medical device usability studies can pose unique challenges. These are understandably related to the type of device to be evaluated, the nature of its use, the number of participants, and the health of the target participants. Medical device usability tests frequently involve moderately large sets of users, in our experience from 50 to 150 participants is not unusual. In addition, users of medical devices may be elderly, infirm, may have more than one disease, condition, or contributing factor (co-morbidity) that affects their treatment regimen and/or use of a medical device.

The criteria associated with identifying users of a specialized device, or even one intended for the general public may be complex and may take significant time to identify and enumerate with clients. Notifying a recruiting partner as early as possible that a study may require patient participants with a specific diagnosis is extremely helpful, so that partner can begin laying groundwork for reaching out to potential study participants. Moreover, identifying patient populations in significant numbers may be difficult, involve unforeseen travel, or require higher honoraria to ensure participation. Recruitment partners, such as external recruiting agencies may also have insights into geographic regions where a greater population of the target audience may be found. Recruiting specialized populations may take significantly longer in the medical arena and can cause unexpected study delays. As always, we recommend open communication with clients about outreach efforts, organizations contacted, and any difficulties encountered. In many cases clients may be legally unable to directly recommend clinicians, institutions, or patients associated with a particular disease, condition, or disability.

When recruiting patients it can be helpful to cultivate relationships with local acute and ambulatory care organizations, as can reaching out to groups that specialize in serving the audience you are seeking. These may include: healthcare institutions, local and national support groups, federal agencies, community support groups, social media, and online crowd-sourcing sites. When reaching out to potential participants, you may discover that acute and ambulatory care providers may be unable to "promote" a study that is not associated with their organization, which can limit access to potential participants. We have also encountered situations where clinical practitioners request a "referral fee" for sharing recruitment flyers with patients. While this appears to be a relatively common practice, it is illegal in the United States and not recommended.

In studies where an IRB is involved, recruitment flyer and screener text will need to be defined early in the project and be approved by the IRB before recruitment may begin. It is worth noting that once a study is in progress, any change in recruitment screener criteria (or methodology) will have to be documented along with a rationale for the change then re-submitted to the IRB for approval. This can add time delays and in some cases additional costs. IRBs will often "stamp" an approved recruitment flyer (and consent form) and the stamp must be present on documents used to support the study, indicating that the documents have not been altered.

The contents of a successful study flyer (to be distributed to clinician's offices or electronically) will include: the purpose of the study, why potential participants would want to participate, compensation details, and recruiter contact information.

Fig. 3. Sample Recruitment Flyer

5   Conducting the Study

5.1   Participant Safety

As with any usability study, safeguarding participants' comfort and safety is of paramount importance. Where medical device usability studies are concerned practitioners should be especially cognizant of participants' health. Will participants need accessibility accommodations? Will their condition/disease affect participation? Will they arrive with an aide or caretaker? Moreover, we recommend ensuring their physical safety by having a robust first aid kit (and in some cases medical personnel) nearby, making water, juice, sugary, and non-sugary snacks available, ensuring that they know whether they will be working with a placebo rather than a medicinal agent, and providing accessible food that may be easily grasped and consumed. Most importantly we establish a plan of action ahead of time for the (hopefully unlikely) event someone is injured. This plan should include a path of notification in the event of injury: reporting it internally, to the client, the IRB, Adverse Event personnel, a regulatory agency (as appropriate), and any other relevant governing agencies.

To prevent participant injury, stress, dehydration, confusion, disorientation, and fatigue, knowledge of the relevant diseases/conditions associated with the medical device is invaluable. Advance reading, interviewing clinical personnel, and consulting subject matter experts may help practitioners to better safeguard their participants.

5.2   Usability Lab Setup

Medical device usability testing can take place in a formal usability lab, on-site at a clinic or care facility, in participants' homes, or any other relevant location. Without delving too deeply into technical setups, we have found the following rules of thumb helpful when conducting medical device usability testing of a physical device:

- Set up cameras to enable data capture from two different angles
  - A close-up view of the device interaction (over the shoulder or capturing hand interactions)
  - Directly in front of the participant to capture the entire field of interaction (including the participant's face as appropriate)
- Have all device supplies at the ready, within reach, and neatly organized
  - Alcohol wipes, extra needles, batteries, loading cartridges, etc.
  - You're likely to need more supplies than you would initially expect
- Have a first-aid kit and nitrile gloves nearby (some people are allergic to latex)
- Have a first aid plan and practice enacting it

5.3   Adverse Event Reporting

One procedural aspect that may be novel to practitioners unfamiliar with medical device usability testing is Adverse Event reporting. An Adverse Event (AE) occurs when a study participant shares information about a side effect or other unusual or negative experience related to device or drug use. Such information must be reported to clients and regulatory bodies immediately. Encountering and reporting an AE in the US is a tightly regulated process. AEs are critical information for medical institutions, pharmaceutical companies, and the FDA. Identifying an AE can be complex and it is not unusual for clients to require usability practitioners to participate in AE training prior to the commencement of research activities. Practitioners should identify to whom AEs should be reported (most often to the client, who will notify their regulatory agencies). A valuable rule of thumb when determining whether a bit of information is an AE or not is: "When in doubt, report it." Typical AE reports may be as simple as an email or phone call communicating:

- The comment or action comprising the AE
- A general description of the scenario where the AE was discovered
- The device or medication involved
- The date and time of the AE
- AE physical symptoms and corrective action taken
- Whether there was injury to a person or not
- Official study codes

Some examples of adverse events are:

- A usability study participant reports that she stopped taking a drug because the blister packs and pills sometimes arrived crushed.
- While testing an infusion pump a participant mentions that the tube "always fell out of" his previous pump (the client's product).

- During a study a participant mentions that her arms started to itch when she stopped taking the client's medication.
- A male participant mentions that his wife became pregnant two weeks after he started taking the client's medication, even though she used birth control pills.

6   Analysis and Reporting

6.1   Data Analysis

One clear benefit of the up-front time spent defining the Usability Specification documents at the start of the study is that if data capture methodologies are well conceived and executed, data analysis should be very straightforward. The process becomes one of distilling the notes grid into summary findings. We cannot understate the value of a cogent data capture methodology. Without it, inevitable data capture inconsistencies and human error may cause significant data analysis difficulties, particularly with clients versed in the precision of clinical trials.

Frequent questions pertaining to missing data include: Was the question asked? Was the behavior observed? Will the recordings verify or find data? (In this case it is vital that you HAVE recordings, of course, and that they offer clear images and sound.) It is not unusual for a client seeking regulatory approval to insist on a perfect notes grid, *i.e.*, that it is entirely complete, reliably reflects the study sessions, and contains no missing data.

For practitioners used to more approximate data capture, this may come as a shock. The amount of time a client may require practitioners to invest in ensuring the perfection of the notes grid is difficult to underestimate. When conducting study research sessions, ensuring that every question is asked, every observation is recorded correctly, and that each session is executed uniformly may be exceedingly difficult. But, this consistency is without a doubt the best defense against a lengthy data analysis phase.

When analyzing quantitative measures practitioners typically benefit from capturing data that answers the following questions:

- What percentage of participants successfully completed the task?
- What ease of use ratings did participants give?
- How many participants committed the most common errors?

6.2   Reporting

Defining reporting requirements up front in the usability specification can bring great benefits as reporting guidelines, formats, and industry standards (e.g., CIF a.k.a. ISO/IEC 25062:2006, other specialized formats [4]) may be extensive and/or complex and raw data may be reviewed many, many, many times by clients paying careful attention to methodology and procedural precision. Moreover, once the Usability Specification documents have been created, reviewed, and ultimately approved, in studies governed by a formal regulatory body, often they may not be changed during the course of the study without being re-examined and approved by all contributing parties, be they client, Internal Review Board, or other regulatory agency. As a result, pre-defining the study risks, procedures, data solicitation and capture methodologies, and the like will often be required.

In our experience, clients sometimes express interest at the close of a study in using the positive study findings as marketing claims, which can raise concerns. To avoid later confusion, be sure to discuss potential data outcomes and follow-on data uses early in the study.

When reporting findings, the reports themselves may be relatively straightforward: a cogent walk-through of the methods utilized and summaries (graphical, statistical, and textual) of the study findings and the researchers' conclusions. However, some clients and regulatory bodies require reports in standardized industry formats (e.g., CIF) or that match existing product documentation. Determining in advance the preferred reporting format again, will save confusion, time, and effort.

7   Conclusion

Conducting a usability study for a medical device is similar to more "typical" studies, except with much stricter protocols and less room for procedural flexibility. Practitioner and participant safety remains paramount, and methodologies that focus on quantitative measures (reporting percentages of participants that did/did not perform an action) are likely to be successful. Careful planning, knowledge of national and international regulations, and open communication with client partners will ensure a smooth and effective research study.

References

1. Association for the Advancement of Medical Instrumentation. ANSI/AAMI HE75:2009: Human Factors engineering – Design of Medical Devices. AAMI, Arlington (2009)
2. Dumas, J.S., Redish, J.C.: A Practical Guide to Usability Testing. Intellect, Portland (1993)
3. International Standards Organization. Medical Devices – Application of usability engineering to medical devices. Geneva, Switzerland: International Electrotechnical Commission (2007)
4. National Institute of Standards and Technology, Common Industry Format for Usability Test Reports. Washington, DC: U.S. Government Printing Office (1999), http://zing.ncsl.nist.gov/iusr/documents/cifv1.1b.htm (retrieved) United States Food & Drug Administration, Quality System (QS) Regulation/Medical Device Good Manufacturing Practices (2011), http://www.fda.gov/medicaldevices/deviceregulationand guidance/postmarketrequirements/qualitysystemsregulations/ default.htm (retrieved)
5. United States Department of Health & Human Services. Health Insurance Portability and Accountability Act of 1996. (US H&HS publication f:publ191.104). Washington, DC: U.S. Government Printing Office (1996)

Exploring the Need for, and Feasibility of, a Web-Based Self-management Resource for Teenage and Young Adult Cancer Survivors in the UK

Louise Moody[1], Andy Turner[2], Jane Osmond[1], Joanna Kosmala-Anderson[2], Louise Hooker[3], and Lynn Batehup[4]

[1] Centre of Excellence in Product & Automotive Design, Coventry University, Coventry, UK
{L.Moody,J.Osmond}@coventry.ac.uk
[2] Applied Research Centre in Health & Lifestyle Interventions, Coventry University, UK
{A.Turner,J.Kosmala-Anderson}@coventry.ac.uk
[3] Teenage & Young Adult Cancer Service, University of Southampton Hospital NHSFT, UK
Louise.Hooker@uhs.nhs.uk
[4] Macmillan Cancer Support, UK
LBatehup@macmillan.org.uk

Abstract. The growth in social networking sites and online forums make the internet a potential platform to be considered for the provision of self-management and e-learning support to young people following cancer treatment. However, the feasibility and potential barriers to this as a post treatment option should be considered. A mixed methods approach was adopted that included an online survey, focus groups and interviews with cancer survivors, their parents, and information technology, clinical and social work professionals to consider the potential of aweb-based self-management resource.Barriers were identified to the delivery of care using this method. Developing such a self-management system requires close working between IT and clinical staff, alongside patient representation and usability expertise. As computer access and use amongst this group is commonplace, there is an expectation that self-management needs will be met at least partially in this way in the future.

Keywords: Web-based self-management, young cancer survivors, online support.

1 Introduction

Due to earlier diagnosis and advanced treatments, it is estimated that nearly three-quarters of British teenage and young adults who develop cancer now survive [1]. Since the population of young cancer survivors is constantly growing, there is an urgent need to develop a range of alternative ways of providing post-treatment support as well as addressing on-going self-management issues [2-3].

The growth in social networking sites and online forums make the internet potentially an ideal platform on which to provide self-management and e-learning

A. Marcus (Ed.): DUXU/HCII 2013, Part II, LNCS 8013, pp. 417–423, 2013.

support to young men and women following cancer treatment [3-6]. The internet can encourage young people with cancer to socialise with others who are going through the same experience, and provide and receiveinformational and emotional support [7-8]. Despite these benefits, there are few in existence that have been developed with a structured self-management approach specifically for teenage and young adult cancer survivorswith the aim of improving quality of life and psychosocial wellbeing.

The aim of this project therefore was to explore the self-management support needs of teenage and young adult cancer survivors; and to investigate the potential for these needs to be met through a web-based self-management resource. The research was undertaken within the context of the National Health Service (NHS) in the UK.

2   Method

A mixed methods approach was undertaken including:

1. Focus groups and interviews with teenage and young adult cancer survivors
2. Online survey with teenage and young adult cancer survivors
3. Interviews with medical, nursing, social and youth workers
4. Interviews with Information Technology (IT) staff

2.1   Participants

To determine the information and support needs of teenage and young adult cancer survivors in relation to self-management two separate focus groups were conducted with five young adult cancer survivors and their parents. A further two individual telephone interviews (for those young people who were unable to attend the focus group) were conducted. There were four female and three male participants with ages ranging from 16-24.

Eleven semi-structured interviews were conducted with medical, nursing, social and youth workers who were working with teenage and young adult cancer survivors.The occupational backgrounds of the respondents included paediatric and adult oncology nursing and medical staff, social and community workers, and a hospital play specialist.

Eight interviews were conducted to establish the IT requirements for the delivery of a web-based, self-management intervention. The participants included individuals working with NHS IT, nursing and social work specialists, as well individuals with experience of other teenage and young adult cancer survivors online web-based support programmes to establish good practice and potential barriers to success.

The survey was piloted with 5 teenage and young adult cancer survivors who each were given £20.00 in gift vouchers for completion of and providing feedback about the survey. 30 responses were received, of which 24 were fully completed surveys. Respondents' mean age was 21 (range 17-26). Most respondents had Hodgkin's lymphoma (n=7), followed by brain cancer (n=6), leukaemia (n=5), osteosarcoma (n=4) and thyroid cancer (n=2).

2.2 Procedure

The interview schedules were developed through consultation with the project steering group. The interviews lasted an average of 30 minutes (range 20-40 minutes). Focus groups were conducted face-to-face, lasted for 2 hours and were held simultaneously in adjacent rooms.The focus groups with teenage and young adult cancer survivors and their parents were conducted separately.Teenage and young adult cancer survivors received a £20.00 gift voucher for taking part. The interviews with professionals were conducted over the telephone. The interviews and the focus groups were recorded, transcribed verbatim and analysed independently by two researchers using thematic analysis [9].

The online survey sought to determine the range of different platforms that young people use, their preferences in terms of interaction methods.and design styles, and any barriers to acceptance. The questions for the online survey were partly selected from the features identified from the literature review and findings of the focus groups with the teenage and young adult cancer survivors and their parents. Additional questions were added after consultation with members of the project steering group.

3   Results

The findings indicated that the stakeholders were supportive of the idea of providing a web-based self-management resource to meet the information and support needs of teenage and young adult cancer survivors. This group are "digital natives" and are comfortable with accessing online resources to obtain cancer-related information and support. Therespondents found that information on the internet was not tailored to young people, or contained distressing information such as mortality rates, or contained irrelevant information such as homeopathic cures. They were also unsure as to whether they could find reliable information "I think there's almost too much on the internet isn't there", and "they're all saying slightly different things, so it's like what do I believe in and what's the right thing" (Teenage and young adult cancer survivor).

The potential role of a self-management system, and the required support needs reflected the age and development priorities of this particular age group. There were some strong common information and support needs around body image, fertility, long-term treatment and side effects, fear of recurrence, returning to school/college/work and emotional (e.g. anxiety and depression) and psychological (e.g. confidence and self-esteem) needs. Having a cancer diagnosis impacted negatively on friendships with healthy peers. Teenage and young adult cancer survivors can feel abandoned and "cast adrift" after treatment completion. They also described the importance of having the opportunity of sharing online or face-to-face their feelings and experiences with age-group peers who are going through similar experiences. As one respondent put it: *"You're not glad that they've got cancer, but it's nice to have someone to speak to about it."*

These teenagers and young adults indicated that they would like a resource to provide clinical, information and social support features including: a summary of treatment and a follow-up plan, organisation and re-scheduling of appointments, live question and answer sessions or secure messaging with a doctor / nurse, the capacity to look up test results, provision of peer support, and case studies, written resources and links to credible and reliable cancer websites.

All of the other stakeholders (e.g. parents of teenage and young adult cancer survivors, medical, nursing, social and youth workers) interviewed were broadly in favour of these features with the exception of having access to medical test results. The potential for misunderstanding and misinterpretation of medical information was felt to pose a risk of creating anxiety and fear among the young people if not explained and contextualised in person by a health-care professional.

Table 1. Perceived benefits and risks of on-line self-management support

Perceived benefits	Perceived risks
— Less resource hungry than face to face contact	— Financial outlay to set-up
— The on-going costs are less	— The tailoring of the content requires heavy clinical input resource
— Hospitals want to be ahead and innovating and there is a general culture shift to interact more through technology	— Online safety and the how to manage safeguarding risks for young people and their families
— Reduced waiting times because patients are not coming in as often	— Young people might see this as something to do instead of clinics and not be followed up properly
— Reduced follow up length	
— Reduced re-admittances after discharge	— Losing contact with people who might be quite vulnerable but will not ask for help
— Early avoidance of problems as self-management is quicker	— Not all young people have a smart phone or access to a PC
— Enables networking / teenage and young adult cancer survivors peer interaction	— Engaging and retaining young people
— Has the potential to be used in other areas e.g. congenital heart defects, allergies etc (transition from child to adult services), different age groups.	— It may be inappropriate for young people with learning difficulties, brain tumours, memory problems, ADHD or who are vulnerable.
— Reaching a wider geographically dispersed group that may not be able to, or want to attend face to face events.	— Having to close down the system down due to resource issues could adversely affect the relationship with the young person
— Help teenage and young adult cancer survivors feel like they are no longer a patient	— Logistical problems with providing a resource for small patient numbers at different parts of treatment pathway
— One central resource	— The time required to develop and moderate content of any forum / posting elements

It was identified that a self-management intervention (in terms of a standard informational and developmental resource)is straightforward to develop, but that working within the NHS in the UK involves issues in terms of information and data governance structures. It was identified that it is advisable to separate out social networking and patient: patient interaction, for example,from clinical support. This would be more straightforward to manage in terms of implementation and governance, but also ensure credibility of the information sources available.

4   Discussion

The results indicated some key content needs for a potential online self-management system including information and support around body image, fertility, long-term treatment and side effects, fear of recurrence, returning to school/college/work and emotional and psychological needs.   Teenage and young adult cancer survivors described the importance of having the opportunity of sharing online or face-to-face, their feelings and experiences with others who are going through similar experiences.

A self-management intervention offering information is straightforward to develop and can offer a reliable and credible web-based resource in addition to individualisedface to face interventions from staff, and contact with peers.   Other potential functionality needs further consideration. The desire amongst young people for online contact with health professionals needs to be further explored; for example in terms of the types of communication, gaps in the current service and the support that professionals may need to use this mode of communication appropriately.The mixed views regarding the desirability and feasibility of accessing medical test results as part of a web resource warrant further work to explore the discrepancies in desirability, and explore how in the longer term teenage and young adult cancer survivors may be helped to interpret results remotely. Equally the mixture and balance of social networking, patient to patient interaction and clinical support within a single system needs further consideration.

Barriers to implementation need further exploration within the context of use, for example whether the system sits within an NHS Trust, a hospital, university, within a charity or independently. There were concerns about the interfacing of a self-management system and existing NHS systems in terms of the maintenance of security and protection of data protocols.   However, such a system could be hosted by an external hosting centre (e.g. a cancer charity), provided it did not hold secure patient / hospital data. This would preclude the desired interactions in terms of appointments and medical records.

Any system developedshould be multi-platform, taking into account widespread use of smartphones amongst young people.   There is a need for close working between information technology and clinical staff to ensure clear communication regarding user and governance needs, system functionality and barriers to development and implementation as well as to share learning from other projects. Computer access and use amongst this group is commonplace, and therefore it is an expectation that self-management needs will be met at least partially in this way in the future.

5   Recommendations

The research led to the following recommendations for future work:

- A self-management intervention (in terms of a standard informational and developmental resource) should be developed to meet the information and support needs of young people and those who support them. This should provide a reliable and credible web-based resource in addition to face to face / direct interaction.
- The format should include key behavior and self- management techniques such as goal setting, action planning, problem solving and self- monitoring presented in a developmentally appropriate manner.
- The features should include online appointment arrangements / alerts, Q & As with medical professionals, and patient to patient communication.
- Social networking functions are best provided separately from clinical functionality. Moderation of social networking features is important to ensure appropriate content and safeguarding vulnerable young people.
- Two complimentary systems are recommended one providing social networking and patient: patient interaction and the second offering clinical support in terms of Q & A sessions with health professionals and access to information resources, and access to appointment information. This should be more straightforward to manage in terms of implementation and governance, but also ensure credibility of the information sources available.
- The desire for online contact with health professionals needs to be further explored for example in terms of the types of communication, that are suitable and the support that professionals may need to use this mode of communication appropriately.
- There are mixed views regarding the desirability and feasibility of accessing medical test results as part of the web resource. This warrants further work to explore the discrepancies in desirability, and explore how in the longer term teenage and young adult cancer survivors may be helped to interpret results remotely.
- Any systems developed should be multi-platform, taking into account widespread use of smartphones amongst young people.
- There is a need for close working between IT and clinical staff to ensure clear communication regarding user and governance needs, system functionality and barriers to development and implementation as well as to share learning from other projects.

References

1. Birch, J.M., Pang, D., Alston, R.D., Rowan, S., Geraci, M., Moran, A., Eden, T.O.: Survival from cancer in teenagers and youngadults in England, 1979-2003. British Journal of Cancer 99(5), 830–835 (2008)
2. Zebrack, B.J.: Psychological, social, and behavioral issues for young adults with cancer. Cancer 117, 2289–2294 (2011)

3. Evan, E.E., Zeltzer, L.K.: Psychosocial dimensions of cancer adolescent and young adults. In: Pediatric Oncology Group of Ontario Symposium: Walking two worlds – Adolescent and Young Adult Oncology, Ontario, Canada (2006)
4. Oeffinger, K.C., Eshelman, D.A., Tomlinson, G.E., Buchanon, G.R.: Programs for adult survivors of childhood cancer. Supportive Care in Cancer 17(4), 349–357 (1998)
5. Aziz, N.M., Oeffinger, K.C., Brooks, S., Turoff, A.J.: Comprehensive Long-Term Follow-Up Programs for Pediatric Cancer Survivors. Cancer 107(4), 841–848 (2006)
6. Blank, T.O., Schmidt, S.D., Vangsness, S.A., Monteiro, A.K., Santagata, P.: Differences among breast and prostate cancer online support groups. Computers in Human Behavior 26(6), 1400–1404 (2010)
7. Hulme, M.: Life Support Young people's needs in a digital age. Institute for Advanced Studies, Lancaster University (2010)
8. Elwell, L., Grogan, S., Coulson, N.: Adolescents living with cancer: The role of computer-mediated support groups. Journal of Health Psychology 16, 236–249 (2011)
9. Braun, V., Clarke, V.: Using thematic analysis in psychology. Qual. Res. Psychol. 3(2), 77–101 (2006)

Avatar Interfaces for Biobehavioral Feedback

Tylar Murray[1], Delquawn Hardy[1]
Donna Spruijt-Metz[2], Eric Hekler[3], and Andrew Raij[1]

[1] USF Electrical Engineering
[2] USC Keck School of Medicine
[3] ASU School of Nutrition and Health Promotion
{tylarmurray,dhardy}@mail.usf.edu, dmetz@usc.edu,
ehekler@asu.edu, raij@usf.edu

Abstract. The combination of inexpensive wearable sensors, powerful mobile phones, and always-connected cloud computing are enabling new, real-time feedback and coaching via mobile technologies. This paper explores the use of avatars - digital representations of the self - as an ideal user interface for mobile health application. Specifically, a justification for using avatars is provided, both based on empirical studies and the psychology of human body interpretation. We then provide an organized, theoretical description of how an avatar's traits (appearance, behavior, and virtual environment) can be manipulated to convey specific health-related behavior change messages.

Keywords: avatars, development, Proteus Effect.

1 Introduction

Through real-time processing of sensor and self-report data, mobile health (mHealth) systems can provide appropriate and timely biobehavioral feedback anytime and anywhere. Indeed, several mHealth systems have changed health behaviors [24] and outcomes [20] with varying levels of success. One under-explored source of feedback are avatars, digital representations of the self. While some research and commercial health systems use avatars [11,12,17,18,28–30], the work to date does not provide a clear explanation for why avatars could be a good tool for behavior change, nor is it clear how to best use avatars for effective behavior change. When the avatar is a more prominent part of the interface, its evaluation is minimal, or there is no discussion of what aspects of the avatar were influential. Direct comparison of systems is difficult due to differences in domain, implementation, and design of previous works. Methods of comparison between implementations are not well explored in this area, and the components which make up an avatar interface are not well defined. In this paper, we begin to address this gap in the literature by providing 1) *a clear motivation for the use of avatars in behavior change applications*, and 2) *a design language and methodology to facilitate more structured design, analysis, and evaluation of avatar-based behavioral change interventions.*

A. Marcus (Ed.): DUXU/HCII 2013, Part II, LNCS 8013, pp. 424–434, 2013.

1.1   Why Use Avatars?

The use of avatars as an interface allows for the use of a visualization primitive which can encode a great deal of information simultaneously and leverages our innate abilities to interpret the human form. The 'bandwidth' of traditional visualization strategies is being strained by the ever-growing influx of data, and an increasing push towards 'affective computing' [21] suggests that the future will call for a retooling of interfaces relying on only informative methods. Avatars are uniquely suited to fill the role of influencing behavior due to their use of the human-like form as a communication medium. Humans constantly communicate using their bodies by changing their appearance and behavior, and understanding the meaning behind these changes - social cognition and perception - is typically hard-wired into humans [19]. The bandwidth of this interaction is immense when contrasted with current data visualizations; humans have evolved to interact with other humans (and we do it very well), whereas graph interpretation must be learned and can only span a few dimensions before becoming convoluted. Thus, manipulating the form of human-like avatars seems to have the potential to be a powerful, effective, and easy-to-understand communication format.

In addition to the theoretical support for avatar interfaces, there is also significant empirical evidence that human-like avatars do influence behavior. Previous research indicates that there are at least two mechanisms whereby digital self-representations can influence individuals: the Proteus Effect and operant conditioning.

The Proteus Effect. The Proteus Effect states that behaviors of an individual will conform to implicit cues from an avatar. Several studies on the Proteus Effect in non-mobile contexts indicate that manipulating an avatar's appearance and behavior affects a user's behavior in the real world. For example: seeing one's avatar running on a treadmill can encourage physical activity [10]; using an elderly avatar improves attitudes towards the elderly and increases saving for retirement [15, 26]; using an avatar to saw virtual trees encourages less paper use [1]; and manipulating an avatar's gaze can make the avatar more persuasive [2, 25]. In these cases, the Proteus Effect demonstrates how an avatar can exert an influence over users' perception of themselves and over their behavior. Although the precise psychological mechanism for this influence requires more investigation, one plausible theory is that users see their avatar as a model for their own behavior [3]. Alternatively, the avatar's influence could be explained by a perceived relationship between the user and his/her avatar (i.e., a shared identity [4] or an empathetic bond [5]).

Operant Conditioning. Secondly, operant conditioning can influence behaviors by having an avatar function as a visual representation of success or failure. Even when avatars do not take an explicitly human form, they appear to influence behavior via this mechanism. For example, previous work has explored the use of an avatar as an operant conditioning agent and feedback mechanism for promoting physical activity. In this work, the physical activity of an individual is mapped to the actions and mood of an anthropomorphized virtual bird avatar [12,17]. As physical activity increases, the bird becomes happier and more playful, flies faster, and sings more songs. Pilot work suggests that this avatar can promote increased physical activity among individuals [17]. Moving one step further from 'user-likeness', Fish'n'Steps translates daily steps into the growth and happiness of a virtual fish [18]. Even more abstract from the concept of 'avatar', UbiFit displays a garden on the background wallpaper of a phone. The garden is similar to a historical avatar, providing feedback on the user's physical activity when glancing at the phone [6].

These examples, though spanning varying degrees of 'avatar-ness', still serve in some sense as virtual representations of the self. Behavior change applications nearer the abstract edge of the user-likeness spectrum allow for more creative designs, but may lose some benefits of innate interpretation. The distinction between avatar and non-avatar systems is not well defined currently, but in future research we may learn that the display must meet some (personalized) criterion of realism, interactivity, self-presence, customization, or abstraction to be considered a 'true' avatar which is fully capable of utilizing user the Proteus or similar effects.

This evidence, when combined with conceptual knowledge of human-avatar interaction, suggests that the use of avatar-like interfaces may create behavior change through motivation, rather than purely informative visualization methods. Thus, avatars may be a powerful new technological medium for providing core methods for behavior change based on behavioral science (i.e., goal-setting, self-monitoring, modeling, and positive reinforcement).

2   The Language of BioBehavioral Feedback

Before we are able to identify guidelines for the use of mobile avatars in biobehavioral feedback, we must first have an abstract model of information flow and interaction in any biobehavioral feedback system (with or without avatars). Figure 1 is a pictorial representation of the components of a generic biobehavioral feedback system and the information flow within it. It is important to note here that we use the term 'feedback' in a loose sense in which it represents any output to the user based on user input which may affect future user behaviors. Starting from the top-left of the figure, a description of the user's current behavior (input) is provided via self-report or sensor. This description of in-the-moment user behavior is passed to a feedback algorithm, along with any relevant historical information. Some examples of historical information which may be taken into account are the previous day's user behavior, feedback given to the user previously, or data on the impact of a particular form of feedback on the user. With in-the-moment and historical information, the algorithm then generates the feedback. Output is then observed which may or may not immediately convey the feedback. As a demonstration of this model, consider a typical time-series

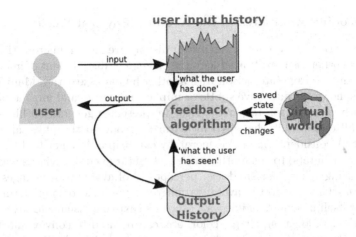

Fig. 1. Information flow diagram for biobehavioral feedback algorithms

feedback visualization which displays level of physical activity inferred from accelerometers. The input in this scenario is the accelerometer data. The feedback algorithm includes the method of inferring physical activity, as well as the mapping of activity level to a 2D plot of timestamps and activity. The graph of past physical activity (created from the mapping, user settings, and/or input parameters for graph creation) makes up the virtual world, and the user navigates the world through a pan/zoom window, which determines the output.

3   Adding Avatars to the BioBehavioral Feedback Model

An avatar-based implementation of the model presented differs from a more traditional visualization system only in the feedback algorithm and the output to the user. Design of the feedback algorithm to map input to output is a complex task, which can not be properly explored without better knowledge of the avatar outputs available.

Guidelines for the outputs of conventional data visualization are well established [16]; *here we aim to identify and organize the wide variety of outputs available to an avatar display and move towards the identification of similar guidelines.* Just as the use of item location, color, and size can be used to convey information in a chart or graph, we propose that characteristics of the avatar display can be altered to convey information. However, the critical difference between innate avatar interpretation and learned graph reading suggests that the most useful encoding attributes of an avatar are based in the psychology of avatar perception.

3.1 Encoding Attributes in the Avatar's Physical World

Encoding attributes available in an avatar display are more numerous than those available in other visualizations due to the extremely vast amount of information humans can gain from interaction with another human-like entity. Many of these attributes, however, may have subtle or implicit influence, and impact can differ significantly from person-to-person. Here we present a generalized hierarchy to describe all conceivable changes which can be made to the physical world of an avatar. A consideration of this hierarchy can help a designer find the proper encoding attribute(s) to ensure that the effect on targeted behavior is maximized while reducing other, undesired user perceptions of avatar trait changes.

Physical - Changes to the avatar primitive in the most obvious form modify the avatar itself in some tangible way. Much like existing visualization strategies, an avatar's size, location, shape, color, etc. can be used to convey information, though in the case of an avatar these encodings often have built-in meaning to a user. For instance, inversely relating the level of daily physical activity into the width of the avatar (so he/she appears to grow thinner with exercise) is intuitive, but encoding the same value proportionally seems to send the wrong message to users, since he/she would appear to grow less fit with additional physical activity.

Behavioral - In addition to the encoding attributes available in an avatar's appearance, avatars provide an additional ability to convey information via a change in their behavior. Changes can be as simple as a change of behavior 'class' for pre-scripted avatars (e.g. from a physically active behavior to a more sedentary behavior) or may involve character attributes that should be reflected in avatar behavior. For example: a case in which an avatar demonstrates increases in strength by an ability to lift heavier objects is more than just a change in avatar behavior (lifting objects); it is a change in avatar traits (strength). Another set of behavioral attributes available to designers are the 'behavioral biometrics' - i.e., the personal characteristics of behavior such as gait, voice timbre, and typing rhythm [23].

Environmental - In addition to manipulation of the avatar primitive, algorithms may manipulate the virtual environment in which the avatar resides in order to affect user perception of the avatar. Changes to the environment can be cosmetic or more complex, and in many cases can have profound impact on the avatar display. For instance: avatar location and surroundings can be manipulated to go along with a behavioral avatar change (e.g., the avatar takes a trip to the beach to encourage the user to relax). Environmental changes can play an even larger role for avatars used in games; changes in the virtual environment can be used as gameplay elements. Location and virtual object removal/addition/manipulation can be used as indicators of progress or accomplishment. Similarly, aspects of the environment may be manipulated to behave differently towards the avatar (e.g., a computer-controlled agent becoming more friendly to one's avatar as a social reward for desired behavior).

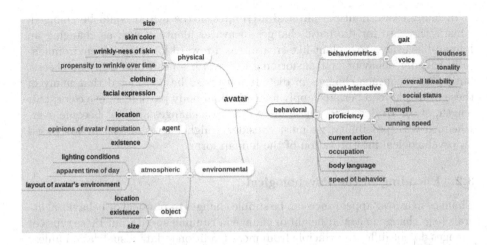

Fig. 2. A hierarchal organization of potential avatar encoding attributes

The hierarchy represented by Figure 2 demonstrates the wide variety of encoding attributes available to visualization designers organized by the categories outlined. This is not intended to be an exhaustive list of possible encoding attributes, but encompasses many possibilities in an organized fashion, so that we may have a language to discuss avatar display changes just as we would discuss changes in shape, color, location, etc. of a traditional data visualization. Though all possible attributes cannot possibly be included, we believe that all possible encoding attributes logically fall within the first-level categories presented (physical, behavior, environment). Some further subdivision is shown, and attributes themselves can in some cases be further broken down (i.e. size subdivided into size of individual body parts).

Each encoding attribute can also be divided into two primary types: 1) *literals* - these changes have a relatively obvious, immediate effect on the avatar and are constantly observable. Examples include height, body shape, facial expression, current behavior, and current avatar location. 2) *traits* - these changes typically have a more subtle effect on the avatar; they are numerical values which describe a certain intangible property of the avatar or virtual environment. Examples include avatar proficiency at a task, behavioral biometric characteristics, and virtual character interaction characteristics. Avatar traits are a common theme in modern games, where a user may achieve a new 'level' or acquire a new 'power up' which will modify their gameplay. Traits typically will trigger a change in the value of a literal, but this change may not be apparent until a certain action is performed or as time passes. Strength, for example, is only observable when performing a strength-dependent behavior, and may display in multiple ways (e.g. speed of lifting, reduced apparent strain of lifting, increased lift height). These primary types of attributes can be found at any place in the formulated hierarchy; more examples of 'traits' and 'literals' can be identified by color as blue and red, respectively, in Figure 2.

In many cases, multiple physical attributes of the avatar could be changed. This is the case for dramatic changes in avatar identity, such as changing an human-like avatar to a plant-like creature as a reward for adopting environmentally friendly behavior or transforming the avatar's head into a greasy cheeseburger to encourage changes in diet. It must also be considered that many of these principles can perhaps apply for individual body parts (e.g., eye color, hair length, etc.). To design for these more dramatic changes and not become overwhelmed with possibility, we must consider a higher level of abstraction based on psychological interpretation of the human form.

3.2   Encoding in the Psychological

Changes in avatar appearance can be simple changes to physical or behavioral literals (e.g. change in avatar height or change in running speed), but these types of changes do not differ in principle from more traditional data visualization unless they can be interpreted without explanation. That is, a non-intuitive encoding strategy such as using avatar height to encode sleep quality is, in principle, a bar graph with human-shaped bars. However, when using an avatar primitive, simple encodings will almost always have a complex psychological effect on the user. For instance, encoding a user's caloric intake in the overall size of an avatar could have the unintended consequence of making the user view the avatar as more attractive as he/she grows taller. This complication arises because the mapping from the user's interpretation of the avatar to the physical or behavioral space of the avatar is not well defined; indeed, a simple change in the physical space almost always creates complex changes in the user's perception of the avatar.

Avatar displays designed to leverage the psychology of avatar interpretation should instead aim to adjust the user's perception of a specific, high-level trait of the avatar which is relevant to the targeted behavior change. For instance, one could aim to change the perceived abilities of the avatar by making it appear frail, weak, or elderly. By attempting to encode values in high-level interpretation rather physical traits, we can utilize heuristic knowledge of human-form interpretation in our intervention design. Figure 3 provides a minimal demonstration of selected 'low-level' physical attributes and 'high-level' psychological encoding attributes.

4   A Guide to Application of Avatar Interface

The work of Yee et al. [27] provides some example of avatar visualization design from the psychological perspective. Experiment designers wished to modify a psychological construct (the attractiveness of the user) and did so by using height as a proxy based on existing research. To further deepen the effect, other modifications could have been made to the avatar in order to modify the perceived attractiveness. For instance, adjusting the facial features [7] could have also been used. Care must be taken not to assume that multiple changes combine linearly, however. In general, adjustment of multiple encoding attributes could cause an entirely different effect than the original two.

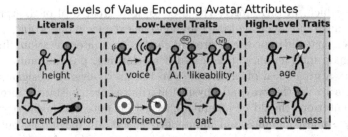

Fig. 3. Various levels of encoding attributes used to modify user perception

Below we describe suggested stages of development for designing an avatar interface. Like many design processes, traversing the stages is iterative in nature; progression through the stages often reveals a need to return to a previous stage to further refine the design. A constant re-checking of past decisions is crucial to creating an avatar interface that is coherent across all dimensions of the system. We present some novel examples as well as some from literature at each suggested stage in Figure 4.

1) *Identify Behavior Change Plan* In this step one must identify our general plan for behavior modification. The targeted behavior must be explicitly defined and a theoretical basis for motivating a change must be found. In this paper we argue that motivation for change is generated with avatars through both the Proteus effect and operant conditioning, but other psychological theories could be applied here as well. Existing literature provides additional guidance on the use of behavioral theories within an HCI context [14], as well as explanation and tools for defining, understanding, and describing behavior change [8,9].

2) *Identify Target Trait in User's Perception* Once we have an overall plan for motivating change, we must identify precisely what part of the user's perception of the avatar we aim to use as the encoding attribute. The resulting 'high-level' trait(s) should come from behavior change literature or designer intuition and not from the hierarchy of low-level traits and literals.

3 *Map the Target to Avatar's Physical Encoding Attributes* Once the targeted high-level encoding attribute is found, the desired effect should be mapped to physical changes in the avatar such as those laid out in Figure 2. At times an easily manipulable physical attribute can act as a proxy for conveying a more psychosocial concept (e.g.: perceived attractiveness could be changed by manipulating height or facial symmetry), but in many cases there may not be significant literature on perception of the targeted attribute. Sometimes this mapping is so intuitive that researchers may (rightfully) not see it worthy of investigation; for example: perceived age can certainly be conveyed via wrinkling of the skin and whiteness of hair. However, it is important to explicitly consider this process of assumption to ensure that the targeted trait is conveyed most effectively. Returning to Figure 3, this process moves us leftwards away from the high-level user-perception space. In fact, encoding attributes must be reduced leftwards completely to the avatar's physical space in order to implement encoding

attributes, which, in turn, forces the user to do a great deal of interpretation. Here an understanding of the target audience is extremely important, since cultural or personal differences can greatly change user interpretation. Just as in human-human interaction, subtleties such as clothing, posture, and body language carry a great deal of information to the user - even if designers do not intend them to. In this way, all physical attributes are constantly interpreted, so implementations should be carefully checked for potential misinterpretation. Ultimately, some confounds and unintended effects are inevitable, but at this stage we minimize potential harm through careful consideration and iterative testing of many possible mappings.

	Outline Behavior Change Plan	Identify targeted trait(s)	map to Avatar's Physical Encoding Attributes
Time to Eat [21]	to improve eating habits subjects are shown a virtual pet with mood determined by the healthiness of breakfast	mood of the pet is the targeted trait	mood of the pet is conveyed on a scale between happy and sad through images with varying facial expression, posture, and text.
MILES [17]	The happiness of a bird avatar is determined by user level of physical activity.	percieved level of happiness of the bird is the targeted avatar trait	the mood of the bird is shown via increased flight speed, and increased song singing.
Yee et al. [24]	hypothesis: increase in avatar attractiveness changes subject's social behavior	Percieved avatar attractiveness is targeted trait.	Avatar height used as a proxy for 'attractiveness'
stressReduce	Desire; reduce overall stress. Motivate behavior change via operant conditioning; users see avatars recieve rewards and experience happiness when avatar is relaxed, unhappiness when avatar is stressed.	levels of stress' and 'levels of happiness' need to be conveyed	level of stress' conveyed via frizzing of avatar's hair, hands placed on temples, bags under eyes, amount of steam coming out of ears. 'level of happiness' via smile achieved through manipulation of mouth and eyes.
ActivitySuggest	to increase user physical activity (PA) via the proteus effect user is presented with PA avatar to increase desire to be PA. Avatar mirrors user level of PA as measure from accelerometers most of the time, but occasionally 'suggests' a higher level by simply displaying it.	Aim is to modify user's percieved level of avatar physical activity	scale of perceived level of PA created using activies of varying intensity. Running, bicycling, swimming are 'high' PA level; walking, playing catch are 'medium' PA level; sleeping and studying are 'low' PA level.

Fig. 4. Example applications (some from literature and some hypothetical) described at each stage of interface development

5   Open Questions and Concerns

The dangers of unintended consequences via misinterpretation may become more serious as we develop systems with more powerful behavior change methods and as we first explore these uncharted methods for providing feedback via avatars. The problem of misinterpretation becomes an even greater concern for the described systems since the method of interpretation for these outputs to the user is no longer something which is taught, but can be entirely dependent on the user's perception of the avatar. For example, a user who may suffer from distorted bodily self-perception may interpret the body shape of the avatar much differently from the norm.

One of the largest challenges remaining for an implementation of human-in-the-loop feedback with avatars is that the method of mapping inputs to outputs (the algorithm itself) may need to vary from application to application and from user to user. Due to the large search space, identifying the best mapping from input to output may require significant iterative design and personalization along with advanced analytic methods such as the use of control systems engineering and dynamical systems modeling [13].

Through the use of described methodology, the design process for avatar interfaces is given some foundation, but much more exploration is needed to address the questions posed throughout this article. Through additional implementations guided by behavior change theory, it is our expectation that avatars will prove an extremely powerful tool for behavior change science.

References

1. Ahn, S.: Embodied Experiences in Immersive Virtual Environments: Effects on Pro-Environmental Attitude and Behavior. Stanford University (2011)
2. Bailenson, J.N., et al.: Transformed Social Interaction, Augmented Gaze, and Social Influence in Immersive Virtual Environments. Human Communication Research 31(4), 511–537 (2005)
3. Bandura, A.: Social learning theory. Prentice Hall, Englewood Cliffs (1977)
4. Behm-Morawitz, E.: Mirrored selves: The influence of self-presence in a virtual world on health, appearance, and well-being. Computers in Human Behavior (2012)
5. Belman, J., et al.: Designing Games to Foster Empathy. International Journal of Cognitive Technology 14(2), 11 (2009)
6. Consolvo, S., et al.: Flowers or a robot army?: encouraging awareness & activity with personal, mobile displays. In: Proceedings of the 10th International Conference on Ubiquitous Computing. ACM (2008)
7. Cunningham, M.R.: Measuring the physical in physical attractiveness: Quasi-experiments on the sociobiology of female facial beauty. Journal of Personality and Social Psychology 50(5), 925–935 (1986)
8. Fogg, B.J.: A behavior model for persuasive design. In: Proceedings of the 4th International Conference on Persuasive Technology. ACM (2009)
9. Fogg, B., et al.: Behavior wizard: A method for matching target behaviors with solutions. Persuasive Technology, 117–131 (2010)
10. Fox, J., et al.: Virtual Self-Modeling: The Effects of Vicarious Reinforcement and Identification on Exercise Behaviors. Media Psychology 12(1), 1–25 (2009)
11. Fujiki, Y., et al.: Neat-O-Games: Blending Physical Activity and Fun in the Daily Routine. Computers in Entertainment (CIE) 6(2), 21 (2008)
12. Hekler, E.B., et al.: A case study of BSUED: Behavior science-informed user experience design. In: Personal Informatics & HCI: Design, Theory & Social Implications, at the ACM SIGCHI Conference on Human Factors in Computing Systems, Vancouver, BC, Canada (2011), http://personalinformatics.org/chi2011/hekler
13. Hekler, E.B., et al.: Exploring Behavioral Markers of Long-term Physical Activity Maintenance: A Case Study of System Identification Modeling within a Behavioral Intervention. In: Submitted for future publication in Health Education and Research (2012)
14. Hekler, E.B., et al.: Mind the Theoretical Gap: Interpreting, Using and Developing Behavioral Theory in HCI Research. In: ACM-CHI Conference, Paris, France (May 2013)
15. Hershfield, H.E., et al.: Increasing Saving Behavior through Age-Progressed Renderings of the Future Self. Journal of Marketing Research 48(SPL), 23–37 (2011)
16. Kelleher, C., et al.: Ten guidelines for effective data visualization in scientific publications. Environmental Modelling & Software 26(6), 822–827 (2011)
17. King, A.C., et al.: Mobile phone applications to promote physical activity increases: Preliminary results of the MILES pilot study. In: Annual Conference for the Society of Behavioral Medicine, New Orleans, LA, USA (2012)

18. Lin, J., et al.: Fish'n'steps: Encouraging Physical Activity with an Interactive Computer Game. In: International Conference on Ubiquitous Computing (UbiComp), pp. 261–278. ACM (2006)
19. Mehrabian, A.: Silent messages: Implicit communication of emotions and attitudes. Wadsworth, Belmont (1981)
20. Newton, K.H., et al.: Pedometers and text messaging to increase physical activity: randomized controlled trial of adolescents with type 1 diabetes. Diabetes care. 32(5), 813–815 (2009)
21. Picard, R.W.: Affective computing (1995)
22. Pollak, J., et al.: It's time to eat! Using mobile games to promote healthy eating. IEEE Pervasive Computing 9(3), 21–27 (2010)
23. Revett, K.: Behavioral biometrics: a remote access approach. Wiley Publishing (2008)
24. Shapiro, J.R., et al.: Use of text messaging for monitoring sugar-sweetened beverages, physical activity, and screen time in children: a pilot study. Journal of Nutrition Education and Behavior 40(6), 385–391 (2008)
25. Turk, M., et al.: Multimodal Transformed Social Interaction. In: International Conference on Multimodal Interfaces, pp. 46–52. ACM (2004)
26. Yee, N., et al.: Walk a Mile in Digital Shoes: The Impact of Embodied Perspective-Taking on the Reduction of Negative Stereotyping in Immersive Virtual Environments. In: Proceedings of PRESENCE, pp. 24–26 (2006)
27. Yee, N., et al.: The Proteus Effect: Implications of Transformed Digital Self-Representation on Online and Offline Behavior. Communication Research 36(2), 285–312 (2009)
28. Ibitz kids avatar application, http://ibitz.com/kidsapp/ (last accessed January 13, 2013)
29. Striiv Smart Pedometer, http://www.striiv.com (last accessed November 9, 2012)
30. Wii Fit avatar, http://wiifit.com/ (last accessed Febuary 15, 2013)

Participatory Interaction Design for the Healthcare Service Field

Takuichi Nishimura[1], M. Kobayakawa[2], M. Nakajima[1], K.C. Yamada[3,1],
T. Fukuhara[1], M. Hamasaki[4], H. Miwa[1], Kentaro Watanabe[1], Y.Sakamoto[3],
T. Sunaga[2], and Yoichi Motomura[1]

[1] Centre for Service Research, National Institute of Advance Industrial Science and
Technology, AIST Waterfront 3F, 2-3-26, Aomi, Koto-ku, Tokyo 135-0065, Japan
[2] Tama Art University
[3] Saga University Hospital
[4] AIST Information Technology Research Unit
takuichi.nishimura@aist.go.jp

Abstract. Innovative service operations in the healthcare field should be cooperative and proactive. However, this is often difficult because separate providers have different ideas and backgrounds and little information of others' practices. For example, we found that workers in a care facility share one notebook for communication and have no incentive to improve the workflow. We also observed that most point-of-care system PDAs in a hospital were not being used to record and share information by the nurses, mainly because the system interface impeded their workflow. In addition, members of a dance sports circle, who want to improve their health, are inactive because of a lack of support. Such healthcare communities should be encouraged to be proactive and collaborate in solving problems. Participatory interaction design is important for this purpose, and so an activity methodology combined with technical systems should be developed. This paper proposes three steps towards participatory interaction design and describes a prototype of the methodology.

Keywords: Participatory interaction design, service engineering, nursing-care service, collaborative system development.

1 Introduction

The national burden of long-term care insurance costs in Japan during FY 2009 rose to 7.7 trillion yen, underscoring a continuously rising trend [1]. It is important to reduce this burden by improving healthcare service productivity and fostering a health-conscious community.

The profitability of many care services is less than 5%. Moreover, healthcare workers bear a large workload. Thus, improving productivity while maintaining the quality of service is an urgent task. Nursing-care services comprise care facility services, visiting services, and assistive device services. This paper examines facility services, because their features are similar to those encountered by nurses in hospitals. Many people from different backgrounds and serving in different roles must

A. Marcus (Ed.): DUXU/HCII 2013, Part II, LNCS 8013, pp. 435–441, 2013.

collaborate to provide nursing-care services for various residents and patients. For these reasons, service processes vary widely depending on the workplace community characteristics related to employees, patients, and the environment. Furthermore, it is difficult to collaborate effectively and gain patients' trust, both of which can greatly improve service productivity.

Given the nature of this work, there is clearly a need for good teamwork among various employees, the sharing of information related to the medical and physical condition of patients and users (especially to ensure a comfortable service process), and for each employee to maintain a high skill level. Indeed, fine-grained services like these are important to foster trust in patients and users. Without trust, user and patient satisfaction will decrease, irrespective of the quality of the service that is offered.

A business analysis of helpers in a care service facility was conducted with the cooperation of an assisted-living paid nursing home in the city of Osaka, Hirano Super Court (SC Hirano). The results, reported herein, indicate that 58% of the helpers' time was spent on work that was not directly related to nursing, and 30% of their time was spent recording and sharing information, especially computer work such as transcription and calculation. Such indirect work does not engender long-term care insurance points. Moreover, it is not directly related to the value of the care received. Therefore, research is being conducted to support the creation and visualization of work records.

To this end, attention is being devoted to the introduction of IT infrastructure to promote cooperation and alignment among employees. This should promote the development of a technological interface to facilitate an efficient workflow and limit the increase in data input work, which is not directly related to care.

This proposal encourages the active participation of employees in real-world environments to develop a system that can be expected to embed itself into the employees' natural workflow (Participatory Interaction Design). In addition, employees should be able to share knowledge in the workplace, using technology to record information whenever a task is completed (point-of-care recording). In the latter case, an input system that enables the ready sharing of necessary workplace-related knowledge should be realized, thereby creating a systematic information database that can be shared among workers.

The situation is similar in mutual-support communities, such as dance circles. Members want to improve their health condition, but some require more support from others instead of trying to change the situation proactively. The members have a varying ability to support the community, and have the potential to find a more adequate solution to activate their fellow members.

Participatory interaction design is important for this purpose, and so an activity methodology combined with technical systems should be investigated. Three steps towards participatory interaction design are proposed, and prototypes for the steps are described herein.

2   Participatory Interaction Design for the Healthcare Service Field

2.1   Characteristics of the Healthcare Service Field

There are various healthcare services, such as hospitals, nursing care homes, home help, gymnasia, and civic circle activities. These services are gradually beginning to collaborate, connecting the entire local community to enhance social capital. There are three main characteristics of such healthcare services:

- Collaboration by various professionals, such as doctors, nurses, and care workers.
- High skill levels and a broad range of knowledge, such as medical, nursing, daily support, biomechanical, education, community management, and legal knowledge.
- Customization, because each individual is different in body, character, health condition, and so on.

The value added will be measured both physically and psychologically, as shown in Figure 1. This relates to not only customers, but also employees because employee satisfaction will influence customer subjectivity.

Therefore, a community spirit between employees and customers should be fostered. This will allow mutual understanding among employees and between employees and customers, leading to the realization of a natural workflow using new IT systems shown in Figure 2. In turn, this will help each worker to share their experience and intuition, and achieve the aims of the service field.

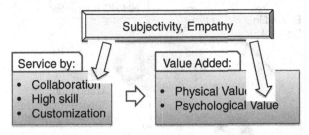

Fig. 1. Characteristics of healthcare services

Fig. 2. Tool for workplace should be developed based on the community

2.2   Participatory Interaction Design

Various system development methodologies have been proposed. Engineering design [2] provides systematic solutions for a given product specification on the condition that the needs are clear. Contextual design [3] and scenario-based design [4] enable system designers to fully understand the users and their environment, but the users do not participate in the design process. System development based on a business process model [5] is efficient for process innovation, but this is also a top-down approach with no responsible participation.

To properly embed new technology into the workflow, we should consider the subjective situation of each employee. This varies among employees, even though the experience is similar, because different characters and health conditions will influence each individual's point of view and reaction. These subjective situations are somewhat restricted, with little information about the whole service field. Inter-subjective is defined as common subjective of each members related to the service field. And the inter-subjective world tends to be small in busy workplaces because the members do not have enough time to share others' subjective. An objective view of the workplace situation can be obtained by a time-and-motion study or position/action sensor data from each employee.

In this report, participatory interaction design for the healthcare service field is proposed. This aims to encourage service field members to develop a better service process by themselves and lead the development of improved IT systems.

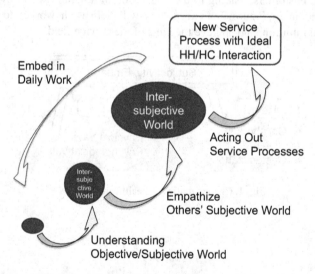

Fig. 3. Participatory interaction design

The following three steps, shown in Figure 3, are used for participatory interaction design:

• *Understanding the Objective/Subjective World.*

If employees are aware of their own actions and those of others, they are often enlightened and begin to improve the workflow. This changes their subjective world, and makes the inter-subjective world larger. By reflecting on their subjective world, employees notice subconscious thoughts and knowledge that will modify the subjective world.

• *Empathize with Others' Subjective Worlds.*

Usually, employees do not have time to express their own subjective world and cannot know others' subjective worlds. If they have the chance to empathize with others' subjective worlds, their inter-subjective world will grow.

• *Acting Out Service Processes.*

Finally, in order to modify employees' behavior and elicit new service processes with ideal human–human or human–computer interaction, service processes should be acted out. This will allow employees to consider other workers' or customers' subjective worlds in the service process, and encourage them to change their behavior to improve the process and use the new IT system proactively.

3   Examples of Each Step

3.1   Understanding the Objective/Subjective World

The characteristics of nursing and the healthcare sector include diverse needs, numerous interruptions, and the necessity of working with others. Moreover, patients receiving the same service often require a process that is unique to their circumstances.

Therefore, it has been difficult to define an appropriate action classification code. The construction of an easily described work process code was proposed [6], and this led to the modeling and analysis of complex nursing processes. Furthermore, the total time required for each operation and process model was obtained. Another example, which shows the contents of hand-over notes, is illustrated in Figure 4. This shows that 66% of hand-over information concerned residents or their families.

These results were presented to employees and employers. Their knowledge and opinions were assessed through discussions of the current state of affairs in the business via a collaborative model.

3.2   Empathize with others' Subjective Worlds

Some complaints related to the teamwork assistance system were found to result from user community malfunctions rather than system configuration problems. User communities are usually extremely busy, and have no opportunities for mutual understanding and discussion of their service mission.

Therefore, as a second step, we held a workshop in which employees could mutually express their subjective world related to the workplace experience. The first workshop was the Zuzie workshop [7], which helped attendees to express their own ideas and those of others. Nurses do not usually express themselves, but they were encouraged to express their feelings and opinions, and found that this, and an insight

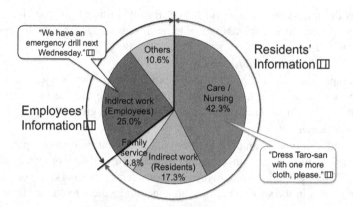

Fig. 4. Contents of hand-over notes

.Fig. 5. Scenes from a reflection, expression, and reconstruction workshop

into others' subjective worlds, was exciting. Participants were also asked to categorize their feelings on each work process and express their own desires, mission, reasons for miscommunication, and so on. Thus, their inter-subjective worlds grew.

4   Conclusion

In this study, the authors proposed the concept of participatory interaction design and showed some examples of the steps necessary for its implementation. In future research, the authors will refine and validate each step by developing an actual system. Embedding the proposed method in the service field will also be studied.

References

1. Ministry of Health, Labour and Welfare (MHLW), Survey Results of Nursing-Care Service Facilities and Companies (2011) (in Japanese)
2. Pahl, G., Beitz, W.: Engineering Design – A Systematic Approach, 2nd edn. Springer, London (1996)
3. Beyer, H., Holtzblatt, K.: Contextual Design: Defining Customer-Centered Systems. Morgan Kaufmann, San Francisco (1998)

4. Carroll, J.M.: Five reasons for scenario-based design. Interacting with Computers 13, 43–60 (2000)
5. van der Aalst, W.M.P., ter Hofstede, A.H.M., Weske, M.: Business process management: A survey. In: van der Aalst, W.M.P., ter Hofstede, A.H.M., Weske, M. (eds.) BPM 2003. LNCS, vol. 2678, pp. 1–12. Springer, Heidelberg (2003)
6. Miwa, H., Fukuhara, T., Nishimura, T.: Service process visualization in nursing care service using state transition model. In: Proceedings of 4th International Conference on Applied Human Factors and Ergonomics, CD-ROM (2012)
7. Nakamura, Y., Kobayakawa, M., Takami, C., Tsuruga, Y., Kubota, H., Hamasaki, M., Nishimura, T., Sunaga, T.: Zuzie: Collaborative Storytelling Based on Multiple Compositions. In: Aylett, R., Lim, M.Y., Louchart, S., Petta, P., Riedl, M. (eds.) ICIDS 2010. LNCS, vol. 6432, pp. 117–122. Springer, Heidelberg (2010)

Virtual Environment to Treat Social Anxiety

Ana Paula Cláudio[1], Maria Beatriz Carmo[1], Tânia Pinheiro[1],
Francisco Esteves[2], and Eder Lopes[1]

[1] LabMAg
Faculty of Sciences, University of Lisbon
Lisbon, Portugal
[2] Mid Sweden University, Östersund, Sweden,
CIS-IUL, University Institute of Lisbon/ISCTE, Portugal
{apc,bc}@di.fc.ul.pt, fc28181@alunos.fc.ul.pt,
francisco.esteves@iscte.pt, fc40571@launos.fc.ul.pt

Abstract. The aim of our work is to propose a Virtual Reality solution to treat social anxiety, applying cognitive-behavioral therapies, that preserves the sense of immersion without requiring the use of expensive special purpose hardware. We have developed an application, called Virtual Spectators, that creates a simulation taking place in a virtual scenario inhabited by animated virtual humans whose behaviors are dynamically controlled by the therapist. To evaluate the effective usefulness of the tool from the point of view of the therapist, we performed an evaluation of the application with a set of these professionals familiarized with the use of exposure therapy. Their feedback was positive and they were enthusiastic about the possibility of using such a tool to support a session of exposure therapy.

Keywords: Virtual reality, virtual humans, social anxiety.

1 Introduction

To experience some level of anxiety in our daily life is natural, and might even have a positive motivational value; nevertheless, in some situations, anxiety may be difficult to deal with, being highly debilitating in extreme cases. If not conveniently treated, these cases can evolve to severe anxiety disorders, such as social phobia or panic attacks.

To treat patients suffering from these conditions, cognitive-behavioral therapies expose patients to situations they fear. This exposure may be carried out either in vivo or by putting the patients imagining their triggering situations.

Some psychotherapists started using Virtual Reality (VR) systems during the 90's to apply exposure therapy to different types of disorders obtaining very encouraging results.

The use of digital platforms to support the therapeutic process has many advantages comparing to traditional techniques: it offers a greater variety of scenarios and reduces the cost of creating situations difficult or impossible to recreate. Additionally, these platforms support automatic data recording, are geographically independent, and

A. Marcus (Ed.): DUXU/HCII 2013, Part II, LNCS 8013, pp. 442–451, 2013.

are able to recreate situations that may be infinitely replicable. A single package of content may be used by many therapists, being available worldwide.

However, the use of VR platforms involves a significant investment: the purchase of sophisticated hardware components (e.g. VR glasses, head-mounted displays, CAVE) and their maintenance, as well as the software contents development. Besides, a considerable number of patients using these VR equipments experience uncomfortable sensations (dizziness or even sickness) that may prevent them to complete the therapy.

The aim of our work is to propose a solution to treat social anxiety, applying cognitive-behavioral therapies, that preserves the sense of immersion induced by VR systems without requiring the purchase of expensive special purpose hardware. Our solution is easy to install and maintain, even for people who do not have special expertise in the field of informatics, as it is the case of the large majority of therapists. Our solution resorts to a common apparatus, and it was designed to have a user-friendly interface that allows therapists to recreate in a controlled manner various types of stimuli.

The implemented application, called Virtual Spectators, involves: i) a simulation, observed by the patient, taking place in a virtual scenario inhabited by virtual humans with dynamically controlled behaviors and ii) an interface, used exclusively by the therapist, to control these behaviors as well as a set of events in the simulation.

The simulation is devoted to the fear of speaking in front of an audience and it attempts to recreate the realism of an audience which induces the sense of immersion in the patient using credible virtual humans and motion capture animations. During a therapy session, the patient will face the challenge of delivering a speech or a presentation before the virtual audience. While the patient is focused on his task and on the simulation, the therapist is observing his reactions and is controlling the stimuli using the interface commands.

The interface is simple and intuitive, giving the therapist a set of configurations of the auditorium and simulation events that can be used to adjust the level of discomfort to which the patient is subjected. This allows a higher level of control over the simulation than the one available in a recreated exposure therapy that involves real scenarios and/or real people, where unexpected events or behaviors may occur. Furthermore, it gives the therapist the possibility to go back and repeat a moment or a sequence in the exposure, in order to better train patients to deal with their specific difficulties.

We use free software tools that support the creation of video-games to create the simulation and a Kinect camera to record natural movements to incorporate in the virtual humans.

The simulations are displayed on a projection screen and in a way that the patient sees the projected elements of the environment with a size similar to their real counterparts; sound is also introduced in the simulations.

To evaluate the effective usefulness of the tool from the point of view of the therapist we performed an evaluation of the application. The feedback of the professionals that participated in the evaluation was positive and they were enthusiastic about the possibility of using such a tool to support a session of exposure therapy. Some of their suggestions were already incorporated in the application and have been considered in our on-going work.

2   Related Work

In the nineties some psychotherapists started using VR systems in exposure therapy for different types of disorders. Most of them seem to agree that VR is a valuable tool in treating phobic disorders [1], [2], [3], [4] and some concluded that VR Exposure Therapy (VRET) presents an efficacy level similar to that of traditional cognitive behavior therapies (CBT) [5].

Klinger (2004) studied, over 12 sessions, the evolution of the fear of public speaking in 36 participants [5]. Participants were divided into 2 groups, one treated with traditional CBT and other with VRET. The VRET was conducted using four virtual environments which simulated social situations involving performance (eg, public speaking), inter-personnel interaction (eg, a dinner conversation), assertiveness (eg, defending an idea) and evaluation (eg, talk while being observed). According to the study, patients in the VRET group showed a larger reduction of its social anxiety than patients in the CBT group. From a clinical point of view and taking into account psychometric criteria, the decrease in symptoms was similar in the two groups.

Herbelin (2005) published a validation study with 200 patients, confirming that his VR platform met the requirements of VRET therapeutic exposure for social phobia. Moreover, he also proved that it is possible to improve the clinical assessment with monitoring tools integrated in the application, such as eye-tracking [6].

However, these publications only present some of the features of VRET. These techniques have become the specialty of clinics and hospitals such as Virtually Better[7], Virtual Reality Medical Center [8] and Duke University Medical Center [9] and are the result of research carried out over many years.

3   Virtual Spectators

The application Virtual Spectators was conceived to be used by therapists to help in the treatment for Social Anxiety. The first implemented simulation is directed to the fear of speaking in front of an audience, taking place in a virtual auditorium populated with animated virtual humans whose behavior is controlled in real-time by the therapist who may also trigger a set of potentially disturbing events.

To overcome public speaking anxiety is a fundamental step towards personal and professional success in our society. However it may be a challenging and demanding goal that needs therapeutic monitoring, most probably using exposure therapy. The most important condition to perform a successful exposure therapy is provoking stimuli in the patient that are similar to those in real situations, causing in the patient the feeling of presence [6]. It is therefore important that the application generates a simulation interactively controlled by the therapist who is responsible for managing the stimuli caused in the patient.

Considering the course of simulation during a therapy session, the therapist has an active role while the patient has a passive one. The patient role is to perform a speech in front of the virtual audience that is facing him, while the therapist performs simultaneously two roles: i) he is aware of the behavior and responses of the patient to the stimuli caused by the audience and ii) interacts with the application to adapt the course of the simulation accordingly, either by changing the behavior of Virtual Humans (VH) or by triggering specific events in the scenario (e.g., turn on/off lights in the auditorium, make a mobile phone ring). The therapist is also responsible for configuring the initial scenario of the simulation, before starting a therapy session.

Our application was conceived to be executed and visualized in widely available equipment: a regular computer that executes the application, one projector and one projection screen and two nearby sound columns. Two separate windows are displayed: one for the simulation (Fig.1), which should be projected on the screen and another one containing the therapist interaction window (Fig. 2) which should be displayed in the computer screen and not visible to the patient.

The interaction window was conceived to be used by the therapist in two different moments: before and during the simulation. Thus, the interface is divided into two zones, with only one active in each of these moments. Before the simulation, the interface allows the configuration of the auditorium (left side of Fig. 2): set the number of male and female VH in the simulation, choose the colors of the physical elements of the room (walls, chairs), set the status of the lights of the auditorium (on/off) and the position of the camera within the 3D scene. The initial position of the camera can be adjusted within certain limits and along three orthogonal directions: zoom in and out (zoom), move to the right and to the left and move up and down. This is a sort of camera calibration, adjusting its position to the height and the position of the patient relative to the screen, so that the virtual elements are projected with a size similar to their real counterparts. Moreover, the virtual characters will also adjust the direction of their look in order to simulate that they are looking at the patient.

After setting up the scene, the therapist begins the simulation by clicking on the "Start Simulation" button. The string on this button changes to "Pause Simulation" and the button thus can be used to suspend the simulation.

During the simulation, the therapist can command the audience behavior (right side of Fig. 2): change the number of attentive or distracted characters, change the number of characters nodding in order to show agreement or the reverse situation, put some to sleep, trigger the occurrence of a whisper in the back of the room or the receiving of a text message on a mobile phone followed by the corresponding action of writing a response. Fig. 1 illustrates some of these situations.

The sound emitted by the columns is synchronized with the events "whisper" or "receive a message" happening in the simulation. There is also a button in the interaction window that triggers the generation of the sound of an airplane flying over the audience.

With this ordinary infrastructure, we have the advantage of using an inexpensive and easy to install equipment, projecting an image on a large screen, inducing in the patient the feeling of immersion. Moreover, it can be observed simultaneously by several persons, which may be valuable, for instance, in educational and training contexts/classes.

Fig. 1. The simulation window illustrating a possible situation during a therapy session: some of the characters are distracted, two of the girls are whispering, and one (on the left side of the scenario) has just received a text message on his mobile phone and is going to reply

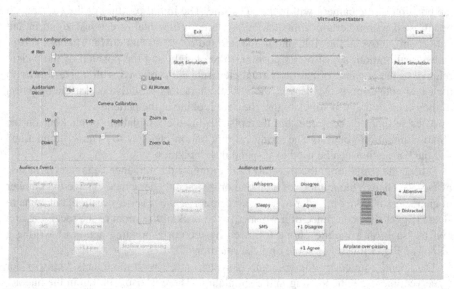

Fig. 2. The therapist interaction window. On the left: the configuration zone is active; on the right: the simulation mode is active.

3.1   Technical Details

The application Virtual Spectators was implemented following the architecture of a video-game; we have chosen Blender[10], a free and open-source tool used for creating 3D animated models and video-games. The Blender game engine manages the graphic content while the logical component of the system is implemented in the programming language Python.

The Virtual Humans and the Auditorium

The application MakeHuman [11] was used for the creation of 3D realistic models of human characters that exports models to Blender format. Resorting to different web-sites with free content for SecondLife and OpenSim and "The Sims 2" [12], [13], [14], [15] we have obtained credible clothing and hair for the characters, thus avoiding to develop them from scratch. With an image editor we produced a variety of clothing and hair by simply changing the base colors. Using this procedure, we have created several distinct VH models, each one with about 2200 vertices.

The animations of the VH body were produced using motion capture data recorded with a Kinect camera [16] and resorting to the software iPiSoft [17].

Due to restrictions of the Kinect camera drivers, animations do not contain the ro-tations of the hands and head. For this we added manually the animations of the head and hands using Blender features and created a set of animations for VH: "be aware", "be distracted" "receive a text message", "sleep", "whisper", "hear the whisper", "wink" and "sleep/wake". The more complex ones such as "being distracted" and "receive a text message", suffered a large number of amendments that were made manually in Blender's animation editor. To produce the "blink" movement in the VH's eyes we created shape keys.

As a proof of concept, one of the virtual characters in the scenario is provided with artificial intelligence, in order to have an autonomous behavior. Its behavior is not controlled by the therapist; the character changes its own level of attention according to the other VH in the auditorium. This feature allows the application to recreate si-mulations that are more similar to an exposure session in front of a real audience. Besides, the variability of the simulations from session to session, potentially reduces the "déjà vu" feeling of a patient subjected to a continuous therapy.

The auditorium was completely modeled and textured in Blender using standard 3D modeling techniques, such as mesh modeling, extrude, sculpting, among other. We have used textures from SecondLife/OpenSim.

All software used to create the auditorium and the animated characters is free ex-cept iPiStudio from iPiSoft; we used a free trial version available for 30 days.

The Interaction Window

To control the VH and trigger events in the simulation we created an interaction win-dow that exchanges information with the simulation using inter-process communica-tion, adopting the module pexpect [18]. To control the flow of messages we imple-mented threads that manage the Input/Output.

Fig. 3 outlines the articulation of our application with the Blender's game engine. The scenario is updated by the 3D game engine and is controlled via our Python script (Main Controller). The game engine is responsible for creating the simulation window while the interaction window communicates with the Main Controller.

The script receives the input from the interaction window and, besides triggering events, manages animations and provides access to objects and modifies properties, which are essential to set up the scenario such as visibility, textures, animations, among others.

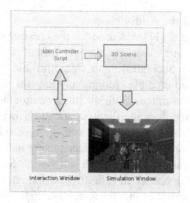

Fig. 3. Architecture of the application

3.2 Evaluation

The application was evaluated from the point of view of the therapists to assess its potential in supporting the realization of an exposure therapy session to treat the anxiety of speaking in front of an audience. Four therapists, one man aged 41 and three women aged 39, 41 and 44 participated in the evaluation. They were all familiarized with the use of exposure therapy and had no prior contact with the application. Moreover, they all felt at ease using the computer and were comfortable with the idea of using a VR tool to support exposure therapy.

For each therapist there was an individual test session in a room with the necessary equipment: a laptop to run the application and to display the interaction interface, a projector, a projection screen and two sound columns. Each session consisted in two successive phases: the first was a familiarization period with the application and the second was an exposure therapy session with a volunteer patient.

The first phase took five to ten minutes and was used by the therapist to explore the available functionalities in the interface, observing their practical effect in the simulation. In the second phase, which took seven to ten minutes, four students volunteered, one for each therapist, to play the role of patient. The therapist played his/her own role using the application to control the level of stimulus induced in the patient.

The therapists were unanimous saying that they would use this application to support a session of exposure therapy. They found no critical aspects in the interface and they all considered that the simulated events are interesting.

The aspects classified as more interesting were the credibility of the behaviors creating situations similar to those of a real auditorium, specially the possibility of having characters nodding in order to show agreement or disagreement, inducing positive or negative reinforcement.

The following improvements/additions were suggested: increase the number of characters (up to the limit of the auditorium capacity); improve the realism of the virtual humans, their animations and the movements of the eyes; increase the number of simulated events (for instance, characters entering and leaving the scenario, talking or speaking loud, using a laptop, taking snapshots or filming with a mobile phone or a camera); include the possibility of choosing different scenarios and the possibility of changing the appearance of the characters (for instance, the clothes, the age).

After the sessions the four volunteer students, aged around 22, gave an informal testimony of their experience. They all reported that, despite they knew the audience is virtual, the fact that the virtual humans move and exhibit variation in their behaviors somehow induces the sense of immersion and really affected them during the session.

This fact suggests that a person suffering from anxiety when talking in front of an audience can really profit from this application in a therapeutic context.

They suggested inserting more sounds in the environment, such as cars honking outside or the sound of the air conditioning system, to introduce more variability in the animations. The main identified problem is the lack of variability in facial expressions which were considered too neutral.

After these tests and from our own experience we conclude that there are important improvements that should be introduced in order to obtain a higher level of realism in the simulation. Some of the flaws are possible to solve in newer Blender versions (for instance, the movement of the eyes looking at the camera), while others may be easily attained or solved if manpower is available (for instance, more animated characters in the auditorium). Nevertheless, the realism can only be improved up to the limit of maintaining the rendering of the simulation in real-time.

4   Virtual Assessment Interview

Currently, we are working in a scenario to support the treatment of the anxiety caused by an assessment situation that is conceived to be used with the same equipment. We are still using Blender to produce the scenario setting but we are using a different technological approach. The simulation is generated by Unity3D game engine [19] that allows the development of video-games that can be played in the web or in the traditional devices such as desktops, mobile devices and consoles.

This simulation has peculiarities that make it significantly different from the simulations described above. These simulations are conceived to contain up to three VH sitting in a table facing and looking at the patient (Fig. 4). The therapist interface will provide functionalities to choose among a set of predefined models from both genders, different ages and wearing formal or informal outfits.

The assessment interview scenario is more intimidating to the patient comparing with the auditorium scenario: despite there are fewer VH, they are closer to the patient and clearly have a decisive evaluation role. Our main focus is the expression of emotions through body and facial poses. An Artificial Intelligence module will be developed in order to simulate distinct states of mind and personalities in VH. Unity supports this integration gracefully. For the time being we are not dealing with automatic speech recognition, but this will be a future challenge.

Fig. 4. Virtual assessment interview simulation

5   Conclusions and Future Work

We propose a low-cost solution to perform exposure therapy using Virtual Reality. During a therapy session, the patient will face the challenge of delivering a speech or a presentation before a virtual audience displayed on a projection screen. While the patient is focused on his task and on the simulation, the therapist is observing his reactions and is controlling the stimuli using the interface commands displayed in the screen of his computer. This interface provides a range of configuration options in the auditorium and a set of controllable events in the simulation.

The simulation tries to represent as realistically as possible an audience that cause "impact" on the patient using VH and accurate animations. For this end, convincing VH models were used and natural animations were developed using motion capture data. However, in this kind of applications, one must always find a balance between the realism of the 3D environment and the need to render the animation in real-time. So, up to some level, we had to sacrifice realism to obtain real-time response to the user interaction.

The development of the application has been closely followed by a therapist who has informally assessed the successive versions and has given clues to the next steps and features to implement.

We have carried out an evaluation process with a group of four therapists with the purpose of assessing if the application can support their work during an exposure therapy session to treat the anxiety of a patient caused by speaking in front of an audience. This evaluation included a configuration of the scenario by the therapist and a simulated session of exposure therapy with a volunteer "patient". The analysis of their answers to a questionnaire has lead us to the conclusion that our solution is not perfect and needs improvements but has a good potential for being useful in these therapies.

Informal testimonies recorded among the volunteer-patients suggest that our solution may be effectively useful in these therapies, inducing in the patients the sense of immersion and really affecting them during the therapy.

More scenarios are being developed to extend the application, e.g., with an assessment interview scene where we want to explore the expression of facial and body emotions. An artificial intelligence module concerning the simulation of emotions will be developed. We consider that this type of scenario might be interesting to use, for example, with graduate or undergraduate students to help some young people suffering from anxiety to speak to an audience or to a more limited set of people in an assessment situation. We are aware that there is a significant number of students that uses the existing psychology offices in colleges to ask for support in these specific situations. We are planning to perform user tests to evaluate the sense of immersion caused by this type of scenarios.

References

1. Brinkman, W.-P., van der Mast, C., Inan, F.: A Virtual Environment to Create Social Situations: First Step to a VRET System for Social Phobia. In: Euromedia 2009, Eurosis-ETIS, Belgium, pp. 103–107 (April 2009)
2. Powers, M., Emmelkamp, P.: Virtual reality exposure therapy for anxiety disorders: A meta-analysis. Journal of Anxiety Disorders 22(3), 561–569 (2008)
3. Roy, S.: State of the art of virtual reality therapy (VRT) in phobic disorders. PsychNology Journal 1(2), 176–183 (2003)
4. Project Virtual Reality and Phobias, http://mmi.tudelft.nl/vret/index.php/Virtual_Reality_and_Phobias
5. Klinger, E., Bouchard, S., Légeron, P., Roy, S., Lauer, F., Chemin, I., Nugues, P.: Virtual Reality Therapy Versus Cognitive Behavior Therapy for Social Phobia: A Preliminary Controlled Study. Cyberpsychology& Behavior 8(1), 76–88 (2005)
6. Herbelin, B.: Virtual reality exposure therapy for social phobia. PhD Thesis, Université Louis Pasteur, Strasbourg (2005)
7. Virtuallybetter website, http://www.virtuallybetter.com
8. Vrphobia website, http://www.vrphobia.com
9. Dukehealth phobia treatment website, http://www.dukehealth.org/services/psychiatry/programs/adult_services/
10. Blender website, http://www.blender.org/
11. Makehuman website, http://www.makehuman.org
12. Second life shirts website, http://www.secondlife-shirts.com
13. Opensim creations website, http://opensim-creations.com
14. Linda kellie website, http://www.lindakellie.com
15. Mod the sims website, http://www.modthesims.info
16. Kinect website, http://www.xbox.com/en-US/kinect
17. ipisoft website, http://www.ipisoft.com/
18. Python pexpect module website, http://www.noah.org/wiki/pexpect
19. Unity3D website, http://unity3d.com/

Development and Evaluation of a Knowledge-Based Method for the Treatment of Use-Oriented and Technical Risks Using the Example of Medical Devices

Simon Plogmann, Armin Janß, Arne Jansen-Troy, and Klaus Radermacher

Helmholtz-Institute for Biomedical Engineering Aachen, Aachen University
Pauwelsstraße 20, Aachen D-52074, Germany
simon.plogmann@rwth-aachen.de, janss@hia.rwth-aachen.de

Abstract. Rapidly evolving technological progress in the field of medical devices not only leads to a potential enhancement of therapeutic results but also to a change of the Human-Machine-Interaction characteristics, causing deficiencies in the use process and bringing along high potential for hazardous human-induced failures. This implicates higher risks for patients, medical professionals and third parties. In order to support the usability engineering and risk management process of medical devices, a new methodology for risk control has been developed and evaluated. The aim is to implement appropriate counteractions in the risk control process, reducing errors in the Human-Machine-Interaction process as well as system-inherent technological risks. Accessing information from the method's knowledge base enables the operator to detect the most suitable countermeasures for the respective problem. 41 approved generic countermeasure principles have been indexed as a resulting combination of root causes and failures that might appear during Human-Machine-Interaction or manufacturing and developmental process. The method has been tested in comparison to conventional approaches. Evaluation of the matrix and reassessment of the risk priority numbers by a blind expert demonstrated a substantial benefit of the new *mAIXcontrol* method.

Keywords: Human Error Taxonomy, Usability Engineering, Human-Machine-Interaction, Risk Control, Human Factors in Risk Management, System Safety, Theory of Inventive Problem Solving (TRIZ), Healthcare/Medical Systems.

1 Introduction

In the field of medical devices, strict regulatory standards exist, defining the development process for medical devices, supporting good manufacturing practices and giving advice for user-centered human device interfaces [8][9]. One important standard is the DIN EN ISO 14971 (Medical devices - Application of risk management to medical devices) which divides the risk management process into four stages: risk identification, risk evaluation, risk control and market observation [10]. In contrast to risk identification or risk evaluation, at present no methodological approach for the generation and selection of countermeasures within risk control process exists.

A. Marcus (Ed.): DUXU/HCII 2013, Part II, LNCS 8013, pp. 452–461, 2013.

Brainstorming – being the most common state-of-the-art method - is a rather simple and unsystematic approach. Moreover, as a quality criterion of a countermeasure, only the recommendation to distinguish between inherent, protective and descriptive security measures makes it possible to compare safety measures on the basis of a common value system [10]. This makes it difficult for developers and risk managers to find, choose, implement and also justify effective and efficient risk control measures when designing a product or setting the alignment for a manufacturing process.

2   State of the Art

2.1   Usability Engineering and Risk Management

Scientific studies in the medical context show that in most of the cases use-oriented or human-induced errors [1] are the cause for critical events concerning the introduction and application of medical devices [2]. Therefore it is indispensable that risk management guidelines are supported by usability specifications (especially for risk sensitive systems as medical devices) such as DIN EN 62366 (Medical devices - Application of usability engineering to medical   devices) [8] or DIN EN ISO 60601-1-6 (Medical electrical equipment - General requirements for basic safety and essential performance – collateral standard: usability) [11] and DIN EN ISO 9241-110 (Ergonomics of human-system interaction: Dialogue Principles) [12]. Whereas general advice for the design of human-machine-interfaces or the composition of environmental working conditions is easily accessible in standards and guidelines, comprehensive methods for the risk control process (especially with a focus on human-induced errors), that offer advice in dependency of the specific problem or context, are rare.

In recent years we implemented and evaluated the risk analysis method mAIXuse for risk analysis of human-machine-systems very successfully (Walter Masing Award 2010 of the German Society for Quality - DGQ (http://www.walter-masing-preis.de/wmp/walter-masing-preis.htm) [18, 19]). On this basis, we developed the concept of *mAIXcontrol*, a risk control tool that fills the methodology-gap within the (use-oriented and technical) risk control process. The methodology harks back to a knowledge-base of so far 14 risk analyses from industry and research and can gradually be fed with further data in the future. The method allows a systematic treatment and control of a particular risk as a function of previously identified weaknesses of the product or use process.

2.2   Theory of Inventive Problem Solving

The new method has been developed on the basis of the contradiction matrix of Genrikh S. Altshuller's TRIZ (Theory of Inventive Problem Solving), which is particularly known in innovation management and mechanical construction design [7]. TRIZ includes a practical methodology, a knowledge base for generating new ideas and solutions for technological contradictions. The problem solving process (shown in 1) has been adapted to the needs of usability engineering and risk management in medical context, mapping typical use deficiencies with interfaces and their potential solutions amongst others, but the general modus operandi of the matrix stays the same. The necessary steps to successfully apply the method to a specific problem are:

1. The specific problem has to be abstracted.
2. The matrix proposes one or several abstract solution approaches, which serve as a thought-provoking impulse.
3. The proposed approach needs to be adapted to the specific case by developers' efforts.

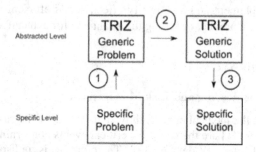

Fig. 1. Schematic Illustration of the Problem Solving Process, Applying TRIZ

In particular the steps one (induction) and three (deduction) require the developer's creative contribution, whereas step two is provided by the matrix.

3   A New Approach for Risk Treatment: mAIXcontrol

The new *mAIXcontrol* methodology accesses experts' knowledge from a database of different risk analyses and maps suitable context-individual countermeasures as a function of failures and failure-causes. On a superordinated level, it structures causes and failures by terms of their error taxonomy. For applying the methodology to a specific problem, the operator has to check the failures and causalities within the axes and has to find the respective failure-causality combination. In consequence the method proposes one or several of the 41 abstract principles of risk control. An excerpt of the new matrix can be seen in Figure 2.

3.1   A Knowledge-Based Matrix for Human Risk Control

In order to detect the most suitable countermeasures, the method has to assess the risk (combination of failure and cause) as precisely as possible on the one hand, proposing a case-tailored approach for the individual case and stay user-friendly on the other hand, avoiding a disaggregation into a catalogue of numerous individual cases. To solve this trade-off, different approaches have been analyzed regarding to their road capability. The approach implicating that principles of risk control can be mapped as a function of causes and failures turned to be the most reasonable. Other approaches, e.g. combining different (root) causes with each other, different failures, or displaying the principles of risk control in dependency on a combination of cause and effect, have been dismissed after a detailed analysis of alternatives. Essential for the final design is the awareness that any harm originates from a combination of a root cause and an (undetected) failure and that this information is available in any risk analysis.

As the commutability of root cause, failure and effect (depending on the abstraction level of analysis) has been proven by several reputable researchers [5,6,1,14,15], we desisted to make a clear distinction between the three elements of the failure chain and put, root causes and failures, as coding information on the mirror-inverted axes of the matrix. In fact, during assessment of the risk analyses we discovered several cases where an incident that has been the failure for an upcoming adverse event, turned out to be the (root) cause for another consequence in a different risk analysis, showing that a distinction between (root) cause and failure is only possible in a very narrow, risk-analysis-dependent context. As we seceded from this in our comprehensive approach, the strict distinction has been dropped.

mAIXcontrol		Insufficient Depiction/ Displaying	Imperfect Joining	Joining impossible
Error by Execution: Confusion Error	Confusion		[8] [3] [8]	
	Wrong Combination			
Error by Execution	Lacking Manual Skills		[22] [27] [29]	
Error by Execution: Qualitative Error	Insufficient Execution of Work Step			[7] [27] [29]
Error by Execution: Timing Error	Execution of Work Step Too Late			
Error by Omission	Forgetfulness		[4]	

[Excerpt]

Fig. 2. Excerpt from the *mAIXcontrol* Matrix

In practical application there is a more complex failure chain at the basis of each cause-failure-effect triple than an average risk analysis is likely to show. Unfortunately, this supports a non-standardized evaluation of risks. Therefore, concerning risk evaluation of technology, manufacturing and use process, it would be meaningful to define different severity levels exclusively for personal injury like affecting health of patient, user or third party.

3.2   Taxonomy of Human Errors

Human and technical failures/causes which appear in the database have been filed and systematized based on the Human-Machine-System approach by Bogner [17]. The taxonomy of error deploys the three categories "Environment", "Human" and "Machine". Human errors in turn have been divided into six different categories, according to Norman's action cycle and Rasmussen's skill, rule and knowledge SRK-based classification [3][4]. Human errors include genotypes of errors as well as phenotypes and range from simple slips, like "unintended actions", over basic personal skills e.g. "lacking manual skills", up to mistakes like "misinterpretation" or "false estimation" (see Figure 3).

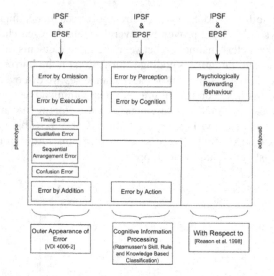

Fig. 3. Employed Categories in Human Error Taxonomy

Technical failures have accordingly been sorted into the two groups "predisposi-tion" and "loss", dividing system faults that are inherent to the design of the product from those that emerge during the use-cycle.

3.3   Principles of Risk Control

In addition to the categorization of causes and failures, the 41 principles of risk control have also been summarized, divided into four categories "Established", "Crea-tive", "Technical" and "Knowledge and Organization" (Figure 4).

Established			
[1] Compatibility	[5] Have Replacement in Store	[9] Exit Strategy	[13] Shift of Competence
[2] Repetition	[6] Maintenance	[10] Redundancy	[14] Wait for Reassurance
[3] Give Constraints	[7] Feedback	[11] Highlighting	[15] Display / Presentation /Illustration
[4] Simplicity	[8] Labeling	[12] Durability	

Technical			
[22] Discrete Adaption Mechanism	[26] Calibration at Beginning of Operation	[30] Thermal Behaviour	[34] Choice of Material
[23] Locking Mechanism	[27] Inseparability	[31] Avoid Lumen	[35] Anti-Adhesion
[24] Tender Velvet	[28] Enable Dismantlement	[32] Enable Free Movement	
[25] Accuracy of Fit	[29] Help for Assembly (Techn. Device)	[33] Alignment and Accessibility	

Creative		Knowledge and Organisation	
[16] Prevent	[20] Eliminate Disturbances	[36] Atention to Details in instructions	[40] Expertise and Culture
[17] Overdo	[21] Resistency	[37] Check and Control	[41] Supply Patient with Information
[18] Divide / Seperate		[38] Standards	
[19] Reduce		[39] Anamnesis of Patient	

Fig. 4. Principles of Risk Control

4   Characteristics of Countermeasures

The counteractions generated with the aid of the method comply with the aims of usability engineering and international risk management norms, concerning risk treatment procedures: inherent safety measures, protective measures or by providing safety information. During development of the methodology, further quality characteristics of counter measures and their graduation have been identified and elaborated: degree of innovation (low-medium-high), costs/effort relation (inexpensive-reasonable-expensive), affected system components (human-environment-machine), development phase (development-manufacture-use), impact on respective components of error chain (cause-failure-effect) and degree of inherence (inherent-protective-descriptive) (Figure 5).

Subsequently, these quality characteristics have been assessed regarding the application for the review process of generated countermeasures in the course of evaluation of *mAIXcontrol*.

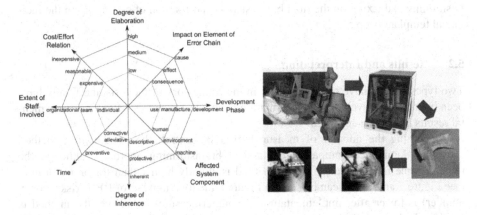

Fig. 5. Characteristics of Countermeasures   **Fig. 6.** Exemplary Planning, Manufacturing and Surgical Process Steps of an Individual Template for Total Knee Replacement Surgery, Finally the Simulated Intraoperative Surgical Process is Used for Evaluation of the Method

5   Evaluation

5.1   Experimental Set-Up

The method has been assessed with medical engineering students. The test population has been divided into two groups of 3 subjects, who had to deal independently from each other with the same exemplary case of total knee replacement within a flexible time frame, but a defined number of risks, which should have been minimized by application of counter measures. Potential risks in the use-process had already been identified and assessed at an earlier stage and information has been given to the participants in an orderly documented way, using the risk analysis software CARAD [16]. The subjects had to use the new methodology and the classical approach (brainstorming) in a first and second run, with the order turned the other way around. This helped to permit detection of memory biases. Homogeneous knowledge about the particular steps of the surgery process had been assured by providing participants with detailed information on the basis of free accessible expert commentaries in the on-hand risk analysis. Finally, participants completed a questionnaire on test-level basis.

Figure 6 shows the planning, manufacturing and the intraoperative surgical process steps of an individual positioning device for individual template (custom jig) guided total knee replacement [20]. Finally, only the surgical process (using the custom jig) has been used for application of the methodology in an evaluation study. The comprehensive process includes inter alia computer-based processing of anatomical data for planning of the patient-specific template (step 1), manufacture of the custom jig (step 2), drill holing and finishing of the individual template (step 3), intraoperative positioning and fixing on the tibia bone (step 4) and fixation of cutting jig to the individual template (step 5).

5.2   Results and Interpretation

Two types of data have been generated in the framework of the tests and finally have been interpreted. Psychometric information from questionnaires as well as experimental results have been collected.

Concerning the number of measures for risk control, the *mAIXcontrol* method shows predominance compared to classical brainstorming approach, although the required time for application of the method is slightly higher than for brainstorming (see Figure 7 and 8). As can be seen in Figure 8 the total number of RPN (risk priority number) is lower after implementation of countermeasures, whenever the method is employed, although the predominance of the method is weaker in the case of group B, where brainstorming was employed after the method. Countermeasures have been reviewed by a blind expert after the tests, in order to reassess the related RPNs. As a risk is typically characterized by the probability of its occurrence (O), the probability of detection (D) and the severity (S) of its outcome, the RPN is defined by:

$$RPN = O \times D \times S \tag{1}$$

As can be seen in Figure 7, risk priority numbers after implementation of countermeasures generated with the new method, are lower than in the case when brainstorming has been employed. This does also apply to the case, when brainstorming was employed after the method. Figure 5 illustrates how group A managed to reduce the total risk priority number from 170 to 145, when working with brainstorming and twice as much (down to 120), when working with the *mAIXcontrol*. In the second run, group B achieved a total RPN of 135, when working with *mAIXcontrol* and 140, when working with brainstorming.

Evaluation by questionnaires shows a "slight advantage" of *mAIXcontrol*, compared to conventional brainstorming. Although users prefer to work with conventional brainstorming, when referring to time/benefit – ratio, higher completeness of matrix-generated results and the potential learning effect for experienced users made 83% of the polled participants state that they would prefer the method, if they were able to choose between method and brainstorming for an equivalent task. Lower risk priority numbers, demonstrate a clear predominance of the *mAIXcontrol* method. The fact that the method significantly outperforms brainstorming in case of group A can be due to memory biases from sequential conduction (*mAIXcontrol* has been applied after brainstorming). Nevertheless, it is striking that the total RPN with application of brainstorming is higher in case of group B, although group B could have been able to benefit from prior experience with the *mAIXcontrol* application.

Test Subjects: Students Medical Engineering	Test Group A		Test Group B	
	Brainstorming	mAIXcontrol	mAIXcontrol	Brainstorming
Number of generated countermeasures	54	64	55	51
Required Time [in minutes]	50	63	80	50
Sum of RPN after Counter-measures and Reassessment of Risk (Reference RPN value: 170)	145	120	135	140

Fig. 7. Results from evaluation based on risk priority numbers

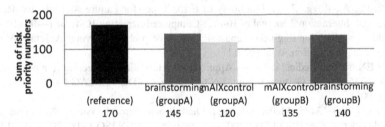

Fig. 8. Risk Priority Numbers Before and After Reassessment

6   Discussion

The first evaluation of the *mAIXcontrol* method in the framework of our feasibility study showed promising results. As observed in each of the two sessions, the use of the matrix requires a certain learning curve. The test subjects needed a learning time of more or less 15 minutes before a working routine had been adopted. This presumes a learning effect that increases time efficiency for experienced users. Best practice has been the approach of task sharing where a moderator (one subject), without any implements, is discussing each risk and potential countermeasures with the matrix-equipped team members. This proceeding enables higher communication rate and synchronicity of work, which turns out to be beneficial for performance.

Additionally, it has been observed that subjects do not always search for a defined cause-error combination on both axes, but run through complete lines of the matrix. The fact that all users have been novice users implicates a naturally higher expenditure of time. However, most participants rate the method as mainly self-explanatory, even for novice users. Additional time required with *mAIXcontrol* is compensated by qualitative advantages in total risk reduction, documentation and justification of counter measures, which in fact could be essential in the context of the official approval process of a medical device.

Acknowledgements. The *mAIXcontrol* methodology has been developed within the AiF/FQS project SysRisk which is funded by the Federal Ministry of Economics and Technology (BMWi).

References

1. Reason, J.: Human Error. Cambridge University Press (1990)
2. Kohn, K.T., Corrigan, J.M., Donaldson, M.: To Err Is Human: Building a Safer Health System. National Academy Press, Washington, DC (1999)
3. Rasmussen, J.: Skills, rules, knowledge; signals, signs, and symbols, and other distinctions in human performance models. IEEE Transactions on Systems, Man and Cybernetics 13, 257–266 (1983)
4. Norman, D.A.: The Design of Everyday Things. Doubleday/Currency, New York (1983)
5. Hollnagel, E.: Reliability and safety analysis: Context and control. Reliability Engineering & System Safety 52(3), 327–337 (1996)
6. Sutcliffe, A., Rugg, G.: A Taxonomy of Error Types for Failure Analysis and Risk Assessment. International Journal of Human-Computer Interaction 10(4), 381–405 (1998)
7. Gadd, K.: TRIZ for Engineers; enabling inventive problem solving. A John Wiley and Sons, Ltd., Publication, Wiley (2011)
8. DIN EN 62366: Medical devices - Application of usability engineering to medical devices (IEC 62366:2007); German version EN 62366:2008, VDE VERLAG GMBH, 10625 Berlin (2008)
9. DIN EN ISO 13485: Medical devices. Quality management systems. Requirements for regulatory purposes (ISO 13485:2003); German version EN ISO 13485:2003, BeuthVerlag GmbH, 10772 Berlin (2003)
10. DIN EN 14971: Medical devices - Application of risk management to medical devices (ISO 14971:2000); German version EN ISO 14971:2001, BeuthVerlag GmbH, 10772 Berlin (2000)
11. DIN EN 60601-1-6: Medical electrical equipment – part 1-6: general requirements for basic safety and essential performance – collateral standard: usability (60601-1-6:2007); VDE VERLAG GMBH, 10625 Berlin (2007)
12. DIN EN ISO 9241-110: Ergonomics of human-system interaction – Part 110: Dialogue principles (ISO 9241-110:2006); German version EN ISO 9241-110:2006, BeuthVerlag GmbH, 10772 Berlin (2006)
13. van der Peijl, J., Klein, J., Grass, C., Freudenthal, A.: Design for risk control: The role of usability engineering in the management of use-related risks. J. Biomed. Inform (2012)

14. Käppler, W.D.: Menschliche Fehler als Unfallursachen: Untersuchungen und Ergebnisse mit ARIADNE. In: Grandt, M. (ed.) Verlässlichkeit der Mensch Maschine-Interaktion: Deutsche Gesellschaft für Luft- und Raumfahrt e. V. Report 04-03, Bonn, S, pp. 197–212 (2004)

15. Rasmussen, J.: Reasons, causes and human errors. In: Rasmussen, J., Duncan, K., Leplar, J. (eds.) A New technology and human error, pp. 53–61. Wiley, Chichester (1987)

16. CARAD: Computer Aided Risk Analysis and Documentation, A Softwaretool for Risk Analysis and Documentation; SurgiTAIX AG (2012),
    `http://www.surgitaix.com/cms/index.php`

17. VDI 4006-2: Menschliche Zuverlässigkeit, Methoden zur quantitativen Bewertung menschlicher Zuverlässigkeit, VDI 4006-Teil2" Zu beziehen durch / Available from Beuth Verlag GmbH, 10772 Berlin (2003)

18. Janß, A., Lauer, W., Radermacher, K.: A New Model-based Approach for the User Interface Design of Medical Devices and Systems. In: Duffy, V.G. (ed.) Advances in Human Factors and Ergonomics in Healthcare, pp. 499–508. CRC Press -Taylor and Francis Group (2010)

19. Janß, A., Lauer, W., ChuembouPekam, F., Radermacher, K.: Using New Model-Based Techniques for the User Interface Design of Medical Devices and Systems. In: Roecker, C., Ziefle, M. (eds.) Human Centered Design of E-Health Technologies: Concepts, Methods and Applications, pp. 234–251. IGI Global, Hershey (2011)

20. Portheine, F., Ohnsorge, J.A.K., Schkommodau, E., Radermacher, K.: CT-Based Planning and Individual Template Navigation in TKA. In: Stiehl, J.B., Konermann, W.H., Haaker, R.G. (eds.) Navigation and Robotics in Total Joint and Spine Surgery, pp. 336–342. Springer, Heidelberg (2003)

Interactive System for Solving Children Communication Disorder

Wafaa M. Shalash, Malak Bas-sam, and Ghada Shawly

Information Technology department, King Abdul Aziz University
P.O Box 42808, Jeddah 21551, Saudi Arabia
Wafaa1@yahoo.com

Abstract. The recent development in information technology contributes significantly in solving special needed people problems. This paper describes an ongoing project to help those children suffering from speech disorder problems. The current application is an interactive game using speech recognition technology; kid can interact with an animated picture using his/her voice. There are several levels for improving the speaking skills of children at different stages. Firstly, by encouraging child just to produce sounds then by improving his/her pronunciation skills by pronouncing short vocal Arabic words. This application solves speech disorder problems such as difficulty producing speech, dysfluency, shuttering and voice disorders. The current work is pioneer in developing an Arabic language application and targeted to children aged from 2 years to 7 years.

Keywords: children speech disorder, speech recognition, interactive applications.

1   Introduction

Children speech or language disorder can be considered as a critical problem not only affecting the child and his own family but also the whole society. If the child doesn't receive the proper therapy in the proper time he/she may suffering from that problem the rest of his/her life not only on educational performance but on his/her opportunity to get good jobs and to communicate with the whole society.

The concept of communication disorders comprises a wide variety of problems in language, speech, and hearing. Speech and language impairments include articulation problems, voice disorders, fluency problems (such as stuttering), aphasia (difficulty in using words, sometimes as a result of a brain injury, viral infections, cardio-vascular accident, mental retardation), and delays in speech and/or language. Hearing impairments include partial hearing and deafness. Deafness refers to a kind of loss sufficient to make auditory communication difficult or impossible without amplification. A good number of communication disorders can equally result from other pathological conditions such as learning disabilities, cerebral palsy, mental retardation, or cleft lip or cleft palate [1].

Different researchers have studied speech and language dysfunctions depending on their disciplines and orientations. Not all speech variations are clinical problems.

A. Marcus (Ed.): DUXU/HCII 2013, Part II, LNCS 8013, pp. 462–469, 2013.

A speech difference is a problem if it is interferes with communicabilities attracts undue or negative, attention or causes the speaker to be emotionally disturbed or socially maladjusted[2].

Freeman & Silver [3] had noted that distinguished speech disorders are typically more difficult in children than adults, and most difficult in cerebral palsied subjects. However, these children are not placed in treatment for speech disorder until it was clear that they were not going to outgrow the problem in addition to limited professional and financial resources. As consequence, most subjects did not receive professional assistance until they were over 7 years old. In these older subjects, deviant speech patterns were firmly established [4].

Children suffering from communication disorders tend to manifest a number of peculiar cognito-behavioural features. For instance, a child with speech or language delays may present a variety of characteristics including the inability to follow directions, slow and incomprehensible speech, and pronounced difficulties in syntax and articulation. Articulation disorders are characterized by the substitution of one sound for another or the omission or distortion of certain sounds. Stuttering or dysfluency is a disorder of speech flow that most often appears between the ages of 3 and 4 years and may progress from a sporadic to a chronic problem. Stuttering may spontaneously disappear by early adolescence, but speech and language therapy should be considered. Typical voice disorders include hoarseness, breathiness, or sudden breaks in loudness or pitch. Voice disorders are frequently combined with other speech problems to form a complex communication disorder [1].

"Speech or Language Impairment" means a communication disorder, such as stuttering, impaired articulation, language impairment, or a voice impairment, that adversely affects a child's educational performance [4].

Types of Speech Disorder Includes:

- Dysfluency: an interruption in the flow of speech, such as stuttering e.g. some person who stutters may repeat the first part of a word (as in wa-wa-wa-water) or hold a single sound for a long time (as in caaaaaaake).
- Articulation or phonological disorders: difficulties with the pitch, volume or quality of the voice while the sound is formed e.g. Substituting a "w" for an "r" ("wabbit" for "rabbit"), omitting sounds ("cool" for "school"), or adding sounds to words ("pinanio" for "piano") are examples of articulation errors.
- Aphasia: is the loss of the ability to understand language, whether spoken or written, and occurs due to disturbances in the areas of the brain that are used in language processing.
- Dysarthria: Dysarthria refers to a difficulty in pronouncing certain sounds or words that is usually due to a problem with muscle control.
- Dyspraxia : is a motor learning difficulty that can affect planning of movements and co-ordination as a result of brain messages not being accurately transmitted to the body.
- Slurred Speech :speech in which words are not enunciated clearly or completely but are run together or partially eliminated

- Speech Disturbance : Difficulty with speech can be the result of problems with the brain or nerves that control the facial muscles, larynx, and vocal cords necessary for speech.
- Speech Impediment.
- The Language Disorders is the situation that the child has a large amount of vocabulary but he/she can't use them at sentences and doesn't use the grammatical patterns for making sentences.

While Types of Language Disorders includes:

- First type: improper use of words and their meanings.
- Second type: inability to express ideas, inappropriate grammatical patterns.
- Third type: reduced vocabulary and inability to follow directions.

As mentioned in the above sections speech disorder is a critical and important problem and it is better to find solutions for it in early stages to overcome its drawbacks. So, in the current work we tried to introduce an easy, cheap, and interactive solution for the families have child suffering from this problem and also for therapists.

The current work is an Arabic language application based on the idea that, a particular beneficial feature of human-computer interaction (HCI) is that children find them a "safe" and enjoyable experience. This can be explained by the fact that interaction with computers does not pose the expectations and judgment issues that are associated with social interaction. Computer systems tend to function in a controlled environment with minimal distractions and this makes them an attractive option for the education of autistic children [5]. Consequently this type of interaction elicits positive feelings, whereas communication with humans is frequently fraught with problems [6]. The positive feelings appear to be generic and uncorrelated with the type of software interface [7].

Out training strategy followed the suggested strategy illustrated on [4] to start by training speech muscles: by slow abdominal respiration to increase expiration and use air amount for speaking; first for voices then letters then words then sentence [4].

The current work is targeted to children ages from 2 years to 7 years.

2   Related Work

Many commercial application deal with speech disorder problems such as Speech-Language Pathologist Package[11] and Bungalow Software [12].

Regarding to Arabic reading applications for communication disorder therapy, there are relatively few software applications that are targeting speech disorder problems.

3   Methodology

Our proposed application consists of several levels in order to help in children speech disorder therapy. This application aims to help kids to learn and improve their communication skills in an easy, interactive manner, like playing a game. The current application main advantage is that it is in Arabic where most of the available commercial applications are in English. This application can be used easily at home, institution or any place. It also helps adults (therapists or parents) to keep tracking of the child progress by recording his/her score each level.

We combine animated picture and speech recognition technologies in order to develop the current system. The first level is very basic to help child to improve his/her speech skills and making sure that the child doesn't have any health problem preventing him from specking. This level aims to encourage the child to produce sounds. It provides an interesting interactive interface shows friendly simple objects. These objects start to animate as the child produces sounds and this behavior changes when sound threshold level increased in an interesting manner. For example, one interface story contains a car starts to move as a child starts to produce sounds and it will stop if he/she stops producing sound. Then, it changes to become a 2 racing cars as the child increases his/her voice (as shown if figure 1). Figure 2 and 3 show another two stories just like the first figure but with different animated object popular to children.

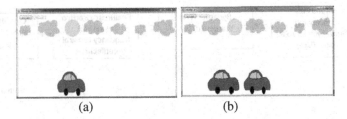

Fig. 1. Sample screenshots of the first level interactive interfaces (car story)

Fig. 2. Sample screenshots of the first level interactive interfaces (bird story)

(a)   (b)

Fig. 3. Sample screenshots of the first level interactive interfaces (girl and boy story)

The second stage is devoted to those children who got the ability to pronounce letters but in a wrong way, this stage aims to correct their language disorder problems by providing short vocal words such as cat or beer in Arabic (قطه – دب) with related pictures and encourage them to pronounce words correctly by producing clapping sounds, saying words in Arabic language such as "Good job" and rewarding children by giving them marks if they saying word correctly. This stage based on a simple speech recognition system   consists of pre-processing stage (Butter worth band-pass filter) for noise removal followed by Dynamic time warpping and feature extraction stage using Mel frequency Sepstral cofffecianat, finally performing classification stage by compaing the distance between   input features with the saved corresponding one from system database as shown in figure 4 [8 - 10].

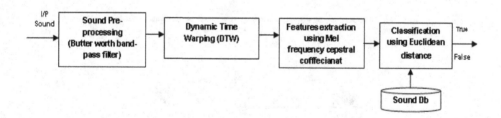

Fig. 4. Level 2 simple speech recognition system

(a)   (b)

Fig. 5. Sample screenshots of the second level interactive interfaces (Cat word)and (tree word)

The third level designed for improving the communication skills by involving the kids into a conversation and asking them to complete it in a right way but we still work on it and didn't finished.

4   Results and Discussion

The test was conducted on two groups of users 5 therapists and 10 parents as one group and 8 children their ages ranges from two and half years to seven years, six of them were girls as second group. The tests started by giving the each group (therapists, parents and children) an overview about our application, and then giving them tasks to perform. While the most three important parts of the system are Registration(for therapists and parents), Playing Level One and Playing Level Two(for children), the testing process will focus on those three parts. Testers observed tests and recorded information about time needed to perform each task and the number of correct clicks and wrong clicks. An interview is conducted with children about the software application and the problems they faced after using it.

The Following Are the Tasks Given to Users:.
Giving a certain users 6 tasks for testing our application that include:

1. Create an account that contains your information as supervisor's account.
2. Log in to your account that u had create it in pervious task.
3. Add a child with this information: (name : Muhammad Husain Ali ,gender : boy , birthday 18/3/2005 ,city : Jeddah , address : Al-Rawdah neighborhood , Phone No. : 02-6666776).
4. Make the child that you registered before start playing with the level that measure the child's ability to issue votes (Level One).
5. Make the child that you registered before start playing with the level that tests the child pronunciation (Level Two).
6. View the child statues from the children.

After observation of the testing process, the results of the usability test shows that all of 5 therapists and 8 of 10 of the parents did all the tasks directly and navigate through the application windows easily without mistakes. The children test results shows that for the first level 7 of 8 children play it in a short time, while in the second level test 6 of 8 play it in a short time. Generally the children impression was good and they like the animated pictures response a lot.

The results of the usability test show promising results for both speech therapist and kids. Most of the users performed the required task in a reasonable time and number of clicking.

After task session completion, participants of first group (therapists and parents) rated the System by six overall measures, these measures include:

1. Ease of use
2. Clarity of the buttons meaning.

3. Clarity of menus and its contents.
4. Clarify of help windows
5. The quality and consistency of colors and fonts.

Table-1 shows analysis of the results from the post test questionnaire.

Table 1. Analysis of post test questionnaire

Question	Answer	Sum	Average
Using the software was	very easy	12	80%
	Easy	2	14%
	Neither easy nor difficult	0	0%
	difficult	1	7%
	very difficult	0	0%
Clarity of button meanings	very clear and understandable	11	73%
	clear and somewhat	2	14%
	not clear	1	13%
Clarity menus and its contents	very clear and understandable	14	93%
	Somewhat clear	1	7%
	not clear	0	0%
Clarity of help windows	very clear and understandable	15	100%
	Somewhat clear	0	0%
	not clear	0	0%
The quality and consistency of fonts and colors	Comfortable and consistent	4	80%
	Somewhat Comfortable and consistent	1	20%
	Inconsistent and Uncomfortable	0	0%

5   Conclusion

We present an ongoing project to produce a software package to be used in the thereby of those children suffering from speech disorder in an interactive game manner. The current work covers two stages in our way to improve children communication skills. The first stage was concerning of encourage children to produce sounds and the second stage improving the pronunciation of letters through short vocal words in an interactive manner. We also provide a record for each child score through levels to help therapists and parents watching the child progress.

The main advantage of this application is that it is in Arabic where most of the applications available in market are in English. The application can be used easily at home, institution or any place so, it is an expensive way to overcome speech disorder problem.

In near future we aim to complete the third stage which helps children to pronounce long vocal words and sentences through long interactive stories combining animated cartoon characters with sound recognition to produce dialog system. We also aim to test the system with much more number of children.

References

1. Agbedo, C.U.: Communication Disorders in Children: A Case Study of Mimo Usama and Sele Yengi. International Journal of Communication: An Interdisciplinary Journal of Communication Studies 8(1) (2008)
2. Daniloff, R. (ed.): Articulation assessment and treatment issues, p. 247. College Hill press, sanDiego (1984)
3. Freeman, F., Silver, L.: Developmental Articulation Disorders compr. In: Kaplan, H., Sadock, B. (eds.) Textb of psychiat II, ch. 36. 3a, pp. 1804–1809 (1989)
4. Nawal, M., Elfiky, M., Basiony, S.: Research Journal of Medicine and Medical Sciences 4(1), 7–13 (2008)
5. Green, S.J.: Computer-based simulations in the education and assessment of autistic children. In: Rethinking the Roles of Technology in Education, Tenth International Conference on Technology and Education, vol. 1, pp. 334–336. Massachusetts Institute of Technology, Cambridge (1993)
6. Hutinger, P., Rippey, R.: How five preschool children with autism responded to computers,
   http://scott.mprojects.wiu.edu/~eccts/articles/autism1.html
7. Konstantinidis, E., Luneski, A., Frantzidis, C., Nikolaidou, M., Hitoglou-Antoniadou, M., Bamidis, P.: Information and Communication Technologies (ICT) for Enhanced Education of Children with Autism Spectrum Disorders. The Journal on Information Technology in Healthcare 7(5), 284–292 (2009)
8. Juang, B.-H., Chou, W., Lee, C.-H.: Minimum classification error rate methods for speech recognition. IEEE Transactions on Speech and Audio Processing 5(3), 257–265 (1997)
9. Molau, S., Pitz, M., Schlüter, R., Ney, H.: Computing Mel-frequency cepstral coefficients on the power spectrum. In: IEEE International Conference on Acoustics, Speech, and Signal Processing (ICASSP 2001), vol. 1, pp. 73–76 (2001)
10. Salvador, S., Chan, P.: FastDTW: Toward Accurate Dynamic Time Warping in Linear Timeand Space. IEEE Transactions on Biomedical. Engineering 43(4) (2007)
11. Special needs software: Speech-Language Pathologist Package (2011),
    http://www.laureatelearning.com/specials/slppack.html
12. Bungalow Software (2010), http://www.bungalowsoftware.com

Game-Based Interactive Media in Behavioral Medicine: Creating Serious Affective-Cognitive-Environmental-Social Integration Experiences

Alasdair G. Thin[1] and Marientina Gotsis[2]

[1] Heriot-Watt University, UK
[2] University of Southern California, USA
a.g.thin@hw.ac.uk, mgotsis@cinema.usc.edu

Abstract. The need to refocus health systems more towards prevention is now widely recognized, since most of the major disease conditions in the developed world have significant behavioral determinants. However, most efforts to date have been limited in their impact as they have generally failed to take account of the complex hierarchy of interacting social and environmental influences. The reality of life in a networked society is such there is now an additional set of corresponding influences that arise in the digital world(s) that an individual inhabits. Concurrent with these developments, the rapid emergence of a wide range of digital technologies offers a whole new set of affordances and potential health applications. We therefore argue for the design of digital supportive environments that utilize mobile devices, sensors, social media, game worlds and mechanics, in order to create transformative experiences that can effect large scale positive health behavior change.

Keywords: health promotion, games, supportive environment, empowerment.

1 Introduction

The obesity epidemic has grown to such an extent that a former US Surgeon General has deemed it to be a threat to US national security [1]. While the need to shift the focus of health systems upstream and devote more effort and resources towards prevention is now widely recognized, efforts to date have generally had limited success. One of the main reasons for this lack of impact is the complex nature of the interactions of a hierarchy of social and environmental factors that influence every individual's health behaviors [2]. Around the same time that concern was being expressed about military preparedness, the US Army, in recognition of the widespread popularity of video games, developed the highly popular video game "America's Army" to increase awareness of the many potential career opportunities in the military [3]. The enormity of the size of many of health behavior issues that need to be tackled means that any proposed solutions will only be viable if they are scalable to a population level. While some specific individuals/issues may need the intervention of trained health professionals, using digital media is maybe the only realistically scalable and cost-effective way forward. There is therefore a clear need for carefully designed

A. Marcus (Ed.): DUXU/HCII 2013, Part II, LNCS 8013, pp. 470–479, 2013.

tools and services that support this endeavor. Many different models of health behavior have been developed over the years [4]. Most tend to focus on the factors that influence the conscious, rational decision making process. Health promotion interventions have then been designed based on these models with the intention of influencing one or more of these in the hope of effecting a positive change in individuals' health behaviors. In a recent study of a weight loss intervention, four leading models were only able to predict a modest proportion of the total variance (20-30%) in the outcome [5]. While this is clearly better than nothing, it starkly illustrates the significant problem with many current approaches.

2   Supportive Environments

As the limited impact of early interventions targeted at individuals' behaviors became apparent, alternative models of health behaviors were proposed that were not solely focused on the individual but including both their immediate and wider social and environmental contexts [6]. This change in perspective has resulted in the recognition of the need to develop "Supportive Environments" that positively support health [7-9]. However, they are generally conceived as being concerned with the creation of physical environmental and social conditions that make the "healthy option" the "easy choice." Sometimes, positive changes can be achieved relatively easily and quickly (e.g. removal of vending machines from schools), other issues will require massive amounts of resources and whole scale changes (e.g. making urban environments conducive to physically active lifestyles). It is therefore, important that such considerations are automatically part of any new development or regeneration projects.

While there is a hierarchy of social and environmental influences surrounding the physical world of a given individual, the reality of life in a networked society is such there is now an additional set of corresponding influences that arise in the digital world(s) that an individual inhabits. In recognition of the many ways in which digital technologies and media have permeated our lives, we have recently proposed an extension to the existing social-ecological model [2] that we have called the *Cyber-Ecological Model* [10]. In addition to the existing concentric spheres of influence in the physical world, our new model adds another parallel set of influences that arise in the digital "world(s)" that people inhabit and that these two sets of influences have at their confluence the individual and their avatar(s). Furthermore, as time progresses, it is anticipated that there will be increasing amounts of interaction between physical and digital influences. However, given the way digital media can transcend physical distance, the impact of more remote digital influences is less likely to be diminished and transnational influences may even have greater significance.

Concurrent with these developments, the rapid emergence of a wide range of digital technologies offers a whole new set of affordances and potential health applications. Mobile location-based media can be used to places digital layers over a current user's surroundings. Such layers have the potential to augment the current environment and provide additional information and/or emphasize aspects positive to health and potentially de-emphasize negative ones. A different approach may be for the layer to present an alternate reality, whereby a game is played out in the real world and involves assigning alternative meanings to real objects such that they become game artifacts. There is also significant potential to use social media to create a supportive social context. By connecting up users, new forms of peer support can be facilitated, especially if they center on a shared goal, or the supporter constitutes a significant other to the user. It may also be possible to shift social norms by making positive health behavior more visible through social media. Given the imperative to act, it has been pointed out that supportive environments based on digital technology [11] could be designed and built in a much short time and at a fraction of the cost. Thus, it is our view that carefully designed digital supportive environments have significant potential for health promotion and warrant serious consideration.

It is worth for a moment considering the factors that appear important for successful behavior change. In order to try and elicit them, a comprehensive study [12] using semi-structured interviews with almost 400 individuals who had achieved varying degrees of positive health behavior changes was undertaken. The two most commonly cited facilitating factors were "feeling better" and "social support" and indicate that particular attention should be paid to affective and social influences when developing an intervention. In the digital realm, perhaps the best example is the Nike+ system which has attracted over 5 million users [13] and has been referred to as the "World's Biggest Running Club" [14]. While not explicitly designed as a health promotion intervention, the system is intended to attract new users and help them to keep physically active and by doing so benefit the company financially via increased sportswear sales. The system uses sensors to track physical activity and combines this with individual and group challenges, personalized feedback, social interaction, and support, and also game elements including status levels. It is evident from even this brief consideration, that there are many potential new avenues to explore to develop more effective forms of health promotion interventions.

3   Games for Health

There is growing interest in using video games for health applications [15] with much of this interest arising from the fact that they are now a mainstream medium, incorporate high levels of interactivity, and are *"fun"* to play. Neurophysiological research has demonstrated the existence of affective (i.e., emotional) brain circuits devoted to play that appear to be conserved in many mammalian species [16] and it has been postulated that the role of play is in providing *"food for thought"* for the brain. From a sociological perspective, Huizinga [17] in his seminal account of the historical development of human culture and institutions, argues that play has acted as a significant cultural force down through the centuries. In historical terms, digital games are a very recent invention. Compared to traditional games, digital games often have a strong narrative aspect [18]. Storytelling is another ancient cultural phenomenon that has acted as a medium to convey knowledge, insight, and wisdom. In digital games players are often on some form of journey or quest, and many games can and are designed to impact emotionally on players [19]. Thus, from both individual (neurophysiological) and social perspectives, play would appear to have significant potential as a catalyst for change.

4   Affective-Cognitive-Environmental-Social Integration

The *Empowerment Approach* [20] to health promotion has been put forward by Tones and Tilford as a more ideologically sound and practical alternative to existing educational and preventative approaches. This new approach has the ultimate aim of ensuring that individuals and communities actually posses *"genuine potential for making choices"* via three distinct strategies: building social capital, empowering individuals, and creating supportive environments. The *Empowerment Approach* is underpinned by the *Health Action Model* (HAM) [21] which Tones developed in the mid 1980s in response to the issues surrounding increased intravenous drug use. The HAM explicitly incorporates affective influences on health behavior, given that drug use can be *"genuinely and powerfully rewarding"* [21]. The HAM includes both cognitive and affective aspects of an individual's mental processes. There is a three way interaction between these two (intra-individual) processes and the surrounding social norms which give rise to discrete behavioral intentions. What determines whether or not a given intention is translated into a discrete action is determined by the balance of facilitating factors and social and environmental barriers. This process is illustrated across the center of Figure 1. Each discrete action will then generate either positive or negative feedback that then modulates future intentions.

An understanding of the nature and characteristics of each of the specific processes in the HAM provide insight into the way the empowerment approach can be implemented and will be discussed shortly. But, first it is necessary to consider other aspects of Figure 1 in more detail. We have previously discussed the reality of life in a networked society and how our *Cyber-Ecological Model* incorporates the associated digital influences. By overlaying these spheres on the HAM in Figure 1, we are acknowledging that social *Norms* arise outside the individual in both the physical and digital worlds. In the physical domain, the degree of influence of more distal sources is shown to taper, whereas the in the digital domain they are assumed not to diminish. With regard to *Facilitators* and *Barriers*, the many new affordances of different digital technologies would appear to offer a whole new set of facilitating factors, but it also has to be pointed out that there may be new types of barriers that arise in this domain too.

Behavioral Intentions arise out of the interactions between an individual's *Belief* and *Motivation Systems* and social *Norms* that the individual is exposed to. The *Belief System* is the cognitive aspect of the HAM comprises beliefs about the costs, benefits and seriousness in relation to specific health issues. However, their influence on behavioral intention is modulated by the *Motivation System*. The *Belief System* has a more stable and enduring aspect (personality) designated *Self-Concept* and include beliefs the person holds their *susceptibility* to specific disease conditions and about their ability to act (i.e., *self-efficacy* and *perceived locus of control*). In a study investigating why playing video games is enjoyable [22] evidence was found to indicate that game play was meeting the three basic psychological needs (Competence, Autonomy, and Relatedness) posited by Self-Determination Theory [23]. Being able to exhibit competence in performing tasks enables an individual to increase *self-efficacy* and having autonomy to act implies an internal *locus of control*. Finally, relatedness has correspondence with the *sense of community* aspect of the motivation system and is discussed in the next section.

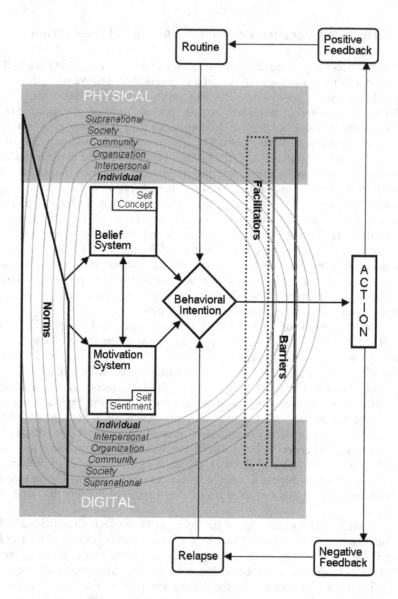

Fig. 1. Combined Cyber-Ecological and Health Action Models

The *Motivation System* involves affective processes and includes an individual's *Values* and *Attitudes*. However, these may be overridden by more basic physiological (e.g. hunger, pain, and sex) or pharmacological (e.g. legal and illegal drugs) drives. Furthermore changing positive or negative affective states (feelings and moods) may have an inhibitory or excitatory influence on behavioral intention. There is also a personality aspect to the motivation system termed *Self-Sentiment* and incorporates the constructs of *self-esteem*, *sense of community*, *existential control*, and *achievement motivation*. Self-esteem concerns how an individual values themselves and how they are valued by others and how well they can achieve goals valued both by themselves and by the people around them. Existential control involves the attribution of meaning to events, normally to diminish the perceived threat [24]. It is very interesting to note that these constructs have correspondence with a large scale survey of 3,000 MMORPG players [25] which revealed three distinct groupings of play factors that motivated them: Achievement, Community, and Immersion. While the first two are self-evident, the third requires some explanation. Play factors that comprised Immersion included Discovery, Role-Playing, Customization and Escapism, all of which involve the player in the process of attributing meaning to game events/artifacts.

The nature of *Norms* in terms of spheres of influence has already been discussed. At this point it is worth adding that it is how an individual perceives the prevalence of a given norm, their strength of their motivation to conform and the actions and attitudes of significant others. *Facilitating* factors at an individual level these include amongst other things supporting skills concerning social interaction and self-regulation. Beyond the individual these include social and environmental support (*making the healthy option the easy choice*). In contrast, *Barriers* represent external factors which block positive behavioral intentions. Feedback after a discrete action can be either positive or negative. *Positive Feedback* will help to reinforce a particular action such that it becomes a routine (habit). Alternatively, *Negative Feedback* will diminish the possibility of habit formation. At the time that the HAM was developed, Tones [21] highlighted the fact that there were then no positive affective approaches (only negative; e.g., shock tactics) available to behavioral health professionals. While that might have been the case 25 years ago, game-based interactive media have now reached a level of advancement and sophistication that they can be used to create compelling combined cognitive and affective experiences.

5   Creating Serious Integration Experiences for Health Promotion

Having considered the comprehensive nature of the *Empowerment Approach*, we therefore wish to argue for the design and development of digital supportive environments that utilize mobile devices, sensors, social media, game worlds and mechanics, in order to create transformative experiences that can effect large scale positive health behavior change. For example attractive, competent role model characters could promote self-esteem [26] and empathic agents could learn about a player's values and reflect back positive attitudes. In contrast, an in-game buddy, or various forms of group interactions could serve to challenge a player's values and characters exhibiting inconsistent behavior and/or disrupting what is comfortable to believe could promote reflection and discussion. Also, an in-game "*Health Economy*" [27] could be designed such that a player's drive for gratification is moderated by realistically reflecting their game actions (both negative and positive) in the penalties and rewards applied to their "*Health Score.*" Finally, a game could maximize appeal by coming across as lighthearted (to overcome any initial apprehension) and heighten impact by using carefully choreographed changes in the emotions elicited.

Designing and developing such digital supportive environments will be a significant undertaking requiring multi-disciplinary teams. In an attempt to demonstrate the wide-ranging potential of such an endeavor, we have listed each of the above model components along with a potential intervention objective and a corresponding design principle or feature in Table 1 (*Intentions*) and Table 2 (*Actions*). This is only a initial attempt at compiling such a list, but we would anticipate that a compendium of relevant design patterns would be developed in the future.

6   Limitations

The empowerment approach involves three distinct strategies of individual empowerment, the development of social capital and environmental improvement. The combined affordances available from integrating sensors, augmented and alternative realities, social media, and games can be used to design experiences that can act in all three strategic areas. While social/environmental barriers can be diminished by constructive an alternative world lens through which to view them by altering their meaning/value/significance, it has to be acknowledged that this will not negate the need for improvements in the physical environment. Of course, there is also the possibility that such interventions can act as mobilizing forces for community action and political lobbying/demand for change. There is also the possibility that game-based health promotion approaches may be taken less seriously precisely because they are games. However, if carefully designed, it seems likely that they would be a significant improvement on current practice. In order, to fully exploit the design approach we are advocating to health promotion approaches there is a clear need for a systematic program of research given the complexity both of human behavior and the approach advocated.

7   Conclusion

Carefully designed digital supportive environments based on an empowerment approach to health promotion and which utilizes mobile devices, sensors, social media, game worlds and mechanics, in order to create transformative experiences would appear to have significant potential both in terms of reach and cost effectiveness to effect large scale positive health behavior change and warrant a comprehensive program of research and development.

Table 1. Example Design Principles and Features aimed at Behavioral Intentions

Model Component		Potential Intervention Objective	Example Design Principle/ Feature
Belief System	Beliefs	clarify beliefs	present dilemmas where player has to make choices based on cost/benefit trade-offs
	Self-Efficacy	increase belief in ability to perform specific actions	fine-graded challenges
	Perceived Locus of Control	shift towards internal locus of control	ensure player is able to exert a high level of control in the game world
	Susceptibility	clarify beliefs about susceptibility	design a selection of game events to occur with varying but discernable probabilities
Motivation System	Values and Attitudes	clarify values and attitudes	dynamically adjust game values (economy) in response to player actions
	Drives	provide alternative forms of gratification	carefully target game rewards
	Self-Esteem -Self Achievement	facilitate achievement	incorporate multiple levels and permit player to have some choice in difficulty level
	Self-Esteem -Social Achievement	facilitate social recognition of achievement	incorporate status badges, social endorsement functions, empathic non-player characters
	Sense of Community	community building	incorporate social media functionality
	Existential Control	opportunities for customization, discovery and role-play	create a coherent game world and avatars that players can customize
	Achievement Motivation	meaningful challenges, progression	balance challenges to ability level of players
Norms	Perceived Prevalence of social norms	increased encounters with positive role models	include several different non-player characters that can act as positive role models to players

Table 2. Example Design Principles and Features aimed at Behavioral Actions

Model Component		Potential Intervention Objective	Example Design Principle/ Feature
Facilitating Factors	Social Interaction Skills	require collaboration	include team challenges
	Self-Regulation Skills	include time management, checklists, reminders, self-monitoring and journaling functions	support personal skill development and integrate supportive functions with players own tools (e.g. SMS reminders, calendar functions)
	Social Support	mentoring/ buddies/ peer support	incorporate mentoring tasks into game play from more experienced players
	Supportive Environment	location/contextual awareness, provision of relevant information/choices	use location sensing to provide additional contextual information
Barriers	Social	altered meaning/ influence	use game narrative to give altered meaning to barrier and/or internal game economy to increase the benefit of overcoming the barrier
	Environmental	altered meaning/ influence	use game narrative to give altered meaning to barrier and/or internal game economy to increase the benefit of overcoming the barrier
Feedback	Positive	where appropriate increase/ supplement	use game rewards to provide additional positive feedback
	Negative	where appropriate decrease or increase/ supplement	modulate negative feedback, although this will need to be done with great care

Acknowledgements. This work has been funded in part by the EU under the FP7, in the Games and Learning Alliance (GALA— http://www.galanoe.eu) Network of Excellence, Grant Agreement no. 258169. The authors would like to acknowledge all the people the world over who have: inspired us to play; taught us how to play; designed and/or organized the games we have played; dared to play with us either as team mates or opponents.

References

1. SFGatecom,
   http://www.sfgate.com/health/article/Obesity-a-threat-to-U-S-security-Surgeon-2686994.php
2. Kok, G., Gottlieb, N.H., Commers, M., Smerecnik, C.: The ecological approach in health promotion programs: a decade later. Am. J. Health Promot. 22, 437–442 (2008)
3. Zichermann, G., Linder, J.: Game-Based Marketing. John Wiley & Sons, Hoboken (2010)

4. U.S. Department of Health and Human Services.: Theory at a Glance. A Guide for Health Promotion Practice. National Institutes of Health, Washington, DC (2005)

5. Palmeira, A.L., Teixeira, P.J., Branco, T.L., et al.: Predicting short-term weight loss using four leading health behavior change theories. Int. J. Behav. Nutr. Phys. Act. 4, 14 (2007)

6. McLeroy, K.R., Bibeau, D., Steckler, A., Glanz, K.: An ecological perspective on health promotion programs. Health Educ. Q. 15, 351–377 (1988)

7. World Health Organization, http://www.who.int/healthpromotion/conferences/previous/ottawa/en/

8. European Commission, http://ec.europa.eu/health/ph_determinants/life_style/nutrition/documents/nutrition_wp_en.pdf

9. U.S. National Physical Activity Plan, http://www.physicalactivityplan.org/theplan.php

10. Palmeira, A.L., Thin, A.G.: Active video games as an example of a cyber-ecological approach to health promotion. In: ISBNPA Annual Conference, Minneapolis, MN (2010)

11. Thin, A.G.: Interactive and exercise-generating gaming/video games, active gaming. In: Diet, Physical Activity and Health – A European Platform for Action, Brussels, Belgium (2008)

12. Currie, C.E., Amos, A., Hunt, S.: The dynamics and process of behavioural change in five classes of health-related behaviour-findings from qualitative research. Health Educ. Res. 6, 443–453 (1991)

13. Cendrowski, S.: Nike's new marketing mojo. Fortune Magazine (February 27, 2012)

14. Wired, http://www.wired.com/medtech/health/magazine/17-07/lbnp_nike

15. Games for Health Project, http://gamesforhealth.org/about/

16. Panksepp, J.: Affective Neuroscience. Oxford University Press, New York (1998)

17. Huizinga, J.: Homo Ludens. Beacon Press, Boston (1955)

18. Juul, J.: Half-Real: Video Games between Real Rules and Fictional Worlds. MIT Press, Cambridge (2005)

19. Mandryk, R.L., Atkins, M.S., Inkpen, K.M.: A continuous and objective evaluation of emotional experience with interactive play environments. In: CHI 2006: Proceedings of the SIGCHI Conference on Human Factors in Computing Systems, pp. 1027–1036 (2006)

20. Tones, K., Tilford, S.: Health Promotion: Effectiveness, Efficiency and Equity, 3rd edn. Nelson Thornes, Cheltenham (2001)

21. Tones, K.: Devising strategies for preventing drug misuse: the role of the Health Action Model. Health Educ. Res. 2, 305–317 (1987)

22. Ryan, R.M., Rigby, C.S., Przybylski, A.: The motivational pull of video games: A self-determination theory approach. Motiv. Emotion. 30, 347–363 (2006)

23. Ryan, R.M., Deci, E.L.: Self-determination theory and the facilitation of intrinsic motivation, social development, and well-being. Amer. Psych. 55, 68–78 (2000)

24. Lewis, F.M.: The concept of control: a typology and health-related variables. Adv. Health Ed. Prom. 2, 277–309 (1987)

25. Yee, N.: Motivations for play in online games. Cyberpsychol. Behav. 9, 772–775 (2006)

26. Lieberman, D.A.: Interactive Video Games for Health Promotion: Effects on Knowledge, Self-Efficacy, Social Support, and Health. In: Street, R.L., Gold, W.R., Manning, T. (eds.) Health promotion and interactive technology: theoretical applications and future directions, Lawrence Erlbaum Associates, Mahwah (1997)

27. Barr, P., Khaled, R., Boyland, J., Biddle, R.: Feeling strangely fine: The well-being economy in popular games. In: IJsselsteijn, W.A., de Kort, Y.A.W., Midden, C., Eggen, B., van den Hoven, E. (eds.) PERSUASIVE 2006. LNCS, vol. 3962, pp. 60–71. Springer, Heidelberg (2006)

A Mobile Prototype for Clinical Emergency Calls

Cornelius Wille[1], Thomas Marx[1], and Adam Maciak[2]

[1] University of Applied Sciences, Bingen, Germany
{wille,marx}@fh-bingen.de
[2] Institute for Neuroradiology, University Hospital of Mainz, Germany
am@avallia.com

Abstract. In case of an emergency within a hospital, all available doctors get alarmed through a central collecting point. Only the doctor arriving first at the patient undertakes the medical treatment. All other doctors needlessly interrupt their current treatments or standby service. This article presents a prototype, to locate and alarm safely the nearest and available doctor. Mobile devices (smartphones und tablets based on Android or iOS) are used for localization, alarming and confirmation. Beside the localization in closed buildings the daily use of the prototype was tested. This incorporated the smooth integration into clinical information systems, the easy to use interface as well as the availability and robustness of the solution.

Keywords: emergency calls, indoor localization, paging, clinical information systems, mobile solution, eHealth.

1 Objectives

All business processes in hospitals are based upon *clinical information systems*. Besides data on the hospital's organization structure and on patients, these information systems encompass more and more context related information, like medical knowledge, guidelines or availability of resources. At night and on weekends 2-3 doctors attend 80 to 120 patients. Today, in case of clinical emergencies a notice is generated and distributed through clinical information systems, informing all doctors with a pager. This pager is an additional device, probably replaced by a smartphone in future.

We designed and evaluated a *prototype for clinical emergency calls* [1] which can be integrated into clinical information systems. This prototype locates and safely pages by smartphone only the nearest doctor depending on his availability.

2 Prototype

2.1 Localization within Buildings

Because of missing GPS signals in buildings, we decided to implement the localization upon Wi-Fi data, assuming complete Wi-Fi coverage for a building. To assure

A. Marcus (Ed.): DUXU/HCII 2013, Part II, LNCS 8013, pp. 480–487, 2013.

quick and safe alarming, all devices were made to send their current position continuously to the server, automatically excluding "lost" devices from the alarming
process on server side.

In order to calculate the most current whereabouts, three different approaches were
tested:

1. *Radio cell method*, blending relative signal strengths from different access points
   together into a location characteristic, see [2].
2. *Triangulation method*, implementing distance measurement via signal propagation
   time or through signal strength, see [3], [4].
3. *Table based methods* using measured reference points, see [5].

The radio cell method showed inaccurate results, especially for different locations
being strongly influenced the same signal. For the triangulation approach the correct
compensation of absorption [5] was probed, induced by the different wall consisten-
cies, furniture and other objects.   While these absorptions make it difficult to produce
accurate results, these phenomena even proved to be helpful for the third method.
Comparing the pros and cons of all three approaches, the table based method finally
showed the best test results.

To apply the table based method, the buildings have to be metered upfront in the
following way:

1. Identify all distinguishing position points within all rooms and floors.
2. Measure and register the Wi-Fi data ("fingerprints") for all reference points
   (weighted signal intensity to "visible" access points, identified by their MAC address). Within out testing we found out that we need 120 seconds per reference
   point to balance out fluctuations (median).
3. Built a graph by connecting reference points (vertices) that interlink directly to
   each other.
4. Annotate the distance between reference points (in meters) to each edge of the
   graph. Distances within staircase are weighted by factor.

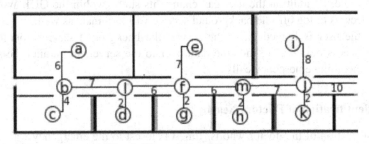

Fig. 1. Floor with weighted graph

We built a tiny app for Android and iOS to support the metering. This app sends the reference point data to the server while the weighted edges have to be added manually on server side.

Fig.1 shows a floor represented by a weighted graph. A positioning service was implemented to run in the background of the mobile app. Test series showed that scan duration of 10 seconds (delivering approx. 11 scan results) provided satisfactory stable values. Unstable access points dropping out of the 11 scans were weighted by 75%. The measured signals are send continuously (e.g. every 2 minutes) to the server and get matched with the fingerprints. To become more tolerant against minor signal aberrations, our table based method applies *Euklid's distance function*, as proposed in [2], see **Fig.2**.

$$\sqrt{\sum \left(s_{ap}^{reference\ tuple} - s_{ap}^{messured} \right)^2}$$

Fig. 2. Euklid's distance function

Within our tests the table based method always identified the correct floor and was off 10 meters in worst case ever observed. We detected no significant differences between iOS and Android based devices. The scans consume only about 2% processor load, leaving the system in energy save mode with no implications to other apps running in parallel.

2.2   Notification of the Current Position

Starting our prototype, the user initially confirms his availability within the Main-Screen of the app (see **Fig. 3**). Herby, the app connects to the server, synchronizes the settings and starts the background service, see **Fig. 4**. The ConnectedScreen is displayed. Running the main functionality in background allows the user to use its mobile device for any other tasks in parallel. The GUI of the prototype in the ConnectedScreen can be put in background without affecting the functionality of the background service. In addition the user can change its status within the GUI. Whenever the user decides to log off, the background service will terminate as well.

While the user is logged on to the server, the background service continuously scans for access points and sends the data over to the server. In parallel the service listens to incoming emergency calls.

2.3   Identification of Doctors Nearby

The identification of the doctor who is (timely) closest to the emergency was understood as a graph problem. Rooms represented vertices while the option to move from one room to another was modeled by vertices plus annotations (distance). To optimize response times the calculation of paths was pre-computed by the *Bellmann-Ford*

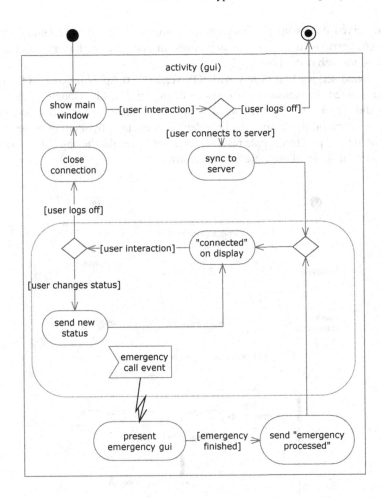

Fig. 3. Front end (activities MainScreen and ImageScreen)

algorithm [6], another option would have been to apply the *all pairs shortest path* algorithm. Obviously the hospital's graph model and the calculated paths have to be updated regularly to reflect changes, like new doors or construction areas.

2.4   Alarming Process

For the alarming process we evaluated two different technologies:

1. Push notification service The push notification service allows to signal incoming messages within an average of 1.4 seconds. It even wakes up iOS devices from version 3.0 and higher from the *enhanced standby mode*. But there are two problems that make the notification service inapplicable: Push notifications are funneled through Apples PUSH server with no guaranteed processing times.

We observed delays up to 6 minutes. Secondly only the iPhone family supports push notifications, iPads have to stay online discharging the battery. In context of Android no such restrictions apply.

2. Background service Fortunately with iOS version 4.0 Apple introduced the option to run (limited) background processes from an app, just like Google's Android always did. With iOS so called *local notifications* must be send to a background process in special mode, to wake up a device from stand by. Putting these kinds of apps onto the App Store, apple reserves the right to revoke the app without reasons. In context of Android there are no such restrictions.

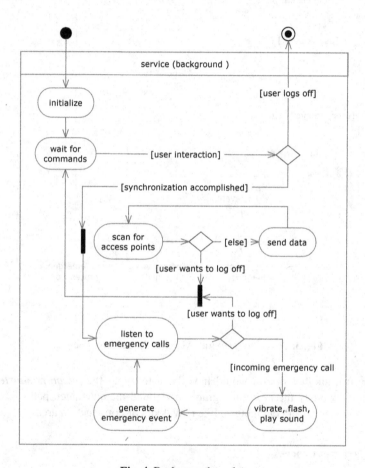

Fig. 4. Background service

The background service of our prototype waits for incoming notifications from *NetworkManager*. In case of arrival, see **Fig. 4**, the user is alarmed (sound, vibration) plus the *EmergencyScreen* is displayed by the front end activity. The background service continues to wait for notifications right after notifying the front end. The *EmergencyScreen* requests the user to accept or decline the call and will only stop after having received an input. The result is given back to the server that may alarm additional doctors.

3   Case Study

3.1   Mobile Devices and Clinical Information Systems

More and more mobile devices are used for so called *mHealth applications* in hospitals. Here, specific demands apply, like the ability to be sanitized, certificate on non-interference, usability, availability, battery performance etc. on to a reasonable price to allow general provisioning.

For our *eHealth prototype* [7] we evaluated standard devices (iPad), dedicated devices (Dell Streak) and design studies (Intel Motion Computing C5). We diagnosed significant differences. Especially the operating system has significant influence on professional use, because vendors of clinical information systems might lack native clients.

3.2   Integration of mHealth-Applications

Specific requirements for *mHealth applications* within clinical use are: complete encryption, strict authentication, authorization, perfect usability and self-explaining interfaces. Medical staff got to be assisted in its daily work, supported by up to date contextual data and operations that are executed directly identically as upon workstations.

In corporation with our partner, the University Hospital Mainz, three different mHealth solutions were evaluated to integrate our prototype: *drchrono iPad app* [8], *checkPAD MED* [9] und *myCare2x* [10].

Besides evaluating the aforementioned criteria the applications were rated upon openness and ease of integration, using common medical standards, like the communication standard *HL7* [11], the image communication standard *DICOM* [12] or the *LOINC-Code-System* [13].

All three products implement well the core requirements for clinical environments. *checkPAD MED* and *drchrono* showed best usability and integration option for our prototype [7], allowing our server to receive information emergency call including the location.

3.3   Testing within the University Hospital of Mainz

For a case study we implemented the following setting: The 5th and 6th floor of the University of Mainz at Staudinger Weg 9 was chosen. All rooms, floors, the staircase, Wi-Fi access points were identified and became part of the building's model. No additional technical infrastructure was added. Reference points were determined by metering the individual Wi-Fi perception plus the distance to nearby reference points. A weighted graph was built upon these reference points. Three testees were equipped with Android devices (different HW and OS versions) plus the prototype app. A note-book running the server engine was added to the network. An inspector constantly compared the testee's location to the reported one on the server. Test alarms were send to different devices and locations. The case study ran on a single day.

The case study delivered the following findings: The app constantly delivered acceptable location data without crashing. Only once we observed a significant fault of 10 meters which was still acceptable. The alarming process, identifying the doctor close by, worked very reliable without any problems. During the complete tests, the doctors approved an easy to use interface. There were brief instructions given before-hand, no tutorial. Neither client nor server software were able to detect connection loss in time (limit set to 3 minutes). Finally the battery consumption of competing apps and phone usage became critical for our test plus we were not able to detect user failures, e.g. whenever a doctor left his device in his jacket.

4   Summary and Outlook

We presented a full functional prototype for an intelligent paging of doctors on clini-cal emergency calls. The prototype worked on Android and iOS devices and inte-grated well with clinical information systems. A case study in a real hospital infra-structure proved that the prototype was able to alarm the doctor being close-by the emergency.

Tests showed that there is still some room for improvement, e.g. on calculating the exact location. Here, the correction of measuring faults and to achieve a better affinity degree *Spearmans rank correlation coefficient* [14] should be investigated on, using different antennas simultaneously. The observed sporadic skipping between rooms might get fixed by including historical data into calculations. Beside these tweaks it is important, that the Wi-Fi fingerprints get regularly update to respect changes.

Future tests should include additional building types, because the tested University Hospital of Mainz is a homogenous, mainly column supported building. In production scenarios the demand of selective alarming should be relaxed to probably three doc-tors at the same time. Features like end-to-end encryption, anonymization of data and battery performance protection have to be added, too.

Besides these improvements there is still one critical problem to solve: it still might take too much time to recognize whenever clients loose server connection. Constant keep alive signals or other brute force approaches will quickly discharge the battery.

References

1. Drchrono Inc., Electronic Medical Records (2012), https://drchrono.com/ (retrieved February 11, 2012)
2. Friedrich, R.: eHealth - KlinischeInformationssysteme (Bachelor Thesis). Mainz: Joh. Gutenberg-University Mainz (2011)
3. Healthcare Consulting GmbH, mycare3x (2007), http://www.mycare2x.de/ (retrieved February 11, 2012)

4. HL7 Deutschland e.V, HL7 (2012),
    http://www.hl7.de/standard/standards.php (retrieved February 11, 2012)
5. Jehl, G.: Deterministic WLAN Position Determination, Universität Freiburg (February 7, 2007), http://de.pdfsb.com/readonline/596c5a416641743057484231 4148356855513d3d-4508901 (retrieved February 11, 2012)
6. Lange, K.: Taschenbuch der Hochfrequenztechnik, 5th edn. Springer, Heidelberg (1992)
7. Leinberger, M.: EinNotrufsystemmit Andoid Smartphones (Bachelor Thesis). Joh. Gutenberg University Mainz, Mainz (2011)
8. Lohmann & Birkner Health Care Consulting GmbH (2012), http://www.lohmann-birkner.de/lohmann/wDeutsch/HP_Checkpad/Index.php (retrieved February 11, 2012)
9. Meyer, M.: Kommunikationstechnik, Friedr. Vieweg & Sohn Verlagsgesellschaft mbH, 2nd edn (2002)
10. National Electrical Manufacturers Association, Digital Imaging and Communications in Medicine (2012), http://medical.nema.org/ (retrieved February 11, 2012)
11. Dornbusch, P., Zündt, M.: Realisierung von Positionsortungen in WLAN. Dresden (2002), http://www.fireflow.de/publikationen.htm (retrieved February 11, 2012)
12. Regenstrief Institute, Inc., Logical Observation Identifiers Names and Codes (2012) http://loinc.org/ (retrieved February 11, 2012)
13. Cormen, T.H., Leiserson, C.E.: Algorithmen – EineEinführung, 2nd edn. Oldenbourg Verlag (2007)

Part IV
Games and Gamification

The Design in the Development of Exergames: A New Game for the Contribute to Control Childhood Obesity

Marina Barros, André Neves, Walter Correia, Marcelo Márcio Soares, and Fábio Campos

Post-Graduate Program in Design / Federal University of Pernambuco
Centre for Arts and Communication - Cidade Universitária – Recife-PE
marinalnbarros@terra.com.br, {andremneves,fc2005}@gmail.com,
ergonomia@me.com, marcelo2@nlink.com.br

Abstract. Obesity is increasing alarmingly worldwide, especially in children's audience, due to the adoption of sedentary habits. The exergames are a new class of digital games that have arisen over the possible use of technology, low cost, to unite physical activity to video games such as Nintendo Wii, X-Box 360, among others. And these have been gaining ground due to immersion of users, working their cognitive skills, attention and memory. This study presents a new game, the PEGGO developed by Federal University of Pernambuco, with data supporting the use for this type of game in order to contribute to help control childhood obesity.

Keywords: Exergame, Design, Ergonomics, Control Obesity.

1 Introduction

Over the years the weight of the child population has increased considerably, and this can be observed due to the statistical data presented by some countries, such as Brazil and the USA. In Brazil the data presented by the Brazilian Institute of Geography and Statistics (IBGE), show the increasing obesity, where between 1974 and 1975, 2.9% of boys and 1.8% of girls aged 5-9 years were obese, already in 2008, those numbers increase to 16.6% of boys and 11.8% of girls of the same age. In the U.S., may also be noted that increasing obesity, which according to the Centers for Disease Control and Prevention (CDC) increased by 6.5% in 1980 to 19.6% in 2008 in children aged 6 -11, this same institute reports that it tripled in 30 years, until 2008. [1, 2]

Obesity is a chronic multifactorial, which may be accompanied by multiple complications and develops through the interaction of genotype and environment, based on several factors, such as social, behavioral, cultural, physiological, metabolic and genetic, is characterized by excessive accumulation of fat in the body to such a degree that compromises the health of the individual, whether child or adult, and elderly regardless of sex. [3]

The increase in obesity has led researchers to study the factors that contributed to this. One of the contributing factors was the increasing number of hours wasted in front of the television or computer, and displays the results of the survey conducted by the CDC, in the United States, because according to it, it was observed that

A. Marcus (Ed.): DUXU/HCII 2013, Part II, LNCS 8013, pp. 491–500, 2013.

children and teenagers, between eight and 18 spend an average of 3 hours per day in front of them. [4, 5]

The body mass index (BMI) is currently the main factor measurement of obesity. BMI is calculated from the relationship between the individual's weight and height squared (weight / height 2). The result of this relationship should be observed according to the table on the following page (Table 1).

Table 1. Reference degree of obesity with BMI. Source: Adapted from Reynolds and Spruijt-Metz [6].

Category	BMI
Extreme thinness	less than 16.5
Underweight	16.5 to 18.5
Healthy	18,5 to 25
Overweight	25 to 30
Obesity	30 to 35
Clinical obesity	35 to 40
Morbid obesity	greater than 40

For children, does not apply directly to this table, the National Center for Health Statistics (NCHS) indicates the age group of seven to nine years following table (Table 2).

Table 2. Reference BMI for children. Source: Adapted from Reynolds and Spruijt-Metz [6].

Age	Gender	Normal BMI
7 to 9 years	male	14 to 24
7 to 9 years	female	13 to 22

As seen in recent researches video games and computer are becoming more popular among all age groups and in various countries around the world, in the U.S. 65% of U.S. households play video games or computer, without distinction between age and sex, showing that can become a public health problem, due to increased inactivity. [7, 8, 9]

Exergame is using video games to perform physical activities. Emerged in the early mid-90s, and in 1998, with the company Konami Dance Revolution, came the first hit, with the aim of helping to control obesity, especially childhood, its playfulness factor, but became today a big profit source. In 2006 came the Nintendo console, the Wii, with various game types and for all ages, managing to reach a wider audience. [10].

Given this growing concern, coupled with the problem of childhood obesity that has reached alarming data in Brazil and abroad, this paper presents a new video game for PC, developed by the Federal University of Pernambuco in partnership with National Research Council (CNPQ) called PEGGO.

2   Exergames

The emergence of a new kind of form of interaction experience has messed with the HCI community. Called effort games or exergames, which are interactive games using players' movements, joins an old idea, where games are used in addition to the social benefits and mental attributes, physical attributes. The ability to interpret human movement is a fundamental task for the computer, this type of game, and it has received much attention in recent years by companies operating in this field. One of the main reasons for the increasing interest in exergames was concern about the significant increase in obesity since it is expected that interest in games, can cause people to exercise in an interactive and playful. Another great strength of exergames is great profit potential, since only U.S. sales of exercise equipment reached $ 5.2 billion last year. [10, 11, 12]

According to the vision of Wollersheim et al (2010) are seen as the exergames simulators for low and medium trust can simulate sports such as skiing, horseback riding, tennis or bowling. While older people can no longer play sports or do not believe they would be able to take part in them, participation in such experiences promote for computer simulators that can give older people a sense of involvement in a once forgotten by exercise limitations physical and still manage to be updated with these new technologies. For children realizes a new way of thinking and improve agility, and the benefits of having a physical activity and less sedentary daily life near the same.

2.1 Benefits of Exergames

There are several benefits that exergames can bring under various spheres. From a social standpoint, the benefits are the most mentioned by the authors in research, as stated by Baranowski et al and Leeu et al, where several respondents demonstrate a high emotional satisfaction, to share power with a physical activity other family members and especially with friends who once only spoken by phone, finding reasons to have a moment of entertainment "physical" that once only possible in parks, when they had time, helping with time, etc. [13, 14]

Under the physical realm, according Leeu et al, in research with a group of women with application of Nintendo Wii games and low-impact, it was found that despite the objective measures do not find evidence of increased physical activity, all participants mentioned the physical nature of the program as one of its strengths. It has been noticed and observed that participants regarded the game as a tool that assisted in maintaining the need to keep active. The Wii encouraged women to engage in an activity that had already perceived to be impossible to be performed during normal execution because of their own health and advanced age. Furthermore, the author also notes, the Wii can be played despite limited mobility, as suggested by several participants. [14]

2.2 Exercise Physiology

Physical activity, from the 1990s, was considered vital for health promotion, health being considered the physical, mental and social. This can be defined as one that promotes body movement through muscle contraction, generating energy expenditure. The importance of this type of activity gains strength as it becomes fundamental for the treatment and prevention of chronic degenerative diseases and other types of disease in general, since there is evidence that this activity helps in improving the immune practitioner. Moreover, physical activity is a major contributor to socialization through sports centers, spaces for walking, bringing health both physical standpoint, as the social and behavioral. [15:16]

There are three types of training, strength, aerobic and anaerobic them. Strength training aims to seek practitioner gain strength, without necessarily gaining muscle hypertrophy. The anaerobic exercises are performed to vigorous physical training, where activities are carried out in a short period of time and intensive, such as sprinting. This system utilizes energy form as the ATP-PCr (Adenosine triphosphate - phosphocreatine) and anaerobic degradation of muscle glycogen (glucose). Aerobic exercise, also called cardiorespiratory endurance training, training is conducted in endurance activities such as hiking and long distance running, uses as energy form ATP, and promotes better transport and utilization of oxygen, and are best explained below.

3   Presentation of the Game - PEGGO

3.1 Description

This game was named "PEGGO," on account of its main objective, to "get" things on the screen while in use. The game consists of six mini games, which contains two to three stages, summing up 30 minutes into the game, where each stage represents a group of exercises that you want to achieve, not being mutually exclusive such exercises.

The game aims to get green icons that appear on the screen, and avoid touching red icons. Besides the character of use as motor physical activity, it has an educational character, which addresses topics widely discussed today, as sexuality, recycling, waste sorting, among others.

3.1.1   Object of the Game
Take green icons and avoid touching red icons to pass phase, according to the theme.

3.1.2   Game Features

1. Catch as many green icons you can;
2. Six mini games with different themes of today;
3. Two different characters to play;

4. It can be played in pairs;
5. Each mini game features several stages;
6. It has several levels of difficulty.

3.1.3 Gender
This game is characterized as a exergame, ie a game of exercise, combining entertainment and application of principles of activity exercise program engines, which also involve aspects of cognition.

3.1.4 Number of Players
Can be played individually or in pairs, depending on the space that has to play. The delimitation is given by the physical area at the site and be observed by the game screen the ability to insert more than one player on the playing field.

3.1.5 Platform
To use a computer with webcam attached to interaction and movement within the game to meet the goals of the same.

3.1.6 Target Audience
School age children 6-12 years. It can also be played by adults and other age groups, but some concepts that are connected with the formation of knowledge about the topics covered in the game may be underestimated by participants above the age required by the game.

3.2 Description of the Screens

Then has some models screen that are present in the game and account for most of actions taken by users for use of the mode PEGGO one.

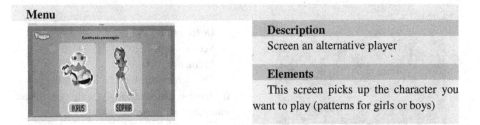

Fig. 1. Screen choice of characters

Mini games

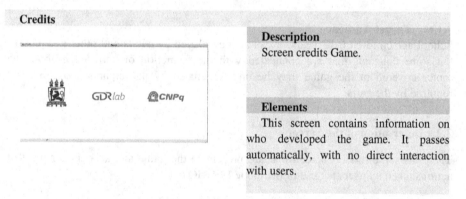

Description

Choice screen game type.

Elements

This screen has the options between mini games: "Nine Months," "Exploring the history," "Okay on the table", "SOS", "Get Rhythm" and "All Along Recycled".

On these screens, there is the option to change profile in the lower right corner cases will be user.

Fig. 2. Screen choice of characters (Female)

Fig. 3. Screenshot of choosing characters (Male)

Credits

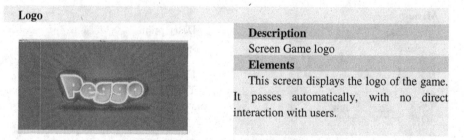

Description
Screen credits Game.

Elements
This screen contains information on who developed the game. It passes automatically, with no direct interaction with users.

Fig. 4. Screen credits for game development

Logo

Description
Screen Game logo
Elements
This screen displays the logo of the game. It passes automatically, with no direct interaction with users.

Fig. 5. Screen with the logo of the game

Adjusting the Screen

Description

Screen adjustment away from the screen to start the game properly

Elements

This screen displays a callout of how to adjust the distance ideal for playing.

This will appear whenever you select the game

Fig. 6. Screen Adjustment

Jogo

Description

This screen shows a representation of how you play the PEGGO

Elements

This screen can be seen the (s) player (s), the icons, the game options and change the profile function.

To disconnect, you must tighten the red dot in the upper left (clicking with the mouse)

Fig. 7. Screen mode game

Icons

Description

Screen with icons of the game in active mode (green and red)

Elements

Appear on the screen, the icons green and red, where they are related to the chosen theme of the game.

Fig. 8. Sample screen with icons of the game

3.3 Mechanisms of the Game

3.3.1 PEGGO

The game consists of six mini games and each mini game features two or three levels, each with an average of 1.30 minutes.

The objective of the game is to capture as many green icons and dodge most of the red icons. Icons are inspired by the theme of the games, where are the green icons that represent the good attitudes and habits and reds are wrong, what should not be done.

The game has a minimum score of 600 points to pass to the next level, it does not reach the minimum score, the player loses and has to start again. There is no maximum score.

3.3.2 Multiplayer
The game can be played in either individual or double, just depends on the area where the game is played and the choice of time, factors of personal entertainment, etc.

3.3.3 Game Mode
Playing individually, the player can choose whether to play the male or female version. In double, players have to play with the same profile.

3.3.4 Controls
The game has no control, the game works with the body's movements, this feature is present in virtually all exergames.

3.3.5 Rules of the Game
You have to move around and try to capture as much green icons and try to dodge the red icons.

3.3.6 Score
You must make as many points as possible, and should not do less than 600 points, minimum requirement to pass the level, and continue to evolve in the game.

4   Experiment

The study had an experimental character, with a scientific slant, where pre-tests were performed to analyze the relevance of PEGGO as agent control childhood obesity. The explanations were given to all users on how to use the game through body movements for their operation, goals, game name, etc.. Was done through check list for each user, and it was necessary to be done only once with each, demonstrating the ease of use and learning.

The experiment was conducted both at the Federal University of Pernambuco, as the home of some of the study participants. Lasted four weeks, adding to 11 days of testing, where six children, of both sexes, attended the same, with the consent of their guardians.

From the first day to the last day of testing were measured Heart Rate (HR), calculating 85% of that, Weight, Height and Waist Circumference in order to have benchmarks. During the tests, were always measured initial FC, FC during the test, with 10 HR and 20 minutes and final weight and initial and final end Caloric Expenditure (Kcal).

At the end of the experiment can be seen that participants who achieved a significant reduction in BMI, as to normalize it, since they did not participate in any program of diet control.

It is also evident that the effects on the users of the game are beneficial in the sense of actually getting to have a reduction of calories after some game time, with the average caloric expenditure of 163 kcal per 30 minutes of play.

5   Conclusion

The childhood obesity epidemic is a reality that is bringing alarming and worrying about global health, given that obese children tend to become obese adults, as already stated above. Aiming to avoid this progression of childhood obesity to adult, as well as other evils ae metabolic syndrome, one must not only teach children to exercise regularly, but encourage this practice. Exercise programs made on a regular basis have a positive effect in preventing and also in the treatment of obesity, either with decreasing body weight or insulin resistance, the root causes of metabolic syndrome.

Exergames as PEGGO, whose purpose is to exercise children without a stated requirement, and still seeks entertainment and knowledge of these, in a fun and inexpensive (considering the hardware that demand), is a simple and effective way of doing this. The number of players in the phase between 5 and 12 years who are joining the "wave" of games in the world is growing at a dizzying line, and not worth even a stage for this steady growth over the next ten years. New technologies are emerging and increasingly attracting this kind of audience, and that generates millions every year. So why not take advantage of this market as assiduous about technology and help keep children and young people healthier through their use.

References

1. IBGE – Istituto Brasileiro de Geografia e Estatística, information,
   http://www.ibge.gov.br/home/presidencia/noticias/
   noticia_visualiza.php?id_noticia=1699&id_pagina=1
2. CDC - Centers for Desease Control and Prevention, information (2010a),
   http://www.cdc.gov/healthyyouth/obesity/index.htm
3. National Institutes of Health, Clinical Guidelines on the Identification, Evaluation, and Treatment of Overweight and Obesity in Adults: The Evidence Report. NIH publication 98-4083 (September 1998)
4. CDC - Centers for Desease Control and Prevention. Morbidity and Mortality Weekly Report. 59 (2010b)
5. Lanningham-Foster, L., Foster, R.C., Mccrady, S.K., Jensen, T.B., Mitre, N., Levine, J.A.: Journal of Pediatrics 154, 819–823 (2009)
6. Reynolds, K., Spruijt-metz, D., Am, J.: Health Behavior, pp. 115–124 (2008)
7. Siegel, S.R., Haddock, B.L., Dubois, A.M., Wilkin, L.D.: International Journal of Exercise Science 2, 165–174 (2009)

8. Ballard, M., Gray, M., Reilly, J., Noggle, M.: Eating Behaviors 10, 161–167 (2009)
9. Van Den Beemt, A., Akkerman, S., Simons, R.J.: Computers in Human Behavior 26, 1158–1165 (2010)
10. Sinclair, J., Hingston, P., Masek, M.: ACM 1 (2007)
11. Finkelstein, S.L., Nickel, A., Barnes, T., Suma, E.A.: IEEE 20, 267–326 (2010)
12. Mueller, F.F., Gibbs, M.R., Vetere, F.: ACM, 263–266 (2008)
13. Baranowski, T., Buday, R., Thompson, D.I., Baranowski, J.: American Journal of Preventive Medicine 34, 74–82 (2008)
14. Leeu, J.R.J., Bruijn, M., Weert-Van Oene, G.H., Schrijvers, A.J.P.B.: Public Health 10, 544 (2010)
15. Mcardle, W., Katch, F.I., Katch, V.L.: Fisiologia do Exercício: Energia Nutrição e Desempenho Humano. Guanabara, São Paulo (2010)
16. Wilmore, J.H., Costill, D.L., Kenney, W.L.: Fisiologia do Esporte e do Exercício. 4 edn. Manole, São Paulo (2009)

Case Study: Identifying Gamification Opportunities in Sales Applications

Joëlle Carignan and Sally Lawler Kennedy

SAP Labs, 3410 Hillview Ave, Palo Alto, CA 94304
{joelle.carignan,sally.lawler.kennedy}@sap.com

Abstract. This paper presents results from interviews aimed at identifying end-users interest in a gamified Sales application, motivations, and information sharing concerns. A promotional video was used to introduce the concept of gamification to participants in order to allow them to form an opinion on the concept. Participants had mixed reactions, ranging from skeptical to positive. For some participants, a game would need to be aligned with their primary work goal, but others were interested in making connections with coworkers or increased sales knowledge. The interviews provided basic information early in the design lifecycle and helped in gaining support from the management team for the validation of a prototype. The paper describes results from the study and provides insights into the design process for the gamification of enterprise software.

Keywords: CRM, Design, Enterprise Software, Gamification, Research Methods, Sales, User Experience.

1 Introduction

Gamification, the "use of game design elements in non-game contexts" (Deterding 2011), has been applied successfully to a number of popular applications[1] and is now being applied to a few business applications. Gamification components such as challenges, leader boards, and rewards are now available commercially and can be integrated into existing business applications[2]. For example, in the context of Sales applications, points could be offered to encourage data entry and sharing amongst colleagues; work that is often not a high priority compared to generating sales yet needed by managers to generate forecasts.

While being a popular topic at the moment, little is known or shared about design best practices or on the outcome of gamification practices in business environments. Nicholson (2012) raises a concern that providing incentives to complete work will create a dependency, and that providing extrinsic rewards could result in decreased motivation. Others believe that adoption, desirability or satisfaction will depend on the suitability of the application and the quality of the execution.

---

[1] Foursquare, Jelli, Waze.
[2] Badgeville, Bunchball.

A. Marcus (Ed.): DUXU/HCII 2013, Part II, LNCS 8013, pp. 501–507, 2013.
© Springer-Verlag Berlin Heidelberg 2013

In *Reality is Broken* (2011), McGonigal defines key design principles for game design, such as defining a goal for the game and ensuring voluntary participation. This work can be used as a starting point for designing gamification in business applications, but additional knowledge is needed to identify which technique can be used to gather information on motivation, given that most users are not familiar with enterprise gamification concepts and that gamification is not a basic necessity to accomplish work.

This paper presents the early process of incorporating gamification concepts into a Sales Application, including the design questions, interviews with users, and findings. A discussion on the usefulness of these results in the context of commercial software development will follow along with recommendations on the design process.

2   Context

SAP is a vendor of business management software and developed a new Sales application recently. The application provides means to document sales accounts, contacts, leads, and sales activities; to exchange updates related to these activities with other employees; to track progress and make sales forecasts. The application was deployed on a Cloud two years ago and new functionality is added on a quarterly basis based on customer requests, usability findings, and market analyses.

The product team was interested in exploring gamification and decided to work on a proof of concept. Initially many questions came to mind, such as: Which game goal should be supported? Should the game support competition or collaboration? What type of rewards would be offered? Would rewarding quantity be a detriment over quality? What would be the business value?

A work session was organized with the Product Manager to compare notes on potential game goals and one proposal was selected by the team, as a candidate for the conceptual design. The game would encourage Sales Representatives to use a sales methodology that is currently offered in the business application. Developing and exposing sales competencies would provide intrinsic rewards, while points which can translate into any compensation by an employer would potentially provide extrinsic rewards.

The team was questioning how this idea would be received and had planned on using the design wireframes to collect feedback from users. However, due to higher priorities, the gamification research project had to be scaled back. As an alternative, the team opted to insert some questions on gamification at the beginning of a usability session scheduled to test the latest release. The focus would be on collecting first impressions on gamification concepts and collecting basic information that could influence the design direction. The team was also interested in collecting ideas for rewards to develop a storyline for the demo and to eventually share best practice with eventual customers.

3   Methodology

A screening questionnaire was provided to a third party vendor for the recruitment of ten Sales Representatives or Account Executives. Selection criteria included at least two years of experience as a Sales Representative, a mix of industries, one year of experience using an on-demand (web-based) CRM[3] application and ability to verbalize well. Two screening questions were added to recruit participants with some exposure to computer games. Participants were asked whether they use any game applications for personal usage and if so, which ones. They were also asked if they used any business applications with gaming aspects to them.

The final sample included nine participants from different industries with knowledge of computer games. The average number of years of sales experience was twelve years; ranging from five to twenty years. All participants had experience with a CRM system, mobile devices and social networking or collaboration tools. All but one played games for personal usage such as Seduko, Chess, Angry Birds (six participants), World of Warcraft, Words with Friends, and x-Box. None of the participants had experience with game applications for business.

The sessions were conducted in a usability lab with a moderator and with one participant at a time. A one minute extract of a video found on the Internet was presented to participants in order to introduce gamification concepts and allow them to form an opinion. The video, a commercial pitch for a project management application, explained how points were associated with completing "important but non-glamorous tasks". It showed badges associated to the user profile and rewards that can be used in exchange for gift cards, sporting tickets, lunches or paid time off.

After seeing the video, the participants were asked the following questions:

- What are your thoughts on incorporating game aspects/concepts into a business application such as your CRM tool?
- What game concepts would you want include?
- What goal would you want to achieve by playing a game?
- What rewards would motivate you to play an online game with your colleagues?
- What information would you share in a game with colleagues and managers?
- Is there any information that you would not want to share?

Based on general knowledge on gamification, one hypothesis was that some participants would not be interested in the concept of gamification. Yet, the team was curious to find out how participants would react and if they would be able to formulate ideas for a game with little context, time or knowledge.

4   Results

The questions provided insight into potential interest, what conditions would make the game interesting, types of game concepts that users would like, types of rewards

---

[3]   Customer Relationship Management.

envisioned, and information that would or would not be shared willingly with co-workers.

4.1   Initial Thoughts

Overall, reactions to the video clip were mixed with some participants reacting positively and others being skeptical.

Participants that had an interest in the game concepts stated:

— "I would like something that is fun, goofy, "ada boy' concept. I dread looking at [the current tool she has to use] everyday."
— "Sales Reps don't like to spend time in CRM systems. If you redeem the points it is like getting paid. That would be fun to have in the CRM system."

Participants that were not interested in the game concepts stated:

— "Business is business. Business is not fun. I play games to take my mind off of business. For me business and games are 180 degrees from each other."
— "If I had a game on my CRM system I wouldn't use it. I come to work not to waste my time. I play games to have fun and for downtime."
— "Other high producing Sales Reps wouldn't care about having game concepts in a CRM system. It is all about the money."

4.2   Game Concepts

Participants were familiar with game mechanics or understood the principle after seeing the video. The following game concepts/mechanics looked interesting to participants:

• Challenges (individual and team), e.g. who can post the most sales in one week.
• Leader board, e.g. show top achievers.
• Badges
• Points, e.g. getting points for reaching milestones or getting points for entering info about a win. This information would help other Sales Representatives.

One participant thought of game rewards and bonuses as a modern day incentive plan.

We noticed that most participants did not understand the term "concept" as in "game concept". Some participants responded to this question by providing game ideas:

• "Share case studies, then have people read and take quizzes on them."
• "Poker game where you could create sub-groups and teams to play one another."

4.3   Game Goals (Purpose)

Aside from the ideas formulated previously, participants responded that the primary purpose of the game should be to support the existing sales goals. They indicated that anything that is not related to supporting the selling process would be a distraction.

— "I have a large revenue quota and my focus is on achieving that. I wouldn't go out of my way (do anything extra) to play a game. The goals (for the game) must align with my sales activities."
— "My whole job is revenue based. I have to make a quota."

Some participants responded that they play games to challenge their minds, for an escape, or to connect with others.

— "I want games to be something that exercise/engages my brain."
— "I want games to be fun and have a social environment/aspect/connection."

4.4   Game Rewards

Two participants indicated that they would only be motivated by money and one participant mentioned donating money to a charity. Other rewards mentioned included:

- Recognition/acknowledgement
- Extra time off
- Gas or Starbucks cards, nice dinners, tickets to sporting events, relaxing activities, things that one can do with spouse, e.g. night out on the town
- Products, e.g. iPod, iPhone, Play Station 3, flat screen TV, DVR, neat gadgets
- Stocks
- Trips

4.5   Information Sharing

Most participants were open to share any sales information related to their work with coworkers while a few would share limited information. Participants were willing to share the following:

- Best practices (selling tactics/strategies, how to overcome objections, how a prospect deal was won, how to beat the competition)
- Competitive information
- Reference customers and accounts
- Recent leads, customers, wins, license deals
- Close ratio and target achievement
- Activities and number of follow-up calls made
- Pipeline and forecast
- Marketing campaigns
- Articles, papers related to business, case studies and training material

Information that would not be shared would be content-related, such as pricing, number of licenses; compensation or commissions; and key reference accounts. One participant wouldn't share details about his customers.

5   Analysis

The interviews provided insights on interests and self-perceived motivational factors. They indicate that some users are receptive to gamification concepts, while others would not be interested in them. This confirmed our hypothesis.

Results also indicated that Sales Representatives would be primarily interested in a game that would be align with their performance goals and help them meet their existing sales targets; an idea that the team had ruled out. More data will be needed to establish the effects and business value if primary tasks are "gamified".

Few participants were able to formulate other ideas for games in the context of interviews, but one participant mentioned an interest in making connections with other coworkers or increasing their sales knowledge. This proposal was in-line with the idea of providing intrinsic rewards.

In terms of rewards, results indicated that participants would be interested in a variety of incentives. Participants had no difficulty imaging points as a currency for tangible rewards. Interestingly, some participants suggested other types of rewards, such as giving. The research suggests that offering a variety of cash and non-cash rewards would meet all aspirations.

In terms of information sharing, very few topics were off limit. Most participants were open to share their database information, except for one participant. Confidential data such as deal size, commissions and reference customers would be off limit.

These results were presented to executives responsible for the product. Knowing that some users had a positive outlook on gamification led to a decision to pursue the research and tap into the internal sales organization for feedback on the existing wireframes. In addition, validating the concept using internal users will also increase the project visibility in an organization where a multitude of innovative ideas are competing for support.

6   Conclusion

This paper presented results from interviews aimed at identifying interest from end-users in a gamified Sales application, motivations, and concerns.

Including interviews in a usability test had advantages and disadvantages: It provided convenient access to Sales professionals at a low-cost, but the sample of participants was limited to Sales Representatives with exposure to computer games. Ideally we would like to conduct a research with a mix of players/non-players and different stakeholders, such as employees/managers, customers/non-customers, etc. In particular, research is needed to define if the ideas generated by employees will match with the ideas generated by managers.

As introduction to the interviews, we avoided showing an example of a gamified sales application, which was an option available to us. This would have shifted the focus on the validation of an existing concept. Using material found on the Internet allowed us to introduce the concept of gamification without much effort and was effective. We avoided selecting material from our competitors to respect internal policies and recommend verifying research policies before conducting studies with public content. Participants were able to relate to the concept without too much difficulty and provided useful insight on most questions, except for the reference to "game concepts" which should be avoided.

The number of questions was limited in this study due to time constraints. More targeted research methods such as a focus group or a card sorting activity can be envisioned to identify original solutions. User validation activities will also be needed as the conceptual design work progresses and if the concept is implemented to evaluate engagement levels.

Finally, interviews helped in gaining support from the management team to pursue research activities with the validation of a prototype. Involving the project management team in the research is valuable, not only to gain resources, but creating momentum for a project in a large organization.

The gamification of enterprise software represents a business opportunity to improve the user experience and engage end-users if done well, but it also carries some risks at the moment due to a lack of knowledge on adoption, which can be mitigated by conducting research activities during the design life-cycle.

References

1. Deterding, S., Khaled, R., Nacke, L.E., Dixon, D.: Gamification: Toward a Definition. In: CHI 2011, Vancouver, BC, May 7-12 (2011)
2. McGonigal, J.: Reality Is Broken: Why Games Make Us Better and How They Can Change the World. Penguin, London (2011)
3. Nicholson, S.: A User-Centered Theoretical Framework for Meaningful Gamification. In: Games + Learning + Society 8.0, Madison, WI (2012)

Interactive Doodles: A Comparative Analysis of the Usability and Playability of Google Trademark Games between 2010 and 2012

Breno José Andrade de Carvalho[1], Marcelo Márcio Soares[2],
Andre Menezes Marques das Neves[2], and Rodrigo Pessoa Medeiros[1]

[1] Course Technology Games Digiais, Catholic University of Pernambuco, Brazil
[2] Post Graduate Program in Design, Federal University of Pernambuco, Brazil
{breno25,andremneves}@gmail.com, marcelo2@nlink.com.br,
prof@rodrigomedeiros.com.br

Abstract. By using artistic mutations, called Doodles, Google has been commemorating important events and personalities. This fun approach started with still images, evolved to increasingly complex interactions, and has resulted in games based on the configurations of its logo. Thus, the company which was born in the digital world has introduced a new interactive approach to its logo in cyberspace, thus offering new experiences to the user. This article sets out to present a comparative analysis of usability and playability of five interactive Doodles by applying the RITE (Rapid Interation Testing and Evaluation) approach so as to investigate ergonomic criteria of invitation, suitability, immediate feedback and user control.

Keywords: Interactive Doodles, Mutated Logo, Google, Game, Playability, Usability.

1 Introduction

In 1999, from a simple drawing of a person behind the second "o" in the word Google, the search engine, born in cyberspace, changed its logo in a humorous way to celebrate important events, which gave rise to the mutations of its logo, better known as Doodles[1] **(Fig. 1.).** What started as a simple joke is now looked forward to by Internet users who access the company´s search page looking for new updates.

Google, in addition to commemorating important events, began developing more elaborate and complex alterations to its logo to broadcast information of a political, social and cultural nature all over the world, by means of visual composition, sometimes in stills, sometimes in animation, of the characters of its logo. However, starting in 2010, Google reinvented a way for its users to interact with their identity. What hitherto had only been done visually for the user, now has a new approach which

---

[1] Doodle "consists of changes in the look of the Google logo in order to celebrate holidays, anniversaries, and the lives of famous artists and scientists" [1].

A. Marcus (Ed.): DUXU/HCII 2013, Part II, LNCS 8013, pp. 508–517, 2013.
© Springer-Verlag Berlin Heidelberg 2013

Fig. 1. A. The Crazy Kid´s birthday; B. Louis Braille's birthday; C. Pi's Day; D. Discovery of the X-Ray; E. Flintstones' 50th birthday; F. Centenary of Czeslaw Milosz (Poland)

provides the netizen with an immersion experience, interfaced by its own logo based on manipulating the company's logo. This manipulation enables creative interaction, thus making it possible for the user to play with the logo.

The aim of this paper is to set out a comparative study of interactive doodles, based on games released on the company´s search page in 2010 (commemorating 30 years of Pac-Man) and 2012 (celebrating the London Olympics). Two aspects of the Human-Computer Interaction in the games were evaluated, viz., the issues of usability and playability, by means of applying the RITE (Rapid Interation Testing and Evaluation) approach, to investigate the ergonomic criteria of invitation, suitability, immediate feedback and user control. Moreover, factors related to playability were measured such as the challenge set, the attention required, loss of self-awareness and changing the perception of time.

2   Doodles: Making the Logo Dynamic so as to Interact with the User

Mankind has always used signs to express an idea. This need to demonstrate meanings and information set off a relentless pursuit to develop mechanisms and graphical and visual elements to transmit the message quickly and efficiently. Brands, at first, were created with the aim of identifying tools, properties and livestock. Subsequently, the signs were transformed into symbols and began to signal an attribute of the quality and reliability of a product [2].

With the development of trade and increasing competition, institutions began to invest in the design of these signs, of these brand names in search of a unique identity that would stand out from the others and which their customers could easily identify. The design of a brand name evolved into a logo so as to create a visual identity, formed, in most cases, by a configuration of alphanumeric characters (logo), whether or not tied to a symbol, in addition to signaling a chromatic standard.

Besides identifying products, logos also convey emotions and keep a memory of moments, thereby serving as a criterion in the choices that people make every day. According to Strunck [3], a logo is the intangible sum of a product; its name, its packaging and price, its history, its reputation and how it is promoted. The logo is also defined by consumers' impressions about the people who use it; as well as because of their own professional experience.

Technological advances and the development of mass communications oblige companies and designers to seek a differential so they may continue to lead the dialogue between the brand and its consumers. According to Purvis [4] the word Zeitgeist "means the spirit of the times and refers to trends and characteristics of cultural preferences was determined." Thus designers need to be connected, incessantly, to social, political and economic society to express with accuracy the Zeitgeist of their time and space, building visual symbols that make the most sense for their users.

The technological advance and the development of mass communications obliges companies and designers to seek a differential so they may continue to lead a dialogue between the logo and its consumers. According to Purvis [4] the word Zeitgeist "means the spirit of the times and refers to trends and cultural preferences that characterize a certain epoch." Thus designers need to be connected, incessantly, to social, political and economic aspects of society in order to express accurately the Zeitgeist of their time and space by constructing visual symbols that make the most sense to its users.

In this context, some designers have constructed logos that are more flexible, dynamic, multishaped and multicolored, thereby producing a new discourse so as to materialize emotions and allure the expectations of the active target public. In a relationship of humans with visual identity, the static view of a univocal image is transformed into a subjective or open identity that makes it possible for the onlooker to identify his/her values in the object observed.

In the globalized world connected to cyberspace, companies need the concept of branding (brand management) to transmit emotions to consumers and entice them to consume such products and/or services. According to Kreutz and Fernández [5], a brand can evoke memories and provoke emotion, and thus maintain a more affective and lasting relationship with its public, thereby allowing them to have a sentimental attachment to the brand, by identifying themselves with it.

The logo interacts with consumers starting with the interface presented by graphical items, namely billboards, packaging, print ads and television commercials. These, for their part, comprise words, images and signs (the message), signaled by the company's visual identity. "The logo, graphically speaking, is always presented to the consumer as a seal in the print and electronic media, a lifeless and passive element." [6].

Born in the dynamic universe of the internet, Google introduced this concept of a mutating logo for brand identity in 1999 when it created its first doodle (**Fig.2.**) to pay tribute to a festival that took place in Nevada, USA, by adding a mannequin (the icon of the *Burning Man* festival) behind the second "o" of the logo. After this experiment, the home page of the Google search engine began to display more elaborate mutations, and to exploit all the possibilities of the hypermedia environment.

Fig. 2. First *doodle* made by Google

Google doodles (**Fig. 3**) are the convergence of interactive and non-sequential multi-media, the fusion of verbal and non-verbal signs with the written text, the audiovisual and computing, i.e., representations of all the matrices of language [7]. In 2010, the company evolved the interaction of its logo with its users by putting a digital game in the interface, namely, the doodle commemorating the 30th anniversary of the Pac-Man game (**Fig. 4**).

Fig. 3. Vídeo *doodle* of John Lennon's 70th birthday, Shown in October 2010

This new approach enabled its users to have a new experience, just by extending the length of stay on the search engine page, but by triggering a strong emotional and communicative appeal. According to the website Olhar Digital (Digital Look) [8], as there were 500 million views on the day, this was one of the most accessed doodles.

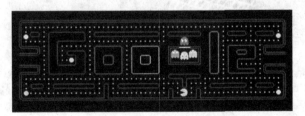

Fig. 4. Doodle for the 30th anniversary of the launch of Pac-Man. Shown in May 2010

For Marc Gobé [9], companies must not only reject conventions, but must also institutionalize innovation, improvisation and imagination in their discourse. "To humanize the logo so that it is reflected in people is crucial to 'bringing to life' the emotions which move the passion of a company's workforce as well as clients' aspirations". [9]

As it had positive feedback from its users, Google began to develop some doodles based on games to convey, in a playful way, information and feelings. In 2012, four different sports (hurdling, football, basketball and canoeing) were launched to celebrate the London Olympics (**Fig. 5.**). These mutant logos require a process of differentiated creation and to pay attention to aspects of usability and playability. For Laitinen [10], on applying heuristic tests of "usability in games, it is common to come across problems in game interfaces such as menus, which are complicated to use, displays the meanings of which are unclear and controls that are difficult to learn". (**Fig. 6.**).

a.   b.

c.   d.

Fig. 5. Doodles of the London Olympics. A. Hurdles; B. Basket-ball; C. Canoeing; D. Football. Shown in August 2012

Fig. 6. Football Doodles. The interaction screen is presented. Shown in August 2012

3   Methodology Used for the Test of Usability and Playability

According to Cybis [11], simply put. the usability of a game is about not presenting challenges not related to the game so that the player is focused only on having fun, viz., nothing in the interface apart from the ergonomic criteria that may make the player lose the focus of his/her objective in the game. The concept of playability is about the player undergoing these challenges with the game while having fun, and understanding the increase in the difficulty and changes of levels.

It is a challenge to conduct a test that is proposed to test both usability as well as playability, mainly because there are no methods that span the two concepts together. Furthermore, according to the author, the focus of the ergonomic interventions changes in games because it is not about developing interfaces that directly and objectively support the performance of a user's given task . According to Cybis [11], the objective is to offer the right number of challenges in an immersive environment. Thus it can be said that in games both issues of usability and those of playability also contribute to the end-user's experience.

Therefore, this study used some guidelines from the RITE (Rapid Interation Testing and Evaluation) approach, the evolutionary assessment method described by Medlock et al [12] who propose a freedom to change the format of the test during interviews with users. That is, instead of conducting only one range of tests, the prototype, process and/or questions may be modified and improved for later tests. **Fig 7** shows the difference of this method compared with the traditional method for a usability test.

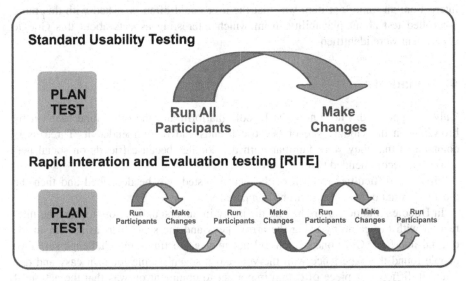

Fig. 7. RITE testing versus "Standard" Usability Testing, based on [13]

10 people were selected from among staff and students of the Center for Communication of the Catholic University of Pernambuco in order to conduct the tests, of whom 8 were men and 2 women aged between 20 and 34 years old, among whom only one user was not familiar with the Doodles. These people had had different experience of using a computer and levels of web browsing that ranges from basic to advanced, which may well generate a range of interesting results for analysis.

The objective of the test was, in a single session with the user, to identify good practice and/or misuse of some ergonomic criteria regarding the game interface. Another goal was also to identify elements that might describe that this Google experience had good or bad playability. Four doodles from the London Olympics and the Pac-Man doodle were chosen for the tests.

Three types of sessions were held (these sessions were different because within the testing process, some flaws were identified and could be corrected and adjusted using the RITE methodology): remote sessions; sessions with users in their work environment; and sessions with users in the laboratory of the institution with an interview that was more focused on playability.

The first two sessions took place remotely using an online questionnaire that people responded to as they interacted with the games. Two of the ten users were monitored in real time using a voice system by means of which they also commented aloud on what was happening during the experience of each game. The third and fourth users had their evaluation conducted in their work environment, with a moderator by their side, while a camera filmed their reactions and there was a system for identifying their navigation on the screen. The six remaining users were monitored by a moderator and a camera in the laboratory of the institution for a face-to-face interview in which they performed tasks proposed within the environment studied so as to complete the actions in the game and/or elements of the interface where the user had interaction; an important item was that the user could often be asked with this more controlled test about playability, from which interesting aspects about this Google experiment were identified.

4   Findings

Only one person did not know the Doodle platform and the other nine found it by browsing on the Google site or because friends had recommended it. Three users commented that they were familiar with the doodles because friends on social networks had recommended them.

First, the difficulties in each of the games tested will be described and then the most important points found will be compared.

In Doodle Athletics, users had no difficulty in understanding how to start the interaction with the game by using the arrow keys and the space bar, as set out in the tutorial interface. Only one person did not manage to finish the challenge set. Two people found the experience with the very easy; seven people found it easy and one found it difficult. A piece of datum important to comment on was that the action of clicking on the buttons quickly and repeatedly to make the character run became tiring for 4 of the users tested.

As to Doodle basketball, all users understood how to start the game. The metaphor of the button to start was well applied in this context. Eight users completed the task set by the game. All users commented that the dynamics of holding the spacebar down to make the basketball gain force when thrown at the basket is tiring. Some users made the comment that their fingers hurt during this process. Another important finding was that users did not have feedback on what force they using to make the ball go farther or less far so as to get the pitch right.

In the game of canoeing all users managed to start the game quickly. However, one point that was criticized was that they did not know the times of other friends in order to see how good or bad they were at the interaction. Six users commented that they did not know how to control the canoe more easily, thus making it difficult for them to control the direction as they wished. Nor was there any feedback during the game when they made a mistake because they had not passed by an item.

In Doodle soccer, all users understood how to start the game. However, only one quickly managed to understand the dynamics of how to start the interaction with the character. Despite this, only 2 users commented that the game was difficult. Eight users commented that playability was flawed and that there was need to increase the difficulty level and to create other levels.

With the Pac-Man doodle this was a bit different: no users had any difficulty in getting started and they also quickly understood the dynamics of playability, and 8 of the 10 users considered this to be very easy. The two users who did not find it easy had had no interaction with the Pac-Man on another console such as Atari.

According to the tests, in general, the experience of using the Doodle as a platform for a game is surprising. However, it is further noted that playability is deficient. Only in the case of Pac-Man were different levels and stages identified. All the other games of the London Olympics had only one way and only one stage to be played.

As to the ergonomic criteria, the one most commented on was user control because the possibilities of interaction with games are minimal and users would like greater freedom to choose elements and improve their performance at the game. In basketball Doodle, users commented most on the control via the space key being tiring and on their not understanding the feedback on increasing ball speed. In Doodle canoeing, the possible keys for interaction with the game confuse players, so although they do understand well the signs and tips on how to start, this confusion makes it difficult for them to achieve a better performance. It was in this Doodle that that the lack of a better leveling of the stages was noted. It clearly could have two or three phases with levels of progressive difficulty.

In the ergonomic criterion of invitation, there were few occurrences of error on starting the interaction with the game, concentrated, in the case of Pac-Man, where the form of initial interaction comes about on clicking the image and not on a button. From the point of view of immediate feedback, the lack of a timer or scoring system in 2 of the 4 Doodles of the London Olympics 2012 made users' interaction with the games difficult. This very often reduced their wish to play and merely encouraged users to finish the task proposed. Incidentally, this was one of the most recurrent criticisms, namely, users would like to spend more time interacting with the game and, moreover, to see what the ranking of their friends with regard to Google is.

From the point of view of the playability, the Doodles of the London Olympics have a serious problem related to the value of something in the game and the players' motivations. An example of this problem is that there are many comments about the scoring not opening up new possibilities for games, and thus the experience ends in an ephemeral process of playability. That is, there are almost no rewards for the effort process on performing the activity of finishing the stage or completing the task requested. In the case of Pac-Man the fact that there are some stages opened up possibilities for the user to build empathy with the game and to want to continue the gameplay to the end. Even though the speed added to the elements is something that makes experiencing it on the website brief.

5   Final Remarks

Since 2010, Google has launched a new phase in the changing configuration of its logo. The interaction goes beyond simply looking and listening, to an immersion in the fun learning universe of the game, which leads some users to lose their way in time and space, as they forget, in some cases, the real objective of accessing the web page of the search engine. This makes it possible not only that the user will remain longer on the company´s homepage but also that the trademark will be broadcast in other cyberspace environments such as news portals and social networks.

It is noticeable that these interactive Doodles created by Google are still experimental initiatives as they use their own trademark to build platforms which have games on them in cyberspace. Even so, this opens up a path to be explored in the construction of games with a view to offering quick and simple experiences.

Just like Cybis [11] who demonstrates the research on video games and experiences that sprout from this universe, this leads researchers on usability to step outside a certain comfort zone by showing that concern only at the interface with the user is not enough to understand what a good experience of using the game is.

As a result of the tests conducted in the study, it is apparent that users had more empathy with the Pac-Man game because it has other phases and levels of difficulty. However, the doodles of the Olympic Games did not provide the same experience for users, whether through lack of other steps in the games or because they did not have some elements of motivation, a timer or a scoring system.

The knowledge made available and the existing techniques and tools to assess usability aspects and playability together need to advance and improve in order to measure and understand other important aspects for the user's experience, such as getting rid of worries and frustrations (and assimilating concerns and frustrations of the games sector), not investigated in this study.

References

1. Google, http://www.google.com/doodle4google/resources/history.html
2. Frutiger, A.: Sinais e símbolos: desenhos, projetos e significados / Adrian Fruiger; tradução Karina Jannini. Martins Fontes, São Paulo (1999)
3. Strunck, Gilberto Luiz Teixeira Leite.: Como criar identidades visuais para marcas de sucesso: Um guia sobre o marketing das marcas e como representar graficamente seus valores. pp. 19, Rio Books, 3 Edição, revista e atualizada, Rio de Janeiro (2007)
4. Meggs, P., Purvis, A.W.: História do design gráfico. 4 edn., Cosac e Naify, São Paulo (2009)
5. Kreutz, E., Fernández, F.J.M.: Google: a narrativa de uma marca mutante. Comunicação Mídia e Consumo, Escola Superior de Marketing 6(16), 89–107 (2009)

6. Carvalo, B.J.A., Santos, F.H.S.: Doodle e a comunicação imersa no design da marca. Rozon y Palabra, n. 79, maio – julho (2012)

7. Santaella, L.: Matrizes da linguagem e pensamento. Sonora visual verbal. Iluminaras, São Paulo (2001)

8. Olhar Digital,
`http://olhardigital.uol.com.br/produtos/digital_news/`
`usuarios-gastaram-4.8-mi-de-horas-no-pac-man-do-google`

9. Gobé, M.: Brandjam: o design emocional na humanização das marcas/ Marc Gobé; tradução Maria Clara Di Biase, pp. 14, pp. 118, Rocco, Rio de Janeiro (2010)

10. Laitinen, S.: Usability and playability expert evaluation. In: Isbister, K., Schaffer, N. (eds.) Game Usability. Advice from the experts for advancing the player experience, p. 93. Morgan Kaufmann Publishers, USA (2008)

11. Cybis, W.: Ergonomia e usabilidade: conhecimentos, métodos e aplicações/ Walter Cybis, Adriana Holtz Betiol, Richard Faust. 2 edn., São Paulo: Novatec Editora (2010)

12. Medlock, M.C., Wixon, D., Terrano, M., Romero, R., Fulton, B.: Using the RITE Method to improve products: a definition and a case study. Usability Professionals Association, Orlando (2002)

13. Bias, R.G., Mayhew, D.J.: Cost-Justifying Usability, Second Edition: An Update for the Internet Age, 2nd edn. Interactive Technologies, pp. 489–518 (2005)

Exploring Adjustable Interactive Rings in Game Playing: Preliminary Results

Leonardo Cunha de Miranda[1], Heiko Hornung[2], Roberto Pereira[2],
and Maria Cecília C. Baranauskas[2]

[1] Department of Informatics and Applied Mathematics,
Federal University of Rio Grande do Norte (UFRN), Natal, Brazil
[2] Institute of Computing, University of Campinas (UNICAMP), Campinas, Brazil
leonardo@dimap.ufrn.br, heix@gmx.com,
{rpereira,cecilia}@ic.unicamp.br

Abstract. In recent years new forms of interaction have been proposed by academia and industry for the contexts of use of interactive Digital Television (iDTV) and games. One of these proposals is called Adjustable Interactive Rings (AIRs), which is a technology resulting from a research project that was originally designed to be used with iDTV applications. Taking into account the design features of the physical artifact of interaction developed, it seems possible to conjecture its use in other contexts then the iDTV. In this paper, we present preliminary results of an experiment conducted with users in order to investigate the suitability of AIRs in the context of playing computer games.

Keywords: AIRs, kinect, wiimote, joystick, gamepad, gesture-based interaction.

1 Introduction

New forms of interaction with electronic games have been recently proposed in literature and the digital entertainment industry. These forms of interaction differ substantially from traditional (joystick/gamepad)-supported interaction with videogames. New technologies or products, such as the Nintendo WiiMote [12] and the Microsoft Kinect [1], enable a different quality of engagement with videogames. That is, instead of just pushing buttons, players can control the game, for example, with gestures and body movements, enabling a different user experience. This study is situated in the area of new ways of interacting with games through new hardware, especifically with the Adjustable Interactive Rings [4] for videogames.

In this work, we present results of an experiment with seven users conducted to investigate the suitability of using the Adjustable Interactive Rings in the context of games. The game used for the experiment is the Meteor Invasion [9]. It was chosen because it has features, such as simple game controls, that make it suitable for a first test of a new hardware artifact in the context of using computer games.

This paper is organized as follows: Section 2 presents the Adjustable Interactive Rings for computer games; Section 3 presents the game that was used in the experiment;

A. Marcus (Ed.): DUXU/HCII 2013, Part II, LNCS 8013, pp. 518–527, 2013.

Section 4 describes in detail the scenario and the methodology employed for this work; Section 5 presents the quantitative results and analysis of the experiment; Section 6 presents our conclusion.

2   Adjustable Interactive Rings for Computer Games

The Adjustable Interactive Rings (AIRs) are a technology [2] resulting from a research project [8] originally developed for the context of use of interactive Digital Television (iDTV). The resulting physical artifact of interaction, as specified and implemented in [4], is affordable, adjustable, ergonomic and ambidextrous. It furthermore supports flexibility of use and features a simple interaction language, conceived to be used by anyone, to the greatest possible extent. The design solution was based on the principles of Universal Design [11] and developed in a participatory manner [10] as presented in [6]. Results of using this prototype, specifically for interaction with a simulated set of iDTV applications are available in [5,7].

The "original" AIRs for the iDTV solution is composed of three different types of AIRs: AIR-A for activation operations, AIR-M for movement operations, and AIR-O for selecting contextual options [4]. Prior to the experiment, AIRs for iDTV have been adapted to function in use context of computer games through a solution composed of only two AIRs: AIR-A and AIR-M, i.e. we explore the use of AIRs with computer games with one AIR less than in your working configuration with iDTV. Therefore, the goal is to evaluate this new configuration of AIRs in the context of use of computer games. In Fig. 1 we present the hardware design of the AIRs.

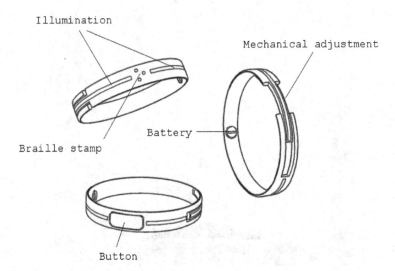

Fig. 1. Hardware design of the AIRs (cf. our patent for physical artifacts of interaction [2])

3   The Computer Game

The single player game chosen to be used in this work is called Meteor Invasion [9], which was chosen because of its characteristics that facilitate the evaluation of the use of AIRs in the context of computer games. The game consists of a single screen and its objective is to save a city from destruction by meteor strikes altering the trajectory of falling meteors by shooting at them with a cannon placed in the city center. Gameplay as well as visual and acoustic design seem to stimulate users to play the game until they reach the final goal, i.e., until saving the city from "meteor invasion". It is worth noting that this game was used in this study with permission of its developer.

This game can be used in three difficulty levels, i.e., easy, normal or hard. The change of difficulty level entails the following changes (in the order of the most easily perceivable to the most subtle change): i) increase in the number of meteors falling; ii) increase in the meteor sizes; and iii) how a shot alters the trajectory of a meteor. Regardless of the difficulty level, the game always has 20 levels, i.e. one wins the game by protecting the city until the end of the last level. As the game has advancing levels, the background scene is darkening, giving the idea of nightfall. After each level, which lasts at most 50 seconds, the complexity of the game increases, i.e. the amount, speed, and sizes of meteors falling on the city increase. Fig. 2 shows the game interface.

Fig. 2. The Meteor Invasion game: (a) level indication, (b) time bar, (c) a shot projectile, (d) hit point bar, (e) a meteor, (f) ammo bar, (g) cannon, and (h) city

The player's mission is to protect the city (Fig. 2h) from the invasion of meteors, i.e. to not let meteors drop on the city. The player, controlling a cannon (Fig. 2g), shoots in the direction of the meteors. The cannon has a limited shot capacity and also requires a period of time in order to reload the ammo (Fig. 2f), so that more shots can be fired. Hitting a meteor with a shot projectile causes a certain shift in its trajectory. The idea, therefore, is to change the meteors' trajectories so that they drop outside the city limits. As the meteors are dropping onto the city, the player's hit points will be reducing. In this game the hit points work as a sort of "life energy" of the player, and for each new level the hit points bar starts at 100%. The player loses the game when the hit points reach zero.

This game runs at 30 frames per second and the time (t) – in frames – between two meteors in the scenario of the game is given by the formula (1):

$$t = 70 * (0,94 - d * 0,01)^{l+d} \tag{1}$$

In the expression (1), d represents the level of difficulty of the game, i.e., easy ($d=1$), normal ($d=2$) or hard ($d=3$), l represents the current level of the game and may vary from one to 20. This expression was used in the game in order to ensure that the amount of meteors dropping from the "sky" is directly related to the level of difficulty and the current phase of the game. In turn, formula (2) specifies the maximum size of meteor (s) that may fall into certain levels of play. There is also a random function that is used to launch meteors in the scenario of the game of a size between $s=1$ and the maximum size described in formula (2).

$$s = 1 + (l + d) * 0,4 \tag{2}$$

Fig. 3 shows the ten different sizes of meteors (all in the same scale). Fig. 3a to Fig. 3h show the eight main sizes (s) in increasing order from left to right. These eight types of meteors appear in all 20 levels of the game according to the random function. There are also two bigger meteors – "bosses" in gaming jargon – that appear only once during level 10 (Fig. 3i) and level 20 (Fig. 3j).

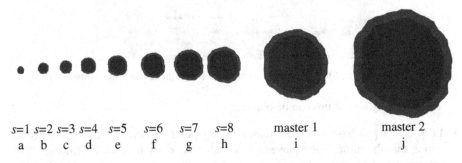

| $s=1$ $s=2$ $s=3$ $s=4$ | $s=5$ | $s=6$ | $s=7$ | $s=8$ | master 1 | master 2 |
| a   b   c   d | e | f | g | h | i | j |

Fig. 3. Meteors used in the game. The eight main meteor sizes are presented in (a) to (h). Meteors "bosses" (i) and (j) are used, respectively, in level 10 and level 20

Different sizes of meteors have different impacts in relation to the hit points when dropping on the city. Formula (3) describes the function of hit point loss (p) in relation to meteor size (s):

$$p = 8 + (s * 5) \tag{3}$$

In expression (3), s represents the size of meteor which can vary from 1 to 8. This expression was used to ensure that the damage caused on the city is neither too small nor too big, because there is a very strong linear growth.

In each of the 20 levels the player can win +4 bonus points. If one level is finished with no loss ("full life"), i.e. no meteor dropped on the city, the player gains an extra bonus point, thus concluding the level with +5 bonus points. Furthermore, depending on the user's performance in the game bonus points won at the end of each level can be "converted" into power-ups (improvements). It is worth noting that the cost of power-ups has no fixed value, but varies depending on the progress of the levels of the game. Fig. 4 shows the interface where power-ups can be acquired.

Fig. 4. Power-ups that can be acquired between the levels of the game

The following power-ups can be obtained:

- **Life:** Every purchase of life increases the hit point capacity by 20%. It is worth noting that the initially the player starts with 100 points in level 1. However, this amount might increase when acquiring additional hit points. As the hit points bar graphically represents the value of a percentage, it always remains the same size, even after several acquisitions of Life.

- **Power:** Force used to deflect the meteor from its initial trajectory. Each purchase of "Power" increases the capacity by 18%.
- **Rate of Fire:** Amount of time between shots of the cannon. Each acquisition of "Rate of Fire" the time between shots is reduced by 20%.
- **Recharge:** Time required to reload the cannon with more "ammo" (ammunition). The formula (4) represents the recharge function (r). In practice, this parameter influences the rate at which the shots are available for use. With the purchase of "Recharge", shots are available for use sooner.

$$r = 35 - (n * 3,6) \tag{4}$$

- **Ammo Capacity:** Amount of the cannon shots that are ready to be fired. The formula (5) represents the function ammo capacity (a). Acquiring the "Ammo Capacity" increases the number of cannon shots.

$$a = 12 + (n * 6) \tag{5}$$

- **Accuracy:** Distance between the point aimed at and the point where the projectile will be fired at. The acquisition of "Accuracy" lowers this distance by 15%. Acquiring "Accuracy" eight times will achieve 100% accuracy.

The first parameter (Life) increases hit points and other five parameters are related to improvements of the cannon. It is worth noting that improvements in these six parameters of the game can be performed up to eight times. The cost of acquisition is increasing and always the same for all parameters: 1, 2, 2, 2, 3, 3, 3, and 4.

Meteor Invasion has simple rules and controls. At the same time, it is an engaging game. These characteristics make it a good choice for evaluating AIRs in the context of use of computer games, since it can be expected that side effects due to unattractive, tedious, complicated or unclear gameplay are minimized. Furthermore, regarding the evaluation of the hardware characteristics of AIRs, Meteor Invasion is a dynamic game that requires short response times from hardware input.

4   Research Scenario and Methodology

For the experiment presented in this paper, we built on the experiences of previous experiments of this nature that had already been carried out by our research team, for example, the experiment that evaluated the interaction of users with the TV via remote control [3] and the experiment that evaluated the interaction of users with an iDTV simulated application via the AIRs [5,7].

The activity was conducted on April 2011 and was recorded with prior consent of participants to facilitate future analyses. The experiment involved the participation of seven users identified in this work by U1, U2, ..., U6, U7. Table 1 presents information about the users who participated in the experiment. It is worth noting that all users of the study are undergraduate or graduate students of Computer Science at

University of Campinas (UNICAMP), Brazil. This audience was chosen for conducting this experiment because of the potential familiarity with videogame consoles and games development.

Table 1. Additional information regarding the participants in the experiment

User	Age	Gender	Handedness	Gaming experience	
				Yes/No	Description
U1	21	M	right-handed	yes	game user, developer and renter
U2	21	M	right-handed	yes	game user only
U3	24	M	right-handed	yes	game user and developer
U4	22	M	left-handed	yes	game user only
U5	22	M	right-handed	yes	game user only
U6	22	M	right-handed	yes	game user only
U7	22	F	right-handed	yes	game user only

At the beginning of the experiment the facilitator, who is also the first author of this paper, gave a presentation explaining the solution of AIRs and how the AIRs had been adapted to function in the context of use of computer games. The facilitator also showed users how to play Meteor Invasion with the mouse and with the AIRs, since the objective was to evaluate the interaction of users with this game by using these two input devices.

The odd-numbered users – i.e., U1, U3, U5, and U7 – started playing the game with the mouse and then switched to the AIRs, while for even-numbered users the reverse sequence was adopted. Despite the small number of participating users, it was possible to conduct a preliminary analysis to evaluate whether the sequence has an effect on the results.

Although Meteor Invasion has 20 levels (each with a maximum of 50 seconds), we chose to limit the experiment to the first two levels, i.e., if the subject successfully completed level 2, the experiment was terminated. This decision was made because the objective of the experiment was to evaluate the suitability of AIRs in the use context of computer games by comparing mouse and AIR performance, i.e. the objective was not to evaluate the learnability of the AIRs' interaction language. In order to guarantee an equal base of comparison for all users, the participants were instructed not to perform any power-up acquisition when the advancing from level 1 to level 2.

The following materials were used during the experiment:

- hardware prototype of AIRs for computer games;
- the Meteor Invasion game;
- one notebook with RGB output;
- one USB mouse;
- one LCD projector;
- one digital camcorder;
- one audio amplifier;
- one stopwatch;
- seven forms of personal data;

- seven terms of consent;
- seven observer forms;
- seven feedback forms for game players;
- seven player self-assessment forms – SAM;
- seven feedback forms for the observer.

For this activity three researchers assumed the following roles:

- **Facilitator:** Responsible for the ongoing dynamics of the experiment;
- **Observer:** Responsible for filling out the observation form, measuring game completion time, and collecting participants' feedback and self-assessment forms;
- **Cameraman:** Responsible for filming the activity and especially the interaction of users with the AIRs hardware prototype and the game.

5   Experiment Results

Table 2 and Table 3 present the quantitative results of the experiment, i.e., the points obtained by the seven participants after the first and the second levels of Meteor Invasion. A dash ("-") means that the respective user lost the game during level 1.

Table 2. Points at the end of each level of the players who started the game using the mouse

Interaction	Hardware	Game level	Users			
			U1	U3	U5	U7
1st	Mouse	1	5	5	4	4
		2	9	9	8	8
2nd	AIRs	1	4	4	4	0
		2	8	8	8	–

Regarding Table 2 it is worth noting that U7 using AIRs during the second interaction lost the game before completing level 1 (49.90s).

Table 3. Points at the end of each level of the players who started the game using AIRs

Interaction	Hardware	Game level	Users		
			U2	U4	U6
1st	AIRs	1	0	4	4
		2	–	8	9
2nd	Mouse	1	0	4	5
		2	–	8	9

Regarding Table 3, it is worth noting that U2 using AIRs in his first interaction lost the game before completing level 1 (47.94s). This same user also lost the game during the second interaction, i.e. using the mouse (25.06s). Fig. 5 presents this data in a single chart.

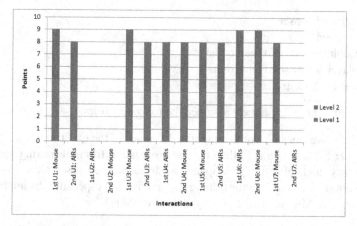

Fig. 5. Points scored in the game by the participants of the experiment

Regarding users whose first interaction with the game was done via mouse, it is worth noting that the results of U1 and U3 suggest that performance (based on points earned in the game) was higher with the use of the mouse. The performance of U7 was lower than both U1 and U3 using the mouse. Using the AIRs, U7 could not complete level 1. U5 had a performance that was similar for both input methods.

As for users whose first interaction with the game was done via the AIRs, U2 could not complete level 1 with neither AIRs nor the mouse. However, it is worth noting that U2 lost the game faster with the mouse (25.06s) than with AIRs (47.94s). Therefore it seems that the performance of that user has not been adversely affected due to the use of the new hardware of interaction. U6 had slightly higher performance using the mouse. U4 showed similar performance for both input types. Independently of the hardware input method (mouse or AIRs), no user lost the game at level 2 after passing level 1.

The result of the performance of the players using AIRs, compared to the performance of the players using the mouse (whether in the first or second stage of interaction with the game), suggests that, despite the users have much more developed skills regarding the mouse use, the AIRs seem appropriate for the context of use of computer games. However, further investigations are required, i.e. conducting activities with a larger number of users and different games, and most importantly also analyzing qualitative data.

Finally, we highlight the good learning curve for the interaction language of the AIRs for the context of electronic games, as well as a good user acceptance. Thus, we gathered evidence that suggest that the AIRs are adequate for playing computer games.

6   Conclusion

This paper presented preliminary results of an experiment conducted in order to evaluate the suitability of Adjustable Interactive Rings in the context of use of computer games. As demonstrated in this work, the performance of the players with the AIRs was similar using the mouse, even for those users who had never used AIRs before the experiment. Moreover, the AIRs' interaction language was quickly learned by users.

As future work, we suggest the use of Adjustable Interactive Rings in other contexts of use to evaluate their suitability in other application domains.

Acknowledgments. This work was partially supported by the State of São Paulo Research Foundation (FAPESP grant #2010/11004-9), by the Brazilian National Council of Scientific and Technological Development (CNPq grant #141058/2010-2), and by the Physical Artifacts of Interaction Research Group (PAIRG) at the Federal University of Rio Grande do Norte (UFRN), Brazil. The authors would also like to thank the Meteor Invasion developer for permitting us to use his game for the experiment described in this paper.

References

1. Kinect: Microsoft Kinect, http://www.xbox.com/kinect/
2. Miranda, L.C., Baranauskas, M.C.C.: UNICAMP: Artefato Físico de Interação de Televisão Digital. BR Patent PI1013466-2 (2010)
3. Miranda, L.C., Hayashi, E.C.S., Baranauskas, M.C.C.: Identifying Interaction Barriers in the Use of Remote Controls. In: 4th Latin American Conference on Human-Computer Interaction / 7th Latin American Web Congress, pp. 97–104. IEEE, Los Alamitos (2009)
4. Miranda, L.C., Hornung, H.H., Baranauskas, M.C.C.: Adjustable Interactive Rings for iDTV. IEEE Transactions on Consumer Electronics 56(3), 1988–1996 (2010)
5. de Miranda, L.C., Hornung, H.H., Baranauskas, M.C.C.: Adjustable Interactive Rings for iDTV: First Results of an Experiment with End-Users. In: Kurosu, M. (ed.) HCD 2011. LNCS, vol. 6776, pp. 262–271. Springer, Heidelberg (2011)
6. de Miranda, L.C., Hornung, H.H., Baranauskas, M.C.C.: Prospecting a New Physical Artifact of Interaction for iDTV: Results of Participatory Practices. In: Marcus, A. (ed.) HCII 2011 and DUXU 2011, Part II. LNCS, vol. 6770, pp. 167–176. Springer, Heidelberg (2011)
7. Miranda, L.C., Hornung, H.H., Baranauskas, M.C.C.: Qualitative Results of an Experiment with Adjustable Interactive Rings for iDTV. In: IADIS International Conference on Interfaces and Human Computer Interaction, pp. 233–240. IADIS Press, Lisbon (2011)s
8. Miranda, L.C.: Artifacts and Languages of Interaction with Contemporary Digital Systems: The Adjustable Interactive Rings for Interactive Digital Television (part in Portuguese). Ph.D. Thesis, University of Campinas (2010)
9. Miranda, Z.C.: Meteor Invasion, http://www.kongregate.com/games/Z_master/meteor-invasion/
10. Schuler, D., Namioka, A.: Participatory Design: Principles and Practices. Lawrence Erlbaum Associates, Hillsdale (1993)
11. Story, M.F.: Maximizing Usability: The Principles of Universal Design. Assistive Technology 10(1), 4–12 (1998)
12. WiiMote: Nintendo WiiMote, http://www.nintendo.com/wii/

Gamification at Work: Designing Engaging Business Software

Janaki Kumar

3410 Hillview Ave., Palo Alto, CA, 94304, USA
janaki.kumar@sap.com

Abstract. Gamification is a buzz word in business these days. In its November 2012 press release, Gartner predicts that "by 2015, 40% of Global 1000 organizations will use gamification as the primary mechanism to transform business operations". In the same report, they also predict that "by 2014, 80% of current gamified applications will fail to meet business objectives, primarily due to poor design".

What is gamification? Does it belong in the workplace? Are there design best practices that can increase the chance of success of enterprise gamification efforts?

Janaki Kumar answers these questions and more in this paper Gamification @ Work. She cautions against taking a "chocolate covered broccoli" approach of simply adding points and badges to business applications and calling them gamified. She outlines a methodology called Player Centered Design which is a practical guide for user experience designers, product managers and developers to incorporate the principles of gamification into their software.

Keywords: Gamification, Enterprise Gamification, Gamification of business software, enterprise software, business software, User experience design, UX, Design, Engagement, Motivation.

1   Introduction

"The opposite of play is not work, it is depression"

– Brian Sutton-Smith

This paper covers the intersection of the worlds of enterprise software and gamification.

Enterprise software refers to software that businesses use to run their day-to-day activities such as finance, sales, human resources, manufacturing, shipping, and procurement. It is typically purchased by companies as off-the-shelf software, customized and configured to meet their business needs, and made available to their employees. Enterprise software provides visibility to executives regarding the health of their organization and enables them to make course corrections as needed.

Gamification is the application of game design principles and mechanics to non-game environments. It attempts to make technology more inviting by encouraging

A. Marcus (Ed.): DUXU/HCII 2013, Part II, LNCS 8013, pp. 528–537, 2013.

users to engage in desired behaviors by showing the path to mastery, and taking advantage of people's innate enjoyment of play.

Gamification is a buzzword in business these days. Both Fortune Magazine and Wall Street Journal have noted this trend in late 2011. In its November 2012 press release, Gartner predicts that "by 2015, 40% of Global 1000 organizations will use gamification as the primary mechanism to transform business operations"[1]. M2 Research predicts that the gamification market will reach 2.8 billion dollars by 2016[2].

There are many reasons for this trend. To name a few, the changing nature of information work, entry into the workforce of digital natives[3]- a new generation that has grown up playing online and video games, and the wide spread adoption of social media and mobile technology. Businesses are turning to gamification both to engage their customers and to motivate their employees.

As with any innovative trend, best practices are still emerging. This paper explores the application of design best practices to gamification to increase the chance of success. It outlines a process called Player Centered Design, which offers a five step approach to gamification that works.

2   Beyond User Centered Design

Designers who adopt the user centered design philosophy in their daily work, pay attention to the user's goals, and strive to build products that help the user achieve them in an efficient, effective, and satisfactory manner.

While effectiveness, efficiency, and satisfaction are worthy goals, gaming and gamification extends and adds increased engagement to these goals. In the context of a game, players voluntarily seek challenges to enhance their playing experience. They seek empowerment over efficiency, delight, and fun over mere satisfaction. These factors increase their level of engagement in the game.

3   Player Centered Design Process

To help designers deal with these changing rules and rising expectations, we introduce a concept called Player Centered Design that puts the player at the center of the design and development process. The figure below illustrates the process of Player Centered Design.

3.1   Understand the Player

The first step in the player centered design approach is to understand the player and their context. The success of your gamification efforts depends on this clear understanding.

---

[1] Gartner November 28th Gamification Trends and Strategies to Help Prepare for the Future. Burke. B.

[2] M2 Research Fall 2011: http://www.m2research.com/

[3] http://en.wikipedia.org/wiki/Digital_native

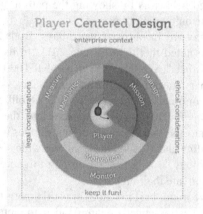

Fig. 1. Player Centered Design Process

Is your player a sales representative, a financial controller, an employee, a supplier, or a customer? Identify them and understand as much as you can about them.

Fig 2 provides a template to capture the multi dimensionality of the player, since this has a direct impact to their gamification preference.

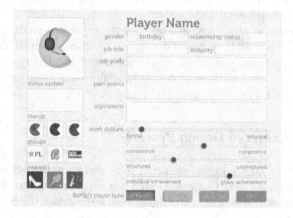

Fig. 2. Player persona template

3.2   Understand the Mission

The next step is to define the Mission. This step involves understanding the current business scenario (what players are doing today), identifying the desired or target business outcome (what management wants to achieve), and setting an appropriate mission for your gamification project.

3.3   Understand Human Motivation

"Gamification is 75% Psychology and 25% Technology."

– Gabe Zichermann

There are two general types of motivations: intrinsic and extrinsic. Intrinsic motivation refers to internal motivations such as autonomy, mastery and meaning. Extrinsic refers to external motivational techniques such as money, trophies etc.

There are a number of theories of human motivation. We recommend you familiarize yourself with the latest research on motivation in order to create effective game mechanics.

Motivational drivers, discussed below, have applicability beyond digital technology. They are based on observations on what motivates people in the real world, and drawing from this knowledge to design engaging experiences in the virtual world.

Here is a curated list of behaviors that drive motivation.

Collecting

We enjoy collecting – trading cards, coins, stamps, antique wristwatches, cars or friends on Facebook. Some collections may have monetary value, e.g. trading cards. While other collections may be symbolic of social status, e.g. friends on Facebook. Once we get started on a collection that comes in a "set", we have the urge for "Set Completion". If the set is infinite, we are motivated to keep collecting for the joy it brings us. In some cases, we may compare our collections to others and feel the urge to compete.

Connecting

We long to be part of something larger than ourselves. This could mean connecting to other people to be part of a community, or connecting to a cause to be part of something larger and meaningful. We join clubs of various sorts to connect with people like us and have meaningful shared experiences. It validates our existence and makes life more enjoyable.

Achievement

We get great satisfaction from achievement, no matter what our Bartle player profile. If we are challenged, we are more likely than not, motivated to try hard to achieve success. When we do, we get a positive psychological feedback that makes us want to do it again. There are some subtle factors to pay attention to. If the challenge is too difficult or too easy, we may not be as motivated by achievement, as we would be if the challenge is the just right level of difficulty.

We do not expect to win every time. A variable schedule of achievement or a chance to win may be enough of a motivator to make us try. Lottery players play for the chance to win even if they know intellectually that the odds of winning are not high.

Feedback

We like to receive feedback. This could be as simple as the small nods we get when we talk to people. It communicates "I heard you. I am paying attention. What you are saying is worth listening to". It motivates us to continue talking to this person. A digital example is Amazon sending us an instant confirmation email when we place an order. It communicates "We received your order. It is safe with us". It enhances our sense of security and wellbeing.

Not receiving any feedback can be extremely demotivating. If you were talking to someone and they remained impassive, you will eventually stop talking, since you are not sure if the other person hears you or understands you. Software that gives you no feedback when you perform an action is significantly less enjoyable to use than one that does.

Self-Expression

We are entering an era of hyper-personalization enabled by technology. Companies like Nike are offering customers the ability to specify the exact size, features, colors, and style of their shoes. Players of online games spend time customizing their avatars, from eye and skin color and body shape to accessories like earrings, hats and gloves, to control how they are viewed by other players.

Reciprocity

Many of us have had the experience of walking into a store, accepting a "free" sample, and feeling compelled to make a purchase out of a sense of reciprocity. Organizations such as the March of Dimes, Cystic Fibrosis Foundation, World Wildlife Fund, Easter Seals and the American Diabetes Foundation send free address labels to potential donors to leverage this motivational driver as a fund raising technique.

Blissful Productivity

Mihaly Csikszentmihalyi (pronounced MEE-hy CHEEK-sent-me-hi-ee), a distinguished professor of Psychology and Management at Claremont Graduate University. He is the director of Quality of Life Research Center and has done pioneering work researching human strengths such as optimism, motivation and responsibility. He defined the concept of Flow as "The mental state of operating in which a person in an activity is fully immersed in the feeling of energized focus, full involvement and the success in the process of the activity". When a task is too difficult, it causes people to be anxious. When a task is to too easy, it causes boredom. When the task it just right, we are in a state of heightened focus and immersion, or in other words a state of Flow.

Video game players experience this sense of flow when the game is the right level of difficulty for their skill. Games offer levels so users can graduate to increasing difficulty levels as their skills improve. Business software can benefit from incorporating the concept of levels to enable their users to achieve this sense of flow.

3.4   Apply Game Mechanics

Armed with a clear understanding of the player and the mission, and the theory behind human motivation, it is time to apply game mechanics, and create a positive flow for your gamification project. Game mechanics refer to the UI elements player interacts with such as badges, points and leaderboards to name a few. Here are a list of game mechanics relevant to enterprise software.

Points

Points are the granular units of measurement in gamification. They are single count metrics. This is the way the system keeps count of the player's actions pertaining to the targeted behaviors in the overall gamification strategy. For example, FourSquare counts each check in, and LinkedIn counts each connection.

Points provide instant feedback to the player, and thus address the feedback motivational driver. Players may also motivated by collection, to see their points count go up.

Badges

Once the player has accumulated a certain number of points, they may be awarded badges. Badges are a form of virtual achievement by the player. They provide positive reinforcement for the targeted behavior.

Foursquare awards badges, when the player has accumulated enough check-ins. Another example of a badge is eBay's top seller virtual "ribbon".

Badges address the motivational driver of collection and achievement.

Leaderboards

Leaderboards bring in the social aspect of points and badges, by displaying the players on a list typically ranked in descending order with the greatest number of points at the top. The possible disadvantage of a leaderboard is that it could be demotivating to a new player. For example, if player A has 10,000 points, and is on top of the leaderboard, and a new player B had 10 points and is at the bottom, it is likely that player B may become demotivated and give up playing the game. They may believe that they are never going to compete with player A, and therefore why should they even try?

Foursquare has a modified leaderboard into a cross-situational leader board. This variant places the logged-in player in the center and shows similar scoring fellow players above and below for context. The ranking (points) is limited to a set of players who are close to the logged-in player. The goal with this variant of leaderboard is to motivate the player to compete with the players closest to them. Note that, a cross-situational leaderboard may be different for each player since it is limited to their context. It does not convey an overall ranking of all players.

The achievement motivational driver is addressed via a leaderboard.

Relationships

Relationships are game mechanics based on the motivational driver of connection. We are social beings, and relationships have a powerful effect on how we feel and what we do.

Peer pressure is not restricted to school age children. Adults succumb to it too. In 2010, the authors did research on personal sustainability and one of the findings was that a trusted person in a participant's network had more impact on their day-to-day choices than the media. For example, participants were more likely to recycle if a trusted member of their community did so, than if they were told to do so by the media.

Relationships reduce stress in people and are positive motivators. People who are trying to quit bad habits such as alcoholism, or deal with a loss of a loved one have found support groups to offer emotional support and encouragement during a time of need. In the technology world, developer communities are a good example of a support group for developers where they offer and receive technical help.

Relationship addresses the motivational driver of connection.

Challenge (with Epic Meaning)

Challenge is a powerful game mechanic to motivate people to action, especially if they believe they are working to achieve something great, something awe-inspiring, and something bigger than themselves.

Scientists at the University of Washington challenged the public to play Foldit a game about protein folding. Folding proteins provides important clues to the scientists on how to prevent or treat diseases such as HIV/AIDS, cancer and Alzheimer's. A team of experts had worked on this problem for over 10 years and had not solved it. Once the scientific challenge was launched in the form of a game, 46,000 volunteer players solved the puzzle in 10 days.

The challenge game mechanic addresses the achievement motivational driver. However, in the case of the Foldit challenge, the feeling of connection and perhaps reciprocity, (if the player had known someone dear to them suffering with the illness the challenge was seeking to cure) may have played a part in it's overwhelming success.

Constraints (with Urgent Optimism)

Interestingly constraints such as deadlines, when combined with urgent optimism, motivates people to action. Urgent Optimism refers to extreme self-motivation. It is the desire to act immediately to tackle an obstacle combined with the belief that we have a reasonable hope of success.

Some registration sites use gamification to reduce the drop off rate by limiting the amount of time the user can take to complete the registration process.

Gilt, a fashion ecommerce site, constrains the time allowed for their customers to bid on items to motivate them to action.

Players are motivated by achievement when they are faced with these constraints and are driven to overcome them.

Journey

The journey game mechanic recognizes that the player is on a personal journey and incorporates this element into the experience. Here are three examples of implementations of this game mechanic.

Onboarding

A new player needs to be on boarded since they are just starting the journey. Offering help, and a brief introduction to the features and functions motivate the player to embark on the journey.

Scaffolding

Scaffolding is a way to help the on-boarded, but yet inexperienced user, prevent errors and feel a sense of positive accomplishment. A product could progressively disclose more features as the player gains more experience using the product.

Progress

Progress refers to providing feedback to the user on where they are in the journey, and encouraging them to take the next step.

Journey addresses the player's need for blissful productivity, by presenting the right set of features appropriate to the player's level in the game.

Narrative

The narrative game mechanic draws the player into a story within the game. Zombie Run, a fitness game, uses narrative to make the player believe that zombies are after them, and they need to run as fast as they can to get away. The object of the game is to motivate the player to get fit without making it explicit.

Narrative offers the player a chance to express themselves via role play. In the case of Zombie run, players are motivated by achievement by out-running the zombies.

Emotion

As Don Norman eloquently argues in his book Emotional Design, our emotions do play a role in how we experience a product.

In many ways, emotional design is a large category in and of itself. In the context of gamification, we are not attempting to cover the topic as a whole. Rather, we want to draw inspiration from it, to enrich our gamification designs.

Game designers have led the way in investing in high quality artwork that appeal to our emotions in their products. Consumer products (iPhones, iPads) and websites (Pinterest) are following this trend. Employees experience emotional delight in the consumer software they use, and have similar expectations with enterprise software.

Humor is another emotion pertinent to game mechanics. The tone of the product can be conveyed in the micro-copy, or the informational text and messages on the user interfaces. Humor has the power to deflect a negative experience into a (somewhat) positive one.

Humorous micro-copy addresses the motivational driver of feedback. While people may choose to use esthetically designed products as an avenue of self-expression.

Game Economy

Garner describes game economy as follows:

There are four basic currencies that players accumulate in game economies — fun, things, social capital and self-esteem — that are implemented through game mechanics, such as points, badges and leaderboards. These game mechanics are simply tokens of different currencies of motivation that are being applied to reward players.

As part of the game plan, you can decide the mechanics you want to use as currencies in your game economy.

3.5   Game Rules

Once you have decided what mechanics to use, the next them is to come up with a set of rules of the game. If you are designing a system to motivate call center employees to undergo training, and you decided to use points in your game economy, you will need to decide how many points you award for the action. If the employee only took 50% of the training, do they receive all the points, none of the points or 50% of the points?

The rules of the game pull together the mechanics into a flow to motivate the player to achieve the mission.

3.6   Engagement Loop

The core engagement loop refers to game mechanics combined with positive reinforcement and feedback loops that keeps the player engaged in the game. This concept has been discussed by both Amy Jo Kim, a renowned game designer.

The four main stages in the loop are:

- Motivate emotion,
- Call to action,
- Re-engage,
- Feedback and reward.

This frequent invitation to interact with the system creates positive reinforcement and the player will be motivated to stay engaged.

3.7   Manage, Monitor and Measure

Gamification is a program and not a project. Therefore, it is important to start small, closely monitor progress, and adjust as needed. The mission needs to be managed, the motivation needs to be monitored, and mechanics need to be measured continuously.

3.8   Other Considerations in the Enterprise Context

There are many legal and ethical consideration that impact gamification in the context of the enterprise. Privacy and worker's protection practices vary across countries, and what may be legal in one country may not be in another.

The ethics of gamification need to be considered as part of any project. Gamification can be used to engage and motivate, and never manipulate.

The ultimate goal of gamification is to engender positive emotions in the player such as fun, trust and delight. It is important not to forget this when working on the serious aspects of gamification.

4   Conclusion

In this paper, we present a process of gamification, which we call Player Centered Design. It is inspired by User Centered Design, but goes beyond UCD to incorporate the concept of engagement. The process begins with a good understanding of the player, and the mission. This is followed by psychological research on motivation. Based on this solid foundation, we advocate a thoughtful application of game mechanics, economy and rules to create a core engagement loop. We recommend you start small, monitor closely for best results. The enterprise context including legal and ethical considerations cannot be ignored. And remember to make it fun!

Stand Up, Heroes! : Gamification for Standing People on Crowded Public Transportation

Itaru Kuramoto, Takuya Ishibashi, Keiko Yamamoto, and Yoshihiro Tsujino

Kyoto Institute of Technology
Matsugasaki, Sakyo-ku, Kyoto, 606-8585 Japan
ent@hit.is.kit.ac.jp

Abstract. There are quite many commuters who are forced to keep standing on crowded public transportation in Japan, and they often feel fatigue and frustration. Stand Up, Heroes! (SUH) is an EELF-based gamification system to motivate commuters to keep standing. In SUH, they have their own avatars which grow according to their time of standing. As the result of a twelve-week practical evaluation, it is found that SUH can stimulate commuters' motivation during first eight weeks. Growing-up avatars are most effective for stimulation and fun. However, some participants cannot feel fun or stimulation for standing from SUH, because their public transportation which they get on is not so crowded that they can seat on the transportation.

Keywords: gamification, EELF, public transportation, motivation, mobile device.

1 Introduction

1.1 Background

In Japan, most of workers commonly use public transportation such as buses and urban trains for commute. There are so many commuters that the transportation is usually crowded, especially at the rush hour. In this situation, they cannot commute comfortably, and must keep standing on the transportation during long time to their offices. They then often feel fatigue and frustration. Such problematic situations have been one of the Japanese social problems.

As usual, commuters on train usually kill time by reading books, playing games, listening to music tunes, and so on. However, on quite crowded transportation at the rush hour, they cannot do most of such activities because they cannot move there. Moreover, such activities are only for time killing, so their feelings of fatigue and frustrations are piled up during commuting even if they could.

In order to solve the problem on the quite crowded public transportation, we propose a method to gamify the commuter rush hours based on EELF [1], which is one of the frameworks of gamification and aims to motivate users for daily dull and monotonous activities. Based on the proposed gamification method, we implement a new game system named "Stand Up, Heroes!" which motivates users for the troublesome crowded public transportation.

A. Marcus (Ed.): DUXU/HCII 2013, Part II, LNCS 8013, pp. 538–547, 2013.
© Springer-Verlag Berlin Heidelberg 2013

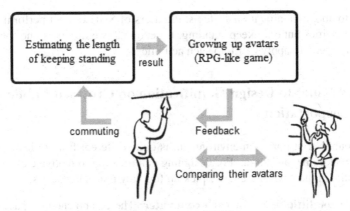

Fig. 1. Concept of SUH

Fig. 1 shows the concept of the game system. "Stand Up, Heroes!" (SUH) recognizes the time and whether to take on public transportation by an accelerometer built in a mobile device such as smartphone, and SUH estimates the level of their effort to keep standing. Then SUH represents an avatar for each commuter which grows up according to his or her estimated subjective effort, and the avatar acts automatically in a fantasy RPG (role playing game) like game system. The longer and harder users keep standing up on public transportation, the stronger their avatars become. Users can compare their avatars' abilities and their finding treasures each other, which leads fun and motivation to keep standing.

1.2   Related Works

SUH is one of the gamification systems, which introduce game mechanism into non-game applications such as office, social networks, and so on [2]. Emotional Flower [3] is one of such systems to enhance social interaction at office. In this system, each office worker has their own virtual flower which grows up according to the time of the owner's positive facial expression. The flowers are shown on a shared display at the office. Weekend Battle [4] is another gamification system in office environment. This system is based on EELF framework. Office workers have their own avatars, and they grow up according to their subjective workload which is estimated based on the number of operations on their PC for work.

Exercise and education is another target of the gamification. GrabApple [5] is an exergame, which means a gamification system for physical exercise, for motivating daily casual exercises. Grammenos et. al propose an exergame for advertising food products [6]. This research aims to make advertisements active so that the exergame can produce positive feeling of the products to players. In education area, Howland et. al propose a language learning system with video game elements such as 3D virtual world, item collection, scoring system, and so on [7]. MIPS (Musical Instrument Practice System) [8] is another one of EELF-based gamification systems for those who practice musical instruments such as piano.

Unlike to above gamification systems, the users of SUH did not perform anything for target activities but only keep standing. In section 2, we discuss some special considerations needed to apply EELF to such activities.

2   Key Issues to Design Gamification on Crowded Public Transportation

Crowded public transportation environment is quite different from ordinal ones such as at office, at home, and so on. For designing gamification to motivate commuters to keep standing in the environment, we pick up four key issues to discuss.

1. **Consider too little space for each commuter:** There is no enough space to manipulate his or her own device and to watch any displays in the environment. The gamification must not require any operations normally, and some non-visible feedbacks, such as audible, touch, and so on, must be provided.
2. **Consider the length of commuting:** In common, a commuter with longer time spent feels much more fatigue than shorter one. The gamification must take time spent in commuting into account.
3. **Consider the difference of commute paths:** Commuters have different paths to their offices each other. If only the time for commuting affects the gamification, some commuters with longer commuting paths always have advantages in game play. In such a case, it is afraid that other commuters with short paths might lose the motivation for using the gamification. It is needed to enable to configure the gamification settings to avoid that the difference of their commute paths has an enormous influence on the fun of the gamification.
4. **Consider the newcomers in the middle of use:** Not all users start using the gamification at the same time, so it should take care of newcomers after introduction.

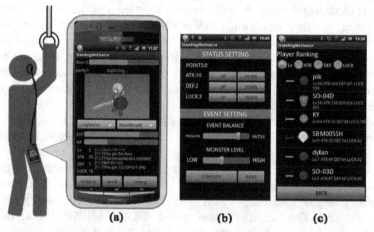

Fig. 2. Implementation of SUH: (a) exploring, (b) strategy configuration, (c) all users' avatars

3   Implementation

SUH (shown in Fig. 2) is implemented as an application on a mobile device such as smartphone. It has two subsystems: transportation-and-standing estimation subsystem and avatar-and-game representation subsystem.

3.1   Transportation and Standing Estimation

At first, this subsystem estimates the type of transportation using an accelerometer and a GPS receiver built in a mobile device. In transportation estimation, the subsystem tries to get the current place of a user, or a mobile device, by GPS receiver. If recognized place is near a station, it decides that the user is on public transportation such as trains or buses. If the place is far from any stations, then it checks the current speed of user's, or a mobile device's, movement. Only when the speed is enough fast as moving on public transportations, it decides the user is now on public transportation. If GPS receiver cannot recognize the current place, for example, when in underground, it reminds the last place where it could recognize successfully. Only if the last place is near a subway station, it decides that he or she is on subway, one of public transportations. This algorithm is shown in Fig. 3. This subsystem samples the current place every one minute, and the threshold of the distance of a "near" station is 30 meters. It means that a certain station is near when the distance between the current place and the station is shorter than 30m.

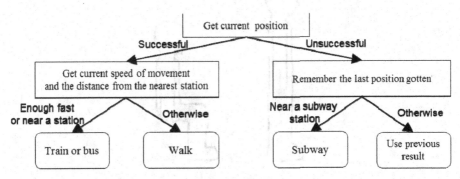

Fig. 3. Estimation algorithm of the type of transportation

We evaluate the accuracy of the estimation method practically. We implemented the estimation method on an Android smartphone as a mobile device, and one of the authors carry the smartphone and move along his commute path, including each 20-minute walk, train, and subway. We gather the log on five round trips of the path. Table 1 shows the result of accuracy, coverage and F-value of the estimation method. These F-values are high, so the subsystem can estimate which type of transportation a commuter uses enough for implementation of SUH.

Table 1. Result of estimating which type of transportation a commuter uses

Type	Accuracy	Coverage	F-value
Walk	.773	.888	.827
Train	.913	.818	.863
Subway	.893	.962	.926

Then, in order to estimate whether a user is standing or not, the subsystem uses the orientation of gravity acceleration (G) of the mobile device in one of the pockets of the user's trousers or pants. The subsystem decides the user standing only when the orientation of G is along to Y-axis. When sitting, the orientation of G moves some different direction which is not along to Y-axis (see Fig. 4). In addition, the subsystem distinguishes walking from standing and sitting, with using the variance of the value of acceleration measured. If we are standing or sitting quietly, our bodies do not move so much, so the acceleration of the mobile device is almost unchanged during standing. By contrast, when we are walking, our bodies continue to move. In such a case, the acceleration value is continuously changing. It means that the valiance on walking is larger than on standing or sitting. This subsystem samples the value of acceleration with 10 Hz frequency, and uses 50 (five second) sampling values for calculating the valiance.

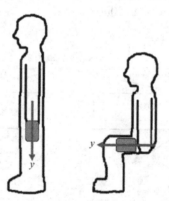

Fig. 4. How to estimate standing by a mobile device with an accelerometer

We evaluated the accuracy of the estimation method practically. We implemented the method on an iPod touch as a mobile device. We recruited eight participants who are undergraduate students, and asked them to commute with the device and to log manually their action below; sitting down on a sheet in public transportation, standing up from the sheet, starting walking, and stopping walking. We consider standing time as the period from standing up or stopping walking to any other action, sitting time as from sitting down to standing up, and walking time as from starting walking to stopping walking. Table 2 shows the result of the accuracy, coverage, and F-value of the estimation method. These F-values are high, so the subsystem can estimate whether a commuter stands, sits, or walks enough for implementation of SUH.

Table 2. Result of estimating a commuter standing, sitting, or walking

Period	Accuracy	Coverage	F-value
Stand up	.790	.868	.827
Sit	.969	.973	.971
Walk	.890	.825	.856

3.2   Avatar and Game Representation

This subsystem automatically executes a RPG-like game and controls each user's avatar. The avatar has abilities shown in Table 3. Experience point is the basic score of the avatar's ability, and the avatar gets the points when the user keeps standing on public transportation. When a certain amount of experience points are gathered, the avatar's level is up, and some other abilities are increased.

Table 3. Abilities of an avatar

Ability	Description
Level	Indicates comprehensive power of the avatar
Experience point	Indicates basic score of the avatar's ability
Vitality	The avatar can keep exploring while Vitality is positive
Attack	Affects the additional experience point when encountering a monster (If Attack is high, the point is increased)
Defense	Affects the decrement of vitality when encountering a monster (If Defense is high, the decrement is small)
Luck	Affects the probability of getting an equipment item when finding a treasure

In the game, the avatar explores a "dungeon," and the subsystem shows the progress of the exploration (see Fig. 2(a)). This progress is represented by audible feedbacks for satisfying the issue 1 mentioned in Section 2.

The avatar explores the dungeon only when the owner of the avatar keeps standing on public transportation. The longer he or she keeps standing, the deeper floor of the dungeon his or her avatar explores in. The avatar gets more experience points when the avatar explores in the deeper floor. It means that the avatar of the user who keeps standing for longer time is naturally stronger than others, which satisfies the issue 2. When the user stops standing because of getting off public transportation or sitting down on a sheet, the avatar returns to the first floor of the dungeon, and takes a rest until he or she stands up again.

An occasional event happens during exploring the dungeon. There are two types of events; encountering a monster and finding a treasure. In "encountering a monster" event, the avatar must fight against a monster. After the battle, the avatar's vitality point is decreased instead of getting additional experience points. If the vitality is below zero, the avatar dies and returns to the first floor of the dungeon. In "finding a treasure" event, the avatar finds either a healing potion, which cures the avatar's vitality point, or an equipment item, which can change the avatar's appearance.

There are commuters with shorter commuting paths, so their avatars might lose every time against the avatars of commuters with longer commute paths. To avoid the unfairness and to satisfy the issue 3, users can configure some settings to change the strategy of avatars' growing-up (see Fig. 2(b)), including:

- Changing the ratio of monster/treasure encounter: when the possibility to encounter monsters is high, an avatar can get more scores for growing up while increasing the possibility of its death.
- Changing the balance of gaining avatars' parameters at their level-up timing.

The avatar's abilities are reset at the beginning of every week to avoid accumulating too much difference of abilities between avatars. This covers the issue 4. However, this restart might make the motivation of long-term users decreased. To avoid this, equipment items are not reset at the beginning of week.

In addition, the subsystem shows all the users' avatars with the results of exploration such as their abilities and treasures via a web server (see Fig.2(c)). This representation is only visual and it is aimed users to watch the results out of public transportation.

4   Evaluation

We conducted an empirical experiment to evaluate the effect of SUH for solving the problem on crowded public transportation. We asked nine participants who commute to their offices or schools everyday by public transportation including trains and subways. We installed SUH to their Android smartphones, and they freely used SUH on their commute for twelve weeks. At the end of each week, we asked them to answer the questionnaire about their motivation for keep standing and the fun of SUH. We also asked them which component of SUH is fun. The questions are shown in Table 4.

Table 4. The questionnaire

Question	Answers
You feel motivation to keep standing with SUH.	From -2 (strongly disagree) to +2 (strongly agree)
You feel fun with SUH.	From -2 (strongly disagree) to +2 (strongly agree)
Which components of SUH is fun?	(A) Watching your avatar's growing-up
	(B) Configuring the strategy of your avatar's growing-up
	(C) Collecting equipment items
	(D) Changing the appearance of your avatar by equipped items
	(E) Comparing others' avatars to yours

The result of the questionnaire is shown in Fig. 5. As the result through the first eight experiment period, the average score of questionnaire about both motivation to keep standing and fun is slightly higher than zero. It indicates that SUH can motivate participants to keep standing and SUH is enough fun to motivate them. However, the average score is not so high. As the result of interviews after the experiment, three of participants whose average score is lower than zero told us that they had not met crowded trains on their commute paths. They had no chances to play with SUH, so they did not stimulate their motivation to keep standing nor feel fun.

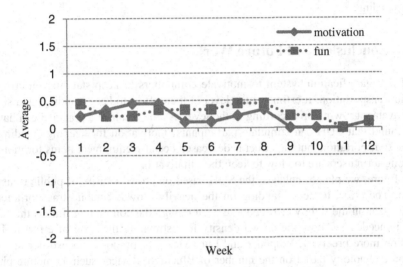

Fig. 5. Result of questionnaire: motivation and fun

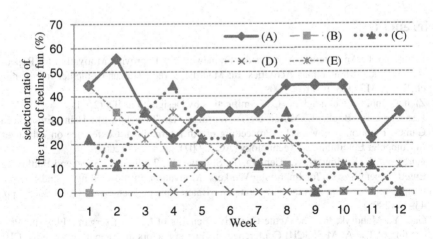

Fig. 6. Result of questionnaire: the reason of feeling fun

Fig. 6 shows the result of components which the participants feel fun from. As opposed to the previous expectation, collecting equipment items (C) stimulate their motivation during only the first half of the experiment. As the result of the interviews, some participants pointed out that they could not get new equipment items at the latter half of the experiment period because they had collected most of them. It indicates that the equipment items are too few to keep their long-term motivation of the participants. By contrast, watching avatars' growing-up (A) affects all through the experiment period. This is the same result of the long-term use of another EELF-based entertainment system [9], so the clear feedback of their effort is important to stimulate their motivation to keep standing.

5   Conclusion and Future Work

SUH is a gamification system to motivate commuters to keep standing on crowded public transportation. It estimates the level of their effort to keep standing, and shows their avatars growing up according to the level. As the result of a practical evaluation, it is found that SUH can stimulate participants' motivation for keeping standing on public transportation, but the effect is decreased because equipment items for motivating long-term users are too few to keep their motivation.

In future, we plan to enhance the SUH based on crowd density of public transportation. The effort to keep standing on the heavily crowded public transportation is higher than on the lightly crowded one even though the commuting time is the same, so it is needed to know the crowd density for estimating the level of effort to keep standing more precisely. Weppner and Lukowicz [10] propose a crowd density estimation technology based on the number of Bluetooth devices such as mobile phone which people have. We will evaluate the technique for SUH enhancement.

References

1. Kuramoto, I.: An Entertainment System Framework for Improving Motivation for Repetitive, Dull and Monotonous Activities. In: Maurtua, I. (ed.) Human-Computer Interaction, ch.18, pp. 317–338. In-TEH (2009)
2. Zichermann, G., Cunningham, C.: Gamification by Design, O'Reilly (2011)
3. Bernhaupt, R., Boldt, A., Mirlacher, T., Wilfinger, D., Tscheligi, M.: Using Emotion in Games: Emotional Flowers. In: Proceeding of 4th International Conference on Advances in Computer Entertainment Technology (ACE 2007), pp. 41–48 (2007)
4. Kuramoto, I., Kashiwagi, K., Uemura, T., Shibuya, Y., Tsujino, Y.: Weekend Battle: An Entertainment System for Improving Workers' Motivation. In: Proceeding of 2nd International Conference on Advances in Computer Entertainment Technology (ACE 2005), pp. 43–50 (2005)
5. Gao, Y., Mandryk, R.: The Acute Cognitive Benefits of Casual Exergame Play. In: Proceeding of The ACM SIGCHI Conference on Human Factors in Computing Systems (CHI 2012), pp. 1863–1872 (2012)

6. Kuramoto, I., Shibata, Y., Shibuya, Y., Tsujino, Y.: An Entertainment System for Improving Motivation in Repeated Practice of Musical Instruments. In: Jacko, J.A. (ed.) HCI 2007. LNCS, vol. 4553, pp. 278–283. Springer, Heidelberg (2007)

7. Grammenos, D., Margetis, G., Koutlemanis, P., Zabulis, X.: 53.090 Virtual Rusks = 510 Real Smiles Using a Fun ExergameInstallation for Advertising Traditional Food Products. In: Nijholt, A., Romão, T., Reidsma, D. (eds.) ACE 2012. LNCS, vol. 7624, pp. 214–229. Springer, Heidelberg (2012)

8. Howland, R., Urano, S., Hoshino, J.: SanjigenJiten: Computer Assisted Language Learning System within a 3D Game Environment. In: Nijholt, A., Romão, T., Reidsma, D. (eds.) ACE 2012. LNCS, vol. 7624, pp. 262–273. Springer, Heidelberg (2012)

9. Kuramoto, I., Katayama, T., Shibuya, Y., Tsujino, Y.: A Virtual Aquarium Based on EELF with Subjective Competition for Keeping Workers' Motivation. IPSJ Journal 50(12), 2807–2818 (2009) (in Japanese)

10. Weppner, J., Lukowicz, P.: Collaborative Crowd Density Estimation with Mobile Phones. In: 9th ACM Conference on Embedded Network Sensor Systems (2011)

Applying Gamification in Customer Service Application to Improve Agents' Efficiency and Satisfaction

Prerna Makanawala, Jaideep Godara, Eliad Goldwasser, and Hang Le

SAP Labs, Palo Alto, 3410 Hillview Ave,
Palo Alto, California, U.S.A. 94304
{prerna.makanawala,j.godara,eliad.goldwasser,h.le}@sap.com

Abstract. Gamification is the idea of applying game mechanics to non-game areas in order to encourage the use of product or service and to help make technology more engaging. This paper discusses approaches to improve agents' productivity, spirit, and engagement at work by introducing gamification into SAP Service OnDemand, an enterprise application running in the cloud, using player-centered design. Customer service domain suffers with low job satisfaction, low employee morale, and high turnover due to the lack of job control and the task variety. We present ideas using gamification elements that could increase the job engagement and make various repetitive tasks more fun resulting in a more efficient and effective customer service. Added benefits would be reduced training needs and higher retention rates.

1 Problem Statement

For the context of this paper, customer service refers to the activities performed to provide satisfaction to customers and facilitate correct use of products. Customer service agents use a variety of tools and media - phone, chat, email, and social applications - to perform these activities. Ironically, customer service agents have one of the least satisfactory jobs in modern economy. They primarily deal with unhappy and angry customers, and are under time pressure - from both their management and their customers - to quickly resolve the issues [1]. In addition, in most instances, this domain of work provides low amounts of job control and variety in tasks performed [2]. Therefore, it is no surprise that a host of studies have found that customer service agents have high rates of turnover due to the lack of job control and low rates of job satisfaction due to the lack of task variety (see [3], [4], [5]). Of course, the ideal solution would be to significantly redesign these jobs in such a way that provides high job control, task variability, and other means of job enrichment. The next best option is to enhance the job quality by improving the job engagement. As Harter et al [6] found that being engaged and emotionally involved in the job tasks can improve the productivity. Throughout the human evolution, games have played a vital role in fostering collaboration and team spirits, enhancing the sense of belonging, developing skills, and engaging people [7]. Because of these qualities, games seem to have qualities that, if imparted in other non-game, may cure many of modern productivity

A. Marcus (Ed.): DUXU/HCII 2013, Part II, LNCS 8013, pp. 548–557, 2013.

ailments. Encouragingly, there has been strong evidence that when these game mechanics are applied to serious work they result in significant improvement in the employee engagement [8].

1.1   The Target Scenario

We want to reach the state where customer service agents can enjoy their work while providing better service. We are not substantially altering their work processes; however, we are employing various game mechanics in their tasks so that they would engage more with their colleagues and the complaints from clients would become quests that they conquer. This idea of applying game mechanics to non-game areas in order to encourage the use of a product or service and help make technology more engaging is called Gamification [9]. Even new agents would recognize the incentive of blending better with the team, and feel that their tasks guide them in working more efficiently and enjoyably. In the end, the company, the agents, and the customer are all satisfied.

2   Game Mission

We want to apply gamification to customer service solutions for the following reasons:

- To provide higher-quality customer service
- Satisfied customers bring increased business, provides incentive for returning clients, and in the end contributes to brand loyalty. Organized and competent agents help to achieve this goal.
- To motivate agents to have fun at work
- By enhancing personal satisfaction through stimulating team interaction, potentially reducing stress, and frequently rewarding agents with summaries and certificates.
- To increase agents' productivity and efficiency by:
  - Encouraging quick resolution of tickets, for instance, a winning rule can involve completing a certain number of tickets within a given time frame.
  - Fostering collaboration amongst agents, for example, the game awards agents who are helping others.
  - Influence agents to follow good practice, such as rewarding agents for keeping clean customer records and notes.

2.1   Motivation

In his seminal work on happiness and how various contexts impact it; Mihaly Csikszentmihalyi [10] says that our best moments - the ones that we enjoy the most - occur when we're voluntarily trying to accomplish something difficult for which we have the right skills. This is mostly due to the superiority of intrinsic motivators (autonomy, mastery, and the sense of belonging) over extrinsic motivators that are more materialistic - rewards, money, etc. To achieve the game mission, we are applying both extrinsic and intrinsic motivators in our games.

Considering our player type, the following motivators will make the most impact:

- For agents to have fun at work
  - Satisfaction
    We help agents achieve a sense of accomplishment; for example, agents get recognized for being efficient at their jobs, or solving the largest number of tickets during a day or week.
  - Rewards / Point / Badges
    Rewards and levels will motivate some agents to do a better job. However, the ultimate goal of the game is to increase agents' performance, not badges. We also do not use badges for performance reviews or bonuses.
- For agents' productivity and efficiency
  - Mastery
    We provide agents an opportunity to excel at work, for example, they get better at certain tasks by repeating them in a fun setting.
  - Connecting
    We facilitate collaborative activities, such as an objective that involves helping other agents to solve complicated tickets.
  - Learning and Training
    We ease the learning curve by encouraging agents to follow and explore good practice, for instance, agents will learn that keeping clean records helps them excel at their job, or encouraging agents to proactively learn about new products and services.
  - Competition
    Small competitions in the team can push service agents in a positive way to do their jobs better. However, competitions also need to be carefully executed as they can cause a negative effect on teams. It is also essential to regularly provide a status report to players as well as making leaderboards available in different granularities to allow multiple winners.

2.2   Applied Game Mechanics

We can borrow certain qualities of games and apply them to serious work contexts. Some of these qualities and elements are:

- Measure and motivate
- Recognition and reward
- Loyalty
- Reputation
- Guiding and amplifying high-value behavior

Game mechanics play an important role in the result of a game. There exists a range of concepts, techniques, know-hows and best practices used to develop successful games. A number of these available game mechanics can be applied to SAP Service OnDemand:

- Achievement
  We provide players with digital or tangible representation of accomplishment, such as badges, levels, or certificates.
- Communal Discovery
  All players work together to solve a challenge or a problem, in this case, agents collaborate to solve tickets.
- Micro-leaderboards
  Players compete as a team and the games objectives vary, where multiple players/teams can win a subcategory, for example, titles can include "winner of channel Y", "winner of product X", "fastest solver of X tickets", "winner of the day", etc.
- Progression Dynamics
  Players are conscious of game milestones and how they are measured through the process of completing tasks or events, such as knowing that they have completed ⅖ objectives.
- Fun Once, Fun Always

The games can be repeatedly played and enjoyed as agents do their work.

We want to handsomely reward the great performance, but not overly punish the poor performance.

2.3   Player Persona

The players are customer service agents who work on customer issues across multiple channels (e-mail, phone, social media and chat). Usually, junior customer service agents are young with not much experience and do not generally stay with one company for long. They take down issues from customers and solve simple issues and pass complex issues to senior agents. Most of the time, their work is repetitive and they can get bored or easily demotivated. Their work is not as creative, fun, or dynamic as other professions such as design or sales. Sometimes, inefficient systems hinder them from being productive. They work in teams and are measured on first call resolution, hold time, abandonment rates, incident handling time, average talk time, response and resolution rates, escalation rates etc. It's a perfect environment for introducing game mechanics. It can make their jobs more fun, increase motivation and help alleviate stress.

Table 1. Summarize the attributes that characterize a typical player persona:

Player Name	Josh
Gender	Male
Birthday	1986

Table 1. *(Continued)*

Relationship Status	Steady 2-year relationship
Hobbies	He took this job because he's tech savvy and there are not too many opportunities in the area. He loves to hang out with friends in cafes downtown or play sports video games together. He's active on Facebook, Twitter and Pinterest.
Job Title	Junior Customer Service Agent
Industry	Department Store Support
Job Goals	Become a product expert and senior support agent, know more about the company, products and colleagues.
Pain-points	Unhappy customer, unsatisfactory work
Aspirations	Own a surfboard shop
Work culture	More formal, More cooperative, Structured, Individual achievement
Bartle's player type (Bartle, 1996)	Socializer [11]

3   Game Examples

After defining players, missions, and game mechanics, we brainstormed a number of game ideas. Out of those, we narrowed it down to the following two that may be beneficial to the customer service environment and meet the stated goals:

1. The first game is "Bingo". Yes, you know what Bingo is...but it's modified a bit to fit the purpose. Here's how it goes...a manager sets up a series of activities for his/her agents to play. Once the agents opt-in to play, they can continue their work as usual. An agent sends a request for information to the customer. After the customer returns the information, he updates his internal records. He receives a "bingo activity winner" notification for keeping clean records. At any point in time, he can see how many activities he has fulfilled and how many more are needed to win. Other activities can include solving a number of tickets in a certain amount of time, requesting collaboration with other agents, helping another agent, or solving a ticket in category X, etc. Upon completing the game, all the players and the manager are notified about the winner. The game can be repeated and a

summary report is provided at the end of the day. "Bingo" focuses on fostering collaboration between agents and providing a fun factor into agents workflow.

2. The second game is a "Training Game". When a company rolls out a new product, managers can introduce games to help ease the learning process. For example, a manager sets up a small 5-question quiz in the first 3 months after the product launch. Once the agents log into the system, they are provided with a quiz of random questions about the new product. The game will repeat every day until agents answer all questions correctly 3 days in a row. "Training Game" focuses on improving agents knowledge by complementing traditional training sessions.

3.1   Game 1: Bingo

Manager or Administrator creates a bingo game. The game has a few predefined activities the agents need to do.

Possible game criteria's

- Speed related – close or reply to a ticket in under certain time
- Product related – close a ticket for product X or category Y
- Geo – close a ticket of a customer from California
- Collaboration – help another agent solve a ticket

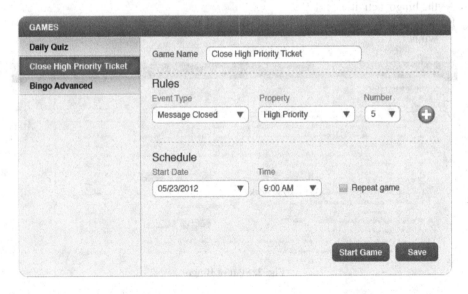

Fig. 1. Customer related - complete customer record or receive positive feedback from customer **Fig. 1** Game setup

Gamification Scenario

Meet Mary, she is the manager of a team of customer service agents at pHoton.

Every day she initiates a bingo game among her agents. She sets up 5 activities and launches the game!

Agent Aaron and Agent Pam opt in to play the game and continue with their daily tasks.

1. Starts to work on the first item
2. He sends a request for information to the customer
3. After customer returns the information he updates his internal records.
4. He receives a "bingo activity winner" notification for keeping clean records.
5. He replies to the customer with a proposed solution and closes the ticket within the same day (under the average time). He again gets another "bingo activity winner" notification for that.
6. The customer is pleased with the solution and sends Aaron a thank you note. He get's another "bingo activity winner" notification for that.
7. Aaron sees on his scorecard that he has won 3 of the 5 activities.
8. Pam (agent 2) has won 4 activities so far.
9. She gets a collaboration request from Aaron. The ticket is high priority as it is about to expire (SLA close to past due)
10. She accepts the request and helps Aaron solve his ticket.
11. They both receive bingo activity winner" notification. Pam has now completed all the bingo activities.
12. A notification is sent to all the players and the manager that Pam is this Bingo winner.

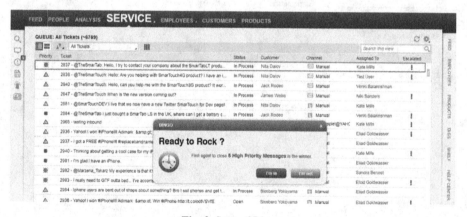

Fig. 2. Start of Bingo

3.2   Game 2: Training

Acme has just rolled out a new product: The camera XXLR3000. Since most agents are not familiar with it, the customer service manager Lucy has decided to include a small quiz in the first 3 months after the product launch.

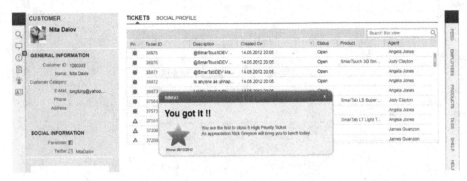

Fig. 3. Agent wins the Bingo game

Possible game criteria

- Knowledge - how many questions need to be answered, randomly generated questions
- Success condition - agents complete their training and get a certificate when they answer all questions correctly 3 days in a row
- Collaboration - ask another team member if player is stuck, helper gets additional points

Gamification Scenario

1. Manager Lucy sets up a 5-question quiz for all agents in her team to complete every morning when they first log into the system.
2. Everyday, all agents in her team answer this quiz. If they answer the question wrong, it pops up an explanation of the correct choice so that they remember if customers ask them next time.
3. Agents Aaron and Pam also take the quiz.
4. Agent Aaron answers all the questions correctly but not agent Pam.
5. During the break, Aaron tells her that he read up on the product specs thoroughly so that he can complete the quiz.
6. Agent Pam is now motivated to read up on the product so she can pass the quiz too.
7. For the next 3 days, she is able to answer all quiz questions correctly. At the end of the 3rd quiz, a notification pops up and lets her know that she has completed the camera XZLR3000 training game, and she doesn't need to go for the formal training session.

   1.   It saves her time by not having to attend all-day training and the company's time and reputation when more issues are resolved quickly. It's a win-win situation!

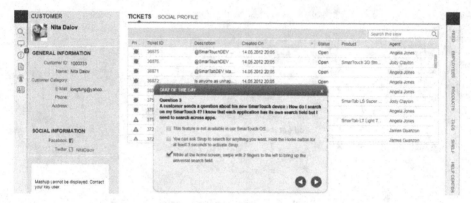

Fig. 4. Agent answers Quiz questions

Fig. 5. Agent answers all questions correctly and receives a badge

4   Challenges

- With the tight schedule of product development, it is very hard to prioritize "gamifying" the software vs. other sets of core product features. The team needs to prove value of adding game mechanics before product management will buy into it.
- Presenting "games" in the context of enterprise software sometimes raises an eyebrow with stakeholders and potential customer.
- Managers need to carefully think about or experiment with rewards. It is important to let the employees know that the games are for fun and not for measuring their performance (this should be reiterated from time to time)
- It is important to monitor and make sure that agents don't focus on the game and focusing on tasks that advance them in their game. There is always a risk of competitive employees wanting to "rule" the game. Their main goal should always be help customers and keep them happy.
- Different service organizations are set up differently and measure different KPI's. Applying game mechanics that will work in a variety of team setups is challenging.

4.1 Next Steps

To refine our game ideas, we plan to conduct user research sessions to know what customer service agents think about gamification at work, and which game approach works better for agents. If we can prove that the game mechanics work in our scenario and possibly partner with a customer to create a proof of concept and test in in a productive environment on a small scale. The ultimate goal is to implement this in the general available product.

References

1. De Ruyter, K., Wetzels, M., Feinberg, R.: Role stress in call centers: its effects on employee performance and satisfaction. Journal of Interactive Marketing 15(2), 23–35 (2001)
2. Jaiswal, A.K.: Customer satisfaction and service quality measurement in Indian call centres. Managing Service Quality 18(4), 405–416 (2008)
3. Baumgartner, M., Good, K., Udris, I.: Call Centers in der Schweiz. Psychologische Untersuchungen in 14 Organisationen (Call Centres in Switzerland. Psychological Investigations in 14 Organizations). Reports from the Institute for Work Psychology, Swiss Federal Institute of Technology, Zurich, Switzerland (2002)
4. Grebner, S., et al.: Working conditions, well-being, and job-related attitudes among call centre agents. European Journal of Work and Organizational Psychology 12(4), 341–365 (2003)
5. Hoekstra, E.J., et al.: Ergonomic, job task, and psychosocial risk factors for workrelated musculoskeletal disorders among teleservice center representatives. International Journal of Human-Computer Interaction 8(4), 421–431 (1996)
6. Harter, J.K., Schmidt, F.L., Keyes, C.L.M.: Well-being in the workplace and its relationship to business outcomes: A review of the Gallup studies. Flourishing: Positive psychology and the life well-lived, 205–224 (2003)
7. McGonigal, J.: Reality is broken: Why games make us better and how they can change the world. Penguin Press HC (2011)
8. Reeves, B., Read, J.L.: Total Engagement: How Games and Virtual Worlds Are Changing the Way People Work and Businesses Compete. Harvard Business Press (2009)
9. Deterding, S., et al.: Gamification: Toward a definition. In: Proceedings of the 2011 Annual Conference Extended Abstracts on Human Factors in Computing Systems. ACM, New York (2011)
10. Csikszentmihalyi, M., Wong, M.M.: The situational and personal correlates of happiness: A cross-national comparison. Subjective well-being: An interdisciplinary perspective 21, 193–212 (1991)
11. Bartle, R.: Hearts, clubs, diamonds, spades: Players who suit MUDs. Journal of MUD research 1(1), 19 (1996)

Perception of Gamification: Between Graphical Design and Persuasive Design

Cathie Marache-Francisco[1,2] and Eric Brangier[2]

[1] SAP France, 157-159 rue Anatole France, 92300 Levallois-Perret, France
cathie.marache-francisco@sap.com
[2] Lorraine University, PErSEUs, UFR SHA, Île du Saulcy, 57006 Metz, France
eric.brangier@univ-lorraine.fr

Abstract. We aim at determining Gamification contribution to non-ludic systems. We analyze HCI design evolution and the theories using game design in that scope to finally introduce Gamification. We state that it is perceived through graphics and persuasion concepts without considering usefulness. To demonstrate that, we ask 10 HCI designers to identify and categorize the elements which induce a ludic spirit on Gamification systems. The results show that Graphics and Persuasion aspects are associated with Perceived Gamification, while Usefulness is not. The content and functions associated with the categories are specified. We state that Gamification can become a decisive factor for the design of a successful human-technology relationship beyond classic theories of technology adoption and use. We then question its contribution.

Keywords: Ergonomics, User Experience, Gamification, Persuasive Technology, Emotional Design, Motivation.

1 Gamification and Perception of Gamification

The aim of this communication is to present and discuss the development of games in professional and non-professional interactive systems, so called Gamification. The upholders of that new HCI design concept envision engaging and motivating interactive systems with *"the use of video game elements in nongaming systems"* [5] (p.2).

Games have been a source of inspiration for HCI way before Gamification (e.g., [9]; funology; playfulness; serious games). [4] have differentiated Gamification through four characteristics: game (as opposed to play), elements (not a full game), design (five levels of game design) and non-game context. [5] have defined it as *"An informal umbrella term for the use of video game elements in nongaming systems to improve User Experience (UX) and user engagement"* (p.2).

The study of the influence of video games at work is quite new. The goal is to understand the mutual influence processes between games and work. Some research [14] noted the existence of two processes. First, some game environments facilitate the transfer of learning from video-games to the professional world. Second, playing

A. Marcus (Ed.): DUXU/HCII 2013, Part II, LNCS 8013, pp. 558–567, 2013.
© Springer-Verlag Berlin Heidelberg 2013

online outside of work energizes employees to work as well. It seems that part of this active learning refers to behaviors that provide the experience of competencies with challenge and risk. According to other studies [7], forms of leadership (or other organizational behaviors) could be transferred from video games – especially since serious games. Thus, video games are not only easy and fun to use: it would favor the development of some organizational learning. However, [6] showed all the difficulties faced by users when confronted to leadership redefinition with emails, writings, electronic notes, web pages, etc. All these new forms of communication involve both a good sense of writing and new knowledge related to digital media.

To sum up, [14] highlighted the fact that the leadership, active learning and collaboration can go beyond game to reach work. But the interest of this spillover depends on kind of game and playing techniques (interfaces and scenarios) chosen which can be more or less effective and thus relevant. There are probably interfaces patterns that facilitate or complicate the spillover process. In this paper, we would like to examine closely what is a "gamified" interface and how it's perceived.

Concerning Gamification methods, [8] have defined a "Gamification Loop" starting with a challenge. Achieving a sub goal triggers a reward system based on a point system. This leads to a leaderboard entry and badges attributions and then a modification of the user's social and network status. The authors also mention a game-like surface. However, from a design specification point of view, this concept is not clear. Indeed, lots of current examples can be related to the Gamification loop while other authors call for a meaningful design. Kim [3] insists on the need to define the users' profiles (social style, expertise) to select game mechanics and to create an evolving interaction while relying on intrinsic motivation with autonomy, mastery and purpose as a motto. [12] calls for a user-centered meaningful Gamification as opposed to points and rewards based Gamification that trigger extrinsic motivation.

According to [10] we think that three main aspects underlie Gamification design:

- **Sensory-motor dimension:** the output modes are specific to this kind of systems. Gamification uses extensively games multimodal coding (visual, audio, haptic) for aesthetic purpose and to communicate an atmosphere, a theme or information;
- **Motivational dimension:** one of its most consensual goals. Gamification drives motivation by triggering emotions with game elements that answer users' needs beyond usability (e.g., accomplishment, social). It also exploits game elements that are part of the Persuasive Technology set of tools in order to create engagement;
- **Cognitive dimension:** some authors use Gamification for goal-resolution with guiding elements which are directly related to the task, helping the users solve it efficiently. It implies adapting the interaction to the user profile and communicating relevant and useful information (goal, mean, feedback and outcome).

We will see that the Gamification elements overlap those categories through their several different meaning and functions. The main goal of Gamification is to motivate and engage the users: designers rely on users' unfulfilled needs. This is a main concern as Gamification is said to be able to turn work into something more interesting and motivating. Its ability to foster productivity is thus interesting to explore as workers' main concern may be about their work outcome. If Gamification does not participate in this, it might be perceived as either not relevant or interfering with the target.

2   Problem and Method

2.1   General Question

What is Gamification added value when applied to casual systems? Does it help motivating the users performing a task? Does it lead to better performances? Does it contribute to the main goal of the system or does it add parallel tasks and motivators?

We state that Gamification creates a link between the user and the systems that goes beyond traditional criteria, generating an attractive and persuasive interaction. Consequently, the Gamification dimension is considered and perceived through two main dimensions: a graphical one and a persuasive one.

- **Graphics:** As mentioned by [8], Gamification implies having a game-like surface. Indeed, games communicate an atmosphere, a theme or information through visual stimulations, touch and audition. Some Gamification platforms have been designed to look-like a game environment (e.g., *Mindbloom*) while others only have parts of it amongst a more professional-looking user interface (e.g., *Nitro by SalesForce*);
- **Persuasion:** First, Games and Gamification fit the dynamic criteria for persuasion set by [11]. Indeed, it implies evolutionary interactions with more demanding tasks through time and motivational messages. Second, a lot of persuasive techniques set by [13] are relevant when talking about Gamification: *Primary Task Support (Tunneling, Self-monitoring, Reduction, Tailoring, Personalization, Rehearsal), Dialogue Support (Praise, Rewards, Social role, Similarity, Reminders, Suggestion, Liking) and Social Support (Competition, Cooperation, Social comparison and facilitation, Recognition and Normative influence).*

Through our study, we try to demonstrate that Perception of Gamification lies between Graphical and Persuasive Design, without taking into account the Usefulness dimension of the interaction or "*the extent to which a person believes that the use of a TIC would increase her professional or domestic productivity*" [2] (p.135, own translation).

2.2   Methodology

Our subjects panel consists of ten employees of a software company: five are Visual and Interaction Designers and five are Interface Developers. Most of them know little about Gamification (three have a quite extensive knowledge about it) and they play video games on a regular basis (2 don't play at all).

Ten screenshots of "gamified" systems have been chosen based on their representativeness of that phenomenon (Table1). They contain classic Gamification elements (e.g., badges, points) and game-like visual effects (more or less prominent).

Table 1. Name and description of the screenshots used for the experiment

Name	Description
Nike+	Website : managing running efforts through time
Nitro	Website for selling team : managing work efforts
Mint	Website : managing one's bank accounts online
Foursquare	Mobile application : sharing knowledge of places in a city
LinkedIn	Professional networking website
MindBloom	Website : setting and monitoring healthy-life goals
Ribbon Hero 2	Microsoft office suite plugin : tutorial modules
The Upstream challenge	Website : online recruiting campain
DevHub	Website : websites/blogs management
HealthMonth	Website : setting and monitoring health goals through time

The experiment consists of two steps. First, the screenshots are presented one by one and the subjects are asked to describe what makes the interface ludic. The "Why?-How?" technique has been used in order to obtain first a free answer followed by a more precise description, the why question revealing the underlying concept, the how question revealing its operationalization [1]. During a second phase, the subjects are asked to summarize the key ideas that arouse out of their analysis by writing it down on blank cards which are then used to perform a conceptual sorting.

The analysis of the outcome of the interview is both quantitative and qualitative: we record the Gamification elements found by the subjects as well as the categories created and its underlying meaning.

2.3   Data Analysis

We conduct a content analysis based on the verbalizations. Content analysis is a systematic and methodical review of texts or transcribed speeches. It is particularly useful in social sciences for the study of social representations.

This method requires every verbalization on the research question (the interviews). We classify all statements and create categories to help differentiating the verbalizations. The categories are related to the content of the document or screens selected. Finally, the interpretation phase aims at giving sense to the categorizations.

3   Results: Gamification Is Perceived through Two Main Dimensions: Graphics and Persuasion

All subjects refer to Graphics and Persuasion (18 and 29 categories). Table 2 sums up the categories created according to our main study dimensions. No subject has explicitly mentioned the classical "Usefulness": they verbalize about persuasion and aesthetics.

Table 2. Subjects categories per subject and main dimensions (non exclusive *in italic*)

Subject	Graphics	Persuasion
1	Visual, *Staging, Immersion System* (3)	Support System, *Staging* (2)
2	Visual, *Performance* (2)	*Performance*, Me (2)
3	Visual, Wording (2)	Point System, Social, Personalization (3)
4	Attractive Graphics (1)	Challenge, Self-Image, Social Image (3)
5	*Metaphorization*, Information Architecture And Graphical Style (2)	*Metaphorization*, Workflow (2)
6	*Environment* (1)	Challenge, Progress, Earnings, *Environment* (4)
7	*Cosmetic* (1)	*Cosmetic*, Concepts (2)
8	*Game Scenario, Personalization*, Game Designer (3)	*Game Scenario, Personalization*, Community, User Control (4)
9	Immersive Experience (1)	Self-Comparison, Social Comparison, Avatarization (3)
10	Global Layout, Ludic Graphics (2)	Progression, Competition, Virtual Money, Immersion (4)

Graphics. This category is mainly about the visual aspect of the gamified systems.

The subjects mention on average 7 elements out of 9 (min.: 5; max.: 9). 10 subjects have mentioned images and colors, 9 have mentioned effects (e.g., comics look and feel, round shapes) while 7 mentioned theme, metaphor, font, vocabulary and global layout. 4 subjects have associated it to interactive external avatar.

— *"to me, the wording part is as important as the the the visual part, the icons. (...) the text it's not really content, I mean I don't I don't see it as content but as hm something to beautify, to hm intensify the the immersion, so that you understand better what you must do"* (s10)

10 exclusive categories of graphical elements have been created while 8 categories that contain graphical elements amongst others have been created (Table3).

Table 3. Graphics categories by content specificity

Exclusive categories	Non Exclusive Categories
Visual, visual, visual, wording, attractive graphics, information architecture and graphical style, game designer, immersive experience, global layout, ludic graphics	Staging, immersion system, performance, metaphorization, environment, cosmetic, game scenario, personalization

Two categories of functions have been associated with the graphical elements: Attractiveness (by all subjects; i.e., emotions, amusement, staging, immersion, fading the feeling of being in touch with reality, appealing, call-for-use) and Legibility (by five subjects; i.e., prominent graphical representation, clear layout).

— *"if it were realistic [visual design], it would be too professional looking and serious"* (s1)
— *"make it as an experience, not as a tool (...) the suspension of belief, you stop to believe, like, when you see a movie, you don't say 'it's not possible' "*(s9)
— *"a gauge versus the accurate figure hm which is more immediately read and which recalls the the game or cockpit environments (...) a bit like 'visual representation at any cost'"* (s3)

Persuasion. The dimension of persuasion consists of three main concepts: self and social competition, self and social image, freedom of choice.
Self and Social Competition: challenging the player and rewarding his efforts.

The subjects mention on average 10 elements out of 16 (min.: 7; max.: 12). 10 subjects mention points, trophies-medals and leaderboards; 9 mention goals, virtual objects gain, virtual money; 8 mention progress images; 7 mention situation inventory; 6 mention badges; finally 5 subjects mention levels. 6 items are mentioned by less than five subjects (greetings, timer, statistics, instructions, accomplishment, external feedback).

The subjects create on average 2 categories (min.:1; max.:3). 12 categories out of 19 are exclusive. They are not homogeneous and 4 of the non-exclusive categories share items with the other two Persuasion categories (Table4).

Table 4. Persuasion „Self and social competition" categories by content specificity

Exclusive categories	Non Exclusive Categories
Support system, point system, Challenge, challenge, Progress, Earnings, concepts, self-comparison, social comparison, Progression, Competition, virtual money	Performance, me, social image, metaphorization, cosmetic, game scenario, avatarization

The function of self and social completion is to support a workflow that consists of three steps: (1) Goals: to take up a challenge; (2) Evaluation elements: to progress, completion needs; (3) rewards: incentive. As suggested by the label of that category, it both concern self and social motivation through competition.

— *"We can feel that it... that they try to prompt the users with points earnings (...) assuming that earning points is ludic"* (s3)
— *"I would say that having this percentage of profile completeness always puts me in a a status of anxiety, I would like to see it 100% so I thought many times to add what's missing, in my case a picture (...) it's a good way to push you to improve your profile"* (s6)
— *"track run : the history allows you to monitor your progress, compare with yourself"* (s10)

Self and Social Image: a gathering of elements which are typical of social websites – linking people together, allowing them to communicate and express themselves.

The subjects mention on average 4 items on 8 (min.:1; max.:6). 6 subjects mention avatars and 5 mention sharing and personalization. Some items are mentioned two times only: taking care of growing artifacts, nickname, newsfeed, comments and social network. The fact that some social platforms elements are not identified by most of the subjects could be due to a generational issue. "Old gamers" are not used to it and are reluctant classifying it ludic as it has spread recently and is not game specific.

— *"I've been playing a lot but, let's say, offline video games (...) For me it's not normal at all to play a game and share my results on Facebook (...) but maybe, ten years ago (...) I would have"* (s6)

The subjects have created on average 1 category (max: 2). 4 categories out of 10 are exclusive. They are not homogeneous and 3 of the non-exclusive categories share items with the other two Persuasion categories (Table5).

Table 5. Persuasion „Social system and self-image" categories by content specificity

Exclusive categories	Non Exclusive Categories
Social, personalization, immersion, self-image	Me, social image, environment, personalization, community, avatarization

9 subjects have identified an identity function behind those elements which can be split into two subcategories: Self-image (about self-identity, expression and existence through it; e.g., personalization elements, verbal expression elements, the caring of growing artifacts) and Social image (about relationship, community, sharing and collaboration, one's image to the group).

— « *you are giving your contribution (...) it is concrete, the proof of your experience, so: the proof of your existence* » (s9)
— *"I have the social part (...)it's also the private part (...) when we have a ludic intent hm we need an account, a name, a picture, an avatar, we often need that personalization part"* (s2)

Freedom of Choice: giving options to a user within a system; the idea of control.

Two kind of freedom of choice are mentioned: Participating willingly (i.e., taking action) on the reward and point system as well as on the social system and Controlling the sequence of events.

— *"We don't have to be competitors, we can be if we want"* (s1)
— *"I control the way I get involved at a ludic level"* (s2)
— *"The start button on the playstation (...) it's either 'I stop' or 'I take a break' (...) notion of game mastery, I have control over the website. I don't feel like I have to go thought 10 pages and if I don't the website is gonna crash and tell me 'no, you shouldn't have done that"* (s8)

Four subjects mention that characteristic. One has created an exclusive category. As for the others, the items associated and the categories are heterogeneous (Table6).

Table 6. Persuasion „Freedom of choice" categories by content specificity

Exclusive categories	Non Exclusive Categories
User Control	Staging, Me, Metaphorization, Workflow

Usefulness. The subjects do not mention explicitly this notion. However, they relate the elements we have classified in "Graphics" and "Persuasion" to the users' tasks.

The "self and social competition" part of "Persuasion" (Table4) is said to motivate the users during task resolution. In here, Gamification does not aim at increasing the performance per se, but at increasing the motivation of the users at getting better at what they do. Indirectly (without modifying the actions needed to perform a task), those Gamification elements are supposed to participate to productivity increase.

However, the attractiveness function of Graphics could be seen as opposite to usefulness as it implies immersion and stepping back from reality.

— *"[nike+ is] the most ludic of all as it seems to be the most useless"* (s4)

4   Discussion

Through that presentation, we have tried to determine the contribution of Gamification to non-ludic systems. We have analyzed HCI design evolution and the theories using game design in that scope to finally introduce Gamification. We state that it is perceived through Graphics and Persuasion concepts and that Usefulness is not part of the scope. In order to demonstrate that, we have asked HCI designers to identify and categorize the elements inducing a ludic spirit on Gamification systems screenshots. We have then presented the results that we will discuss on that next section.

The results of that study are consistent with our hypothesis. Indeed, the Graphics and Persuasion aspects of the interfaces have been associated with a ludic spirit and thus Perceived Gamification (Figure1). Usefulness has not been mentioned explicitly.

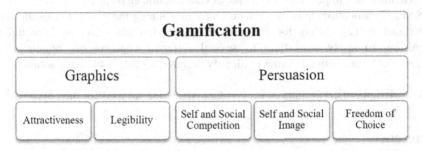

Fig. 1. The Two dimensions of Gamification Design

Graphics.   Every subject has mentioned that component. It mainly concerns the visual aspect of the interfaces and it carries two functions: Attractiveness (triggering emotions, leading to appealing and immersive experience) and Legibility (through a clear user interface). Some subjects have mentioned a potential infantilization.

— *"It's immersive, offbeat, sometimes even childish"* (s8)
— *"What's that?! Is it for kids?"* (s5)

Persuasion. Again, that component of Gamification has been pointed at by every subject. Three sub-dimensions have been mentioned:

- Self and social competition: motivation through a workflow that foster self and social competition and that rely on three steps: (1) Goals and challenge; (2) Evaluation elements; (3) Rewards;
- Self and social image : motivation through identity and expression elements;
- Freedom of choice: engagement through voluntary participation and the control of the sequence of event [11].

Perception of Gamification. These results give weight to the concept of "Perception of Gamification" that introduces persuasive technologies and graphic design to explain the interfaces appearance and users commitment.

To a certain extent, Gamification will increase the use of professional software. It would thus appear as a decisive factor for the design of a successful human-technology relationship beyond classic theories of technology adoption and use.

However, it relies on motivators dealing with nonfunctional needs; the usefulness of a system is not covered despite its importance, notably on work context. It thus questions the contribution of Gamification to casual systems, especially considering the kind of motivation triggered [12]. We state that Gamification is about creating an interactive universe that would be simple, beautiful, appealing and engaging. It implies a will to mislead the user by modifying the core meaning of work: the conflicting relationship between men and work.

Two limitations of that study have been identified. First, our choice of Gamification systems implies a vision of what it consists of which could constitute a bias despite our will to be neutral. Second, screenshots cannot render the interactive and acoustic part of the systems which impoverish our sample of Gamification elements.

Some Gamification upholders are currently mentioning the concept of meaningful Gamification [12], calling for user-centered game elements selection. It would be interesting to apply our study to several different contexts of application of meaningful Gamification in order to identify design rules that could be generalized.

Acknowledgments. The authors would like to thank the subjects for their insight.

References

1. Bisseret, A., Sebillotte, S., Falzon, P.: Techniques pratiques pour l'étude des activités expertes. OCTARES, Toulouse (1999)
2. Brangier, E., Hammes-Adelé, S., Bastien, J.-M.C.: Analyse critique des approches de l'acceptation des technologies: de l'utilisabilité à la symbiose humain-technologie-organisation. Revue Européenne de Psychologie Appliquée 60(2), 129–146 (2010)
3. Casual Games Association. Smart Gamification: Seven Core Concepts for Creating Compelling Experiences (2012),
   http://casualconnect.org/lectures/business/smart-
   Gamification-seven-core-concepts-for-creating-compelling-
   experiences-amy-jo-kim (retrieved February 2, 2012)

4. Deterding, S., Khaled, R., Nacke, L., Dixon, D.: Gamification: Toward a Definition. In: Proceedings of CHI 2011 Workshop Gamification: Using Game Design Elements in Non-Game Contexts, pp. 6–9 (2011)
5. Deterding, S., Sicart, M., Nacke, L., O'Hara, K., Dixon, D.: Gamification: Using Game Design Elements in Non-Gaming Contexts. In: Proceedings of CHI 2011 Workshop Gamification: Using Game Design Elements in Non-Game Contexts, Vancouver, pp. 2–5 (2011)
6. Fayard, A.-L., Metiu, A.: The Power of Writing in Organizations: From Letters to Online Interactions, Routledge. Series in Organization and Management, 226 p. (2012)
7. Korteling, H., Helsdinger, A., Theunissen, C.M.: Serious gaming @ work. In: Derks, D., Bakker, A.B. (eds.) Digital Media at Work, pp. 102–122. Psychology Press, New York (2012)
8. Liu, Y., Alexandrova, T., Nakajima, T.: Gamifying intelligent environments. In: Proceedings of the 2011 International ACM Workshop on Ubiquitous Meta User Interfaces, Ubi-MUI 2011, pp. 7–12. ACM, NY (2011)
9. Malone, T.W.: Heuristics for designing enjoyable user interfaces: Lessons from computer games. In: Thomas, J.C., Schneider, M.L. (eds.) Human Factors in Computer Systems, pp. 1–12. Ablex, Norwood (1984)
10. Marache-Francisco, C., Brangier, E.: Gamification experience: UXD with gamification background. In: Blashki, K., Isaias, P. (eds.) Emerging Research and Trends in Interactivity and the Human-Computer Interface, IGI-GLobal (2013, accepted)
11. Némery, A., Brangier, E., Kopp, S.: First validation of persuasive criteria for designing and evaluating the social influence of user interfaces: Justification of a guideline. In: Marcus, A. (ed.) HCII 2011 and DUXU 2011, Part II. LNCS, vol. 6770, pp. 616–624. Springer, Heidelberg (2011)
12. Nicholson, S.: A User-Centered Theoretical Framework for Meaningful Gamification. Paper Presented at Games+Learning+Society 8.0, Madison, WI (June 2012)
13. Oinas-Kukkonen, H., Harjumaa, M.: Persuasive Systems Design: Key Issues, Process Model, and System Features. Communications of the Association for Information Systems 24(1), 485–500 (2009)
14. Xanthopoulou, D., Papagiannidis, S.: Games-work interaction: The beneficial effects of computer games for work behaviors. In: Derks, D., Bakker, A.B. (eds.) Digital media at work, pp. 102–122. Psychology Press, New York (2012)

Interactive Rock Climbing Playground Equipment: Modeling through Service

Mikiko Oono[*], Koji Kitamura, Yoshifumi Nishida, and Yoichi Motomura

National Institute of Advanced Industrial Science and Technology (AIST), Japan
{mikiko-oono,k.kitamura,y.nishida,y.motomura}@aist.go.jp

Abstract. Rock-climbing is a tool for investigating a full-body interaction. To design physical and psychological interaction with rock-climbing equipment, it is critical that scientific data on children's interaction with the equipment be collected. We developed a rock-climbing wall with embedded sensors to record the physical behavior of children while playing on the wall. Over 1000 children participated in this study. With the aim of creating an evidenced-based interaction design of climbing, we formulated a climbing behavior model to see the relationship among influencing variables that describe climbing activities.

Keywords: embedded sensor network, full-body interaction, children's behavior model, playground equipment.

1 Introduction

Physical activity is essential for all children to grow healthy [1]. According to the American College of Sports Medicine recommendation, children between the ages of 5 and 18 years old need to have 60 minutes of moderate to vigorously intense physical activity a day [2]. Rock-climbing has become a popular sport worldwide to get physically active. The difficulty of a climb is determined based on a grading system developed around the world [3]. Many studies on rock-climbing have researched on the relationship between physiological responses such as oxygen consumption, heart rate, blood pressure and the level of climbing difficulty [3], anthropometric factors [4], rock-climbing related injury [5].

From a human-interaction point of view, rock-climbing is a tool for investigating a full-body interaction. Sibella et al. gathered data on climbing movements using an optoelectronic system with six infrared cameras to research on common patterns and different climbing strategies in a group of recreational climbers [6]. Quaine and Martin conducted to study on the vertical and the horizontal force distribution on the holds and its distribution changes after a hold had been released based on the principles of Newtonian mechanics [7].

In the present study, we deal with the full-body interaction of children when they play with rock-climbing equipment. In this study, we focused on the following points:

1. Collect children's climbing behavior data to develop a climbing model
2. Understand what influences children's climbing behaviors

---

[*] Corresponding author.

A. Marcus (Ed.): DUXU/HCII 2013, Part II, LNCS 8013, pp. 568–576, 2013.

3. Discuss the possibilities of designing evidence-based interactive playground equipment

In trying to understand how children interact with rock-climbing wall, we conducted two types of experiment. The first experiment was to develop a climbing behavior model by observing children while they played with outdoor climbing wall. The second experiment was to understand which factors related to climbing behavior. We developed the rock-climbing wall equipped with sensors to record children's climbing activities while playing on the wall. The climbing holds with sensors enable the measurement of children's climbing behavior in a natural situation. We discuss what variables influence climbing behavior based on the developed climbing behavior models.

2   The First Attempt to Develop a Children's Climbing Behavior Model, Using the Outdoor Climbing Wall

We first attempted to develop a children's climbing behavior model by observing how children play on the rock climbing wall, as shown in Figure 1.

Fig. 1. Rock climbing wall in Kawawa Kindergarten

To collect children's climbing behavior data, we set up cameras to records the process of children's playing on the wall. We worked with 47 three to six year-old boys and girls enrolled in Kawawa Kindergarten in Yokohama, Japan. As a very first step to formulate a climbing behavior model, we decided to employ the following variables: age, weight, height, the rock depth that a child touched, and a child's posture. We considered a child's climbing posture as a link structure as shown in Figure 2 and calculate the distance based on the following definitions:

1. Relative distance between the left hand and right hand (L1)
2. Relative distance between the right hand and right foot (L2)
3. Relative distance between the right foot and left foot (L3)
4. Relative distance between the left foot and left hand (L4)
5. Relative distance between the left hand and right foot (L5)
6. Relative distance between the right hand and left foot (L6)

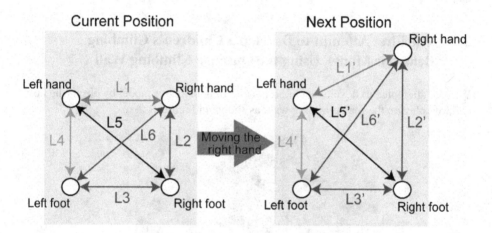

Fig. 2. Link structure for expressing body movements as a child scales the rock-climbing equipment

We extracted children's behavior data each time a child changed his or her climbing posture and generated a cross-tabulation table. The structure of the Bayesian network is computed based on the cross-tabulation table of organized data from 20 children, using custom-developed software [8]. We determine conditional probabilities by providing each node with the node's parent variables. The Bayesian network is constructed using a stepwise method based on AIC [9] in order to determine a set of proper parent nodes and to construct the model. We can find a relationship among chosen variables from a Bayesian network model.

A model of a child's climbing behavior for the right hand is presented in Figure 3. The line width indicates the strength of the relationship between nodes. The model can estimate the distance a child covers when changing from their current position to next position. The model indicates current positions influenced next positions, and children's characteristics such as weight, age, and height influenced current positions. In addition, the rock depth strongly affected the current position. However, we could not formulate a precise climbing behavior model because the real phenomenon of climbing was very complex. From this experience, we learned that we should understand how one variable influenced the others first before explaining the phenomenon of climbing behavior as a whole. Thus, we decided to start over from scratch to develop a climbing behavior model.

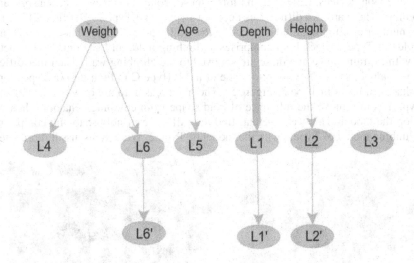

Fig. 3. A model of a child's climbing behavior for the right hand

3   Development of a Children's Climbing Model, Using a Sensor-Embedded Rock Climbing Equipment

To understand the whole phenomenon of outdoor climbing, we started with the development of a climbing model, using an artificial climbing wall with embedded force sensors. The benefit of an artificial climbing wall is that we can manipulate variables that affect climbing behavior. This way, we can develop a precise climbing model and understand what influences climbing. Based on a scientific understanding of climbing behavior, it will be possible to develop artifactually-produced playground equipment. Moreover, as we will discuss shortly, LEDs and force sensors are embedded in our developed rock-climbing equipment. This interactive equipment allows us to collect a variety of children's climbing movements because a target that a child climbs up is programmed by software. On the other hand, when we gathered data using the outdoor climbing wall, we could not obtain good data of various movements since children tended to climb some particular fixed routes they preferred. In this section, we discuss the development of a rock-climbing wall and the construction of a child climbing model.

3.1   Development of Rock-Climbing Equipment with Sensors

To gather children's behavioral data, we developed two rock-climbing equipments which embedded force sensors as shown in Figure 4. Every time children put their hands or feet on the climbing holds, the sensors collect load data. The colors of holds changes using the sensor data. The rock-climbing equipment is 2.7m high, 1.8m wide. The hardware of the rock-climbing equipment comprises a main control device, four data collection devices, LED-unit and force-sensor control devices, force sensors, and LED units. There are two differences between Type 1 and Type 2. The first difference is the number of climbing hold attached to the wall. There are 50 holds in Type 1 and 54 holds in Type 2. Each hold comprises a climbing hold, an LED unit, and a metal case with a strain gauge and these are screwed to the climbing wall. The other difference was a hold shape. We use one shape of holds (type C in Figure 5) in Type 1 and five shapes of holds in Type 2 (Figure 5). The main reason to use only one hold shape in Type 1 is to remove the influence of hold shape from climbing behavior when we develop the model. This way, we can find the influence of hold shape by comparing the climbing model of Type 1 with the model of Type 2. We will discuss it more later.

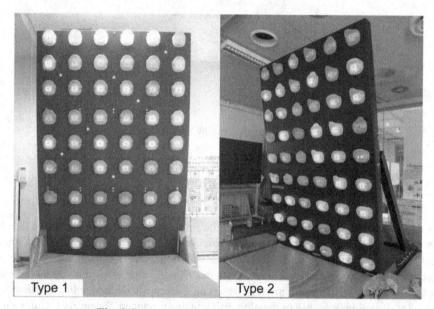

Fig. 4. Sensor-embedded rock-climbing equipment

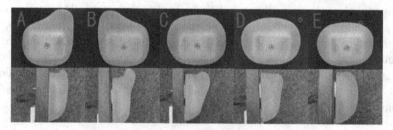

Fig. 5. Hold shapes

3.2   Collecting Climbing Behavior Data, Using the Rock-Climbing Equipment

We conducted experiments for measuring the children's playing behavior, using Type 1 and Type 2 climbing equipments in cooperation with four events in 2009-2010.

So far, we collected 1226 children's behavior data (Table 1).

Table 1. The number of participants per event

Events	The event duration	Number of participants
Yokohama's 150th year in 2009	3 days	188 children
Kids Design Award 2009	4 days	435 children
Kids Create 2010	3 days	398 children
Childhood Injury Prevention Project in 2010	3 days	205 children

The instructions for playing were provided to participants as follows:

1. Climbing up to the two holds that turn to red. These red holds are your target.
2. When you reach these two targets, two new targets will activate.
3. Climbing to these new targets for 90 seconds.

Fig. 6. The snapshots of children playing on the rock-climbing equipment

The targets appear at random since the positioning of targets is programmed by software. Children were not allowed to touch the targets with their foot. When the game was over, children got their game scores based on the number of targets reached. All participants were recorded using two video cameras. Snapshots of the experiments in progress during the events are shown in Figure 6.

3.3   Constructing a Climbing Model

A Climbing Model, Using Type 1 Equipment. To formulate the model of Type 1 equipment, we employ the following variables in the model: sex, age, height, weight, target direction (to top or to bottom), a child posture, and the distance a child advances in a step. This time, we particularly looked at how target direction influences children's climbing behavior. Since only one hold shape was used in Type 1 equipment, we can find how target direction influences a child's posture.

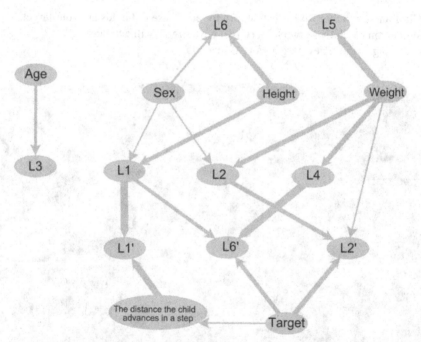

Fig. 7. Climbing behavioral model when a right hand moves (Type 1)

A children's climbing behavior model for Type 1 is shown in Figure 7. This is the right hand's model. It predicts how and where a child will climb when given the height of a child, target direction and his or her current posture. The developed model indicates that the next position was influenced by the current position, target direction, and the distance the child advances in a step. In addition, the current position was influenced by age, sex, height, and weight. The climbing model of Type 1 became more precise compared to the model of outdoor climbing wall shown in

Figure 3 because of the following reasons. First, unlike the outdoor climbing wall, there is a limitation of where children hang onto. Second, children need to climb up to a direction where targets appeared when they play with Type 1. This means how children climb is controlled. Thus, a direction of climbing is an important factor to describe the phenomenon of rock-climbing behavior.

A Climbing Model, Using Type 2 Equipment. To develop a climbing model, using Type 2 equipment, we used eight variables: sex, age, height, weight, target direction (to top or to bottom), a child posture, the distance a child advances in a step, and hold shape. There are 5 types of shape as already shown in Figure 5. The definition of the hold shape is a hold shape that a child actually touched.

A children's climbing behavior model for Type 2 is shown in Figure 8. This is also the right hand's model. The model indicates that a hold shape for a child's four appendages strongly affects his or her current position, and target direction influences the next position. Hold shape influences the current position more strongly than children's physical characteristics such as sex and age. This means that the current position (or more specifically the relative distance between appendages) was strongly influenced by hold shape that each appendage touched. The interaction between the current position and hold shape then affects the next position. For this reason, hold shape is also a critical factor that describes the phenomenon of rock-climbing behavior.

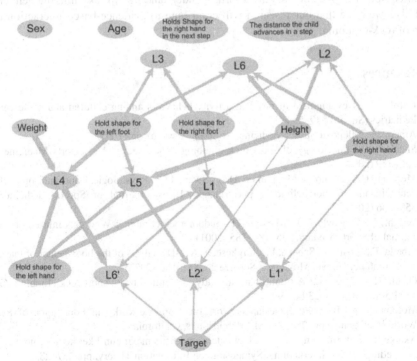

Fig. 8. Climbing behavioral model when a right hand moves (Type 2)

4   Conclusion

In this paper, based on the result of the climbing model of outdoor climbing wall, we developed an artificial rock-climbing equipment to understand what factors influence children's climbing behavior. We gathered data on how children climb while they play with the developed equipment. So far, 1226 children participated in this study, and we constructed two climbing behavioral models to determine influencing variables of climbing behavior. The model of Type 1 showed that the next position was influenced by the current position and target direction, and the current position was influenced by children's physical characteristics. We developed the model of Type 2 to see how hold shape influenced climbing behaviors. The model of Type 2 showed that the next position was influenced by target direction, and the current position was strongly influenced by hold shape that each appendage touched.

As a result of our present study, we conclude that rock-climbing is a hypercomplex interactive phenomenon that was created from the combination of three things: 1. the abundance of hold shape which four appendages can use is intricately allocated, 2. the current position is affected by hold shape, and its position affects the next position, and 3. a direction in which a child is supposed to climb keeps changing over time. Most importantly, our research revealed that the hypercomplex interactive phenomenon can be modeled and quantitatively described through creating the artificial sensorized equipments. We hope to gain a further understanding of rock-climbing behavior, and also we hope that our research will contribute to evidence-based interaction design of rock-climbing.

References

1. Harold, W.: Development of physical activity behaviors among children and adolescents. Pediatrics (Suppl.) 549–554 (1998)
2. American College of Sports Medicine, http://www.acsm.org/
3. Sheel, A.W.: Physiology of sport rock climbing. British Journal of Sports Medicine 38, 355–359 (2004)
4. Mermier, C.M., Janot, J.M., Parker, D.L., Swan, J.G.: Physiological and anthropometric determinants of sport climbing performance. British Journal of Sports Medicine 34, 359–366 (2000)
5. Wright, D.M., Royle, T.J., Marshall, T.: Indoor rock climbing: Who gets injured? British Journal of Sports Medicine 35, 181–185 (2001)
6. Sibella, F., Frosio, I., Schena, F., Borghese, N.A.: 3D analysis of the body center of mass in rock climbing. Human Movement Science 26, 841–852 (2007)
7. Quaine, F., Martin, L.: A biomechanical study of equilibrium in sport rock climbing. Gait and Posture 10, 233–239 (1999)
8. Motomura, Y.: Bayonet: Bayesian network on neural network. In: Foundation of Real-World Intelligence, pp. 28–37. CSLI Publications, California
9. Akaike, H.: Information theory and an extension of the maximum likelihood principle. In: Proceedings of 2nd International Symposium on Information Theory, pp. 267–281

Work and Gameplay in the Transparent 'Magic Circle' of Gamification

Insights from a Gameful Collaborative Review Exercise

Răzvan Rughiniş

University Politehnica of Bucharest, Splaiul Independenţei 313, Bucharest, Romania
razvan.rughinis@cs.pub.ro

Abstract. We analyze the 'Revision Fever' gamification exercise and the challenges of adjusting the logic of gameplay to the logic of the non-game activity. We rely on 'instrumental genesis' theory (Béguin & Rabardel, 2000) and a conceptualization of the 'magic circle' of gameplay (Stenros, 2012) to highlight points of divergence and possibilities of adjustment on two dimensions: the gamification artifact, including the rules of the game layer and the organization of the arena of play, and players' activity schemes, especially their play strategies and their engagement with the game layer. The work of adjustment is collective and distributed across roles, participants, and time. Gamification involves the design and continuous enactment of a 'magic circle' that is transparent towards the associated non-game activity.

Keywords: Gamification, magic circle, collaborative work, distributed work, instrumental genesis theory.

1   Introduction

Gamification consists in framing a non-game activity as a gameplay experience, using game design methods and mechanics (Deterding, Dixon, Khaled, & Nacke, 2011). While the idea of transforming work through play is not new (Nelson, 2012), the concept of "gamification" is a recent neologism (Hagglund, 2012), usually referring to digital game mechanics applied to online services. The "gamification" movement developed mostly in business, education, and health care, in a broader social context including the transformation of video games into a mainstream medium for entertainment, and the diffusion of gaming into non-game contexts through serious games, pervasive games, games with a purpose etc. As gaming became more widespread across demographic and social strata, and gaming experiences were more and more common in varied situations of life, the use of game design elements to create value for customers, service beneficiaries (including students or patients), and employees has also increased. In recent years the concept of gamification has gained increased acceptance as a design instrument and as a research topic.

Deterding et al. (2011) define gamification as the "use of game elements in non-game contexts" (p. 2), distinguishing gamefulness from playfulness and, consequently,

A. Marcus (Ed.): DUXU/HCII 2013, Part II, LNCS 8013, pp. 577–586, 2013.

differentiating gameful from playful design; along these lines we can formulate a narrower of gamification as distinctive from 'playification' (Nicholson, 2012). Still, as Deterding et al. also observe, gamification often gives rise to playful behaviors and attitudes. We consider that the 'gameful' vs. 'playful' distinction is important in analysis, but should not restrain concept extension; gameplay involves elements of play, unless it becomes pure rule-bound competition. Therefore, we discuss gamification as the process of inviting gameplay through gameful and playful design of non-game (and non-play) activities.

The concept and the practices of gamification have been criticized for the promise of quasi-mechanical motivational efficiency of game elements, seen as degrading for users and also for games as sophisticated cultural creations. Bogost (2011) translates the concept rhetorically as "exploitationware", denouncing unfair deals in which valuable customer information and engagement is exchanged for simplistic, empty imitations of games, while Robertson (2012) comments on the use of "pointsification" as design panacea. Indeed, the addition of points, badges and leaderboards, three of the most often used game mechanics, do not automatically give rise to gamefulness and improved engagement: *there is nothing algorithmic about motivating through gameful design.* Reflecting on this controversy, we study gamification in practical, situated use, and we observe participants' work in sustaining meaningful gamefulness in their activity.

Gamification does not involve exclusively digital gaming (Deterding et al., 2011); for example, Foster, Sheridan, Irish, & Frost (2012) use a card-based game layer to stimulate safety awareness, reflection, and engagement in an Engineering Design course. We also discuss a gamification initiative that mostly relies on face-to-face gameful interaction. Our design is also simple and low-cost, allowing replication (and variations) with little effort, in similar activity settings.

Our objectives in the present study[1] are:

- To present the "Revision Fever" (RF) gamification exercise, and to discuss its challenges in attending to divergent logics of gameplay and work;
- To examine the solutions put in place by RF designers and participants, before and during gameplay;
- At a more general level, to highlight the specificity of gamification projects as 'transparent magic circles' that require collective, distributed work for balancing divergent logics of gameplay and non-game activity.

2   Gamification: A 'Magic Circle' Transparent-By-Design

Gamification is yet another type of situation that explicitly challenges the distinction between game and non-game worlds, similar with other types of ambiguous, borderline activities such as pervasive games or dark play. Gamification is openly *instrumental*: while games often extend invitations to autotelic play (which are then taken over by participants in various configurations of play-bound or ulterior motives),

[1] This research has been supported by the program EXCEL, grant POSDRU/89/1.5/S/62557.

gamification extends an openly ambivalent invitation: to pursue non-game goals with a (partially) 'lusory' attitude (Salen & Zimmerman, 2004). Gamification may be fruitfully conceptualized as a specific strategy of *configuring the 'magic circle' of play as transparent-by-design*.

The concept of "magic circle" has been introduced by Huizinga (1938) in his discussion of the rupture between the world of gameplay and the real world that surrounds it, but does not assimilate it. The concept has been re-created in academic scholarship through Salen and Zimmerman's work (2004), generating substantial debate on the distinction between play and non-play (Stenros, 2012). On the one hand, play is often shaped by real-world, non-play considerations, including matters of money, social status and relationships with significant others (Juul, 2008; Malaby, 2007; Stenros, 2012). On the other hand, the creation (often through negotiation) of a boundary between play and non-play remains, in each empirical instance of play, a core activity of participants. Both Juul (2008) and Stenros (2012) indicate that the 'magic circle' is a concept of heuristic value if we do not take it as a binary distinction. The establishment of a "magic circle" is a defining feature of gameplay, which has, each and every time, a different shape that should be empirically observed in order to understand what is going on: "the magic circle is best understood as *the boundary that players negotiate*" (Juul, 2008, p. 64, emphasis in original).

Stenros (2012) distinguishes three dimensions of this boundary: the "psychological bubble", the "magic circle", and the "arena of play" (pp. 10-14). As we find this differentiation useful for our discussion, we present it succinctly.

The "arena of play" refers to the spatial and temporal arrangements created to host players and play, such as sports fields, Carnival periods, and game products. At any given moment arenas may be populated or empty, used playfully or with other orientations (ibid.). Pervasive games and pervasive play (such as flash mobs) are challenging because they stage gameplay in arenas that are socially understood as serious.

The "psychological bubble" refers to players' attitude towards their activities in the game; the ideal-type of playful attitude combines a feeling of *safety* and disposition to take risks in the gameworld, with the *intention* to pursue game goals, and with *disattention* to elements of the situation that are not marked as relevant in the game (ibid.). The ambivalence of dark play is visible on this dimension: participants' awareness that they are playing (in) a game may be dim, oscillating, or even absent. This sort of duality is also visible in the case of gamers that play for money or other real-world rewards (Dibbell, 2007).

The "magic circle" refers to the socially shaped and agreed-upon set of rules and relevancies of a particular instance of gameplay (Stenros, 2012). Participants may participate in this magic circle with full engagement, or with ulterior motives or half-beliefs. Still, in any situation of gameplay, participants establish some rules of what counts as valuable and relevant, and what is to be ignored in the game. By communicating these rules, they frame their activity, symbolically, as "just play" – to some extent.

Gamification projects are openly dual, attending to the logic of their non-game activity (such as working, learning, improving one's physical condition, consuming, buying etc.) and to the logic of a game layer that affords simple gameplay. This ambivalence can be observed on all three dimensions introduced by Stenros (2012).

As regards the arena of play, gamified activities often include heterogeneous sets of equipment – some with in-game value, some with real world value. For example, gamified education combines fictive, playful, and educational messages. Work tools are used alongside gameplay instruments. Space and time arrangements must be devised to invite gameplay, but also to afford efficiency in the non-game activity.

As regards the 'magic circle' understood as a set of locally settled rules of engagement, gamification mixes practices of 'serious', non-game activity (such as work or learning) with practices of gameplay. Trouble may arise when one practice overrides the other, because then the composite activity turns into something else than expected by designers and organizers. For example, in-game competition may disrupt work collaboration; the value of fictional resources may confound the values of real-world resources. This difficulty is also shared by serious games, which attempt to cultivate a 'serious' competence or achievement through gameplay. In-game skills often do not overlap completely with the real-world skills sought after (Rughiniş, 2012).

Last but not least, participants' attitudes towards the activity may vary from playful to gameful to instrumental, changing through time, or from one person to another. Gamified applications, such as Foursquare, may be "played" by some but "used" by others (Deterding et al., 2011). For example, Frank discusses the "gamer mode" in educational gaming, a style of playing serious games without regard to the non-game logic which they aim to cultivate (Frank, 2012). Moral stakes and interpretations depend on participants' attitudes: the more playful may be more tolerant of cheating and rule bending (Berne, 2012; Glas, 2011) than those oriented more gamefully (rule-bound) or instrumentally (towards real-world value).

This ambivalent attention towards gameplay and 'serious' activity means that gamification requires a 'transparent' magic circle, by introducing signals of gameplay and game-relevant resources, while at the same time keeping participants' eyes open to non-game relevancies. Unlike activities in serious games, that are ultimately accountable to the gameworld rules, activities in gamified projects remain accountable to two logics:1) the gameplay order and 2) the real-world value system of the non-game activity. We propose that this is a useful dimension on which we can differentiate serious games from gamification – namely, the degree to which participants are invited to be 'nothing but players', or to remain "user/players" attentive to two structures of relevance.

Both in serious games and in gamified projects, designers must accommodate two potentially divergent sets of requirements: the gameplay and the 'serious' activity. Still, in gamified projects this adjustment work is required not only from designers, but also from participants: the gamified 'magic circle' is sketched such as to draw their attention, but not to engage them completely. Non-game elements remain visible and demanding. In what follows we study designers' and participants' work of balancing conflicting orientations in the Revision Fever exercise, on three dimensions: 1) establishing the 'magic circle' of gameplay rules and relevancies, 2) subjectively engaging the gamified activity, and 3) configuring the play arena.

3   Gamification as Instrument

Gamification may be fruitfully studied through the theoretical lens of "instrumental genesis" (Béguin & Rabardel, 2000; Longchamp, 2012). Béguin and Rabardel observe that an instrument cannot be conceptualized only as an artifact, because it is a *composite* entity with two main elements: "artifact structures", including material and symbolic resources that facilitate action, and "psychological structures", including users' schemes for organizing and conducting the mediated activity. Béguin and Rabardel also highlight the *developmental* nature of the instrument: both artifact structures and psychological structures emerge and change through activity, in the very process of using the instrument. The process of change in artifact structures is called "instrumentalization", while the process of change in users' activity schemes is called "instrumentation"; both represent dimensions in the genesis and evolution of an instrument (Béguin & Rabardel, 2000).

We conceptualize gamification as a socio-technical instrument consisting of an *artifact* and participants' *activity schemes*. This approach maps well with Stenros' (2012) three dimensions, introduced above:

1. The *gamification artifact* includes the set of symbolic and material elements that define the game layer: stories, rules, messages, material requisites for play, etc. We also include here the *accessory set* of elements (hardware, software, furniture, consumables) that support implementation, making the play arena practicable and hospitable. For example, the rules of the game may not explicitly require food and drinks for participants, but they may be essential resources for actual gameplay. The gamification artifact, therefore, includes the locally established 'magic circle' of in-game relevance, and the play arena.
2. We distinguish two types of *users' schemes*, following Glas (2011): a) gameplay styles, including ways of cheating, and b) players' degrees of engagement with the game frame. Each game opens the possibility for multiple strategies within a given rule system, and multiple interpretations of the rules themselves – including what may seem to be, to some or to all, rule-bending or outright cheating. Participants' engagement with the game, their identification with in-game characters and goals, is also variable, both within players, who change their attitudes in time, and between players. Participants may play from within the "psychological bubble" or, alternatively, take a more mundane orientation.

There are situations in which an instrument involves different categories of users. For example, Longchamp (2012) discusses CSCL solutions that involve "teachers" and "students" as two types of roles. Flexible design may include differential rights and incentives of adjustment work for such categories of users; Longchamp differentiates "teacher-instrumentalizable" versus "learner-instrumentalizable" systems (ibid.). Games often include privileged roles, such as game masters, arbiters, judges etc. Gamification projects may, therefore, be "arbiter-instrumentalizable" or "player-instrumentalizable", to different degrees.

4   Case Study

We study the implementation of "Revision Fever" (RF), a gamified exercise of collaborative review, in two sessions of play, through observation and 11 interviews with
project participants (designers, players, and judges).

Each year, instructors from the Cisco Networking Academy of University Politehnica of Bucharest[2] review last year's course presentations. In previous years instructors revised materials individually, working wherever and whenever they wanted in
the limits of a given period, discussing with colleagues freely, through any means
they chose. This review work was not particularly cherished, being rather defined as
tedious. In order to address what seemed to be an attention and motivation deficit in
revising the curriculum, in the fall of 2012 we initiated a collaborative review exercise. We designed a flexible instrument that would adapt through use, and through
feedback in-between sessions. The main idea was to transform individual reviewing
into a competition between teams, organized and supervised in a play arena organized
to this purpose.

The RF *gamification artifact* included three main *gameful interactional devices*
(some elements were modified in the 2nd session, organized one week later):

1. *Competition between teams*: reviewers were grouped in three teams of five, sending 'error tickets' ('typo', 'graphic design', 'rewording', 'missing concept', and
   'wrong concept') to a judge committee via an issue tracker. In the first edition, the
   actual corrections based on the approved error tickets were done by reviewers individually, after the game – for fear that, in hurry, teams would introduce additional
   errors into presentations. This has proven to be cumbersome, defying the purpose
   of transforming individual review work in playful teamwork. In the 2nd session,
   teams implemented repairs prior to sending the tickets. With their approved tickets
   teams gained points, which they could spend (on various items detailed below) or
   re-invest by 'buying' more presentations to review, more computers to work on, or
   an additional member (in the 2nd edition). The highest scoring team at the end of
   the 3-hour review session was the winner.
2. *Limited resources*: each team started with only one computer (increased to 2 computers in the 2nd session), one chair, and two presentations; they could buy additional ones, as well as water, pizza, and they could bid to include a supplementary
   expert team member for 15 minutes (in the 2nd session), on the game market.
3. *Tempo*: a combination of mediated communication via Trac v.1 and Dropbox with
   face-to-face communication, supported by organization of the work space (Figure 1),
   evolved to support a fast paced gameful interaction (Rughiniş, 2013).

The play arena was organized in a training room. In Fig. 1 we present the spatial organization of participants; while there were available chairs for everybody, the rules
of limited resources meant that, at least in the beginning, some were not occupied.
When lacking chairs, reviewers could stand, sit on the floor, or sit in pairs on the same
chair. In retrospect, a few of them also decided to "bend the rules" and sit on chairs
they did were not entitled to.

---

[2] http://www.ccna.ro/

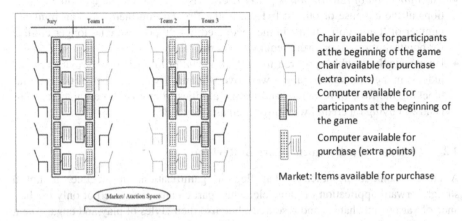

Fig. 1. The play arena in Revision Fever gamification exercise: spatial arrangements encouraged collaboration across team borders

4.1 Convergence and Divergence between Work and Gameplay Profiles

The game layer of the Revision Fever exercise introduced significant changes in the previous organization of the review activity: teamwork and competition instead of individual independent work; a clear allocation of space and time; a fast tempo; a division of labor between players and arbiters; strategies for division of labor within reviewer teams; a classification of corrections in five types, with points that indicated their relative value; more intense communication and public visibility of one's work.

Some RF elements were explicitly gameful and signaled that the exercise invites gameplay: the competition, the rules of limited resources, and the game market. The 'magic circle' was particularly signaled by those elements that countered the work logic. The rules of limited resources were in manifest divergence from requirements of effective work: teams did not have enough chairs and computers to work as they chose, but had to "buy" them through points gained by reviewing presentations. Of course, the fact that reviewers worked hard, in the game, in order to be able to work even more added to the overall sense of playfulness and humor, at least for most participants. (A couple of instructors did not see the point of this gamified arrangement and, more or less explicitly, chose to review presentations individually, on computers outside the play arena.)

Besides the collectively self-imposed limitation of resources, other elements of the gamification exercise also had the potential to conflict with the logic of revision work:

- *Competition between teams* could interfere with review work productivity, if it hampered communication between reviewers in different teams; comments and advice from senior instructors, distributed across adversary teams, were essential for correcting more subtle errors and for proposing improvements in structure and choice of relevant topics;

- The *allocation of reward points* per type of revision could encourage some corrections at the expense of others. Indeed, in the first edition there were an immense number of 'typo' corrections; in the second edition 'typos' were no longer eligible for points, but reviewers were required to correct them "for free".
- Unexpectedly, trouble appeared from the *division of labor* between reviewers and judges: in the first edition judges were overwhelmed by the number of tickets, thus blocking the flow of resources and teams' abilities to buy new presentations. This is how "buying on credit" was introduced as a new rule.

4.2   Distributed Adjustment Work in Revision Fever

A close examination indicates that flexible gamification, in practice, is not a straightforward application of game elements: participants fine tune not only the balance of various mechanics and resources, but also their styles of play and engagement with the game frame.

We focus on the locally problematic divergence of the game logic versus the review activity logic. There is a constant work of adjustment, through which participants modify the gamification artifact (*instrumentalization*) and their schemes of play and engagement (*instrumentation*), to support the flow of gamified activity. As discussed, there were many instances of conflict between the game logic and the review work logic – some by design, some unintended. For example, players initially sent 'typo' tickets in large numbers, ignoring more substantive errors; the initial restriction of 1 computer per team seriously restricted the productivity of the review process.

Participants pursued convergence by three types of solutions:

- *Re-designing the gamification artifact,* including game rules and the play arena (such as: declaring 'typos' ineligible; giving teams 2 computers·to start with, in the 2nd edition; adjusting the tempo and duration of the event; spatial reorganization of participants);
- *Shaping play styles,* which included forms of cheating (such as spiriting away a glass of water or a chair) or the division of labor between participants in a team (by instructing junior instructors to focus on typo and graphic style errors, and senior instructors to look for missing concepts and other technical errors);
- *Fine-tuning engagement* with the game frame: participants alternatively observed and ignored the game frame; most of them managed the relative priorities of game and non-game objectives through an attitude of *half-engagement*. For example, players constantly collaborated with members of competing teams and the judge committee, thus entering and exiting the game frame according to the task at hand.

It is also important to observe here that the work of adjustment between the game layer and work requirements is *distributed* across multiple participants, and there is a division of labor across various types of participants. By design, changes in the RF gamification artifact during gameplay were allowed for the judge committee, but not for players – although they could make suggestions; designers also changed the gamification artifact from one edition to the second. Players developed and changed their activity schemes, by alternatively observing and ignoring gameplay requirements, by cheating, and by searching for productive work / play strategies.

5   Conclusions

On the basis of our case study, we conclude that a flexible gamification instrument may develop considerably by adjustment in use. The conceptual framework proposed by Stenros (2012) and the theory of instrumental genesis (Béguin & Rabardel, 2000) draws our attention to the fact that troubles and adjustments can appear in different *dimensions*: in participants' psychological orientations, in the 'magic circle' of locally established game rules and relevancies, and in the play arena, which includes gameplay requisites as well as various accessories. For example, face-to-face communication is shaped by the spatial disposition of players and the temporal organization of their interaction. Adjustment work is *distributed:* a) across different *types* of participants (such as designers, judges and players); b) across *time* (players were more engaged in the first edition and more work-oriented in the second edition) and c) across *participants* themselves (some "played" the Review Fever, while others "worked" within its arena).

In a generalization attempt, we can identify three types of gamification solutions, according to strategies for distributing adjustment work:

- *No adjustment* during gameplay: rules in the game layer remain formally unchanged during gameplay; this does not prevent players from modifying their strategies, interpretations, and degrees of involvement – but, formally, the game does not change;
- *Role-bound adjustment*: privileged participants (instructors, judges) are allowed to change the rules of the game during gameplay, in order to accommodate conflicts and maladjustments. Privileged participants see through the 'magic circle' in order to monitor work effectiveness and to translate work requirements into elements of gameplay; the other participants may carry on their activity without minding divergences between the game layer and the non-game activity;
- Delegated adjustment: all participants have a certain degree of autonomy in configuring their gameplay, and they are in charge of monitoring work success while playing; the 'magic circle' is transparent for everybody.

Some instances of divergence between the game logic and the work logic are introduced by design in order to frame the activity as gameplay; some others are unintended, or just partially expected. Such divergent elements and their consequences for the gamified activity may not be fully visible at a glance; given that gamification openly invites and thrives on such dual logics, it is recommendable that designers and organizers of gamified projects also plan for *debriefing sessions* or other types of qualitative evaluations, involving all types of participants.

References

1. Berne, P.: I cheat at Foursquare. Slash Gear (2012),
   http://www.slashgear.com/i-cheat-at-foursquare-25219923/
   (retrieved November 3, 2012)
2. Bogost, I.: Persuasive Games: Exploitationware. Gamasutra (2011),
   http://www.gamasutra.com/view/feature/6366/persuasive_
   games_exploitationware.php/ (retrieved January 18, 2012)
3. Béguin, P., Rabardel, P.: Designing for instrument-mediated activity. Scandinavian Journal
   of Information Systems 12(1), 173–190 (2000)
4. Deterding, S., Dixon, D., Khaled, R., Nacke, L.: From Game Design Elements to Gamefulness: Defining "Gamification". In: MindTrek 2011, pp. 9–15. ACM Press, Tampere (2011)
5. Dibbell, J.: The Life of the Chinese Gold Farmer. The New York Times, June 17 (2007)
6. Foster, J.A., Sheridan, P.K., Irish, R., Frost, G.S.: Gamification as a Strategy for Promoting Deeper Investigation in a Reverse Engineering Activity. In: 2012 ASEE Annual Conference, pp. 1–15. ASEE, San Antonio (2012)
7. Frank, A.: Gaming the Game: A Study of the Gamer Mode in Educational Wargaming.
   Simulation & Gaming 43(1), 118–132 (2012)
8. Glas, R.: Breaking Reality: Exploring Pervasive Cheating in Foursquare. In: DiGRA 2011
   Think Design Play, pp. 1–15 (2011)
9. Hagglund, P.: Taking gamification to the next level. Umea University (2012),
   http://ojs.library.dal.ca/index.php/djim/article/download/
   2012vol8Chorney/518 (retrieved)
10. Huizinga, J.: Homo Ludens: A Study of Play Element in Culture. Beacon Press, Boston
    (1938)
11. Juul, J.: The Magic Circle and the Puzzle Piece. In: Gunzel, S., Liebe, M., Mersch, D.
    (eds.) Conference Proceedings of the Philosophy of Computer Games 2008, pp. 56–67.
    Potsdam University Press (2008)
12. Longchamp, J.: An instrumental perspective on CSCL systems. International Journal of
    Computer-Supported Collaborative Learning 7(2), 211–237 (2012)
13. Malaby, T.M.: Beyond Play: A New Approach to Games. Games and Culture 2(2), 95–113
    (2007)
14. Nelson, M.J.: Soviet and American Precursors to the Gamification of Work. In: MindTrek
    2012. ACM, Tampere (2012)
15. Nicholson, S.: A User-Centered Theoretical Framework for Meaningful Gamification A
    Brief Introduction to Gamification Organismic Integration Theory Situational Relevance and
    Situated Motivational Affordance. Games+Learning+Society 8.0. Madison (2012),
    http://scottnicholson.com/pubs/meaningfulframework.pdf (retrieved)
16. Robertson, M.: Can't play, won't play. Hide&Seek (2012),
    http://www.hideandseek.net/2010/10/06/cant-play-wont-play/
    (retrieved April 4, 2012)
17. Rughini, R.: Serious games as input versus modulation: different evaluations of utility. In:
    BCS-HCI 2012, ACM, Birmingham (2012)
18. Rughini, R.: Time as a heuristic in serious games for engineering education. In: 5th Inter-
    national Conference on Computer Supported Education CSEDU 2013. INSTICC, Aachen
    (2013)
19. Salen, K., Zimmerman, E.: Rules of play. MIT Press, Cambridge (2004)
20. Stenros, J.: In Defence of a Magic Circle: The Social and Mental Boundaries of Play. In:
    DiGRA Nordic 2012 Conference, pp. 1–18. Tampere, Finland (2012)

Augmenting Yu-Gi-Oh! Trading Card Game as Persuasive Transmedia Storytelling

Mizuki Sakamoto and Tatsuo Nakajima

Department of Computer Science and Engineering
Waseda University, Japan
{mizuki,tatsuo}@dcl.cs.waseda.ac.jp

Abstract. In this paper, we present *Augmented Trading Card Game* that enhances remote trading card game play with virtual characters used in the fictional stories of popular animations and games. We show our observations about the way players use the system, realizing the game, and what their feelings and impressions about the game are. We believe the obtained results would be useful to consider how to use empathetic virtual characters and the fictional story that the characters are used in, in the real world activities for future information services. We also discuss how our approach can be extended to design a new type of transmedia storytelling by considering *Augmented Trading Card Game* as one form of transmedia storytelling. From the experiences we propose a framework for designing transmedia story telling aiming to change people's attitude and behavior named persuasive transmedia storytelling. The framework called value-based design framework is a first step to design persuasive transmedia storytelling.

Keywords: Storytelling, Augmented Reality, Trading Card Game, Virtual Character.

1 Introduction

Virtual characters are widely used in our daily life, recently. For example, famous Disney characters like *Mickey Mouse* and *Donald Duck* provoke our empathetic feelings easily anytime and anywhere, and *Kitty* and *Pokémon* are now found all over the world. In animations and games, each virtual character has its own personality and story, which can be used as a medium to convey special information and messages to people. If people are familiar with the fictional story of an animation or a game, then the story's characters are able to recall the leitmotif of the story easily without much additional information but by just performing some action/interaction with the story's character. Especially, many Japanese animation and game stories contain serious ideological messages that are important to make our daily life more desirable. We believe that this observation is very important when considering how to use virtual characters in various future information services in the real world.

In the contemporary Japanese society, several posters for public service announcements have adopted the idea to use virtual characters from recent popular

A. Marcus (Ed.): DUXU/HCII 2013, Part II, LNCS 8013, pp. 587–596, 2013.

animation stories. For example, Japanese popular animation K-ON! has been used for promoting a national survey in Japan[1]. Also, NFGD that promotes guide dogs' training has created two posters using popular characters from Puella Magi Madoka Magica, which is recently very popular in Japan[2]. These examples show the effectiveness of using virtual characters that have their background stories to attract people. Moreover, they are good evidences that virtual characters could be used to convey ideological messages that might play significant role in changing people's current attitude. In Japan, the majority of young people have been enjoying animation and game stories for a long time and they know the popular animation and game characters and their stories very well. This we believe is a good prerequisite for using virtual characters to enhance emotional feelings and successfully convey ideological messages through the characters' stories.

This paper presents Augmented Trading Card Game (Augmented TCG) for playing the Yu-Gi-Oh! Trading Card Game[3] (Yu-Gi-Oh! TCG) between two players who are located in different places. The system, realizing the game, supports the remote trading card game play with virtual characters. In Augmented TCG, we use virtual characters used in Yu-Gi-Oh! comic and animation. Yu-Gi-Oh! TCG has been originally introduced in the Yu-Gi-Oh! comic and animation. One of the reasons why Yu-Gi-Oh! TCG is popular in Japan is the fact that almost all young people have first enjoyed the comic and the animation story and then learnt how to play the game from that story. The story also teaches some important ideological concepts such as the importance of justice, friendship, bravery, positivity, and thoughtfulness. That is why we believe that the characters of the Yu-Gi-Oh! animation story can be used to enhance the playing style of the game through the stories they carry and recall. In this research we are interested in investigating the impact of the presence and behavior of the 3D virtual characters on the players' emotions and feelings, and the play style of the game. We discuss that Augmented TCG is considered as one form of transmedia storytelling. Transmedia storytelling is the technique of telling a single story or story experience across multiple platforms and formats using current digital technologies [2]. Our approach enhances an original fictional story in corporation with a real world game to create a new story that a player of the game participants.

From the experiences with *Augmented TCG* as transmedia storytelling, we also propose a value-based design framework for designing persuasive transmedia storytelling aiming to change people's attitude and behavior. Persuasive transmedia storytelling consists of *Augmented TCG* as a real world game and a fictional story, where the fictional story enhances the game play by reminding ideological messages in the story while playing the game, and this encourages a player to change his/her attitude and behavior. The framework uses six values, *informative value*, *economic value*, *empathetic value*, *aesthetic value*, *persuasive value*, and *ideological value* that are extracted from our experiences with designing *Augmented TCG*. The proposed framework shows how the four (*informative, economic, empathetic, aesthetic*) values

---

[1] http://www.youtube.com/watch?v=IdAkKZKEfGU
[2] http://www.nkoku.jp/pos
[3] http://www.yugioh-card.com/en/

are used in a real world game to increase people's extrinsic motivation by offering adequate feedback to them. On the other hand, the *ideological value* offered in a fictional story makes people's dream and expectation explicit to teach how changing a player's attitude realizes his/her dream. Also, the *persuasive value* in the story increases human self-efficacy. The values enhance their intrinsic motivation and makes people think more positively. Therefore, the hurdles for people to solve hard problems become lower, and they become more confident and enthusiastic in taking an action to solve the problem through their increased self-efficacy and positive thinking.

2   An Overview of Augmented Trading Card Game

Augmented TCG enhances the remote trading card play performed by two persons. The basic design approach is similar to the one of the augmented reality games introduced in [9], which integrates physical items and virtual items. As shown in Fig. 1, the two players are located in different places. Each player's cards, in his/her duel field on the table in front of him/her, are captured by a camera and projected on the opponent player's table.

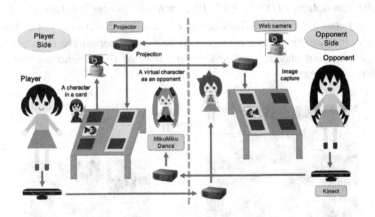

Fig. 1. Augmented Trading Card Game System

Also, each player is represented by the 3D model of a virtual character used in popular animations and games, and this character is shown to the opponent player. In the current implementation, *MikuMikuDance*[4] is used to show the 3D models of the virtual characters. *MikuMikuDance* is free software for creating 3D movies by using virtual characters. The virtual character is controlled using *MS Kinect* and its movement is synchronized with the movement of the opponent player. In the current *Augmented TCG*, a player can choose one of three virtual characters that are *Yugi* and

---

[4] http://www.geocities.jp/higuchuu4

Kaiba from the *Yu-Gi-Oh!* animation story, and *Link* from The *Legend of Zelda*[5]. *Yugi* is always surrounded by many friends and his winning success is a result of his strong bonds with his friends who love the trading card game. *Kaiba* is a lonely hero and he always seeks the strength in the game, but he does not accept other people's help even if he is in a critical situation. However, in the story he also finally understands the importance of friendship. Most young boys want to follow either of these two characters because of their typical, very attractive and ideal personalities. The reason to choose *Link* as the third character in our experiment is that we would like to investigate how a popular character from another unrelated to TCG story affects the attitude of a player.

Furthermore, while playing the game, another virtual character, which has been depicted on one of the player's cards in advance, appears on a small display near the player once that card is drawn out of the deck, and supports and encourages him/her to win the game until the end of the game. In the current prototype system, we cannot show characters depicted in any cards of players. In our experiments, we have chosen one special card, and show the character in the card on a small display for evaluating our approach.

We have selected *Dead Master* from *Black★Rock Shooter*[6] as a character to be depicted on the card because we feel that the character does not contradict with or violate the atmosphere of *Yu-Gi-Oh!*. *Black★Rock Shooter* has two worlds. *Dead Master* is an enemy of *Black★Rock Shooter* in another dimension world, but in the daily world, they are very close friends. This becomes a persuasive message conveying the meaning that players need to keep and develop their friendship even if they fight seriously in a game.

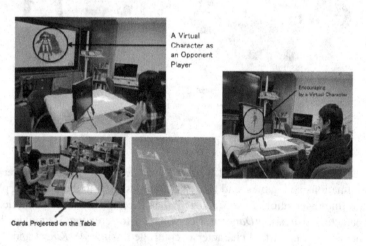

Fig. 2. Current Prototype Configuration

---

[5] http://zelda.com/
[6] http://blackrockshooter.wikia.com/

Fig. 2 shows the current prototype configuration for a participant. On a large display, a virtual character, which movement is synchronized with the movement of the person who imitates the opponent player, is shown. A camera is setup behind the small display near the participant, and captures the image of the cards. The opponent player's cards are projected on the table by a projector.

3   Augmented TCG as Transmedia Storytelling

Enhancing games played in the real world like TCG with fictional stories is a promising direction to design a new form of transmedia. In this section, we discuss some design implications of *Augmented TCG* that will be considered as one form of future transmedia storytelling from our experiences with designing and experimenting *Augmented TCG*.

In the current *Augmented TCG*, its animation and game story is explicitly not shown during the play. A player needs to recall the story during his/her play. More tight integration of the game play, and the animation and game story offers a new possibility to design transmedia. The movement of a virtual character from the virtual world to the real world offers a tight integration between the fictional story and the TCG game play. Transversal interfaces [1] offer a way to move between the worlds seamlessly. The approach offers a stronger association between a fictional story in the virtual world and the real world through a virtual character than the current approaches, and the boundary between the two worlds becomes more blurred.

We believe that a participant would be more excited to play the game if a character drawn on a card from his/her favorite deck is shown to encourage him/her. Cards are considered as one piece of transmedia to construct a fictional story. However, the preferences for that character are different according to the player's gender. A female player usually likes a card depicting a pretty girl. In this case, encouraging cheerfully the player with gestures by that character would be natural and meaningful. On the other hand, a male player usually likes a powerful card that may depict a strong monster. In such a case, the encouragement by the character should be more powerful and adding special effects to show the superior ability of the character would be more suitable and more effective to motivate the player. Thus, if the character is one of the player's favorite characters, then the encouragement would be a powerful tool to increase the player's motivation and excitement of the game.

When playing with a virtual character from animation and game story, the player also tries to mimic the character's behavior in the animation story. This can be a useful and successful approach to teach players how to improve their gaming skills. If players follow the skillful character's way of playing in the story, then they can learn new skills and techniques from that character's experience in the animation. Of course, a skillful friend is a good coach for improving players' skills, but if there is no good coach available around the player, then they need to learn by themselves and doing it following the experience of the character would be a promising and exciting approach to exploit future transmedia storytelling.

In our experiments, we could not find the rigorous evidence that the stories of the virtual characters could always strongly affect the attitude of the players. One of the reasons is that in our current research we focus on a game. For most people, the purpose of a game is just for fun. Of course, the duel against *Yugi* and *Kaiba* makes players play the game more seriously, but it is hard to make players braver when *Link* is shown as an opponent player. *Link* is a character in an RPG game, and a male player considers that the character is just like his avatar in the game, so his story does not have strong ideological messages in the game. Also, the presence of *Dead Master* does not have a strong impact on a player, since the character itself is very popular, but its story is not so well known yet. This means that well known stories that contain strong ideological messages and characters that have powerful and distinctive personalities are important to make virtual characters be used as metaphors. We also consider that the music used in the popular stories could also become a metaphor for the stories because in Japanese animations, their music sometimes becomes more popular than their characters. We believe that designing metaphors that use the popular stories in animations and games is a promising future direction to convey complex ideological messages to people without presenting a large amount of information to them.

One of the problems in using virtual characters is their copyright. There are many free 3D models for *MikuMikuDance*, but some of them are deleted on the Web due to the copyright violation. However, freely available models offer new possibilities to enhance games because the models can be easily customized. In Japan, it is a popular culture to create new characters and stories from existing ones. Using a customizable virtual character in *Augmented TCG* may create a new playing style of TCG, and the new stories of the character can be used to enhance its role as a metaphor.

As already described, virtual characters used in animations and game stories are widely used in multiple media channels. In *Pokémon,* a synergy among games, movies, and TV programs is used to make the *Pokémon* story more popular, and make the story pervasive in its fan's daily life. Also, in the *Yu-Gi-Oh!* animation story, the animation story teaches its game players how to play the TCG game and why the game is attractive while they are watching the animation story. Using multiple channels to communicate messages among people is a very effective way to convey the messages among people because each channel can convey the message in a special partial way. This is also a typical approach in the current advertisement because only one medium cannot deliver the advertisement to a large audience of people.

4 Value-Based Design Framework for Designing Persuasive Transmedia Storytelling

The important power of *Augmented TCG* as persuasive transmedia storytelling is to change a user's attitude and behavior. In *Augmented TCG*, we adopted the idea to show virtual characters as opponent players. The virtual characters are used to remind their background fictional story, in which these characters play an important role. The story contains some ideological messages and makes a player to believe that the ideological messages are important in his/her daily life. In the *Yu-Gi-Oh!* animation story,

Yugi and *Kaiba* always think that they can overcome the current problem and all problems will be overcome if they work very hard. Then, a player becomes to think positively that his/her skills in the game will be increased and he/she will play a TCG game much better than before.

In our daily life, there are many social issues that we need to take into account. These issues will be solved if we can work hard in order to overcome them. However, we usually do not feel the self-efficacy to overcome the issues. The results of the positive psychology teach us that the positive thinking plays a very important role to increase our self-efficacy to solve hard problems [4, 5].

In our approach, the fictional story offered with *Augmented TCG* makes it possible to change a user's attitude and behavior. The story first teaches us how playing *Augmented TCG* is effective in our daily life. Then, the ideological message in the story also makes a user believe that changing his/her attitude and behavior is essential to achieve an ideological goal that will lead to overcoming some serious social problems. Finally, the positivity in the story increases the user's self-efficacy to overcome the problems.

Recently, the promotion of a commercial product becomes very complicated because consumers are fragmented to use various social media, and there is not only one medium that is useful to advertise a target commercial product. Persuasive transmedia storytelling will be useful to promote the attractiveness of the products. The story offered as transmedia reminds us the product's attractiveness. Modern advertisement methods use various media, not only traditional television and newspaper commercials, but also *Twitter* and *Facebook*. The advertisement delivers the story about the product or its brand through these various media. The reality of the story increases the empathy on the story. Also, the ideological message contained in the story makes a user believe the effectiveness of the product, where the product helps to overcome some social issues in our daily life by using the product and by changing the user's habit or thinking. Finally, the positivity in the story can increase the self-efficacy to overcome the social issue. Our experiences with *Augmented TCG* show that using fictional stories can be extended to design ordinal consumer products as persuasive transmedia storytelling.

For considering the above issues, we need a design framework to show a guideline to design persuasive transmedia storytelling. Fig. 3 shows our basic approach to use the proposed six values to increase people's intrinsic motivation and to make them think positively when incorporating a fictional story into persuasive transmedia storytelling[7]. The *empathetic*, *economic*, and *aesthetic values* offer people extrinsic incentives, and the *informative value* shows the reason to change human's attitude or tips and tactics for making a better decision. Our framework is based on the *transtheoretical model* that is a psychological model to change human's attitude [10]. The four values are used as tools in the model to change a user's current behavior by reminding the importance of changing his/her behavior and encouraging this change at an early stage. On the other hand, the *ideological value* makes people's dreams and

---

[7] The values are originally proposed in [7]. The current definition of the values is enhanced from the experiences with *Augmented TCG*.

expectations explicit and teaches how changing a user's attitude realizes his/her dream. Also, the *persuasive value* delivers the importance of the *ideological value* to a user. The values are used to increase the intrinsic motivation to change his/her attitude in the latter stage of the *transtheoretical model*. In our approach, we assume that a user already knows the story so the persuasion in the latter phase becomes faster than using traditional ways.

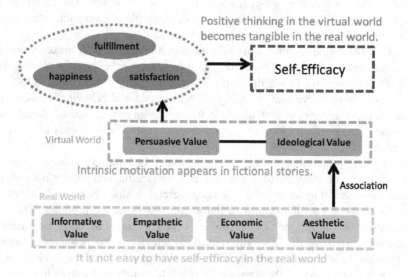

Fig. 3. Value-based Design Framework

The combination of the extrinsic motivation and the *ideological value*, and the *persuasive value* strongly enhances the intrinsic motivation and changes people's way of thinking. At first, the four values are used to increase a user' extrinsic motivation, but after a user understands the ideological messages represented as the ideological value in stories, the persuasive value makes him/her believe that he/she needs to achieve the ideological message in the real world through the association between the real world and the virtual world in the fictional story. In this step, the *pervasive value* changes the extrinsic motivation of the four values to the intrinsic motivation. For example, playing against a favorite virtual character becomes a player's extrinsic motivation. However, during understanding the background story of the character well, the empathy on the character becomes the intrinsic motivation because the user can know how the character tried to realize the ideological message in the fictional story. Also, the tangibility of a trading card as the *economic value* becomes a player's extrinsic motivation. However, while collecting trading cards, a player increases his/her self-esteem by constructing his/her own personalized and unique card deck, and this becomes his/her intrinsic motivation because the process also constructs his/her firm personality.

The story' positivity makes people think more aggressively by increasing their self-efficacy. Thus the hurdles for people to solve some hard social problems become lower, and they become more confident and enthusiastic in taking an action to solve the problem through their increased self-efficacy and positive thinking.

5   Related Work

The Alternative Reality Game (ARG) is a promising approach to convey messages to people using multiple channels. Fictional stories are embedded into a pervasive game that can use multiple channels [6, 8]. The channels offered in the game are used to exploit the game's fictional story. For example, in Perplex City[8], trading cards are used to introduce its characters and story. Web sites, emails, phone calls, and SMS messages are cooperatively used to solve riddles in the mystery story. Our approach is also a useful way to design the transmedia story telling. Especially, the form to represent a story affects how an ideological message is conveyed to a user. The transmedia storytelling divides a story across multiple media so that it is a possibility to choose the most suitable form to attract a user and to convey a message to a user.

Designing a user's experience [3] is related to the value based design framework. In the current approach, we extracted and analyzed values from a newly designed artifact, but it may be desirable to investigate how the values are emerged by analyzing a user's activities. Since designing values strongly depends on a user's experience, in the next step, it is an important research question to explore how values affect the user's experience, and how the values designed in the artifacts interact with the values emerged in the user's experience.

Popular Japanese games such as *the Legend of Zelda* and *Kid Icarus*[9] offer rich fictional stories incorporating the persuasive and ideological value. However, the games cannot make the values tangible in the real world because the games do not offer associations between the real world and the virtual world.

"Seichi Junrei" is a typical geek culture in Japan, especially related to Japanese animation, manga and game, in which people tend to visit famous locations from animation, manga and game. *"Seichi"* means *"Holy Land"*, *"Junrei"* means *"Pilgrimage"*. Anime fans arrive at that location, and take pictures with the same screen/angle of the animation, and upload them to their blogs. The most important aspect of *"Seichi Junrei"* is to bring something from the fictional story to the real world. The fans create new stories with these pictures and the virtual characters appearing in the fictional stories, and co-construct the stories to share them within their communities. This is a very interesting phenomenon to harmonize the real world and the fictional world. We believe that interactive pervasive games or social information services based on fictional stories are very promising tools to increase the reality of the fictional world, and the tools enhance the *"Seichi Junrei"* phenomena by realizing more tight integration between the fictional world and the real world. The experiences described in the paper will offer useful insights to design tools that will realize new types of transmedia storytelling.

---

[8] http://perplexcitywiki.com/wiki/Main_Page
[9] http://kidicarus.nintendo.com/

6   Conclusion

This paper presented some observations on the usage and the design of *Augmented TCG* that enhances remote trading card game play against empathetic virtual characters. We discussed that *Augmented TCG* can be considered as a one form of transmedia storytelling, and proposed the value-based design framework for designing persuasive transmedia storytelling.

Our approach is also useful to enhance gamification [11] with transmedia storytelling. The current gamification design focuses on how to offer incentives by using game mechanics. Such approach is useful to increase extrinsic motivation, but it is hard to increase intrinsic motivation. Our finding is that a virtual character can be used as a medium to convey ideological concepts efficiently, and this can be used to change a user's attitude to keep his/her obtained good habits for a long time.

References

1. André, E., Dorfmüller-Ulhaas, K., Rehm, M.: Engaging in a Conversation with Synthetic Characters Along the Virtuality Continuum. In: Butz, A., Fisher, B., Krüger, A., Olivier, P. (eds.) SG 2005. LNCS, vol. 3638, pp. 1–12. Springer, Heidelberg (2005)
2. Dena, C.: Transmedia Practice: Theorising the Practice of Expressing a Fictional World across Distinct Media and Environments, Dissertation Thesis, University Sydney (2009)
3. Forlizzi, J., Battarbee, K.: Understanding Experience in Interactive Systems. In: Proceedings of the 5th International Conference on Designing Interactive Systems (2004)
4. Fredrikson, B.L.: Positivity: Top-Notch Research Reveals the 3 to 1 Ratio That Will Change Your Life. Three Rivers Press (2009)
5. McGonigal, J.: ENGAGEMENT ECONOMY: The Future of Massively Scaled Collaboration and Participation, September 2008 I SR-1183 Institute For The Future (2008)
6. McGonigal, J.: Reality Is Broken: Why Games Make Us Better and How They Can Change the World. Penguin Press (2011)
7. Sakamoto, M., Nakajima, T., Alexandrova, T.: Digital-Physical Hybrid Design: Harmonizing the Real World and the Virtual World. In: Proceedings of the 7th International Conference and Workshop on the Design & Semantics of Form & Movement, DesForm 2012 (2012)
8. Szulborski, D.: This Is Not a Game: A Guide to Alternate Reality Gaming, http://Lulu.Com (2005)
9. Yamabe, T., Nakajima, T.: Playful Training with Augmented Reality Games: Case Studies towards Reality-Oriented System Design. Multimedia Tools and Applications 62(1), 259–286 (2012)
10. Velicer, W.F., Prochask, J.O., Fava, J.L., Norman, G.L., Redding, C.A.: Smoking Cessation and Stress Management: Applications of the Transtheoretical Model of Behavior Change. Homeostasis in Health and Disease 38(5-6), 216–233 (2008)
11. Zicbermann, G., Cunningham, C.: Gamification by Design. O'Reilly (2011)

How Gamification and Behavior Science Can Drive Social Change One Employee at a Time

Susan Hunt Stevens

Founder & CEO, Practically Green

Abstract. This paper discusses the use of interactive technology and gamification at companies to drive positive behavior change at scale around the topic of sustainability and corporate responsibility. While game and social based learning is still a relatively new concept for companies, our research and experience in the marketplace has shown that it can be effectively used to bridge the education gap among employees to help translate complex environmental science and ideas into a framework that people can understand as well as understand their own personal impact.

Keywords: Behavioral science, gamification, corporate sustainability, persuasive technology, game design.

1 Introduction

Practically Green is a pioneer in the use of interactive technology and gamification to drive positive behavior change. As a leading provider of sustainability engagement programs in North America and around the world, Practically Green motivates, empowers and quantifies the real-time impact of employee sustainability efforts both in the workplace and the communities where they live. Practically Green's clients include Fortune 500 companies, as well as sustainability leaders like EnerNOC and Seventh Generation.

Started in 2010, Practically Green was built with the goal of providing a solution to help motivate people to change their behavior associated with daily choices related to health and sustainability. For example, saving energy, saving water, reducing waste, and participating in the local and shared economy. Unlike weight loss or fitness, there are no official guidelines or shared scale for personal sustainability, As a result, Practically Green is at the forefront of pioneering the use of persuasive technology, social mechanics and game mechanics to drive positive behavior change at scale, and bringing it to a subject matter—sustainability—which was previously seen as something difficult and hard rather than measurable and fun.

The Practically Green platform was originally designed for individual networks, but about a year into the consumer program, companies saw the promise of using the platform at their company and approached Practically Green about creating a corporate version that would motivate and engage employees to help them meet their

A. Marcus (Ed.): DUXU/HCII 2013, Part II, LNCS 8013, pp. 597–601, 2013.

sustainability goals. In 2011, Practically Green tailored the platform to be used in an enterprise, software as a service (SaaS) model to help companies achieve sustainability success.

2   The Importance of Sustainability Employee Engagement

With the rise in corporate sustainability initiatives over the past five years, companies are quickly looking to their employees to help them meet the challenges of innovating and incorporating more sustainable business practices into their daily operations. Everything from their product pipeline to how they run their facilities. In the last year, nearly 50 percent of companies changed their business models as a result of sustainability opportunities, and in that same time, the percentage of companies reporting a profit from their sustainability efforts rose 23 percent to 37 percent, according to research by the *MIT Sloan Management Review* (*MIT SMR*) and the Boston Consulting Group (BCG).

As companies work to meet their corporate and financial sustainability goals, a knowledgeable and engaged workforce can lead to innovation around solving for business challenges. And yet, most employers are just starting to engage employees broadly in their sustainability mission and goals. One study by the National Environmental Education Foundation found that nearly 50 percent were planning to start an employee education initiative; however, that same NEEF survey found that most companies are not happy with the existing choices, which range from lunch-n-learns to workshops to sustainability fairs. They were often custom-built and difficult to maintain, provided no metrics and were challenging to scale in large organizations. Must most importantly, they tended to only reach the "already interested" rather than engaging a broad swath of the workforce.

The Practically Green platform has helped to bridge this education gap and barrier to engagement by pairing the best of interactive technology with the power of outstanding environmental content, which helps translate complex environmental science into a framework that people can understand.   In addition, by being available in mobile and web, a broader portion of the workforce can use it and the sustainability team can measure the impact. Finally, the mechanics used make it both engaging and effective.

3   About the Practically Green for Business Platform

Practically Green is a configurable web and mobile application that allows companies to engage employees to take actions, work together as groups, earn rewards, track their personal environmental impact—as well as the impact of their colleagues—and earn points, badges and receive social recognition for their actions via leaderboards and working through various levels of green-expertise.

Fig. 1. The Practically Green platform (Source: Practically Green, www.practicallygreen.com)

The platform includes:

- Newsfeed to help users stay up to date on actions their colleagues are taking and provide positive feedback and comments
- A recommendation engine that suggests actions for each user to complete based on personal preferences, social graph, company priorities and action history
- Recognition elements including badges, leaderboards
- Communication tools like newsletters and alerts to enable communication between program coordinators and users
- 500 science-backed actions that have been scored with a proprietary points system by our staff scientists for environmental impact
- Comprehensive dashboard that can track and provide real-time environmental metrics

4   Behavior Design Models

Practically Green takes influences from the two main behavior design models set out by BJ Fogg of the Stanford Persuasive Technology Lab, and Robert Cialdini, Professor of Psychology and Marketing at Arizona State University and author of *Influence The Psychology of Persuasion.*

At the crux of the Practically Green platform are Cialdini's two principles of "social proof" and "liking." By making actions visible, the commitments people make helps bring visibility to everyday sustainability actions that may otherwise go unnoticed. It is helping to foster new social norms within the workplace and provides positive feedback for the individuals that participate.

Motivation within the platform takes influences from Fogg's Behavior Grid. People can enter the platform at varying sustainability abilities and map their own path to success. This includes one-time behaviors, which Fogg calls "Dot" behaviors (e.g., buying a reusable mug), behaviors that have duration, called "Span" behaviors (e.g., taking public transportation for one month), and behaviors that provide a lasting change, called "Path" (e.g., installing solar panels).

The triggers for re-engagement and continued behavior change come from the ability to like, comment, invite others to join the platform (and earn a badge for doing so), customized notifications, weekly summaries. Users are also able to share their success stories, which increases

5   Gamification in Action

In order for these behavior principles to work, however, there needs to be incentives and an element of fun for the user. This is where applying game design techniques and social tools have been introduced into the platform. Practically Green has structured the experience so that it continues to be engaging for users at all levels and areas of expertise.

1. By creating a points system based on impact, people can track their own journey and progress over time against a shared set of levels. This enables people to both celebrate their own milestones, ie "I'm now a level 5 Solidly Green!!" as well as compare themselves to others. They can also see where they are relative to other colleagues and at the group level, groups can have the same comparisons. So I may individually be top of the leaderboard, but my group may be in the middle. This can inspire an individual to start influencing others to move up the overall group.
2. By creating shared achievements, primarily in the form of badges, corporate clients are providing digital monikers of success—and in some cases they even create offline versions to award status to employee participants. For example, one client has a certified green office program and participants who earn the Green Office Badge get a sticker that goes on their nameplate. As the stickers proliferate in the workplace, more employees are encouraged to participate and take action.
3. Using the feature that can group actions and create a time-based challenge, corporations can emphasize what's important to the company and encourage much broader participation by rewarding span-based participation, not just 'path' based change. An example of a clients challenge was a "ditch the cup" day that asked employees to use a reusable cup, but for just one day. Participants were all rewarded with free coffee if it was in a reusable mug. The metric for success was both overall participation and quantifying the total cups saved.

Applying game design techniques in conjunction with the behavior design principles has lead to real-time results for our clients.

6   Sustainability at Work: Is It Different from Personal Efforts

In our experience, there are aspects of being in a workplace that make elements of utilizing a digital, social platform more successful, and there are other aspects that make it challenging.

In terms of success, companies that are using the Practically Green platform have recognized the importance of sustainability and have made it a priority for their company and for the employees to participate it. When this happens, we see the social stigma of joining in sustainability efforts go away—people are less inclined to feel judged about participating, or even having their political beliefs be questioned. The company has articulated that this effort is good for business so people feel "safe" inviting others. Whereas in a personal setting, users have expressed more reluctance to invite others because they worry that people will think they are being judgmental about the person's lifestyle.

The challenge in a workplace is that participants may be there who are not intrinsically motivated or interested in the topic, but experience the social norming pressure to participate. As a result, the game design has to make fewer assumptions about inherent interest, especially during the first time user experience. It has also prompted our design team to think more about how we uncover what areas of sustainability might be most appealing to each user so the focus can be there. We are starting this work by developing different personas and thinking about the optimal design for each user archetype.

7   Conclusion

Although game and social based learning is still a relatively new concept, our research and experience in the marketplace has shown that behavior change at scale, across companies is possible by leveraging interactive technology. We believe that similar to the rise of wellness programs, within five years, digital sustainability engagement programs will become a core program for any responsible, innovative company.

Bridging the Gap between Consumer and Enterprise Applications through Gamification

Tim Thianthai and Bingjun Zhou

SAP Labs, Palo Alto, 3410 Hillview Ave,
Palo Alto, California, 94304, U.S.A.
{tim.thianthai,eric.zhou}@sap.com

Abstract. Consumer and enterprise applications are often perceived as the opposites in user-experience spectrum. One seemed serious, complex, and dull, while the other seemed fun, simple, and visually stimulating. Through gamification, these differences in perception can change, and the line between consumer and enterprise applications can be blurred. Some may think that applying the gamification concept to enterprise application is much harder than applying it to consumer application where the limitations are not as prominent. Thus, some may have already given up before they started. When analyzed closely based on our experience, these two types of application are quite similar.

Keywords: Gamification, Enterprise, SAP.

1   Introduction

As User Experience designers at SAP, we are familiar with designing enterprise applications. However, our design team also had the opportunity to work on consumer-oriented Global Business Incubator project called Apollo in the past year. Apollo, which is also known as **SAP Precision Retailing**, is the technology that provides:

- **Complete, Dynamic View of the Consumer** by combining information about a consumer's profile, purchase history and preferences with data about their current shopping context.
- **1-1 Targeted Offers in Real-Time** by delivering targeted offers and content, optimized in real-time on a 1-to-1 basis, to consumers across mobile, social and online channels.
- **Deep Insights to Optimize Campaign Performance** by providing access to insights on consumer behavior and offer performance, at any moment and any level of detail, to help optimize campaigns.

Based on this advanced retailing technology, we have designed a few consumer applications that spread across various industries such as grocery shopping (Casino, a supermarket franchise in France), banking (Bank of America), cosmetics (L'Oréal),

A. Marcus (Ed.): DUXU/HCII 2013, Part II, LNCS 8013, pp. 602–607, 2013.

and public transportation (Société de transport de Montréal, a public transportation company in Montreal, Canada). By having our hands on both enterprise and consumer applications, we learned that today's consumer and enterprise applications shared similarities in terms of the *design process, architectural structure,* and *design challenges.*

2   Design Process

Gamification needs a purpose. While "Fun" is a desirable complement to the gamification experience, it is certainly not the ultimate goal for either consumer or enterprise applications.

Before we started gamifying our application, first we needed to identify the task pain points and the task opportunities within the applications; gamification is not always a problem-solver, but it can be an opportunity-grabber in an area of application that is underachieved as well. After we found the pain point or the area of opportunity, we can look for the action(s) that we want to encourage our user to perform to counteract the pain point or best use the opportunity. We called this action(s) our "mission." Then the next step is to find the right gamification mechanics to complete this mission. This process is applicable to both consumer and enterprise application design.

On-boarding experience is a great example to illustrate how we integrated this gamification design process into our work. On-boarding experience is also what consumer and enterprise applications have in common. Though the process length and complexity varies from application to application.

On-boarding procedure often involves registering or filling out information about the user, which can be tedious but necessary. Too long or too complex of an on-boarding process can leave the user with a bad impression and turn the user off right away. The worst-case scenario is that the user may discontinue using the application because he or she does not want to go through the on-boarding process.

Sometimes simplifying the on-boarding process by minimizing the steps or questions can work. However, some applications do require asking the user many inevitable questions from the start. This is where gamification will come in handy.

For an on-boarding process, the paint point in most of our applications usually involves the user not answering all of the questions because the list of questions seemed tedious and endless (thus they avoided using the application). With this pain point in mind, the next step is to imagine the action(s) that we want to encourage the user to perform, which is to answer all of the questions completely and thoroughly. Once we identified both the pain point and the targeted behavior, then we can think about the gamification mechanics that we can use to complete this mission; in other words, what we can do to make the user *wants* to complete the on-boarding process.

As part of Apollo Casino project's (grocery store franchise in France) on-boarding process, the user has to fill out his or her information via the Consumer Web Portal. In this Web Portal, we included the gamification mechanic such as "points" system to encourage the user to fill out more information; the more information the user filled out, the more points the user gets. Another possible issue with the form is that the user does not know when he or she will be done. Hence, we also capped the points' limit to 100 and presented the number right next to the user's current points, as an indication of the user's location in relation to the finished line. Displaying the user's progress in the registration process may seem minimal, but its visual and psychological effect played a major role in guiding and persuading users to completely fill out the registration form.

3   Architectural Structure

By designing consumer applications like Apollo, we also learned the reason why gamifying enterprise applications is a challenge for some designers; it is because of their seemingly complex architectural structure. Most consumer applications, regardless of which industry they belong, are designed for a single scenario. Apollo applications are no different (i.e. Casino app is only for grocery shopping, L'Oréal app is only for cosmetics shopping). With the limited number of tasks in a single scenario application, it is easier to apply gamification since we can set up a clear gamified goal. Most of the time, the gamified goal will match the goal of the application. An example in Apollo STM app, the business goal for the app is to encourage people to take public transportation, and we gamified this goal by using "Tree Saving" as the measure to indicate the emission reduction by taking public transportation.

Most enterprise applications, on the other hand, always involved a holistic approach; one application is designed to have multiple functionalities, and more functions would also be added to accommodate identified scenarios. At a glance, applying gamification to the enterprise application with multiple goals, scenarios, and features may be challenging because every single activity or added element will simply make the application more complicated. It may also increase the implementation cost and potentially cause the performance issue.

When we looked closely at how average users use the enterprise application, they only use it for very few tasks most of the time. Based on the enterprise application's complex architectural structure, the key to gamification is to look at the user as an individual, and dissect the enterprise application into multiple consumer applications. If we could adapt activity-base design approach to break down an enterprise application into small, manageable parts (which we called "Mini App"), then we could easily start the gamification process from there. In other words, once we focused on each (type of) user and their specific tasks, and not what everything that the enterprise application can do, then the scope of architectural structure for enterprise applications would be manageable. For each of the Mini App, we can disregard the pattern-based design since consistency is less concerned, and we can pick the right gamification mechanic for that works best for its designated use case.

4   Challenges

Besides the architectural structure and the gamification process, gamifying consumer and enterprise applications also shared similar challenges. For instance, we needed to have adequate domain knowledge about the field of application to identify the sweet spot to gamify without lowering the work efficiency. If we lacked sufficient domain knowledge, gamification would not bring significant changes or meaningful results in how the user behaved. It could even bring negative effects such as adding an unnecessary step to an already-complex task.

Finding an appropriate level of information that is digestible for the user is not easy. We have to keep in mind that gamification is an on-going process. Gamification can improve user experience, but too much gamification all at once can be intimidating; we do not want to drastically change the user's behavior or bombard the user with a number of gamification elements that they are not familiar in one day.

We have to keep in mind that gamification is not the same as gaming. Our applications are not games. Inserting full-fledged gamification mechanics into our application from the beginning may not be the right idea, as the mechanics can overshadow the main features of the applications. Instead, lightweight gamification can be used as an experiment to gain the user's loyalty and see if we are designing in the right direction before we add more gamification elements. We also have to think about gamification as a long-term plan, and how we can change the user's behavior progressively over time since many applications do have multiple versions.

Designing Apollo STM application is where our lightweight-gamification strategy came in handy. Our ultimate goal for Apollo STM application is to persuade people in Montreal to use public transportation, but it has to be done methodically step by step, little by little. In the first version of the application, our mission was to encourage the general public to register their transit card called OPUS. We rewarded these users with benefits from STM's partnered retail stores (e.g. promotion or product discounts for people who registered their card). In order to register OPUS card, view the store's promotion, or navigate to the store, the user would have to download and use the application that we designed for them. Once the user became acquainted with the application, then we could add more gamification mechanics to make sure that the user would find value in using the application often (thus, using public transportation often).

One of the gamification mechanics we added in the second version of the Apollo STM application is the concept of "tree saving". We created the system in which STM would calculate the number of trees that the user saved based on the distance that the user travelled via public transportation. This virtual "tree" works in many levels; it works an analogy that objectified the concept of saving the environment, as the user who uses public transportation more can save more fuel and reduce more pollution caused by personal vehicles. It also works as "points" that the user can collect, and a measurable monetary system in which the user can trade for other benefits in the latter versions of the application. Without the tree saving mechanic, the user would only use the application when, for example, they want to go shopping with discount. With the tree saving mechanic, the user would feel the need to use public transportation often, so that they can collect more trees, and eventually gain more benefit from the application.

Once the user is both acquainted with the core feature of the application and the "tree saving" system, then we could polish this gamification mechanism even more. For this reason, we designed the leaderboard. In this leaderboard, the user can see how many trees they have saved as well as how many trees have other users saved in comparison. What is a must when designing a leaderboard is to make sure the user can feel relatable to the people in it. If the user knows the people in his/her leaderboard (e.g. Friends on Facebook, employees of the same department), or if the user sees how many trees that the person ranked right above him/her in the leaderboard has saved, then it will give the user a reachable incentive to collect more trees.

Not everything has to be about competition. Teamwork and cooperation can positively influence the user performance as well. Another feature that we showed in our leaderboard's screen is the number of trees that the user's community has saved. We learned from our experience that competition might work well for some user groups, but not the others. For many users, they wanted to save more trees because they wanted to see themselves as part of something bigger, and wanted to see how their actions can affect the prosperity of their community. For them, cooperative aspect of gamification is more important than the personal achievement and competition. Similar to the competition aspect of the leaderboard, we should limit the scope of this "community" to be something that is reachable and relatable to the user. Thus, this "community" should not represent, for example, the population of the whole planet, but a community that is small enough for the user to relate such as the user's circle of friends or the user's neighborhood.

One thing that we have to keep in mind when we design each gamification mechanic is to always remember our mission. We do not want to encourage the user to do the type of action that is out of our scope, even if they have fun doing it. By doing so, we will potentially decrease the user's efficiency in completing the tasks we want them to complete, or lose the focus of our application. This is extremely important in enterprise applications because the user's performance efficiency means the company's money. When we created our leaderboard for Apollo STM application, we had to be very specific about what we wanted the user to compete. Because we wanted the user to use more public transportation, the leaderboard only illustrated the number of trees that the user saved, which represented the distance that the user has traveled via public transportation. We did not want the user to compete in, for example, the number of promotions that the user has used, or the amount of money the user has saved from promotions in comparison to others.

If gamification is executed well in the application, it can increase loyalty. It is quite evident how consumer application needs high level of loyalty to prolong. In actuality, enterprise application needs loyalty as much as consumer application. If users are not loyal to the enterprise application, they will likely try to avoid or minimize using it. This may cause various problems depends on the user's field of work. High level of user loyalty, on the other hand, can increase the application usage and allow the application to reach its full potential.

5   Conclusion

We learned from our gamification experience with both consumer applications and enterprise applications that the number-one difference that distinguishes these applications is merely the user experience and the public perception towards them. Consumer applications are always fun, simple, and visually stimulating, but that does not mean they lack significance towards a consumer's life than the seemingly more serious enterprise application. Even though enterprise applications are used for "work", their user experience does not need to be a hair-pulling one. Through gamification, this general perception can change.

Ideally, the best kind of gamification for enterprise application is the one that makes the user completely forgets that they are working, and motivates them to keep "playing" the application for long hours or multiple times a day. Today, this can hardy be achieved, as gamification is still an emerging field. Today, gamification by itself cannot solve every single problem and turn the enterprise application into an addictive game. To change the nature of enterprise application and redefine "work", the core concept or the main feature of the each application, whether it be consumer or enterprise, will need to be thought out with the word like "play" or "fun" in mind from the start. In other words, not only the gamification mechanic, but also the application itself will need to be well designed to engage the user.

Gamification: When It Works, When It Doesn't

Erika Noll Webb

Oracle Corporation, Broomfield CO
erika.webb@oracle.com

Abstract. The concept of using game mechanics to attract and retain customers in the consumer space is now well accepted. However, the use of gamification in the enterprise space is still catching on. There are a number of reasons to believe that acceptance of gamification will grow in the enterprise space. The most likely reason is that companies are increasingly concerned about the effect of employee engagement on productivity. But, there are circumstances where gamification can be successful and circumstances where gamification can fail.

Keywords: Gamification, Game Mechanics, Enterprise Software, User Experience, User-centered design.

1   Introduction

Gamification as defined by Deterding, S., et al [1] is the use of game mechanics in non-gaming environments, such as websites, education, and social networks. The concept of using game mechanics to attract and retain customers in the consumer space is now well accepted, however the use of gamification in the enterprise space is still catching on. The idea is that you can use game mechanics in a way that captures the advantages of games while integrating those mechanics into actual work flow. It has been said that gamification is the way you can uncover the game within work and there are a number of reasons to believe that gamification will grow in the enterprise space. The most likely reason is that companies are increasingly concerned about the effect of employee engagement on productivity. But, there are circumstances where gamification can be successful and circumstances where gamification can fail.

Gamification has become a hot topic in a variety of areas from consumer sites to enterprise software. In 2011 and 2012, Gamification was included in the Gartner Hype Cycles for Emerging Technologies, in both cases just at the edge of the peak of inflated expectations (see Fig. 1).

Gartner has pointed out some of the potential hazards in the use of gamification. In late 2012, a separate Gartner report concluded that 80% of current gamified applications would fail to meet business objectives, primarily due to poor design [2]. In that report, the author states: "The focus is on the obvious game mechanics, such as points, badges and leader boards, rather than the more subtle and more important game design elements, such as balancing competition and collaboration, or defining a meaningful game economy, as a result, in many cases, organizations are simply counting points, slapping meaningless badges on activities and creating gamified applications that are simply not engaging for the target audience. Some organizations are already beginning to cast off poorly designed gamified applications."

A. Marcus (Ed.): DUXU/HCII 2013, Part II, LNCS 8013, pp. 608–614, 2013.

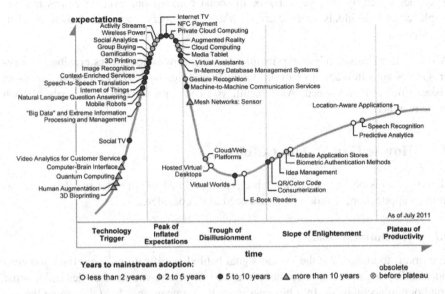

Fig. 1. The 2011 Gartner Hype Cycle (http://www.gartner.com/hc/images/215650_0001.gif)

2   Main Problem

To understand the potential conflict that was described in the Gartner report, it's important to understand the essence of games. Deterding created a set of game principles [3] which are adapted here. Games typically have a number of features.

- Games have SMART goals. That is, games have goals that are specific, measurable, achievable, realistic and time bound. If you play a game, you know that your goal in a game is to move from Level 1 to Level 2 in the short term, but in the long term, you want to get to level 15. You know what you need to do conceptually to make progress on these goals.
- Games have actions and choices that are easy to see. If you are playing a game, you can fairly easily see what actions and choices are available. In addition, there is a clear relationship between actions/choices available and goals you are trying to achieve. This combination of SMART goals, clear actions and choices, and obvious relationships between my actions/choices and goals make games very appealing.
- Games provide a lot of feedback. In a game, you get a lot of feedback about what you are doing, when you are successful, and when you are not. At any point, you can tell where you are in the game, because your current status is obvious.
- Games involve increasing challenges for growing skills. Most games have layers to them, where the game can become increasingly challenging as the player gets better and more skilled at the game.

- Games generally involve a degree of social comparison. Even in games that are played as individuals, often there is an aspect of social comparison such as a leaderboard.

A simple transference of game principles to work flow is not always possible, however. Games are often about emotion, intensity and duration. Work, however, is about tasks, efficiency and speed. As a result, you can't always make the goals of each come together.

3   How to Gamify Successfully

Gamification is not just about applying points and badges. In order to effectively gamify an application, several key issues need to be considered.

3.1   The Business Goal

The first is to understand the business goal behind gamification. Every time you consider adding a gamification element to a business flow, you need to determine what you hope to accomplish. In a business case, the company needs to determine the answer to a few key questions. Will gamification improve productivity in a particular product or business flow? Will it make the tasks involved in that product or flow more interesting to the end user involved? Will it improve employee engagement in that product or flow? For example, if you know that end users are not completing a task that you would like them to do, would gamification make them more likely to complete that activity?

Customer Relationship Management (CRM) tools are a good example of a product that a company would like their sales teams to use, but encounter resistance. Sales people often do not see the value of the CRM application to them. The company, however, would like to collect as much sales data as possible to better understand who their sales people are talking to, how often, and what makes some sales people more effective than others. Sales people, on the other hand, often feel that time spent entering information into a CRM tool is time spent not selling. Since they get rewarded financially on the basis of sales completed, the CRM tool is considered overhead by many. As a result, CRM tools are a good example of where gamification might be used to engage users in activities that the company values but that the end user does not. There are a number of examples of how CRM tools can be gamified available on the web [4-5].

3.2   Measurement

Once a business goal has been identified, the next step is to define how the company can determine whether gamification is successful in driving user behavior to meet these goals. What part of the product does the company want to gamify? Not all areas of a product may be good candidates for gamification. It is essential to select areas where outcomes can be measured [6-7]. In that regard, it is essential to make each goal as specific and discrete as possible. If the goal is too large, it will be difficult to determine whether the specific game mechanics utilized are successful in altering the behavior of the end user.

The business goals for gamification need to be based on areas in which metrics can be attained both before gamifying and after gamification is applied. Ideally, gamification would be applied and measured with A/B testing, or other test methods, in which some users work with the gamified system while others use the non-gamified system [8].

3.3   Understanding Your User

One of the most important aspects of successful gamification is understanding what motivates the system user. It is crucial to understand the users and their motivations before blindly slapping points and badges on interactions that many have no meaning to them. For example, outgoing, competitive types may want to see how they compare to others while more introverted, quiet types might be turned off by the same mechanics.

Some gamification experts recommend that you start with Bartle's 4 player types [9] to decide if your users fit best into the categories of Killers, Achievers, Explorers or Socializers. While this may have some value, Bartle was describing types of players of a multi-player online games. Enterprise software users may not fit neatly into a set of categories developed for people playing an online game, although some have tried to modify the descriptions for employees (see Fig. 2). But when trying to define a worker whose main job responsibility is General Ledger accounting, it may be difficult to decide which of these descriptions adequately captures their motivations.

Fig. 2. A matrix of employee types based on Bartle's 4 player types. (http://frankcaron.com/Flogger/?p=1732)

In the case of enterprise software, the end user of a system is often described by a user profile or persona [10] for the purpose of helping develop the software flow. A persona is a fictional representative of the users of your software or system based on research about that user type. It often includes details about their demographics, job responsibilities, goals and tasks as well as the environment in which they work. Taking the time to research the user and their context of use is one aspect of the user-centered design (UCD) process that helps ensure that the software is designed around the users' needs and work process. Just as with the UCD process to develop software, understanding the end user of a system is critical to gamification as well. By developing an understanding of what your user is trying to accomplish, their motivations and what they find rewarding will help you to apply appropriate game mechanics to an enterprise software flow.

3.4   Bringing the Business Goal and User Considerations Together

Once you have considered what your business goal is and have developed an understanding of your user and their motivations, the next step is to consider what game mechanics would help you accomplish your goal. Consider the Fogg Behavior Model [11], which posits that persuasive designs get behaviors to occur because they merge a trigger prompting the behavior, with the motivation to do something and the ability to do it. Take the CRM example from earlier. If you have a business goal to have users enter more sales information into the CRM system, you can consider what might make that behavior more likely. The first might be to establish a trigger that prompts the behavior that plays on some other motivation they may have and at a time that they have the ability to perform the behavior. According to Gabe Zicherman [12], people are motivated by Status, Achievement, Power and Stuff, in approximately that order.

Since sales people as a general rule are gregarious and social, they may be motivated by elements that play on status and achievement more than they are by material goods. Therefore it may be useful to consider more social aspects of game mechanics such as points and leaderboards. As a behavior trigger, you might consider a challenge to the sales groups which involves entering more complete information into the CRM system which they see when they log in, which is the time they have the ability to enter the information. You might also consider prompting them with reminders of the challenge while they are on the pages you want them to fill out more completely.

3.5   Avoiding the Unintended Outcome

One key consideration in gamification is to consider the unintended outcome in your design. Put another way, people will always try to game the system if they see a way to do it. Your gamification model needs to consider what you can do to ensure that the data they put in satisfies your real requirements in order to win. For example, if your business goal is to increase the number of invoices a user completes per hour, you may increase speed (intended) at the expense of accuracy (unintended). In some cases, such as invoicing, it is impossible to know immediately whether the information is accurate and may be several days before errors are uncovered. So how can you achieve the balance you need between speed/accuracy? In adding game mechanics to that process, you might consider a reward for speed that is balanced with a loss of points if accuracy drops below some baseline measure. In this way, you may achieve your ultimate goal, which is to have invoices processed as quickly as possible while maintaining accuracy at an acceptable level.

3.6   Test, Test and Test again

In the end, it is important to test design concepts with prospective end users and be willing to modify your design. Again, a standard process in UCD is to research, design, and evaluate, continually iterating the to improve the product. If gamification is considered as another aspect of the user experience, involving many of the same ideas of good usability, then gamification should be approached in the same manner. Prior to creating a gamified system, it is useful to test the concepts with end users of the system. This process can be as simple as creating paper prototypes and asking end users to evaluate the suggested flows and specific game mechanics.

Once gamification has been employed, a company needs to be willing to test whether they are effective in making changes to the business goal and be willing to modify and adapt. Gartner's suggestion that 80% of gamified applications will fail due to poor design can be avoided by early testing but also by evaluating whether the application of game mechanics has succeeded in achieving the business goal. Using the earlier example of sales people and the CRM system, after the application of game mechanics, the company needs to determine if users are entering more information. This requires knowing what the behavior was prior to the application of the game mechanics to ensure that you have, in fact, moved the needle on the dial. For any gamified system, analytics are essential.

If the game mechanics have achieved the business goal in the short term, the goal is now to make this a sustainable process. As anyone familiar with Foursquare can attest, once you have earned badges for a while, you can lose interest in the game. Returning to Deterding's description of games, it is essential to consider a key aspect, which is that games involve increasing challenges for growing skills. As the users attain new levels, the gamification layer should evolve to increase the challenges. This can be accomplished in a variety of ways, either by updating the challenges for the users or increasing the rewards within the system.

4   Conclusions

Gamification can be a powerful way to increase employee engagement and productivity within an enterprise software system. However, as with any UCD process, successful gamification requires a thorough understanding of the end user of the system, design based on that user's motivations and goals, and testing both during development and following release. Just as other areas of good usability practice, a gamified user experience should be reviewed, evaluated and updated regularly to ensure that it continues to meet the goals of both the users and the companies.

References

1. Deterding, S., Sicart, M., Nacke, L., O'Hara, K., Dixon, D.: Gamification. Using game-design elements in non-gaming contexts. In: Proceedings of CHI Extended Abstracts, pp. 2425–2428. ACM (2011)
2. Burke, B.: Gartner Says by 2014, 80 Percent of Current Gamified Applications Will Fail to Meet Business Objectives Primarily Due to Poor Design, Gartner.com (November 27, 2012), http://www.gartner.com/technology/research/gamification/ (Cited: January 6, 2013)
3. Deterding, S.: Just add points? What UX can (and cannot) learn from games. SlideShare (June 1, 2010), http://www.slideshare.net/dings/just-add-points-what-ux-can-and-cannot-learn-from-games (Cited: December 15, 2011)
4. Paharia, R.: Gamification = Motivation by Rajat Paharia, CPO, Bunchball.com. Slideshare (May 24, 2012), http://www.slideshare.net/Vator/gamification-motivation-by-rajat-paharia-cpo-bunchballcom (Cited: March 7, 2013)
5. Badgeville Solutions. Badgeville.com, http://badgeville.com/solutions/sales (Cited: March 6 , 2013)
6. Duggan, K., Shoup, K.: Business Gamification for Dummies. John Wiley & Sons, Inc., Hoboken (2013)
7. Werbach, K., Hunter, D.: For the Win: How Game Thinking Can Revolutionize Your Business. Wharton Digital Press, Philadelphia (2012)
8. Kohavi, R., Longbotham, R., Sommerfield, D., Henne, R.: Controlled experiments on the web: survey and practical guide. Data Min. Knowl. Disc. 18, 141–180 (2009)
9. Bartle, R.: Hearts, Clubs, Diamonds, Spades: Players Who Suit Muds (April 1996), http://www.mud.co.uk/richard/hcds.htm (Cited: March 6, 2013)
10. Develop Personas. Usability.gov, http://usability.gov/methods/analyze_current/personas.html (Cited: March 6, 2013)
11. Fogg, B.J.: A Behavior Model for Persuasive Design. Persuasive. ACM, Claremont (2009)
12. Zicherman, G.: Cash is for SAPS. Gamification Co. (October 18, 2010), http://www.gamification.co/2010/10/18/cash-is-for-saps/ (Cited: March 6, 2013)

Author Index

Abascal-Mena, Rocío   IV-231
Abdelnour-Nocera, José   II-161
Abromowitz, Scott   III-130, III-140
Abu-Hnaidi, Malak   II-342
Abujarad, Fuad   III-3
Abulkhair, Maysoon F.   II-3, III-130
Aderhold, Andreas   II-321
Adikari, Sisira   I-3
Adukaite, Asta   IV-163
Ahn, DaeSung   III-316
Ahram, Tareq   IV-325
Alacam, Ozge   IV-334
Al-Arifi, Bayan   II-333
Albatati, Reem   III-85
Alelis, Genevieve   III-429
Al-Ghamdi, Amal   II-296
Alhafzy, Maram S.   II-3
Al-Harbi, Shatha   II-342
Abo Al Laban, Tsneem   III-85
Almeida, Ana   III-169
Almirall, Magí   II-180
Al-Ofisan, Ghadah   II-333
Alomari, Ebtesam A.   II-3
Alpkaya, Seda   IV-84
Al-Romi, Norah   II-333
Al-Rubaian, Arwa   II-333
Al-Saggaf, Reem   II-296
Al-Sahafi, Sultana   II-296
Al-Semairi, Ghadeer   II-342
Altakrouri, Bashar   III-327
Al-Tayari, Hadeel   II-342
Al-Wabil, Areej   II-333
Al-Zebaidi, Maha   II-296
Andersen, Kristina   III-548
Andrade, Ana   IV-121
Ang, Chee Siang   III-429
Ang, Kevin Z.Y.   III-120
Aoyama, Hisae   IV-506
Arning, Katrin   I-439, III-10
Asano, Kaho   II-11
Asthana, Siddhartha   I-183
Atkinson, Robert K.   II-276
Attisano, Roby   III-20
Aurelio, David   IV-469

Austin, Ann   II-161
Avery, Josh   IV-601
Ayanoğlu, Hande   III-30

Bakeer, Mai   III-85
Bamasak, Omaima   II-342
Banic, Amy Ulinski   II-209
Baranauskas, Maria Cecília C.   I-459,
    II-518
Barattin, Daniela   I-242
Barnes, Tiffany   II-189
Baroni, Ilaria   III-558
Barros, Helda O.   III-337
Barros, Marina   I-379, II-491
Bas-sam, Malak   II-462
Batehup, Lynn   II-417
Batawil, Samah   III-85
Baurley, Sharon   IV-424
Bavelier, Daphne   II-352
Bayliss, Jessica D.   II-352
Bazo, Alexander   IV-248
Belden, Jeffery L.   II-381
Bellini, Sara   III-558, III-594
Bellows, Brooke G.   I-13, I-144
Bengler, Klaus-Josef   II-89, IV-359
Berlin, Dan   II-407
Biersack, Peter   II-20
Bilgin, Gökhan   IV-651
Blankl, Martin   II-20
Blondon, Katherine S.   II-361
Blustein, Jamie   I-162
Bobrowicz, Ania   III-429
Böhm, Stephan   IV-631
Bordegoni, Monica   I-242
Bouwmeester, Ruben   IV-575
Braik, Roa'a   II-342
Brandenburg, Stefan   I-449
Brangier, Eric   II-558
Brazinskas, Mantas   III-179
Breiner, Kai   I-193
Breuer, Henning   IV-3
Breyer, Felipe   II-266, III-227
Brockmann, Tobias   I-340
Buchdid, Samuel B.   I-459

Burghardt, Manuel   IV-248, IV-432
Byrne, Daragh   II-276
Bystřický, Jiří   I-22

Çağıltay, Kürşat   IV-334
Cai, Guowei   III-120
Çakır, Tuğba   IV-173
Calado, Alexana Vilar Soares   III-345
Campbell, John   I-3
Camplone, Stefania   IV-23
Campos, Fábio   I-203, I-379, II-491,
     III-337, III-345, IV-113, IV-257
Cantoni, Lorenzo   IV-163, IV-696
Cappiello, Cinzia   IV-641
Carignan, Joëlle   II-501
Carlson, Darren   III-327
Carmo, Maria Beatriz   II-442
Cavalcanti, Aline   II-266, III-227
Cavalcanti, Virginia   IV-121
Champagnat, Ronan   I-74
Chang, Chia-Ling   I-469
Chang, Chih-Kai   II-28
Chang, Teng-Wen   IV-402
Chelnokova, Polina   IV-221
Chen, Ben M.   III-120
Chen, Bo-Sheng   II-304
Chen, Chaomei   IV-601
Chen, Frank (Ming-Hung)   I-545
Chen, Kuo-Pin   III-446
Chen, Ting-Han   III-246
Chen, Yuanyuan   I-479
Chiou, Megan   IV-67
Chisnell, Dana   IV-193
Chiu, Shu-Chuan   I-593
Cho, Yen-Ting   IV-478
Choensawat, Worawat   II-171
Choi, Jung-Min   III-40
Choi, Young Mi   III-75
Chou, Hsin-Yin   II-304
Chou, Wen-Huei   III-446
Chu, Sauman   II-371
Chuang, Miao-Hsien   III-455
Chung, Wei-Ming   III-306
Chung, WonJoon   I-29, I-125
Chynał, Piotr   I-212
Clarke, Martina A.   II-381
Clarkson, P. John   IV-457
Cláudio, Ana Paula   II-442
Combe, Nicola   III-49
Conn Welch, Karla   III-105

Conti, Antonia S.   IV-359
Cordeiro, Erimar   IV-121
Correia, Walter   I-203, I-379, II-491,
     III-337, III-345, IV-113, IV-257
Corte, Joao   IV-113
Coursaris, Constantinos K.   IV-274
Coutinho, Solange   II-219
Cugini, Umberto   I-242
Cui, Jinqiang   III-120

Damásio, Manuel José   IV-13
Danylak, Roman   III-465
da Silva, Daliton   II-266
da Silva, Fernando Moreira   III-419
da Silva, José Carlos P.   IV-265
Da Silva, Régio Pierre   I-330
da Silva, Tiago Silva   I-599
da Silva Augusto, Lia Giraldo   III-150
da Silveira, Dierci Marcio Cunha   I-409
das Neves, Andre Menezes Marques
     II-508
de Carvalho, Breno José Andrade   II-508
de França, Ana Carol Pontes   I-68
de Lemos Meira, Luciano Rogério   I-68
de Lera, Eva   II-180
Demetrescu, Emanuel   IV-238
de Miranda, Leonardo Cunha   II-518
Dennis, Toni A.   III-3
de Oliveira Passos, Marcel   II-286
de Souza, Clarisse Sieckenius   I-115
D´Garcia, Germannya   IV-121
Dias, Patrícia   IV-13
Di Bucchianico, Giuseppe   IV-23
Dinis, Susana   III-475
Dong, Hua   I-171, III-49
Dong, Miaobo   III-120
Dong, Xiangxu   III-120
Donovan, Jared   III-352
Dorey, Jonathan   II-79
Drewitz, Uwe   I-449
Drexler, David   IV-533
Du, Shiau-Yuan   III-246
Duarte, Emília   III-30, III-189, III-205,
     III-362, III-419, III-475
Duckworth, Jonathan   II-391
Dumas, Joseph   I-349

Eibl, Maximilian   III-411
Ekşioğlu, Mahmut   IV-173
El Said, Ghada R.   II-38

Erbil, Mehmet Ali   III-179
Erdal, Feride   IV-334
Eriksson, Joakim   I-262, IV-238
Esteves, Francisco   II-442
Eugene, Wanda   II-189
Evans, Andrea L.   I-222

Fabri, Marc   III-484, III-585
Falcão, Christianne Soares   IV-342
Faroughi, Arash   I-38
Faroughi, Roozbeh   I-38
Febretti, Alessandro   I-232
Fei, Qian   II-44
Feijs, Loe   III-494
Fernandes, Fabiane R.   IV-265
Ferrise, Francesco   I-242
Fesenmaier, Daniel R.   IV-212
Filgueiras, Ernesto   III-205
Filho, Epitácio L. Rolim   III-337
Filippi, Stefano   I-242
Fineman, Andrea   IV-193
Fischer, Holger   I-252
Flanagan, Patricia J.   I-48, I-58, III-439
Følstad, Asbjørn   I-506
Ford, Rebecca   I-312, IV-486
Ford, Treschiel   II-209
Ford, Yelena   IV-424
Fortier, Sara   I-29
Francis, Jon   III-372
Fukatsu, Yoshitomo   III-255
Fuks, Hugo   III-237, III-439
Fukuda, Yutaka   IV-506
Fukuhara, T.   II-435
Fukumoto, Makoto   III-264
Furbach, Ulrich   III-270

Gabriele, Felipe   II-257
Gandhi, Rajeev   III-372
Gao, Jie   IV-183, IV-352
Gao, Yi   III-504
Garduno, Elmer   III-372
Gasser, Jochen   III-513
Gençer, Merve   IV-651
Ghinea, Gheorghita   II-401
Gisbert, Mercè   II-180
Gockel, Bianca   I-262
Godara, Jaideep   II-548
Göktürk, Mehmet   III-57
Goldwasser, Eliad   II-548
Gong, Yida   III-75

Gotsis, Marientina   II-470
Götze, Martin   IV-359
Gouda, Sara   II-105
Gould, Emilie W.   IV-496
Gower, Andy   IV-140, IV-150
Graf, Holger   I-262, II-321, IV-238
Greenspan, Steven   IV-581
Greenwood, Kristyn   I-273
Grønli, Tor-Morten   II-401
Guo, Xiaopeng   IV-183, IV-352
Gurgel, Andrei   II-286
Güvendik, Merve   IV-173
Guy, Olivier   I-74
Gyoda, Koichi   III-65

Hachimura, Kozaburo   II-171
Hama, Daiki   I-283
Hamasaki, M.   II-435
Han, Junghyun   III-316
Hansen, Jarle   II-401
Hao, Yu   III-75
Hardt, Wolfram   III-411
Hardy, Delquawn   II-424
Harrell, Cyd   IV-193
Harrison, David   III-49
Hass, Chris   II-407
Hattori, Kanetoshi   IV-560
Hayashida, Kousuke   III-280
Heemann, Adriano   IV-414
Heidt, Michael   II-54
Heikkilä, Päivi   IV-660
Heimgärtner, Rüdiger   II-20, II-62,
    II-95, II-139
Hekler, Eric   II-424
Henriques, Sara   IV-13
Higgins, Jordan F.   I-13
Hirako, Hajime   IV-506
Hirao, Akemi   IV-560
Holme, Thomas   I-389
Hooker, Louise   II-417
Hornung, Heiko   II-518
Hsieh, Ming-Hsuan   I-488
Hsieh, Yi-Ta   I-564
Hsu, Hung-Pin   IV-666
Huang, Cheng-Yong   I-488
Huang, Chiwu   III-455
Huang, Scottie Chih-Chieh   IV-367

Ibrahim, Lamiaa F.   III-85
Ienaga, Takafumi   III-264

Igler, Bodo IV-673
Iitaka, Toshikazu IV-682
Imamura, Ken I-283
Inoue, Satoru IV-506
Inoue, Sozo III-280
Inversini, Alessandro IV-163
Ishibashi, Takuya II-538
Ishii, Hirotake III-530
Islam, Muhammad Nazrul I-84

Jaimes, Luis G. III-520
Jakobs, Eva-Maria I-439
Jang, Yung Joo IV-30
Jansen-Troy, Arne II-452
Janß, Armin II-452
Järventie-Ahonen, Heli IV-660
Jeong, Eunseong IV-274
Jiang, Nan I-294
Jimenez, Yerika IV-376
Johnson, Andrew E. I-232
Johnson, Ian I-417
Johnson, Steven L. IV-212
Johnston, Angela I-273
Joyce, Mary I-303
Ju, Da Young IV-103
Jung, Eui-Chul II-199, IV-30, IV-385,
    IV-515
Jung, Yvonne II-321

Kakara, Hiroyuki III-95
Kang, Namgyu I-498
Kang, Shin Jin I-322
Kao, Chih-Tung II-129
Kao, Hsin-Liu III-306
Karahasanović, Amela I-506
Karlin, Beth I-312, IV-486
Karwowski, Waldemar IV-325
Kato, Mariko I-283
Keenan, Gail M. I-232
Keinath, Andreas IV-359
Kelner, Judith II-266, III-227
Khashman, Nouf II-79
Kierkels, Jeanine III-494
Kijkhun, Chommanad II-171
Kim, Chang Hun I-322
Kim, Jeongmi (Jamie) IV-212
Kim, Kyong-ho III-393
Kim, Min Soon II-381
Kim, Si-Jung IV-740
Kim, Sunyoung II-199

Kim, Yeolib IV-203
Kim, Young Bin I-322
Kim, Youngtae IV-515
Kirakowski, Jurek I-303
Kırış, Esin IV-173, IV-581
Kistmann, Virgínia IV-414
Kitamura, Koji I-516, II-568
Kitamura, Satoru I-516
Kitamura, Takayoshi III-530
Kitamura, Yoshinobu IV-560
Klasnja, Predrag II-361
Knolmayer, Gerhard F. IV-221
Kobayakawa, M. II-435
Kohno, Izumi I-525
Komischke, Tobias IV-691
Kondo, Akira IV-525
Kondo, Naoko IV-525
Koopman, Richelle J. II-381
Kosmala-Anderson, Joanna II-417
Kouroupetroglou, Georgios IV-575
Koyutürk, Efsane D. IV-173
Ku, Vincent (I-Hsun) I-545
Kulkarni, Anand S. III-105
Kulpa, Cínthia Costa I-330
Kumar, Janaki II-528
Kuno, Yuki III-255
Kuramoto, Itaru II-538
Kurani, Kenneth S. III-578
Kurioka, Mai I-283
Kurosu, Masaaki I-94

Lai, Ih-Cheng IV-402
Lam, Miu-Ling III-290
Lamontagne, Valérie III-296
Langdon, Patrick IV-457
Langhorne, Anna L. III-112
Lawler Kennedy, Sally II-501
Lawrence, Kira II-209
Le, Hang II-548
Le, Nguyen-Thinh IV-533
Leão, Crystian II-266
Lecca, Nicola II-247
Lee, Douglas IV-37
Lee, Lin-Chien IV-392
Lee, Tong H. III-120
Leitão, Carla Faria I-115
Levi, Dennis II-352
Li, Kun III-120
Liang, Rung-Huei I-610, III-306
Liang, Zhi-Hong IV-450

Lin, Feng   III-120
Lin, Ming-Huang   IV-392
Lin, Tsen-Ying   III-306
Lin, Tz-Ying   IV-47
Lincoln, Dino   I-203
Lindemann, Udo   I-554, IV-130
Liu, Haibin   I-294
Liu, Qing   IV-543
Liu, Zhengjie   I-479
Lo, Chia-Hui Nico   IV-402
Loi, Daria   IV-57
Lopes, Eder   II-442
Lopez, Karen Dunn   I-232
López-Ornelas, Erick   IV-231
Lourenço, Daniel   II-219
Lu, Chia-Chen   I-535
Lu, Haind   I-340
Lucci Baldassari, Guido   IV-238
Luh, Ding-Bang   I-469, I-488, I-535,
    I-545, IV-47, IV-450
Luo, Delin   III-120

Ma, Chia-Hsiang   I-488
Maas, Alisa   II-209
Maciak, Adam   II-480
Maciel, Francimar Rodrigues   II-229
Madhavan, Krishna P.C.   IV-543
Mahdy, Hind H.   II-3
Maier, Florian   IV-94
Makanawala, Prerna   II-548
Mankodiya, Kunal   III-372
Mankovskii, Serge   IV-581
Marache-Francisco, Cathie   II-558
Marchetti, Emanuela   II-238, II-311
Marcus, Aaron   II-72, II-247, III-130,
    III-140, IV-67, IV-696
Maron, Markus   III-270
Martins, Edgard Thomas   III-150,
    III-160
Martins, Isnard Thomas   III-150, III-160
Martins, Laura B.   II-257
Martins, Rolando   III-372
Marx, Thomas   II-480
Matera, Maristella   IV-641
Matey, Luis M.   I-583
Matthiessen, Neil   I-100
McDonald, Craig   I-3
McGee, Mick   I-349
McKenna, Ann F.   IV-543

Medeiros, Rodrigo Pessoa   II-508
Meenowa, Joshan   IV-140, IV-150
Meier, Florian   IV-248
Mejia, G. Mauricio   II-371
Melo, André R.   IV-257
Melo, Claudia de O.   I-599
Melo, Miguel   III-169
Memon, Mohsin Ali   IV-706
Ménard, Elaine   II-79
Mendonca, Saul   IV-113
Michaelides, Mario   II-161
Michailidou, Ioanna   I-554, IV-130
Mielniczek, Witold   III-179
Mikkonen, Jussi   I-564
Milewski, Allen E.   IV-37
Min, Kyung-Bo   IV-385
Miwa, H.   II-435
Mizoguchi, Hiroshi   I-516, III-95
Mizoguchi, Riichiro   IV-560
Moallem, Abbas   I-107
Modi, Sunila   II-161
Mont'Alvão, Claudia Renata   IV-714
Monteiro, Ingrid Teixeira   I-115
Moody, Louise   II-417
Moore, Joi L.   II-381
Morreale, Patricia   IV-376
Motomura, Yoichi   II-435, II-568
Moura, Guilherme   II-266
Muehlhans, Heike   III-10
Murray, Tylar   II-424, III-520

Nahum, Mor   II-352
Nakajima, M.   II-435
Nakajima, Tatsuo   II-587
Nakamura, Akemi   IV-560
Nakamura, Masato   III-280
Nakanishi, Miwa   I-283
Nakashima, Naoki   III-280
Narasimhan, Priya   III-372
Narula, Chirag   IV-67
Nebe, Karsten   I-252
Neves, André   II-491, IV-113
Neves, Maria   I-203
Newby, Ethan   IV-193
Niebuhr, Sabine   IV-533
Nishida, Yoshifumi   I-516, II-568, III-95
Nishikawa, Masahiro   I-525
Nishimura, Satoshi   IV-560
Nishimura, Takuichi   II-435

Nohara, Yasunobu   III-280
Noriega, Paulo   III-30, III-205, III-362, III-419, III-475
Nunes, Isabel L.   I-359, I-620

Obermeier, Martin   IV-568
Ocak, Nihan   IV-334
Oe, Tatsuhito   III-255
Oettli, Michael   IV-77
Ogaick, Tara   I-125
Okazawa, Naoya   IV-408
Okimoto, Maria Lúcia L.R.   II-89, IV-414
Olaverri Monreal, Cristina   II-89
Oliveira, Sabrina   IV-414
Oono, Mikiko   II-568
Orehovački, Tihomir   I-369
Osen, Martin   III-383
Osmond, Jane   II-417
Öztürk, Özgürol   IV-284, IV-623

Pagano, Alfonsina   I-262
Pakkan, Ali   III-57
Panagis, Tasos   IV-77
Park, Hyesun   III-393
Parzianello, Luiz Claudio   I-599
Paschoarelli, Luis Carlos   IV-265
Peng, Kemao   III-120
Peng, Yuan   II-247
Penha, Marcelo   I-379
Pereira, Roberto   I-459, II-518
Pescarin, Sofia   I-262, IV-238
Petersson Brooks, Eva   II-238, III-504
Peterson, Matthew S.   I-144
Phang, Swee King   III-120
Phillips, Robert   IV-424
Picciani, Stefano   IV-23
Picozzi, Matteo   IV-641
Pierce, Graham L.   IV-274
Pinheiro, Tânia   II-442
Pinkwart, Niels   IV-533
Plogmann, Simon   II-452
Pohlmeyer, Anna Elisabeth   III-540
Post, Lori A.   III-3
Pradhan, Neera   II-209
Prata, Wilson   IV-714
Prior, Stephen D.   III-179, IV-304
Prisacari, Anna   I-389
Propst, Dennis B.   IV-274
Provost, Gabrielle   I-399

Quaresma, Manuela   IV-714
Quesenbery, Whitney   IV-193

Radermacher, Klaus   II-452
Rafelsberger, Walter M.   IV-553
Raij, Andrew   II-424, III-520
Raison, Colette   I-573
Rebelo, Francisco   III-30, III-169, III-189, III-205, III-362, III-419, III-475
Redish, Janice (Ginny)   IV-294
Reis, Bernardo   III-227
Reis, Lara   III-189
Riihiaho, Sirpa   IV-660
Rızvanoğlu, Kerem   IV-284, IV-623
Robert, Jean-Marc   I-399
Roberts, Michael   IV-581
Rosca, Daniela   IV-37
Rosi, Alice   III-558, III-594
Rughiniş, Răzvan   II-577

Sadauskas, John   II-276
Sade, Gavin   III-352
Sadler, Karl   IV-424
Said, Tarek   IV-359
Sakae, Ken-Ichiro   I-516
Sakamoto, Mizuki   II-587
Sakamoto, Y.   II-435
Sakarya, Cem   IV-84
Salazar, Jorge H.   III-215
Samson, Audrey   III-548
Sandino, Diego   I-583
Sanna, Alberto   III-558, III-594
Santa Rosa, José Guilherme   II-286
Sapkota, Nabin   IV-325
Sasajima, Munehiko   IV-560
Sasaki, Toshiya   IV-506
Schaffzin, Gabriel Y.   I-134
Schieder, Alex   III-199
Schieder, Theresa Karolina   IV-696
Schmidt, Snezna   I-573
Schneidermeier, Tim   IV-94, IV-432
Schoper, Yvonne   II-95
Schrader, Andreas   III-327
Schricker, Johannes   IV-94
Schulz, Christian   III-401
Schütz, Daniel   IV-568
Seevinck, Jennifer   III-352
Shalash, Wafaa M.   II-462
Shawly, Ghada   II-462

Shen, Siu-Tsen   III-179, IV-304
Shieh, Meng-Dar   III-568
Shilli, Rudainah   III-85
Shimoda, Hiroshi   III-530
Shin, Hyunju   III-316
Shin, Min   IV-103
Shinker, Jacqueline   II-209
Shizuki, Buntarou   III-255
Shum, David   II-391
Silva, Luiz Bueno   III-169
Silve, Sarah   IV-424
Silveira, Milene Selbach   I-599
Simões-Marques, Mário   I-359
Singh, Amarjeet   I-183
Singh, Pushpendra   I-183
Sini, Viola   IV-221
Smith, Melissa A.B.   I-144
Smythe, Kelli C.A.S.   IV-441
Soares, Marcelo Márcio   I-68, I-203,
    I-379, II-491, II-508, III-150, III-160,
    III-337, III-345, IV-113, IV-257,
    IV-342
Sobecki, Janusz   I-212
Sonntag, Daniel   III-401
Sookhanaphibarn, Kingkarn   II-171
Spiliotopoulos, Dimitris   IV-575
Spinillo, Carla Galvão   IV-441
Spruijt-Metz, Donna   II-424
Spyridonis, Fotios   II-401
Stavropoulou, Pepi   IV-575
Steege, Linsey M.   II-381
Stevens, Susan Hunt   II-597
Stieglitz, Stefan   I-340
Stifter, Janet   I-232
Stillwater, Tai   III-578
Strenge, Benjamin   I-252
Strube, Gerhard   II-105
Sturm, Christian   II-105
Su, Chih-Sheng   I-610
Sugawara, Satoshi   I-525
Sun, Huatong   II-115
Sun, Vincent C.   II-129
Sunaga, T.   II-435
Suto, Hidetsugu   I-498
Swierenga, Sarah J.   III-3, IV-274
Szwec, Lee   IV-631
Szymański, Jerzy M.   I-212

Tabosa, Tibério   IV-121
Taileb, Mounira   II-296

Takahashi, Hiroe   IV-560
Takamatsu, Asao   III-530
Takaoka, Yoshiyuki   IV-560
Tallig, Anke   III-411
Tanaka, Jiro   III-255, IV-706
Tanaka-Ishii, Kumiko   I-152
Tang, Da-Lung   II-129
Teixeira, Fábio Gonçalves   I-330
Teixeira, João Marcelo   II-266, III-227
Teixeira, Luís   III-30, III-205, III-362,
    III-419, III-475
Teixeira-Botelho, Inês   IV-13
Teles, Júlia   III-362
Thianthai, Tim   II-602
Thin, Alasdair G.   II-470
Thomas, Patrick R.   II-391
Thomas, Robert L.   I-417
Tomimatsu, Kiyoshi   I-593
Toyama, Takumi   III-401
Trapp, Marcus   IV-723
Trevisan, Bianka   I-439
Trevorrow, Pip   III-484, III-585
Tseng, Jin-Han   IV-450
Tsonos, Dimitrios   IV-575
Tsuei, Mengping   II-304
Tsujino, Yoshihiro   II-538
Turner, Andy   II-417
Tussyadiah, Iis P.   IV-733

Umbach, Elisabeth   IV-3

Vainio, Juhani   I-479
Valente, Andrea   II-311
Valverde, Llorenç   II-180
van Lieshout, Marjolein   III-494
van Schijndel, Nicolle H.   III-494
Vasconcelos, Luis Arthur   II-266, III-227
Vaughan, Misha   I-349
Vedamurthy, Indu   II-352
Vega, Katia Fabiola Canepa   I-48,
    III-237, III-439
Vélez, Gorka   I-583
Velez-Rojas, Maria C.   IV-581
Vicini, Sauro   III-558, III-594
Vilar, Elisângela   III-205, III-362,
    III-419, III-475
Vinagre, Pedro   I-620
Vogel, Marlene   I-449
Vogel-Heuser, Birgit   IV-568

von Saucken, Constantin   I-554, IV-130
Vorvoreanu, Mihaela   IV-543
Voyvodaoğlu, Tansel   IV-651

Wakeling, Jon   IV-140, IV-150
Waldron, Julie A.   III-215
Wall, Andrew   III-484
Walser, Kate   I-427
Wang, Biao   III-120
Wang, Fei   III-120
Wang, Man-Ying   II-129
Wang, Pi-Fen   II-121
Watanabe, Kentaro   II-435
Webb, Erika Noll   II-608
Weber, Markus   III-401
Welch, Shelly   IV-740
Wilkie, Diana J.   I-232
Wilkinson, Christopher R.   IV-457
Wilkosinska, Katarzyna   II-321
Wille, Cornelius   II-480
Williams, Doug   IV-140, IV-150
Wilson, Jennifer   II-189
Wilson, Peter H.   II-391
Windl, Helmut   II-139
Wolff, Christian   IV-248, IV-432
Wolze, Zeno   IV-3

Xu, Tao   IV-601
Xu, Yu-Jie   II-149

Yamada, K.C.   II-435
Yamamoto, Keiko   II-538
Yamaoka, Toshiki   IV-408
Yamazaki, Kazuhiko   II-11, IV-506
Yang, Beiqing   III-120
Yantaç, Asım Evren   I-630
Yasmin, René   IV-723
Yasu, Hiroko   I-525
Yasuda, Junko   I-516
Yılmaz, Merve   IV-173
Yin, Mingfeng   III-120
You, Manlai   II-149
Youmans, Robert J.   I-13, I-144
Yu, Allan   IV-67
Yuan, Xiaojun   IV-591, IV-601
Yule, Daniel   I-162

Zahabi, Liese   IV-611
Žajdela Hrustek, Nikolina   I-369
Zan, Özgür   IV-651
Zeng, Yujing   IV-183, IV-352
Zepeda-Hernández, J. Sergio   IV-231
Zhang, Bin   I-171
Zhang, Tao   IV-313
Zhang, Xiangmin   IV-601
Zhang, Zhenghua   IV-183, IV-352
Zhao, Shiyu   III-120
Zhou, Bingjun   II-602
Ziefle, Martina   I-439, III-10
Zillner, Sonja   III-401